Zabbix Network Monitoring
Second Edition

Gather detailed statistics and data while monitoring the performance and availability of network devices and applications using the all-new Zabbix 3.0

Rihards Olups

[PACKT] open source*
PUBLISHING   community experience distilled

BIRMINGHAM - MUMBAI

Zabbix Network Monitoring
Second Edition

First published: March 2010

Second edition: August 2016

Production reference: 1030816

Published by Packt Publishing Ltd.
Livery Place
35 Livery Street
Birmingham B3 2PB, UK.

ISBN 978-1-78216-128-8

www.packtpub.com

Credits

Author
Rihards Olups

Reviewers
Werner Dijkerman
Volker Fröhlich
Adail Horst
Raymond Kuiper
Julien Recurt

Acquisition Editor
Sonali Vernekar

Content Development Editor
Samantha Gonsalves

Technical Editor
VIshal K. Mewada

Copy Editor
Madhusudan Uchil

Project Coordinator
Devanshi Doshi

Proofreader
Safis Editing

Indexer
Mariammal Chettiyar
Monica Ajmera Mehta

Graphics
Disha Haria

Production Coordinator
Nilesh Mohite

Cover Work
Nilesh Mohite

About the Author

Rihards Olups has over 15 years of experience in information technology, most of it with open source solutions. His foray into Zabbix, one of the leading open source enterprise-class monitoring solutions, was with the first public release back in 2001, which has allowed him to gain considerable knowledge on the subject. Previously employed by a government agency, Rihards was mostly involved in open source software deployment, ranging from server to desktop-grade software, with a big emphasis on Zabbix. Later, he joined Zabbix SIA, the company behind the software that this book is about, which allowed him to gain even more experience with the subject.

While at Zabbix, he helped Zabbix users and customers get the most value out of the monitoring tool and was responsible for delivering Zabbix training sessions that have been described by some participants as extremely practical and quite challenging.

He started working on the very first book on Zabbix, *Zabbix 1.8 Network Monitoring*, before joining Zabbix, and he finalized that book with even more in-depth details while helping advance Zabbix.

Rihards departed from Zabbix SIA and ended up seeing more of the user side again, including deployments of Zabbix in real-world environments.

Acknowledgments

I would like to thank my family and friends. Not spotlighting here—but if you think whether this includes you, yes, it does.

I would also like to thank all the people I have worked with. It was a great experience at the State Social Insurance Agency, and it was helped by being surrounded by nice people.

A huge thank you goes to everybody at Zabbix. Besides being experts in their own and many other fields, my Zabbix team members were extremely friendly, helpful, and welcoming. And it is true for everybody in the team. You are all great and will achieve a lot.

The Zabbix community deserves an extra mention. I have met a lot of wonderful people through the Zabbix community, and it is such a pleasure to meet them again every year in Riga, at the Zabbix conference. It is the community that takes Zabbix from the pure product level to something more.

And all you great people at Packt Publishing—thank you for dealing with the delays in Zabbix releases, my own schedule delays, and all the other small things. If you are reading this before the book is out, you know you have helped a lot.

Thank you all.

About the Reviewers

Werner Dijkerman is a systems engineer from the Netherlands. He has more than 10 years of experience in IT operations departments of different organizations. He started working with a leading online retailer in the Netherlands and continued in one of the leading software companies for general practitioners. He now works for iWelcome, the only established IDaaS provider in Europe.

With experience as a Windows and Linux admin, he also know his way around Java applications servers such as Tomcat and Jboss, (No)SQL databases, and monitoring systems. He started with Nagios in the early days and has even tried other tools such as Cacti, but Zabbix has been his main monitoring tool for several years now, with him finding ways and writing (Python) scripts to monitor everything it can.

He is also the author of the most popular Puppet module for Zabbix, `wdijkerman-zabbix`. It can be found at `https://forge.puppetlabs.com/wdijkerman/zabbix` on Puppet Forge. Besides this Puppet module, he has also created several Ansible roles under his alias `dj-wasabi` for four Zabbix components, which can be found on `https://galaxy.ansible.com/detail#/role/7626`.

Adail Horst is a free software evangelist, Zabbix translator, Zabbix documentation translator, and a lecturer on monitoring in various free software events (such as FISL, Latinoware, and Zabbix Conference). He has authored a book on the tool (De a Zabbix, in Portuguese), created Zabbix-Extras, and has experience in large IT environments monitored by Zabbix.

He is also one of the authors of the book *A to Zabbix*.

Raymond Kuiper is an IT infrastructure specialist with a strong focus on monitoring, networks, and operations. Raymond started using Zabbix 1.1.3 in 2006, when the company he was working for needed a flexible, integrated solution to monitor infrastructure availability and performance. Over the years, Raymond has become a keen supporter of Zabbix and has implemented monitoring with the tool for various organizations. He also likes to hang out on `#zabbix` on the Freenode IRC network to help out other Zabbix users.

Julien Recurt is an engineer who has multiples roles depending on the occasion. In the beginning, he worked for SUPINFO to enhance a complex and multisite infrastructure and reduce global costs. His big break was working with Ceph at Cloud-Solution, a French startup, to provide low-cost, scalable storage. Now, he works at Waycom, an Internet and web services provider, and manages about 1200 servers and virtual machines using Ansible.

I would like to thank everybody that contributes to open source software and also my coworkers who supported me in this job.

www.PacktPub.com

eBooks, discount offers, and more

Did you know that Packt offers eBook versions of every book published, with PDF and ePub files available? You can upgrade to the eBook version at `www.PacktPub.com` and as a print book customer, you are entitled to a discount on the eBook copy. Get in touch with us at `customercare@packtpub.com` for more details.

At `www.PacktPub.com`, you can also read a collection of free technical articles, sign up for a range of free newsletters and receive exclusive discounts and offers on Packt books and eBooks.

PACKTLiB™

`https://www2.packtpub.com/books/subscription/packtlib`

Do you need instant solutions to your IT questions? PacktLib is Packt's online digital book library. Here, you can search, access, and read Packt's entire library of books.

Why subscribe?

- Fully searchable across every book published by Packt
- Copy and paste, print, and bookmark content
- On demand and accessible via a web browser

Table of Contents

Preface

Imagine you're celebrating the start of the weekend with Friday-night drinks with a few friends. And then suddenly, your phone rings—one of the servers you administer has gone down, and it needs to be back up before tomorrow morning. So you drag yourself back to the office, only to discover that some logfiles have been growing more than usual over the past few weeks and have filled up the hard drive. While this scenario is very simplistic, something similar has happened to most IT workers at one or another point in their careers. To avoid such situations, this book will teach you to monitor your network's hardware, servers, and web performance using Zabbix, an open source system monitoring and reporting solution.

This book will guide you through setting up almost every feature in Zabbix. With step-by-step instructions, anybody should be able to configure monitoring. You could even say that this is an idiot's guide to Zabbix—but only because we all have had moments of not understanding something. In order to not leave you confused, throughout this book, I will try to hold your hand, push you forward, and explain everything in so much detail that you won't get frustrated at all.

What this book covers

Chapter 1, Getting Started with Zabbix, covers Zabbix installation from scratch, including the initial database, server and agent daemons, and web frontend, all running on the same machine. We will also configure the Zabbix web frontend, using PHP to access the database.

Chapter 2, Getting Your First Notification, covers configuring Zabbix using the frontend to set up data gathering, triggering upon specified conditions, and informing us by sending an e-mail for a single data source.

Chapter 3, Monitoring with Zabbix Agents and Basic Protocols, takes you through setting up the most widely used and basic data-gathering methods—Zabbix agents and simple checks, such as ICMP ping and direct TCP service checking.

Chapter 4, Monitoring SNMP Devices, teaches you how to set up the industry-standard monitoring protocol, SNMP. We will explore both polling by Zabbix and receiving SNMP traps, which will allow us to monitor a large variety of devices, including printers, switches, UPSes, and routers.

Chapter 5, Managing Hosts, Users, and Permissions, covers hosts, users, and permissions, including host and user group functionality and their impact on permissions. We will also explore related topics, including host and host group maintenance.

Chapter 6, Detecting Problems with Triggers, looks at ways to define which conditions are noteworthy by crafting expressions to detect values outside of the normal range, and other cases.

Chapter 7, Acting upon Monitored Conditions, helps you figure out how to react to triggers firing by sending an e-mail, launching an external script, opening a report in a separate bug tracker, or even restarting a faulty service. We will also learn to configure escalations in Zabbix and figure out how hysteresis works.

Chapter 8, Simplifying Complex Configuration with Templates, tells us how we did it all wrong before and teaches us to improve our configuration using templates that allow us to apply uniform configuration to a bunch of hosts while customizing thresholds per host with user macros. We'll also explore template nesting, which allows creating very flexible configuration in a large and mixed environment.

Chapter 9, Visualizing the Data with Graphs and Maps, explains how to create visual elements to display gathered data, including several types of graphs and interactive network maps.

Chapter 10, Visualizing the Data with Screens and Slideshows, helps you configure screens that collect various types of elements to display and slideshows that allow cycling through several screens in an automated fashion.

Chapter 11, Advanced Item Monitoring, explores more advanced ways to gather information using external, calculated, aggregate, and custom item types to retrieve any information.

Chapter 12, Automating Configuration, teaches us how to discover filesystems, network interfaces, and other entities on hosts with low-level discovery. On a higher level, we will explore the ability to automatically manage hosts via network discovery and active agent autoregistration.

Chapter 13, Monitoring Web Pages, takes us through monitoring the accessibility, performance, and availability of web pages using the built-in web scenario feature of Zabbix.

Chapter 14, Monitoring Windows, covers Windows monitoring by installing Zabbix agents, using performance counters, and retrieving data over WMI.

Chapter 15, High Level Business Service Monitoring, demonstrates the "IT services" feature, which allows aligning monitored services in a tree and calculating SLA conformity. We will fake some data to see how this feature actually looks.

Chapter 16, Monitoring IPMI Devices, teaches us how to set up yet another industry-standard protocol, IPMI. Monitoring both analog and discrete IPMI sensors will be covered.

Chapter 17, Monitoring Java Applications, a separate daemon called Zabbix Java gateway is set up and used to retrieve basic information over JMX.

Chapter 18, Monitoring VMware, covers the built-in VMware monitoring support. We will explore the ability to automatically discover and monitor hypervisors and virtual machines.

Chapter 19, Using Proxies to Monitor Remote Locations, explores the usage of passive and active Zabbix proxies that collect the data on behalf of the Zabbix server and then transmit it back to the server, which helps with remote locations that can't be accessed directly because of firewall concerns and also reduces the load on the Zabbix server.

Chapter 20, Encrypting Zabbix Traffic, looks into one of the major new features in Zabbix 3.0: the ability to encrypt traffic between the Zabbix server, proxies, agents, and the get and sender utilities.

Chapter 21, Working Closely with Data, helps us figure out some details about how data is stored in the Zabbix database and how we can interact with it directly as well as using Zabbix's native XML import and export functionality to more easily create large amounts of configuration. We will also get started with the Zabbix API for more advanced automation needs.

Chapter 22, Zabbix Maintenance, teaches us about the Zabbix upgrade procedure, how different components of various versions can interact, and what database patching between versions involves. We will also explore the internal monitoring options available, discuss backup strategies, and talk in detail about all the configuration parameters Zabbix daemons have.

Appendix A, Troubleshooting, covers common pitfalls with installation, connectivity, configuration, and other areas.

Appendix B, Being Part of the Community, tells us how we are not alone and there's a community around the Zabbix monitoring solution, which we can reach via IRC, forums, and the community wiki.

What you need for this book

You will need at least one Linux system, which could be a virtual machine as well. Depending on specific features discussed, you might also benefit from the following:

- Access to an SMTP (e-mail) server
- More Linux systems
- A device with SNMP support
- A Windows system
- A device with IPMI support
- A Java virtual machine
- A VMware instance

Some of these can be replicated on the same Linux box—for example, running snmpd or a Java VM will allow you to try out all the monitoring solutions without a separate system.

Who this book is for

This book is perfect for system admins who are new to Zabbix and are interested in creating simple monitoring reports. This book assumes knowledge of basic system administration tasks. Zabbix has added quite a lot of new features over the years, and many features new to 3.0 will be covered, so even experienced users of previous versions should be able to find new information.

Conventions

In this book, you will find a number of text styles that distinguish between different kinds of information. Here are some examples of these styles and an explanation of their meaning.

Code words in text, database table names, folder names, filenames, file extensions, pathnames, dummy URLs, and user input are shown as follows: "One of the first monitoring solutions most administrators implement is a simple `shell` script invoked from a `crontab` that checks some basic parameters such as disk usage or some service state, such as an Apache server."

A block of code is set as follows:

```
memory_limit = 128M
post_max_size = 16M
max_execution_time = 300
max_input_time = 300
upload_max_filesize = 2M
```

When we wish to draw your attention to a particular part of a code block, the relevant lines or items are set in bold:

```
memory_limit = 128M
post_max_size = 16M
max_execution_time = 300
max_input_time = 300
upload_max_filesize = 2M
```

Any command line input or output is written as follows:

```
# rpm -ivh http://repo.zabbix.com/zabbix/3.0/rhel/7/x86_64/zabbix-release-3.0-1.el7.noarch.rpm
```

New terms and **important words** are shown in bold. Words that you see on the screen, for example, in menus or dialog boxes, appear in the text like this: "This screen doesn't offer us much to configure, so just click on **Next step**."

> Warnings or important notes appear in a box like this.

> Tips and tricks appear like this.

Reader feedback

Feedback from our readers is always welcome. Let us know what you think about this book—what you liked or disliked. Reader feedback is important for us as it helps us develop titles that you will really get the most out of.

To send us general feedback, simply e-mail feedback@packtpub.com, and mention the book's title in the subject of your message.

If there is a topic that you have expertise in and you are interested in either writing or contributing to a book, see our author guide at www.packtpub.com/authors.

Customer support

Now that you are the proud owner of a Packt book, we have a number of things to help you to get the most from your purchase.

Downloading the example code

You can download the example code files for this book from your account at http://www.packtpub.com. If you purchased this book elsewhere, you can visit http://www.packtpub.com/support and register to have the files e-mailed directly to you.

You can download the code files by following these steps:

1. Log in or register to our website using your e-mail address and password.
2. Hover the mouse pointer on the **SUPPORT** tab at the top.
3. Click on **Code Downloads & Errata**.
4. Enter the name of the book in the **Search** box.
5. Select the book for which you're looking to download the code files.
6. Choose from the drop-down menu where you purchased this book from.
7. Click on **Code Download**.

You can also download the code files by clicking on the **Code Files** button on the book's web page at the Packt Publishing website. This page can be accessed by entering the book's name in the **Search** box. Please note that you need to be logged in to your Packt account.

Once the file is downloaded, please make sure that you unzip or extract the folder using the latest version of:

- WinRAR / 7-Zip for Windows
- Zipeg / iZip / UnRarX for Mac
- 7-Zip / PeaZip for Linux

The code bundle for the book is also hosted on GitHub at https://github.com/PacktPublishing/Zabbix-Network-Monitoring-Second-Edition. We also have other code bundles from our rich catalog of books and videos available at https://github.com/PacktPublishing/. Check them out!

Downloading the color images of this book

We also provide you with a PDF file that has color images of the screenshots/
diagrams used in this book. The color images will help you better understand the
changes in the output. You can download this file from `https://www.packtpub.com/`
`sites/default/files/downloads/ZabbixNetworkMonitoringSecondEdition_`
`ColorImages.pdf`.

Errata

Although we have taken every care to ensure the accuracy of our content, mistakes
do happen. If you find a mistake in one of our books — maybe a mistake in the text or
the code — we would be grateful if you could report this to us. By doing so, you can
save other readers from frustration and help us improve subsequent versions of this
book. If you find any errata, please report them by visiting `http://www.packtpub.`
`com/submit-errata`, selecting your book, clicking on the **Errata Submission Form**
link, and entering the details of your errata. Once your errata are verified, your
submission will be accepted and the errata will be uploaded to our website or added
to any list of existing errata under the Errata section of that title.

To view the previously submitted errata, go to `https://www.packtpub.com/books/`
`content/support` and enter the name of the book in the search field. The required
information will appear under the **Errata** section.

Piracy

Piracy of copyrighted material on the Internet is an ongoing problem across all
media. At Packt, we take the protection of our copyright and licenses very seriously.
If you come across any illegal copies of our works in any form on the Internet, please
provide us with the location address or website name immediately so that we can
pursue a remedy.

Please contact us at `copyright@packtpub.com` with a link to the suspected
pirated material.

We appreciate your help in protecting our authors and our ability to bring you
valuable content.

Questions

If you have a problem with any aspect of this book, you can contact us at
`questions@packtpub.com`, and we will do our best to address the problem.

Getting Started with Zabbix
1

It's Friday night, and you are at a party outside the city with old friends. After a few beers, it looks as if this is going to be a great party, when suddenly your phone rings. A customer can't access some critical server that absolutely has to be available as soon as possible. You try to connect to the server using SSH, only to discover that the customer is right—it can't be accessed.

As driving after those few beers would quite likely lead to an inoperable server for quite some time, you get a taxi—expensive because of the distance (while many modern systems have out-of-band management cards installed that might have helped a bit in such a situation, our hypothetical administrator does not have one available). After arriving at the server room, you find out that some log files have been growing more than usual over the past few weeks and have filled up the hard drive.

While the preceding scenario is very simplistic, something similar has probably happened to most IT workers at one or another point in their careers. Most will have implemented a simple system monitoring and reporting solution soon after that.

We will learn how to set up and configure one such monitoring system—Zabbix. In this very first chapter, we will:

- Decide which Zabbix version to use
- Set up Zabbix either from packages or from the source
- Configure the Zabbix frontend

The first steps in monitoring

Situations similar to the one just described are actually more common than desired. A system fault that had no symptoms visible before is relatively rare. A subsection of UNIX Administration Horror Stories (`http://www-uxsup.csx.cam.ac.uk/misc/horror.txt`) that only contains stories about faults that weren't noticed in time could probably be compiled easily.

As experience shows, problems tend to happen when we are least equipped to solve them. To work with them on our terms, we turn to a class of software commonly referred to as **network monitoring software**. Such software usually allows us to constantly monitor things happening in a computer network using one or more methods and notify the persons responsible, if a metric passes a defined threshold.

One of the first monitoring solutions most administrators implement is a simple shell script invoked from a `crontab` that checks some basic parameters such as disk usage or some service state, such as an Apache server. As the server and monitored-parameter count grows, a neat and clean script system starts to grow into a performance-hogging script hairball that costs more time in upkeep than it saves. While the do-it-yourself crowd claims that nobody needs dedicated software for most tasks (monitoring included), most administrators will disagree as soon as they have to add switches, UPSes, routers, IP cameras, and a myriad of other devices to the swarm of monitored objects.

So, what basic functionality can one expect from a monitoring solution? Let's take a look:

- **Data gathering**: This is where everything starts. Usually, data is gathered using various methods, including **Simple Network Management Protocol (SNMP)**, agents, and **Intelligent Platform Management Interface (IPMI)**.

- **Alerting**: Gathered data can be compared to thresholds and alerts sent out when required using different channels, such as e-mail or SMS.

- **Data storage**: Once we have gathered the data, it doesn't make sense to throw it away, so we will often want to store it for later analysis.

- **Visualization**: Humans are better at distinguishing visualized data than raw numbers, especially when there's a lot of data. As we have data already gathered and stored, it is easy to generate simple graphs from it.

Sounds simple? That's because it is. But then we start to want more features, such as easy and efficient configuration, escalations, and permission delegation. If we sit down and start listing the things we want to keep an eye out for, it may turn out that that area of interest extends beyond the network, for example, a hard drive that has Self-Monitoring, Analysis, and Reporting Technology (SMART) errors logged, an application that has too many threads, or a UPS that has one phase overloaded. It is much easier to manage the monitoring of all these different problem categories from a single configuration point.

In the quest for a manageable monitoring system, wondrous adventurers stumbled upon collections of scripts much like the way they themselves implemented obscure and not-so-obscure workstation-level software and heavy, expensive monitoring systems from big vendors.

Many went with a different category — free software. We will look at a free software monitoring solution, Zabbix.

Zabbix features and architecture

Zabbix provides many ways of monitoring different aspects of your IT infrastructure and, indeed, almost anything you might want to hook up to it. It can be characterized as a semi-distributed monitoring system with centralized management. While many installations have a single central system, it is possible to use distributed monitoring with proxies, and most installations will use Zabbix agents.

What features does Zabbix provide? Let's have a look:

- A centralized, easy to use web interface
- A server that runs on most UNIX-like operating systems, including Linux, AIX, FreeBSD, OpenBSD, and Solaris
- Native agents for most UNIX-like operating systems and Microsoft Windows versions
- The ability to directly monitor SNMP (SNMPv1, SNMPv2c, and SNMPv3) and IPMI devices
- The ability to directly monitor Java applications using Java Management Extensions (JMX)
- The ability to directly monitor vCenter or vSphere instances using the VMware API
- Built-in graphing and other visualization capabilities

- Notifications that allow easy integration with other systems
- Flexible configuration, including templating
- A lot of other features that would allow you to implement a sophisticated monitoring solution

If we look at a simplified network from the Zabbix perspective, placing the Zabbix server at the center, the communication of the various monitoring aspects matters. The following figure depicts a relatively simple Zabbix setup with several of the monitoring capabilities used and different device categories connected:

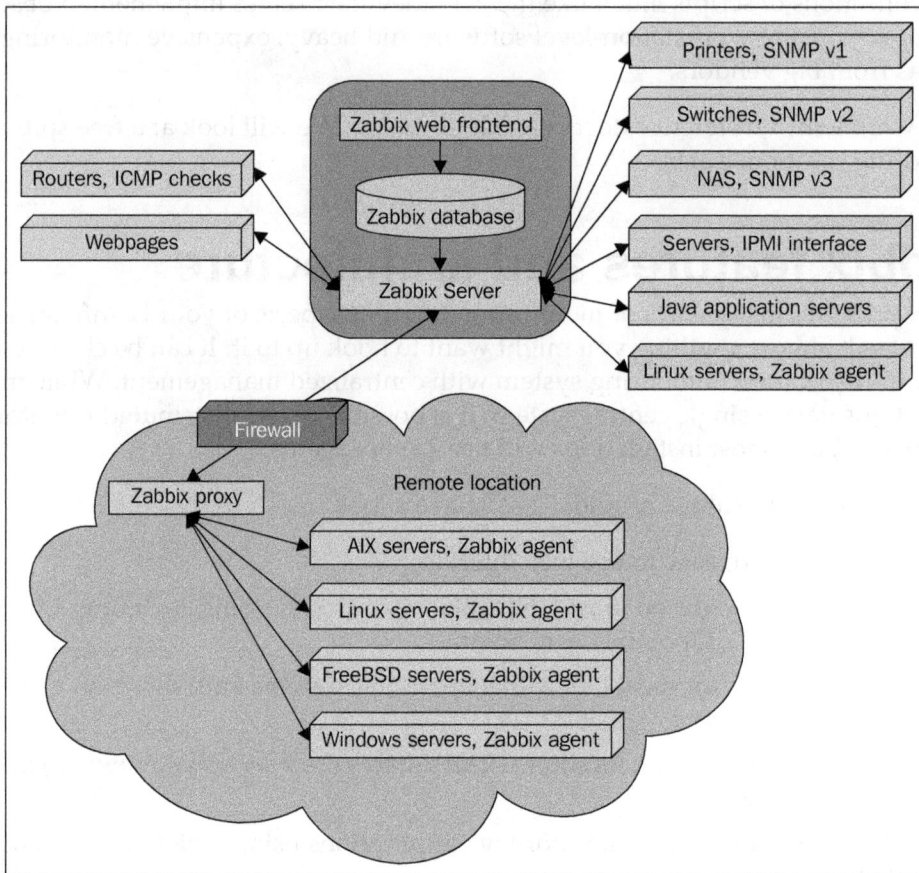

The **Zabbix server** directly monitors multiple devices, but a remote location is separated by a firewall, so it is easier to gather data through a **Zabbix proxy**. The **Zabbix proxy** and **Zabbix agents**, just like the server, are written in the C language.

Our central object is the **Zabbix database**, which supports several backends. The **Zabbix server**, written in the C language, and the **Zabbix web frontend**, written in PHP, can both reside on the same machine or on another server. When running each component on a separate machine, both the **Zabbix server** and the **Zabbix web frontend** need access to the **Zabbix database**, and the **Zabbix web frontend** needs access to the **Zabbix server** to display the server status and for some additional functionality. The required connection directions are depicted by arrows in the following figure:

While it is perfectly fine to run all three server components on a single machine, there might be good reasons to separate them, such as taking advantage of an existing high-performance database or web server.

In general, monitored devices have little control over what is monitored — most of the configuration is centralized. Such an approach seriously reduces the ability of a single misconfigured system to bring down the whole monitoring setup.

Installation

Alright, enough with the dry talk—what use is that? Let's look at the dashboard screen of the Zabbix web frontend, showing only a very basic configuration:

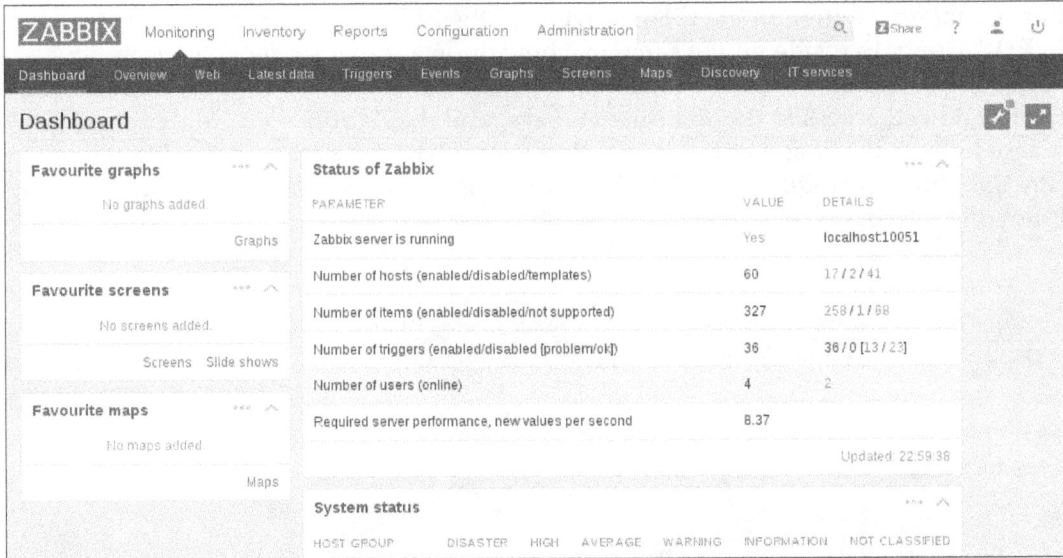

The Zabbix dashboard shows you a high-level overview of the overall status of the monitored system, the status of Zabbix, some of the most recent problems, and a few more things. This particular dashboard shows a very tiny Zabbix setup. Eventually, your Zabbix installation will grow and monitor different devices, including servers of various operating systems, different services and the hardware state on those servers, network devices, UPSes, web pages, other components of IT, and other infrastructure.

The frontend will provide various options for visualizing data, starting from lists of problems and simple graphs and ending with network maps and reports, while the backend will work hard to provide the information that this visualization is based on and send out alerts. All of this will require some configuration that we will learn to perform along the course of this book.

Before we can configure Zabbix, we need to install it. Usually, you'll have two choices—installing from packages or setting it up from the source code. Zabbix packages are available in quite a lot of Linux distribution repositories, and it is usually a safe choice to use those. Additionally, a Zabbix-specific repository is provided by SIA Zabbix (the company developing the product) for some distributions.

> It is a good idea to check the latest installation instructions at https://www.zabbix.com/documentation/3.0/manual/installation.

Choosing the version and repository

At first, we will set up the Zabbix server, database, and frontend, all running on the same machine and using a MySQL database.

Should you use the packages or install from source? In most cases, installing from the packages will be easier. Here are a few considerations that might help you select the method:

- There are certain benefits of using distribution packages. These include the following:
    - Automated installation and updating
    - Dependencies are usually sorted out

- Compiling from source also has its share of benefits. They are as follows:
    - You get newer versions with more features and improvements
    - You have more fine-grained control over compiled-in functionality

But which version to choose? You might see several versions available in repositories, and those versions might not be equal. Since Zabbix 2.2, the concept of a **Long-Term Support (LTS)** release has been introduced. This determines how long support in the form of bug fixes will be available for. An LTS release is supported for 5 years, while a normal release is supported until a month after the release date of the next version. Zabbix 2.2 and 3.0 are LTS releases, while 2.4 and 3.2 are normal releases. Choose an LTS release for an installation that you don't plan to upgrade for a while and a normal release for something you intend to keep up to date. In this book, we will use Zabbix version 3.0.

> This policy might change. Verify the details on the Zabbix website: http://www.zabbix.com/life_cycle_and_release_policy.php.

The most widely used Zabbix architecture is a server that queries agents. This is what we will learn to set up initially so that we can monitor our test system.

As with most software, there are some prerequisites that we will need in order to run Zabbix components. These include requirements of hardware and other software that the Zabbix server and agent depend on. For the purpose of our installation, we will settle for running Zabbix on Linux, using a MySQL database. The specific Linux distribution does not matter much — it's best to choose the one you are most familiar with.

Hardware requirements

Hardware requirements vary wildly depending on the configuration. It is impossible to provide definite requirements, so any production installation should evaluate them individually. For our test environment, though, even as little RAM as 128 MB should be enough. CPU power in general won't play a huge role; Pentium II-class hardware should be perfectly capable of dealing with it, although generating graphs with many elements or other complex views could require more powerful hardware to operate at an acceptable speed. You can take these as a starting point as well when installing on a virtual machine.

Of course, the more resources you give to Zabbix, the snappier and happier it will be.

Installing from the packages

If you have decided to install Zabbix from the packages, package availability and the procedure will differ based on the distribution. A few distributions will be covered here — read the distribution-specific instructions for others.

RHEL/CentOS

RedHat Enterprise Linux or CentOS users have two repositories to choose from: the well-known **Extra Packages for Enterprise Linux** (**EPEL**) and the Zabbix repository. EPEL might be a safer choice, but it might not always have the latest version.

EPEL

If EPEL is not set up already, it must be added. For RHEL/CentOS 7, the command is similar to this:

```
# rpm -Uvh http://ftp.colocall.net/pub/epel/7/x86_64/e/epel-release-7-5.noarch.rpm
```

> Check the latest available version at http://download.fedoraproject.org/pub/epel/7/x86_64/repoview/epel-release.html.

Once the repository has been set up, you may install the packages:

```
# yum install zabbix22-agent zabbix22-dbfiles-mysql zabbix22-server-mysql
zabbix22-web-mysql
```

The Zabbix repository

First, the package that will define the Zabbix repository should be installed:

```
# rpm -ivh http://repo.zabbix.com/zabbix/3.0/rhel/7/x86_64/zabbix-
release-3.0-1.el7.noarch.rpm
```

Once the repository has been set up, you may install the packages:

```
# yum install zabbix-server-mysql zabbix-web-mysql zabbix-agent
```

OpenSUSE

For OpenSUSE, Zabbix is available in the `server:monitoring` repository. First, the repository should be added and its package list downloaded (you might have to change the distribution version):

```
# zypper addrepo http://download.opensuse.org/repositories/
server:monitoring/openSUSE_Leap_42.1/server:monitoring.repo
# zypper refresh
```

Once the repository has been set up, you may install the packages:

```
# zypper install zabbix-server-mysql zabbix-agent zabbix-phpfrontend
```

Installing from source

If you have decided to install Zabbix from source, you will need to obtain the source, configure it, and compile it. After the daemons are put in place, the frontend will have to be set up manually as well.

The server and agent

At first, we will only set up the Zabbix server and agent, both running on the same system. We will set up additional components later during the course of this book.

Software requirements

Now, we should get to compiling the various components of Zabbix, so make sure to install the minimum required packages to get Zabbix working with MySQL. Here they are:

- **GCC**
- Automake
- MySQL (http://www.mysql.com/)

Depending on your distribution and the desired functionality, you might also need some or all of the following packages:

- `zlib-devel`
- `mysql-devel` (for MySQL support)
- `glibc-devel`
- `curl-devel` (for web monitoring)
- `libidn-devel` (`curl-devel` might depend on it)
- `openssl-devel` (`curl-devel` might depend on it)
- `net-snmp-devel` (for SNMP support)
- `popt-devel` (`net-snmp-devel` might depend on it)
- `rpm-devel` (`net-snmp-devel` might depend on it)
- `OpenIPMI-devel` (for IPMI support)
- `libssh2-devel` (for direct SSH checks)
- `libxm2-devel` (for VMware monitoring)
- `unixODBC-devel` (for database monitoring)
- Java SDK (for Java gateway/JMX checks)

Downloading the source

There are several ways of downloading the source code of Zabbix. You can get it from a **Subversion** (**SVN**) repository, which will be discussed in *Appendix A, Troubleshooting*, however, for this installation procedure, I suggest you download version 3.0.0 from the Zabbix homepage, http://www.zabbix.com/. While it should be possible to use the latest stable version, using 3.0.0 will allow you to follow instructions more closely. Go to the **Download** section and grab the compressed source package. Usually, only the latest stable version is available on the download page, so you might have to browse the source archives, but do not take a development or beta version, which might be available.

To make further references easy, I suggested you choose a directory to work in, for example, ~/zabbix (~ being your home directory). Download the archive into this directory.

Compilation

Once the archive has finished downloading, open a terminal and extract it:

```
$ cd ~/zabbix; tar -zxvf zabbix-3.0.0.tar.gz
```

I suggest you install the prerequisites and compile Zabbix with external functionality right away so that you don't have to recompile as we progress.

For the purpose of this book, we will compile Zabbix with server, agent, MySQL, curl, SNMP, SSH, ODBC, XML (VMware), and IPMI support.

To continue, enter the following in the terminal:

```
$ cd zabbix-3.0.0
$ ./configure --enable-server --with-mysql --with-net-snmp --with-libcurl
--with-openipmi --enable-agent --with-libxml2 --with-unixodbc --with-ssh2
--with-openssl
```

In the end, a summary of the compiled components will be printed. Verify that you have the following enabled:

```
    Enable server:          yes
  Server details:
    With database:          MySQL
    WEB Monitoring:         cURL
    SNMP:                   yes
    IPMI:                   yes
    SSH:                    yes
    TLS:                    OpenSSL
    ODBC:                   yes
    Enable agent:           yes
```

If the configuration completes successfully, it's all good. If it fails, check the error messages printed in the console and verify that all prerequisites have been installed. A file named config.log might provide more detail about the errors. If you can't find out what's wrong, check *Appendix A, Troubleshooting*, which lists some common compilation problems.

To actually compile Zabbix, issue the following command:

```
$ make
```

You can grab a cup of tea, but don't expect to have much time — Zabbix compilation doesn't take too long; even an old 350-MHz Pentium II compiles it in approximately five minutes. On a modern machine, give it less than a minute. After the make process has finished, check the last lines for any error messages. If there are none, congratulations, you have successfully compiled Zabbix!

Now, we should install it. I suggest you create proper packages, but that will require some effort and will be distribution dependent. Another option is to run make install. This will place the files in the filesystem but will not register Zabbix as an installed package — removing and upgrading such software is harder.

If you have experience with creating distribution packages, do so — it is a better approach. If this is just a test installation, run the following:

```
# make install
```

> Here and later in the book, a $ prompt will mean a normal user, while a # prompt will mean the root user. To run commands as root, su or sudo are commonly used.

But remember that test installations have the tendency of becoming production installations later — it might be a good idea to do things properly from the very beginning.

Dash or underscore?

Depending on the method of installation, you might get Zabbix binaries and configuration files using either a dash (minus) or an underscore, like this:

* zabbix_server **versus** zabbix-server
* zabbix_agentd **versus** zabbix-agentd
* zabbix_server.conf **versus** zabbix-server.conf

While Zabbix itself uses an underscore, many distributions will replace it with a dash to follow their own guidelines. There is no functional difference; you just have to keep in mind the character that your installation uses. In this book, we will reference binaries and files using an underscore.

Initial configuration

After compilation, we have to configure some basic parameters for the server and agent. Default configuration files are provided with Zabbix. The location of these files will depend on the installation method you chose:

- Source installation: /usr/local/etc
- RHEL/CentOS/OpenSUSE package installation: /etc

On other distributions, the files might be located in a different directory. In this book, we will reference binaries and configuration files using relative names, except in situations where the absolute path is recommended or required.

To configure the Zabbix agent, we don't have to do anything. The default configuration will do just fine for now. That was easy, right?

For the server, we will need to make some changes. Open the zabbix_server.conf file in your favorite editor (you will need to edit it as the root user) and find the following entries in the file:

- DBName
- DBUser
- DBPassword

DBName should be zabbix by default; we can leave it as is. DBUser is set to root, and we don't like that, so let's change it to zabbix. For DBPassword, choose any password. You won't have to remember it, so be creative.

> In UNIX-like solutions, a hash character or # at the beginning of a line usually means that the line is commented out. Make sure not to start lines you want to have an effect with a hash.

Creating and populating the database

For the Zabbix server to store the data, we have to create a database. Start a MySQL client:

```
$ mysql -u root -p
```

Enter the root user's password for MySQL (you will have set this during the installation of MySQL, or the password could be something that is the default for your distribution). If you do not know the password, you can try omitting -p. This switch will tell the client to attempt to connect without a password (or with an empty password).

> If you are using MySQL Community Edition from the
> packages and the version is 5.7.6 or higher, it generates a
> random password that is stored in `logfiles`. Check out
> the MySQL documentation at `http://dev.mysql.com/`
> `doc/refman/5.7/en/linux-installation-rpm.`
> `html` for more details.

Now, let's create the database. Add the user that Zabbix would connect to the
database as, and grant the necessary permissions to this user:

```
mysql> create database zabbix character set utf8 collate utf8_bin;
Query OK, 1 row affected (0.01 sec)
mysql> grant all privileges on zabbix.* to 'zabbix'@'localhost'
identified by 'mycreativepassword';
Query OK, 0 rows affected (0.12 sec)
```

Use the password you set in the `zabbix_server.conf` file instead of
`mycreativepassword`.

Quit the MySQL client by entering the following command:

```
mysql> quit
```

Let's populate the newly created database with a Zabbix schema and initial data.
The following commands refer to the files as they appear in the Zabbix source.
When installing from packages, these files could be located in a directory such as `/usr/share/doc/zabbix-server-mysql-3.0.0/create/` or `/usr/share/zabbix-server-mysql`:

```
$ mysql -u zabbix -p zabbix < database/mysql/schema.sql
$ mysql -u zabbix -p zabbix < database/mysql/images.sql
$ mysql -u zabbix -p zabbix < database/mysql/data.sql
```

All three importing processes should complete without any messages. If there are
any errors, review the messages, fix the issue, and retry the failed operation. If
the import is interrupted in the middle of the process, you might have to clear the
database—the easiest way to do this is to delete the database by typing this:

```
mysql> drop database zabbix;
Query OK, 0 rows affected (0.00 sec)
```

> Be careful not to delete a database with important
> information! After deleting the Zabbix database,
> recreate it as we did before.

By now, we should have the Zabbix server and agent installed and ready to start.

Starting up

You should never start the Zabbix server or agent as root, which is common sense for most daemon processes. If you installed Zabbix from distribution packages, system users should have been created already — if not, let's create a new user to run these processes. You can use tools provided by your distribution or use the most widely available command — useradd, which we need to execute as root:

```
# useradd -m -s /bin/bash zabbix
```

> For production systems, consider using different user accounts for the Zabbix server and agent. Otherwise, users with configuration rights will be able to discover Zabbix database credentials by instructing the agent to read the server configuration file. Some distribution packages, such as the EPEL and OpenSUSE ones, already use a separate user account called zabbixsrv or zabbixs by default.

This will create a user named zabbix with a home directory in the default location, /home/zabbix usually, and a shell at /bin/bash.

> While using bash on a test system will make it easier to debug issues, consider using /bin/nologin or /bin/false on production systems.

If you installed from source, let's try the direct approach — running the binaries. The location of the binaries will depend on the chosen method of installation. Installing from the source without any extra parameters will place agent and server binaries in /usr/local/sbin; distribution packages are likely to place them in /usr/sbin. Assuming they are in your path, you can determine where the binaries are by running this:

```
# which zabbix_server
```

> Keep in mind the potential use of a dash or minus instead of an underscore.

This will show something similar to the following:

```
/usr/sbin/zabbix_server
```

Alternatively, the `whereis` command can also list configuration and other related files:

```
# whereis zabbix_server
```

This would likely list the binary, the configuration file, and the manpage:

```
zabbix_server: /usr/sbin/zabbix_server /usr/local/etc/zabbix_server.conf
/usr/share/man/man3/zabbix_server
```

Once you know the exact location of the binaries, execute the following as `root` user:

```
# <path>/zabbix_agentd
```

> We are using `zabbix_agentd`, which runs as a daemon. Older versions also had the `zabbix_agent` executable, which provided an option to be run within **internet service daemon (inetd)**; it did not support active items and, in most cases, had worse performance than the agent daemon.

This will start the Zabbix agent daemon, which should start up silently and daemonize. If the command produces errors, resolve them before proceeding. If it succeeds, continue by starting the Zabbix server:

```
# <path>/zabbix_server
```

> Check the Zabbix server logfile, configurable in `zabbix_server.conf`. If there are database-related errors, fix them and restart the Zabbix server.

If you installed from the packages, execute this:

```
# service zabbix-agentd start
Starting zabbix agent daemon
done
# service zabbix-server start
Starting zabbix server daemon
done
```

That should get the agent and server started. On OpenSUSE, you can also use a different, shorter syntax:

```
# rczabbix-agentd start
# rczabbix-server start
```

Feel free to experiment with other parameters, such as `stop` and `restart` — it should be obvious what these two do.

You can verify whether services are running with the `status` parameter. For a service that is not running, you would get the following:

```
# service zabbix-server status
Checking for service Zabbix server daemon
unused
```

A running service would yield the following:

```
# service zabbix-agentd status
Checking for service Zabbix agent daemon
running
```

> On some distributions, this might return more verbose output, including all of the running processes.

Some distributions might have another parameter called `probe`. This will check whether the corresponding service has been restarted since the last configuration file changes.

If it has been restarted, no output will be produced. If the service has not been restarted (thus possibly missing some configuration changes), the `reload` string will be output.

While it's nice to have Zabbix processes running, it's hardly a process one expects to do manually upon each system boot, so the server and agent should be added to your system's startup sequence. This is fairly distribution specific, so all possible variations can't be discussed here. With RHEL or CentOS, a command like this should help:

```
# chkconfig --level 345 zabbix-agent on
# chkconfig --level 345 zabbix-server on
```

This will add both services to be started at `runlevels` 3, 4, and 5. For OpenSUSE, the following should work:

```
# chkconfig -s zabbix-server 35
# chkconfig -s zabbix-agentd 35
```

This will add both services to be started at runlevel 3 and runlevel 5, which are used for multiuser and networked environments. The previous commands might work on other distributions, too, although some distributions might use runlevel 4 instead of runlevel 5 for a graphical environment—consult your distribution's documentation when in doubt. There's usually no need to start Zabbix in single-user or non-networked runlevels (1 and 2), as data gathering requires network connectivity.

> If installing from source, consider taking just the init scripts from the distribution packages.

With some init scripts in some distributions, it is even simpler than that:

```
# chkconfig -a zabbix_server zabbix_agentd
```

This will add both services as specified in the corresponding init scripts, which in our case should be runlevels 3 and 5, configured by the Default-Start parameter in the init script. If the command succeeds, you'll see the following output:

```
zabbix_server        0:off  1:off  2:off  3:on  4:off  5:on  6:off
zabbix_agentd        0:off  1:off  2:off  3:on  4:off  5:on  6:off
```

Using systemd

It is possible that your distribution uses the systemd boot manager to manage services. We won't dig into that much, but here's a quick, convenient lookup for the most common systemd alternatives to service-management commands:

- Starting a service: systemctl start service_name
- Stopping a service: systemctl stop service_name
- Restarting a service: systemctl restart service_name
- Enabling a service to start upon system startup: systemctl enable service_name

A nice summary can be found at https://fedoraproject.org/wiki/SysVinit_to_Systemd_Cheatsheet.

Verifying the service's state

While the `init` script method is a nice way to check a service's state for some distributions, it's not available everywhere and isn't always enough. Sometimes, you might want to use these other methods to check whether the Zabbix server or agent is running:

- Checking running processes: The most common method to check whether a particular process is running is by looking at the running processes. You can verify whether the Zabbix agent daemon processes are actually running using this command:

    ```
    $ ps -C zabbix_agentd
    ```

- Output from the `netstat` command: Sometimes, an agent daemon might start up but fail to bind to the port, or the port might be used by some other process. You can verify whether some other process is listening on the Zabbix port or whether the Zabbix agent daemon is listening on the correct port by issuing this command:

    ```
    $ netstat -ntpl
    ```

    - Process names won't be printed for other users' processes unless you are the `root` user. In the output, look for a line similar to this:

        ```
        Proto Recv-Q Send-Q Local Address          Foreign Address
        State          PID/Program name
        tcp       0        0 0.0.0.0:10050          0.0.0.0:*
        LISTEN         19843/zabbix_agentd
        ```

    - This indicates that the `zabbix_agentd` process is running and listening on all addresses on port `10050`, just what we need.

- Telnetting to the port: Even when a service starts up and successfully binds to a port, there might be some connectivity issues, perhaps due to a local firewall. To quickly check connectivity on the desired port, you can try this:

    ```
    $ telnet localhost 10050
    ```

    This command should open a connection to the Zabbix agent daemon, and the daemon should not close the connection immediately. All of this applies to the Zabbix server as well, except that it uses a different port by default: `10051`.

The web frontend

Now that we have the Zabbix server and agent either compiled and installed or installed from the distribution packages, and both daemons are running, you probably have a feeling that something's missing. We have only configured some low-level behavior, so where's the meat?

That's what the frontend is for. While, in theory, Zabbix can have multiple frontends, the only one with full functionality so far is the Zabbix web frontend, which is written in PHP. We have to set it up to configure Zabbix and get to those nice graphs everybody likes.

Prerequisites and setting up the environment

Of course, being a Zabbix web frontend, it will require a platform to run on: a web server with a PHP environment. We will need the following installed:

- A web server that is supported by PHP; Apache is the most common choice
- PHP version 5.4.0 or higher

> The following instructions apply when installing from source. Installing from packages usually sets up the Zabbix frontend as well.

It is easiest to install these from the distribution packages. For PHP, we'll also need the following functionality:

- gd
- mysqli
- bcmath
- mbstring
- gettext

> Some distributions split out the core PHP modules. These might include ctype, net-socket, libxml, and others.

Once you have all these installed, it's time to set up the frontend. Again, there's a choice of using packages or installing from source. If you decided to go with the packages, you should have the frontend installed already and should be able to proceed with the configuration wizard section explained next. If you went with the source installation, it's just a simple copying of some files.

First, you have to decide where the frontend code has to go. Most distributions that package web servers use /srv/www/htdocs or /var/www. If you compiled the Apache web server from source, it would be /usr/local/apache2/htdocs (unless you manually changed the prefix or installed an older Apache version). We will place the frontend in a simple subdirectory, zabbix.

Assuming you have Apache distribution packages installed with the web root directory at /srv/www/htdocs, placing the frontend where it is needed is as simple as executing the following as the root user:

```
# cp -r frontends/php /srv/www/htdocs/zabbix
```

Using the web frontend configuration wizard

The web frontend has a wizard that helps you to configure its basics. Let's go through the simple steps it offers.

Now, it's time to fire up a browser and navigate to Zabbix's address: http://<server_ip_or_name>/zabbix. It should work just fine in the latest versions of most browsers, including Firefox, Chrome, Safari, Opera, Konqueror, and Internet Explorer.

Step 1 – welcome

If everything has been configured properly, you should be greeted by the installation wizard:

If you are not, there are several things that could have gone wrong.

If the connection fails completely, make sure Apache is started up and there is no firewall blocking access. If you see a blank page or some PHP code, make sure that PHP is properly installed and configured to parse files ending with the .php extension through the AddType application/x-httpd-php directive. If you see a file and directory listing instead of the installation wizard, make sure you have added index.php to the DirectoryIndex directive. If these hints do not help, check the PHP documentation at http://www.php.net/manual/en/.

This screen doesn't offer us much to configure, so just click on **Next step**.

Step 2 – PHP prerequisites

In this step, the installation wizard checks PHP-related prerequisites. If you are lucky, all will have been satisfied, and you will be greeted with all green entries:

ZABBIX	Check of pre-requisites	CURRENT VALUE	REQUIRED	
Welcome	PHP version	5.4.20	5.4.0	OK
Check of pre-requisites				
Configure DB connection	PHP option "memory_limit"	128M	128M	OK
Zabbix server details	PHP option "post_max_size"	32M	16M	OK
Pre-installation summary	PHP option "upload_max_filesize"	16M	2M	OK
Install	PHP option "max_execution_time"	600	300	OK
	PHP option "max_input_time"	600	300	OK
	PHP option "date.timezone"	Europe/Riga		OK
	PHP databases support	MySQL		OK
	PHP bcmath	on		OK

Back   Next step

If so, just click on the **Next step** button to continue to *Step 3*.

However, more often than not, one or more entries will have a red **Fail** warning listed next to them. This is where things get more interesting. Problems at this point fall into two categories: **PHP installation** or **configuration**.

Entries such as **PHP version, PHP databases support, PHP bcmath, PHP mbstring, PHP gd, PHP gd PNG/JPEG/FreeType support**, and others that are not listed as an **option** are PHP installation problems. To solve these, either install the appropriate distribution packages (sometimes called **php5-bcmath, php5-gd, php5-mysql**, and so on), or recompile PHP with the corresponding options.

PHP option "memory_limit", PHP option "post_max_size", PHP option "upload_ max_filesize", PHP option "max_execution_time", PHP option "max_input_ time", and **PHP time zone** are configuration issues that are all set in the php.ini configuration file. This file is usually located at /etc/php5 or similar for distribution packages and /usr/local/lib for PHP source installations. Set the following options:

```
memory_limit = 128M
post_max_size = 16M
max_execution_time = 300
max_input_time = 300
upload_max_filesize = 2M
```

> The code bundle for the book is also hosted on GitHub at https://github.com/PacktPublishing/Zabbix-Network-Monitoring-Second-Edition. We also have other code bundles from our rich catalog of books and videos available at https://github.com/PacktPublishing/. Check them out!

For the time zone, set the date.timezone option to a time zone that best matches your environment. The default for Zabbix is Europe/Riga, and you can see valid options at http://www.php.net/manual/en/timezones.php.

Make sure you restart Apache after changing the PHP configuration file. If you can't find php.ini, or you make changes but the installation wizard does not pick them up, create a file named test.php in the htdocs directory with only this content:

```
<?php phpinfo() ?>
```

Navigate to this file using your browser and check the value for a **Configuration File (php.ini) Path** entry—this is where you should look for php.ini.

Once everything is fixed, click on the **Next step** button to continue.

Step 3 – database access

Remember the database we created earlier? That's the information we'll supply here:

ZABBIX

Welcome

Check of pre-requisites

Configure DB connection

Zabbix server details

Pre-installation summary

Install

Configure DB connection

Please create database manually, and set the configuration parameters for connection to this database. Press "Next step" button when done.

Database type MySQL ▼

Database host localhost

Database port 0   0 - use default port

Database name zabbix

User zabbix

Password

Back   Next step

We already configured database credentials for the Zabbix server, but the Zabbix frontend uses a different configuration file. The default **Database type**, **Database host**, and **Database port** values should work for us. Set both **Database name** and **User** to zabbix. If you have forgotten the **Password**, just look it up or copy it from zabbix_server.conf. After entering the data, click on the **Next step** button. If all the information is correct, the wizard should proceed to the next step.

Step 4 – Zabbix server details

The next screen lets you specify the Zabbix server's location:

The defaults for the host and port are suitable for us, but we could benefit from filling in the **Name** field. The contents of this field will be used for page titles and a label in the upper-right corner of the Zabbix interface — this could be really handy if we had multiple Zabbix installations. Feel free to enter any name here, but for this book, we'll call the server **Zabbix One**. When you're done, it's over to the **Next step** again. The next screen is a summary of the choices made in the previous screens.

Step 5 – summary

If you left the defaults where appropriate and your database connection test was successful, it should be safe to continue by clicking on **Next step**:

Step 6 – writing the configuration file

It is quite likely that in the next screen, you will be greeted with failure:

ZABBIX

Install

Details   Cannot create the configuration file.

Unable to create the configuration file.

Welcome

Check of pre-requisites

Configure DB connection

Zabbix server details

Pre-installation summary

Install

Alternatively, you can install it manually:

1. Download the configuration file

2. Save it as "/srv/www/htdocs/zabbix/conf/zabbix.conf.php"

Back   Finish

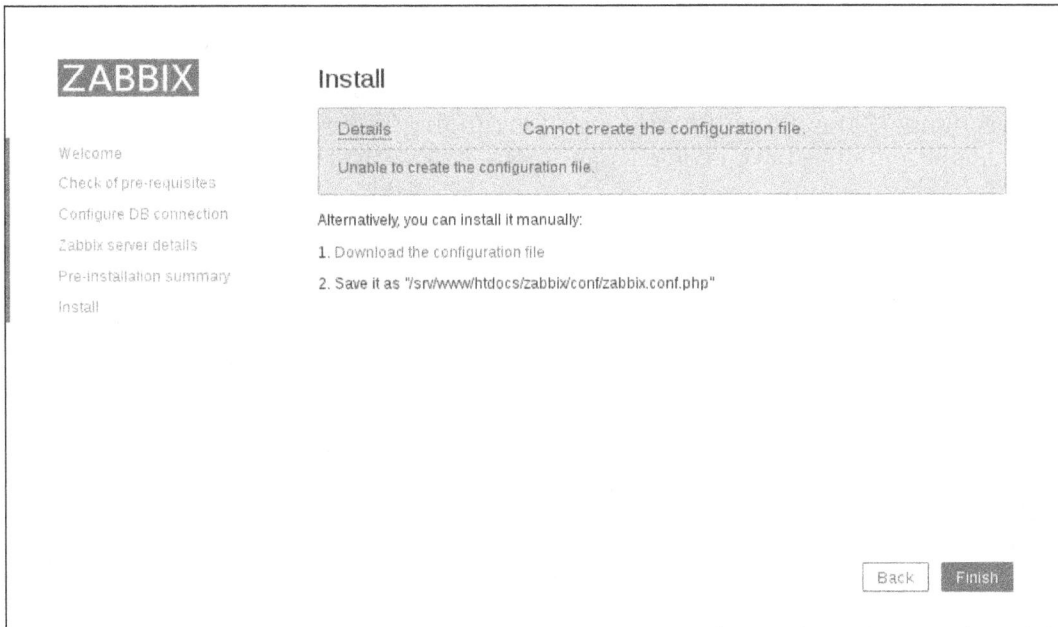

The installation wizard attempted to save the configuration file, but with the access rights that it has, it should not be possible. Previous versions of Zabbix explained two alternatives for proceeding. Unfortunately, Zabbix 3.0 has lost the explanation for one of those. The two possible solutions are as follows:

1. Click on **Download the configuration file** and manually place this file in the `htdocs/zabbix/conf` directory.

2. Make the `htdocs/zabbix/conf` directory writable by the web server user (execute as `root`). Use these commands:

    ```
    # chown <username> /path/to/htdocs/zabbix/conf
    # chmod 700 /path/to/htdocs/zabbix/conf
    ```

Obviously, we need to insert the correct username and directory in these commands. Remember, common locations are `/srv/www/htdocs` and `/usr/local/apache2/htdocs` — use the one you copied the Zabbix frontend code to. Common users are `wwwrun`, `www-data`, `nobody`, and `daemon` — you can find out which one the correct user is for your system by running this:

```
$ ps aux | grep http
```

You could also run this:

```
$ ps aux | grep apache
```

The username that most `httpd` processes are running under will be the correct one. Once the permissions have been changed, click on **Finish**. That should successfully save the configuration file.

> You can also skip the configuration wizard by copying `zabbix.conf.php.example` in the `conf` directory to `zabbix.conf.php` and editing it directly. In this case, you should manually verify that the PHP installation and configuration requirements have been met.

It is suggested that you restrict the permissions on this file afterwards to be readable only by the web server user, by issuing these commands as `root`:

```
# chmod 440 /path/to/htdocs/zabbix/conf/zabbix.conf.php
# chown root /path/to/htdocs/zabbix/conf/
```

The file contains the database password, which is best kept secret.

Step 7 – finishing the wizard

Congratulations, this is the last wizard screen, which only wants you to be friendly to it and press **Finish**:

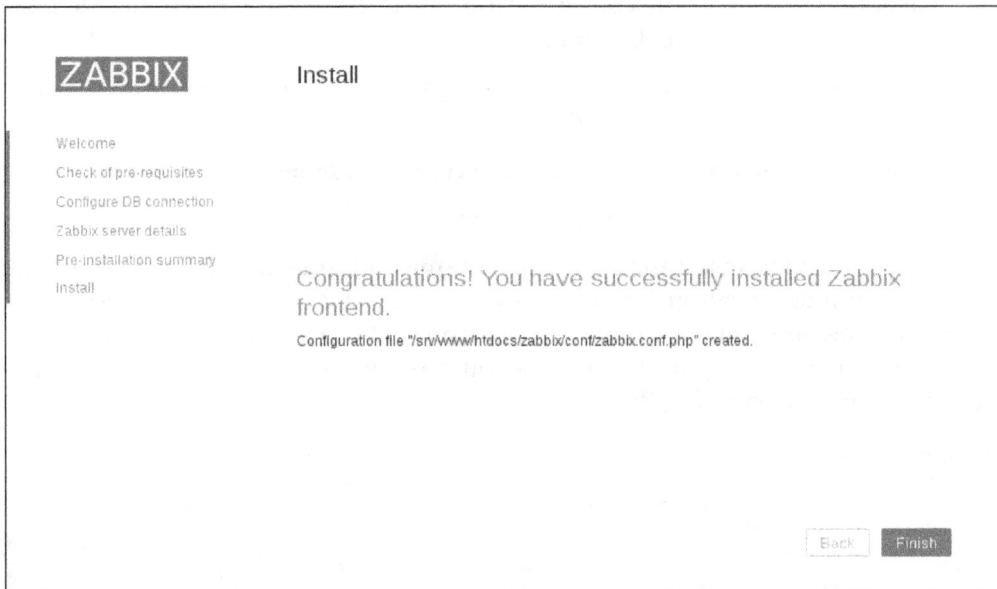

ZABBIX   Install

Welcome
Check of pre-requisites
Configure DB connection
Zabbix server details
Pre-installation summary
Install

Congratulations! You have successfully installed Zabbix frontend.

Configuration file "/srv/www/htdocs/zabbix/conf/zabbix.conf.php" created.

Back   Finish

Step 8 – logging in

Immediately after clicking on **Finish**, you should see a login form:

The Zabbix database data that we inserted previously also supplied the default username and password. The default credentials are as follows:

- **Username**: Admin
- **Password**: zabbix

That should get you to the initial frontend screen, which drops you into a quite empty dashboard:

Congratulations! The web frontend is now set up and we have logged in.

> It is possible to easily change the Zabbix frontend configuration later. The zabbix.conf.php configuration file can be edited to change database access details, the Zabbix server host and port, and the server name that we entered in the fourth step as well. Most of the parameters in that file should be self-explanatory; for example, $ZBX_SERVER_NAME will change the server name.

If you take a closer look at the upper-right corner, you'll spot something familiar — it's the server name we entered earlier in the configuration wizard. This makes it easier to distinguish this installation from other Zabbix instances, for example, if you had a testing and a production instance. Additionally, this name is also used in the page title — and thus in the tab title in most modern browsers. When multiple tabs are open, you should be able to see the instance name right there in the tab. There's no need to click on each tab individually and check the URL or upper-right corner of the Zabbix frontend:

The dashboard isn't too exciting right now, except maybe for that table, labeled **Status of Zabbix**. The same view is also available somewhere else, though — click on **Reports** and then click on **Status of Zabbix**, the very first report:

PARAMETER	VALUE	DETAILS
Zabbix server is running	Yes	localhost:10051
Number of hosts (enabled/disabled/templates)	39	0 / 1 / 38
Number of items (enabled/disabled/not supported)	0	0 / 0 / 0
Number of triggers (enabled/disabled [problem/ok])	0	0 / 0 [0 / 0]
Number of users (online)	2	1
Required server performance, new values per second	0	

Now we can concentrate on this widget. The frontend successfully sees that the Zabbix server is running and displays the host and port to which it is trying to connect. It also knows some basic things about Zabbix's configuration—there are 39 hosts configured in total. Wait, what's that? We have only set it up and have not configured anything; how can there be 39 hosts already? Let's take a closer look at the **DETAILS** column. These values correspond to the descriptions in parentheses located in the **PARAMETER** column. So, there are 0 monitored hosts, 1 that is not monitored, and 38 templates. Now that makes more sense—38 of those 39 are templates, not actual hosts. Still, there's one host that isn't monitored, what's up with that?

Click on **Configuration** and choose **Hosts**. You should see this:

NAME ▲	APPLICATIONS	ITEMS	TRIGGERS	GRAPHS	DISCOVERY	WEB
Zabbix server	Applications 11	Items 63	Triggers 42	Graphs 10	Discovery 2	Web

> The first thing to do here: click on that large **Filter** button in the middle of the page. In older versions of Zabbix, it was a very tiny button that was hard to spot. Unfortunately, the Zabbix team overshot with solving that problem—the button is now huge, and all filters are open by default. We will discuss and use filters later. For now, whenever you see a huge filter preceding the information we came for, just close it.

So, there it is. It turns out that the default Zabbix database already has one server configured: the local Zabbix server. It is disabled by default, as indicated in the **Status of Zabbix** screen and here by the **Disabled** string in the **STATUS** column.

> There's a lot of technical detail in the Zabbix online manual at https://www.zabbix.com/documentation/3.0/.

Summary

In this chapter, we set up a fresh Zabbix installation consisting of a database, a server, and an agent daemon, all running on the same machine. We also installed and configured the Zabbix web frontend, based on PHP, to access the database.

We will use the results of this work in all of our future chapters. To see how we can get from a monitored metric to an alert e-mail, we'll go through a simple scenario in the next chapter—think of it as sort of a quick start guide.

2
Getting Your First Notification

We have now installed Zabbix, but it's not doing much—this is what we'd expect. Software that starts doing something on its own would probably be a bit undesirable, at least for now. The promise of Zabbix is to inform you about problems as soon as possible, preferably before your users and management notice them. But how do we get data, where do we place it, and how do we define what a problem is? We will try to quickly get Zabbix working and alerting us on a single monitored item, which is the most common scenario. Before we can tell Zabbix who to send notifications to, we will have to explore and use some basic Zabbix concepts. They are as follows:

- Navigating around the frontend
- Creating a host and item (the Zabbix term for a monitored metric)
- Looking at the gathered data and finding out how to get it graphed
- Defining a problem threshold with a trigger
- Telling Zabbix that it should send an e-mail when this threshold is exceeded
- Causing a problem in order to actually receive the notification

Exploring the frontend

Although we have already looked at some data provided by the frontend, we should get a bit more familiar with it before attempting some more configuration tasks.

Configuration steps will be followed by verifying results in the **Monitoring** section. We will then explain some generic **item** terms used in Zabbix and their uses. Items, being the basis of information gathering, have a fair amount of configuration possibilities.

In your browser, open Zabbix's root URL (`http://<server_ip_or_name>/zabbix`), and log in again if you have been logged out. You should now see a pretty empty dashboard with little information:

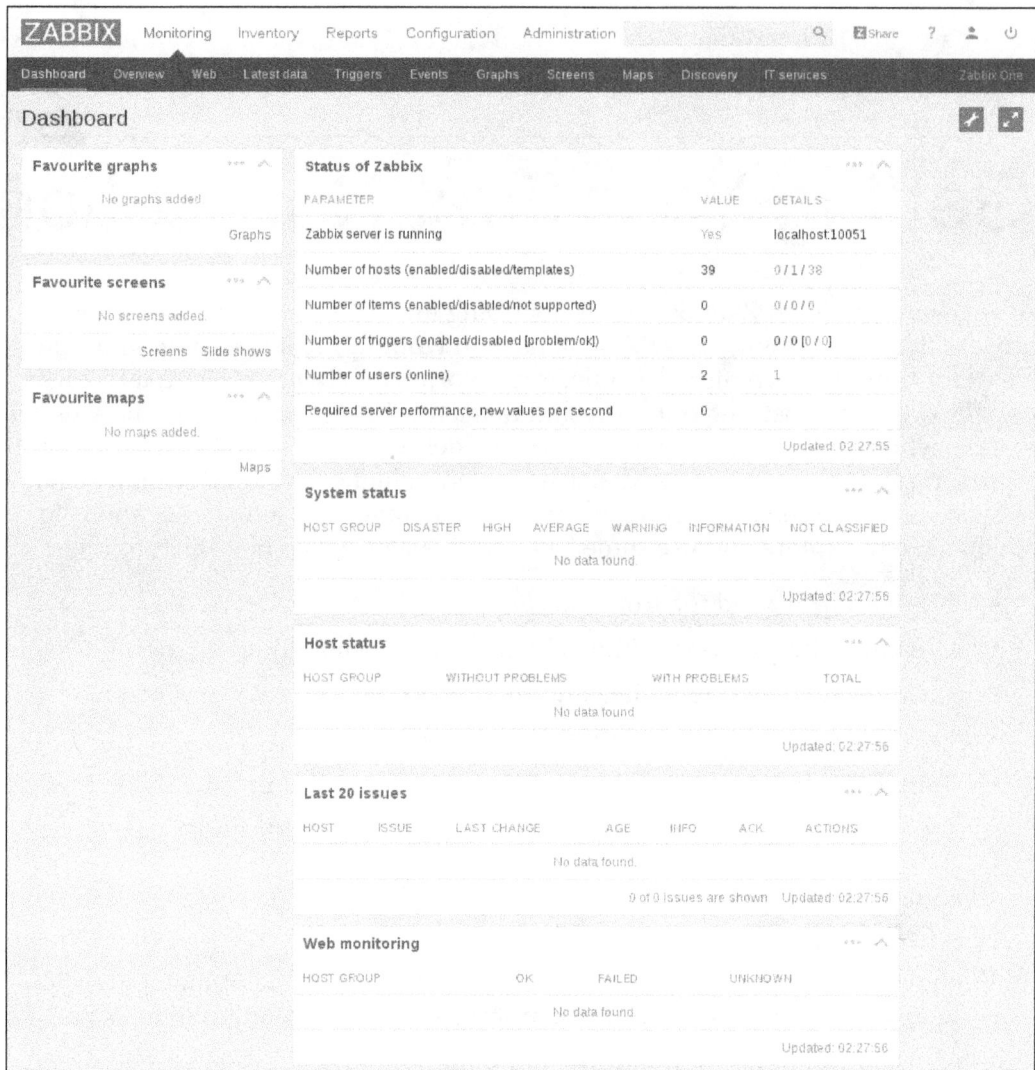

| ZABBIX | Monitoring | Inventory | Reports | Configuration | Administration | | 🔍 | 🔗 Share | ? | 👤 | ⏻ |

| Dashboard | Overview | Web | Latest data | Triggers | Events | Graphs | Screens | Maps | Discovery | IT services | Zabbix One |

Dashboard

Favourite graphs ••• ∧

No graphs added

Graphs

Favourite screens ••• ∧

No screens added

Screens   Slide shows

Favourite maps ••• ∧

No maps added

Maps

Status of Zabbix ••• ∧

PARAMETER	VALUE	DETAILS
Zabbix server is running	Yes	localhost:10051
Number of hosts (enabled/disabled/templates)	39	0 / 1 / 38
Number of items (enabled/disabled/not supported)	0	0 / 0 / 0
Number of triggers (enabled/disabled [problem/ok])	0	0 / 0 [0 / 0]
Number of users (online)	2	1
Required server performance, new values per second	0	

Updated: 02:27:55

System status ••• ∧

HOST GROUP	DISASTER	HIGH	AVERAGE	WARNING	INFORMATION	NOT CLASSIFIED

No data found

Updated: 02:27:56

Host status ••• ∧

HOST GROUP	WITHOUT PROBLEMS	WITH PROBLEMS	TOTAL

No data found

Updated: 02:27:56

Last 20 issues ••• ∧

HOST	ISSUE	LAST CHANGE	AGE	INFO	ACK	ACTIONS

No data found

0 of 0 issues are shown   Updated: 02:27:56

Web monitoring ••• ∧

HOST GROUP	OK	FAILED	UNKNOWN

No data found

Updated: 02:27:56

Click on the entries of the top menu bar and observe how the lower menu bar shows subentries of the chosen category. Click on **Configuration**, and then click on **Host groups** in the second-level menu—here, all configured host groups are shown. You will be using these menus a lot, so in the future, we'll refer to the action we just performed as **Configuration | Host groups**. (Whenever you see such a notation, the first is the main category, and the second is the entry under it.)

As you can see in the following screenshot, there are five main categories, and they are as follows :

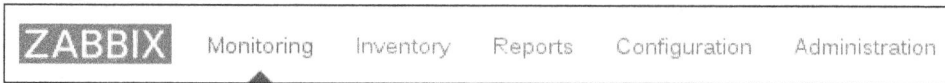

- **Monitoring**: This category contains most of the monitoring-related pages. You will be able to view data, problems, and graphs here.
- **Inventory**: Here, inventory data for monitored systems can be viewed.
- **Reports**: This section contains some simple reports.
- **Configuration**: Setting up everything related to the monitoring of systems, parameters, notification sending, and so on happens here.
- **Administration**: This section allows you to set up more of the Zabbix internals, including authentication methods, users, permissions, and global Zabbix configuration.

The user profile

Before we venture deeper into these categories, it might be worth visiting the profile section—see the person-like icon in the upper-right corner:

Clicking on it should open your profile:

Here, you can set some options concerning your user account, for example, changing the password, the frontend language, or the frontend theme. As we will be using an **English (en_GB)** frontend, I suggested you to leave that at the default. Previous Zabbix versions shipped with four different themes, but that has been reduced in Zabbix 3.0; now, there are only the *Blue* and *Dark* themes. We'll stick with the default theme, but both of the themes shipped with Zabbix 3.0 seem to be visually pretty.

Notice that you can find out the user account you are currently connected as by moving the mouse cursor over the profile icon in the upper-right corner. A tooltip will show your username, as well as name and surname, as configured in the user profile. When you are not logged in, no profile icon is shown.

There are two options related to logging in: **Auto-login**, which will automatically log the user in using a cookie saved by their browser, and **Auto-logout**. By default, **Auto-login** should be enabled, and we will not change these options.

> At the time of writing this, any background operation in the frontend will reset the **Auto-logout** timer, essentially making it useless. You can follow the issue ZBX-8051 in the Zabbix issue tracker, described in more detail in *Appendix B, Being Part of the Community*.

We won't change the **URL** option at present, but we'll discuss the benefits of setting a custom default URL for a particular user later. The **Refresh** option sets the period in seconds after which some pages in the frontend will refresh automatically to display new data. It might be beneficial to increase this parameter for huge screens, which we do not yet have.

The **Rows per page** option will limit the amount of entities displayed at a time. In larger installations, it might be useful to increase it, but making it too large can negatively affect performance of the frontend.

Let's make another change here—switch over to the **Messaging** tab:

User	Media	Messaging

Frontend messaging ☐

Message timeout (seconds) 60

Play sound Once ▼

Trigger severity ☐ Recovery   alarm_ok ▼   Play   Stop

☐ Not classified   no_sound ▼   Play   Stop

☐ Information   alarm_information ▼   Play   Stop

☐ Warning   alarm_warning ▼   Play   Stop

☐ Average   alarm_average ▼   Play   Stop

☐ High   alarm_high ▼   Play   Stop

☐ Disaster   alarm_disaster ▼   Play   Stop

Update   Cancel

It allows you to configure frontend messages. For now, just mark the **Frontend messaging** option to enable them and change **Message timeout (seconds)** to 180. We will discuss what the various options do later in this chapter, when the messages start to appear.

> Verify that all the checkboxes in the **Trigger severity** section are marked: if you saved the user profile before, they might have a different default state.

After you have changed the theme and enabled frontend messages, click on the **Update** button.

Monitoring quickstart

Now that we have a basic understanding of the frontend navigation, it's time to look at the basis for data gathering in Zabbix—items. In general, anything you want to gather data about will eventually go into an *item*.

> An item in Zabbix is a configuration entity that holds information on gathered metrics. It is the very basis of information flowing into Zabbix, and without items, nothing can be retrieved. An item does not hold any information on thresholds—that functionality is covered by triggers.

If items are so important in Zabbix, we should create some. After all, if no data retrieval is possible without items, we can't monitor anything without them. To get started with item configuration, open **Configuration | Hosts**. If it's not selected by default, choose Zabbix servers in the **Group** drop-down menu (in the top-right corner). This is a location we will visit quite a lot, as it provides easy access to other entity configurations, including **Items** and **Triggers**. Let's figure out what's what in this area. The most interesting functionality is the host list:

Zabbix server   Applications 13   Items 77   Triggers 43   Graphs 12   Discovery 2   Web 1

Primarily, it provides access to host details in the very first column, but that's not all. The usefulness of this screen comes from the other columns, which not only provide access to elements that are associated with hosts but also list the count of those elements. Further down the host entry, we can see a quick overview of the most important host configuration parameters as well as status information, which we will explore in more detail later:

INTERFACE	TEMPLATES	STATUS	AVAILABILITY	AGENT ENCRYPTION INFO
127.0.0.1: 10050	Template App MySQL, Template App Zabbix Server, Template OS Linux (Template App Zabbix Agent)	Disabled	ZBX SNMP JMX IPMI NONE	

We came here looking for items, so click on **Items** next to the Zabbix server. You should see a list similar to the one in the following screenshot:

NAME ▲	TRIGGERS	KEY	INTERVAL	HISTORY	TRENDS	TYPE	APPLICATIONS	STATUS	INFO
Template App Zabbix Agent: Agent ping	Triggers 1	agent.ping	1m	7d	365d	Zabbix agent	Zabbix agent	Enabled	
Template OS Linux: Available memory	Triggers 1	vm.memory.size[available]	1m	7d	365d	Zabbix agent	Memory	Enabled	
Template OS Linux: Checksum of /etc/passwd	Triggers 1	vfs.file.cksum[/etc/passwd]	1h	7d	365d	Zabbix agent	Security	Enabled	
Template OS Linux: Context switches per second		system.cpu.switches	1m	7d	365d	Zabbix agent	CPU, Performance	Enabled	

Note the method we used to reach the items list for a particular host—we used convenience links for host elements, which is a fairly easy way to get there and the reason why we will use **Configuration | Hosts** often.

Back to what we were after, we can see a fairly long list of already existing items. But wait, didn't the Zabbix status screen that we saw in the first screenshot claim there's a single host and no items? That's clearly wrong! Return to **Reports | Status of Zabbix** (or **Monitoring | Dashboard**, which shows the same data). It indeed shows zero items. Now move the mouse cursor over the text that reads **Number of items (enabled/disabled/not supported)**, and take a look at the tooltip:

Status of Zabbix		
PARAMETER	VALUE	DETAILS
Zabbix server is running	No	localhost:10051
Number of hosts (enabled/disabled/templates)	39	0 / 1 / 38
Number of items (enabled/disabled/not supported)	0	0 / 0 / 0
Number of triggers (enabled/disabled [problen Only items assigned to enabled hosts are counted	0	0 / 0 [0 / 0]
Number of users (online)	2	1
Required server performance, new values per second	0	

Aha! so it counts only those items that are assigned to enabled hosts. As this example host, Zabbix server, is disabled, it's now clear why the Zabbix status report shows zero items. This is handy to remember later, once you try to evaluate a more complex configuration.

Creating a host

Instead of using this predefined host configuration, we want to understand how items work. But items can't exist in an empty space—each item has to be attached to a host.

> In Zabbix, a host is a logical entity that groups items. The definition of what a host is can be freely adapted to specific environments and situations. Zabbix in no way limits this choice; thus, a host can be a network switch, a physical server, a virtual machine, or a website.

If a host is required to attach items to, then we must create one. Head over to **Configuration | Hosts** and click on the **Create host** button, located in the top-right corner. You will be presented with a host creation screen. This time, we won't concern ourselves with the details, so let's input only some relevant information:

- **Name**: Enter A test host.

- **Groups**: Select **Linux servers** from the right-hand listbox, named **Other groups**; press the ◂ button to add this group. Then, select Zabbix servers from the **In groups** listbox and press the ▸ button to remove our new host from this predefined group.

> Why did we have to select a group for this host? All permissions are assigned to host groups, not individual hosts, and thus, a host must belong to at least one group. We will cover permissions in more detail in *Chapter 5, Managing Hosts, Users and Permissions*.

The fields that we changed for our host should look as follows:

Host name	A test host
Visible name	

Groups	In groups		Other groups
	Linux servers	◂ ▸	Database servers Discovered hosts Hypervisors Network devices Templates UPS devices Virtual machines Web servers Windows servers Zabbix servers

When you are ready, click on the **Add** button at the bottom.

Creating an item

So, we have created our very own first host. But given that items are the basis of all the data, it's probably of little use right now. To give it more substance, we should create items, so select **Linux servers** from the **Groups** dropdown, and then click on **Items** next to the host we just created, A test host. This host has no items to list—click on the **Create item** button in the upper-right corner.

There's a form, vaguely resembling the one for host creation, so let's fill in some values:

- **Name**: Enter CPU load into this field. This is how the item will be named — basically, the name that you will use to refer to the item in most places.

- **Key**: The value in this field will be system.cpu.load. This is the "technical name" of the item that identifies what information it gathers.

- **Type of information**: Choose Numeric (float). This defines which formatting and type the incoming data will have.

After filling in all the required information, you will be presented with the following screen:

Name	CPU load
Type	Zabbix agent ▼
Key	system.cpu.load Select
Host interface	127.0.0.1 : 10050 ▼
Type of information	Numeric (float) ▼

We will look at the other defaults in more detail later, so click on the **Add** button at the bottom.

> More information on item keys is provided in *Chapter 3, Monitoring with Zabbix Agents and Basic Protocols.*

You should now see your new item in the list. But we are interested in the associated data, so navigate to **Monitoring | Latest data**. Notice the filter that takes up half the page? This time, we will want to use it right away.

Starting with Zabbix 2.4, the **Latest data** page does not show any data by default for performance reasons; thus, we have to set the filter first:

		Filter ▲		
Host groups	type here to search	Select	Name	
Hosts	type here to search	Select	Show items without data	☑
Application		Select	Show details	☐
		Filter Reset		

In the **Filter**, type `test` in the **Hosts** field. Our new host should appear. Click on it, then click on the **Filter** button. Below the filter, expand the **- other -** section if it's collapsed. You might have to wait for up to a minute to pass after saving the item, and then you should see that this newly created item has already gathered some data:

NAME ▲	LAST CHECK	LAST VALUE
- other - (1 Item)		
CPU load	2016-02-16 20:44:55	0.05

What should you do if you don't see any entries at all? This usually means that data has not been gathered, which can happen for a variety of reasons. If this is the case, check for these common causes:

* Did you enter item configuration exactly as in the screenshot? Check the item key and type of information.

* Are both the agent and the server running? You can check this by executing the following as `root`:

```
# netstat -ntpl | grep zabbix
```

* The output should list both the server and agent daemons running on the correct ports:

```
tcp        0       0 0.0.0.0:10050          0.0.0.0:*
            LISTEN          23569/zabbix_agentd
tcp        0       0 0.0.0.0:10051          0.0.0.0:*
            LISTEN          23539/zabbix_server
```

If any one of them is missing, make sure to start it.

* Can the server connect to the agent? You can verify this by executing the following from the Zabbix server:

```
$ telnet localhost 10050
```

If the connection fails, it could mean that either the agent is not running or some restrictive firewall setting is preventing the connection. In some cases, SELinux might prevent that connection, too.

If the connection succeeds but is immediately closed, then the IP address that the agent receives the connection from does not match the one specified in `zabbix_agentd.conf` configuration file for the `Server` directive. On some distributions, this can be caused by IPv6 being used by default, so you should try to add another comma-delimited value to the same line for the IPv6 localhost representation to this directive, `::1`.

The Zabbix server reads into cache all the information on items to monitor every minute by default. This means that configuration changes such as adding a new item might show an effect in the data collected after one minute. This interval can be tweaked in `zabbix_server.conf` by changing the `CacheUpdateFrequency` parameter.

Once data starts arriving, you might see no value in the **Change** column. This means you moved to this display quickly, and the item managed to gather a single value only; thus, there's no change yet. If that is the case, waiting a bit should result in the page automatically refreshing (look at the page title—remember the 30-second refresh we left untouched in the user profile?), and the **Change** column will be populated. So, we are now monitoring a single value: the UNIX system load. Data is automatically retrieved and stored in the database. If you are not familiar with the concept, it might be a good idea to read the overview at `https://en.wikipedia.org/wiki/Load_(computing)`.

Introducing simple graphs

If you went away to read about system load, several minutes should have passed. Now is a good time to look at another feature in Zabbix—**Graphs**. Graphs are freely available for any monitored numeric item, without any additional configuration.

You should still be on the **Latest data** screen with the **CPU load** item visible, so click on the link named **Graph**. You'll get something like this:

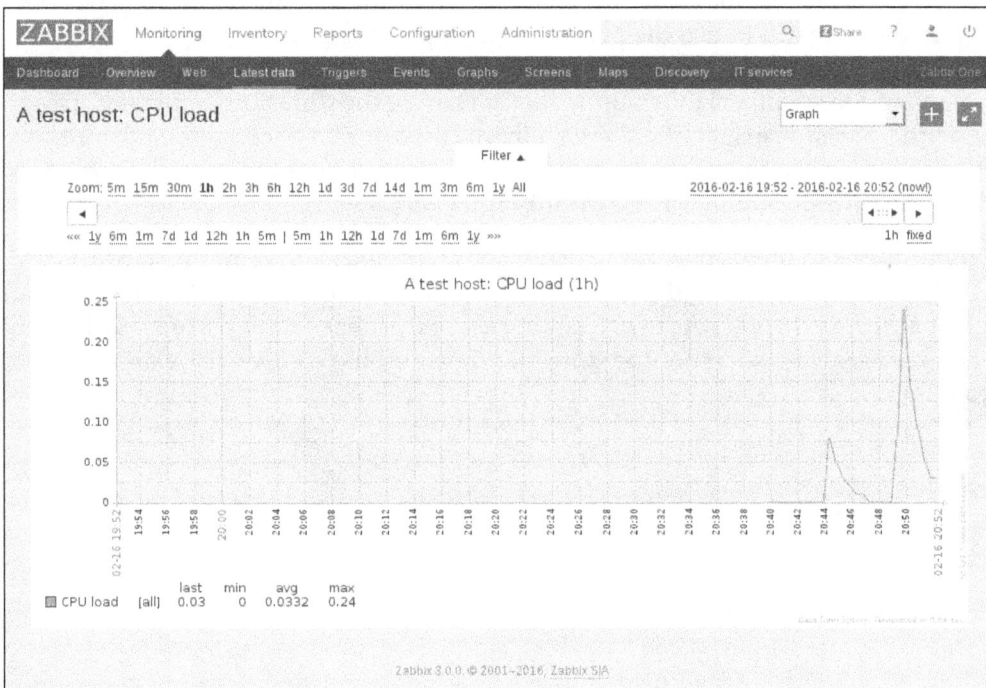

While you will probably get less data, unless reading about system load took you more than an hour, your screen should look very similar overall. Let's explore some basic graph controls.

[🔆 If you don't see any data even after several minutes have passed, try dragging the scrollbar above the graph to the rightmost position.]

The **Zoom** controls in the upper-left corner allow you to quickly switch the displayed period. Clicking on any of the entries will make the graph show data for the chosen duration. At first, Zabbix is a bit confused about us having so little data; it thus shows all the available time periods here. As more data is gathered, only the relevant periods will be shown, and longer zoom periods will gradually become available.

Zoom: 5m 15m 30m **1h** 2h 3h 6h 12h 1d 3d 7d 14d 1m 3m 6m 1y All

◄

«« 1y 6m 1m 7d 1d 12h 1h 5m | 5m 1h 12h 1d 7d 1m 6m 1y »»

Below these controls are options that seek through time periods; clicking on them will move the displayed period by the exact time period that was clicked on.

The *scrollbar* at the top allows you to make small changes to the displayed period: drag it to the left (and notice the period at the top of the graph changing) and then release, and the graph is updated to reflect the period changes. Notice the arrows at both ends of the scrollbar: they allow you to change the duration displayed. Drag these with your mouse just like the scrollbar. You can also click on the buttons at both ends for exact adjustments. Using these buttons moves the period back and forth by the time period that we currently have displayed.

The date entries in the upper-right corner show the start and end times for the currently displayed data, and they also provide calendar widgets that allow a wider range of arbitrary period settings. Clicking on one of these time periods will open a calendar, where you can enter the time and date and have either the start or end time set to this choice:

2016-02-16 20:05 - 2016-02-16 21:05 (now!)

	◄		2016		►	
	◄		February		►	
M	T	W	T	F	S	S
1	2	3	4	5	6	7
8	9	10	11	12	13	14
15	16	17	18	19	20	21
22	23	24	25	26	27	28
29	1	2	3	4	5	6
7	8	9	10	11	12	13

Time 21 : 05

Now   Done

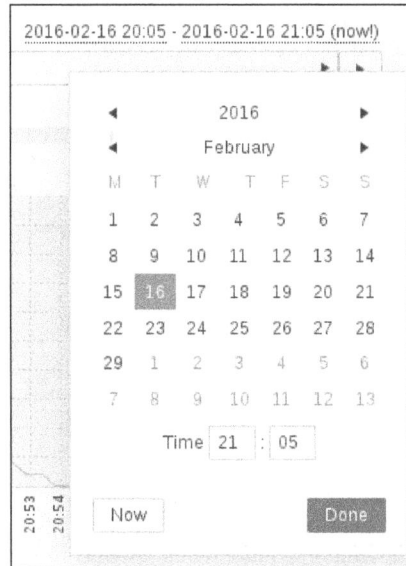

Try entering a time in the past for the starting (leftmost) calendar. This will move the displayed period without changing its length. This is great if we are interested in a time period of a specific length, but what if we want to look at a graph for the previous day, from 08:30 till 17:00? For this, the control **(fixed)** in the lower-right corner of the scrollbar will help. Click on it once—it changes to **(dynamic)**. If you now use calendar widgets to enter the start or end time for the displayed period, only this edge of the period will be changed.

For example, if a 1-hour period from 10:00 to 11:00 is displayed, setting the first calendar to 09:00 while in **(fixed)** mode will display the period from 09:00 till 10:00. If the same is done while in **(dynamic)** mode, a two-hour period from 09:00 till 11:00 will be displayed. The end edge of the period is not moved in the second case.

> Depending on the time at which you are looking at the graphs, some areas of the graph might have a gray background. This is the time outside of working hours, as defined in Zabbix. We will explore this in more detail later.

Clicking and dragging over the graph area will zoom in to the selected period once the mouse button is released. This is handy for a quick drilldown to some problematic or interesting period:

The yellow area denotes the time period we selected by clicking, holding down the mouse button, and dragging over the graph area. When we release the mouse button, the graph is zoomed to the selected period.

> The graph period can't be shorter than one minute in Zabbix. Attempting to set it to a smaller value will do nothing. Before version 3.0, the shortest possible time period was one hour.

Creating triggers

Now that we have an item successfully gathering data, we can look at it and verify whether it is reporting as expected (in our case, that the system is not overloaded). Sitting and staring at a single parameter would make for a very boring job. Doing that with thousands of parameters doesn't sound too entertaining, so we are going to create a trigger. In Zabbix, a trigger is an entry containing an expression to automatically recognize problems with monitored items.

> An item alone does nothing more than collect the data. To define thresholds and things that are considered a problem, we have to use triggers.

Navigate to **Configuration | Hosts,** click on **Triggers** next to **A test host,** and click on **Create trigger.**

Here, only two fields need to be filled in:

- **Name**: Enter `CPU load too high on A test host for last 3 minutes`
- **Expression**: Enter `{A Test Host:system.cpu.load.avg(180)}>1`

Name	CPU load too high on A test host for last 3 minutes	
Expression	{A Test Host:system.cpu.load.avg(180)}>1	Add

It is important to get the expression correct down to the last symbol. Once done, click on the **Add** button at the bottom. Don't worry about understanding the exact trigger syntax yet; we will get to that later.

Notice how our trigger expressions refer to the item key, not the name. Whenever you have to reference an item inside Zabbix, it will be done by the item key.

The trigger list should be now displayed, with a single trigger—the one we just created. Let's take a look at what we just added: open **Monitoring | Triggers**. You should see our freshly added trigger, hopefully already updated, with a green **OK** flashing in the **STATUS** column:

SEVERITY	STATUS	INFO	LAST CHANGE ▼	AGE	ACK	HOST	NAME
Not classified	OK		2016-02-16 22:28:55	13s	Yes	A test host	CPU load too high on A test host for last 3 minutes

You might see **PROBLEM** in the **STATUS** field. This means exactly what the trigger name says—the `CPU load too high on A test host for last 3 minutes`.

Notice the big filter?

Filter ▲		
Triggers status	Recent problem	Filter by application
Acknowledge status	Any	Filter by host inventory
Events	Hide all	
Minimum trigger severity	Not classified	Show hosts in maintenance
Age less than	14 days	Show details
Filter by name		

Filter Reset

We can filter displayed triggers, but why is our **OK** trigger displayed even though the default filter says **Recent problem**? The thing is, by default, Zabbix shows triggers that have recently changed their state with the status indicator flashing. Such triggers show for 30 minutes, and then they obey normal filtering rules. Click on **Filter** to close the filter. We will explore this filter in more detail later.

You could take a break now and notice how, in 30 minutes, there are no triggers displayed. With the filter set to only show problems, this screen becomes quite useful for a quick overview of all issues concerning monitored hosts. While that sounds much better than staring at plain data, we would still want to get some more to-the-point notifications delivered.

Configuring e-mail parameters

The most common notification method is e-mail. Whenever something interesting happens in Zabbix, some action can be taken, and we will set it up so that an e-mail is sent to us. Before we decide when and what should be sent, we have to tell Zabbix how to send it.

To configure the parameters for e-mail sending, open **Administration | Media types** and click on **Email** in the **NAME** column. You'll get a simple form to fill in with appropriate values for your environment:

Name	Email
Type	Email
SMTP server	mail.company.com
SMTP server port	25
SMTP helo	company.com
SMTP email	zabbix@company.com
Connection security	None STARTTLS SSL/TLS
Authentication	None Normal password
Enabled	

Update Clone Delete Cancel

Change the **SMTP server**, **SMTP helo**, and **SMTP email** fields to use a valid e-mail server. The **SMTP email** address will be used as the **From address**, so make sure it's set to something your server will accept. If needed, configure the SMTP authentication, and then click on the **Update** button.

We have configured the server to send e-mail messages and set what the **From address** should be, but it still doesn't know the e-mail addresses that our defined users have, which is required to send alerts to them. To assign an e-mail address to a user, open **Administration | Users**. You should see only two users: **Admin** and **Guest**. Click on **Admin** in the **ALIAS** column and switch to the **Media** tab:

User	Media	Permissions					
	Media	TYPE	SEND TO	WHEN ACTIVE	USE IF SEVERITY	STATUS	ACTION
		Add					

Update Delete Cancel

Click on the **Add** button:

Type	Email ▼
Send to		
When active	1-7,00:00-24:00
Use if severity	▣ Not classified ▣ Information ▣ Warning ▣ Average ▣ High ▣ Disaster
Enabled	▣

Add Cancel

The only thing you have to enter here is a valid e-mail address in the **Send to** textbox—preferably yours. Once you are done, click on **Add** and then **Update** in the user properties screen.

That finishes the very basic configuration required to send out notifications through e-mail for this user.

Creating an action

And now, it's time to tie all this together and tell Zabbix that we want to receive e-mail notifications when our test box is under heavy load.

Things that tell the Zabbix server to do something upon certain conditions are called **actions**. An action has three main components:

- **Main configuration**: This allows us to set up general options, such as the e-mail subject and the message.

- **Action operations**: These specify what exactly has to be done, including who to send the message to and what message to send.

- **Action conditions**: These allow us to specify when this action is used and when operations are performed. Zabbix allows us to set many detailed conditions, including hosts, host groups, time, specific problems (triggers) and their severity, as well as others.

To configure actions, open **Configuration | Actions** and click on **Create action**. A form is presented that lets you configure preconditions and the action to take:

Action	Conditions	Operations

Name	
Default subject	{TRIGGER.STATUS}: {TRIGGER.NAME}
Default message	Trigger: {TRIGGER.NAME} Trigger status: {TRIGGER.STATUS} Trigger severity: {TRIGGER.SEVERITY} Trigger URL: {TRIGGER.URL} Item values: 1. {ITEM.NAME1} ({HOST.NAME1}:{ITEM.KEY1}): {ITEM.VALUE1}
Recovery message	
Enabled	

Add   Cancel

First, enter a **NAME** for our new action, such as Test action, and check the **Recovery message** checkbox. Next, we should define the operation to perform, so switch to the **Operations** tab. In the **Operation** tab, insert 3600 in **Default operation step duration**, as shown in the following screenshot:

Default operation step duration	3600	(minimum 60 seconds)			
Action operations	STEPS New	DETAILS	START IN	DURATION (SEC)	ACTION

In here, click on **New** in the **Action operations** block. This will open the **Operation details** block:

In the **Send to Users** section, click on the **Add** control. In the resulting popup, click on the **Admin** user. Now, locate the **Add** control for the **Operation details** block. This can be a bit confusing as the page has four controls or buttons called **Add** right now. The correct one is highlighted here:

Click on the highlighted **Add** control. Congratulations! You have just configured the simplest possible action, so click on the **Add** button in the **Action** block.

Information flow in Zabbix

We have now configured various things in the Zabbix frontend, including data gathering (**Item**), threshold definition (**Trigger**), and instructions on what to do if a threshold is exceeded (**Action**). But how does it all work together? The flow of information between Zabbix entities can be non-obvious at first glance. Let's look at a schematic showing how the pieces go together:

In our Zabbix server installation, we created a host (A test host), which contains an item (CPU load). A trigger references this item. Whenever the trigger expression matches the current item value, the trigger switches to the **PROBLEM** state. When it ceases to match, it switches back to the **OK** state. Each time the trigger changes its state, an event is generated. The event contains details of the trigger state change: when it happened and what the new state is. When configuring an action, we can add various conditions so that only some events are acted upon. In our case, we did not add any, so all events will be matched. Each action also contains operations, which define what exactly has to be done. In the end, some operation is actually carried out, which usually happens outside of the Zabbix server, such as sending an e-mail.

A trigger can also be in the **UNKNOWN** state. This happens if there is not enough data to determine the current state. As an example, computing the average value for the past 5 minutes when there's no data for the past 10 minutes will make the trigger go into the **UNKNOWN** state. Events that cause a change to or from the **UNKNOWN** state do not match normal action conditions.

Let's create some load

Right, so we configured e-mail sending. But it's not so interesting until we actually receive some notifications. Let's increase the load on our test system. In the console, launch this:

```
$ cat /dev/urandom | md5sum
```

This grabs a pseudorandom, never-ending character stream and calculates its MD5 checksum, so system load should increase as a result. You can observe the outcome as a graph—navigate to **Monitoring | Latest data** and click on **Graph** for our single item again:

Notice how the system load has climbed. If your test system can cope with such a process really well, it might not be enough—in such a case, you can try running multiple such MD5 checksum calculation processes simultaneously.

Allow **3 minutes** to pass and there should be a popup in the upper-right corner, accompanied by a sound alert:

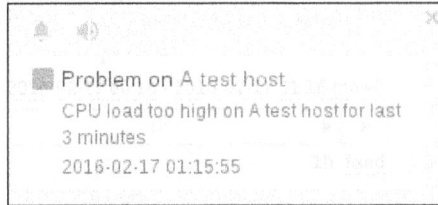

There is one of the frontend messages we enabled earlier in our user profile. Let's look at what is shown in the message window:

- The small grey rectangle ■ represents trigger severity. For recovery messages, it is green. We will discuss triggers in *Chapter 6, Detecting Problems with Triggers*.
- The first link leads to the **Monitoring | Triggers** page, displaying the current problems for the host that are causing the message.
- The second link leads to the **Monitoring | Events** page, displaying the problem history for the trigger in question. In this case, it is wrapped in two lines.

The third link leads to the event details, displaying more information about this particular occurrence.

The window itself can be repositioned vertically, but not horizontally — just drag it by the title bar. At the top of the window, there are three buttons:

These buttons also have tooltips to remind us what they do, which is as follows:

- The snooze button ■ silences the alarm sound that is currently being played.
- The mute/unmute ■ button allows to disable/enable all sounds.
- The clear button ✕ clears the currently visible messages. A problem that is cleared this way will not show up later unless it is resolved and then happens again.

The frontend messaging is useful as it provides:

- Notifications of new and resolved problems when you aren't explicitly looking at a list of current issues
- Sound alarms
- Quick access to problem details

Now is a good time to revisit the configuration options of these frontend messages. Open the profile again by clicking on the link in the upper-right corner, and switch to the **Messaging** tab:

Here is what these parameters mean:

- **Frontend messaging**: This enables/disables messaging for the current user.
- **Message timeout (seconds)**: This is used to specify how long a message should be shown. It affects the message itself, although it may affect the sound alarm as well.
- **Play sound**: This dropdown has the options **Once**, **10 seconds**, and **Message timeout**. The first one will play the whole sound once. The second one will play the sound for 10 seconds, looping if necessary. The third will loop the sound for as long as the message is shown.

- **Trigger severity**: This lets you limit messages based on trigger severity (see *Chapter 6, Detecting Problems with Triggers*, for more information on triggers). Unmarking a checkbox will not notify you about that specific severity at all. If you want to get the message but not the sound alert, choose no_sound from the dropdown.

> Adding new sounds is possible by copying .wav files to the audio subdirectory in the frontend directory.

Previously, when configuring frontend messaging, we set the message timeout to 180 seconds. The only reason was to give us enough time to explore the popup when it first appeared; it is not a requirement for using this feature.

Now, let's open **Monitoring | Triggers**. We should see the CPU load too high on A test host for last 3 minutes trigger visible with a red, flashing **PROBLEM** text in the **STATUS** column:

SEVERITY	STATUS	INFO	LAST CHANGE ▼	AGE	ACK	HOST	NAME
Not classified	PROBLEM		2016-02-17 01:27:25	5m 54s	No 3	A test host	CPU load too high on A test host for last 3 minutes

> The flashing indicates that a trigger has recently changed state, which we just made it do with that increased system load.

However, if you have a new e-mail notification, you should already be aware of this state change before opening **Monitoring | Triggers**. If all went as expected, you should have received an e-mail informing you about the problem, so check your e-mail client if you haven't yet. There should be a message with the subject **PROBLEM: CPU load too high on A test host for last 3 minutes**.

Did the e-mail fail to arrive? This is most often caused by some misconfiguration in the mail delivery chain preventing the message from passing. If possible, check your e-mail server's log files as well as network connectivity and spam filters. Going to **Reports | Action** log might reveal a helpful error message.

You can stop all MD5 checksum calculation processes now with a simple *Ctrl + C*. The trigger should then change status to **OK**, though you should allow at least the configured item interval of 30 seconds to pass.

Again, check your e-mail: there should be another message, this time informing you that it's alright now, having the subject **OK: CPU load too high on A test host for last 3 minutes**.

Congratulations, you have set up all required configuration to receive alerts whenever something goes wrong as well as when things go back to normal. Let's recall what we did and learned:

- We created a host. Hosts are monitored device representations in Zabbix that can have items attached.

- We also created an item, which is a basic way of obtaining information about a Zabbix system. Remember: the unique item identifier is key, which is also the string specifying what data will actually be gathered. A host was required to attach this item to.

- We explored a simple graph for the item that was immediately available without any configuration. The easy-to-use time-period selection controls allowed us to view any period and quickly zoom in for drilldown analysis.

- Having data already is an achievement in itself, but defining what a problem is frees us from manually trying to understand a huge number of values. That's where triggers come in. They contain expressions that define thresholds.

- Having a list of problems instead of raw data is a step forward, but it would still require someone looking at the list. We'd prefer being notified instead — that's what actions are for. We were able to specify who should be notified and when.

Basic item configuration

We rushed through the configuration of our simple item, so you might have gotten curious about the parameters we didn't change or talk about. Let's take a quick look at what can be monitored and what we can configure for each item.

Zabbix can monitor quite a wide range of system characteristics. Functionally, we can split them into categories, while technically, each method used corresponds to an item type.

Monitoring categories

Let's take a look at the generic categories that we can keep an eye on. Of course, this is not an exhaustive list of things to monitor — consider this as an example subset of interesting parameters. You'll soon discover many more areas to add in your Zabbix configuration.

Availability

While the simplified example we started with (the unlucky administrator in a party—remember him?) might not frighten many, there are more nightmare scenarios available than we'd want to think about. Various services can die without a sign until it's too late, and a single memory leak can bring the system down easily.

We'll try to explore the available options for making sure such situations are detected as early as possible in order to, say, help our administrator deal with disk space problems during the working day and find out that an important service has died because of a database hiccup just as he goes through the door.

Performance

Performance is one of several holy grails in computing. Systems are never fast enough to accommodate all needs, so we have to balance desired operations with available resources. Zabbix can help you both with evaluating the performance of a particular action and monitoring the current load.

You can start with simple things, such as network performance, indicated by a ping roundtrip or the time it takes for a website to return content, and move forward with more complex scenarios, such as the average performance of a service in a cluster coupled with the disk array throughput.

Security

Another holy grail in computing is security, a never-ending process where you are expected to use many tools, one of which can be Zabbix.

Zabbix can, independently of other verification systems, check simple things such as open ports, software versions, and file checksums. While these would be laughable as the only security measures, they can turn out to be quite valuable additions to existing processes.

Management

System management involves doing many things, and that means following a certain set of rules in all of those steps. Good system administrators never fail at that, except when they do.

There are many simple and advanced checks you can use to inform you about tasks to perform or problems that arise when configuring systems: cross-platform notifications about available upgrades, checking whether the DNS serial number has been updated correctly, and a myriad of other system-management pitfalls.

Efficiency

While generally considered a subset of availability or performance, some aspects of efficiency do not quite fit in there. Efficiency could be considered the first step to improved availability and performance, which increases the importance of knowing how efficient your systems are.

Efficiency parameters will be more service-specific than others, but some generic examples might include Squid hit ratios and MySQL query cache efficiency. Other applications, including custom in-house ones, might provide other efficiency-measuring methods.

Item types

As explored before, Zabbix gathers all its data within items. But surely, we'll want to get information in more ways than just through the Zabbix agent. What are our options? Let's have a look:

```
Zabbix agent
Zabbix agent (active)
Simple check
SNMPv1 agent
SNMPv2 agent
SNMPv3 agent
SNMP trap
Zabbix internal
Zabbix trapper
Zabbix aggregate
External check
Database monitor
IPMI agent
SSH agent
TELNET agent
JMX agent
Calculated
```

This is the item type configuration dropdown when editing an item. We pretty much skipped this selection when creating our item because the default value suited us. Let's take a quick look at the types available now:

- **Zabbix agent**: This is the default type. The server connects to the agent and gathers data.

- **Zabbix agent (active)**: This can be considered as the opposite of the previous type. The Zabbix agent gathers data and connects to the server as required.

- **Simple check**: As the name implies, this type groups simple checks that are performed by server. This includes checking for open TCP ports, ICMP ping, and so on. We will discuss both Zabbix agent types and simple checks in *Chapter 3, Monitoring with Zabbix Agents and Basic Protocols*.

- **SNMP agents**: These three types deal with gathering SNMP data. Versions, obviously, denote the protocol version to use when connecting to the monitored host.

- **SNMP trap**: While still relying on Net-SNMP's snmptrapd to obtain traps from the network, Zabbix offers the functionality of receiving SNMP traps easily. This item type allows you to do that, including automatic sorting per host. We will cover SNMP polling and trapping in *Chapter 4, Monitoring SNMP Devices*.

- **Zabbix internal**: This groups items that gather information about the internal state of Zabbix. We will discuss the internal monitoring in *Chapter 3, Monitoring with Zabbix Agents and Basic Protocols*.

- **Zabbix trapper**: This item type accepts incoming data instead of querying for it. It is useful for any data you might want to feed into Zabbix that is obtained using other tools, customs scripts, or any other method.

- **Zabbix aggregate**: These items aggregate values across a host group. This is mostly useful for clusters or server farms where the overall state is more important than the state of individual machines.

- **External check**: External checks allow the Zabbix server to execute external commands and store the returned values in the item. This allows it to pass along any information that isn't accessible using any of the other item types. We will use Zabbix trapper items, aggregate items, and external checks in *Chapter 11, Advanced Item Monitoring*.

- **Database monitor**: This type includes built-in native checks for querying various database parameters.

- **IPMI agent**: The **Intelligent Platform Management Interface (IPMI)** is a specification for managing and monitoring (which we're mostly after) systems, especially for out-of-band solutions. The IPMI item type allows direct access to this data. We will cover IPMI monitoring in *Chapter 16, Monitoring IPMI Devices*.

- **SSH agent**: It is possible to directly query a host with SSH and retrieve shell-command output. This check supports both password and key-based authentication.

- **TELNET agent**: For some systems where SSH is unavailable, direct a Telnet check can be used. While insecure, it might be the only way to access some devices, including older-generation switches or UPSes. We will discuss SSH and Telnet items in items in *Chapter 11, Advanced Item Monitoring*.

- **JMX agent**: Zabbix provides a component called the Zabbix Java gateway. It allows you to monitor JMX-capable applications directly. JMX monitoring will be discussed in *Chapter 17, Monitoring Java Applications*.

- **Calculated**: These are advanced items that allow you to create new values from other, pre-existing Zabbix items without duplicate data retrieval. We will use these items in *Chapter 11, Advanced Item Monitoring*.

While all these types might look a bit confusing at this point, an important thing to remember is that they are available for your use, but you don't have to use them. You can have a host with a single ICMP ping item, but if you want to monitor more, the advanced functionality will always be there.

As you might have noticed, the item type is set per individual item, not per host. This allows great flexibility when setting up monitored hosts. For example, you can use ICMP to check general availability, a Zabbix agent to check the status of some services and simple TCP checks for others, a trapper to receive custom data, and IPMI to monitor parameters through the management adapter — all on the same host. The choice of item type will depend on network connectivity, the feature set of the monitored host, and the ease of implementation. Zabbix will allow you to choose the best fit for each item.

How items can be monitored

While that covered categories and item types, we skipped some other parameters when creating the item, so it might be helpful to learn about basic values that will have to be set for most item types. Let's take a quick look at the fields in the item creation/editing window:

- **Name**: A user-level item name. This is what you will see in most places where data is shown to users.

- **Type**: This is the main property, affecting other fields and the way item data is gathered, as discussed previously.

- **Key**: This is the property that explicitly specifies what data has to be gathered for this item. It is sort of a technical name for the item. The key value must be unique per host. For certain other item types, the field that is actually identifying collected data might be Simple Network Management Protocol Object Identifiers (SNMP OID) or IPMI sensor, and the key will be only used to reference the item.

- **Type of information**: This allows you to choose the data type that will be gathered with the item. You'll have to set it according to the values provided: integers, decimals, and so on.

- **Data type** : This property provides a way to query data in hexadecimal or octal format and convert it to decimal values automatically. Some SNMP-capable devices (mostly printers) send information in these formats. There's also the Boolean data type that converts several inputs to 1 or 0.

- **Units**: This property allows you to choose the unit to be displayed besides data, and for some units, Zabbix will calculate corresponding conversions as required (called "human-readable" in many tools, so you get 32.5 GB instead of the same value in bytes).

- **Use custom multiplier**: This property multiplies incoming data with the value specified here and stores the result. This is useful if data arrives in one unit but you want to store it as another (for example, if the incoming data is in bytes but you want it in bits, you'd use a multiplier of 8).

- **Update interval**: This sets the interval between data retrieval attempts.

- **Custom intervals**: This setting allows you to modify the update interval during specific times or use cron-like item scheduling — either because you have no need for a particular item during the night or because you know some particular service will be down, for example, during a backup window.

- **History storage period**: This sets the time period for which actual retrieved values are stored in the database.

- **Trend storage period**: This does the same as the **History storage period** option, but for trends. Trends are data calculated from history and averaged for every hour to reduce long-term storage requirements.

- **Store value**: This property is for numeric data only and allows the Zabbix server to perform some basic calculations on the data before inserting it into the database, such as calculating the difference between two checks for counter items.

- **Show value**: In this dropdown, a value map may be selected. It allows you to show human-readable values for numeric codes, for example, as returned by the SNMP interface status. Refer to *Chapter 3, Monitoring with Zabbix Agents and Basic Protocols*, for more information on value mapping.

- **Applications**: This property makes it possible to perform logical grouping of items, for example, on the **Monitoring | Latest data** screen.

- **Populates host inventory field**: Allows you to place collected item values in an inventory field (explored in *Chapter 5, Managing Hosts, Users and Permissions*).

- **Description**: This field, available for several entities in Zabbix 3.0, allows you to describe an item. You may explain the way data is collected, manipulated, or what it means.

- **Enabled**: This allows you to enable or disable the item.

Don't worry if these short descriptions didn't answer all of your questions about each option. We'll dig deeper into each of these later, and there are more options available for other item types as well.

Using global search

So far, we have navigated to a host or its items and other entities by going to specific pages in the frontend and then looking up the group and host. This is a convenient enough method in smaller installations, and it's also what we will mostly use in this book. In a larger installation, navigating like this could be very time consuming; thus, a feature called **global search** becomes very useful. Actually, many users almost completely skip the classic navigation method and use search exclusively.

The global search field is available in the upper-right corner of the Zabbix frontend. In there, type a single letter, a. Anything entered here is matched against the beginnings of hostnames, and results are shown in a dropdown. In our case, **A test host** matches:

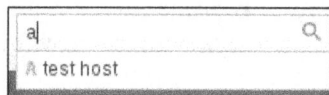

You can choose one of the dropdown entries with your keyboard or mouse or search using your original string. Let's choose the single entry in the dropdown by either clicking on it with the mouse or highlighting it with the keyboard and hitting *Enter*. In the search results, we can see three blocks that correspond to the three types of entities that can be searched in Zabbix:

- Hosts
- Templates
- Host groups

This is how the entry looks:

Search: A test host

Hosts

HOST	IP	DNS	LATEST DATA	TRIGGERS	EVENTS	GRAPHS	SCREENS	WEB	APPLICATIONS	ITEMS	TRIGGERS	GRAPHS	DISCOVERY	WEB
A test host	127.0.0.1		Latest data	Triggers	Events	Graphs	Screens	Web	Applications	Items 1	Triggers 1	Graphs	Discovery	Web

Displaying 1 of 1 found

Host groups

HOST GROUP	LATEST DATA	TRIGGERS	EVENTS	GRAPHS	WEB	HOSTS	TEMPLATES

No data found.

Displaying 0 of 0 found

Templates

TEMPLATE	APPLICATIONS	ITEMS	TRIGGERS	GRAPHS	SCREENS	DISCOVERY	WEB

No data found.

Displaying 0 of 0 found

For all of them, searching by name is possible. Additionally, for hosts, a search can also be performed by **IP** address and **DNS**.

In the search results, clicking on the host name will open the host's properties. There are also additional links for each host, but the column headers can be confusing: **TRIGGERS**, **GRAPHS**, and **WEB** are duplicated. While it's not very intuitive, the difference is the use of a number next to the links: if there's a number, this is a link to the configuration section. If there's no number, it is a link to the monitoring section, or maybe there are no entities of that type configured. In that case, you sort of have to remember that the rightmost column with the same name is for configuration. The number for the configuration links, if present, is the count of the entities.

Summary

This was the chapter where we finally got some real action: monitoring an item, creating a trigger, and getting a notification on this trigger. We also explored the Zabbix frontend a bit and looked at the basic item parameters. Let's review what basic steps were required to get our first alert:

- We started by creating a host. In Zabbix, everything to be monitored is attached to a logical entity called a **host**.

- Next, we created an item. Being the basis of information gathering, items define parameters about monitored metrics, including what data to gather, how often to gather it, how to store the retrieved values, and other things.

- After the item, we created a trigger. Each trigger contains an expression that is used to define thresholds. For each trigger, a severity can be configured as well. To let Zabbix know how to reach us, we configured our e-mail settings. This included specifying an e-mail server for the media type and adding media to our user profile.

- As the final configuration step, we created an action. Actions are configuration entities that define actual operations to perform and can have conditions to create flexible rules for what to do about various events.

- Well, we actually did one more thing to make sure it all works — we *created a problem*. It is useful to test your configuration, especially when just starting with Zabbix. Our configuration was correct, so we were promptly notified about the problem.

While this knowledge is already enough to configure a very basic monitoring system, we'll have to explore other areas before it can be considered a functional one. In the next chapter, we will figure out what the difference between passive and active items is and what the important things to keep in mind are when setting up each of them. We'll also cover basic ICMP items and other item properties such as positional parameters, value mapping, units, and custom intervals.

3
Monitoring with Zabbix Agents and Basic Protocols

Now that we have explored the basics of information gathering and acting upon it in Zabbix, let's take a closer look at two simple and widely used methods for obtaining data: the already mentioned Zabbix agents and so-called **simple checks**. Simple checks include **TCP connectivity** and **ICMP checks**. In this chapter, we will cover the following:

- Understanding and using Zabbix agents
- Creating a simple check
- Binding it all together

Using the Zabbix agent

Previously, we installed the Zabbix agent on the same host and monitored a single item for it. It's now time to expand and look at how inter-host connectivity works.

To continue, install the Zabbix agent on another host. The easiest way might be installing from the distribution packages—or you may choose to compile it from the source. If installing from the packages on RHEL/SUSE-based systems, refer to *Chapter 1, Getting Started with Zabbix*, for repository instructions. Potential agent package names could be:

- `zabbix30-agent`
- `zabbix-agent`

Compiling the agent only from the source is done in a similar way to how all components were included for compilation in *Chapter 1, Getting Started with Zabbix*. Instead of the full configure line, we will use a single flag this time:

```
$ ./configure --enable-agent
```

Configuration should complete successfully, and the following summary lines are important:

```
Enable server:        no
Enable proxy:         no
Enable agent:         yes
```

If the output you see matches the preceding output, continue by issuing the following command:

```
$ make install
```

Compilation should complete without any errors, and it should do so relatively quickly.

If you install distribution packages on a distribution different from where the server is installed, don't worry when the agent daemon has an older version than the server. This is supported and should work well. In fact, the version 1.0 Zabbix agent daemon works quite well with a version 3.0 server. The other way might not work and is not supported. You should avoid using an older server with new agents.

> Staying with an older agent can be more convenient as you already have one installed and working well. When setting up new ones, it is suggested you go with the latest one, as it might have bugs fixed, improved performance, more supported items for a particular platform, and other benefits.

With the agent installed, now is the time to start it up. How exactly this is done depends on the installation method—and if you installed from the packages, it depends on the distribution as well. For examples on how to start up the agent, refer to *Chapter 1, Getting Started with Zabbix*. As a quick reminder, if you installed from packages on an RHEL/SUSE-based system, the agent daemon can likely be started up like this:

```
# service zabbix-agentd start
```

If you installed from the source, directly execute the binary:

```
# <path>/zabbix_agentd
```

Once the agent has been started, we also have to add this new host to the configuration, so go to **Configuration | Hosts**. Make sure that the **Group** dropdown in the upper-right corner says **Linux servers**. Click on the **Create** host button and fill in this form:

Host name	Another host
Visible name	

Groups — In groups / Other groups

In groups:
- Linux servers

Other groups:
- Database servers
- Discovered hosts
- Hypervisors
- Network devices
- Templates
- UPS devices
- Virtual machines
- Web servers
- Windows servers
- Zabbix servers

New group:

Agent interfaces

IP ADDRESS	DNS NAME	CONNECT TO	PORT	DEFAULT
192.168.56.11		IP DNS	10050	◉ Remove

Add

Here are some tips on filling out the form:

- **Host name**: Feel free to choose a descriptive name, or simply enter **Another host**
- **Agent interfaces**: Fill in either **IP ADDRESS** or **DNS NAME** depending on which connection method you want to use
- **CONNECT TO**: If you decide to go with **DNS NAME**, switch to **DNS**

When you're done, click on the **Add** button at the bottom.

Passive items

The item we created before was a so-called passive item, which means that the Zabbix server initiates a connection to the agent every time a value has to be collected. In most locations, they are simply referred to as being of the Zabbix agent type.

An easy way to remember what's passive or active in Zabbix is to think from the agent's perspective. If the agent connects to the server, it's active. If not, it's passive:

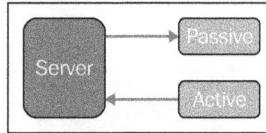

Let's create another passive item to check for the remote host. Go to **Configuration | Hosts**, click on **Items** next to the host you just created, click on the **Create item** button, and fill in these values:

- **Name**: Enter **Web server status**
- **Key**: Enter net.tcp.service[http,,80] (that's two subsequent commas preceding 80)
- **Update interval (in sec)**: Change to 60 from the default (30)—once a minute should be more than enough for our needs
- **History storage period (in days)**: Change to 7 from the default (90)—that's still a whole week of exact per-minute service status records kept

The end result should be as follows:

But what's up with that `, , 80` added to the service name? Click on the **Select** button next to the **Key** field. This opens a window with a nice list of keys to choose from, along with a short description of each:

Standard items	Type Zabbix agent
KEY	NAME
agent.hostname	Agent host name. Returns string
agent.ping	Agent availability check. Returns nothing - unavailable; 1 - available
agent.version	Version of Zabbix agent. Returns string
kernel.maxfiles	Maximum number of opened files supported by OS. Returns integer
kernel.maxproc	Maximum number of processes supported by OS. Returns integer
net.dns[<ip>,zone,<type>,<timeout>, <count>,<protocol>]	Checks if DNS service is up. Returns 0 - DNS is down (server did not respond or DNS resolution failed); 1 - DNS is up

The **Type** dropdown in the upper-right corner will allow you to switch between several item types—we'll discuss the other types later. For now, find `net.tcp.service` in the list and look at the description. There are two things to learn here: firstly, we didn't actually have to add that `80`—it's a port, and given that the default already is `80`, adding it was redundant. However, it is useful if you have a service running on a nonstandard port. Secondly, there's a key list just one click away to give you a quick hint in case you have forgotten a particular key or what its parameters should be like.

This key, `net.tcp.service`, is a bit special: it tries to verify that the corresponding service actually does respond in a standard manner, which means the service must be explicitly supported. As of writing this, Zabbix supports the following services for the `net.tcp.service` key:

- FTP
- HTTP
- HTTPS
- IMAP
- LDAP
- NNTP
- POP
- SMTP
- SSH
- TCP
- Telnet

The TCP service is a bit special in its own way. While others perform service-specific checks, TCP is not really a service; it just checks the TCP connection. It's closer to a key you can see a couple of rows above in the item list, net.tcp.port. As the description says, this one just tries to open a TCP connection to any arbitrary port without performing any service-specific checks on the returned value. If you try to use an arbitrary service string that is not supported, you would simply get an error message saying that such an item key is not supported.

> There's also a net.udp.service key that currently supports only one service—**Network Time Protocol (NTP)**.

Feel free to look at the other available keys—we will use a couple of them later as well—then close this popup and click on the **Add** button at the bottom.

You have probably already noticed the green strip at the top of the screen when some operation successfully completes. This time, there's also a control called **Details** available; click on it to expand the details:

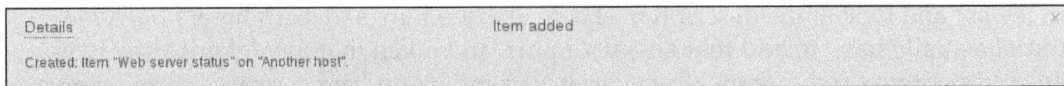

Details	Item added	×
Created: Item "Web server status" on "Another host".		

You can click on **Details** again to collapse the contents. Of course, this can be done whenever the **Details** link is available after some operation.

Now, we could go over to **Monitoring | Latest data** and wait for the values appearing there, but that would be useless. Instead, after a couple of minutes, you should visit **Configuration | Hosts**. Depending on your network configuration, you might see a red **ZBX** marker next to this host. This icon represents errors that have occurred when attempting to gather data from a passive Zabbix agent.

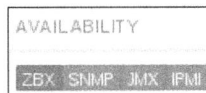

AVAILABILITY

ZBX SNMP JMX IPMI

To see the actual error message, move your mouse cursor over the icon, and a tooltip will open. Clicking on the error icon will make the tooltip permanent and allow you to copy the error message.

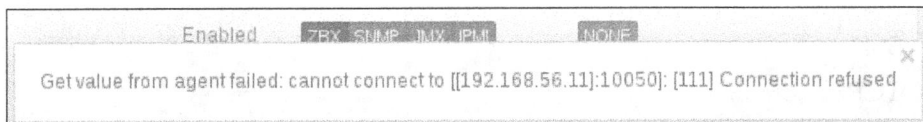

Enabled	ZBX SNMP JMX IPMI	NONE	×
Get value from agent failed: cannot connect to [[192.168.56.11]:10050]: [111] Connection refused			

> The three additional entries represent the SNMP, JMX, and IPMI data-gathering statuses. We will monitor SNMP devices in *Chapter 4, Monitoring SNMP Devices*, IPMI devices in *Chapter 16, Monitoring IPMI Devices*, and JMX applications in *Chapter 17, Monitoring Java Applications*.

If you see an error message similar to **Get value from agent failed: cannot connect to [[192.168.56.11]:10050]: [111] Connection refused** (most likely with a different IP address), it means that the Zabbix server was unable to connect to the agent daemon port. This can happen because of a variety of reasons, the most common being a firewall—either a network one between the Zabbix server and the remote host or a local one on the remote host. Make sure to allow connections from the Zabbix server to the monitored machine on port `10050`.

If you did this correctly (or if you did not have a firewall blocking the connection), you could again go to **Monitoring | Latest data**—only that would be pointless, again. To see why, refresh the host list. Soon, you should see the Zabbix agent status icon turn red again, and moving your mouse cursor over it will reveal another error message, **Received empty response from Zabbix Agent at [192.168.56.11]**, assuming that the agent dropped the connection because of access permissions. Now that's different. What access permissions is it talking about, and why did they work for our first host?

From the Zabbix server, execute this:

```
$ telnet 192.168.56.11 10050
```

> You should always verify network connectivity and access permissions from the Zabbix server. Doing it from another machine can have wildly differing and useless results.

Replace the IP address with the one of your remote host. You should see the following output, and the connection should immediately be closed:

```
Trying 192.168.56.11...
Connected to 192.168.56.11.
Escape character is '^]'.
Connection closed by foreign host.
```

Now, try the same with localhost:

```
$ telnet localhost 10050
Trying 127.0.0.1...
Connected to localhost.
Escape character is '^]'.
```

Notice how this time the connection is not closed immediately, so there's a difference in the configuration. The connection will most likely be closed a bit later—3 seconds later, to be more specific. If this does not happen for some reason, press *Ctrl+]*, as instructed, then enter quit—this should close the connection:

```
^]
telnet> quit
Connection closed.
```

It turns out that configuring the Zabbix agent daemon on another machine is going to be a tiny bit harder than before.

As opposed to the installation on the Zabbix server, we have to edit the agent daemon configuration file on the remote machine. Open zabbix_agentd.conf as root in your favorite editor and take a look at the **Server** parameter. It is currently set to 127.0.0.1, which is the reason we didn't have to touch it on the Zabbix server. As the comment states, this parameter should contain the Zabbix server IP address, so replace 127.0.0.1 with the correct server address here.

> If you have older Zabbix agent instances in your environment, make sure to use and edit zabbix_agentd.conf, with d in the name. The other file, zabbix_agent.conf, was used by the limited-functionality zabbix_agent module, which has been removed in Zabbix 3.0.

Save the file and restart the agent daemon. How exactly this is done depends on the installation method, again. If you installed from the distribution packages, the following will most likely work:

```
# service zabbix-agentd restart
```

If you installed from the source and did not create or adapt some init scripts, you will have to manually stop and start the agent process:

```
# killall -15 zabbix_agentd; sleep 3; zabbix_agentd
```

The preceding command will stop all processes called zabbix_agentd on the system. This should not be used if multiple agents are running on the system. Additionally, the delay of 3 seconds should be more than enough in most cases, but if the agent does not start up after this, check its logfile for potential reasons.

> Never use `kill -9` with Zabbix daemons. Just don't. Even if
> you think you could, do not do it. Signal 15 is SIGTERM—it tells
> the daemon to terminate, which means writing any outstanding
> data to the database, writing out and closing the logfiles, and
> potentially doing other things to shut down properly. Signal 9 is
> SIGKILL—the process is brutally killed without allowing it
> to say goodbye to the loved database and files. Unless you
> really know what you are doing, you do not want to do
> that—seriously, don't.

To verify the change, try telnetting to the remote machine again:

```
$ telnet 192.168.56.11 10050
```

This time, the outcome should be the same as we had with the localhost: the
connection should be opened and then closed approximately 3 seconds later.

> While some host interface must be specified for all hosts, even
> for those only using active items, it is only used for passive
> Zabbix agent checks. If such items are not configured, this
> interface is simply ignored.

Finally, it should be worth opening **Monitoring** | **Latest data**. We will only see our
previously created item, though; the reason is the same filter we changed earlier. We
explicitly filtered for one host; thus, the second host we created does not show up at
all. In the filter, which should still be expanded, clear the host field and select **Linux
servers** in the **Host groups** field, and then click on **Filter**:

		Filter ▲		
Host groups	Linux servers ✕	Select	Name	
	type here to search			
			Show items without data ▨	
Hosts	type here to search	Select		
			Show details ☐	
Application		Select		
		Filter Reset		

> In many filter fields in Zabbix, we can either start typing and
> get a list of matching entries or click on the **Select** button to
> see a list of all available entities. Typing in is a very convenient
> way when we know at least part of the name. Being able to see
> the list is helpful when working in an environment we are less
> familiar with.

We should see two monitored hosts now, each having a single item:

	HOST	NAME ▲	LAST CHECK	LAST VALUE	CHANGE
▼					
▼	Another host	**- other -** (1 Item)			
		Web server status	2016-02-20 00:58:56	1	Graph
▼	A test host	**- other -** (1 Item)			
		CPU load	2016-02-20 00:58:55	0	Graph

Notice how we can click the triangle icon next to each entry or in the header to collapse and expand either an individual entry or all of the entries.

Cloning items

Let's try to monitor another service now, for example, the one running on port 22, SSH. To keep things simple for us, we won't create an item from scratch this time; instead, go back to **Configuration | Hosts**, click on **Items** next to **Another host**, and click on **Web server status** in the **NAME** column. This will open the item editing screen, showing all the values we entered before. This time, there are different buttons available at the bottom. Among other changes, instead of the **Add** button, there's an **Update** one.

> Notice how one of the previously seen buttons is different. What was labeled **Add** previously is **Update** now. This change identifies the operation that we are going to perform: either adding a new entity or updating an existing one. One might open a configuration form intending to clone the entity, scan the fields, change some values, but forget to click on the **Clone** button. In the end, the existing item will be changed. The difference in the labels of the **Add** and **Update** buttons might help spot such mistakes before they are made.

There's also **Delete**, which, obviously, deletes the currently open item. We don't want to do that now. Instead, click on **Clone**:

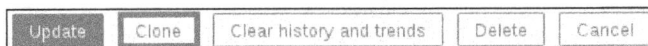

| Update | Clone | Clear history and trends | Delete | Cancel |

Notice how the opened form proposes to create a new item, but this time, all values are set to those that the original item we cloned had. The **Update** button is changed to **Add** as well. Click on the **Add** button—it should fail. Remember, we talked about the key being unique per host; that's what the error message says as well:

Details	Cannot add item	×
Item with key "net.tcp.service[http,,80]" already exists on "Another host".		

The item editing form is still open, so we can correct our mistake. Make the following modifications:

- **Name**: Change it to `SSH server status`
- **Key**: Change `http,,80` to `ssh` so that it looks like this—`net.tcp.service[ssh]`

That's all we have to do for now, so click on the **Add** button at the bottom again. This time, the item should be added successfully. Now, navigate to **Monitoring | Latest data**, where **Another host** should have two items listed: **SSH server status** and **Web server status**. Their status will depend on which services are running on the remote host. As it's remote, SSH most likely is running (and thus has a value of 1), but whether or not the web server is running will be specific to your situation.

HOST	NAME ▲	LAST CHECK	LAST VALUE
Another host	- **other** - (2 Items)		
	SSH server status	2016-02-20 01:17:57	1
	Web server status	2016-02-20 01:17:56	1

> The monitoring of a port is often done to make sure the service on it is available, but that is not a strict requirement. If some system is not supposed to have SSH available through the Internet, we could use such a check to verify that it has not been accidentally exposed either by the inadvertent starting of the SSH daemon or an unfortunate change in the firewall.

Manually querying items

Adding items to the frontend and waiting for them to update is one way of seeing whether you got the item key right. It is not a very quick method, though—you have to wait for the server to get to checking the item. If you are not sure about the parameters or would like to test different combinations, the easiest way to do this is with a utility called `zabbix_get`. When installing from source, it is installed together with the Zabbix agent. When installing from the packages, it could be installed together with the Zabbix agent, or it could also be in a separate package. Using it is very simple: if we want to query the agent on the Zabbix server, we will run this:

```
$ zabbix_get -s 127.0.0.1 -k system.cpu.load
```

This will obtain the value in the exact same way as the server would do it. If you would like to get values like this from Another host, you could run `zabbix_get` on the Zabbix server. Attempting to run it from the same host on which the agent runs will fail as we changed the **Server** parameter to accept connections from the Zabbix server only. If you would like to query the agent from the localhost for debugging purposes, `127.0.0.1` can be added to the **Server** parameter via a comma—this is sometimes done on all systems when deploying the agent.

This covers the basics of normal, or passive, Zabbix items, where the server queries agents. Let's move on to other item types.

Active items

Passive Zabbix items are fine if you can connect to all the monitored hosts from the Zabbix server, but what if you can't allow incoming connections to the monitored hosts because of security or network topology reasons?

This is where active items come into play. As opposed to passive items, for active items, it's the agent that connects to the server; the server never connects to the agent. When connecting, the agent downloads a list of items to check and then reports the new data to the server periodically. Let's create an active item, but this time, we'll try to use some help when selecting the item key.

Go to **Configuration | Hosts**, click on **Items** next to **Another host**, and click on **Create item**. For now, use these values:

- **Name**: Incoming traffic on interface $1
- **Type**: Zabbix agent (active)
- **Update interval (in sec)**: 60
- **History storage period (in days)**: 7

Name	Incoming traffic on interface $1
Type	Zabbix agent (active) ▼
Key	[ ] Select
Type of information	Numeric (unsigned) ▼
Data type	Decimal ▼
Units	
Use custom multiplier	☐ 1
Update interval (in sec)	60
History storage period (in days)	7

We'll do something different with the **Key** field this time. Click on the **Select** button, and in the upcoming dialog that we saw before, click on net.if.in[if,<mode>]. This will fill in the chosen string, as follows:

net.if.in[if,<mode>]	Incoming traffic statistics on network interface. Returns integer

> Replace the content in the square brackets with eth0 so that the field contents read net.if.in[eth0]. When you're done, click on the **Add** button at the bottom. Never leave placeholders such as <mode> — they will be interpreted as literal values and the item will not work as intended.

If your system has a different network interface name, use that here instead of eth0. You can find out the interface names with the ifconfig or ip addr show commands. In many modern distributions, the standard ethX naming scheme has been changed to one that will result in various different interface names. Further, replace any occurrences of eth0 with the correct interface name.

Go to **Monitoring | Latest data** and check whether new values have arrived:

HOST	NAME ▲	LAST CHECK	LAST VALUE
Another host	**- other -** (3 Items)		
	Incoming traffic on interface eth0		

Well, it doesn't look like they have. You could wait a bit to be completely sure, but most likely, no data will appear for this new active item, which means we're in for another troubleshooting session.

First, we should test basic network connectivity. Remember: active agents connect to the server, so we have to know which port they use (by default, it's port 10051). So, let's start by testing whether the remotely monitored machine can connect to the Zabbix server:

```
$ telnet <Zabbix server IP or DNS name> 10051
```

This should produce output similar to the following:

```
Trying <Zabbix server IP>...
Connected to <Zabbix server IP or DNS name>.
Escape character is '^]'.
```

Press *Ctrl +]* and enter quit in the resulting prompt:

```
telnet> quit
Connection closed.
```

Such a sequence indicates that the network connection is working properly. If it isn't, verify possible network configuration issues, including network firewalls and the local firewall on the Zabbix server. Make sure to allow incoming connections on port 10051.

> Both agent and server ports for Zabbix are registered with the **Internet Assigned Numbers Authority (IANA)**.

So, there might be something wrong with the agent—let's take a closer look. We could try to look at the agent daemon's logfile, so find the LogFile configuration parameter. If you're using the default configuration files from the source archive, it should be set to log to /tmp/zabbix_agentd.log. If you installed from packages, it is likely to be in /var/log/zabbix or similar. Open this logfile and look for any interesting messages regarding active checks. Each line will be prefixed with a PID and timestamp in the syntax PID:YYYYMMDD:HHMMSS. You'll probably see lines similar to these:

```
15794:20141230:153731.992 active check configuration update from
[127.0.0.1:10051] started to fail (cannot connect to [[127.0.0.1]:10051]:
[111] Connection refused)
```

The agent is trying to request the active check list, but the connection fails. The attempt seems to be wrong — our Zabbix server should be on a different system than the localhost. Let's see how we can fix this. On the remote machine, open the `zabbix_agentd.conf` configuration file and check the `ServerActive` parameter. The default configuration file will have a line like this:

`ServerActive=127.0.0.1`

This parameter tells the agent where it should connect to for active items. In our case, the localhost will not work as the Zabbix server is on a remote machine, so we should modify this. Replace `127.0.0.1` with the IP address or DNS name of the Zabbix server, and then restart the agent either using an init script or the manual method `killall`.

While you have the configuration file open, take a look at another parameter there — `StartAgents`. This parameter controls how many processes are handling incoming connections for passive items. If set to `0`, it will prevent the agent from listening on incoming connections from the server. This enables you to customize agents to support either or both of the methods. Disabling passive items can be better from a security perspective, but they are very handy for testing and debugging various problems. Active items can be disabled by not specifying (commenting out) `ServerActive`. Disabling both active and passive items won't work; the agent daemon will complain and refuse to start up, and it's correct — starting with both disabled would be a pointless thing to do. Take a look:

`zabbix-agentd [16208]: ERROR: either active or passive checks must be enabled`

We could wait for values to appear on the frontend again, but again, they would not. Let's return to the agent daemon logfile and see whether there is any hint about what's wrong:

`15938:20141230:154544.559 no active checks on server [10.1.1.100:10051]: host [Zabbix server] not monitored`

If we carefully read the entry, we will notice that the agent is reporting its hostname as `Zabbix server`, but that is the hostname of the default host, which we decided not to use and left disabled. The log message agrees: it says that the host is not monitored.

If we look at the startup messages, there's even another line mentioning this:

`15931:20141230:154544.552 Starting Zabbix Agent [Zabbix server]. Zabbix 3.0.0 (revision 58567).`

> You might or might not see the SVN revision in this message depending on how the agent was compiled. If it's missing, don't worry about it as it does not affect the ability of the agent to operate.

As that is not the host name we want to use, let's check the agent daemon configuration file again. There's a parameter named `Hostname`, which currently reads `Zabbix server`. Given that the comment for this parameter says `"Required for active checks and must match hostname as configured on the server."`, it has to be what we're after. Change it to **Another host**, save and close the configuration file, and then restart the Zabbix agent daemon. Check for new entries in the `zabbix_agentd.log` file—there should be no more errors.

While we're at it, let's update the agent configuration on **A test host** as well. Modify `zabbix_agentd.conf` and set Hostname=A test host and restart the agent daemon.

If there still are errors about the host not being found on the server, double-check that the hostname in the Zabbix frontend host properties and agent daemon configuration file (the one we just changed) match.

> This hostname is case sensitive.

It's now time to return to the frontend and see whether data has started flowing in at the **Monitoring | Latest data** section:

HOST	NAME ▲	LAST CHECK	LAST VALUE	CHANGE
Another host	- **other** - (3 Items)			
	Incoming traffic on interface enp0s8	2016-02-20 01:45:20	173013	+1296

> Notice how the system in this screenshot actually has an interface named enp0s8, not eth0. We will find out how to allow Zabbix to worry about interface names and discover them automatically in *Chapter 12, Automating Configuration*.

If you see no data and the item shows up unsupported in the configuration section, check the network interface name.

Great, data is indeed flowing, but the values look really weird. If you wait for a while, you'll see how the number in the LAST VALUE column just keeps on increasing. So what is it? Well, network traffic keys gather data from interface counters, that is, the network interface adds up all traffic, and this total data is fed into the Zabbix database. This has one great advantage: even when data is polled at large intervals, traffic spikes will not go unnoticed as the counter data is present, but it also makes data pretty much unreadable for us, and graphs would also look like an ever-growing line (if you feel like it, click on the **Graph** link for this item). We could even call them "hill graphs". Luckily, Zabbix provides a built-in capability to deal with data counters like this. Go to **Configuration | Hosts**, then click on **Items** next to **Another host**, and click on **Incoming traffic on interface eth0** in the **NAME** column. Change the **Store value** dropdown to read **Delta (speed per second)**, and then click on **Update**.

We will have to wait a bit for the changes to take effect, so now is a good moment to discuss our choice for the **Type of information** option for this item. We set it to **Numeric (unsigned)**, which accepts integers. The values that this item originally receives are indeed integers—they are counter values denoting how many bytes have been received on this interface. The **Store value** option we changed to **Delta (speed per second)**, though, will almost always result in some decimal part being there—it is dividing the traffic between two values according to the number of seconds passed between them. In cases where Zabbix has a decimal number and has to store it in an integer field, the behavior will differ depending on how it got that decimal value, as follows:

- If the decimal value arrived from a Zabbix agent source like a system.cpu. load item, the item will turn up unsupported
- If Zabbix received an integer but further calculations resulted in a decimal number appearing, like with our network item, the decimal part will be discarded

This behavior is depicted in the following figure:

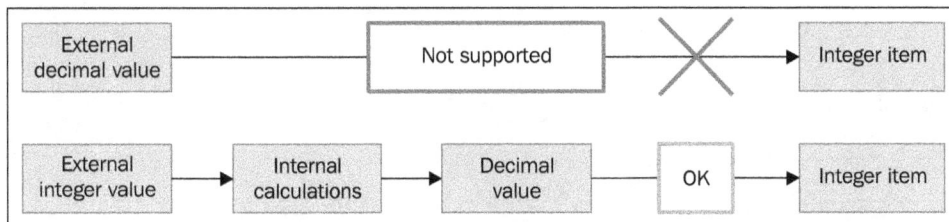

Why is there a difference like this, and why did we leave this item as an integer if doing so results in a loss of precision? Decimal values in the Zabbix database schema have a smaller number of significant digits available before the decimal point than integer values. On a loaded high-speed interface, we might overflow that limit, and it would result in values being lost completely. It is usually better to lose a tiny bit of precision—the decimal part—than the whole value. Note that precision is lost on the smallest unit: a byte or bit. Even if Zabbix shows 5 Gbps in the frontend, the decimal part will be truncated from this value in bits; thus, this loss of precision should be really, really insignificant. It is suggested to use integers for items that have a risk like this, at least until database schema limits are increased.

Check out **Monitoring | Latest data** again:

HOST	NAME ▲	LAST CHECK	LAST VALUE	CHANGE
Another host	**- other -** (3 Items)			
	Incoming traffic on interface enp0s8	2016-02-20 01:50:20	29	-177700

> Keep in mind that in the worst case, configuration changes might take up to 3 minutes to propagate to the Zabbix agent: 1 minute to get into the server configuration cache and 2 minutes until the agent refreshes its own item list. On top of this delay, this item is different from the others we created: it needs to gather two values to compute per second, one of which we are interested in; thus, we will also have to wait for whatever the item interval is before the first value appears in the frontend.

That's better; Zabbix now automatically calculates the change between every two checks (that's what the delta is for) and stores it, but the values still don't seem to be too user friendly. Maybe they're better in the graph—let's click on the **Graph** link to find out:

Another host: Incoming traffic on interface enp0s8 (1h)

	last	min	avg	max
■ Incoming traffic on interface enp0s8 [all]	20	20	124.75 K	177.73 K

Ouch. While we can clearly see the effect our change had, it has also left us with very ugly historical data. The Y axis of that graph represents the total counter value (thus showing the total since the monitored system was started up), but the X axis represents the correct (delta) data. You can also take a look at the values numerically — go to the dropdown in the upper-right portion, which currently reads **Graph**. Choose **500 latest values** from there. You'll get the following screen:

Another host: Incoming traffic on interface enp0s8	500 latest values ▾ As plain text ↗
TIMESTAMP	VALUE
2016-02-20 01:56:19	29
2016-02-20 01:55:19	20
2016-02-20 01:54:19	29
2016-02-20 01:53:19	21
2016-02-20 01:52:19	27
2016-02-20 01:51:19	20
2016-02-20 01:50:20	29
2016-02-20 01:48:20	177729

In this list, we can nicely see the change in data representation as well as the exact time when the change was performed. But those huge values have come from the counter data, and they pollute our nice, clean graph by being so much out of scale — we have to get rid of them. Go to **Configuration | Hosts** and click on **Items** next to **Another host**, then mark the checkbox next to the **Incoming traffic on interface eth0** item, and look at the buttons positioned at the bottom of the item list:

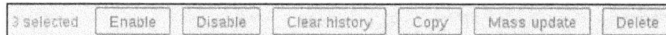

3 selected	Enable	Disable	Clear history	Copy	Mass update	Delete

The third button from the left, named **Clear history**, probably does what we want. Notice the *3 selected* text to the left of the activity buttons — it shows the amount of entries selected, so we always know how many elements we are operating on. Click on the **Clear history** button. You should get a JavaScript popup asking for confirmation to continue. While history cleaning can take a long time with large datasets, in our case, it should be nearly instant, so click on the OK button to continue. This should get rid of all history values for this item, including the huge ones.

Still, looking at the Y axis in that graph, we see the incoming values being represented as a number without any explanation of what it is, and larger values get K, M and other multiplier identifiers applied. It would be so much better if Zabbix knew how to calculate it in bytes or a similar unit. Right, so navigate to **Configuration | Hosts** and click on **Items** next to **Another host**, and then click on the **Incoming traffic on the eth0** interface in the **NAME** column. Edit the **Units** field and enter Bps, and then click on **Update**.

Let's check whether there's any improvement in the **Monitoring | Latest data**:

Incoming traffic on interface enp0s8	2016-02-20 02:02:19	27 Bps

Wonderful; data is still arriving. Even better, notice how Zabbix now automatically calculates KB, MB, and so on where appropriate. Well, it would in our example host if there were more traffic. Let's look at the network traffic; click on **Graph**:

Take a look at the Y axis — if you have more traffic, units will be calculated there as well to make the graph readable, and unit calculations are retroactively applied to the previously gathered values.

> Units do not affect stored data like the **Store value** option did, so we do not have to clear the previous values this time.

One parameter that we set, the update interval, could have been smaller, thus resulting in a better-looking graph. But it is important to remember that the smaller the intervals you have on your items, the more data Zabbix has to retrieve, and each second, more data has to be inserted into the database and more calculations have to be performed when displaying this data. While it would have made no notable difference on our test system, you should try to keep intervals as large as possible.

So far, we have created items that gathered numeric data—either integers or decimal values. Let's create another one, a bit different this time. As usual, go to **Configuration | Hosts** and click on **Items** next to **Another host**. Before continuing with item creation, let's look at what helpful things are available in the configuration section, particularly for items. If we look above the item list, we can see the navigation and information bar:

| All hosts / Another host | Enabled | ZBX SNMP JMX IPMI | Applications | Items 3 | Triggers | Graphs | Discovery rules | Web scenarios |

This area provides quick and useful information about the currently selected host: the hostname, whether the host is monitored, and its availability. Even more importantly, on the right-hand side, it provides quick shortcuts back to the host list and other elements associated with the current host: applications, items, triggers, graphs, discovery rules, and web scenarios. This is a handy way to switch between element categories for a single host without going through the host list all the time. But that's not all yet—click on the **Filter** button to open the filter we got thrown in our face before. The sophisticated filter appears again:

	Filter ▲						
Host group	type here to search	Select	Type	all	Type of information	all	State	all
Host	Another host X	Select	Update Interval (in sec)		History (in days)		Status	all
Application		Select			Trends (in days)		Triggers	all
Name like							Template	all
Key like								

Filter   Reset

Using this filter, we can make complex rules about what items to display. Looking at the top-left corner of the filter, we can see that we are not limited to viewing items from a single host; we can also choose a **Host group**. When we need to, we can make filter choices and click on the **Filter** link underneath. Currently, it has only one condition: the **Host** field contains **Another host**, so the **Items** link from the host list we used was the one that set this filter. Clear out the **Host** field, choose **Linux servers** from the **Host group** field, and click on the **Filter** button below the filter.

> Host information and the quick link bar is only available when items are filtered for a single host.

Now, look right below the main item filter — that is a **Subfilter**, which, as its header informs, only affects data already filtered by the main filter.

```
Subfilter affects only filtered data

TYPES
Zabbix agent 3   Zabbix agent (active) 1


TYPE OF INFORMATION
Numeric (float) 1   Numeric (unsigned) 3


WITH TRIGGERS
Without triggers 3   With triggers 1


HISTORY
7 3   90 1


INTERVAL
30 1   60 3
```

The entries in the subfilter work like toggles — if we switch one on, it works as a filter on the data in addition to all other toggled subfilter controls. Let's click on **Zabbix agent (active)** now. Notice how the item list now contains only one item — this is what the number 1 represented next to this Subfilter toggle. But the subfilter itself now also looks different:

```
TYPES
Zabbix agent +3   Zabbix agent (active) 1


TYPE OF INFORMATION
Numeric (float) 0   Numeric (unsigned) 1
```

The option we enabled, **Zabbix agent**, has been highlighted. **Numeric (float)**, on the other hand, is greyed out and disabled, as activating this toggle in addition to already active ones results in no items being displayed at all. While the **Numeric (unsigned)** toggle still has **1** listed next to it, which shows that enabling it will result in those many items being displayed, the **Zabbix agent** toggle instead has **+3** next to it. This form represents the fact that activating this toggle will display three more items than are currently being displayed, and it is used for toggles in the same category. Currently, the subfilter has five entries, as it only shows existing values. Once we have additional and different items configured, this subfilter will expand. We have finished exploring these filters, so choose **Another host** from the **Host** field, click on the **Filter** button under the filter, and click on **Create item**.

When you have many different hosts monitored by Zabbix, it's quite easy to forget which version of the Zabbix agent daemon each host has, and even if you have automated software deploying in place, it is nice to be able to see which version each host is at, all in one place.

Use the following values:

- **Name**: Enter **Zabbix agent version**
- **Type**: Select **Zabbix agent (active)** (we're still creating active items)
- **Key**: Click on **Select** and then choose the third entry from the list—agent. version
- **Type of information**: Choose **Character**
- **Update interval (in sec)**: Enter 86400

When done! Click on the **Add** button. There are two notable things we did. Firstly, we set the information type to **Character**, which reloaded the form, slightly changing available options. Most notably, fields that are relevant for numeric information were hidden, such as units, multiplier, and trends.

Secondly, we entered a very large update interval, 86400, which is equivalent to 24 hours. While this might seem excessive, remember what we will be monitoring here—the Zabbix agent version, so it probably (hopefully) won't be changing several times per day. Depending on your needs, you might set it to even larger values, such as a week.

To check out the results of our work, go to **Monitoring | Latest data**:

Zabbix agent version	2016-02-24 20:59:45 3.0.0

If you don't see the data, wait a while; it should appear eventually. When it does, you should see the version of the Zabbix agent installed on the listed remote machine, and it might be a higher number than displayed here, as newer versions of Zabbix have been released. Notice one minor difference: while all the items we added previously have links named **Graph** on the right-hand side, the last one has one called **History**. The reason is simple: for textual items, graphs can't be drawn, so Zabbix does not even attempt to do that.

Now, about that waiting—why did we have to wait for the data to appear? Well, remember how active items work? The agent queries the server for the item list it should report on and then sends in data periodically, but this checking of the item list is also done periodically. To find out how often, open the `zabbix_agentd.conf` configuration file on the remote machine and look for the `RefreshActiveChecks` parameter. The default is 2 minutes, which is configured in seconds, thus listing 120 seconds. So, in the worst case, you might have had to wait for nearly 3 minutes to see any data as opposed to normal or passive items, where the server would have queried the agent as soon as the configuration change was available in its cache. In a production environment with many agents using active items, it might be a good idea to increase this value. Usually, item parameters aren't changed that often.

An active agent with multiple servers

The way we configured `ServerActive` in the agent daemon configuration file, it connects to a single Zabbix server and sends data on items to the server. An agent can also work with multiple servers at the same time; we only have to specify additional addresses here as a comma-separated list. In that case, the agent will internally spawn individual processes to work with each server individually. This means that one server won't know what the other server is monitoring—values will be sent to each of them independently. On the other hand, even if several servers request data on individual items, this data will be collected several times, once for each server.

> Always check comments in the configuration files; they can be very useful. In the case of `ServerActive`, the comment shows that an agent may also connect to non-default ports on each server by using syntax like this: `server1:port, server2:port`.

Working with multiple servers in active mode can be useful when migrating from one Zabbix instance to another. For a while, an agent could report to both the old and new servers. Yet another case where this is useful is a customer environment where the customer might have a local Zabbix server performing full-fledged monitoring, while an external company might want to monitor some aspects related to an application they are delivering.

For passive items, allowing incoming connections from multiple Zabbix servers is done the same way: by adding multiple IP addresses to the `Server` parameter.

Supported items

We created some items that use the Zabbix agent in both directions and gather data. But those are hardly the only ones available. You could check out the list while creating an item again (go to **Configuration | Hosts**, click on **Items** for any host, and click on the **Create item** button, followed by the **Select** button next to the **Key** field) in order to see which items are built in for Zabbix agents, along with a short description for most of them.

> Not all Zabbix agent items are available as both passive and active items. For example, **log** and **event log** items (for gathering logfile and Windows event log information, respectively) are only available as active items. Log monitoring is covered in *Chapter 11, Advanced Item Monitoring*, and Windows-specific items in *Chapter 14, Monitoring Windows*.

Looking at the list, we can find out which categories of items Zabbix agents support natively: system configuration, network traffic, network services, system load and memory usage, filesystem monitoring, and others. But that does not mean everything you see there will work on any system that the Zabbix agent daemon runs on. As every platform has a different way of exposing this information and some parameters might even be platform-specific, it isn't guaranteed that every key will work on every host.

For example, when the disk drive statistics report changes to the userspace, the Zabbix agent has to specifically implement support for the new method; thus, older agent versions will support fewer parameters on recent Linux systems. If you are curious about whether a specific parameter works on a specific version of a specific operating system, the best way to find out is to check the Zabbix manual and then test it. Some of the most common agent item keys are as follows:

- agent.ping: This returns 1 when the agent is available and nothing at all when the agent is not available
- net.if.in/out: This provides incoming/outgoing traffic information
- net.tcp.service: This tries to make a simplistic connection to a TCP service
- proc.num: This counts the number of processes and can filter by various parameters
- vfs.fs.size: This provides filesystem usage information
- vm.memory.size: This provides memory usage information

- `system.cpu.load`: This provides CPU load information in a standard decimal representation

- `system.cpu.util`: This provides CPU utilization information, for example, `iowait`

For most of these, various parameters an be specified to filter the result or choose a particular piece of information. For example, `proc.num[,zabbix]` will count all processes that the Zabbix user is running.

Choosing between active and passive items

Even though we discussed Zabbix agents being active or passive, an agent really is neither one nor the other: the direction of the connections is determined by the item level. An agent can (and, by default, does) work in both modes at the same time. Nevertheless, we will have to choose which item type—active or passive—to use. The short version: active items are recommended.

To understand why, let's compare how the connections are made. With a passive agent, it is very simple:

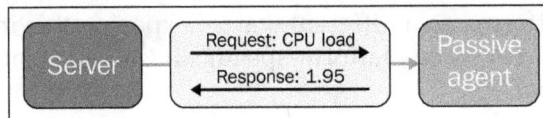

[The arrow direction denotes how connections are made.]

One value means one connection. An active agent is a bit more complicated. Remember: in the active mode, the agent connects to the server; thus, the agent first connects to the Zabbix server and asks for a list of items to be monitored. The server then responds with items, their intervals, and any other relevant information:

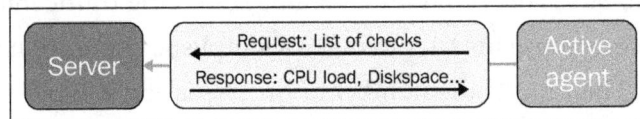

At this point, the connection is closed and the agent starts collecting the information. Once it has some values collected, it sends them to the server:

Note that an active agent can send multiple values in one connection. As a result, active agents will usually result in a lower load on the Zabbix server and a smaller amount of network connections.

The availability icon in the host list represents passive items only; active items do not affect it at all. If a host has active items only, this icon will stay grey. In previous Zabbix versions, if you added passive items that failed and then converted them all to active items, this icon would still stay red. Zabbix 3.0.0 is the first version in which the icon is automatically reset back to grey.

Of course, there are some drawbacks to active items and benefits to passive items too. Let's try to summarize what each item type offers and in which situation they might be better.

The benefits of active items are as follows:

- They have a smaller number of network connections
- They cause lower load on the Zabbix server
- They will work if the network topology or firewalls do not allow connecting from the server to the agent (for example, if the monitored hosts are behind a NAT)
- Items such as log or Windows event log monitoring are supported

Here are the benefits of passive items:

- They are easier to set up for beginners
- Custom intervals are supported (they are not supported by active items)
- Polling a virtual IP address on a cluster allows you to always query the active cluster node
- The default templates use passive items; thus, no modification or other configuration is required to use them

We will discuss using and modifying templates in *Chapter 8, Simplifying Complex Configuration with Templates*.

Item scheduling

Earlier, we discussed what introduces delay before a new item is checked: the Zabbix server configuration cache was mentioned. For passive items, there is another factor involved as well, and it is the way Zabbix schedules items to be polled. Each item is scheduled to be polled at a certain time, and the time between two polls is always constant. Even more, a specific item is always scheduled the same way, no matter when the Zabbix server was started. For example, if an item has a 60-second interval, it could be configured to be polled at second 13 of every minute. If the Zabbix server is restarted, this item will still be polled at second 13 of every minute. This scheduling is based on an **internal item ID**; thus, a specific item will not get this timing changed during its lifetime unless it is deleted and recreated or the item interval is changed.

> This logic is similar for all polled item types and will be relevant when we configure SNMP and other item types.

Active items get their polling started upon agent startup; thus, the specific time when values arrive will change based on when the agent was started. Additionally, active items are processed in a serial fashion; thus, one slow item can delay the values for other items from the same agent.

To summarize, after we add a new passive item, it is saved in the database — the Zabbix server does not know about it yet. This item is then loaded into the configuration cache. The configuration cache is refreshed every 60 seconds by default. After the server finds out about the new item, it schedules the item to be polled for the first time at some point between that moment and the item interval.

This means that with the default interval of 30 seconds, it may take from 30 to 90 seconds before the first value arrives for the item. If the item has a very long interval, such as a serial number or agent version configured earlier, it may take a very long time until the first value appears automatically. There is no way to speed up item polling except by adding it with a short interval at first and then increasing the interval when the item has been verified to work as expected.

After a new active item is added, it is saved in the database again and the Zabbix server does not know about it yet. The active Zabbix agent periodically connects to the server to gather information about items it is supposed to monitor, but as it is not in the configuration cache yet, the server does not tell the agent about the item. This item is then loaded into the configuration cache. The configuration cache is refreshed every 60 seconds by default. After the server finds out about the new item, the item is available to the agent, but the agent connects to the server every 2 minutes by default. Once the agent finds out about the new item, it immediately attempts to collect the first value for it.

> Refer *Chapter 22, Zabbix Maintenance*, for details on how to tune these intervals.

In both cases, if an item is set to delta, we have to obtain two values before we can compute the final value that will be stored in the database and displayed in the frontend—we can't compute the difference from just one value.

Simple checks

The previously created items all required the Zabbix agent daemon to be installed, running, and able to make a connection in either direction. But what if you can't or don't want to install the agent on a remote host and only need to monitor simple things? This is where simple checks can help you. These checks do not require any specialized agent running on the remote end and only rely on basic network protocols such as **Internet Control Message Protocol (ICMP)** and TCP to query monitored hosts.

> Host-availability icons only cover the Zabbix agent, SNMP, JMX, and IPMI status, that is, things where we expect the response to arrive. Our expectations for simple checks could go both ways—an open port could be good or bad. There is no status icon for simple checks.

Let's create a very basic check now. Go to **Configuration | Hosts**, click on **Items** next to **Another host**, and click on **Create item**. Use the following values:

- **Name**: Enter SMTP server status
- **Type**: Select **Simple check**
- **Key**: Click on the **Select** button

The **Type** dropdown at the upper-right corner should already say **Simple check**. If it doesn't, change it to that. In the **Key** list, click on the net.tcp. service[service,<ip>,<port>] key and then edit it. Replace service with smtp and remove everything after it in the square brackets so that it becomes net.tcp. service[smtp], like so:

Name	SMTP server status	
Type	Simple check ▾	
Key	net.tcp.service[smtp]	Select

> When configuring simple checks in Zabbix, beware of "paranoid" network security configurations that might trigger an alert if you check too many services too often.

When done, click on the **Add** button at the bottom. To check the result, go to **Monitoring | Latest data** — our new check should be there and, depending on whether you have the SMTP server running and accessible for the Zabbix server, should list either **1** (if running and accessible) or **0**.

Setting up ICMP checks

What if we care only about the basic reachability of a host, such as a router or switch that is out of our control? ICMP ping (echo request and reply) would be an appropriate method for monitoring in that case, and Zabbix supports such simple checks. Usually, these won't work right away; to use them, we'll have to set up a separate utility, fping, which Zabbix uses for ICMP checks. It should be available for most distributions, so just install it using your distribution's package-management tools. If not, you'll have to download and compile fping manually; it's available at http://fping.sourceforge.net/.

> At the time of writing this, Zabbix 3.0 still does not fully support fping 3. Most notably, setting the source IP for the server will break ICMP ping items. Such support is currently planned for version 3.0.2. For any later version, check compatibility information in the manual. Installing `fping` from distribution packages is likely to provide version 3, and it is also available at `http://fping.org/`.

Once `fping` is properly installed, Zabbix server must know where to find it and be able to execute it. On the Zabbix server, open `zabbix_server.conf` and look for the `FpingLocation` parameter. It is commented out by default, and it defaults to `/usr/sbin/fping`. You can quickly find the `fping` binary location with this command:

```
$ which fping
```

If one of the results is `/usr/sbin/fping`, you don't have to change this parameter. If not, modify the parameter to point to the correct `fping` location and restart the Zabbix server so that it knows about the configuration change. That's not it yet. Zabbix also needs to be able to run `fping` with administrative privileges, so execute the following as `root`:

```
# chgrp zabbix /usr/sbin/fping
# chmod 4710 /usr/sbin/fping
```

> Permissions are usually already correct in Fedora/RHEL-based distributions. If you're using distribution packages, don't execute the previous commands; they might even disallow access for the Zabbix server, as it might be running under a different group.

As the `fping` binary should have been owned by `root` before, this should be enough to allow its use by the Zabbix group as required; let's verify that.

As usual, navigate to **Configuration | Hosts,** click on **Items** next to **Another host,** and click on **Create item.** Set the following details:

- **Name:** `ICMP ping performance`
- **Type: Simple check**
- **Key:** Click on the **Select** button; in the list, click on the `icmppingsec` key, and then remove everything inside the square brackets — and the brackets themselves
- **Type of information:** `Numeric (float)`
- **Units:** `ms`

- **Use custom multiplier**: Select the checkbox and enter `1000`

Name	ICMP ping performance
Type	Simple check ▾
Key	icmppingsec[<target>,<packets>,<interval>,<size>,<t Select
Host interface	192.168.56.11 : 10050 ▾
User name	
Password	
Type of information	Numeric (float) ▾
Units	ms
Use custom multiplier	▦ 1000

When all fields have been correctly set, click on the **Add** button at the bottom. Perform the usual round trip to **Monitoring | Latest data** — ICMP ping should be recording data already. If you wait for a few minutes, you can also take a look at a relatively interesting graph to notice any changes in the network performance.

ICMP ping performance	2016-02-25 20:30:34 0.59 ms

Here, we set up ICMP ping measuring network latency in seconds. If you wanted to simply test host connectivity, you would have chosen the `icmpping` key, which would only record whether the ping was successful or not. That's a simple way to test connectivity on a large scale, as it puts a small load on the network (unless you use ridiculously small intervals). Of course, there are things to be aware of, such as doing something different to test Internet connectivity — it wouldn't be enough to test the connection to your router, firewall, or even your provider's routers. The best way would be to choose several remote targets to monitor that are known to have a very good connection and availability.

For ICMP ping items, several parameters can be specified. For example, the full `icmpping` key syntax is as follows:

```
icmpping[<target>,<packets>,<interval>,<size>,<timeout>]
```

By default, `target` is taken from the host this item is assigned to, but that can be overridden. The `packets` parameter enables you to specify how many packets each invocation should issue — usually, the `fping` default is `3`. The `interval` parameter enables you to configure the interval between these packets — usually, the `fping` default is 1 second against the same target, specified in milliseconds. As for `size`, here, the default of a single packet could differ based on the `fping` version, architecture, and maybe other parameters. And the last one — `timeout` — sets individual target timeouts, with a common default being `500` milliseconds.

> These defaults are not Zabbix defaults — if not specified, `fping` defaults are used.

Note that one should not set ICMP ping items with very large timeouts or packet counts; it can lead to weird results. For example, setting the packet count to 60 and using a 60-second interval on an item will likely result in that item missing every second value.

If you set up several ICMP ping items against the same host, Zabbix invokes the `fping` utility only once. If multiple hosts have ICMP ping items, Zabbix will invoke `fping` once for all hosts that have to be pinged at the same time with the same parameters (such as `packet`, `size`, and `timeout`).

Tying it all together

So, we found out that a normal or passive agent waits for the server to connect, while an active agent connects to the server, grabs a list of items to check, and then reconnects to the server periodically to send in the data. This means that using one or the other kind of Zabbix agent item can impact performance. In general, active agents reduce the load on the Zabbix server because the server doesn't have to keep a list of what and when to check. Instead, the agent picks up that task and reports back to the server. But you should evaluate each case separately: if you only have a few items per host that you monitor very rarely (the update interval is set to a large value), converting all agents to active ones that retrieve the item list more often than the items were previously checked won't improve Zabbix server performance.

> It is important to remember that you can use a mixture of various items against a single host. As we just saw, a single host can have normal or passive Zabbix agent items, active Zabbix agent items, and simple checks assigned. This allows you to choose the best fit for monitoring every characteristic to ensure the best connectivity and performance and the least impact on the network and the monitored host. And that's not all yet — we'll explore several additional item types, which again can be mixed with the ones we already know for a single configured host.

Key parameter quoting

Zabbix key parameters are comma-delimited and enclosed in square brackets. This means that any other character can be used in the parameters as is. If your parameters include commas or square brackets, they will have to be in quote marks. Here are a few examples:

- `key[param1,param2]`: This key has two parameters, `param1` and `param2`
- `key["param1,param2"]`: This key has one parameter, `param1` and `param2`
- `key[param1[param2]`: This is an invalid key
- `key['param1,param2']`: This key has two parameters, `'param1` and `param2'`

What's up with the last one ? Well, Zabbix item keys are not shell-interpreted. Zabbix specifically supports double quotes for key parameter quoting. Single quotes are treated like any other character.

Positional parameters for item names

While we're working with items, let's explore some more tricks. Go to **Configuration | Hosts**, click on **Items** next to **Another host**, and then click on **Incoming traffic on interface eth0** in the **NAME** column. In the item-editing form, click on the **Clone** button at the bottom. In the new form, modify the **Key** field so that it reads `net.if.in[lo]`, and then click on the **Add** button at the bottom.

You might notice it right away, or go to **Monitoring | Latest data** and look at the list. Despite the fact that we only modified the key, the item name was updated accordingly as well:

Incoming traffic on interface enp0s8	2016-02-25 20:43:58	64 Bps
Incoming traffic on interface lo	2016-02-25 20:43:58	40 Bps

That's what the `$1` part in the item **Name** field is doing. It's working like a common positional parameter, taking the first parameter of the item key. If we had more parameters, we could access those for inclusion in the name with `$2`, `$3`, and so on. This is mostly useful in cases where you want to create several items that monitor different entities so that when cloning the items, you have to change only a single instance of the identifier. It's easier than it seems to miss some change when there are multiple locations, thus creating items with mismatched configuration.

Now that we have some more items configured, it's worth looking at another monitoring view. While we spent most of our time in **Monitoring | Latest data**, this time, navigate to **Monitoring | Overview**. The **Type** dropdown in the upper-right corner currently lists **Triggers**, which does not provide a very exciting view for us: we only have a single trigger created. But we did create several items, so switch this dropdown to **Data**:

Overview		Group all ▾	Type Data ▾	Hosts location Top ▾
			ANOTHER HOST	A TEST HOST
ITEMS				
CPU load				0.21
ICMP ping performance			0.48 ms	
Incoming traffic on interface enp0s8			74 Bps	
Incoming traffic on interface lo			40 Bps	
SMTP server status			1	
SSH server status			1	
Web server status			1	
Zabbix agent version			2.5.1	

This time, the overview page is a bit more interesting: we can see which hosts have which items and item values.

Using mass update

Now this looks quite good—we can see all of the monitored data in a compact form. Those 1 results that denote the status for various servers—what do they mean? Was 1 for a running state, or was it an error, like with exit codes? They surely aren't intuitive enough, so let's try to remedy that. Go to **Configuration | Hosts**, and click on **Items** for **Another host**. Select all three server status items (**SMTP**, **SSH**, and **Web**), and then look at the buttons at the bottom of the item list:

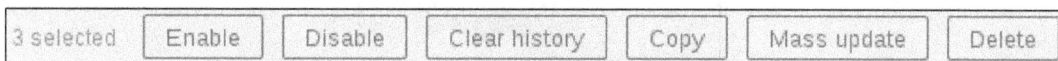

3 selected	Enable	Disable	Clear history	Copy	Mass update	Delete

This time, we will want to make a single change for all the selected items, so the second button from the right looks like what we need—it says **Mass update**. Click on it:

Type	Original
Host interface	Original
SNMP community	Original
Context name	Original
Security name	Original
Security level	Original
Authentication protocol	Original
Authentication passphrase	Original
Privacy protocol	Original
Privacy passphrase	Original
Port	Original
Type of information	Original
Data type	Original
Units	Original
Authentication method	Original
User name	Original
Public key file	Original
Private key file	Original
Password	Original
Custom multiplier (0 - Disabled)	Original
Update interval (in sec)	Original
Custom intervals	Original
History storage period (in days)	Original
Trend storage period (in days)	Original
Status	Original
Log time format	Original
Store value	Original
Show value	Original
Allowed hosts	Original
Replace applications	Original
Add new or existing applications	Original
Description	Original

Update   Cancel

Now that's an interesting screen—it allows us to change some parameters for multiple items at once. While doing that, only changes that are marked and specified are performed, so we can change some common values for otherwise wildly differing items. It allows us to set things such as the **Update interval** or any other parameter together for the selected items.

Value mapping

This time, we are interested in only one value—the one that decides how the value is displayed to us. Mark the checkbox next to the **Show value entry** to see the available options.

Looks like somebody has already defined entries here, but let's find out what it actually means before making a decision. Click on the **Show value mappings** link to the right on the same line:

Value mapping	
NAME ▲	VALUE MAP
APC Battery Peplacement Status	1 ⇒ unknown 2 ⇒ notInstalled 3 ⇒ ok 4 ⇒ failed 5 ⇒ highTemperature 6 ⇒ replaceImmediately 7 ⇒ lowCapacity
APC Battery Status	1 ⇒ unknown 2 ⇒ batteryNormal 3 ⇒ batteryLow
Dell Open Manage System Status	1 ⇒ Other 2 ⇒ Unknown 3 ⇒ OK 4 ⇒ NonCritical 5 ⇒ Critical 6 ⇒ NonRecoverable

Looking at the list, we can see various names, each of them having a list of mapped references. Look at the **NAME** column, where the predefined entries have hints about what they are good for. You can see UPS-related mappings, generic status/state, SNMP, and Windows service-related mappings. The **VALUE MAP** column shows the exact mappings that are assigned to each entry. But what exactly are they? Looking at the entries, you can see things such as **0 => Down** or **1 => Up**. Data arriving for an item that has a value mapping assigned will expose the descriptive mappings. You are free to create any mapping you desire. To create a new category of mapped data, you need to use the button in the upper-right corner called **Create value map**. We won't do that now, because one of the available mappings covers our needs quite well. Look at the entries—remember the items we were curious about? They were monitoring a service and they used 1 to denote a service that is running and 0 to denote a service that is down. Looking at the list, we can see an entry, **Service state**, which defines 0 as **Down** and 1 as **Up**—exactly what we need. Well, that means we don't have to create or modify any entries, so simply close this window.

> You can access the value map configuration screen at any time by navigating to **Administration** | **General** and choosing **show value mappings** from the dropdown in the upper-right corner.

Back in the mass-update screen, recall the mapping entries we just saw and remember which entry fit our requirements the best. Choose **Service state** from the dropdown for the only entry whose checkbox we marked—**Show value**:

Show value ▣	Service state	▾	show value mappings

When you are done, click on the **Update** button. This operation should complete successfully. You can click on the **Details** control in the upper-left corner to verify that all three items we intended were updated.

Let's see how our change affected information display. Configured and assigned value mappings are used in most Zabbix frontend locations where it makes sense. For example, let's visit that old friend of ours, **Monitoring** | **Latest data**. Take a close look at the various server status entries—Zabbix still shows numeric values for the reference, but each has conveniently listed an appropriate "friendly name" mapped value:

SMTP server status	2016-02-25 21:20:00	Down (0)
SSH server status	2016-02-25 21:19:57	Up (1)
Web server status	2016-02-25 21:19:56	Up (1)

We have currently stopped the SMTP server to verify whether both **1 => Up** and **0 => Down** mappings work—as we can see, they do. Value mapping will be useful for returned data that works like code values—service states, hardware states (such as batteries), and other similar monitored data. We saw some predefined examples in the value-mapping configuration screen before, and you are free to modify or create new mappings according to your needs.

Value mapping can be used for integers, decimal values (floats), and strings. One use case for strings could be the mapping of different backup levels that a backup software might return:

- I => Incremental
- D => Differential
- F => Full

Navigate back to **Monitoring | Overview** and again, look at the various server status entries for **ANOTHER HOST**:

While value mapping doesn't seem too useful when you have to remember a single monitored characteristic with only two possible states, it becomes very useful when there are many different possible states and many possible mappings so that in most locations, you will have a quick hint about what each numeric value means and you are always free to invent your own mappings for custom-developed solutions.

Units

We previously configured units for some items, using values such as B or ms. While the effect was visible in the monitoring section quite easily, there are some subtle differences in the handling of different units.

Units is a freeform field. You can type anything in there, but some units will change their behavior when data is displayed:

- **B/Bps**: By default, when applying **K**, **M**, **G**, **T** and other unit prefixes, Zabbix will use a multiplier of 1,000. If the unit is set to **B** or **Bps**, the multiplier used will be changed to 1,024

- **s**: An incoming value in seconds will be translated to a human-readable format

- **uptime**: An incoming value in seconds will be translated to a human-readable format

- **unixtime**: An incoming Unix timestamp will be translated to a human-readable format

Interestingly, for our ICMP ping item, we did not use any of these; we used ms instead. The reason is that in certain cases of a very small roundtrip, a value in seconds might be too small to properly store in the Zabbix database schema. By applying the multiplier of 1,000 in the item configuration, we converted the incoming value in seconds to milliseconds, which should never exceed the limits of the database schema. One downside would be that if a ping takes a long time, the value will not be displayed in seconds—we will have to figure it out from the millisecond value.

> Units do not affect the stored values, only what gets displayed. We may safely change them back and forth until we get them right.

Custom intervals

Another item property that we just briefly discussed was custom intervals. Most item types have their intervals configurable, which determines how often the item values should be collected. But what if we would like to change this interval based on the day of the week or the time of day? That is exactly what custom intervals enable us to do. There are two modes for custom intervals:

- Flexible intervals
- Custom scheduling

Flexible intervals

Flexible intervals override the normal interval for the specified time. For example, an item could collect values every 60 seconds, but that item might not be important during the weekend. In that case, a flexible interval could be added with an interval of 3600 and time specification of 6-7,00:00-24:00. During Saturdays and Sundays, this item would only be checked once an hour:

Custom intervals	TYPE		INTERVAL	PERIOD	ACTION
	Flexible	Scheduling	3600	6-7,00:00-24:00	Remove
	Add				

> Up to seven flexible intervals may be added for a single item.

Days are represented with the numbers 1-7 and a 24-hour clock notation of HH:MM-HH:MM is used.

> In case you were wondering, the week starts with a Monday here.

It is also possible to set the normal interval to 0 and configure flexible intervals. In this case, the item will only be checked at the times specified in the flexible intervals. This functionality can be used to check some item on a specific weekday only or even to simulate a crude scheduler. If an item is added with a normal interval of 0, a flexible interval of 60 seconds, and a time specification of 1,09:00-09:01, this item will be checked on Monday morning at 9 o'clock.

> **Overlapping flexible intervals**
>
> If two flexible intervals with different values overlap, during the overlap period, the smallest value is used. For example, if flexible intervals with periods 1-5,00-24:00 and 5-6,12:00-24:00 are added to the same item, during Friday, from 12:00 to 24:00, the one that has the smallest interval will be used.

Custom scheduling

The example of having a flexible interval of 1 minute works, but it's not very precise. For more exact timing, the other custom interval type can be used: **scheduling**. This enables you to obtain item values at an exact time. It also has one major difference from flexible intervals. Flexible intervals change how an item is polled, but custom scheduling does not change the existing polling. Scheduled checks are executed in addition to the normal or flexible intervals.

It may sound a lot like `crontab`, but Zabbix custom scheduling uses its own syntax. The time prefix is followed by a filter entry. Multiple time prefix and filter values are concatenated, going from the biggest to the smallest. The supported time prefixes are:

- `md`: month days
- `wd`: weekdays
- `h`: hours
- `m`: minutes
- `s`: seconds

For example, an entry of `m13` will schedule this item to be polled every hour at the beginning of minute 13. If it is combined with a weekday specification as `wd3m13`, it will be polled every hour at the beginning of minute 13 on Wednesdays only. Changing the weekday reference to the month day — or date — reference as `md13m13` would make this item be polled every hour at the beginning of minute 13 on the thirteenth day only.

The example of polling the item on Monday morning at 09:00 we looked at before would be `wd1h9`:

Custom intervals	TYPE		INTERVAL	PERIOD ACTION
	Flexible	Scheduling	wd1h9	Remove
	Add			

The filter can also be a range. For example, polling an item at 09:00 on Monday, Tuesday, and Wednesday would be done as `wd1-3h9`.

At the end of the filter, we can also add a step through a slash. For example, `wd1-5h6-10/2` would poll the item from Monday to Friday, starting at 06:00 every other hour until 10:00. The item would get polled at 06:00, 08:00 and 10:00. To make an item be polled every other hour all day long on all days, the syntax of `h/2` can be used.

Multiple custom intervals may also be specified by separating them with a semicolon—`wd1-5/2` and `wd1;wd3;wd5` would both poll an item at the beginning of Monday, Wednesday, and Friday.

Copying items

Looking at the same overview screen, the data seems easier to understand with textual hints provided for previously cryptic numeric values, but there's still a bit of not-so-perfect displaying. Notice the dashes displayed for the **CPU load** item for **Another host** and all other values for **A test host**. We didn't create corresponding items on both hosts, and item data is displayed here, which means missing items should be created for each host to gather the data. But recreating all items would be very boring. Luckily, there's a simple and straightforward solution to this problem.

Go to **Configuration** | **Hosts** and click on **Items** next to **A test host**. We had only a single item configured for this host, so mark the checkbox next to this item. Let's look at the available buttons at the bottom of the list again:

This time, we don't want to update selected items, but copy them to another host, so click on the **Copy** button. We want to copy these items to a specific host, so choose **Hosts** in the **Target type** dropdown and select **Linux servers** in the **Group** dropdown, which should leave us with a short list of hosts. We are copying from **A test host** to **Another host**; mark the checkbox next to the **Another host** entry and click on the **Copy** button:

When the operation has completed, change the **Host filter** field (expand the filter if it is closed) to **Another host**, and then click on **Filter** below the filter itself. Notice how the **CPU load** item has appeared in the list. This time, mark all the items except **CPU load**, because that's the only item **A test host** has. You can use the standard range selection functionality here—mark the checkbox next to the ICMP ping performance item (the first item in the range we want to select), hold down *Shift* on the keyboard, and click on the checkbox next to the Zabbix agent version (the last item in the range we want to select). This should select all the items between the two checkboxes we clicked on.

> Using *Shift* and clicking works to both select and unselect arbitrary entry ranges, including items, hosts, triggers, and other entries in the Zabbix frontend. It works both upwards and downwards. The result of the action depends on the first checkbox marked—if you select it, the whole range will be selected, and vice versa.

With those items selected, click on **Copy** below the item list. Choose **Hosts** in the **Target type** dropdown, choose **Linux servers** in the **Group** dropdown, mark only the checkbox next to **A test host**, and click on **Copy**. After that, click on the **Details** link in the upper-right corner. Notice how all the copied items are listed here. Let's take another look at **Monitoring | Overview**:

ITEMS	ANOTHER HOST	A TEST HOST
CPU load	0	0.19
ICMP ping performance	0.76 ms	0.07 ms
Incoming traffic on interface enp0s8	53 Bps	859 Bps
Incoming traffic on interface lo	41 Bps	194 Bps
SMTP server status	Down (0)	Up (1)
SSH server status	Up (1)	Up (1)
Web server status	Up (1)	Up (1)
Zabbix agent version	3.0.0	3.0.0

Great, that's much better! We can see all the data for the two hosts, with the numeric status nicely explained. Basically, we just cross-copied items that did not exist on one host from the other one.

But it only gets better—mouseover to the displayed values. Notice how the chosen row is highlighted. Let's click on one of the **CPU load** values:

As you can see, the overview screen not only shows you data in a tabular form, it also allows quick access to common timescale graphs and the **Latest values** for the item. Feel free to try that out.

When you have looked at the data, click on one of the Zabbix agent version values:

Notice how this time there are no entries for graphs. Remember: graphs were only available for numeric data, so **Monitoring | Latest data** and these overview screen pop-up menus offer the value history only.

Summary

This time, we created a new host and added several normal or passive agent items and active agent items.

We learned that it is good practice to disable active items if they are not used by commenting out the `ServerActive` parameter. If passive items are not used, they can be disabled by setting `StartAgents` to `0`, although leaving them enabled can help with testing and debugging.

We set up simple checks on two different hosts and explored many tricks and mechanisms to ease managing in the frontend, such as item cloning, copying, and value mapping.

It might be worth remembering how connections are made for active and passive Zabbix agent item types—that's important when you have to decide on monitoring mechanisms based on existing network topology and configuration.

Let's look at the following diagram, summarizing those connections. The arrow direction denotes how connections are made:

Discussing benefits and drawbacks, we found that active items are recommended over passive items in most cases.

Listed here are the default ports that can be changed if necessary:

- Normal or passive items: The Zabbix server connects to a Zabbix agent, which in turn gathers the data
- Active items: The Zabbix agent connects to a Zabbix server, retrieves a list of things to monitor, gathers the data, and then periodically reports back to the server
- Simple checks: The Zabbix server directly queries the exposed network interfaces of the monitored host; no agent is required

The simple checks were different: they never used the Zabbix agent and were performed directly from the Zabbix server. Simple checks included TCP port checking.

This covers the two basic, most commonly used check types: a Zabbix agent with bidirectional connection support and simple checks that are performed directly from the server.

In the next chapter, we will look at SNMP monitoring. We'll start with a quick introduction to the Net-SNMP tools and basic **Management Information Base (MIB)** management and will set up SNMP polling with fixed and dynamic OIDs. We will also receive SNMP traps and map them to hosts and items both using the built-in method and a very custom approach.

4
Monitoring SNMP Devices

Now that we are familiar both with monitoring using Zabbix agents and an agentless method, let's explore an additional method that does not require Zabbix agent installation, even though it needs an agent of some kind anyway. Simple Network Management Protocol, commonly called SNMP, is a well-established and popular network-monitoring solution. We'll learn to configure and use SNMP with Zabbix, including SNMP polling and trap receiving.

Being more than two decades old, SNMP has had the time to become widespread across a whole range of networked devices. Although the name implies management functionality, it's mostly used for monitoring. As the first versions had security drawbacks, the ability to modify configuration over SNMP did not become as popular as its read-only counterpart.

SNMP as the primary monitoring solution is especially popular in embedded devices, where running a complete operating system and installing separate monitoring agents would be overkill. Two of the most popular device categories implementing SNMP out of the box are printers and various network devices, such as switches, routers, and firewalls. SNMP allows the easy monitoring of these otherwise quite closed devices. Other devices with SNMP agents provided include UPSes, **network-attached storage** (**NAS**) devices, and computer rack temperature/humidity sensors. Of course, SNMP is in no way restricted to devices with limited processing power — it's perfectly fine to run a generic SNMP agent instead of a specialized monitoring agent on standard servers. Reasons to use SNMP agents instead of Zabbix agents might include already installed and set up SNMP agents, no access to monitored hosts to install Zabbix agents, or a desire to keep systems relatively free from dependencies on monitoring software.

Given the prevalence of SNMP, it's no wonder Zabbix supports it out of the box. SNMP support in Zabbix builds upon another quality open source product — Net-SNMP (http://net-snmp.sourceforge.net/).

In this chapter, we will:

- Look at basic Net-SNMP tools
- Learn how to add **Management Information Base (MIB)** files so that Zabbix recognizes them
- Configure both SNMP polling and trap receiving

Using Net-SNMP

If you installed Zabbix from the distribution packages, SNMP support should be already included. If you compiled Zabbix from source, it should still have SNMP support, as we included that in the configure flags. All that's left to do is set up SNMP monitoring configuration. Before we do that, we'll need a device that has an SNMP agent installed. This is where you can choose between various options—you can use any networked device that you have access to, such as a manageable switch, network printer, or a UPS with an SNMP interface. As SNMP agents usually listen on port 161, you will need the ability to connect to such a device on this port over **User Datagram Protocol (UDP)**. Although TCP is also supported, UDP is much more widely used.

If you don't have access to such a device, you could also start up an SNMP daemon on a computer. For example, you could easily use **Another host** as a test bed for SNMP querying. Many distributions ship with the SNMP daemon from the Net-SNMP package, and often it is enough to simply start the snmpd service. If that's not the case for your chosen distribution, you'll either have to find one of those networked devices with an SNMP agent already available or configure snmpd manually.

For testing, it may be enough to have a line like the following in /etc/snmp/snmpd. conf:

```
rocommunity public
```

This allows full read access to anybody who uses the public community string.

[Do not use such a configuration in production.]

Whichever way you choose, you will have to find out what data the device actually provides and how to get it. This is where Net-SNMP comes in, providing many useful tools to work with SNMP-enabled devices. We will use several of these tools to discover information that is required to configure SNMP items in Zabbix.

Let's start by verifying whether our SNMP device is reachable and responds to our queries.

While SNMPv3 has been the current version of SNMP since 2004, it is still not as widespread as SNMPv1 and SNMPv2. There are a whole lot of old devices in use that only support older protocol versions, and many vendors do not hurry with SNMPv3 implementations.

To complicate things further, SNMPv2 also isn't widely used. Instead, a variation of it, the community-based SNMPv2, or SNMPv2c, is used. While devices can support both v1 and v2c, some only support one of these. Both use so-called **community authentication**, where user authentication is performed based on a single community string. Therefore, to query a device, you would have to know which protocol version it supports and the community string to use. It's not as hard as it sounds. By default, many devices use a common string for access, public, as does the Net-SNMP daemon. Unless you explicitly change this string, you can just assume that's what is needed to query any host.

> In some distributions, the Net-SNMP daemon and tools can be split out in separate packages. In such cases, install the tool package as well.

If you have installed and started Net-SNMP daemon on **Another host**, you can perform a simple query to verify SNMP connectivity:

```
$ snmpstatus -v 2c -c public <IP address>
```

If the daemon has been started correctly and network connectivity is fine, you should get some output, depending on the system you have:

```
[UDP: [<IP address>]:161->[0.0.0.0]:51887]=>[Linux another
3.11.10-29-default #1 SMP Thu Mar 5 16:24:00 UTC 2015 (338c513) x86_64]
Up: 10:10:46.20
```

```
Interfaces: 3, Recv/Trans packets: 300/281 | IP: 286/245
```

We can see here that it worked, and by default, communication was done over UDP to port 161. We can see the target system's operating system, hostname, kernel version, when was it compiled and what hardware architecture it was compiled for, and the current uptime. There's also some network statistics information tacked on.

If you are trying to query a network device, it might have restrictions on who is allowed to use the SNMP agent. Some devices allow free access to SNMP data, while some restrict it by default and every connecting host has to be allowed explicitly. If a device does not respond, check its configuration—you might have to add the IP address of the querying machine to the SNMP permission list.

Looking at the `snmpstatus` command itself, we passed two parameters to it: the SNMP version (`2c` in this case) and community (which is, as discussed before, `public`).

If you have other SNMP-enabled hosts, you can try the same command on them. Let's look at various devices:

```
$ snmpstatus -v 2c -c public <IP address>
[UDP: [<IP address>]:161]=>[IBM Infoprint 1532 version NS.NP.N118 kernel
2.6.6 All-N-1] Up: 5 days, 0:29:53.22
Interfaces: 0, Recv/Trans packets: 63/63 | IP: 1080193/103316
```

As we can see, this has to be an IBM printer. And hey, it seems to be using a Linux kernel.

While many systems will respond to version `2c` queries, sometimes you might see the following:

```
$ snmpstatus -v 2c -c public <IP address>
Timeout: No Response from <IP address>
```

This could of course mean network problems, but sometimes SNMP agents ignore requests coming in with a protocol version they do not support or an incorrect community string. If the community string is incorrect, you would have to find out what it has been set to; this is usually easily available in the device or SNMP daemon configuration (for example, Net-SNMP usually has it set in the `/etc/snmp/snmp.conf` configuration file). If you believe a device might not support a particular protocol version, you can try another command:

```
$ snmpstatus -v 1 -c public <IP address>
[UDP: [<IP address>]:161]=>[HP ETHERNET MULTI-ENVIRONMENT,SN:CNBW71B06G,F
N:JK227AB,SVCID:00000,PID:HP LaserJet P2015 Series] Up: 3:33:44.22
Interfaces: 2, Recv/Trans packets: 135108/70066 | IP: 78239/70054
```

So this HP LaserJet printer did not support SNMPv2c, only v1. Still, when queried using SNMPv1, it divulged information such as the serial number and series name.

Let's look at another SNMPv1-only device:

```
$ snmpstatus -v 1 -c public <IP address>
[UDP: [<IP address>]:161]=>[APC Web/SNMP Management Card (MB:v3.6.8
PF:v2.6.4 PN:apc_hw02_aos_264.bin AF1:v2.6.1 AN1:apc_hw02_sumx_261.bin
MN:AP9617 HR:A10 SN: ZA0542025896 MD:10/17/2005) (Embedded PowerNet SNMP
Agent SW v2.2 compatible)] Up: 157 days, 20:42:55.19
Interfaces: 1, Recv/Trans packets: 2770626/2972781 | IP: 2300062/2388450
```

This seems to be an APC UPS, and it's providing a lot of information stuffed in this output, including serial number and even firmware versions. It also has considerably longer uptime than the previous systems: over 157 days.

But surely, there must be more information obtainable through SNMP, and also this looks a bit messy. Let's try another command from the Net-SNMP arsenal, `snmpwalk`. This command tries to return all the values available from a particular SNMP agent, so the output could be very large — we'd better restrict it to a few lines at first:

```
$ snmpwalk -v 2c -c public 10.1.1.100 | head -n 6
SNMPv2-MIB::sysDescr.0 = STRING: Linux zab 2.6.16.60-0.21-default #1 Tue
May 6 12:41:02 UTC 2008 i686
SNMPv2-MIB::sysObjectID.0 = OID: NET-SNMP-MIB::netSnmpAgentOIDs.10
DISMAN-EVENT-MIB::sysUpTimeInstance = Timeticks: (8411956) 23:21:59.56
SNMPv2-MIB::sysContact.0 = STRING: Sysadmin (root@localhost)
SNMPv2-MIB::sysName.0 = STRING: zab
SNMPv2-MIB::sysLocation.0 = STRING: Server Room
```

> This syntax did not specify OID, and `snmpwalk` defaulted to `SNMPv2-SMI::mib-2`. Some devices will have useful information in other parts of the tree. To query the full tree, specify a single dot as the OID value, like this:
>
> `snmpwalk -v 2c -c public 10.1.1.100`

As we can see, this command outputs various values, with a name or identifier displayed on the left and the value itself on the right. Indeed, the identifier is called the **object identifier** or **OID**, and it is a unique string, identifying a single value.

Calling everything on the left-hand side an **OID** is a simplification. It actually consists of an **MIB**, **OID**, and **UID**, as shown here:

```
SNMPv2-MIB::sysDescr . 0

    MIB          OID    UID
```

Nevertheless, it is commonly referred to as just the OID, and we will use the same shorthand in this book. Exceptions will be cases when we will actually refer to the MIB or UID part.

Looking at the output, we can also identify some of the data we saw in the output of snmpstatus—SNMPv2-MIB::sysDescr.0 and DISMAN-EVENT-MIB::sysUpTimeInstance. Two other values, SNMPv2-MIB::sysContact.0 and SNMPv2-MIB::sysLocation.0, haven't been changed from the defaults, and thus aren't too useful right now. While we are at it, let's compare this output to the one from the APC UPS:

```
$ snmpwalk -v 1 -c <IP address> | head -n 6

SNMPv2-MIB::sysDescr.0 = STRING: APC Web/SNMP Management Card (MB:v3.6.8
PF:v2.6.4 PN:apc_hw02_aos_264.bin AF1:v2.6.1 AN1:apc_hw02_sumx_261.bin
MN:AP9617 HR:A10 SN: ZA0542025896 MD:10/17/2005) (Embedded PowerNet SNMP
Agent SW v2.2 compatible)

SNMPv2-MIB::sysObjectID.0 = OID: PowerNet-MIB::smartUPS450

DISMAN-EVENT-MIB::sysUpTimeInstance = Timeticks: (1364829916) 157 days,
23:11:39.16

SNMPv2-MIB::sysContact.0 = STRING: Unknown

SNMPv2-MIB::sysName.0 = STRING: Unknown

SNMPv2-MIB::sysLocation.0 = STRING: Unknown
```

The output is quite similar, containing the same OIDs, and the system contact and location values aren't set as well. But to monitor some things, we have to retrieve a single value per item, and we can verify that it works with another command, snmpget:

```
$ snmpget -v 2c -c public 10.1.1.100 DISMAN-EVENT-MIB::sysUpTimeInstance
DISMAN-EVENT-MIB::sysUpTimeInstance = Timeticks: (8913849) 1 day,
0:45:38.49
```

We can add any valid OID, such as DISMAN-EVENT-MIB::sysUpTimeInstance in the previous example, after the host to get whatever value it holds. The OID itself currently consists of two parts, separated by two colons. As discussed earlier, the first part is the name of a **Management Information Base** or **MIB**. MIBs are collections of item descriptions, mapping numeric forms to textual ones. The second part is the OID itself. There is no UID in this case. We can look at the full identifier by adding a -Of flag to modify the output:

```
$ snmpget -v 2c -c public -Of 10.1.1.100 DISMAN-EVENT-
MIB::sysUpTimeInstance

.iso.org.dod.internet.mgmt.mib-2.system.sysUpTime.sysUpTimeInstance =
Timeticks: (8972788) 1 day, 0:55:27.88
```

> To translate from the numeric to the textual form, an MIB is needed. In some cases, the standard MIBs are enough, but many devices have useful information in vendor-specific extensions. Some vendors provide quality MIBs for their equipment, some are less helpful. Contact your vendor to obtain any required MIBs. We will discuss basic MIB management later in this chapter.

That's a considerably long name, showing the tree-like structure. It starts with a no-name `root` object and goes further, with all the values attached at some location to this tree. Well, we mentioned numeric form, and we can make `snmpget` output numeric names as well with the `-On` flag:

```
$ snmpget -v 2c -c public -On 10.1.1.100 DISMAN-EVENT-
MIB::sysUpTimeInstance
```

```
.1.3.6.1.2.1.1.3.0 = Timeticks: (9048942) 1 day, 1:08:09.42
```

So, each OID can be referred to in one of three notations: short, long, or numeric. In this case, `DISMAN-EVENT-MIB::sysUpTimeInstance`, `.iso.org.dod.internet. mgmt.mib-2.system.sysUpTime.sysUpTimeInstance`, and `.1.3.6.1.2.1.1.3.0` all refer to the same value.

> Take a look at the `snmpcmd` man page for other supported output-formatting options.

But how does this fit into Zabbix SNMP items? Well, to create an SNMP item in Zabbix, you have to enter an OID. How do you know what OID to use? Often, you might have the following choices:

- Just know it
- Ask somebody
- Find it out yourself

More often than not, the first two options don't work, so finding it out yourself will be the only way. As we have learned, Net-SNMP tools are fairly good at supporting such a discovery process.

Using SNMPv3 with Net-SNMP

The latest version of SNMP, version 3, is still not that common yet, and it is somewhat more complex than the previous versions. Device implementations can also vary in quality, so it might be useful to test your configuration of Zabbix against a known solution: Net-SNMP daemon. Let's add an SNMPv3 user to it and get a value. Make sure Net-SNMP is installed and that snmpd starts up successfully.

To configure SNMPv3, first stop snmpd, and then, as root, run this:

```
# net-snmp-create-v3-user -ro zabbix
```

This utility will prompt for a password. Enter a password of at least eight characters—although shorter passwords will be accepted here, it will fail the default length requirement later. Start snmpd again, and test the retrieval of values using version 3:

```
$ snmpget -u zabbix -A zabbixzabbix -v 3 -l authNoPriv localhost SNMPv2-
MIB::sysDescr.0
```

This should return data successfully, as follows:

```
SNMPv2-MIB::sysDescr.0 = STRING: Linux another 3.11.10-29-default #1 SMP
Thu Mar 5 16:24:00 UTC 2015 (338c513) x86_64
```

We don't need to configure versions 1 or 2c separately, so now we have a general SNMP agent, providing all common versions for testing or exploring.

The engine ID

There is a very common misconfiguration done when attempting to use SNMPv3. According to RFC 3414 (https://tools.ietf.org/html/rfc3414), each device must have a unique identifier. Each SNMP engine maintains a value, snmpEngineID, which uniquely identifies the SNMP engine.

Sometimes, users tend to set this ID to the same value for several devices. As a result, Zabbix is unable to successfully monitor those devices. To make things worse, each device responds nicely to commands such as snmpget or snmpwalk. These commands only talk to a single device at a time; thus, they do not care about snmpEngineID much.

In Zabbix, this could manifest as one device working properly but stopping when another one is added to monitoring.

If there are mysterious problems with SNMPv3 device monitoring with Zabbix that do not manifest when using command line tools, snmpEngineID should be checked very carefully.

Authentication, encryption, and context

With SNMPv3, several additional features are available. Most notably, one may choose strong authentication and encryption of communication. For authentication, Zabbix currently supports the following methods:

- **Message-Digest algorithm 5 (MD5)**
- **Secure Hash Algorithm (SHA)**

For encryption, Zabbix supports these:

- **Data Encryption Standard (DES)**
- **Advanced Encryption Standard (AES)**

While it seems that one might always want to use the strongest possible encryption, keep in mind that this can be quite resource intensive. Querying a lot of values over SNMP can overload the target device quite easily. To have reasonable security, you may choose the `authNoPriv` option in the **Security level** dropdown. This will use encryption for the authentication process but not for data transfer.

Another SNMPv3 feature is context. In some cases, one SNMP endpoint is responsible for providing information about multiple devices— for example, about multiple UPS devices. A single OID will get a different value, depending on the context specified. Zabbix allows you to specify the context for each individual SNMPv3 item.

Adding new MIBs

One way to discover usable OIDs is to redirect the full SNMP tree output to a file, find out what interesting and useful information the device exposes, and determine what the OIDs are from that. It's all good as long as the MIB files shipped with Net-SNMP provide the required descriptors, but SNMP MIBs are extensible—anybody can add new information, and many vendors do. In such a case, your file might be filled with lines like this:

```
SNMPv2-SMI::enterprises.318.1.1.1.1.2.3.0 = STRING: "QS0547120198"
```

That's quite cryptic. While the output is in the short, textual form, part of it is numeric. This means that there is no MIB definition for this part of the SNMP tree. Enterprise number 318 is assigned to APC and, luckily, APC offers an MIB for download from their site, so it can be added to Net-SNMP configured MIBs. But how?

> Getting SNMP MIBs isn't always easy. A certain large printer manufacturer representative claimed that they do not provide SNMP MIBs, and everybody should use their proprietary printer-management application. Most manufacturers do provide MIBs, though, and in some cases, freely accessible MIB collection sites can help better than official vendor sites.

After downloading a new MIB, you have to place it in a location where Net-SNMP will search for MIB files and configure them as well. Net-SNMP searches for MIBs in two locations: `.snmp/mibs` in the user's home directory and `/usr/share/snmp/mibs`; which one you use is your decision. If you want something for the current user only, or don't have access to the `/usr` directory, you can use `.snmp/mibs`; otherwise, use `/usr/share/snmp/mibs`. Whichever you choose, that's not enough—you also have to instruct tools to include this MIB.

> While Zabbix server uses the same directory to look for MIBs, specifying MIBs to be used is only required for the Net-SNMP tools—Zabbix server loads all MIBs found.

The first method is to pass MIB names directly to the called command. But hey, we don't know the MIB name yet. To find out what a particular name in some file is, open the file in a text editor and look for `MIB DEFINITIONS ::= BEGIN` near the beginning of the file. The string before this text will be the MIB name we are looking for. Here's an example:

```
PowerNet-MIB DEFINITIONS ::= BEGIN
```

So, APC has chosen to name its MIB `PowerNet-MIB`. Armed with this knowledge, we can instruct any command to include this file:

```
$ snmpget -m +PowerNet-MIB -v 1 -c public <IP address> SNMPv2-SMI::enterp
rises.318.1.1.1.1.2.3.0
```

```
PowerNet-MIB::upsAdvIdentSerialNumber.0 = STRING: "QS0547120198"
```

Excellent; `snmpget` included the correct MIB and obtained the full textual string, which confirms our suspicion that this might be a serial number. You can now use the same flag for `snmpwalk` and obtain a file with much better value names. Quite often, you will be able to search such a file for interesting strings such as `serial number` and find the correct OID.

> The + sign instructs us to include the specified MIBs in addition to otherwise configured ones. If you omit the +, the MIB list will be replaced with the one you specified.

Feel free to look at the MIB files in the `/usr/share/snmp/mibs` directory. As you can see, most files here have their filename the same as their MIB name without the extension, which is not required. Actually, the filename has nothing to do with the MIB name; thus, sometimes, you might have to resort to tools such as `grep` to find out which file contains which MIB.

While passing individual MIB names on the command line is nice for a quick one-time query, it gets very tedious once you have to perform these actions more often and the MIB list grows. There's another method, somewhat more durable—the MIB's environment variable. In this case, the variable could be set like this:

```
$ export MIBS=+PowerNet-MIB
```

In the current shell, individual commands do not need the MIB names passed to them anymore. All the MIBs specified in the variable will be included upon every invocation.

Of course, that's also not that permanent. While you can specify this variable in profile scripts, it can get tedious to manage for all the users on a machine. This is where a third method comes in: configuration files.

Again, you can use per-user configuration files, located in `.snmp/snmp.conf` in their home directories, or you can use the global `/etc/snmp/snmp.conf` file.

> The location of the global configuration file and MIB directory can be different if you have compiled Net-SNMP from source. They might reside in `/usr/local`.

The syntax to add MIBs is similar to the one used in the environment variable—you only have to prefix each line with `mibs`, like so:

```
mibs +PowerNet-MIB
```

If you want to specify multiple MIB names in any of these locations, you have to separate them with a colon. Let's say you also need a generic UPS MIB; in that case, the MIB name string would be as follows:

```
+PowerNet-MIB:UPS-MIB
```

> In some Net-SNMP versions, lines in configuration files might be silently cut at 1024 characters, including newline characters. You can specify multiple `mibs` lines to get around this limitation.

And if you feel lazy, you can make Net-SNMP include all the MIB files located in those directories by setting `mibs` to `ALL` — this works in all three locations. Beware that this might impact performance and also lead to some problems if some parts are declared in multiple locations, including warnings from Net-SNMP tools and incorrect definitions being used.

> Zabbix server always loads all available MIBs. When a new MIB is added, Zabbix server must be restarted to pick it up.

Polling SNMP items in Zabbix

Armed with this knowledge about SNMP OIDs, let's get to the real deal — getting SNMP data into Zabbix. To make the following steps easier, you should choose an entry that returns string data. We could use a UPS serial number, such as the one discovered previously to be `PowerNet-MIB::upsAdvIdentSerialNumber.0`. Do the same for some network printer or manageable switch; if you don't have access to such a device, you can choose a simple entry from the Net-SNMP enabled host, such as the already mentioned system description, `SNMPv2-MIB::sysDescr.0`.

Now is the time to return to the Zabbix interface. Go to **Configuration | Hosts**, and click on **Create host**. Then, fill in the following values:

- **Host name**: Enter `SNMP device`.
- **Groups**: If in the **In groups** listbox there's a group, select it and click on the ▸ button.
- **New group**: Enter `SNMP devices`.
- **SNMP interfaces**: Click on **Add**.
- **DNS NAME** or **IP ADDRESS**: Enter the correct DNS name or IP address next to the SNMP interfaces we just added. If you have chosen to use an SNMP-enabled device, input its IP or DNS here. If you don't have access to such a device, use the **Another host** IP address or DNS name.
- **CONNECT TO**: Choose **DNS** or **IP**, according to the field you populated.

| Host name | SNMP device | | | | | |

| Visible name | | | | | | |

Groups   In groups   Other groups

SNMP devices

                                        Database servers
                                        Discovered hosts
                                        Hypervisors
     ◄   Linux servers
                                        Network devices
     ►   Templates
                                        UPS devices
                                        Virtual machines
                                        Web servers
                                        Windows servers

New group   [   ]

Agent interfaces

IP ADDRESS	DNS NAME	CONNECT TO	POPT	DEFAULT
127.0.0.1		IP DNS	10050	⊙ Remove

Add

SNMP interfaces

IP ADDRESS	DNS NAME	CONNECT TO	POPT	DEFAULT
192.168.56.11		IP DNS	161	⊙ Remove
✔Use bulk requests				

Add

> 💡 If no agent items will be created for this host, the agent interface will be ignored. You may keep it or remove it.

When you are done, click on the **Add** button at the bottom. It's likely that you won't see the newly created host in the host list. The reason is the **Group** dropdown in the upper-right corner, which probably says **Linux servers**. You can change the selection to **All** to see all configured hosts or to **SNMP devices** to only see our new device. Now is the time to create an item, so click on **Items** next to **SNMP devices** and click on the **Create item** button. Fill in the following values:

- **Name**: Enter something sensible, such as Serial number, if you are using an OID from an SNMP agent, or System description if you are using the Net-SNMP daemon.

- **Type**: Change to the appropriate version of your SNMP agent. In the displayed example, SNMPv1 agent is chosen because that's the only version our device supports.

- **Key**: This is not restricted or too important for SNMP items, but required for references from triggers and other locations. You can choose to enter the last part of the textual OID, such as upsAdvIdentSerialNumber.0 or sysDescr.0.

- **SNMP OID**: This is where our knowledge comes in. Paste the SNMP OID you have found out and chosen here. In the example, `PowerNet-MIB::upsAdvIdentSerialNumber.0` is entered. If you are using the Net-SNMP daemon, enter `SNMPv2-MIB::sysDescr.0`

- **SNMP community**: Unless you have changed it, keep the default `public` value.

- **Type of information**: Select **Character**.

- **Update interval (in sec)**: This information doesn't really change that often, so use some large value, such as `86400`.

Name	Serial number
Type	SNMPv1 agent
Key	upsAdvIdentSerialNumber.0 Select
Host interface	192.168.56.11 : 161
SNMP OID	zomgPowerNet-MIB::upsAdvIdentSerialNumber.0
SNMP community	public
Port	
Type of information	Character
Update interval (in sec)	86400

> If you left the agent interface in place, notice how it cannot be chosen for this item—only the SNMP interface can. While some item types can be assigned to any interface type, SNMP items must be assigned to SNMP interfaces.

When you are done, click on the **Add** button at the bottom.

Now, the outcome will depend on several factors. If you are lucky, you will already see the incoming data in **Monitoring | Latest data**. If you have chosen some vendor-specific OID, like in our example, it is possible that you will have to go back to **Configuration | Hosts**, click on **Items** next to **SNMP device**, and observe the status of this item:

TYPE	APPLICATIONS	STATUS	INFO
SNMPv1 agent		Not supported	
snmp_parse_oid(): cannot parse OID "PowerNet-MIB::upsAdvIdentSerialNumber.0".			

Now what's that? How could it be? We saw in our tests with Net-SNMP command line tools that there actually is such an OID. Well, one possible situation when this error message appears is when the specified MIB is not available, which could happen if you tried SNMP queries previously from a different host.

Zabbix server works as if ALL is set for MIB contents; thus, you don't have to do anything besides copying the MIB to the correct directory (usually /usr/share/snmp/mibs) on the Zabbix server and restarting the server daemon. If you did not copy the OID, instead deciding to retype it, you might have made a mistake. Verify that the entered OID is correct.

> The error message in the Zabbix frontend might be misleading in some cases. Check the server log to be sure.

After fixing any problems, wait until Zabbix server refreshes the item configuration and rechecks the item. With the item configured, let's see what data we can get in Zabbix from it. Navigate to **Monitoring | Latest data**, expand the filter, clear the **Host groups** field, and start typing SNMP in the **Host** field — **SNMP device** should appear, so choose it and click on **Filter**. Expand the other category if needed, and look for the serial number. You should see something like this:

| Serial number | 2016-03-16 22:27:40 | XA123PO |

The serial number has been successfully retrieved and is visible in the item listing. This allows us to automatically retrieve data that, while not directly tied to actual availability or performance monitoring, is still quite useful. For example, if a remote device dies and has to be replaced, you can easily find the serial number to supply in a servicing request, even if you neglected to write it down beforehand.

Translating SNMP OIDs

In case you can't or don't want to copy vendor-specific MIB files to the Zabbix server, you can always use numeric OIDs, like we did before. While not being as descriptive, they are guaranteed to work even if the copied MIBs are not available for some reason or are removed during a system upgrade.

But how do we derive the corresponding numeric OID from a textual one? While we could use snmpget to retrieve the particular value and output it in numeric form, that requires the availability of the device and network roundtrip. Fortunately, there's an easier way: the snmptranslate command. To find out the numeric form of the OID, we can use PowerNet-MIB::upsAdvIdentSerialNumber.0:

```
$ snmptranslate -On PowerNet-MIB::upsAdvIdentSerialNumber.0
.1.3.6.1.4.1.318.1.1.1.1.2.3.0
```

You must have MIBs placed correctly and pass their names to Net-SNMP tools for translation to work.

The default output format for Net-SNMP tools is the short textual one, which only outputs the MIB name and object name. If you would like to find out the corresponding textual name, use the following:

```
$ snmptranslate .1.3.6.1.2.1.1.1.0
SNMPv2-MIB::sysDescr.0
```

You can also use the -Of flag to output an OID in full notation:

```
$ snmptranslate -Of PowerNet-MIB::upsAdvIdentSerialNumber.0
.iso.org.dod.internet.private.enterprises.apc.products.hardware.ups.
upsIdent.upsAdvIdent.upsAdvIdentSerialNumber.0
```

Dynamic indexes

Previously, we monitored incoming traffic on the eth0 device using an active Zabbix agent daemon item. If we have snmpd set up and running, we can also try retrieving outgoing traffic, but this time, let's try to use SNMP for that.

Monitoring network traffic using the Zabbix agent daemon is usually easier, but SNMP monitoring is the only way to obtain this information for many network devices, such as switches and routers. If you have such a device available, you can try monitoring it instead, though the network interface name will most likely differ.

One way to find the item we are interested in would be to redirect the output of snmpwalk to a file and then examine that file. Looking at the output, there are lines such as these:

```
IF-MIB::ifDescr.1 = STRING: lo
IF-MIB::ifDescr.2 = STRING: eth0
```

Great, so the desired interface, eth0 in this case, has an index of 2. Nearby, we can find actual information we are interested in — traffic values:

```
IF-MIB::ifOutOctets.1 = Counter32: 1825596052

IF-MIB::ifOutOctets.2 = Counter32: 1533857263
```

So, theoretically, we could add an item with the OID IF-MIB::ifOutOctets.2 and name it appropriately. Unfortunately, there are devices that change interface index now and then. Also, the index for a particular interface is likely to differ between devices, thus potentially creating a configuration nightmare. This is where dynamic index support in Zabbix comes into use.

Let's look at what a dynamic index item OID would look like in this case:

IF-MIB::ifOutOctets[	"index",	"ifDescr",	"eth0"]
Database OID	Literal string "index"	Index-based OID	Index string

- **Database OID**: This is the base part of the OID that holds the data we are interested in, that is, without the actual index. In this case, it's the OID leading to ifOutOctets, in any notation.
- **Literal string "index"**: This is the same for all dynamic index items.
- **Index-based OID**: This is the base part of the OID that holds the index we are interested in. In this case, it's the OID leading to ifDescr, in any notation.
- **Index string**: This is the string that the index part of the tree is searched for. This is an exact, case-sensitive match of all OIDs from the previous base OID. Here, the name of the interface we are interested in, eth0, will be searched for. No substring or other matching is allowed here.

The index that this search will return will be added to the database OID, and the following queries will gather values from the resulting OID.

You can easily view the index to determine the correct string to search for with Net-SNMP tools:

```
$ snmpwalk -v 2c -c public localhost .iso.org.dod.internet.mgmt.mib-2.
interfaces.ifTable.ifEntry.ifDescr

IF-MIB::ifDescr.1 = STRING: lo

IF-MIB::ifDescr.2 = STRING: eth0

IF-MIB::ifDescr.3 = STRING: sit0
```

As can be seen, this machine has three interfaces: **loopback**, **Ethernet**, and a **tunnel**. The picture will be very different for some other devices. For example, an HP ProCurve switch would return (with the output shortened) the following:

```
$ snmpwalk -v 2c -c public 10.196.2.233 .iso.org.dod.internet.mgmt.mib-2.
interfaces.ifTable.ifEntry.ifDescr

IF-MIB::ifDescr.1 = STRING: 1

IF-MIB::ifDescr.2 = STRING: 2

...

IF-MIB::ifDescr.49 = STRING: 49

IF-MIB::ifDescr.50 = STRING: 50

IF-MIB::ifDescr.63 = STRING: DEFAULT_VLAN

IF-MIB::ifDescr.4158 = STRING: HP ProCurve Switch software loopback
interface
```

Now that we know the OID to use for dynamic index items, let's create one such item in Zabbix. Navigate to **Configuration | Hosts**, click on **Items** next to the correct host you want to create the item for, and click on **Create item**. Fill in the following values:

- **Name**: Outgoing traffic on interface $1
- **Type**: **SNMPv2 agent**
- **Key**: ifOutOctets[eth0]
- **SNMP OID**: IF-MIB::ifOutOctets["index","ifDescr","eth0"]
- **Units**: Bps
- **Store value**: **Delta (speed per second)**

Same as before, replace eth0 with an interface name that exists on the target system. When you are done, click on the **Add** button at the bottom.

> Make sure that the compound OID is entered correctly, paying close attention to quotes and spelling. We discussed the reason to use the **Numeric (unsigned)** type of information in *Chapter 3, Monitoring with Zabbix Agents and Basic Protocols.*

The newly added item should start gathering data, so let's look at **Monitoring | Latest data**. If you don't see this item or the data for it, navigate back to **Configuration | Hosts** and click on **Items** next to the corresponding host—there should be an error message displayed that should help with fixing the issue. If you have correctly added the item, you'll see the traffic data, as follows:

LAST CHECK	LAST VALUE	CHANGE
2016-03-18 19:40:07	37 Bps	-2 Bps

> Remember that the index matches the exact string—a substring match will not work here.

Dynamic index items are quite common. Many network devices have fixed port names but varying indexes. Host-based SNMP agents place things such as disk usage and memory statistics in dynamic indexes; thus, if you have such devices to monitor, Zabbix support for them will be handy.

Using dynamic index items can slightly increase overall load, as two SNMP values are required to obtain the final data. Zabbix caches retrieved index information, so the load increase should not be noticeable.

A dynamic SNMP index enables us to easily monitor a specific interface or other entity by name, but it would not be a very efficient method for monitoring a larger number of interfaces. We will discuss an automated solution, low-level discovery, in *Chapter 11*, *Advanced Item Monitoring*.

SNMP bulk requests

You might have spotted the checkbox next to the **SNMP interfaces** section, **Use bulk requests**:

SNMP interfaces	
	192.168.56.11
	✔Use bulk requests

When requesting values from SNMP hosts, Zabbix may request one value at a time or multiple values in one go. Getting multiple values in one go is more efficient, so this is what Zabbix will try to do by default—it will ask for more and more values in one connection against a device until all SNMP items can be queried in one go or the device fails to respond. This approach enables us to find the number of values that a device is configured to return, or is technically capable of returning, in one go. No more than 128 values will be requested in one attempt, however.

Only items with identical parameters on the same interface will be queried at the same time—for example, if the community or the port is different, Zabbix will not try to get such values in one attempt.

There are quite a lot of devices that do not work properly when multiple values are requested; thus, it is possible to disable this functionality per interface.

Receiving SNMP traps

While querying SNMP-capable devices is a nice method that requires little or no configuration of each device in itself, in some situations, information flow in the reverse direction is desired. For SNMP, these are called **traps**. Usually, traps are sent upon some condition change, and the agent connects to the server or management station on port 162 (as opposed to port 161 on the agent side, which is used for queries). You can think of SNMP traps as being similar to Zabbix active items; as with those, all connections are made from monitored machines to the monitoring server.

The direction of the connections isn't the only difference—SNMP traps have some other pros and cons when compared to queries. For example, SNMP traps are usually more capable of detecting short-lived problems that might have been missed by queries. Let's say you are monitoring incoming voltages on a UPS. You have decided on a reasonable item interval that would give you useful data and wouldn't overload the network and Zabbix server—let's say some 120 seconds, or 2 minutes. If the input voltage suddenly peaks or drops for a minute, your checks might easily miss this event, thus making it impossible to correlate it with problems with other devices that are not connected to the UPS. Another benefit that traps provide is reduced network and Zabbix server load as the information is only sent when an event occurs and there is no constant querying by the server. One drawback is partial decentralization of the configuration. SNMP trap-sending conditions and parameters have to be set for each device or device group individually. Another drawback is a lack of the guaranteed sending of the traps. Almost all SNMP implementations will use UDP, and trap information might get lost without any trace.

As such, SNMP traps aren't used to replace SNMP queries. Instead, they supplement them by leaving statistical information-gathering to the queries and providing notifications of various events happening in the devices, usually notifying us of emergencies.

In Zabbix, SNMP traps are received by snmptrapd, a daemon again from the Net-SNMP suite. These traps then have to be passed to the Zabbix daemon with some method. There are several ways of doing it, and we will explore two different approaches:

- Using the built-in ability of Zabbix to receive traps from the Net-SNMP trap daemon
- Using a custom script to push SNMP values to Zabbix

The first method, especially when using the embedded Perl code approach, is the most simple one and will offer the best performance. A custom script will provide the most flexibility but will also require more effort.

Using embedded Perl code

Using embedded Perl code in snmptrapd is the easiest method to set up. Unless you need extra functionality, it is suggested to stick with this method.

We'll start by configuring snmptrapd to pass information to Zabbix. There is an example script in the Zabbix sources called misc/snmptrap/zabbix_trap_ receiver.pl. Place this file in some reasonable location—perhaps a bin subdirectory in the Zabbix home directory. If the directory does not exist, create it, as follows:

```
# mkdir -p /home/zabbix/bin; chown zabbix /home/zabbix
```

> If using distribution packages, you might have to use a different username. Check your distribution packages for details.

Place the zabbix_trap_receiver.pl file in this directory:

```
# cp misc/snmptrap/zabbix_trap_receiver.pl /home/zabbix/bin
```

> On some distributions, Net-SNMP Perl support could be split out into a separate package, such as net-snmp-perl.

Now, on to instructing `snmptrapd` to use that script. We only need to tell the trap daemon to process all the received traps with this script. To do this, you'll have to find the location where your distribution places the Net-SNMP configuration files—usually, `/etc/snmp/`. In this directory, look for a file named `snmptrapd.conf`. If it's there, edit it (create a backup copy before you do anything); if it's missing, create it. Edit it as root and make it look as follows:

```
authCommunity execute public
perl do "/home/zabbix/bin/zabbix_trap_receiver.pl";
```

This will accept all traps that have the community set to `public` and pass them to the Perl receiver script.

> If you expect to receive traps with various community strings that are not known in advance, you could disable the authorization or checking of the community string with the `disableAuthorization yes` option in `snmptrapd.conf`.

Start or restart the trap daemon. It might be worth taking a quick look at the `zabbix_trap_receiver.pl` file. Notice the line that specifies the path:

```
$SNMPTrapperFile = '/tmp/zabbix_traps.tmp';
```

Behind the scenes, traps are passed to the Zabbix server through a temporary file. We'll discuss this in a bit more detail later in this chapter.

Filtering values by received data

Now on to the items on the Zabbix side. To test the most simple thing first, we will try to send values from the Zabbix server. Navigate to **Configuration | Hosts**, click on **A test host** in the **NAME** column, and click on **Add** in the **SNMP interfaces** section. Click on the **Update** button at the bottom, and then click on **Items** next to **A test host**. Click on **Create item** and enter these values:

- **Name:** `SNMP trap tests`
- **Type: SNMP trap**
- **Key:** `snmptrap[test]`
- **Type of information: Character**

When you're done, it should look like this:

Name	SNMP trap tests
Type	SNMP trap
Key	snmptrap[test] Select
Host interface	192.168.56.11 : 161
Type of information	Character

This item will collect all traps that this host gets, if the traps contain the string `test`. We have the trap daemon configured to place traps in a file, and we have the item to place these traps in. What's left is telling the Zabbix server where to get the traps. Open `zabbix_server.conf` and modify the `StartSNMPTrapper` parameter:

```
StartSNMPTrapper=1
```

There is a special process in Zabbix that reads traps from a temporary file. This process is not started by default, so we changed that part of the configuration. Take a look at the parameter just above this one:

```
SNMPTrapperFile=/tmp/zabbix_traps.tmp
```

Notice how it matches the file in the Perl script. A change in the script should be matched by a change in this configuration file and vice versa. At this time, we will not change the location of this temporary file.

After these changes have been made, restart the Zabbix server daemon.

Now, we are ready to test this item. Let's send a trap by executing the following from the Zabbix server:

```
$ snmptrap -Ci -v 2c -c public localhost "" "NET-SNMP-
MIB::netSnmpExperimental" NET-SNMP-MIB::netSnmpExperimental s "test"
```

This slightly non-optimal Net-SNMP syntax will attempt to send an SNMP trap to `localhost` using the `public` community and some nonsense OID. It will also wait for a response to verify that `snmptrapd` has received the trap successfully — this is achieved by the `-Ci` flag. It uses the default port, 162, so make sure the port is open in your firewall configuration on the Zabbix server to receive traps.

> Waiting for confirmation also makes `snmptrap` retransmit the trap. If the receiving host is slow to respond, the trap might be received multiple times before the sender receives confirmation.

If the command is successful, it will finish without any output. If it fails with the snmpinform: Timeout error message, then several things could have gone wrong. As well as double-checking that UDP port 162 is open for incoming data, verify that the community in the /etc/snmp/snmptrapd.conf file matches the one used in the snmptrap command and that the snmptrapd daemon is actually running.

If everything goes well, we should be able to see this item with a value on the latest data page:

SNMP trap tests	2016-03-18 23:17:48	23:17:46 2016/03/18 PDU INF…

Now, let's send a different trap. Still on the Zabbix server, run this:

```
$ snmptrap -Ci -v 2c -c public localhost "" "NET-SNMP-
MIB::netSnmpExperimental" NET-SNMP-MIB::netSnmpExperimental s "some other
trap"
```

This trap will not appear in the item we created. What happened to it? As the value that we sent did not contain the string test, this value did not match the one in the item. By default, such traps are logged in the server logfile. If we check the logfile, it should have something similar to the following:

```
9872:20160318:232004.319 unmatched trap received from "127.0.0.1":
23:20:02 2016/03/18 PDU INFO:
  requestid                253195749
  messageid                0
  transactionid            5
  version                  1
  notificationtype         INFORM
  community                public
  receivedfrom             UDP: [127.0.0.1]:54031→[127.0.0.1]:162
  errorindex               0
  errorstatus              0
VARBINDS:
  DISMAN-EVENT-MIB::sysUpTimeInstance type=67 value=Timeticks:
(2725311) 7:34:13.11
  SNMPv2-MIB::snmpTrapOID.0        type=6   value=OID: NET-SNMP-
MIB::netSnmpExperimental
  NET-SNMP-MIB::netSnmpExperimental type=4  value=STRING: "some other
trap"
```

This is not so easy to trigger on, or even see in, the frontend at all. We will improve the situation and tell Zabbix to handle such unmatched traps for this host by placing them in a special item. Navigate to **Configuration** | **Hosts**, click on **Items** next to A test host, click on **Create item**, and then fill in these values:

- **Name:** SNMP trap fallback
- **Type: SNMP trap**
- **Key:** snmptrap.fallback
- **Type of information: Character**

When you're done, click on the **Add** button at the bottom.

The key we used here, snmptrap.fallback, is a special one. Any trap that does not match any of the snmptrap[] items will be placed here. Retry sending our previously unmatched trap:

```
$ snmptrap -Ci -v 2c -c public localhost "" "NET-SNMP-
MIB::netSnmpExperimental" NET-SNMP-MIB::netSnmpExperimental s "some other
trap"
```

Let's check the latest data page again:

SNMP trap fallback	2016-03-18 23:33:04	23:33:03 2016/03/18 PDU INF...
SNMP trap tests	2016-03-18 23:17:48	23:17:46 2016/03/18 PDU INF...

The fallback item got the value this time. To see what the value looks like, let's click on the **History** link next to one of these items:

TIMESTAMP	VALUE	
2016-03-18 23:33:04	23:33:03 2016/03/18 PDU INFO: community receivedfrom errorindex errorstatus requestid	public UDP: [127.0.0.1]:54642->[127.0.0.1]:162 0 0 108168159

It contains quite a lot of information, but it also looks a bit strange, almost as if the value was cut. Turns out, with this method, the trap information that is recorded in the database is quite verbose and the character information type does not offer enough space for it—this type is limited to 255 characters. We cannot even see the string we sent in the trap that matched or failed to match the filter. Let's try to fix this with the mass update functionality again. Go to **Configuration | Hosts** and click on **Items** next to **A test host**. Mark the checkboxes next to both SNMP trap items and click on the **Mass update** button. In the resulting form, mark the checkbox next to **Type of information** and choose **Text**:

Type of information ✔	Text	▾

Click on the **Update** button. This should have fixed it, but we don't know that for sure yet. Let's verify—send both of these traps again:

```
$ snmptrap -Ci -v 2c -c public localhost "" "NET-SNMP-
MIB::netSnmpExperimental" NET-SNMP-MIB::netSnmpExperimental s "test"
```

```
$ snmptrap -Ci -v 2c -c public localhost "" "NET-SNMP-
MIB::netSnmpExperimental" NET-SNMP-MIB::netSnmpExperimental s "some other
trap"
```

If we look at the history of one of these items now, we will see that this change has indeed helped, and much more information is displayed—including the custom string we used for distributing these values across items:

```
TIMESTAMP             VALUE

                      00:14:55 2016/03/19 PDU INFO:
                        messageid                0
                        transactionid            11
                        requestid                973564866
                        notificationtype         INFORM
                        version                  1
2016-03-19 00:14:56     receivedfrom             UDP: [127.0.0.1]:40852->[127.0.0.1]:162
                        community                public
                        errorstatus              0
                        errorindex               0
                      VARBINDS:
                        DISMAN-EVENT-MIB::sysUpTimeInstance type=67 value=Timeticks: (3054527) 8:29:05.27
                        SNMPv2-MIB::snmpTrapOID.0      type=6  value=OID: NET-SNMP-MIB::netSnmpExperimental
                        NET-SNMP-MIB::netSnmpExperimental type=4  value=STRING: "some other trap"
```

> If the value is still cut, you might have to wait a bit more for the configuration cache to be updated and resend the trap.

The first item we created, with the `snmptrap[test]` key, can actually have a regular expression as the item parameter. This allows us to perform more advanced filtering, such as getting a link up and down traps in a single item. If a trap matches expressions from multiple items, it would get copied to all of those items.

Filtering values by originating host

We figured out how to get values in specific items, but how did Zabbix know that it should place these values in A test host? This happens because the address of the host that the trap came from matches the address in the SNMP interface for these items. To test this, let's copy the trap items to **Another host**. Navigate to **Configuration | Hosts** and click on **Items** next to **A test host**. Mark the checkboxes next to both SNMP trap items and click on the **Copy to** button. Choose **Hosts** from the **Target type** dropdown and mark the checkbox next to **Another host**. Then, click on **Copy**.

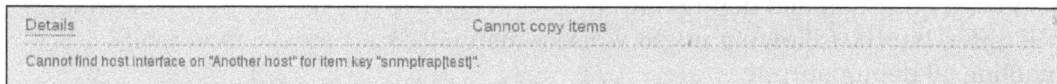

Details	Cannot copy items	x
Cannot find host interface on "Another host" for item key "snmptrap[test]".		

[💡 If you added an SNMP interface to Another host earlier, this operation might succeed.]

Looks like that failed, and Zabbix complains that it can not find an interface. **Another host** did not have an SNMP interface; thus, these items can not be attached to any interface at all. Go to **Configuration | Hosts**, click on **Another host**, then add a new SNMP interface with the address that this host has, and click on **Update**. Try to copy the SNMP trap items from A test host to **Another host** the same way as done previously, and it should succeed now:

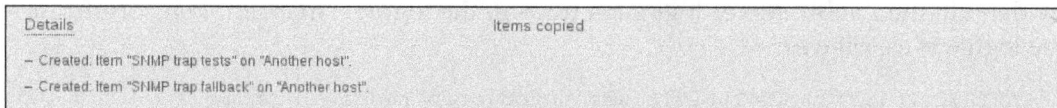

Details	Items copied	x
— Created: Item "SNMP trap tests" on "Another host".		
— Created: Item "SNMP trap fallback" on "Another host".		

With the items in place, let's test them. Send two test traps from **Another host**, the same way we sent them from the Zabbix server before:

```
$ snmptrap -Ci -v 2c -c public <Zabbix server> "" "NET-SNMP-
MIB::netSnmpExperimental" NET-SNMP-MIB::netSnmpExperimental s "test"
```

```
$ snmptrap -Ci -v 2c -c public <Zabbix server> "" "NET-SNMP-
MIB::netSnmpExperimental" NET-SNMP-MIB::netSnmpExperimental s "some other
trap"
```

Replace <Zabbix server> with the IP or DNS name of the Zabbix server. These commands should complete without any error messages.

The traps should be placed properly in the items on **Another host**.

Debugging

If traps do not arrive at all or do not fall into the correct items, there are a few things to check. If the traps do not appear when sent from a remote host, but work properly when sent from the Zabbix server, check the local firewall on the Zabbix server and make sure incoming UDP packets on port 162 are allowed. Also make sure that the IP address the Zabbix server sees in the incoming traps matches the address in the SNMP interface for that host.

Sometimes, one might see that traps arrive at the SNMP trap daemon but do not seem to be passed on. It might be useful to debug snmptrapd in this case—luckily, it allows a quite detailed debug output. Exact values to use for various file locations will differ, but the following might work to manually start the daemon while enabling all debug output:

```
# /usr/sbin/snmptrapd -A -Lf /var/log/net-snmpd.log -p /var/run/
snmptrapd.pid -DALL
```

Here, -Lf specifies the file to log to and -DALL tells it to enable full debug.

If the received trap is in a numeric format and not very readable, you might have to add specific MIBs to the /etc/snmp/snmp.conf file so that they are found by snmptrapd.

What happens if Zabbix decides that a trap does not belong to any item on any host? This could happen because there are no trap items at all, the fallback item is missing, or the address in the incoming trap is not matched with any of the SNMP interfaces. By default, the Zabbix server logs such traps in the logfile. An example record from the logfile is as follows:

```
    2271:20150120:124156.818 unmatched trap received from
[192.168.168.192]: 12:41:55 2015/01/20 PDU INFO:
    errorindex                0
    transactionid             1
    requestid                 1752369294
    messageid                 0
    receivedfrom              UDP: [192.168.168.192]:45375-
>[192.168.1.13]:162
    errorstatus               0
    version                   1
    notificationtype          INFORM
```

```
community                          public
VARBINDS:
  DISMAN-EVENT-MIB::sysUpTimeInstance type=67 value=Timeticks:
(77578087) 8 days, 23:29:40.87
  SNMPv2-MIB::snmpTrapOID.0       type=6  value=OID: NET-SNMP-
MIB::netSnmpExperimental
  NET-SNMP-MIB::netSnmpExperimental type=4  value=STRING: "non-
matching trap"
```

The logging of non-matching traps can be controlled. If we go to **Administration |
General** and choose **Other** from the dropdown in the upper-right corner, the last
checkbox there is **Log unmatched SNMP traps**. Unmarking it will stop logging
such traps:

And what if you would like to try out Zabbix's SNMP trap handling without setting
up an SNMP trap daemon, perhaps on some development server? That should be
very easy as you can simply append trap information to the temporary file. It's a
plaintext file, and Zabbix does not know who added content, the trap daemon, user,
or somebody else. Just make sure to add all the data for a single trap in one go.

Handling the temporary file

The temporary file to pass traps from the trap daemon to Zabbix is placed in /tmp by
default. This is not the best practice for a production setup, so I suggest you change it
once you are satisfied with the initial testing.

Note that the temporary file can grow indefinitely—Zabbix only reads data from it,
and never rotates or removes the file. Rotation should be set up separately, probably
with the logrotate daemon.

SNMP Trap Translator

Zabbix may also receive traps that are parsed by **SNMP Trap Translator** (**SNMPTT**, http://www.snmptt.org/). This method uses the same temporary file and internal process approach as the embedded Perl trap receiver solution. SNMPTT can be useful for making received data human-readable.

Remember that it changes passed data, so depending on how things are set up, adding SNMPTT might require changes to item mapping, triggers, or other configuration.

Using a custom script

The method covered earlier, the embedded Perl receiver, is easy to set up and performs well. If it is not possible to use it for some reason or some advanced filtering is required, a custom script could push trap values to items. This subsection will use an example script shipped with Zabbix to demonstrate such a solution.

We'll place the example SNMP trap parsing script in the Zabbix user's home directory:

```
# cp misc/snmptrap/snmptrap.sh /home/zabbix/bin
```

Let's take a look at that script now. Open the file we just copied to /home/zabbix/bin/snmptrap.sh. As you can see, this is a very simplistic script, which gets passed trap information and then sends it to the Zabbix server, using both host snmptrap and key snmptrap instances. If you are reading carefully enough, you've probably already noticed one problem: we didn't install any software as ~zabbix/bin/zabbix_sender, so that's probably wrong.

First, let's find out where zabbix_sender is actually located:

```
$ whereis zabbix_sender
zabbix_sender: /usr/local/bin/zabbix_sender
```

On this system, it's /usr/local/bin/zabbix_sender. It might be a good idea to look at its syntax by running this:

```
$ zabbix_sender --help
```

This allows you to send a value to the Zabbix server, specifying the server with the -z flag, port with -p, and so on. Now let's return to the script. With our new knowledge, let's look at the last line — the one that invokes zabbix_sender. The script seems to pass values retrieved from the SNMP trap as parameters to zabbix_sender; thus, we can't make any decisions and information transformation between snmptrapd and Zabbix. Now, let's fix the problem we noticed:

- Change ZABBIX_SENDER to read /usr/local/bin/zabbix_sender (or another path if that's different for you)
- Additionally, change the last line to read $ZABBIX_SENDER -z $ZABBIX_ SERVER -p $ZABBIX_PORT -s "$HOST" -k "$KEY" -o "$str" — this way, we are also quoting host and key names, just in case they might include spaces or other characters that might break command execution

Save the file. Let's prepare the Zabbix side now for trap receiving. On the frontend, navigate to **Configuration | Hosts** and click on **Create host**. Fill in the following values:

- **Name**: snmptraps
- **Groups**: Click on **SNMP devices** in the **Other groups** box, then click on the ◂ button; if there are any other groups in the **In groups** listbox, remove them

Click on the **Add** button at the bottom. Notice that the hostname used here, snmptraps, must be the same as the one we configured in the snmptrap.sh script; otherwise, the traps won't be received in Zabbix.

Now, click on **Items** next to the **snmptraps** host, and then click on **Create item**. Enter these values:

- **Name**: Received SNMP traps
- **Type**: **Zabbix trapper**
- **Key**: snmptraps
- **Type of information**: **Character**

> We used the **Character** type of information here as our script is expected to pass less information to the item. If large amounts of information would have had to be passed, we would have set this parameter to **Text** again.

When you are done, click on the **Add** button at the bottom. Again, notice how we used the exact same key spelling as in the snmptrap.sh script.

We're done with configuring Zabbix for SNMP trap receiving, but how will the traps get to the script we edited and, in turn, to Zabbix? The same as before, this is where `snmptrapd` steps in.

Let's create a simplistic configuration that will pass all the received traps to our script. To do this, we will edit `snmptrapd.conf`. If you created it earlier, edit it (you may comment out the lines we added previously); if it's missing, create the file. Edit it as root and make it look as follows:

```
authCommunity execute public
#perl do "/home/zabbix/bin/zabbix_trap_receiver.pl";
traphandle default /bin/bash /home/zabbix/bin/snmptrap.sh
```

We commented out the Perl receiver line and added a line to call our new script. The default keyword will make sure that all received traps go to this script (that is, unless we have other `traphandle` statements with OIDs specified, in which case only those received traps will get to this script that don't match any other `traphandle` statement). Save this file, and then start or restart the `snmptrapd` daemon as appropriate for your distribution.

Now, we should be able to receive SNMP traps through all the chain links. Let's test that by sending a trap same the way as before from the Zabbix server:

```
$ snmptrap -Ci -v 2c -c public localhost "" "NET-SNMP-
MIB::netSnmpExperimental" NET-SNMP-MIB::netSnmpExperimental s "test"
```

Once the command completes successfully, check the frontend for the results. Go to **Monitoring | Latest data** and select **SNMP devices** in the filter:

Received SNMP traps	2016-03-19 00:41:52	localhost "test" NET-SNMP-MI...

Great, data from our test trap has been received here. It's trimmed in the table view, though, so click on **History** to view all of it:

TIMESTAMP	VALUE
2016-03-19 00:41:52	localhost "test" NET-SNMP-MIB::netSnmpExperimental

Excellent, we can see our trap in its entirety. Notice how with this custom script we decided to parse out only the specific string, instead of pushing all the details about the trap to Zabbix. Let's check what it looks like with several traps received one after another. From the console again, execute the following:

```
$ snmptrap -Ci -v 2c -c public localhost "" "NET-SNMP-
MIB::netSnmpExperimental" NET-SNMP-MIB::netSnmpExperimental s "another
test"
```

Refresh the **History** screen we had open in the browser and check whether the result is satisfactory:

TIMESTAMP	VALUE
2016-03-19 00:44:31	localhost "another NET-SNMP-MIB::netSnmpExperimental
2016-03-19 00:41:52	localhost "test" NET-SNMP-MIB::netSnmpExperimental

Our latest trap is nicely listed, with entries being ordered in descending order.

> If the trap did not arrive, refer to the *Debugging* subsection earlier in this chapter.

But wait, everything after the first space is missing from the informative text. That's not desirable, so let's try to fix this problem. As root, open the /home/zabbix/bin/snmptrap.sh file and look for the line that strips out addresses from received information:

```
oid=`echo $oid|cut -f2 -d' '`
address=`echo $address|cut -f2 -d' '`
community=`echo $community|cut -f2 -d' '`
enterprise=`echo $enterprise|cut -f2 -d' '`
```

As seen here, when using a space as the separator, only the second field is grabbed. We want the full details captured instead, as otherwise, A Very Important Failure would simply show up as A for us. Let's add a dash to the field parameter so that all trailing fields are captured as well:

```
address=`echo $address|cut -f2- -d' '`
```

This should solve the problem, so let's test it again:

```
$ snmptrap -Ci -v 2c -c public localhost "" "NET-SNMP-
MIB::netSnmpExperimental" NET-SNMP-MIB::netSnmpExperimental s "A Very
Important Failure"
```

Return to the frontend and refresh the history listing:

TIMESTAMP	VALUE
2016-03-19 00:47:09	localhost "A Very Important Failure" NET-SNMP-MIB::netSnmpExperimental
2016-03-19 00:44:31	localhost "another NET-SNMP-MIB::netSnmpExperimental
2016-03-19 00:41:52	localhost "test" NET-SNMP-MIB::netSnmpExperimental

Finally! The data from our important traps won't be lost anymore.

Filtering the traps

While that is great for receiving all traps in a single location, it also makes traps harder to correlate to particular hosts, and especially hard to observe if you have lots and lots of trap-sending hosts. In such a case, it becomes very desirable to split incoming traps in some sort of logical structure, similar to the way we did with the Perl receiver solution earlier. At the very least, a split based on existing hosts can be performed. In this case, all received traps would be placed in a single item for that host. If there are particular traps or trap groups that are received very often or are very important, these can be further split into individual items.

For example, if a network switch is sending various traps, including link up and down ones, we'll probably want to place these in a single item so they do not obscure other traps that much. If the switch has many workstations connected that are constantly switched on and off, we might even want to drop these traps before they reach Zabbix. On the other hand, if this switch has very important connections that should never go down, we might even go as far as creating an individual item for notifications coming from each port.

All the methods work by either replacing, improving, or hooking into the handler script, snmptraps.sh.

Custom mapping

One way to approach trap distribution is to create custom mappings that choose an appropriate destination for the trap depending on any parameters, including source host, OID, and trap details. Such mapping, while being relatively cumbersome to set up, is also the most flexible, as you can perform all kinds of specific case handling. It also requires double configuration—most changes have to be made both to the Zabbix configuration and to these mappings.

Custom mapping can use file-based lookup, a separate database, or any other kind of information storage.

Database lookups

Another method is to tap into existing knowledge, through the Zabbix database. As the database already holds information on host/IP address relationships, we can simply look up the corresponding hostname. Let's modify `snmptraps.sh` so that all traps coming from hosts defined in Zabbix end up in an `snmptraps` item for that specific host, but other traps are collected in the generic `snmptraps` host instead.

Start by modifying `/home/zabbix/bin/snmptraps.sh` and adding two lines:

```
oid=`echo $oid|cut -f11 -d'.'`
community=`echo $community|cut -f2 -d'"'`
zabbixhost=$(HOME=/root mysql -N -e "select host from zabbix.hosts
left join zabbix.interface on zabbix.hosts.hostid=zabbix.interface.
hostid where ip='$hostname' order by 'hostid' limit 1;" 2>/dev/null)
[[ $zabbixhost ]] && HOST=$zabbixhost
str="$hostname $address $community $enterprise $oid"
$ZABBIX_SENDER $ZABBIX_SERVER $ZABBIX_PORT -s "$HOST" -k "$KEY" -o
"$str"
```

So what do these do? The first line queries the MySQL database and checks whether a host is defined with the same IP as the trap source. If it is, the Zabbix host variable gets the hostname, as defined in Zabbix, assigned. Returned results are sorted by host ID and only the first match is taken. Thus, if there are multiple hosts with the same IP address (which is perfectly fine in Zabbix), only the oldest entry is selected. Any error output is discarded (redirected to `/dev/null`), so in case of a database misconfiguration, traps are not lost but end up in the generic trap-handling host.

The second line simply sets the host used for sending data to Zabbix to the entry returned from the database, if it exists.

But what's that HOME variable in the first line? The `mysql` command used there does not specify user, password, or any other connection information, so for the command to succeed, it would have to get this information from somewhere. For MySQL, this information can be placed in the `.my.cnf` file located in the user's HOME directory. Given that `snmptrapd` runs as root, but services often do not get all the environment variables normal logins do, we are directing further commands to look in `/root` for that file.

This means we're not done yet; we have to create the `/root/.my.cnf` file and fill it with the required information. As root, create `/root/.my.cnf` and place the following content in it:

```
[client]
user=zabbix
password=mycreativepassword
```

For the password, use the same one you used for the Zabbix server and frontend (if you don't remember this password, you can look it up in `zabbix_server.conf`).

Now, we should prepare for trap receiving on the Zabbix side. Open **Configuration | Hosts**, click on **Items** next to **Another host**, and then click on the **Create item** button. Enter these values:

- **Name**: snmptraps
- **Type**: **Zabbix trapper**
- **Key**: snmptraps
- **Type of information**: **Character**

When you are done, click on the **Add** button at the bottom.

Before we send a test trap, let's do one more thing: make sure that `snmptrapd` does not perform reverse lookups on received traps. While that might slightly decrease the prettiness of the data, we want to keep this script simple for now and this will also improve performance a bit. To do this, add the `-n` flag for `snmptrapd` to the startup scripts and restart it. This procedure is distribution specific.

Finally, we are ready to test our tricky setup. From **Another host**, execute this:

```
$ snmptrap -Ci -v 2c -c public <Zabbix server> "" "NET-SNMP-
MIB::netSnmpExperimental" NET-SNMP-MIB::netSnmpExperimental s "test"
```

Replace `<Zabbix server>` with the IP or DNS name of the Zabbix server. This command should complete without any error messages.

> This won't work with `A test host` — the oldest host with the IP address of `127.0.0.1` would be the Zabbix server example host.

Back in the frontend, navigate to **Monitoring | Latest data**:

Another host	- **other** - (1 Item)		
	snmptraps	2016-03-19 11:35:34	192.168.56.11 "test" NET-SNM...

Great, `snmptrap` instances are now successfully sorted by host, if present.

In case this trap was not sorted properly and still went into the **snmptraps** host, it could be caused by different output in some Net-SNMP versions. Instead of passing the IP address or hostname of the incoming connection as the first value, they pass a string like this:

```
UDP: [192.168.56.11]:56417->[192.168.56.10]:162
```

In that case, try adding another line before the `zabbixhost` assignment:

```
oid=`echo $oid|cut -f11 -d'.'`
community=`echo $community|cut -f2 -d'"'`
hostname=$(echo "$hostname" | awk -F'[] []' '{print $2}')
```

It will extract the first string enclosed in square brackets from the `hostname` variable. After making this change to the script, send the trap again.

That took us some time to set up, but now it's very simple. If we want traps from some host to be handled by a specific host, we create that host and an `snmptraps` item for it. All other traps go to the generic **snmptraps** host and **snmptraps** item.

But what about item lookup? The database holds information on item keys as well, so perhaps we could try using that.

We need to retrieve the item key from any database field based on the information received in the trap. As traps include SNMP OIDs, they are the best candidates to map traps against items. Now, the OID can be in numeric or textual form. In the Zabbix configuration, we have two fields that could be used:

- **Name**: While pretty much a freeform field, it is a "friendly name," so we'd better keep it human-readable.

- **Key**: This field has more strict rules on the characters it accepts, but OIDs should be fine. While not used by humans much, this field is still referred to in the trigger expressions.

That means we will use the **Key** field. To keep it both short enough and somewhat human-readable, we'll set it to the last part of the received textual-form OID. As the trap will be received by `snmptraps.sh`, it will try to match the received OID to the item key and based on that decide where to send the data.

> Remember that specific MIBs might have to be added to `/etc/snmp/snmp.conf` so that they are found by `snmptrapd`.

Again, as root, edit the `/home/zabbix/bin/snmptraps.sh` script. Replace the two lines we just added, so that it looks like this:

```
community=`echo $community|cut -f2 -d' '`
enterprise=`echo $enterprise|cut -f2 -d' '`
oid=`echo $oid|cut -f11 -d'.'`
community=`echo $community|cut -f2 -d'"'`
hostname=$(echo "$hostname" | awk -F'[][]' '{print $2}')
zabbixhostid=$(HOME=/root mysql -N -e "select hosts.hostid,host from
zabbix.hosts left join zabbix.interface on
zabbix.hosts.hostid=zabbix.interface.hostid where ip='$hostname' order
by 'hostid' limit 1;" 2>/dev/null)
zabbixhost=$(echo $zabbixhostid | cut -d" " -f2-)
[[ "$zabbixhost" ]] && {
    zabbixid=$(echo $zabbixhostid | cut -d" " -f1)
    trapoid=$(echo $oid | cut -d: -f3)
    if [ "$trapoid" ]; then
        zabbixitem=$(HOME=/root mysql -N -e "select key_ from
zabbix.items where key_='$trapoid' and hostid='$zabbixid';" 2> /dev/
null)
        if [ "$zabbixitem" ]; then
            HOST=$zabbixhost
            KEY=$zabbixitem
        fi
    fi
}
[[ $KEY = snmptraps ]] && {
    if [ "$(HOME=/root mysql -N -e "select key_ from zabbix.items
where
key_='snmptraps' and hostid='$zabbixid';" 2> /dev/null)" ]; then
        HOST=$zabbixhost
    fi
}
str="$hostname $address $community $enterprise $oid"
```

Save the file. Functionally, for our current configuration, it will work exactly the same as the previous version, with one minor improvement: if you look at the previous version carefully, you'll see it only checks for host availability, so if you created a host but forgot to create an item with the `snmptraps` key for it, the sent trap would be lost. This version will check whether an item with such a key exists for that host. If not, the generic host, `snmptraps`, will receive the trap.

Note that this is one benefit of the custom-script solution over the embedded Perl trap receiver we configured earlier. It is easier to have triggers for traps landing in this fallback host than checking for them in the Zabbix server logfile.

Additionally, it will now check whether the host also has an item with a key, matching the last part of the OID received. A simple decision flow representation is shown in the following figure:

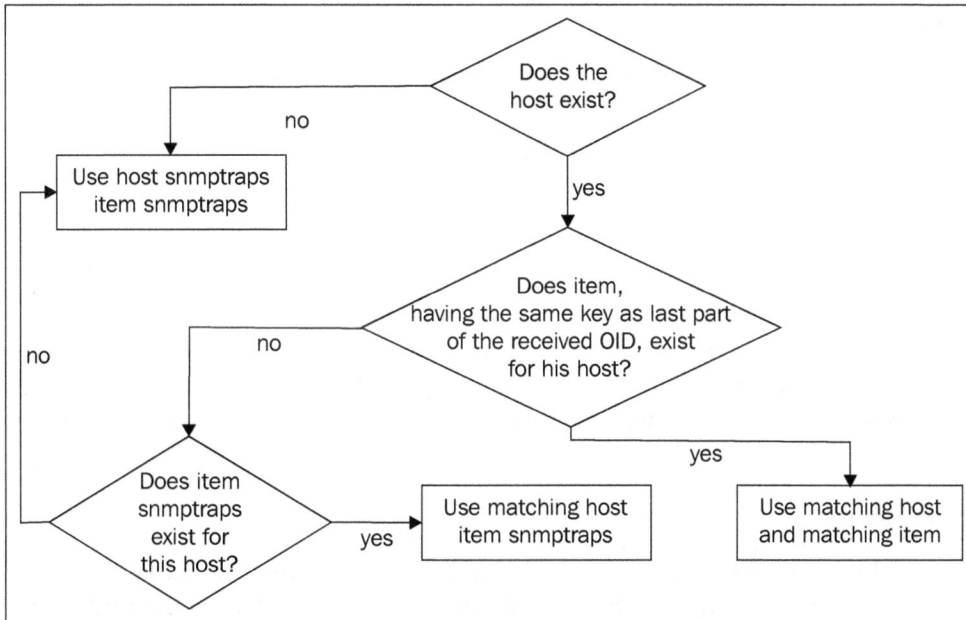

To test this, send an SNMP trap from **Another host** (there is no need to restart snmptrapd):

```
$ snmptrap -Ci -v 2c -c public <Zabbix server> "" "NET-SNMP-
MIB::netSnmpExperimental" NET-SNMP-MIB::netSnmpExperimental s "test"
```

Replace <Zabbix server> with the Zabbix server's IP or DNS name. If you now check **Monitoring | Latest data** for **Another host**, the trap should be correctly placed in the snmptraps item for this host. A trap sent from any other host, including the Zabbix server, should be placed in the snmptraps host and snmptraps item—feel free to try this out. Previously, a trap sent from the Zabbix server would be lost, because the script did not check for the snmptraps item's existence—it would find the host and then try to push the data to this nonexistent item.

Let's try out our item mapping now. Go to the Zabbix interface, **Configuration | Hosts,** click on **Items** next to **Another host,** and click on the **Create item** button. Fill in these values:

- **Name**: Experimental SNMP trap
- **Type: Zabbix trapper**

- **Key**: `netSnmpExperimental`
- **Type of information: Character**

When you're done, click on the **Add** button at the bottom. Again, send a trap from **Another host**:

```
$ snmptrap -Ci -v 2c -c public <Zabbix server> "" "NET-SNMP-
MIB::netSnmpExperimental" NET-SNMP-MIB::netSnmpExperimental s "test"
```

In the frontend, look at **Monitoring | Latest data**. If all went right, this time the trap data should have been placed in yet another item — the one we just created:

Experimental SNMP trap	2016-03-20 03:12:07	192.168.56.11 "test" NET-SNM...

Now, whenever we have a host that will be sending us traps, we will have to decide where we want its traps to go. Depending on that, we'll decide whether it needs its own host with an `snmptraps` item, or perhaps even individual items for each trap type.

Summary

Having explored basic monitoring with a Zabbix agent before, we looked at a major agentless monitoring solution in this chapter — SNMP. Given the wide array of devices supporting SNMP, this knowledge should help us with retrieving information from devices such as printers, switches, UPSes, and others, while also listening and managing incoming SNMP traps from those.

Beware of starting to monitor a large number of network devices, especially if they have many interfaces. For example, adding 10 switches with 48 ports, even if you monitor a single item per switch once a minute only, will make Zabbix poll eight new values per second (480 ports once a minute results in 480/60=8 new values per second). Usually, more values per port are monitored, so such an increase can bring a Zabbix server down and severely impact network performance even when SNMP `bulk get` is used.

While we have created several hosts by now, we only paid attention to the host properties that were immediately useful. In the next chapter, we will look some more into what we can control on hosts, including host and host group maintenance. We'll also discover how we can provide access for other users to what we have been configuring so far, using user and permission management.

5
Managing Hosts, Users, and Permissions

We created some hosts and host groups earlier, thus exploring the way items can be grouped and attached to hosts. Now is the time to take a closer look at these concepts and see what benefits they provide. We will:

- Explore host inventory and ways to automatically populate it
- Take a look at host and host group maintenance, which enables us to stop collecting data or suppress alerts
- Find out about the permission system in Zabbix so that you are able to allow partial access to other users as necessary

Hosts and host groups

A host can be considered as a basic grouping unit in Zabbix configuration. As you might remember, hosts are used to group items, which in turn are basic data-acquiring structures. Each host can have any number of items assigned, spanning all item types: Zabbix agents, simple checks, SNMP, IPMI, and so on. An item can't exist on its own, so hosts are mandatory.

Zabbix does not allow a host to be *left alone*, that is, not belong to any group. Let's look at what host groups we have currently defined — from the frontend, open **Configuration | Host groups**:

The first thing that catches the eye is that the **Templates** group seems to have a large number of templates already. These are provided as examples so that you can later quickly reference them for some hints on items. We'll ignore these for now. We can also see an empty **Discovered hosts** group and the Zabbix servers group, which contains a single example host. The interesting part is in the first half of the table — we can see both groups we used along the way, with all the corresponding members. This table is fairly simple, with just a group name, a count of the number of group members (individually denoting hosts and templates contained in the group), and individual members being listed.

As can be seen, individual members are color coded, in the following convention:

- **Green**: Normal, enabled host
- **Red**: Normal, disabled host
- **Gray**: Template

Let's create **Another Host** group and assign some hosts to it. Click on the **Create host group** button. Enter `Test group` in the **Group name** field, and then select **Linux servers** from the **Group** dropdown above the **Other hosts** listbox. From the filtered list, select our custom-created hosts: **A test host** and **Another host**. You can use the *Ctrl* and *Shift* keys to select multiple entries. When you have these hosts selected, click on the ◄ button.

Now, select **SNMP devices** from the **Group** dropdown and select **SNMP device**; then, click on the ◄ button again:

Group name	Test group		
Hosts	Hosts in		Other hosts | Group SNMP devices ▾
	Another host A test host SNMP device	◄ ►	snmptraps
	Add Cancel		

This form allows the easy selection of any number of hosts to add when a new group is created. You can freely move hosts from one box to another until you are satisfied with the result. When you are done, click on **Add**.

A new group will now appear in the list. As you can see, it contains the three hosts we just added:

Test group	Hosts 3	Templates	Another host, A test host, SNMP device

But wait! The **Linux servers** and **SNMP devices** groups have two hosts each:

Linux servers	Hosts 2	Templates	Another host, A test host
SNMP devices	Hosts 2	Templates	SNMP device, snmptraps

Right, we forgot to add the snmptraps host. Move your mouse cursor over it—notice how this (and every other host on this page) is a link. Clicking on it will take you to host details, so do that now. As we can see on the host editing form, it is already in one group: **SNMP devices**. Click on **Test group** in the **Other groups** listbox, and then click on the ◄ button:

Host name	snmptraps		
Visible name			
Groups	In groups		Other groups
	SNMP devices		Discovered hosts
	Test group	◄	Hypervisors
		►	Linux servers
			Templates
			Virtual machines
			Zabbix servers

When you are done, click on **Update**.

You have probably guessed by now that a host can belong to any number of groups. This allows you to choose grouping based on any arbitrary decision, such as having a single host in groups called **Linux servers, Europe servers**, and **DB servers**.

Now, we are back in the host list, so return to the host group list by navigating to **Configuration | Host groups**. **Test group** contains four hosts, as it should. Let's say you want to disable a whole group of hosts, or even several host groups. Perhaps you have a group of hosts that are retired but which you don't want to delete just yet, or maybe you want to disable hosts created for testing when creating an actual production configuration on the Zabbix server. The group listing provides an easy way to do that: mark the checkboxes next to the **Linux servers** and **SNMP devices** entries, click on the **Disable hosts** button at the bottom of the list, and confirm the popup.

After this operation, all green hosts should be gone—they should be red now, indicating that they are in a disabled state.

This time, you could also have only marked the checkbox next to **Test group**, as **Linux servers** and **SNMP devices** are subsets of **Test group**, and the final effect would be the same. After doing this, we should remember that **snmptraps** is a generic SNMP trap-receiving host, which probably should be left enabled. Again, click on it to open the host details editing page.

While we have the host details page open, we can take a quick look at the interface section. As you can see, there are four different interface types available. For each of them, a single IP and DNS field is available, along with **Connect to** controls, which are used for checks initiated from the server side. We've already used **Agent** and **SNMP** interfaces. We will also use IPMI and JMX interfaces when configuring monitoring using those protocols.

Mark the **Enabled** checkbox and click on **Update**:

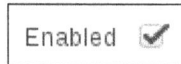

Enabled ☑

You should now see a host list with one disabled host (indicated by red text saying **Disabled** in the **STATUS** column) and one enabled host (indicated by green text saying **Enabled** in the **STATUS** column). Let's re-enable the **SNMP device** — click on the **Disabled** text next to it and confirm the popup. That leaves us with two enabled devices on the list. Select **Linux servers** from the **Group** dropdown, mark the checkboxes next to the two still-disabled hosts, click on the **Enable** button at the bottom of the list, and confirm the popup. Finally, we are back to having all the hosts enabled again. We used four methods to change the host state here:

- Changing the state for the whole group in the **Configuration | Host groups** area
- Changing the state for a single host using the **Enabled** checkbox in that host's properties page
- Changing the state for a single host using controls for each host in the **STATUS** column in the host configuration list
- Changing the state for a single host or multiple hosts by marking the relevant checkboxes in the host configuration list and using the buttons at the bottom of the list

We created the previous host group by going through the group configuration screen. As you might remember, another way is to use the **New group** field when creating or editing a host — this creates the group and simultaneously adds the host to that group.

The host list on the configuration screen is also useful in another way. It provides a nice and quick way of seeing which hosts are down. While the monitoring section gives us quite extensive information on the state of specific services and the conditions of each device, sometimes you will want a quick peek at the device status, for example, to determine the availability of all the devices in a particular group, such as printers, routers, or switches. The configuration provides this information in a list that contains almost no other information to distract you. If we were to now select **All** from the **Group** dropdown, we would see all the hosts this installation has:

NAME ▲	APPLICATIONS	ITEMS	TRIGGERS	GRAPHS	DISCOVERY	WEB	INTERFACE	TEMPLATES	STATUS	AVAILABILITY
Another host	Applications	Items 12	Triggers	Graphs	Discovery	Web	192.168.56.11: 10050		Enabled	ZBX SNMP JMX IPMI
A test host	Applications	Items 10	Triggers 1	Graphs	Discovery	Web	127.0.0.1: 10050		Enabled	ZBX SNMP JMX IPMI
SNMP device	Applications	Items 2	Triggers	Graphs	Discovery	Web	127.0.0.1: 10050		Enabled	ZBX SNMP JMX IPMI
snmptraps	Applications	Items 1	Triggers	Graphs	Discovery	Web	127.0.0.1: 10050		Enabled	ZBX SNMP JMX IPMI
Zabbix server	Applications 13	Items 77	Triggers 43	Graphs 12	Discovery 2	Web 1	127.0.0.1: 10050	Template App MySQL, Template App Zabbix Server, Template OS Linux (Template App Zabbix Agent)	Disabled	ZBX SNMP JMX IPMI

This time, we are interested in two columns: **STATUS** and **AVAILABILITY**. From the previous screenshot, we can see that we have one host that is not monitored, and this information is easily noticeable—printed in red, it stands out from the usual green entries. The **AVAILABILITY** column shows the internal state, as determined by Zabbix, for each host and polled item type. If Zabbix tries to get data from a host but fails, the availability of that host for this specific type of information is determined to be absent, as has happened here with **Another host**. Both the availability status and error message are preserved for the following four separate types of items polled by the Zabbix server:

- Zabbix agent (passive)
- SNMP
- JMX
- IPMI

On the other hand, the availability of the snmptraps host is unknown for all polled item types, as Zabbix has never tried to retrieve any data from it (that is, there are no items configured for it that the Zabbix server polls). Again, both unknown and unavailable hosts visually differ from the available ones, providing a quick overview.

> Remember that the availability icon in the host list represents passive Zabbix agent items only—active items do not affect it at all. If a host has active items only, this icon will stay gray. If you add passive items that fail and then convert them all to active items, the icon should turn back to gray. This is an improvement in Zabbix 3.0; in previous versions, the icon would stay red throughout.

Availability information is aimed more at Zabbix administrators—it shows problems related to gathering data from a host, not information such as resource usage, process status, or performance metrics.

That just about wraps it up for host and host group management in Zabbix. Host group usefulness extends a bit past frontend management, though—we'll see how exactly later in this chapter, when we talk about permissions.

Host inventory

We looked at managing hosts, but there's one area of host properties that warrants a slightly longer view. Go to **Configuration** | **Hosts**, and make sure **Linux servers** has been selected in the **Group** dropdown. Then, click on **A test host**, and switch to the **Host inventory** tab. By default, the inventory is set to **Disabled**:

All hosts / A test host	Enabled	ZBX SNMP JMX IPMI	Applications	Items 10

Host	Templates	IPMI	Macros	Host inventory	Encryption

	Disabled	Manual	Automatic
Type			
Type (Full details)			

Editing inventory data manually

Click on **Manual** to enable the inventory fields. Notice how there are a lot of fields, starting with simple things such as type, name, operating system, and hardware, and ending with hardware maintenance dates, location data, and point-of-contact information. In the **Type** field, enter test, and then click on **Update**:

	Disabled	Manual	Automatic
Type	test		
Type (Full details)			

Now click on **Another host**, switch to the **Host inventory** tab, and click on **Manual**. Then, enter the same `test` string in the **Type** field again. Click on **Update**. Now, let's switch to **SNMP devices** in the **Group** dropdown. Mark the checkboxes next to both hosts and click on **Mass update** at the bottom of the list. In the **Mass update** form, switch to the **Inventory** tab and mark the checkbox next to **Inventory mode**. Switch to **Manual**, mark the checkbox next to **Type**, and enter `snmp` in that field:

Inventory mode ✔	Disabled	Manual	Automatic
Type ✔	snmp		
Type (Full details) ☐	Original		

Click on **Update**. With some inventory data populated, let's go to **Inventory | Overview**. Choose **All** from the **Group** dropdown and **Type** from the **Grouping by** dropdown. Notice how we can see all the available values for this field and how many hosts we have for each of them:

TYPE	HOST COUNT ▼
test	2
snmp	2

Click on the number **2** in the **HOST COUNT** column next to **snmp**. Here, we can see individual hosts and some of the inventory fields, including the field that we used, **TYPE**:

HOST ▲	GROUP	NAME	TYPE	OS	SERIAL NUMBER A
SNMP device	SNMP devices, Test group		snmp		
snmptraps	SNMP devices, Test group		snmp		

This list was filtered to show only those hosts that have the exact string `snmp` in the **Type** field. You can verify that by looking at the filter:

Filter ▲		
Field	Type ▾	exactly ▾	snmp

Filter Reset

Collapse the filter and click on **SNMP device** in the **HOST** column. This will open the host overview page, displaying some basic configuration information. Notably, host interfaces are displayed here. While users without configuration permissions on hosts are not able to open host properties in the configuration section, they may see this host overview page and see the host interfaces this way:

Overview	Details				
Host name	SNMP device				
Agent interfaces	IP ADDRESS	DNS NAME		CONNECT TO	PORT
	127.0.0.1			IP	10050
SNMP interfaces	192.168.56.11			IP	161
Monitoring	Web Latest data Triggers Events Graphs Screens				
Configuration	Host Applications Items 2 Triggers Graphs Discovery Web				
	Cancel				

There are also two lines of links at the bottom of this form: **Monitoring** and **Configuration**. As one might expect, they provide quick access to various monitoring and configuration sections for this host, similar to the global search we discussed in *Chapter 2, Getting Your First Notification*. Clicking on **Host name** will provide access to global scripts. We will explore and configure those in *Chapter 7, Acting upon Monitored Conditions*.

Let's return to **Configuration | Hosts** and click on **SNMP device**. Switch to the **Host inventory** tab, and in the **OS** field, enter Linux (http://www.kernel.org) and click on **Update**. Let's go directly to **Inventory | Hosts** this time—notice how this was the page we ended at when we clicked on the host count from the inventory overview. Looking at the **OS** column, we can see that Zabbix recognized the URL and made it clickable:

HOST ▲	GROUP	NAME	TYPE	OS	SERIAL NUMBER A	TAG	MAC ADDRESS A
SNMP device	SNMP devices, Test group		snmp	Linux (http://www.kernel.org)			
snmptraps	SNMP devices, Test group		snmp				
							Displaying 2 of 2 found

> At this time, the columns displayed on this page cannot be customized.

This allows you to link to websites that provide more information or to web management interfaces for various devices. Note that other than recognizing URLs, fields are not interpreted in any way; for example, **Location latitude** and **Location longitude** fields are just text fields.

Populating inventory data automatically

Manually populated inventory data is useful, but doing that on a large scale may not be very feasible. Zabbix can also collect some inventory values automatically for us. This is possible as any item may populate any inventory field. We will use one of our existing items and create a new one to automatically populate two inventory fields.

Let's start by adding the new item. Navigate to **Configuration | Hosts**, switch to **Linux servers** from the **Group** dropdown, and click on **Items** for **A test host**. Then, click on **Create item**. Fill in the following values:

- **Name**: The full OS name
- **Key**: system.uname
- **Type of information**: **Text**
- **Update interval**: 300

When you're done, click on the **Add** button at the bottom. Let's modify another item to place data in yet another inventory field. Click on the Zabbix agent version, then choose **Software application A** from the **Populates host inventory** field dropdown, and click on **Update**. We now have two items configured to place data in inventory fields, but this alone won't do anything—we have our inventory set to manual mode. From the navigation bar above the item list, click on **A test host** and switch to the **Host inventory** tab. Then, choose **Automatic**. Notice how something changed—a couple of fields here got disabled, and links appeared to the right of them:

Host	Templates	IPMI	Macros	Host inventory	Encryption

	Disabled	Manual	Automatic

Type	test
Type (Full details)	
Name	
Alias	
OS	
OS (Full details)		← Full OS name

These are the fields we chose during the item configuration earlier. The links show which items are supposed to populate these fields and allow convenient access to the configuration of those items. Note that the field we manually populated earlier, **Type**, did not lose the value. Actually, the automatic mode can be said to be a hybrid one. Fields that are configured to obtain their values automatically do so; other fields may be populated manually. Click on **Update**.

Values from items are placed in the inventory whenever an item gets a new value. For the full OS version item, we set the interval to a fairly low one: 300 seconds. The agent one, on the other hand, has a large interval. This means that we might have to wait for a long time before the value appears in that inventory field. To make it happen sooner, restart the agent on **A test host**.

The inventory field we chose, **Software application A**, is not very representative, but there is no way of customizing inventory fields at this time. If you have data that does not match existing inventory fields well, you'll have to choose the best fit — or just use something not very much related to the actual data.

With two items supposed to have their values placed in the inventory fields, let's return to **Inventory | Overview** and choose **Software application A** from the **Grouping by** dropdown. This should display only one host, for the agent version **3.0.0**. Click on **1** in the **HOST COUNT** column, and you should be able to see that, as expected, it is **A test host**. The column we chose is not listed in the current view, though. Click on **A test host** in the **HOST** column and switch to the **Details** tab:

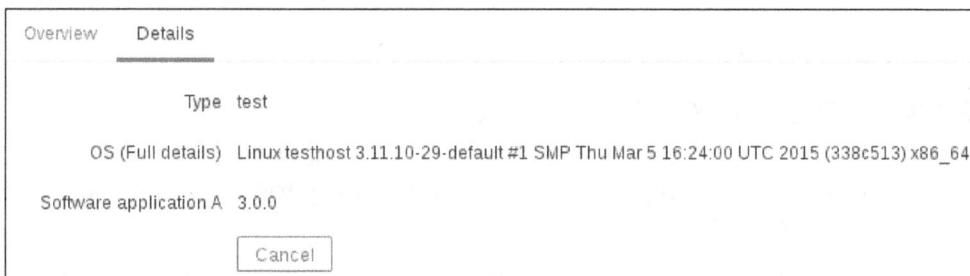

Overview	Details
Type	test
OS (Full details)	Linux testhost 3.11.10-29-default #1 SMP Thu Mar 5 16:24:00 UTC 2015 (338c513) x86_64
Software application A	3.0.0
	Cancel

Here, we can see system information from the `system.uname` item and the agent version from the `agent.version` item.

We used both the overview and host pages of the inventory section. The overview is useful to see the distribution of hosts by inventory field. The host page allows seeing individual hosts while filtering by host group and filtering by a single inventory field. When we ended up on the hosts page, the filter was preset for us to match an exact field value, but we may also search for a substring. For example, if we have systems with OS information containing CentOS 5.5 and CentOS 6.2, we may filter just by `CentOS` and obtain a list of all the CentOS systems, no matter which exact version they are running.

While being able to access inventory data in the frontend is useful sometimes, faster and easier access might be preferred. It is also possible to include inventory data in notifications. For example, sent e-mail could include system location, whom to contact when there's any problem with the system, and some serial numbers among other things. We will discuss notifications in *Chapter 7, Acting upon Monitored Conditions*.

Host maintenance

We want to know about problems as soon as possible, always. Well, not always—there are those cases when we test failover or reconfigure storage arrays. There is also maintenance—the time when things are highly likely to break and we do not want to send loads of e-mails, SMS messages, and other things to our accounts or to other people. Zabbix offers host group and host-level maintenance that enables us to avoid excessive messaging during such maintenance periods.

Hosts being under maintenance can result in three main consequences:

- Data is not collected for these hosts
- Problems for these hosts are hidden or not shown in the frontend
- Alerts are not processed for these hosts

These consequences can also be customized in quite some detail per host group, host, and other factors. We will explore most of those customization possibilities in this chapter, except alert processing—we will discuss that in *Chapter 7, Acting upon Monitored Conditions*.

Creating maintenance periods

We will create a couple of maintenance periods and see how they affect several views in the frontend. We will discuss the available time period options and set up two different maintenance periods:

- One that will not affect data collection
- One that stops data collection

> Before working with maintenance periods, ensure that the time zones configured for the PHP and Zabbix server hosts match. Otherwise, the time displayed in the frontend will differ from the time the actual maintenance takes place.

Collecting data during maintenance

Navigate to **Configuration | Maintenance** and click on **Create maintenance period**. In the resulting form, fill in these values:

- **Name**: Enter `Normal maintenance`

- **Active since**: Make sure this is set to the start of your current day or earlier

- **Active till**: Make sure this is set to a year or so in the future

- **Description**: Enter `We keep data during this maintenance`

Maintenance	Periods	Hosts & Groups

Name	Normal maintenance
Maintenance type	With data collection ▾
Active since	2016 - 03 - 23 00 : 00
Active till	2017 - 03 - 24 00 : 00
Description	We keep data during this maintenance

Add   Cancel

What's that, are we really creating a year-long maintenance period? Not really. Switch to the **Periods** tab.

Here, Zabbix terminology is a bit confusing. The main tab has since–till fields, which allow us to set what we could call the main period. The **Periods** tab allows us to add individual periods, and we could call them subperiods. Any maintenance entry in Zabbix must have at least one subperiod defined. Maintenance in Zabbix is active when the main period overlaps with the subperiods. Let's repeat that:

> Maintenance in Zabbix is active when the main period overlaps with the subperiods.

We should not add a maintenance entry without any subperiods defined. Zabbix 3.0.0 has a minor regression where this is actually possible — it is hoped that this will be fixed in further releases. No subperiods are defined here yet, so let's click on **New**. To keep things simple here, let's add a one time period. In the **Date** field, set the date and time to the current values. We can leave the **Maintenance period** length at the default, which is 1 hour:

Maintenance period		
	Period type	One time only ▾
	Date	2016 - 03 - 23 02 : 45 ▦
	Maintenance period length	0 Days 1 ▾ Hours 0 ▾ Minutes
	Add Cancel	

When you're done, click on the small **Add** link below the **Maintenance period** section — do not click on the **Add** button yet. Only after clicking on that small **Add** link should you click on the **Add** button — an error should appear:

Details	Cannot add maintenance	×
At least one host or group should be selected.		

That didn't seem to work too well — apparently, a maintenance entry without any hosts or groups assigned to it can not be created. Switch to the **Hosts & Groups** tab. For our first maintenance period, make sure the **Group** dropdown in the **Other hosts** section says **Linux servers**, and choose **A test host**. Then, click on the ◄ button:

Hosts in maintenance	In maintenance		Other hosts	Group Linux servers ▾
	A test host	◄ ►	Another host

> You may freely add any number of hosts and host groups, and they may overlap. Zabbix will correctly figure out which hosts should go into maintenance.

With the problem—a missing host or host group—solved, let's click on **Add** again. The maintenance entry should appear in the list:

NAME ▲	TYPE	ACTIVE SINCE	ACTIVE TILL	STATE	DESCRIPTION
Normal maintenance	With data collection	2016-03-23 00:00	2017-03-24 00:00	Active	We keep data during this maintenance

> The reminder to click on the small **Add** link was not repeated several times for no reason—it is too easy to forget to click on it and actually miss your changes in some cases. For example, if you were adding the second subperiod and forgot to click on the small link, it would be silently discarded. Watch out for similar traps in other forms.

With the maintenance entry added, let's try to see the effect this has on several sections in the frontend. In the console, run this:

```
$ cat /dev/urandom | md5sum
```

Navigate to **Monitoring | Triggers** and wait for the trigger to fire. When it shows up, look at the **HOST** column—this time, there's an orange wrench indicator. This shows us that maintenance is currently active for this host. Move the mouse cursor over this indicator:

HOST	NAME	DESCRIPTION
A test host	CPU load too high on A test host for last 3 minutes	Add
	Normal maintenance [Maintenance with data collection] We keep data during this maintenance	1 found

> You may click on the indicator to keep the message open, as with other popup messages in Zabbix.

The message shows the name of the maintenance we used: **Normal maintenance**. It also tells us that this maintenance is configured to keep collecting data, and below, that the description of the maintenance is shown. This allows us to easily inform other users about why this maintenance is taking place. Still on the trigger page, look at the filter. Notice how the **Show hosts in maintenance** checkbox is marked by default. Unmark it and click on **Filter**. All problems for **A test host** should disappear—well, from this view at least. To avoid being confused later, mark that checkbox and click on **Filter** again. Remember, most filter options are remembered between visits to a specific page, so we will not see hosts in maintenance in this view later if we leave it marked.

Let's check how another page looks when a host is in maintenance. Navigate to **Monitoring | Dashboard** and check the **Last 20 issues** widget:

Last 20 issues						
HOST	ISSUE	LAST CHANGE	AGE	INFO	ACK	ACTIONS
A test host	CPU load too high on A test host for last 3 minutes	2016-03-23 02:55:55	6m 33s		No	
			1 of 1 issue is shown		Updated: 03:02:28	

The host that is under maintenance is denoted here in the same way. Again, moving the mouse cursor over the orange icon will reveal the maintenance name, type, and description. We can also hide hosts in maintenance from the dashboard—click on the wrench icon in the upper-right corner to open the dashboard filter. In the filter, click on **Disabled** at the top, and then unmark the checkbox labeled **Show hosts in maintenance**:

Dashboard filter	Enabled
Host groups	All
Hosts	☐ Show hosts in maintenance
Triggers with severity	☑ Not classified ☑ Information ☑ Warning ☑ Average ☑ High ☑ Disaster
Trigger name like	
Problem display	All
	Update Cancel

When done, click on **Update**. Notice how the problem is gone from the **Last 20 issues** widget. Click on the wrench icon again (it has a green dot now to indicate that this filter is active), click on **Enabled** to disable it, and then click on **Update**.

The maintenance status can also be seen in other frontend sections. We will review some of them in *Chapter 9, Visualizing the Data with Graphs and Maps*.

We created and checked one maintenance entry. During this maintenance, data from our host was still collected, and triggers were checking that data. The status was shown in the frontend, and we could choose to hide hosts that were in maintenance. Now, let's try something different—maintenance that also stops data from coming in.

Not collecting data during maintenance

Navigate to **Configuration | Maintenance** and click on **Create maintenance period**. In the resulting form, fill in these values:

- **Name**: Enter `Maintenance with all data dropped`
- **Maintenance type**: Choose **No data collection**
- **Active since**: Make sure this is set to the start of your current day or earlier
- **Active till**: Make sure this is set to a year or so in the future
- **Description**: Enter `We don't need no data`

Name	Maintenance with all data dropped
Maintenance type	No data collection ▼
Active since	2016 - 03 - 23 00 : 00
Active till	2017 - 03 - 24 00 : 00
Description	We don't need no data

Update   Clone   Delete   Cancel

Switch to the **Periods** tab and click on **New**. In the **Date** field, set the date and time to the current values:

Maintenance period		
Period type	One time only ▾	
Date	2016 - 03 - 23 11 : 48 🗓	
Maintenance period length	0 Days 1 ▾ Hours 0 ▾ Minutes	
Add Cancel		

Click on the small **Add** link—again, that one first, not the **Add** button. Now, switch to the **Hosts & Groups** tab. Make sure the **Group** dropdown in the **Other hosts** section says **Linux servers**, and choose **Another host**. Then, click on the ◂ button. Now, click on the large **Add** button. There should be two maintenance entries in the list now:

NAME ▲	TYPE	ACTIVE SINCE	ACTIVE TILL	STATE	DESCRIPTION
Maintenance with all data dropped	No data collection	2016-03-23 00:00	2017-03-24 00:00	Active	We don't need no data
Normal maintenance	With data collection	2016-03-23 00:00	2017-03-24 00:00	Active	We keep data during this maintenance

Go to **Monitoring | Latest data,** and make sure **Linux servers** is selected in the **Host groups** field in the filter. Notice how data stopped coming in for the items in **Another host**—the timestamp is not being updated anymore. That's because of the maintenance without data collection that we created. As such, triggers will not fire, and problems for such hosts will not appear in the frontend, no matter what the filter settings are.

Let's take a quick look at **Configuration | Hosts**. This is another location where the maintenance status can be seen. Hosts that are in maintenance will have **In maintenance** listed in the **STATUS** column—this replaces the normal **Enabled** text:

NAME ▲	APPLICATIONS	ITEMS	TRIGGERS	GRAPHS	DISCOVERY	WEB	INTERFACE	TEMPLATES	STATUS
Another host	Applications	Items 12	Triggers	Graphs	Discovery	Web	192.168.56.11: 10050		In maintenance

We discovered the way maintenance can affect data collection and the displaying of problems. Another important reason to use it is skipping or modifying notifications. We will discuss notifications in *Chapter 7, Acting upon Monitored Conditions*.

Maintenance period options

So far, the only type of maintenance subperiods we've used is one-time maintenance. We decided to call those periods that were configured in a separate tab "subperiods" to distinguish then from the main period, configured in the first tab, **Maintenance**. We also discovered that maintenance would be active only during the time for which the main period overlaps with the subperiods. But what's the point of defining the same thing twice; couldn't the one-time period be the only thing to specify? The benefit of the main period becomes more apparent when configuring recurring maintenance, so let's explore the options available for subperiods. You may navigate to **Configuration | Maintenance**, start creating a new maintenance, and play with the available subperiods as we explore them.

One-time only maintenance

This is the maintenance subperiod type we've already used. It starts at the specified date and time, proceeds for the amount of time specified in minutes, hours, and days, and that's it. This type of subperiod must still overlap with the main period.

Daily maintenance

For daily maintenance, we have to specify the starting time and the length of the maintenance period:

Maintenance period		
Period type	Daily ▾	
Every day(s)	1	
At (hour:minute)	13 : 0	
Maintenance period length	0 Days 1 ▾ Hours 0 ▾ Minutes	
Add Cancel		

During the main period, maintenance will start every day at the specified time. It will start every day with the **Every day(s)** option set to the default, 1. We can change this and make the maintenance only happen every second day, third day, and so on.

Weekly maintenance

For weekly maintenance, we have to specify the starting time and the length of the maintenance period, the same as for daily maintenance:

Maintenance period	Period type	Weekly ▼
	Every week(s)	1
	Day of week	☐ Monday
		☐ Tuesday
		☐ Wednesday
		☐ Thursday
		☐ Friday
		☐ Saturday
		☐ Sunday
	At (hour:minute)	13 : 0
	Maintenance period length	0 Days 1 ▼ Hours 0 ▼ Minutes
	Add Cancel	

We also have to choose on which days of the week the maintenance will take place—we can choose one or more. During the main period, maintenance will start every specified day of the week at the specified time. It will start every week with the **Every week(s)** option set to the default, 1. We can change this and make the maintenance only happen every second week, third week, and so on.

Monthly maintenance

Monthly maintenance has two modes:

* By day (or by date)
* By day of week

For both of these, we have to specify the starting time and the length of the maintenance period, the same as in daily and weekly maintenance modes. Additionally, we have to choose which months the maintenance will happen in—we may choose one month or more. In the day or date mode (option **Date** set to **Day**), we have to enter a date in the **Day of month** field. Maintenance will happen on that date only in each of the months we select:

Maintenance period		
	Period type	Monthly ▾
	Month	☐ January ☐ July
		☐ February ☐ August
		☐ March ☐ September
		☐ April ☐ October
		☐ May ☐ November
		☐ June ☐ December
	Date	**Day** Day of week
	Day of month	13
	At (hour:minute)	13 : 0
	Maintenance period length	0 Days 1 ▾ Hours 0 ▾ Minutes
	Add Cancel	

In the day-of-week mode (option **Date** set to **Day of week**) we have to choose which days of the week the maintenance will take place on—we may choose one or more:

Maintenance period		
	Period type	Monthly ▾
	Month	☐ January ☐ July
		☐ February ☐ August
		☐ March ☐ September
		☐ April ☐ October
		☐ May ☐ November
		☐ June ☐ December
	Date	Day **Day of week**
	Day of week	First ▾
		☐ Monday
		☐ Tuesday
		☐ Wednesday
		☐ Thursday
		☐ Friday
		☐ Saturday
		☐ Sunday
	At (hour:minute)	13 : 0
	Maintenance period length	0 Days 1 ▾ Hours 0 ▾ Minutes
	Add Cancel	

As this has to happen monthly, not weekly, we also have to choose whether this will happen on the **First**, **Second**, **Third**, **Fourth**, or **Last** such weekday in any of the selected months:

```
First
Second
Third
Fourth
Last
```

In addition to these, we may also ask Zabbix to run this maintenance on the last such day in the selected months, for example, every April, August, and December, to run the maintenance on the last Wednesday that month.

With all these recurring maintenance modes, it is possible to create nearly any scenario—one thing that might be missing is the ability to run monthly maintenance on the last day of every month.

So, the benefit of having this sort of a double configuration, this overlap between the main period and the subperiods, is that we can have a recurring maintenance that starts at some point in the future and then stops at some point later completely automatically—we don't have to remember to add and remove it at a specific date.

Ad-hoc maintenance

The maintenance functionality in Zabbix is aimed at a well-planned environment where maintenance is always planned in advance. In practice, people often enough want to place a host in maintenance quickly and then simply remove it manually a bit later. With all the periods and other things maintenance entry requires, it's not quick enough. A slightly hackish workaround is to create a new host group and maintenance period that is always active (make sure to set its end date far enough in the future). Include that host group in the maintenance entry, and then, adding a host to the chosen host group will add that host to maintenance. Of course, one will have to remember to remove the host from the host group afterwards.

Users, user groups, and permissions

Hosts manage monitored entity (host) information and are used to group basic information-gathering units—**items**. User accounts in Zabbix control access to monitored information.

Authentication methods

Before we look at more detailed user configuration, it might be helpful to know that Zabbix supports three authentication methods. Navigate to **Administration | Authentication** to taka a look at authentication configuration:

Default authentication	Internal LDAP HTTP
LDAP host	
Port	389
Base DN	
Search attribute	
Bind DN	Admin
Bind password	●●●●●●
Test authentication	[must be a valid LDAP user]
Login	Admin
User password	
	Update Test

As can be seen here, these are the three authentication methods:

- **HTTP**: Users are authenticated with web server HTTP authentication mechanisms. Support for HTTP authentication basically allows the use of any of the authentication methods for Zabbix that the web server supports, and in the case of the Apache HTTPD daemon, there are many.

- **LDAP**: Users are authenticated using an LDAP server. This can be handy if all enterprise users that need access to Zabbix are already defined in an LDAP structure. Only user passwords are verified; group membership and other properties are not used. A Zabbix user account must also exist for the login to be successful.

- **Internal**: With this method, users are authenticated using Zabbix's internal store of users and passwords. We will use this method.

Creating a user

The initial Zabbix installation does not contain many predefined users—let's look at the user list. Navigate to **Administration | Users**:

ALIAS ▲	NAME	SUPNAME	USER TYPE	GROUPS	IS ONLINE?	LOGIN	FRONTEND ACCESS	DEBUG MODE	STATUS
Admin	Zabbix	Administrator	Zabbix Super Admin	Zabbix administrators	Yes (2016-03-24 12:15:03)	Ok	System default	Disabled	Enabled
guest			Zabbix User	Guests	No (2016-03-23 02:35:08)	Ok	System default	Disabled	Enabled

That's right; only two user accounts are defined: **Admin** and **guest**. We have been logged in as **Admin** all the time. On the other hand, the **guest** user is used for unauthenticated users. Before we logged in as **Admin**, we were **guest**. The user list shows some basic information about the users, such as which groups they belong to, whether they are logged in, when their last login was, and whether their account is enabled.

> By granting access permissions to the **guest** user, it is possible to allow anonymous access to resources.

Let's create another user for ourselves. Click on the **Create user** button located in the upper-right corner. We'll look at all available options for a user account, while filling in the appropriate ones:

- **Alias**: Enter monitoring_user. This is essentially a username.
- **Name**: Enter monitoring. In this field, you would normally enter the user's real name.
- **Surname**: Enter user. Obviously, this field normally contains the user's real surname.
- **Groups**: Just like hosts, user accounts can be grouped. A user must belong to at least one group, so let's assign our new user to some group at least temporarily. Click on the **Add** button next to the **Groups** field, and mark the checkbox next to **Zabbix administrators**. Then, click on **Select**:

☐ No access to the frontend
☑ Zabbix administrators
Select

- **Password**: Choose and enter a password, and then retype it in the next field.

- **Language**: The frontend has translations in various levels of maturity, and each user can choose their own preference. We'll leave this at **English (en_GB)**:

```
English (en_GB)
English (en_US)
Czech (cs_CZ)
French (fr_FR)
Italian (it_IT)
Korean (ko_KR)
Japanese (ja_JP)
Polish (pl_PL)
Portuguese (pt_BR)
Russian (ru_RU)
Slovak (sk_SK)
Ukrainian (uk_UA)
```

> If a language you would like to use is not listed, it might still be there—just incomplete. See *Appendix B, Being Part of the Community*, for more details on how to enable it and contribute to Zabbix translations.

- **Theme**: The Zabbix frontend supports theming. Currently, there are only two themes included, though. We'll leave the theme to be **System default** (which is **Blue**):

```
System default
Blue
Dark
```

- **Auto-login**: Marking this option will automatically log the user in after they have logged in at least once manually. Automatic login is performed with browser cookies. We won't be using automatic login for this user.

- **Auto-logout**: You can make a particular account automatically log out after a specific time of inactivity. The minimum time period that can be set is 90 seconds, and the maximum is about 166 minutes. There is no need to set automatic logout here.

> What's more, at the time of writing this, this option does not work as expected and should not be relied on.

- **Refresh**: This is the time in seconds between page refreshes when in the **Monitoring** section. While smaller values might be nice to look at when first setting up and having items with short check intervals, they somewhat increase the load on the server, and if the page contains a lot of information, then it might sometimes not even finish loading before the next refresh kicks in. Let's set this to 60 for this user—after all, they can always refresh manually when testing something. Note that some pages do not perform a full page refresh; instead, they just reload some elements on that page. A graph page, for example, only reloads the graph image.

- **Rows per page**: Each user can have an individual maximum rows-per-page setting. If the returned data exceeds this parameter, the interface splits the data into multiple pages. We won't change this parameter.

- **URL (after login)**: A user might wish to always see a specific page after logging in—be it the overview, trigger list, or any other page. This option allows the user to customize that. The URL entered is relative to the Zabbix directory, so let's make this user always see **Monitoring | Triggers** when they log in, by entering tr_status.php here.

The final result should look as follows:

User Media Permissions	
Alias	monitoring_user
Name	monitoring
Surname	user
Groups	Zabbix administrators Add
	Delete selected
Password	Change password
Language	English (en_GB) ▼
Theme	System default ▼
Auto-login	▨
Auto-logout (min 90 seconds)	900
Refresh (in seconds)	60
Rows per page	50
URL (after login)	tr_status.php
	Update Delete Cancel

If it does, click on the **Add** button at the bottom.

Now, it would be nice to test this new user. It is suggested that you launch another browser for this test so that any changes are easy to observe. Let's call the browser where you have the administrative user logged in "Browser 1" and the other one "Browser 2." In Browser 2, open the Zabbix page and log in as monitoring_user, supplying whatever password you entered before. Instead of the dashboard, the **Monitoring | Triggers** page is opened.

Also, the page is notably different than before — the main menu entries **Configuration** and **Administration** are missing here. Despite the **Host** and **Group** dropdowns both being set to **All**, no issues are visible, and the dropdowns themselves don't contain any host or host group. Go to **Monitoring | Overview**. The **Group** dropdown is set to all, but the **Details** view claims that there's **No data found**. Why so?

By default, users don't have access to any systems. When our new user logs in, nothing is displayed in the monitoring section, because we did not grant any privileges, including read-only. We did assign this user to the **Zabbix administrators** group, but that group has no permissions set by default. Back in Browser 1, click on **monitoring_user** in the **ALIAS** column. One minor thing to notice: instead of a **Password** input field this time a button that says **Change password** is visible. If you ever have to reset a password for some user, clicking on this button will reveal the password input fields again, allowing a password update along with any other changes that might have been made:

Password	Change password

But there's a tab we still haven't used: **Permissions**. Let's switch to it.

> There's also a **Media** tab. There, users can have various media assigned so that Zabbix knows how to alert them. Media types include e-mail addresses or numbers to send SMS messages to. We will discuss notification functionality in *Chapter 7, Acting upon Monitored Conditions*.

The first thing to notice is the **User type** dropdown. It offers three user types. We'll leave it at **Zabbix User** for this user:

Zabbix User
Zabbix Admin
Zabbix Super Admin

For reference, these types have the following meanings:

- **Zabbix User**: These are normal users that only have access to the **Monitoring, Inventory,** and **Reports** sections in the **Main** menu
- **Zabbix Admin**: These users, in addition to the previous three sections, have access to the **Configuration** section, so they are able to reconfigure parts of Zabbix
- **Zabbix Super Admin**: These users have full access to Zabbix, including the **Monitoring, Configuration,** and **Administration** sections

The following is a section that looks very close to what we are looking for. There are **Hosts** and **Host groups**, split among **READ-WRITE, READ-ONLY,** and **DENY** permissions:

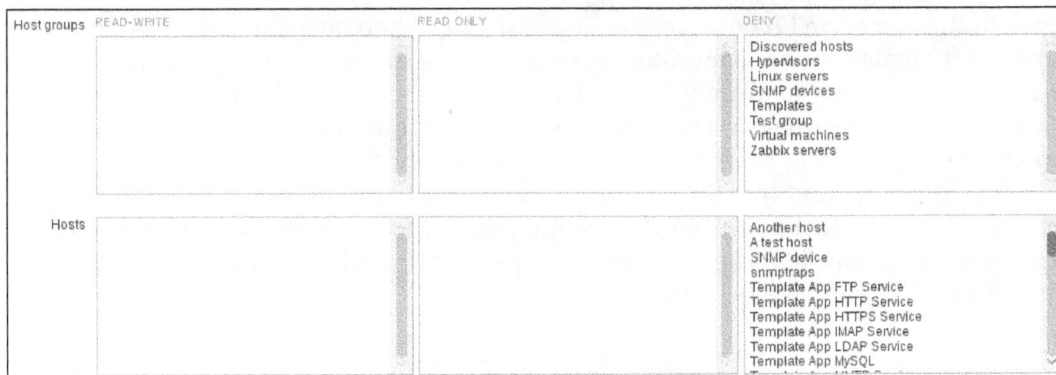

Host groups	READ-WRITE	READ ONLY	DENY
			Discovered hosts Hypervisors Linux servers SNMP devices Templates Test group Virtual machines Zabbix servers
Hosts			Another host A test host SNMP device snmptraps Template App FTP Service Template App HTTP Service Template App HTTPS Service Template App IMAP Service Template App LDAP Service Template App MySQL

There's just one problem: there is no way to change these permissions.

A helpful message at the bottom of the page explains why. It says **Permissions can be assigned for user groups only**.

We conveniently skipped adding or configuring any groups and permissions, so now is a good time to fix that.

Creating user groups

Instead of modifying the default user groups, we will add our own. Navigate to **Administration | User groups**, and take a look at the list of current user groups:

NAME ▲	#	MEMBERS	FRONTEND ACCESS	DEBUG MODE	STATUS
Disabled	Users		System default	Disabled	Disabled
Enabled debug mode	Users		System default	Enabled	Enabled
Guests	Users 1	guest	System default	Disabled	Enabled
No access to the frontend	Users		Disabled	Disabled	Enabled
Zabbix administrators	Users 2	Admin (Zabbix Administrator), monitoring_user (monitoring user)	System default	Disabled	Enabled

As can be seen, there are already a few predefined groups, giving you some idea of how users could be organized. That organization can be based on system categories, systems, management roles, physical locations, and so on. For example, you might have a group of administrators in headquarters and some in a branch location. Each group might not be interested in the UPS status in the other location, so you could group them as HQ admins and Branch admins. A user can belong to any number of groups, so you can create various schemes as real-world conditions require.

Let's create a new group for our user. Click on **Create user group** in the upper-right corner. Let's fill in the form and find out what each control does:

- **Group name**: Enter Our users.

- **Users**: Here, we can add users to the group we are creating. Our current installation has very few users, so finding the correct username with all users displayed is easy. If we had many users, we could use the **Other groups** dropdown to filter the user list and more easily find what we are looking for. Select **monitoring_user** and click on the ◄ button.

- **Frontend access**: This option allows us to choose the authentication method for a specific group. It allows a configuration where most users are authenticated against LDAP, but some users are authenticated against the internal user database. It also allows us to set no GUI access for some groups, which can then be used for users that only need to receive notifications. We'll leave this option at **System default**.

If your Zabbix installation uses LDAP for user authentication, setting **Frontend access** to `Internal` for a user group will make all users in that group authenticate against the internal Zabbix password storage. It is not a failover option—internal authentication will always be used. This is useful if you want to provide access to users that are not in the LDAP directory, or create emergency accounts that you can pull out of a safe when LDAP goes down. Such an approach will not work with HTTP authentication, as it happens before Zabbix gets to decide anything about the authentication backend.

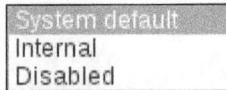

- **Enabled**: With a single option, all the users in this group can be disabled or enabled. As the predefined groups might tell you, this is a nice way to easily disable individual user accounts by simply adding them to a group that has this checkbox unmarked. We want our user to be able to log in, so this option will stay marked.
- **Debug mode**: This option gives users access to frontend debug information. It is mostly useful for Zabbix developers. We will discuss debug mode in *Appendix A, Troubleshooting*.

With the main settings covered, let's switch to the **Permissions** tab:

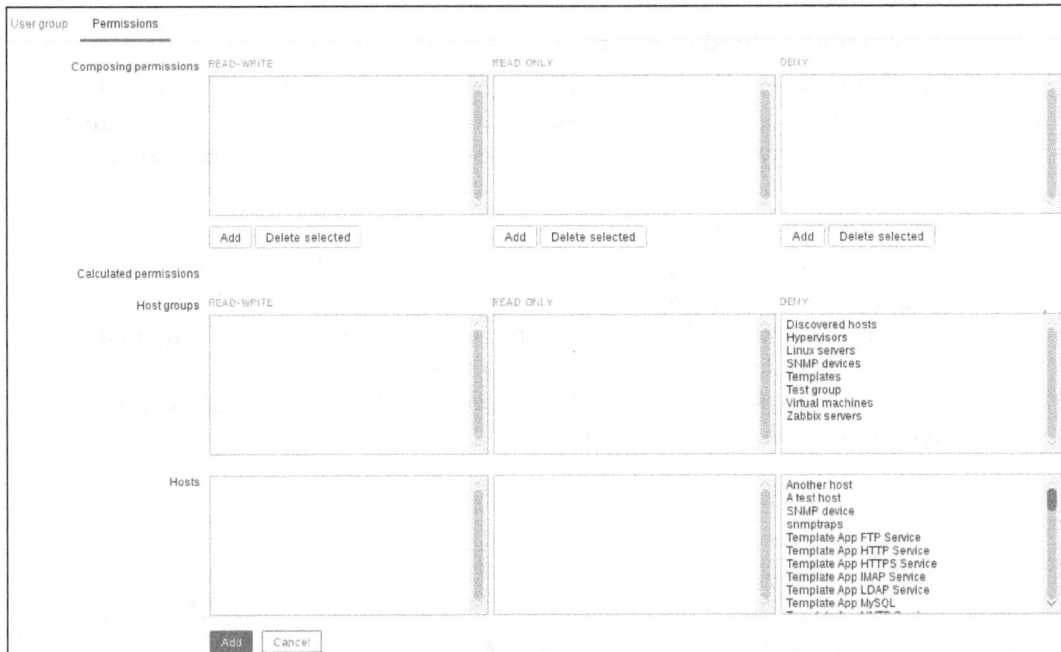

Now that's more like it! We can finally see controls for various permission levels. There are three sections, labeled **READ-WRITE**, **READ ONLY**, and **DENY**. Each has buttons named **Add** and **Delete** selected, which seem to modify the respective permission. Our user had no permissions to see anything, so we will want to add some kind of permissions to the first two boxes. Click on **Add** below the **READ-WRITE** box. This opens a new window with some options.

It also provides us with another valuable bit of information. If you look at the window contents carefully, you'll notice something common for all of these entries: they are all **host groups**. We finally have got the essential information together — in Zabbix, permissions can be set for user groups on host groups only.

Mark the checkbox next to **SNMP devices**, and click on the **Select** button.

We can now see **SNMP devices** added to the **READ-WRITE** box. Next, click on **Add** below the **READ ONLY** box. A popup identical to the previous one will open. This time, mark the checkbox next to the **Linux servers** entry, and then click on **Select**.

Now, the **READ ONLY** box has **Linux servers** listed. The final form should look like this:

Composing permissions	READ-WRITE	READ ONLY	DENY
	SNMP devices	Linux servers	
	Add Delete selected	Add Delete selected	Add Delete selected

Let's look at the **Calculated permissions** section, just below the controls we used:

Calculated permissions			
Host groups	READ-WRITE	READ ONLY	DENY
	SNMP devices	Linux servers	Discovered hosts Hypervisors Templates Test group Virtual machines Zabbix servers
Hosts	SNMP device snmptraps	Another host A test host	Template App FTP Service Template App HTTP Service Template App HTTPS Service Template App IMAP Service Template App LDAP Service Template App MySQL Template App NNTP Service Template App NTP Service Template App POP Service Template App SMTP Service

This view shows effective user rights. We can see what the exact access permissions will look like: which hosts will be allowed read and write access, which will have read only, and for which there will be no access at all. This looks about right, so click on the **Add** button at the bottom. The group will be successfully added, and we will be able to see it in the group list:

Our users	Users 1	monitoring_user (monitoring user)	System default	Disabled	Enabled

Let's get back to Browser 2. Navigate to **Monitoring | Latest data**. Click on **Select** next to the **Host groups** field. Great, both of the groups we selected when configuring the permissions are available. Mark the checkboxes next to them and click on **Select**. Then, click on **Filter**. Now, our new user can view data from all the hosts. But we also added write permissions to one group for this user, so what's up with the **Configuration** menu? Let's recall the user-creation process—wasn't there something about user types? Right, we were able to choose between three user types, and we chose **Zabbix user**, which, as discussed, was not allowed to access configuration.

> It is important to keep in mind that, at this time, a Zabbix user that has write access granted will not be able to configure things in the frontend, but they will get write access through the API. This could cause security issues. We will discuss the API in *Chapter 21, Working Closely with Data*.

To continue exploring user permissions, we'll create another, more powerful user. In Browser 1, go to **Administration | Users**, and click on the **Create user** button. Fill in these values:

- **Alias**: Enter advanced_user.
- **Name**: Enter advanced.
- **Surname**: Enter user.
- **Groups**: Click on **Add**, mark the checkbox next to **Zabbix administrators**, and click on **Select**.
- **Password**: Enter a password in both fields. You can use the same password as for monitoring_user to make it easier to remember.
- **Refresh**: Enter 60.
- **URL (after login)**: Let's have this user view a different page right after logging in. Event history might do—enter events.php here.

Now, switch to the **Permissions** tab and select **Zabbix Admin** from the **User type** dropdown. This is will make quite a large difference, as we will soon see:

User type	Zabbix Admin ▾

When done, click on the **Add** button.

Let's use Browser 2 now. In the upper-right corner, click the logout ⏻ icon, and then log in as `advanced_user`. This user will land in the event history page, and this time, we can see the **Configuration** section. That's because we set the user type to `Zabbix Admin`. Let's check out what we have available there—open **Configuration | Hosts**:

ZABBIX	Monitoring	Inventory	Reports	Configuration				🔍	❷ Share	?	👤	⏻

Host groups	Templates	Hosts	Maintenance	Actions	Discovery	IT services		Zabbix One

Hosts   Group | all ▾ | Create host   Import

Filter ▾

	NAME ▲	APPLICATIONS	ITEMS	TRIGGERS	GRAPHS	DISCOVERY	WEB	INTERFACE	TEMPLATES	STATUS	AVAILABILITY	AGENT ENCRYPTION	INFO

No data found

Displaying 0 of 0 found

0 selected   Enable   Disable   Export   Mass update   Delete

How could there be no hosts available? We set this user as the `Zabbix Admin` type. We probably should look at the user list back in Browser 1:

ALIAS ▲	NAME	SURNAME	USER TYPE	GROUPS	IS ONLINE?	LOGIN	FRONTEND ACCESS	DEBUG MODE	STATUS
Admin	Zabbix	Administrator	Zabbix Super Admin	Zabbix administrators	Yes (2016-03-24 16:01:12)	Ok	System default	Disabled	Enabled
advanced_user	advanced	user	Zabbix Admin	Zabbix administrators	No	Ok	System default	Disabled	Enabled
guest			Zabbix User	Guests	No	Ok	System default	Disabled	Enabled
monitoring_user	monitoring	user	Zabbix User	Our users, Zabbix administrators	Yes (2016-03-24 16:01:08)	Ok	System default	Disabled	Enabled

Here, we can easily spot our mistake—we added `advanced_user` to the **Zabbix administrators** group, but we set permissions for the **Our users** group. We'll fix that now, but this time, we'll use the user properties form. Click on **advanced_user** in the **ALIAS** column, and in the resulting form, click on **Add** next to the **Groups** field. Mark the checkbox next to **Our users**, and then click on **Select**:

Groups	Our users Zabbix administrators		Add

When done, click on **Update**. In Browser 2, simply refresh the host's **Configuration** tab—it should reveal two hosts, **SNMP device** and **snmptraps**, which **advanced_user** can configure.

Suddenly, we notice that we have granted configuration access to the `snmptraps` host this way, which we consider an important host that should not be messed with and that neither of our two users should have access to anyway. How can we easily restrict access to this host while still keeping it in the **SNMP devices** group?

In Browser 1, navigate to **Configuration | Host groups** and click on **Create host group**. Enter the following details:

- **Group name**: Enter `Important SNMP hosts`
- **Hosts**: Filter the **Other hosts** listbox with the **Group** dropdown to display **SNMP devices**, select **snmptraps**, and then click on the ◄ button

When done, click on **Add**.

Open **Administration | User groups**, click on **Our users** in the **NAME** column, and switch to the **Permissions** tab. In the group details, click on the **Add** button below the **DENY** box. In the resulting window, mark the checkbox next to **Important SNMP hosts**, click on **Select**, and then click on the **Update** button.

Now is the time to look at Browser 2. It should still show the host configuration with two hosts. Refresh the list, and the `snmptraps` host will disappear. After our changes, `advanced_user` has configuration access only to the **SNMP device** host, and there will be no access to the monitoring of the `snmptraps` host at all, because we used deny. For `monitoring_user`, nothing has changed—there was no access to the **SNMP devices** group before.

Permissions and maintenance

The maintenance configuration that we looked at in this chapter follows the rules of host group permissions in its own way. Host group permissions impact the way Zabbix admins can configure maintenance entries:

- Zabbix admins may create new maintenance entries and include host groups and hosts they have write permissions on

- Zabbix admins may edit existing maintenance entries if they have write permissions on all the hosts and host groups included in those maintenance entries

Summary

We explored another aspect of host properties in Zabbix: host inventory. Host inventory may be manually populated, but the more useful aspect of it is its ability to receive values from any item in any inventory field. This still allows manually editing inventory fields that do not receive values from items.

Host and Host group maintenance allows us to create on-time or recurring maintenance entries on a daily, weekly, and monthly basis. Problems on hosts that are in maintenance are distinguished visually in the frontend, and in many views, we can also choose not to show such problems at all.

It's important to remember the main rules about permissions in Zabbix:

- Permissions can be assigned to user groups only
- Permissions can be granted on host groups only

This means that for fancy permission schemes, you might have to do some planning before starting to click around. We can also safely say that to avoid mysterious problems in the future, every host should be in at least one host group, and every user should be in at least one user group. Additionally, there were two factors that combined to determine effective permissions: the permissions set for groups and user type. We can try summarizing the interaction of these two factors:

Zabbix user type / Permissions	Zabbix User	Zabbix Admin	Zabbix Super Admin
Read-write	Read only	Full	Full
Read only	Read only	Read only	Full
Deny	None	None	Full

Looking at this table, we can see that the Zabbix Super Admin user type cannot be denied any permissions. On the other hand, Zabbix User cannot be given write permissions. Still, it is very important to remember that at this time, they would gain write privileges through the Zabbix API.

With this knowledge, you should be able to group hosts and manage host inventories and host maintenance, as well as creating and groups, and users, along with assigning fine-grained permissions.

In the next chapter, we'll look at a way to check whether item values indicate a problem or not. While we have items collecting data, items in Zabbix are not used to configure thresholds or any other information to detect bad values. Items don't care what the values are as long as the values are arriving. To define what a problem is, a separate configuration entity, called a trigger, is used. Trigger logic, written as an expression, can range from very simple thresholds to fairly complex logical expressions.

6
Detecting Problems with Triggers

We have gained quite comprehensive knowledge of what kind of information we can gather using items. However, so far, we only have a single thing we are actively monitoring—we only have a single trigger created (we did that in *Chapter 2, Getting Your First Notification*). Triggers can do way more. Let's recap what a trigger is.

A trigger defines when a condition is considered worthy of attention. It "fires" (that is, becomes active), when item data or lack of it matches a particular condition, such as too high system load or too low free disk space.

Let's explore both of these concepts in more detail now. In this chapter, we will:

- Get to know more about the trigger-and-item relationship
- Discover trigger dependencies
- Construct trigger expressions
- Learn about basic management capabilities on the Zabbix frontend with global scripts

Triggers

Triggers are things that fire. They look at item data and raise a flag when the data does not fit whatever condition has been defined. As we discussed before, simply gathering data is nice, but awfully inadequate. If you want any past historical data gathering, including notifications, there would have to be a person looking at all the data all the time, so we have to define thresholds at which we want the condition to be considered worth looking into. Triggers provide a way to define what those conditions are.

Earlier, we created a single trigger that was checking the system load on **A test host**. It checks whether the returned value is larger than a defined threshold. Now, let's check for some other possible problems with a server, for example, when a service is down. The SMTP service going down can be significant, so we will try to look for such a thing happening now. Navigate to **Configuration | Hosts**, click on any of the **Triggers** links and click on the **Create trigger** button. In the form that opens, we will fill in some values, as follows:

- **Name**: The contents of this field will be used to identify the trigger in most places, so it should be human readable. This time, enter SMTP service is down. Notice how we are describing what the problem actually is. As opposed to an item, which gathers statuses, a trigger has a specific condition to check; thus, the name reflects it. If we have a host that should never have a running SMTP service, we could create a trigger named SMTP service should not be running.

- **Expression**: This is probably the most important property of a trigger. What is being checked, and for what conditions, will be specified here. Trigger expressions can vary from very simple to complex ones. This time, we will create a simple one, and we will also use some help from the frontend for that. Click on the **Add** button next to the **Expression** field to open the expression building dialog. It has several fields to fill in as well, so let's look at what those are:

  - **Item**: Here, we can specify which item data should be checked. To do that, click on the **Select** button. Another popup will open. Select **Linux servers** from the **Group** dropdown, and then select **Another host** from the **Host** dropdown. We are interested in the SMTP service, so click on **SMTP server status** in the **NAME** column. The popup will close, and the **Item** field will be populated with the name of the chosen item.

  - **Function**: Here, we can choose the actual test to be performed. Perhaps we can try remembering what the SMTP server status item values were—right, 1 was for the server running, and 0 was for the server being down. If we want to check when the last value was 0, the default function **Last (most recent)** seems to fit quite nicely, so we won't change it.

  - **Last of (T)**: This is a function parameter if the function supports a time period. We used 180 in seconds for our first trigger to check the values during the previous 3 minutes, but when taking the last item value, a time period would make no sense.

  - **Time shift**: We will discuss this functionality later in this chapter, in the *Relative thresholds or time-shift* section.

- ◦ **N**: This field allows us to set the constant used in the previous function. We want to find out whenever an SMTP server goes down (or the status is 0), so here, the default of 0 fits as well.

Item	Another host: SMTP server status	Select
Function	Last (most recent) T value is = N	▾
Last of (T)		Time ▾
Time shift		Time
N	0	
	Insert Cancel	

With the values set as illustrated in the previous screenshot, click on the **Insert** button. The **Expression** field will now be populated with the {Another host:net.tcp.service[smtp].last()}=0 trigger expression.

- **Severity**: There are five severity levels in Zabbix, and an additional **Not classified** severity, as shown here:

Severity	Not classified	Information	Warning	Average	High	Disaster

We will consider this problem to be of average severity, so click on **Average**:

Trigger Dependencies	
Name	SMTP service is down
Expression	{Another host:net.tcp.service[smtp].last()}=0 Add
	Expression constructor
Multiple PROBLEM events generation	☐
Description	
UPL	
Severity	Not classified Information Warning Average High Disaster
Enabled	▣
	Add Cancel

Before continuing, make sure that the SMTP server is running on **Another host**, and then click on **Add**. Let's find out what it looks like in the overview now: go to **Monitoring | Overview**, and make sure the **Type** dropdown has **Triggers** selected. Then, expand the filter, choose **Any** in the **Triggers status** dropdown, and click on **Filter**:

TRIGGERS	ANOTHER HOST	A TEST HOST
CPU load too high on A test host for last 3 minutes		
SMTP service is down		

Great, we can see that both hosts now have a trigger defined. Since the triggers differ, we also have two unused cells:

```
{Another host : net.tcp.service[smtp] . last(        )}    =    0
```

| Host name | Item key with parameters | Trigger function with parameters (empty here) | Operator and comparison value |

Let's look at the `trigger` expression in more detail. It starts with an opening curly brace, and the first parameter is the hostname. Separated with a colon is the item key—`net.tcp.service[smtp]` here. The item key must be replicated exactly as in the item configuration, including any spaces, quotes, and capitalization. After the exact item key comes a dot as a separator, which is followed by the more interesting and trigger-specific thing: the trigger function. Used here is one of the most common functions, `last()`. It always returns a single value from the item history. There are trigger functions that require at least some parameter to be passed, but for the `last()` function, this is optional, and if the first parameter is just a number, it is ignored.

> Older versions of Zabbix required some parameter to be passed, even if it would have been ignored. It is still common to see syntax such as `last(0)` being used. Thus, `last(300)` is the same as `last(0)` and `last()` — they all return a single last value for one item.

On the other hand, if the first parameter is a number prefixed with a hash, it is not ignored. In that case, it works like an *n*th value specifier. For example, last(#9) would retrieve the 9th most recent value. As we can see, last(#1) is equal to last(0) or last(). Another overlapping function is prev. As the name might suggest, it returns the previous value; thus, prev() is the same as last(#2).

> Hostname, item key, trigger function, operators—they all are case sensitive.

Continuing with the trigger expression, curly braces are closed to represent a string that retrieves some value, that is, host and item reference, followed by the trigger function. Then we have an operator, which in this case is a simple equals sign. The comparison here is done with a constant number, 0.

> If item history is set to 0, no values are stored and no triggers are evaluated, even if those triggers would only check the last value. This is different from the previous versions of Zabbix, where triggers, referencing the last value only, would still work.

The trigger-and-item relationship

You might have noticed how items in Zabbix do not contain any configuration on the *quality* of the data—if the CPU load values arrive, the item does not care whether they are 0 or 500. Any definition of a problem condition happens in a trigger, whether it's a simple threshold or something more complex.

And when we created this trigger, we could click on any of the **Triggers** links, but we paid attention to the host selected in the dropdowns when choosing the item. It actually does not matter which of those **Triggers** links we click on, as long as the proper host is selected in that popup or we manually enter the correct hostname.

> A trigger does not belong to a host like an item does. A trigger is associated with any number of hosts it references items from.

If we clicked on **Triggers for host A** and then chose an item from host **B** for that trigger, the created trigger would not appear for host **A**, but would appear for host **B**.

This decoupling of problem conditions from the value collection has quite a lot of benefits. Not only is it easy to check for various different conditions on a single item, a single trigger may also span multiple items. For example, we could check CPU load on a system in comparison with the user session count. If the CPU load is high and there are a lot of users on the system, we could consider that to be a normal situation. But if the CPU load is high while there are a small number of users on the system, it is a problem. An example trigger could be this:

```
{host:system.cpu.load.last()}>5 and {host:user.sessions.last()}<100
```

This would trigger if CPU load is above 5, but only if there are fewer than 100 users on this system.

> Remember that we cannot just start referencing items in trigger expressions and expect that to work. Items must exist before they can be used in trigger expressions.

A trigger could also reference items from multiple hosts. We could correlate some database statistic with the performance of an application on a different host, or free disk space on file servers with the number of users in **Lightweight Directory Access Protocol (LDAP)**.

We will discuss and configure some slightly more advanced trigger expressions later in this chapter.

Trigger dependencies

We now have one service being watched. There are some more being monitored, and now we can try to create a trigger for an HTTP server. Let's assume that our host runs software that is a bit weird—the web service is a web e-mail frontend, and it goes down whenever the SMTP server is unavailable. This means the web service depends on the SMTP service.

Go to **Configuration | Hosts**, click on **Triggers** next to **Another host**, and then click on **Create trigger**. Fill in the following values:

- **Name:** Web service is down.
- **Expression:** Click on **Add**, and then again on **Select** next to the **Item** field. Make sure **Linux servers** is selected in the **Group** dropdown and **Another host** in the **Host** dropdown, and then click on **Web server status** in the **NAME** column. Both the function and its parameter are fine, so click on **Insert**:

Item	Another host: Web server status		Select
Function	Last (most recent) T value is = N		
Last of (T)		Time ▼	
Time shift		Time	
N	0		
	Insert	Cancel	

This inserts the `{Another Host:net.tcp.service[http,,80].last()}=0` expression:

- **Severity**: **Average**
- **Description**: Trigger expressions can get very complex. Sometimes, the complexity can make it impossible to understand what a trigger is supposed to do without serious dissection. Comments provide a way to help somebody else, or yourself, understand the thinking behind such complex expressions later. While our trigger is still very simple, we might want to explain the reason for the dependency, so enter something such as `Web service goes down if SMTP is inaccessible`.

Now, switch to the **Dependencies** tab. To configure the dependency of the web frontend on the SMTP service, click on the **Add** link in the **Dependencies** section. In the resulting window, make sure **Linux servers** is selected in the **Group** dropdown and **Another host** is selected in the **Host** dropdown, and then click on the only entry in the **NAME** column: **SMTP service is down**.

Trigger	Dependencies		
Dependencies	NAME		ACTION
	Another host: SMTP service is down		Remove
	Add		
	Add	Cancel	

When done, click on the **Add** button at the bottom. Notice how, in the trigger list, trigger dependencies are listed in the **NAME** column. This allows a quick overview of any dependent triggers without opening the details of each trigger individually:

SEVERITY	NAME ▲	EXPRESSION
Average	SMTP service is down	{Another host:net.tcp.service[smtp].**last()**}=0
Average	Web service is down **Depends on:** Another host: SMTP service is down	{Another host:net.tcp.service[http,,80].**last()**}=0

Both triggers in the dependency list and items in the **EXPRESSION** column act as links, allowing easy access to their details.

> Item name colors in the **EXPRESSION** column match their state: green for **OK**, red for **Disabled**, and grey for **Unsupported**.

With the dependency set up, let's find out whether it changes anything in the frontend. Navigate to **Monitoring | Overview**, make sure **Type** is set to **Triggers**, expand the filter, then switch **Triggers status** to **Any**, and click on **Filter**:

TRIGGERS	ANOTHER HOST	A TEST HOST
CPU load too high on A test host for last 3 minutes		
SMTP service is down	↑	
Web service is down	↓	

The difference is visible immediately. Triggers involved in the dependency have arrows drawn over them. So, an upward arrow means something depends on this trigger — or was it the other way around? Luckily, you don't have to memorize that. Move the mouse cursor over the **SMTP service is down** trigger for **Another host**, the upper cell with the arrow:

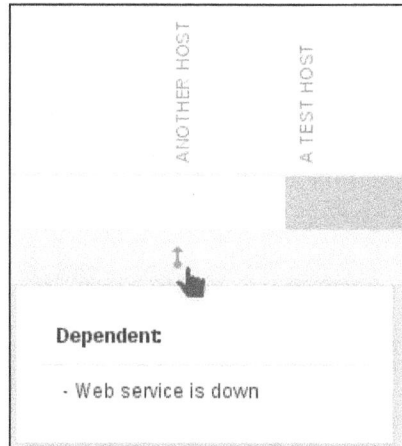

A popup appears, informing us that there are other triggers dependent on this one. Dependent triggers are listed in the popup. Now, move the mouse cursor one cell below, over the downward-pointing arrow:

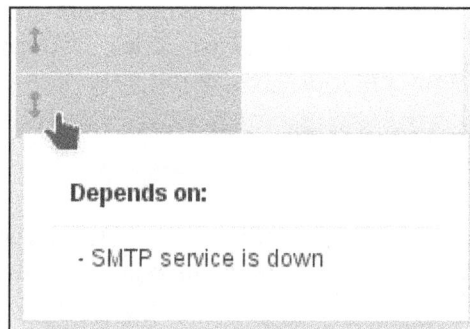

Let's see what effect, other than the arrows, this provides. Go to **Monitoring | Triggers**, and make sure both **Host** and **Group** dropdowns say **all**. Then, bring down the web server on **Another host**. Wait for the trigger to fire, and look at the entry. Notice how an arrow indicating dependency is displayed here as well. Move the mouse cursor over it again, and the dependency details will be displayed in a popup:

SEVERITY	STATUS	INFO	LAST CHANGE ▼	AGE	ACK	HOST	NAME	DESCRIPTION
Average			2016-04-05 15:49:01	3s	No 1	Another host	↕ Web service is down	Show

But what's up with the **Show** link in the **DESCRIPTION** column? Let's find out; click on it. The description we provided when creating the trigger is displayed. This allows easy access to descriptions from the trigger list, both for finding out more information about the trigger and updating the description. Click on cancel (×) to return to the trigger list. Now, stop the SMTP service on **Another host**. Wait for the trigger list to update, and look at it again. The web server trigger has disappeared from the list and is replaced by the SMTP server one. That's because Zabbix does not show dependent triggers if the dependency upstream trigger is in the **PROBLEM** state. This helps keep the list short and concentrate on the problems that actually cause the downtime.

SEVERITY	STATUS	INFO	LAST CHANGE ▼	AGE	ACK	HOST	NAME		DESCRIPTION
Average	PROBLEM		2016-04-05 15:51:00	3s	No 8	Another host	↕ SMTP service is down		Add
							Dependent: - Web service is down		×

Trigger dependencies are not limited to a single level. We will now add another trigger to the mix. Before we do that, we'll also create an item that will provide an easy way to manually change the trigger state without affecting system services. In the frontend, navigate to **Configuration | Hosts**, click on **Items** next to **Another host**, and then click on **Create item**. Fill in the following values:

- **Name**: `Testfile exists`
- **Key**: `vfs.file.exists[/tmp/testfile]`

When you are done, click on the **Add** button at the bottom. As the key might reveal, this item simply checks whether a particular file exists and returns `1` if it does, and `0` if it does not.

> Using a constant filename in /tmp in real-life situations might not be desirable, as any user could create such a file.

In the bar above the **Item** list, click on **Triggers**, and then click on the **Create trigger** button. Enter these values:

- **Name**: `Testfile is missing.`
- **Expression**: Click on **Add** and then on **Select** next to the **Item** field. In the item list for **Another host**, click on **Testfile exists** in the **NAME** column, and then click on **Insert** (again, the default function works for us). The **Expression** field is filled with the following expression:

  `{Another Host:vfs.file.exists[/tmp/testfile].last()}=0`

- **Severity**: **Warning**.

When you are done, click on the **Add** button at the bottom. Let's complicate the trigger chain a bit now. Click on the **SMTP service is down** trigger in the **NAME** column, switch to the **Dependencies** tab, and click on **Add** in the **Dependencies** section. In the upcoming dialog, click on the **Testfile is missing** entry in the **NAME** column. This creates a new dependency for the **SMTP service** trigger:

Dependencies	NAME	ACTION
	Another host: Testfile is missing	Remove
	Add	

Click on **Update**. Now, we have created a dependency chain, consisting of three triggers: **Web service is down** depends on **SMTP service is down**, which in turn depends on "**Testfile is missing**". Zabbix calculates chained dependencies, so all upstream dependencies are also taken into account when determining the state of a particular trigger — in this case, "**Web service is down**" depends on those two other triggers. This means that only a single trigger will be displayed in the **Monitoring | Triggers** section. If we place the *most important* trigger at the bottom and the ones depending on it above, we would get a dependency chain like this:

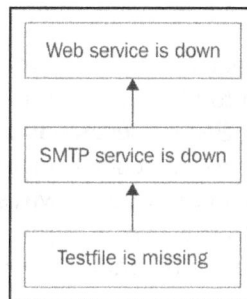

Now, we should get to fixing the problems the monitoring system has identified. Let's start with the one at the top of the dependency chain — the missing file problem. On "Another host", execute this:

```
$ touch /tmp/testfile
```

This should deal with the only trigger currently on the trigger list. Wait for the trigger list to update. You will see two triggers, with their statuses flashing. Remember that, by default, Zabbix shows triggers that have recently changed state as flashing, and that also includes triggers in the "**OK**" state:

SEVERITY	STATUS	INFO	LAST CHANGE ▼	AGE	ACK	HOST	NAME	DESCRIPTION
Warning	OK		2016-04-05 16:12:25	1m 4s	No 1	Another host	↕ Testfile is missing	Add
Average	PROBLEM		2016-04-05 15:51:00	22m 29s	No 8	Another host	↕ ↕ SMTP service is down	Add

Looking at the list, we can see one large difference this time: the SMTP trigger now has two arrows, one pointing up and the other pointing down. Moving your mouse cursor over them, you will discover that they denote the same thing as before: the triggers that this particular trigger depends on or that depend on this trigger. If a trigger is in the middle of a dependency chain, two arrows will appear, as has happened for the **SMTP service is down** trigger here.

The arrows here are shown in the same direction as in our previous schematic. We could say that the dependent trigger is "supported" by the "more important" trigger, as if we had bricks placed one on top of another. If any of the bricks disappears, the bricks above it will be in trouble.

Our testfile trigger worked as expected for the chained dependencies, so we can remove that dependency now. Go to **Configuration | Hosts**, click on **Triggers** next to `Another host`, and click on the **SMTP service is down** trigger in the **NAME** column. Switch to the **Dependencies** tab, click on **Remove** in the **ACTION** column, and click on the **Update** button. Note that you always have to save your changes in the editing form of any entity. In this case, simply removing the dependency won't be enough. If we navigate to some other section without explicitly updating the trigger, any modifications will be lost. Now, you can also restart any stopped services on "`Another host`".

Constructing trigger expressions

So far, we have used only very simple trigger expressions, comparing the last value to some constant. Fortunately, that's not all that trigger expressions can do. We will now try to create a slightly more complex trigger.

Let's say we have two servers, **A test host** and **Another host**, providing a redundant **SSH File Transfer Protocol (SFTP)** service. We would be interested in any one of the services going down. Navigate to **Configuration | Hosts,** and click on **Triggers** next to either **A test host** or **Another host**. Then, click on the **Create trigger** button. Enter these values:

- **Name:** One SSH service is down.

- **Expression:** Click on the **Add** button. In the resulting popup, click on **Select** next to the **Item** field. Make sure **Another host** is selected in the **Host** dropdown, click on the **SSH server status** item in the **NAME** column, and then click on **Insert**. Now, position the cursor at the end of the inserted expression and enter " or " without quotes (that's a space, or, and a space). Again, click on the **Add** button. In the resulting popup, click on **Select** next to the **Item** field. Select **A test host** from the **Host** dropdown, click on the **SSH server status** item in the **NAME** column, and click on **Insert**.

- **Severity: Average** (remember, these are redundant services).

The final trigger expression should look like this:

```
{Another host:net.tcp.service[ssh].last()}=0 or {A test host:net.tcp.
service[ssh].last()}=0
```

When you are done, click on the **Add** button at the bottom.

> In Zabbix versions preceding 2.4, a pipe character, |, was used instead of a lowercase " or ".

The process we followed here allowed us to create a more complex expression than simply comparing the value of a single item. Instead, two values are compared, and the trigger fires if either of them matches the comparison. That's what the or operator does. Another logical operator is and. Using the SSH server as an example trigger, we could create another trigger that would fire whenever both SSH instances go down. Getting the expression is simple, as we just have to modify that single operator, that is, change or to and, so that the expression looks like this:

```
{Another host:net.tcp.service[ssh].last()}=0 and {A test host:net.tcp.
service[ssh].last()}=0
```

> Trigger expression operators are case sensitive, so AND would not be a valid operator—a lowercase and should be used.

Trigger expressions also support other operators. In all the triggers we created, we used the most common one: the equality operator, =. We could also be using the inequality operator, <>. That would allow us to reverse the expression, like this:

```
{A test host:net.tcp.service[ssh].last()}<>1
```

> Zabbix versions preceding 2.4 used the hash mark # instead of <> for the "not equal" comparison.

While not useful in this case, such a trigger is helpful when the item can have many values and we want the trigger to fire whenever the value isn't the expected one.

Trigger expressions also support the standard mathematical operators +, -, *, and /, and comparison operators <, >, <=, and >=, so complex calculations and comparisons can be used between item data and constants.

Let's create another trigger using a different function. In the frontend section **Configuration | Hosts**, choose **Linux servers** from the **Group** dropdown, click on **Triggers** next to **A test host**, and click on the **Create trigger** button. Then, enter these values:

- **Name**: Critical error from SNMP trap
- **Expression**: {A test host:snmptrap.fallback.str(Critical Error)}=1
- **Severity**: **High**

When you are done, click on the **Add** button at the bottom.

This time, we used another trigger function, str(). It searches for the specified string in the item data and returns 1 if it's found. The match is case sensitive.

This trigger will change to the **OK** state whenever the last value for the item does not contain the string specified as the parameter. If we want to force this trigger to the **OK** state manually, we can just send a trap that does not contain the string the trigger is looking for. Sending a success value manually can also be useful when some other system is sending SNMP traps. In a case where the problem trap is received successfully but the resolving trap is lost (because of network connectivity issues, or for any other reason), you might want to use such a fake trap to make the trigger in question go back to the **OK** state. If using the built-in trap-processing functionality, it would be enough to add trap information to the temporary file. If using the scripted solution with Zabbix trapper items, zabbix_sender could be used. SNMP trap management was discussed in *Chapter 4, Monitoring SNMP Devices*.

Preventing trigger flapping

With the service items and triggers we wrote, the triggers would fire right away as soon as the service is detected to be down. This can be undesirable if we know that some service will be down for a moment during an upgrade because of log rotation or backup requirements. We can use a different function to achieve a delayed reaction in such cases. Replacing the function `last()` with `max()` allows us to specify a parameter and thus react only when the item values have indicated a problem for some time. For the trigger to fire only when a service has not responded for 5 minutes, we could use an expression such as this:

```
{A test host:net.tcp.service[ssh].max(300)}=0
```

> For this example to work properly, the item interval must not exceed 5 minutes. If the item interval exceeds the trigger function's checking time, only a single value will be checked, making the use of a trigger function such as `max()` useless.

Remember that for functions that accept seconds as a parameter, we can also use the count of returned values by prefixing the number with #, like this:

```
{A test host:net.tcp.service[ssh].max(#5)}=0
```

In this case, the trigger would always check the five last-returned values. Such an approach allows the trigger period to scale along in case the item interval is changed, but it should not be used for items that can stop sending in data.

Using trigger functions is the easiest and most-applied solution to potential trigger flapping. The previous service example checked that the maximum value over the last 5 minutes was 0; thus, we were sure that there are no values of 1, which would mean "service is up".

For our CPU load trigger, we used the `avg(180)` function, checking the average value for the last 3 minutes. We could also have used `min(180)` — in this case, a single drop below the threshold would reset the 3-minute timer even if the overall average were above the threshold. Which one to use? That is entirely up to you, depending on what the functional requirements are. One way is not always better than the others.

Checking for missing data

Some items are always expected to provide values, such as the CPU load item. The problem condition for this item usually is "value too large". But there are some items that are different, for example, an item with the agent.ping key. This item only tells us whether the agent is available to the server, and it only returns 1 when the agent is up. And yes, that's it—it does not send 0 when the agent is down; there is no value at all. We can't write a trigger with the last() function, as the last value is always 1. The same goes for min(), max(), and avg(). Luckily, there is a function we can use in this case: nodata(). It allows the trigger to fire if an item is missing data for some period of time. For example, if we created an agent.ping item on "A test host", the trigger could look like this:

```
{A test host:agent.ping.nodata(300)=1}
```

Here, the nodata() function is checking whether this item is missing data for 300 seconds, or 5 minutes. If so, the trigger will fire. What's the comparison with 1? All trigger functions in Zabbix return some number. The nodata() function returns 1 if the item is missing data and 0 if there's at least one value in the specified time period. Note that it might not be a good idea to try and guess what return values are available for some trigger function—if you are not sure, better check the manual for details at https://www.zabbix.com/documentation/3.0/manual/appendix/triggers/functions.

The nodata() function is said to be time based. "Normal" trigger functions are evaluated when an item receives a new value. This makes a lot of sense for triggers against items such as the CPU load item we created earlier—when a value arrives, we compare it to the threshold. It wouldn't work that well with our agent.ping item, though. If values were coming in, everything would be good—the trigger expression would be evaluated, and this function would return 0. If values stopped coming in, it would not get evaluated and would never fire. Then, if a new value arrived, the function would get evaluated and would see that new value and declare that everything was perfect.

So in this case, the trigger is not evaluated only when a new value comes in. Instead, this function is evaluatede very 30 seconds. This interval is hardcoded. To be more specific, any trigger that includes at least one time-based function in the expression is recalculated every 30 seconds. With the 30-second interval, one should never use a parameter lower than 30 for the nodata() function. To be safe, never use a parameter lower than 60 seconds. In Zabbix version 3.0.0, the following trigger functions are time-based:

- date()
- dayofmonth()

- `dayofweek()`
- `nodata()`
- `now()`
- `time()`

Refer to the Zabbix manual if using a later version—there might be changes to this list.

Triggers that time out

There are systems that send a trap upon failure, but no recovery trap. In such a case, manually resetting every single case isn't an option. Fortunately, we can construct a trigger expression that times out by using the function we just discussed: `nodata()`. An expression that would make the **PROBLEM** state time out after 10 minutes looks like this:

```
{Another host:snmptrap.fallback.str(Critical Error)}=1 and
{Another host:snmptrap.fallback.nodata(600)}=0
```

For now, we want to have more precise control over how this trigger fires, so we won't change the trigger expression to the previous example's.

Note that adding the `nodata()` function to a trigger will make that trigger reevaluate every 30 seconds. Doing this with a large amount of triggers can have a significant impact on the performance of the Zabbix server.

Triggers with adaptable thresholds

There are monitored metrics that have rather different threshold needs depending on the possible range of the value, even when measuring in percentage instead of absolute values. For example, using bytes for a disk-space trigger will not work that well when disks might range from a few dozen megabytes to hundreds of terabytes or even petabytes. Applying our knowledge of trigger expressions, we could vary our threshold depending on the total disk size. For this, we will have to monitor both free and total disk space:

```
(
    {host:vfs.fs.size[/,total].last()}<=100GB
        and
    {host:vfs.fs.size[/,pfree].last()}<10
) or (
    {host:vfs.fs.size[/,total].last()}>100GB
        and
    {host:vfs.fs.size[/,pfree].last()}<5
)
```

A trigger that requires item values like this with the last function will only work when all involved items have collected at least one value. In this case, two items are referenced, each twice.

The previous expression has been split for readability. In Zabbix versions before 2.4, it would have to be entered on a single line, but since Zabbix 2.4, newlines and tab characters are supported in trigger expressions.

This expression will make the trigger act differently in two cases of disk configuration:

- Total disk space being less than or equal to 100 GB
- Total disk space being more than 100 GB

Depending on the amount of total disk space, a different threshold is applied to the free disk space in percentage—10% for smaller disks and 5% for larger disks.

One might easily expand this to have different thresholds for disks between 100 MB, 10 GB, 100 GB, 10 TB, and higher.

Triggers with a limited period

We discussed hosts and host group maintenance in *Chapter 5*, *Managing Hosts, Users, and Permissions*. That allowed us to stop alerting, but when doing so, the smallest entity the maintenance could affect was a host; we could not create a maintenance for a specific trigger. While this is slightly different functionally, we could limit the time for which a trigger is active on the trigger level, too. To do so, we can use several of those time-based trigger functions. Taking our CPU load trigger as an example, we could completely ignore it on Mondays (perhaps there's some heavy reporting done on Mondays?):

```
{A test host:system.cpu.load.avg(180)}>1 and
{A test host:system.cpu.load.dayofweek()}<>1
```

The dayofweek() function returns a number with Monday starting at 1, and the previous expression works unless the returned value is 1. We have to append a trigger function to some item even if it does not take item values at all, such as in this case. It is quite counterintuitive seeing the dayofweek() function after the CPU load item, but it's best practice to reuse the same item.

We could also make this trigger ignore weekend mornings instead:

```
{A test host:system.cpu.load.avg(180)}>1 and
{A test host:system.cpu.load.dayofweek()}>5 and
{A test host:system.cpu.load.time()}<100000
```

Here, we are checking for the day value to be above 5 (with 6 and 7 being Saturday and Sunday). Additionally, the trigger `time()` function is being used. This function returns the time in the HH:MM:SS format, so our comparison makes sure it is not 10:00:00 yet.

Note that this method completely prevents the trigger from firing, so we won't get alerts, won't see the trigger on the frontend, and there won't be any events generated.

We will also discuss a way to limit alerts themselves based on time in *Chapter 7, Acting upon Monitored Conditions*.

Relative thresholds or time shift

Normally, trigger functions look at the latest values — `last()` gets the last value and `min()`, `max()`, and `avg()` look at the specified time period, counting back from the current moment. For some functions, we may also specify an additional parameter called **time shift**. This will make the function act as if we had traveled back in time; in other aspects, it will work exactly the same. One feature this allows is creating a trigger with relative thresholds. Instead of a fixed value such as 1, 5, or 10 for a CPU load trigger, we can make it fire if the load has increased compared to a period some time ago:

```
{A test host:system.cpu.load.avg(3600)} /
{A test host:system.cpu.load.avg(3600,86400)}
>3
```

In this example, we have modified the time period that we are evaluating — it has been increased to one hour. We have stopped comparing the result with a fixed threshold; instead, we are looking at the average values from some time ago — specifically, 86400 seconds, or one day, ago. Functionally, this expression checks whether the average CPU load for the last hour exceeds the average CPU load for the same hour one day ago more than 3 times.

This way, the CPU load can be 1, 5, or 500 — this trigger does not care about the absolute value, just whether it has increased more than thrice.

The second parameter for the avg() function we used was the time shift. To understand how it gets the values, let's assume that we have added a new item and the time shift is set to 1 hour. It is 13:00:00 now, and a new value for the item has come in. We had previous values for 1 hour at 12:10:00, 12:20:00, and so on up to 12:50:00. The time shift of one hour would get no values at all, as it would first step 1 hour back to 12:00:00 and then look for all the values 1 hour ago—but the first value we had was at 12:10:00:

As of Zabbix version 3.0.0, the following functions support the time shift parameter:

* avg()
* band()
* count()
* delta()
* last()
* max()
* min()
* percentile()
* sum()

> Triggers always operate on history data, never on trend data. If history is kept for one day, a time shift of one day should not be used, as it is likely to miss some values in the evaluation.

Verifying system time

Zabbix can verify a huge number of things, among which is the current time on monitored systems. Let's create a quick configuration to do just that. We will create an item to collect the current time and then a trigger to compare that time with the current time on the Zabbix server. Of course, for this to work properly, the clock on the Zabbix server must be correct—otherwise, we would complain that it is wrong on all the other systems.

The first thing is the item to collect: the current time. Go to **Configuration | Hosts**, click on **Items** next to **Another host**, and then click on **Create item**. Fill in the following values:

- **Name**: Local time
- **Key**: system.localtime
- **Units**: unixtime

When you are done, click on the **Add** button at the bottom. This item returns the current time as a Unix timestamp. While a unit is not required for our trigger, we entered unixtime there. This will translate the timestamp to a human-readable value in the frontend. We discussed item units in more detail in *Chapter 3, Monitoring with Zabbix Agents and Basic Protocols*.

In the bar above the item list, click on **Triggers**, then click on the **Create trigger** button. Enter these values:

- **Name**: Incorrect clock on {HOST.NAME}.

- **Expression**: Click on **Add** and then on **Select** next to the **Item** field. In the item list for **Another host**, click on **Local time** in the **NAME** column and click on **Insert**. The **Expression** field is filled with this expression: {Another host:system.localtime.last()}=0. This isn't actually what we need, but we tried to avoid the function dropdown here, so we will edit the expression manually. Change it to read this: {Another host:system.localtime. fuzzytime(30)}=0.

- **Severity**: Select Warning.

When you're done, click on the **Add** button at the bottom. The fuzzytime() function accepts a time period as a parameter. This makes it compare the timestamp of the item with the current time on the Zabbix server. If the difference is bigger than the time specified in the parameter, it returns 0, which is the problem condition we wanted to catch. Again, if you are not sure about the return value of some trigger function, better check the Zabbix manual.

> Don't forget that an incorrect time on the Zabbix server can result in a huge number of alerts about all other systems.

Human-readable constants

Using plain numeric constants is fine while we're dealing with small values. When an item collects data that is larger, such as disk space or network traffic, such an approach becomes very tedious. You have to calculate the desired value, and from looking at it later, it is usually not obvious how large it really is. To help here, Zabbix supports so-called **suffix multipliers** in expressions—the abbreviations **K, M, G, T,** and so on are supported. This results in shorter and way more easy-to-read trigger expressions. For example, checking disk space for a host called **host** looks like this at first:

```
{host:vfs.fs.size[/,free].last()}<16106127360
```

With suffix multipliers, it becomes this:

```
{host:vfs.fs.size[/,free].last()}<15G
```

This is surely easier to read and modify if such a need arises.

Another type of constant is time based. So far, we've only used time in seconds for all the trigger functions, but that tends to be a bit unreadable. For example, 6 hours would be 21600, and it just gets worse with longer periods. The following time-based suffixes are supported:

- s: seconds
- m: minutes
- h: hours
- d: days
- w: weeks

The s suffix would simply be discarded, but all others would work as multipliers. Thus, 21600 would become 6h, which is much more readable. The SSH service trigger example we looked at earlier would also be simpler:

```
{A test host:net.tcp.service[ssh].max(5m)}=0
```

We have now covered the basics of triggers in Zabbix. There are many more functions allowing the evaluation of various conditions that you will want to use later on. The frontend function selector does not contain all of them, so sometimes you will have to look them up and construct the expression manually. For a full and up-to-date function list, refer to the official documentation at https://www.zabbix.com/documentation/3.0/manual/appendix/triggers/functions.

Customizing trigger display

With all the details explored regarding trigger configuration, we should be able to create powerful definitions on what to consider a problem. There are also several configuration options available to customize the way triggers are displayed.

Trigger severities

Navigate to **Administration | General** and choose **Trigger severities** in the dropdown in the upper-right corner:

Trigger severities		
Not classified	Not classified	97AAB3
Information	Information	7499FF
Warning	Warning	FFC859
Average	Average	FFA059
High	High	E97659
Disaster	Disaster	E45959
Info	Custom severity names affect all locales and require manual translation!	
	Update Reset defaults	

In this section, we may customize severity labels and their colors. As the **Info** box at the bottom of this page says, changing severity labels will require updating translations that anybody might be using in this Zabbix instance.

Trigger display options

Navigate to **Administration | General** and choose **Trigger displaying options** in the dropdown in the upper-right corner:

Trigger displaying options			
Unacknowledged PROBLEM events	▨	DC0000	▨ blinking
Acknowledged PROBLEM events	▨	DC0000	▨ blinking
Unacknowledged OK events	▨	00AA00	▨ blinking
Acknowledged OK events	▨	00AA00	▨ blinking
Display OK triggers for	1800	seconds	
On status change triggers blink for	1800	seconds	
	Update	Reset defaults	

It's not just trigger severity labels that we can modify; we can even change the default red and green colors, used for the **PROBLEM/OK** states. Even better, the color can be different, depending on whether the problem has been acknowledged or not. We discussed trigger state blinking in **Monitoring | Triggers** and other frontend sections for 30 minutes. On this page, we can selectively enable or disable blinking based on the trigger state and acknowledgement status, as well as customize the length of time for which a trigger change is considered recent enough to blink—the default can be seen here defined in seconds: 1800.

Event details

After we have configured triggers, they generate events, which in turn are acted upon by actions.

> We looked at a high-level schema of information flow inside Zabbix, including item, trigger, and event relationships in *Chapter 2, Getting Your First Notification*.

But can we see more details about them somewhere? In the frontend, go to
Monitoring | Events, and click on date and time in the **TIME** column for the latest
entry with **PROBLEM** status.

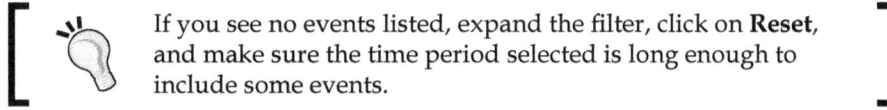

> If you see no events listed, expand the filter, click on **Reset**,
> and make sure the time period selected is long enough to
> include some events.

This opens up the **Event details** page, which allows us to determine the event flow
with more confidence. It includes things such as event and trigger details and action
history. The **Event list** in the lower-right corner, which includes the **previous 20**
events, itself acts as a control, allowing you to click on any of these events and see the
previous 20 events from the chosen event backward in time. As this list only shows
events for a single trigger, it is very handy if one needs to figure out the timeline of
one, isolated problem:

Event details

Event source details

Host	Another host
Trigger	Incorrect clock on Another host
Severity	Warning
Expression	{Another host:system.localtime.**fuzzytime(30)**}=0
Event generation	Normal
Disabled	No

Event details

Event	Incorrect clock on Another host
Time	2016-04-08 00:26:56
Acknowledged	No

Acknowledges

TIME	USER	MESSAGE
	No data found.	

Message actions

STEP	TIME	TYPE	STATUS	RETRIES LEFT	RECIPIENT(S)	MESSAGE	INFO
1	2016-04-08 00:26:57	Email	Sent		Admin (Zabbix Administrator) user@company.tld	PROBLEM: Incorrect clock on Another host Trigger: Incorrect clock on Another host Trigger status: PROBLEM Trigger severity: Warning Trigger URL: Item values: 1. Local time (Another host:system.localtime): 2016.04.07 13:29:23 2. "UNKNOWN" ("UNKNOWN":"UNKNOWN"): "UNKNOWN" 3. "UNKNOWN" ("UNKNOWN":"UNKNOWN"): "UNKNOWN" Original event ID: 335	

Command actions

STEP	TIME	STATUS	COMMAND	ERROR
		No data found.		

Event list [previous 20]

TIME	STATUS	DURATION	AGE	ACK	ACTIONS
2016-04-08 00:26:56	PROBLEM	32m 9s	32m 9s	No	1

Event generation and hysteresis

Trigger events are generated whenever a trigger changes state. A trigger can be in one of the following states:

- **OK**: The normal state, when the trigger expression evaluates to `false`
- **PROBLEM**: A problem state, when the trigger expression evaluates to `true`
- **UNKNOWN**: A state when Zabbix cannot evaluate the trigger expression, usually when there is missing data

> Refer to *Chapter 22, Zabbix Maintenance*, for information on how to notify about triggers becoming **UNKNOWN**.

No matter whether the trigger goes from **OK** to **PROBLEM**, **UNKNOWN**, or any other state, an event is generated.

> There is also a way to customize this with the **Multiple PROBLEM events generation** option in the trigger properties. We will discuss this option in *Chapter 11, Advanced Item Monitoring*.

We found out before that we can use certain trigger functions to avoid changing the trigger state after every change in data. By accepting a time period as a parameter, these functions allow us to react only if a problem has been going on for a while. But what if we would like to be notified as soon as possible, while still avoiding trigger flapping if values fluctuate near our threshold? Here, a specific Zabbix macro (or variable) helps and allows us to construct trigger expressions that have some sort of hysteresis—the remembering of state.

A common case is measuring temperatures. For example, a very simple trigger expression would read like this:

```
server:temp.last()>20
```

It would fire when the temperature was `21` and go to the **OK** state when it's `20`. Sometimes, temperature fluctuates around the set threshold value, so the trigger goes on and off all the time. This is undesirable, so an improved expression would look like this:

```
({TRIGGER.VALUE}=0 and {server:temp.last()}>20) or
({TRIGGER.VALUE}=1 and {server:temp.last()}>15)
```

A new macro, TRIGGER.VALUE, is used. If the trigger is in the **OK** state, this macro returns 0; if the trigger is in the **PROBLEM** state, it returns 1. Using the logical operator or, we are stating that this trigger should change to (or remain at) the **PROBLEM** state if the trigger is currently in the **OK** state and the temperature exceeds 20 or when the trigger is currently in the **PROBLEM** state and the temperature exceeds 15.

One may also think of this as the trigger having two thresholds—we expect it to switch to the **PROBLEM** state when the values pass the upper threshold at 20 degrees but resolve only when they fall below the lower threshold at 15 degrees:

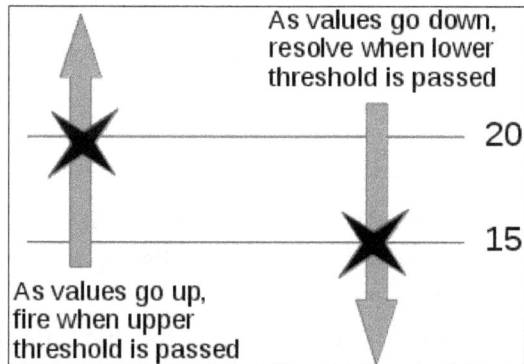

How does that change the situation when compared to the simple expression that only checked for temperatures over 20 degrees? Let's have a look:

In this example case, we have avoided two unnecessary **PROBLEM** states, and that usually means at least two notifications as well. This is another way of preventing trigger flapping.

Summary

This chapter was packed with concepts concerning reacting to events that happen in your monitored environment. We learned to describe conditions that should be reacted to as trigger expressions. Triggers themselves have useful functionality with dependencies, and we can make them depend on each other. We also explored several ways of reducing trigger flapping right in the trigger expression, including using functions such as min(), max(), and avg(), as well as trigger hysteresis.

Among other trigger tricks, we looked at:

- Using the nodata() function to detect missing data
- Using the same nodata() function to make a trigger time out
- Creating triggers that have different used disk space threshold values based on the total disk space
- Creating triggers that only work during a specific time period
- Having a relative threshold, where recent data is compared with the situation some time ago

> Remember that if item history is set to 0, no triggers will work, even the ones that only check the very last value.

Trigger configuration has a lot of things that can both make life easier and introduce hard-to-spot problems. Hopefully, the coverage of the basics here will help you to leverage the former and avoid the latter.

With the trigger knowledge available to us, we will take the time in the next chapter to see where we can go after a trigger has fired. We will explore actions that will allow us to send emails or even run commands in response to a trigger firing.

7
Acting upon Monitored Conditions

Now that we know more about triggers, let's see what we can do when they fire. Just seeing some problem on the frontend is not enough; we probably want to send notifications using e-mail or SMS, or maybe even attempt to remedy the problem automatically.

Actions make sure something is done about a trigger firing. Let's try to send notifications and automatically execute commands.

In this chapter, we will:

- Learn how to limit conditions when alerts are sent
- Send notifications
- Escalate once a threshold is reached
- Use scripts as media
- Integrate with issue manager
- Understand global scripts

Actions

The trigger list would be fine to look at, way better than looking at individual items, but that would still be an awful lot of manual work. That's where actions come in, providing notifications and other methods to react upon condition change.

The most common method is e-mail. If you had an action set up properly when we first configured a fully working chain of item-trigger-action in *Chapter 2, Getting Your First Notification*, you received an e-mail whenever we started or stopped a service, created the test file, and so on. Let's look at what actions can do in more detail.

Limiting conditions when alerts are sent

Our previous action, created in *Chapter 2, Getting Your First Notification*, matched any event, as we had not limited its scope in any way. Now we could try matching only a specific condition. Navigate to **Configuration | Actions**, then click on **Create action**.

> The following activities rely on a correctly configured e-mail setup (done in *Chapter 2, Getting Your First Notification*), and a user group Our users (added in *Chapter 5, Managing Hosts, Users, and Permissions*).

In the **Name** field, enter SNMP action. Now switch to the **Conditions** tab. By default, there are two conditions already added—why so?

Action	Conditions	Operations		
Type of calculation	And/Or ▼	A and B		
Conditions	LABEL	NAME		ACTION
	A	Maintenance status not in *maintenance*		Remove
	B	Trigger value = *PROBLEM*		Remove
New condition	Trigger name ▼	like ▼		
	Add			
	[Add] [Cancel]			

The conditions here are added because they are likely to be useful for a new action for most users:

- **Maintenance status not in maintenance**: This condition ensures that during active maintenance, no operations will be performed. It can be safely removed to ignore maintenance. For example, technical experts might want to receive notifications even during active maintenance, but helpdesk members may not.

- **Trigger value = PROBLEM**: This condition ensures that the action will only do something when the problem happens. The trigger value would also have been **OK** when the trigger resolves, but this condition will make the action ignore the recovery events. While it might seem tempting to remove this condition to get notifications when problems are resolved, it is not suggested. We will discuss a better recovery message option later in this chapter.

Would somebody want to remove the trigger value condition? Yes, there could be a case when a script should be run both when a problem happens and when it is resolved. We could remove this condition, but in that case escalations should not be used. Otherwise, both problem and recovery events would get escalated, and it would be very, very confusing:

Conditions	LABEL	NAME	ACTION
	A	Maintenance status not in *maintenance*	Remove
	B	Trigger value = *PROBLEM*	Remove
	C	Host group = *Important SNMP hosts*	Remove

For our action right now, let's leave the default conditions in place and move to operations. Operations are the actual activities that are performed. Switch to the **Operations** tab and click on the **New** link in the **Action operations** block. To start with, we will configure a very simple action—sending an e-mail to a single **USER GROUP**. This form can be fairly confusing. Click on **Add** in the **Send to User groups** section, and in the upcoming window click on **Our users**. The result should look like this:

	USER GROUP	ACTION
	Our users	Remove
	Add	
Send to User groups		

> Early Zabbix 3.0 versions had a label misalignment in this form—make sure to use the correct section.

Now click on the main **Add** link in the **Operation details** block (just below the **Conditions** section). Finally, click on the **Add** button at the bottom. As we want to properly test how e-mails are sent, we should now disable our previously added action. Mark the checkbox next to the **Test** action, click on the **Disable** button at the bottom, then confirm disabling in the popup.

Now we need triggers on our **SNMP trap** items. Navigate to **Configuration | Hosts**, click on **Triggers** next to **snmptraps**, and click on **Create trigger**. Enter the following:

- **Name:** SNMP trap has arrived on {HOST.NAME}
- **Expression:** {snmptraps:snmptraps.nodata(30)}=0
- **Severity: Information**

Such a trigger will fire whenever a trap arrives, and clear itself approximately 30 seconds later. We discussed the nodata() trigger function in *Chapter 6, Detecting Problems with Triggers*. When done, click on the **Add** button at the bottom.

We will also want to have a trigger fire on **Another host**. Let's copy the one we just created—mark the checkbox next to it and click on **Copy**. Choose **Hosts** in the **Target type** dropdown, **Linux servers** in the **Group** dropdown and select **Another host**:

Target type	Hosts ▾
Group	Linux servers ▾
Target	▨ Another host A test host
	Copy Cancel

When done, click on **Copy**.

> To prevent our trap going in the item that has no trigger against it, go to **Configuration | Hosts**, click on **Items** next to **Another host**, and either remove the **Experimental SNMP trap** item, or change its item key.

There's still one missing link—none of the two users in the Our users group has user media defined. To add media, navigate to **Administration | Users** and click on **monitoring_user** in the **ALIAS** column. Switch to the **Media** tab and click **Add**, enter the e-mail address in the **Send to** field, then close the popup by clicking on **Add**. We now have to save this change as well, so click on **Update**.

Now we have to make a trigger fire. Execute the following from Another host:

```
$ snmptrap -Ci -v 2c -c public <Zabbix server> "" "NET-SNMP-
MIB::netSnmpExperimental" NET-SNMP-MIB::netSnmpExperimental s "Critical
Error"
```

> See *Chapter 4, Monitoring SNMP Devices*, for information on receiving SNMP traps.

Replace `<Zabbix server>` with the IP or DNS name of the Zabbix server. This value should end up in the `snmptraps` item in `Another host` and make the associated trigger fire. You can verify that the trigger fires in the **Monitoring | Triggers** section:

> To make our next trap end up in the `snmptraps` host, go to **Configuration | Hosts**, click on **Items** next to **Another host** and either remove the **snmptraps** item, or change its item key.

Then send another trap from `Another host`:

```
$ snmptrap -Ci -v 2c -c public <Zabbix server> "" "NET-SNMP-
MIB::netSnmpExperimental" NET-SNMP-MIB::netSnmpExperimental s "Critical
Error"
```

As `Another host` has no `snmptraps` item anymore, this value should go to the `snmptraps` host instead. By now, we should have received an e-mail from our new action. Let's check out another view — the event view. Open **Monitoring | Events** and, take a look at the last few entries:

TIME	HOST	DESCRIPTION	STATUS	SEVERITY	DURATION	ACK	ACTIONS
2016-04-13 04:02:56	snmptraps	SNMP trap has arrived on snmptraps	PROBLEM	Information	34s	No	
2016-04-13 04:02:30	Another host	SNMP trap has arrived on Another host	OK	Information	1m 25s	No	
2016-04-13 04:00:56	Another host	SNMP trap has arrived on Another host	PROBLEM	Information	1m 34s	No	1	1

> If you don't see the SNMP events, make sure that both **Group** and **Host** dropdowns have **all** selected.

We can see that three events have been successfully registered by now — first, the SNMP trap item reporting an error on **Another host**, then resolving it, and last, trigger on the **snmptraps** host has fired. But the last column, titled **ACTIONS**, is notably different. While the first **PROBLEM** event has some numbers listed, the most recent one has nothing. So here's why.

> In Zabbix, only users that have at least read-only access to at least one of the systems, referenced in the trigger, receive notifications.

The `snmptraps` host was in the important **SNMP host group**, and permissions on it for our user group were explicitly set to `deny`.

That allows us to overlap **host group** permissions with action conditions to create quite sophisticated notification scenarios.

Additional action conditions

So far, we have only used the two default action conditions. Actually, Zabbix provides quite a lot of different conditions that determine when an action is invoked. Let's look at some examples of what other conditions are available:

- **Application**: Allows us to limit actions to specific applications. For example, an action could only react when items belonging to the MySQL application are involved. This is a freeform field, so it must match the actual application name. We may also match or negate a substring.

- **Host**: Allows us to single out an important (or unimportant) host for action invocation.

- **Host group**: Similar to the **Host** condition, this one allows us to limit based on the host group membership.

- **Trigger**: This condition allows us to match individual, specific triggers.

- **Trigger name**: A bit more flexible than the previous one, with this condition we can limit invocation based on trigger name — for example, only acting upon triggers that have the string database in their names.

- **Trigger severity**: We can limit the action to only happen for the highest two trigger severities, or maybe only for a couple of the lowest severities.

- **Time period**: Operations can be carried out only if a problem has happened in a specified time period, or they can be suppressed for a specified time period instead.

There are more action conditions that are useful in specific use cases — check the list in the action condition configuration to be able to use them later.

Complex conditions

In the action properties, in the **Conditions** tab, there was also a **Type of calculation** dropdown at the very top. It appears when the action has two or more conditions, thus for us it was always present — the default action came with two conditions already. Let's find out what functionality it offers:

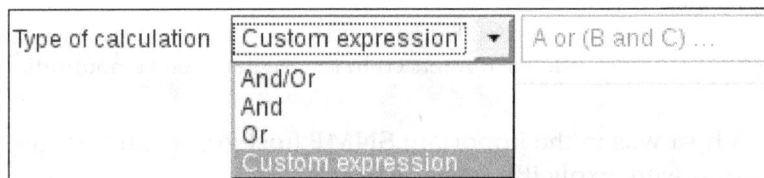

- **And**: All the conditions must be true for the action to match
- **Or**: It is enough for one condition to be true for the action to match
- **And/Or**: Conditions of the same type are evaluated as Or; conditions of different types are evaluated as And
- **Custom expression**: Full freedom option—you write a formula to define how the conditions should be evaluated

The first two options are clear enough. **And/Or** automatically creates the expression and the logic is based on condition types. For example, if we have the following conditions:

- **A**: Application = MySQL
- **B**: Application = PostgreSQL
- **C**: Trigger severity = High
- **D**: Host group = Database servers

Option **And/Or** would create a formula (A or B) and C and D. This works in a lot of situations, but we might now add another condition for a **Host group** like this:

- **E**: Host group = Production servers.

> Actual placeholder letters are likely to be different in the Zabbix frontend as the conditions are ordered. Adding or removing a condition can change the letters of the existing conditions—be careful when using custom expressions and conditions are changed.

The formula would be (A or B) and C and (D or E). The new **Host group** condition, being the same type, is "or-ed" with the previous **Host group** condition. It is probably not what the user intended, though. In this case, the desired condition was *hosts that are both in the database server and production server groups*. The **and/or** option does not help here anymore, so we can use a **Custom expression**. In this case, we would simply type the formula in the provided input field:

```
(A or B) and C and (D and E)
```

Grouping for **D** and **E** here is optional; we added it only for clarity.

The situation is even more complicated when negating some conditions. If one would like to skip an action in case some problem happens for a host either in group A or group B, having two not host group conditions such as (A and B) wouldn't work — it would only match if a host was in both groups at the same time. Making the expression check for (A or B) would match unless a host is in both host groups again. For example, if the problem happens on a host that's in group A, Zabbix would check that the host matched the first condition. It would tell that the action shouldn't be performed — but there's the second part with or. The host wouldn't be part of group B, and thus the action would be performed. Unfortunately, there's no simple solution for such cases. Creating two actions, each only negating a single host group, would work.

Dependencies and actions

Another way to limit the notifications sent is trigger dependencies, which come in really handy here. If a trigger that is dependent on an already active trigger fires, we have seen the effect on the frontend — the dependent trigger did not appear in the list of active triggers. This is even better with actions — no action is performed in such a case. If you know that a website relies on a **Network File System (NFS)** server, and have set a corresponding dependency, the NFS server going down would not notify you about the website problem. When there's a problem to solve, not being flooded with e-mails is a good thing.

There's a possible race condition if the item for the dependent trigger is checked more often. In such a case, the dependent trigger might fire first, and the other one a short time later, thus still producing two alerts. While this is not a huge problem for the trigger displaying in the frontend, this can be undesirable if it happens with actions involved. If you see such false positives often, change the item intervals so that the dependent one always has a slightly longer interval.

Media limits for users

We looked at what limits an action can impose, but there are also possible limits per media. Navigate to **Administration | Users** and click on **Admin** in the **ALIAS** column. Switch to the **Media** tab and click on **Edit** next to the only media we have created here:

Type	Email ▾
Send to	admin@company.tld
When active	1-7,00:00-24:00
Use if severity	▨ Not classified ▨ Information ▨ Warning ▨ Average ▨ High ▨ Disaster
Enabled	▨

> Admin level users may change their own media. Normal users cannot change their own media.

When considering limits, we are mostly interested in two sections here—**When active** and **Use if severity**.

As the name indicates, the first of these allows us to set a period when media is used. Days are represented by the numbers 1-7 and a 24-hour clock notation of HH:MM-HH:MM is used. Several periods can be combined, separated by semicolons. This way it is possible to send an SMS to a technician during weekends and nights, an e-mail during workdays, and an e-mail to a helpdesk during working hours.

> In case you are wondering, the week starts with Monday.

For example, a media active period like this might be useful for an employee who has different working times during a week:

```
1-3,09:00-13:00;4-5,13:00-17:00
```

Notifications would be sent out:

- Monday to Wednesday from 09:00 till 13:00
- Thursday and Friday from 13:00 till 17:00

> This period works together with the time period condition in actions. The action for this user will only be carried out when both periods overlap.

Use if severity is very useful as well, as that poor technician might not want to receive informative SMS messages during the night, only disaster ones.

Click on **Cancel** to close this window.

Sending out notifications

As both of the users specified in the action operations have explicitly been denied access to the snmptraps host, they were not considered valid for action operations.

Let's give them access to this host now. Go to **Administration | User groups** and click on **Our users** in the **NAME** column. Switch to the **Permissions** tab, then mark **Important SNMP hosts** in the **DENY** box, click on **Delete selected** below, then click on **Update**. Both users should have access to the desired host now.

Out triggers have been deactivated by now, so we can send another trap to activate the one on the snmptraps host.

> Notice how no messages were sent when the triggers deactivated, because of the Trigger value = PROBLEM condition. We will enable recovery messages later in this chapter.

Run the following commands on Another host:

```
$ snmptrap -Ci -v 2c -c public <Zabbix server> "" "NET-SNMP-
MIB::netSnmpExperimental" NET-SNMP-MIB::netSnmpExperimental s "Critical
Error"
```

Wait for a while so that the trigger fires again. Check your e-mail, and you should have received a notification about the host that we previously were not notified about, snmptraps. Let's see the event list again—open **Monitoring | Events** and look at the latest entry:

TIME	HOST	DESCRIPTION	STATUS	SEVERITY	DUPATION	ACK	ACTIONS
2016-04-13 08:16:04	snmptraps	SNMP trap has arrived on snmptraps	PROBLEM	Information	56s	No	1 1

> If the **ACTIONS** column shows a number in an orange color, wait a couple more minutes. We will discuss the reason for such a delay in *Chapter 22, Zabbix Maintenance*.

Oh, but what's up with the weird entry in the **ACTIONS** column? Those two differently colored numbers look quite cryptic. Let's try to find out what they could mean—open **Reports | Action log** and look at the last few entries:

RECIPIENT(S)	MESSAGE	STATUS	INFO
monitoring_user (monitoring user) monitoring_user@company.tld	**Subject:** PROBLEM: SNMP trap has arrived on snmptraps **Message:** Trigger: SNMP trap has arrived on snmptraps Trigger status: PROBLEM Trigger severity: Information Trigger URL: Item values: 1. Received SNMP traps (snmptraps:snmptraps): 192.168.56.11 "Critical Error" NET-SNMP-MIB::netSnmpExperimental 2. "UNKNOWN" ("UNKNOWN":"UNKNOWN"): "UNKNOWN" 3. "UNKNOWN" ("UNKNOWN":"UNKNOWN"): "UNKNOWN" Original event ID: 374	Sent	
advanced_user (advanced user)	**Subject:** PROBLEM: SNMP trap has arrived on snmptraps **Message:** Trigger: SNMP trap has arrived on snmptraps Trigger status: PROBLEM Trigger severity: Information Trigger URL: Item values: 1. Received SNMP traps (snmptraps:snmptraps): 192.168.56.11 "Critical Error" NET-SNMP-MIB::netSnmpExperimental 2. "UNKNOWN" ("UNKNOWN":"UNKNOWN"): "UNKNOWN" 3. "UNKNOWN" ("UNKNOWN":"UNKNOWN"): "UNKNOWN" Original event ID: 374	Not sent ☒	

> If you don't see any entries, increase the displayed time period.

The **STATUS** column says that sending the message succeeded for the monitoring_user, but failed for the advanced_user. Thus, green numbers in the event list mean successfully sent notifications, while red numbers mean failures. To see why it failed, move the mouse cursor over the red **X** in the **INFO** column:

No media defined for user "advanced user (advanced_user)"

> You can click the red **X** to make the popup stay when the mouse cursor moves away, which allows us to copy the error text.

Excellent, that clearly explains what the error is—our advanced_user had no media entries defined. We can easily deduce that numbers in the event list represent notification counts—green for successful ones and red for unsuccessful ones. It also shows us that actions should not be configured to send messages for users that do not have media correctly set, as such entries pollute the action log and make it harder to review interesting entries.

While the Action log provides more detail, we could have found out the error in the event list as well. Return to **Monitoring | Events**, and move the mouse cursor over the red, rightmost number 1 in the **ACTIONS** column. A popup appears. Click on the number 1 to make the popup stay and move the mouse cursor over the red **X** in the **INFO** column—the same informative popup will appear, in this case telling us that there's no media defined for this user.

Using macros

Let's take a careful look at the e-mails we received (if you have already deleted them, just send a couple more SNMP traps). The subject and body both mention the trigger name SNMP trap has arrived on snmptraps. Looks like it was a good idea to include the host name macro in the trigger name. While there's another solution we will explore right now, a general suggestion is to always include the host name in the trigger name. Doing so will avoid cases when you receive an alert, but have no idea which host has the problem. For example, if we had omitted the host name macro from our trigger, the e-mail alerts would have said SNMP trap has arrived.

Another solution is possible for the aforementioned problem—we can use the macro in the action to help in this particular case. To proceed, navigate to **Configuration | Actions**, click on **SNMP action** in the **NAME** column, then change the Default subject field contents to:

```
{TRIGGER.STATUS}: {TRIGGER.NAME} on {HOST.NAME}
```

> The use of the word macros can be confusing here—Zabbix calls them macros, although they might be more correctly be considered to be variables. In this book, we will follow Zabbix terminology, but feel free to read macro as variable.

The field already contained two macros — {TRIGGER.STATUS} and {TRIGGER.NAME}. The benefit of a macro is evident when we have a single action covering many cases. We don't have to create a myriad of actions to cover every possible situation; instead we use macros to have the desired information, related to the particular event, replaced. Macro names usually provide a good idea of what a macro does. In this case, we improved the existing subject line, which already contained trigger name and status macros, by adding the host name macro, though it is still recommended to include the host name in trigger names.

To confirm your changes, click on **Update**. Make the trigger change state by sending SNMP traps like before, then check your e-mail. The subject now includes the host name. But wait, now the host name is included twice — what have we done? The subject is now:

```
PROBLEM: SNMP trap has arrived on snmptraps on snmptraps
```

We used the same macro in the trigger name and in the action subject. You should decide where you would like to specify the host name and always follow that rule.

There's also something else slightly strange in the e-mails — at the end of the message body, there are some lines with **UNKNOWN** in them:

```
Received SNMP traps (snmptraps:snmptraps): 192.168.56.11 "Critical Error"
NET-SNMP-MIB::netSnmpExperimental

*UNKNOWN* (*UNKNOWN*:*UNKNOWN*): *UNKNOWN*

*UNKNOWN* (*UNKNOWN*:*UNKNOWN*): *UNKNOWN*
```

If we now look at the corresponding action configuration:

```
Item values:
{ITEM.NAME1} ({HOST.NAME1}:{ITEM.KEY1}): {ITEM.VALUE1}
{ITEM.NAME2} ({HOST.NAME2}:{ITEM.KEY2}): {ITEM.VALUE2}
{ITEM.NAME3} ({HOST.NAME3}:{ITEM.KEY3}): {ITEM.VALUE3}
```

The number that is appended in these macros, such as in {ITEM.NAME1}, is the sequential number of the item in the trigger expression. The trigger that sent the notifications for us referenced a single item only, thus the first reference works, referencing the second and third items fails, and that outputs *UNKNOWN* in the message. The default action is meant to be used as an example — in this case, demonstrating the ability to reference multiple items. If most of your triggers reference only a single item, it might be desirable to remove the second and the third lines. At this time, there is no way to conditionally print the item value, if it exists.

Sometimes, the receiver of the message might benefit from additional information that's, not directly obtainable from event-related macros. Here, an additional class of macros helps—the ones used in trigger expressions also work for macro contents. Imagine a person managing two servers that both rely on an NFS server, which is known to have performance problems. If the system load on one of these two servers increases enough to fire a trigger, the alert receiver would want to know the load on the second server as well, and also whether the NFS service is running correctly. That would allow them to do a quick evaluation of where the problem most likely lies—if the NFS service is down or is having performance problems of its own, then the system load on these two servers most likely has risen because of that, and the NFS server admin will have to take care of that. For this person to receive such information, we can add lines these to the e-mail body:

```
CPU load on Another host: {Another host:system.cpu.load.last()}
NFS service is: {NFS Server:nfs.service.last()}
```

> Make sure to adjust item intervals and trigger expressions to avoid race condition for these items.

Note, there is no built-in NFS service item—one has to create proper hosts and items to be able to reference them like this.

As can be seen in the example, the same syntax is used as in trigger expressions, including the functions supported. This also allows the receiver to be immediately informed about average load over a period of time by adding a macro such as this:

```
Average CPU load on Another host for last 10 minutes: {Another
host:system.cpu.load.avg(600)}
```

You can find a full list of supported macros in the official Zabbix documentation at https://www.zabbix.com/documentation/3.0/manual/appendix/macros/ supported_by_location.

Sending recovery messages

The setup we used only sent out messages when the problem happened. That was ensured by the `Trigger value = PROBLEM` condition, which was added by default. One way to also enable the sending of messages when a trigger is resolved would be to remove that condition, but it will not be useful when escalation functionality is used. Thus it is suggested to leave that condition in place and enable recovery messages on the action level instead.

Let's enable recovery messages for our SNMP trap action. Go to **Configuration |
Actions**, click on **SNMP action** in the **NAME** column, and mark the **Recovery message**
checkbox. Notice how this gives us two additional fields—we can customize the
recovery message. Instead of sending similar messages for problems and recoveries,
we can make recoveries stand out a bit more. Hey, that's a good idea—we will be
sending out e-mails to management, let's add some "feel good" thing here. Modify the
Recovery subject field by adding `Resolved:` in front of the existing content:

Recovery message	▨
Recovery subject	Resolved: {TRIGGER.STATUS}: {TRIGGER.NAME}

> Do not remove the trigger value condition when enabling recovery
> messages. Doing so can result in recovery messages being escalated,
> and thus generate a huge amount of useless messages.

Click on the **Update** button. This will make the outgoing recovery messages have
a sort of a double-affirmation that everything is good—the subject will start with
`Resolved: OK:`. To test the new configuration, set the trap to generate a problem
and wait for the problem to resolve. This time, two e-mails should be sent, and the
second one should come with our custom subject.

In the e-mail that arrives, note the line at the very end that looks similar to this:

```
Original event ID: 1313
```

The number at the end of the line is the event ID—a unique identifier of the
occurrence of the problem. It is actually the so-called **original event ID**. This is
the ID of the original problem, and it is the same in the problem and recovery
notifications. A very useful approach is automatically matching recovery messages
with the problem ones when sending this data to an issue management or ticketing
system—recovery information can be used to automatically close tickets, or provide
additional information for them.

This ID was produced by a macro {EVENT.ID}, and, as with many other macros, you
can use it in your actions. If you would want to uniquely identify the recovery event,
there's yet another macro for that—{EVENT.RECOVERY.ID}.

There are a lot of macros, so make sure to consult the Zabbix manual for a full list
of them.

Escalating things

We know how to perform an action if a threshold is reached, such as the temperature being too high, the available disk space being too low, or a web server not working. We can send a message, open a ticket in a tracker, run a custom script, or execute a command on a remote machine. But all these are simple if-then sequences — if it's this problem, do this. Quite often the severity of the problem depends on how long the problem persists. For example, a couple-of-minutes-long connection loss to a branch office might not be critical, but it's still worth noting down and e-mailing IT staff. The inability to reach a branch office for five minutes is quite important, and at this point we would like to open a ticket in the helpdesk system and send an SMS to IT staff. After 20 minutes of the problem not being fixed, we would e-mail an IT manager. Let's look at what tools Zabbix provides to enable such gradual activities and configure a simple example.

In the frontend, navigate to **Configuration | Actions** and click on **Disabled** next to the **Test action** in the **STATUS** column to enable this action, then click on **Enabled** next to the **SNMP action**. Now click on **Test action** in the **NAME** column. Currently, this action sends a single e-mail to user Admin whenever a problem occurs. Let's extend this situation:

- Our first user, Admin, will be notified for five minutes after the problem happens, with a one-minute interval. After that, they would be notified every five minutes until the problem is resolved.

- advanced_user is lower-level management who would like to receive a notification if a problem is not resolved within five minutes.

- monitoring_user is a higher-level manager who should be notified in 20 minutes if the problem still is not resolved, and if it has not yet been acknowledged.

While these times would be longer in real life, here we are interested in seeing escalation in action.

Now we are ready to configure escalations. Switch to the **Operations** tab.

> Do not remove the Trigger value = PROBLEM condition when using escalations. Doing so can result in a huge amount of useless messages, as **OK** state messages get escalated.

Looking at the operations list, we can see that it currently contains only a single operation — sending an e-mail message to the Admin user immediately and only once — which is indicated by the **STEPS DETAILS** column having only the first step listed:

Action operations	STEPS DETAILS	START IN	DURATION (SEC)	ACTION	
	1 **Send message to users:** Admin (Zabbix Administrator) via all media	Immediately	Default	Edit	Remove
	New				

The first change we would like to perform is to make sure that Admin receives notifications every minute for the first five minutes after the problem happens. Before we modify that, though, we should change the default operation step duration, which by default is 3600 and cannot be lower than 60 seconds. Looking at our requirements, two factors affect the possible step length:

- The lowest time between two repeated alerts — 1 minute in our case.
- The biggest common divisor for the starting time of delayed alerts. In our case, the delayed alerts were needed at 5 and 20 minutes, thus the biggest common divisor is 5 minutes.

Normally, one would set the default step duration to the biggest common divisor of both these factors. Here, that would be 60 seconds — but we may also override step duration inside an operation. Let's see how that can help us to have a simpler escalation process.

Enter 300 in the **Default operation** step duration — that's five minutes in seconds. Now let's make sure Admin receives a notification every minute for the first five minutes — click on **Edit** in the **Action operations** block.

Notice how the operation details also have a **Step duration** field. This allows us to override action-level step duration for each operation. We have an action level step duration of 300 seconds, but these steps should be performed with one minute between them, so enter 60 in the **Step duration** field. The two **Steps** fields denote the step this operation should start and end with. Step 1 means immediately, thus the first field satisfies us. On the other hand, it currently sends the message only once, but we want to pester our administrator for five minutes. In the **Steps** fields, enter 6 in the second field.

> Step 6 happens 5 minutes after the problem happened. Step 1 is right away, which is 0 minutes. Step 2 is one minute, and so on. Sending messages for 5 minutes will result in six messages in total, as we send a message both at the beginning and the end of this period.

The final result should look like this:

Steps	1	·	6
Step duration	60	(minimum 60 seconds, 0 - use action default)	

If it does, click on **Update** in the **Operation details** block — not the button at the bottom yet. Now to the next task — Admin must receive notifications every five minutes after that, until the problem is resolved.

We have to figure out what values to put in the **Steps** fields. We want this operation to kick in after five minutes, but notification at five minutes is already covered by the first operation, so we are probably aiming for 10 minutes. But which step should we use for 10 minutes? Let's try to create a timeline. We have a single operation currently set that overrides the default period. After that, the default period starts working, and even though we currently have no operations assigned, we can calculate when further steps would be taken:

Step	Operation	Interval (seconds)	Time passed
1	Send message to user Admin	Operation, 60	0
2	Send message to user Admin	Operation, 60	1 minute
3	Send message to user Admin	Operation, 60	2 minutes
4	Send message to user Admin	Operation, 60	3 minutes
5	Send message to user Admin	Operation, 60	4 minutes
6	Send message to user Admin	Operation, 60	5 minutes
7	none	Default, 300	6 minutes
8	none	Default, 300	11 minutes

> Operation step duration overrides periods for the steps included in it. If an operation spans steps 5-7, it overrides periods 5-6, 6-7, and 7-8. If an operation is at step 3 only, it overrides period 3-4.

We wanted to have 10 minutes, but it looks like with this configuration that is not possible — our first operation puts step 7 at 6 minutes, and falling back to the default intervals puts step 8 at 11 minutes. To override interval 6-7, we would have to define some operation at step 7, but we do not want to do that. Is there a way to configure it in the desired way? There should be. Click on **Edit** in the **ACTION** column and change the second **Steps** field to 5, then click on **Update** in the **Operation details** block — do not click on the main **Update** button at the bottom.

Now click on **New** in the **Action operations** block. Let's configure the simple things first. Click on **Add** in the **Send to Users** section in the **Operation details** block, and click on **Admin** in the resulting popup. With the first operation updated, let's model the last few steps again:

Step	Operation	Interval (seconds)	Time passed
...	...	...	...
5	Send message to user Admin	Operation, 60	4 minutes
6	none	Default, 300	5 minutes
7	none	Default, 300	10 minutes
8	none	Default, 300	15 minutes

With the latest modifications, it looks like we can send a message after 10 minutes have passed—that would be step 7. But we actually removed message sending on step 6, at 5 minutes. The good news—if we now add another operation to start at step 6, that finishes the first five-minute sending cycle and then keeps on sending a message every 5 minutes—just perfect.

Enter 6 in the first **Steps** field. We want this operation to continue until the problem is resolved, thus 0 goes in the second **Steps** fields. When done, click on the **Add** control at the bottom of the **Operation details** block.

We can see that Zabbix helpfully calculated the time when the second operation should start, which allows us to quickly spot errors in our calculations. There are no errors here; the second operation starts at 5 minutes as desired:

Default operation step duration	300 (minimum 60 seconds)		
Action operations	STEPS DETAILS	START IN	DURATION (SEC)
	1 - 5 **Send message to users:** Admin (Zabbix Administrator) via all media Immediately	60	
	6 - 0 **Send message to users:** Admin (Zabbix Administrator) via all media 00:05:00	Default	
	New		

With that covered, our lower-level manager, advanced_user, must be notified after five minutes, but only once. That means another operation—click on **New** in the **Action operations** block. Click on **Add** in the **Send to Users** section and in the popup, click on **advanced_user** in the **ALIAS** column. The single message should be simple—we know that step 6 happens after five minutes have passed, so let's enter 6 in both **Steps** fields, then click on **Add** at the bottom of the **Operation details** block. Again, the **START IN** column shows that this step will be executed after five minutes, as expected.

> If two escalation operations overlap steps, and one of them
> has a custom interval and the other uses the default, the
> custom interval will be used for the overlapping steps. If
> both operations have a custom interval defined, the smallest
> interval is used for the overlapping steps.

We are now left with the final task—notifying the higher-level manager after 20 minutes, and only if the problem has not been acknowledged. As before, click on **New** in the **Action operations** block, then click on **Add** in the **Send to Users** section, and in the popup, click on **monitoring_user** in the **ALIAS** column. Let's continue with our planned step table:

Step	Operation	Interval (seconds)	Time passed
...	...	...	...
7	none	Default, 300	10 minutes
8	none	Default, 300	15 minutes
9	none	Default, 300	20 minutes

As steps just continue with the default period, this shows us that step 9 is the correct one. As we want only a single notification here, enter 9 in both of the **Steps** fields.

> It is not required to fill all steps with operations. Some steps
> in between can be skipped if the planned schedule requires
> it, just like we did here.

An additional requirement was to notify this user only if the problem has not been acknowledged. To add such a restriction, click on **New** in the **Conditions** area. The **Operation condition** block is displayed, and the default setting already has **Not Ack** chosen, so click on **Add** in the **Operation condition** block. The form layout can be a bit confusing here, so make sure not to click on **Add** in the **Operation details** block instead. While we're almost done, there's one more bit we can do to make this notification less confusing for upper management. Currently, everybody receives the same message—some trigger information and the last values of items that are being referenced in triggers. Item values might not be that interesting to the manager, thus we can try omitting them from those messages. Untick the **Default message** checkbox and notice how we can customize subject and message for a specific operation. For the message, remove everything that goes below the `Trigger URL` line. For the manager, it might also be useful to know who was notified and when. Luckily, there's another helpful macro, `{ESC.HISTORY}`. Let's modify the message by adding an empty line and then this macro. Here's what the final result for this operation should look like:

Operation details		
Steps	9 - 9	
Step duration	0	(minimum 60 seconds, 0 - use action default)
Operation type	Send message ▾	
	USER GROUP	ACTION
	Add	
Send to User groups		
	USER	ACTION
	monitoring_user (monitoring user)	Remove
	Add	
Send to Users		
Send only to	- All - ▾	
Default message	☐	
Subject	{TRIGGER.STATUS}: {TRIGGER.NAME}	
Message	Trigger: {TRIGGER.NAME} Trigger status: {TRIGGER.STATUS} Trigger severity: {TRIGGER.SEVERITY} Trigger URL: {TRIGGER.URL} {ESC.HISTORY}	
	LABEL NAME	ACTION
	A Event acknowledged = *Not Ack*	Remove
	New	
Conditions		
Add Cancel		

It's all fine, so click on **Add** at the bottom of the **Operation details** block. We can now review action operations and verify that each operation starts when it should:

STEPS	DETAILS	START IN	DURATION (SEC)
1 - 5	**Send message to users:** Admin (Zabbix Administrator) via all media	Immediately	60
6 - 0	**Send message to users:** Admin (Zabbix Administrator) via all media	00:05:00	Default
6	**Send message to users:** advanced_user (advanced user) via all media	00:05:00	Default
9	**Send message to users:** monitoring_user (monitoring user) via all media	00:20:00	Default

Everything seems to match the specification. Let's switch back to the **Action** tab and, similar to the **SNMP action**, change the **Recovery subject** to Resolved: {TRIGGER. NAME}. This time we wanted to avoid Resolved: OK:, opting for a single mention that everything is good now. We can finally click on **Update**. With this notification setup in place, let's break something. On Another host, execute:

```
$ rm /tmp/testfile
```

It will take a short time for Zabbix to notice this problem and fire away the first e-mail to the Admin user. This e-mail won't be that different from the ones we received before. But now let's be patient and wait for 20 minutes more. During this time, the Admin user will receive more messages. What we are really interested in is the message content in the e-mail to the monitoring_user. Once you receive this message, look at what it contains:

```
Trigger: Testfile is missing

Trigger status: PROBLEM

Trigger severity: Warning

Trigger URL:


Problem started: 2016.04.15 15:05:25 Age: 20m

1. 2016.04.15 15:05:27 message sent        Email admin@company.tld
"Zabbix Administrator (Admin)"

2. 2016.04.15 15:06:27 message sent        Email admin@company.tld
"Zabbix Administrator (Admin)"

3. 2016.04.15 15:07:27 message sent        Email admin@company.tld
"Zabbix Administrator (Admin)"

4. 2016.04.15 15:08:27 message sent        Email admin@company.tld
"Zabbix Administrator (Admin)"

5. 2016.04.15 15:09:27 message sent        Email admin@company.tld
"Zabbix Administrator (Admin)"

6. 2016.04.15 15:10:27 message failed        "advanced user (advanced_
user)" No media defined for user "advanced user (advanced_user)"

6. 2016.04.15 15:10:27 message sent        Email admin@company.tld
"Zabbix Administrator (Admin)"

7. 2016.04.15 15:15:28 message sent        Email admin@company.tld
"Zabbix Administrator (Admin)"

8. 2016.04.15 15:20:28 message sent        Email admin@company.tld
"Zabbix Administrator (Admin)"
```

> As in all other notifications, the time here will use the local time on the Zabbix server.

It now contains a lot more information than just what happened — the manager has also received a detailed list of who was notified of the problem. The user Admin has received many notifications, and then... hey, advanced_user has not received the notification because their e-mail address is not configured. There's some work to do either for this user, or for the Zabbix administrators to fix this issue. And in this case, the issue is escalated to the monitoring_user only if nobody has acknowledged the problem before, which means nobody has even looked into it.

> The current setup would cancel escalation to the management user if the problem is acknowledged. We may create a delayed escalation by adding yet another operation that sends a message to the management user at some later step, but does so without an acknowledgement condition. If the problem is acknowledged, the first operation to the management user would be skipped, but the second one would always work. If the problem is not acknowledged at all, the management user would get two notifications.

If we look carefully at the prefixed numbers, they are not sequential numbers of entries in the history, they are actually the escalation step numbers. That gives us a quick overview of which notifications happened at the same time, without comparing timestamps. The Email string is the name of the media type used for this notification.

Let's fix the problem now; on Another host execute:

```
$ touch /tmp/testfile
```

In a short while, two e-mail messages should be sent — one to the Admin user and one to monitoring_user. As these are recovery messages, they will both have our custom subject:

```
Resolved: Testfile is missing
```

Our test action had escalation thresholds that are too short for most real-life situations. If reducing these meant creating an action from scratch, that would be very inconvenient. Let's see how easily we can adapt the existing one. In the frontend, navigate to **Configuration | Actions**, then click on **Test action** in the **NAME** column and switch to the **Operations** tab. We might want to make the following changes, assuming that this is not a critical problem and does not warrant a quick response—unless it has been there for half an hour:

*   Increase the interval between the further repeated messages the `Admin` user gets
*   Increase the delay before the messages to the `advanced_user` and `monitoring_user` are sent
*   Start sending messages to the `Admin` user after the problem has been there for 30 minutes

> In the next few steps, be careful not to click on the **Update** button too early—that will discard the modifications in the operation that we are currently editing.

Let's start by changing the **Default operation** step duration to 1800 (30 minutes). Then let's click on **Edit** in the **ACTION** column next to the first entry (currently spanning steps 1-5). In its properties, set the **Steps** fields to 2 and 6, then click on the **Update** control in the **Operation details** block.

For both operations that start at step 6, change that to step 7. For the operation that has 6 in both of the **Steps** fields, change both occurrences the same way as before—and again, be careful not to click on the **Update** button yet.

The final result here should look like this:

Default operation step duration		1800	(minimum 60 seconds)		
Action operations	STEPS	DETAILS		START IN	DURATION (SEC)
	2 - 6	**Send message to users:** Admin (Zabbix Administrator) via all media		00:30:00	60
	7 - 0	**Send message to users:** Admin (Zabbix Administrator) via all media		00:35:00	Default
	7	**Send message to users:** advanced_user (advanced user) via all media		00:35:00	Default
	9	**Send message to users:** monitoring_user (monitoring user) via all media		01:35:00	Default
	New				

If it does, click on that **Update** button.

The first change for the default operation step spaced all steps out—except the ones that were overridden in the operation properties. That mostly achieved our goals to space out notifications to the Admin user and delay notifications to the two other users. By changing the first step in the first operation from 1 to 2, we achieved two goals. The interval between steps 1 and 2 went back to the default interval for the action (as we excluded step 1 from the operation that did the overriding with 60 seconds), and no message was sent to the Admin user right away. Additionally, we moved the end step a bit further so that the total number of messages the Admin user would get with 1-minute intervals would not change. That resulted in some further operations not being so nicely aligned to the 5-minute boundary, so we moved them to step 7. Let's compare this to the previous configuration:

Before				After
STEPS	DETAILS	START IN	DURATION (SEC)	START IN
1 - 5	**Send message to users:** Admin (Zabbix Administrator) via all media	Immediately	60	00:30:00
6 - 0	**Send message to users:** Admin (Zabbix Administrator) via all media	00:05:00	Default	00:35:00
6	**Send message to users:** advanced_user (advanced user) via all media	00:05:00	Default	00:35:00
9	**Send message to users:** monitoring_user (monitoring user) via all media	00:20:00	Default	01:35:00

This allows us to easily scale notifications and escalations up from a testing configuration to something more appropriate to the actual situation, as well as adapting quickly to changing requirements. Let's create another problem. On Another host, execute:

```
$ rm /tmp/testfile
```

Wait for the trigger to fire and for a couple of e-mails arrive for the Admin user, then "solve" the problem:

```
$ touch /tmp/testfile
```

That should send a recovery e-mail to the Admin user soon. Hey, wait—why for that user only? Zabbix only sends recovery notifications to users who have received problem notifications. As the problem did not get escalated for the management user to receive the notification, that user was not informed about resolving the problem either. A similar thing actually happened with advanced_user, who did not have media assigned. As the notification was not sent when the event was escalated (because no e-mail address was configured), Zabbix did not even try to send a recovery message to that user. No matter how many problem messages were sent to a user, only a single recovery message will be sent per action.

So in this case, if the Admin user resolved or acknowledged the issue before monitoring_user received an e-mail about the problem, monitoring_user would receive neither the message about the problem, nor the one about resolving it.

As we can see, escalations are fairly flexible and allow you to combine many operations when responding to an event. We could imagine one fairly long and complex escalation sequence of a web server going down to proceed like this:

1. E-mail administrator
2. Send SMS to admin
3. Open report at helpdesk system
4. E-mail management
5. Send SMS to management
6. Restart Apache
7. Reboot the server
8. Power cycle the whole server room

Well, the last one might be a bit over the top, but we can indeed construct a fine-grained stepping up of reactions and notifications about problems.

Runner analogy

Did that escalation thing seem terribly complicated to you? If so, we can try an analogy that was coined near Salt Lake City.

Imagine there's a runner running through a forest, with a straight route. On this route, there are posts. The runner has a preferred speed (we might call it a **default speed**), which means that it normally takes T seconds for the runner to go from one post to the next one.

On the posts, there may be instructions. The runner starts from the very first post, and checks for instructions there. Instructions can order the runner to do various things:

- Send SMS to somebody at this post only
- Send SMS to somebody from this post until post N
- Change speed from this post until the next post to arrive sooner or later
- Change speed from this post until post N

The route is taken by the runner no matter what—if there are no instructions at the current post, the runner just continues to the next post.

If this analogy made how the action escalation steps are processed by the "runner" clearer, it might be worth reviewing this section and possibly gaining better understanding of the details, too.

Using scripts as media

While Zabbix supports a decent range of notification mechanisms, there always comes a time when you need something very specific and the default methods just don't cut it. For such situations, Zabbix supports custom scripts to be used as media. Let's try to set one up. Open **Administration | Media types** and click on **Create media** type. Enter these values:

- **Name**: Test script
- **Type**: **Script**
- **Script name**: testscript
- **Script parameters**: Click on the **Add** control and enter {ALERT.MESSAGE} in the new field:

Name	Test script	
Type	Script ▾	
Script name	testscript	
Script parameters	PARAMETER	ACTION
	{ALERT.MESSAGE}	Remove
	Add	
Enabled	▨	
	Add Cancel	

> The {ALERT.MESSAGE} macro will be expanded to the message body from the action configuration. Currently, two additional macros are supported in the script parameters — {ALERT.SENDTO} and {ALERT.SUBJECT}. Consult the Zabbix manual to check whether any new macros are added in later versions at https://www.zabbix.com/documentation/3.0/manual/config/notifications/media/script.

When you are done, click on the **Add** button at the bottom. Now we should make sure this media is used at some point. Go to **Administration | Users**, click on **monitoring_user** in the **ALIAS** column, and switch to the **Media** tab. Click on **Add** in the **Media** section. In the **Type** dropdown, select **Test script** and in the **Send to** field, enter `user@domain.tld`:

Type	Test script ▾
Send to	user@domain.tld
When active	1-7,00:00-24:00
Use if severity	▨ Not classified ▨ Information ▨ Warning ▨ Average ▨ High ▨ Disaster
Enabled	▨
	Add Cancel

> The e-mail address won't be passed to our script, but Zabbix does not allow us to save a media entry with an empty **Send to** field.

When you are done, click on **Add** and confirm the changes by clicking on **Update** in the user editing form. Before we continue with the script itself, navigate to **Configuration | Actions** and click on **Disabled** next to **SNMP action** to enable this action.

We entered the script name, but where should the script be placed? Now is the time to return to where we haven't been for some time—take a look at `zabbix_server.conf` and check what value the `AlertScriptsPath` option has. The default location will vary depending on the method of installation. If you installed from source, it will be `/usr/local/share/zabbix/alertscripts`. Distribution packages are likely to use some other directory. As `root`, create a file called `testscript` in that directory:

```
# touch /path/to/testscript
# chmod 755 /path/to/testscript
```

Populate it with the following content:

```
#!/bin/bash
for i in "$@"; do
    echo "$i" >> /tmp/zabbix_script_received.log
done
```

As you can see, we are simply logging each passed parameter to a file for examination. Now generate SNMP traps so that the `snmptraps` trigger switches to the **PROBLEM** state. Wait for the e-mail to arrive, then check the `/tmp/zabbix_script_received.log` file. It should have content similar to this:

```
Trigger: SNMP trap has arrived on snmptraps

Trigger status: PROBLEM

Trigger severity: Information

Trigger URL:


Item values:


1. Received SNMP traps (snmptraps:snmptraps): 192.168.56.11 "Critical
Error"    NET-SNMP-MIB::netSnmpExperimental

2. *UNKNOWN* (*UNKNOWN*:*UNKNOWN*): *UNKNOWN*

3. *UNKNOWN* (*UNKNOWN*:*UNKNOWN*): *UNKNOWN*


Original event ID: 397
```

We can see that the whole message body from action properties is passed here with newlines intact. If we wanted to also know the user media **Send to** value to identify the Zabbix user who received this data, we would also pass the {ALERT.SENDTO} macro to our alertscript. Similarly, to get the subject from the action properties, we would use the {ALERT.SUBJECT} macro.

> If you see message content losing newlines, check the quoting in your script — all newlines are preserved by Zabbix.

From here, basically anything can be done with the data: passing it to issue management systems that do not have an e-mail gateway, sending it through some media not supported directly by Zabbix, or displaying it somewhere.

Let's revisit action configuration now—open **Configuration | Actions** and click on **Test action** in the **NAME** column. Now we have a script executed whenever `monitoring_user` receives a notification. But what if we would like to skip the script for notification, and only use it in a specific action? Thankfully, we don't have to create a separate user just for such a scenario. Switch to the **Operations** tab and in the **Action operations** block, click on **Edit** next to the last operation—sending a message to `monitoring_user`. Take a look at the dropdown **Send only to**. It lists all media types, and allows us to restrict a specific operation to a specific media type only. In this dropdown, choose **Email**. Click on the **Update** link at the bottom of the **Operation details** block, then the **Update** button at the bottom.

By using the **Send only to** option, it is possible to use different notification methods for different situations without creating multiple fake user accounts. For example, a user might receive e-mail for the first few escalation steps, then an SMS would be sent.

Integration with issue management systems

Sending out messages to technicians or the helpdesk is nice, but there are times and conditions when it is desirable to automatically open an issue in some management system. This is most easily achieved by using two main integration methods:

- E-mail gateways
- APIs that decent systems provide

To implement such an integration, the following steps should be taken:

1. Create a Zabbix user for the ticketing system notifications.
2. Configure media for this user (the e-mail address that the system receives e-mail at, or the script to run).
3. Assign read-only access for resources tickets should be automatically created for (remember, no alerts are sent or scripts run if the user does not have access to any of the hosts involved in the event generation).
4. Create a separate action, or add this user as a recipient to an existing action operation with a custom message (by unmarking the **Default message** checkbox when editing the operation).

There's also a *step 5*—either proper message contents should be formatted so that the receiving system knows what to do with the message, or a script created to access the ticketing system API. This is specific to each system, but let's look at a few examples. These examples provide only basic information—for added bonus points you can add other macros such as last or average value ones. Note that the specific syntax might change between ticketing system versions, so check the documentation for the version you are using.

Bugzilla

Bugzilla is famous free bug tracker, sometimes abused as a general issue management system. Still, Zabbix can monitor the status of software tests and open new tickets if, for example, compilation fails. The following would be configured as the message body:

```
@{TRIGGER.NAME}
@product = <some existing product>
@component = <some existing component>
@version = 1.8
{DATE} - {TIME}
{TRIGGER.NAME}.
```

The `From` address is used to determine the user account that is creating the bug report.

Computer Associates Unicenter Service Desk Manager

CA Service Desk Manager (formerly Unicenter Service Desk), from Computer Associates, is a solution that provides a ticketing system, among other features. The following would be configured as the message body:

```
"start-request"
%CUSTOMER= <some existing user account>
%DESCRIPTION= {DATE} - {TIME}
{TRIGGER.NAME}.
%SUMMARY= {TRIGGER.NAME}.
%PRIORITY= {TRIGGER.NSEVERITY}
%CATEGORY= <some existing category>
"end-request"
```

> Use the {TRIGGER.NSEVERITY} macro here—that's numeric trigger severity, with Not classified being 0 and Disaster being 5.

Atlassian JIRA

Atlassian JIRA is a popular ticketing system or issue tracker. While it also supports an e-mail gateway for creating issues, we could look at a more advanced way to do that—using the API JIRA exposes. Media type and user media would have to be created and configured, similar to what we did in the *Using scripts as media* section earlier in this chapter, although it is suggested to create a special user for running such scripts.

As for the script itself, something like this would simply create issues with an identical summary, placing the message body from the action configuration in the issue summary:

```
#!/bin/bash
json='{"fields":{"project":{"key":"PROJ"},"summary":"Issue
automatically created by Zabbix","description":"'"$1"'","issuetype":{"
name":"Bug"}}}'
curl -u username:password -X POST --data "$json" -H "Content-Type:
application/json" https://jira.company.tld/rest/api/2/issue/
```

For this to work, make sure to replace the project key, username, password, and URL to the JIRA instance—and possibly also the issue type.

> For debugging, add the curl flag -D-. That will print out the headers.

This could be extended in various ways. For example, we could pass the subject from the action properties as the first parameter, and encode the trigger severity among other pipe-delimited things. Our script would then parse out the trigger severity and set the JIRA priority accordingly. That would be quite specific for each implementation, though—hopefully this example provided a good starting point.

Remote commands

The script media type is quite powerful, and it could even be used to execute a command in response to an event. For the command to be executed on the monitored host, though, it would require some mechanism to connect, authorize, and such like, which might be somewhat too complicated. Zabbix provides another mechanism to respond to events—remote commands. Remote commands can be used in a variety of cases, some of which might be initiating a configuration backup when a configuration change is detected, or starting a service that has died. We will set up the latter scenario.

Navigate to **Configuration | Actions**, click on **Create action**. In the **Name** field, enter Restart Apache. Switch to the **Conditions** tab and in the **New condition** block choose **Host** in the first dropdown and start typing another. In the dropdown that appears, click on **Another host**. Click on **Add** control (but do not click on the **Add** button yet).

Let's create another condition—in the **New condition** block, in the first dropdown, choose **Trigger name**. Leave the second dropdown at the default value. In the input field next to this, enter Web service is down, then click on **Add** control. The end result should look as follows:

Conditions	LABEL	NAME	ACTION
	A	Maintenance status not in *maintenance*	Remove
	B	Trigger value = *PROBLEM*	Remove
	C	Host = *Another host*	Remove
	D	Trigger name like *Web service is down*	Remove

Now switch to the **Operations** tab. In the **Action operations** block, click on **New**. In the **Operation details** block that just appeared, choose **Remote command** in the **Operation type** field. Zabbix offers five different types of remote command:

- Custom script
- IPMI
- SSH
- Telnet
- Global script

We will discuss SSH and telnet items in *Chapter 10, Advanced Item Monitoring*. We will discuss IPMI functionality in *Chapter 13, Monitoring IPMI Devices*. Global scripts will be covered later in this chapter—and right now let's look at the custom script functionality.

For custom scripts, one may choose to run them either on the Zabbix agent or the Zabbix server. Running on the agent will allow us to gather information, control services, and do other tasks on the system where problem conditions were found. Running on the server will allow us to probe the system from the Zabbix server's perspective, or maybe access the Zabbix API and take further decisions based on that information.

> The interface here can be quite confusing and there may be several buttons or links with the same name visible at the same time – for example, there will be three different things called **Add**. Be very careful which control you click on.

For now, we will create an action that will try to restart the Apache webserver if it is down. Normally, that has to be done on the host that had the problem. In the **Target list** section, click on the **New** link. The dropdown there will have **Current host** selected, which is exactly what we wanted, so click on the **Add** control just below it.

In the **Commands** textbox, enter the following:

```
sudo /etc/init.d/apache2 restart
```

> This step and the steps that come later assume the existence and usability of the /etc/init.d/apache2 init script. If your distribution has a different control script, use the path to it instead. If your distribution uses systemd exclusively, you will probably have to use a command such as /usr/bin/systemctl restart apache2 or /usr/bin/systemctl restart httpd.service. Note that the name of the service can be different, too.

We are restarting Apache just in case it has stopped responding, instead of simply dying. You can also enter many remote actions to be performed, but we won't do that now, so just click on the **Add** control at the bottom of the **Operation details** block. To save our new action, click on the **Add** button at the bottom.

> When running remote commands, the Zabbix agent accepts the command and immediately returns 1 – there is no way for the server to know how long the command took, or even whether it was run at all. Note that the remote commands on the agent are run without timeout.

Our remote command is almost ready to run, except on the agent side there's still some work to be done, so open zabbix_agentd.conf as root and look for the EnableRemoteCommands parameter. Set it to 1 and uncomment it, save the config file, and restart zabbix_agentd.

That's still not all. As remote commands are passed to the Zabbix agent daemon, which is running as a zabbix user, we also have to allow this user to actually restart Apache. As evidenced by the remote command, we will use sudo for this, so edit /etc/sudoers on Another host as root and add the following line:

```
zabbix  ALL=NOPASSWD: /etc/init.d/apache2 restart
```

> For additional safety measures, use the visudo command – it should also check your changes for syntax validity.

> On some systems, sudo is only configured to be used interactively. You might have to comment the requiretty option in /etc/sudoers.

Again, change the script name if you need a different one. This allows the zabbix user to use sudo and restart the Apache web server—just restart it, don't stop or do any other operations.

> Make sure the SMTP server is running on Another host, otherwise the web service trigger will not be triggered as we had a dependency on the SMTP trigger. Alternatively, remove that dependency.

Now we are ready for the show. Stop the web server on Another host. Wait for the trigger to update its state and check the web server's status. It should start again automatically.

> By default, all actions get two conditions. One of them limits the action to fire only when the trigger goes into the **PROBLEM** state, but not when it comes back to the **OK** state. For this action, it is a very helpful setting; otherwise the webserver would be restarted once when it was found to be down, and then restarted again when it was found to be up. Such a configuration mistake would not be obvious, so it might stay undetected for a while. One should also avoid enabling recovery messages for an action that restarts a service.

Note that remote commands on agents only work with passive agents—they will not work in active mode. This does not mean that you cannot use active items on such a host—you may do this, but remote commands will always be attempted in passive mode by the server connected directly to that agent. There might be a situation where all items are active and thus a change in configuration that prevents server-to-agent connection from working is not noticed—and then the remote command fails to work. If you have all items active and want to use remote commands, it might be worth having a single passive item to check whether that type of item still works.

While the need to restart services like this indicates a problem that would be best fixed for the service itself, sometimes it can work as an emergency solution, or in the case of an unresponsive proprietary software vendor.

Global scripts

Looking at values and graphs on the frontend is nice and useful, but there are cases when extra information might be needed right away, or there might be a need to manually invoke an action, such as starting an upgrade process, rebooting the system, or performing some other administrative task. Zabbix allows us to execute commands directly from the frontend—this feature is called **global scripts**. Let's see what is available out of the box—navigate to **Monitoring | Events** and click on the host name in any of the entries:

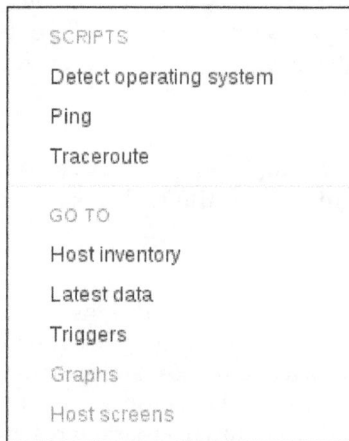

```
SCRIPTS

Detect operating system

Ping

Traceroute

GO TO

Host inventory

Latest data

Triggers

Graphs

Host screens
```

The second part of this menu has convenience links to various sections in the frontend. The first part, labeled **SCRIPTS**, is what we are after. Currently, Zabbix ships with three preconfigured scripts—operating system detection, ping, and traceroute. We will discuss them in a bit more detail later, but for now just click on **Ping**. A pop-up window will open with the output of this script:

```
PING 192.168.56.11 (192.168.56.11) 56(84) bytes of data.
64 bytes from 192.168.56.11: icmp_seq=1 ttl=64 time=0.293 ms
64 bytes from 192.168.56.11: icmp_seq=2 ttl=64 time=0.268 ms
64 bytes from 192.168.56.11: icmp_seq=3 ttl=64 time=0.363 ms

--- 192.168.56.11 ping statistics ---
3 packets transmitted, 3 received, 0% packet loss, time 1998ms
rtt min/avg/max/mdev = 0.268/0.308/0.363/0.040 ms
```

Notice the slight delay—the target host was pinged three times, and we had to wait for that to finish to get the output.

Global scripts are available by clicking on the host in several locations in the frontend from such a context menu. These locations are as follows:

- **Monitoring | Dashboard** (in the **Last 20 issues** widget)
- **Monitoring | Overview** (when hosts are located on the left-hand side)
- **Monitoring | Latest data** (when showing data from more than one host)
- **Monitoring | Triggers**
- **Monitoring | Events**
- **Monitoring | Maps**
- **Inventory | Hosts**, where clicking on the **Host name** will open the inventory overview
- **Reports | Triggers top 100**

Calling those three scripts **preconfigured** hinted at an ability to configure our own. Let's do just that.

Configuring global scripts

We can start by examining the existing scripts. Navigate to **Administration | Scripts**:

NAME ▲	TYPE	EXECUTE ON	COMMANDS	USER GROUP	HOST GROUP	HOST ACCESS
Detect operating system	Script	Server	sudo /usr/bin/nmap -O {HOST.CONN} 2>&1	Zabbix administrators	All	Read
Ping	Script	Server	/bin/ping -c 3 {HOST.CONN} 2>&1	All	All	Read
Traceroute	Script	Server	/usr/bin/traceroute {HOST.CONN} 2>&1	All	All	Read

The same three scripts we saw in the menu can be seen here. Let's see what they do:

- **Detect operating system**: This script calls `nmap` and relies on `sudo`
- **Ping**: Uses the `ping` utility, and pings the host three times
- **Traceroute**: Calls the `traceroute` utility against the host

These three scripts are all are executed on the Zabbix server, so they should work for any host—a server with a Zabbix agent, a switch, a storage device, and so on.

> Zabbix versions before 3.0 discarded `stderr` by default. If you see global scripts redirecting `stderr` to `stdout` by appending `2>&1` after the script command, it was a very important thing to configure in those versions, because otherwise, error messages from scripts would be silently lost. It is not required anymore since Zabbix 3.0, but it does not do any harm either.

We will discuss other options in a moment, but for now let's see whether all of these scripts work. Ping should work for most people. Traceroute will require the `traceroute` utility installed. As for operating system detection, it is unlikely to work for you out of the box. Let's try and make that one work.

> If Zabbix administrators are not supposed to gain `root` shell access to the Zabbix server, do not configure `sudo` as shown here. There's a feature in `nmap` that allows the execution of commands. Instead, create a wrapper script that only allows the `-O` parameter with a single argument.

Start by making sure `nmap` is installed on the Zabbix server. As the script uses `sudo`, edit `/etc/sudoers` (or use `visudo`) and add a line like this:

```
zabbix  ALL=NOPASSWD: /usr/bin/nmap
```

> In distribution packages, Zabbix server might run as the `zabbixs` or `zabbixsrv` user instead—use that username in the `sudoers` configuration.

Adapt the `nmap` path if necessary. Similar to restarting the Apache web server, you might have to uncomment the `requiretty` option in `/etc/sudoers`. Again, all of these changes have to be done on the Zabbix server. When finished, run the operating system detection script from the menu—use one of the locations mentioned earlier:

```
Starting Nmap 6.40 ( http://nmap.org ) at 2016-04-16 02:27 EEST
Nmap scan report for 192.168.56.11
Host is up (0.00042s latency).
Not shown: 996 filtered ports
PORT    STATE  SERVICE
22/tcp  open   ssh
25/tcp  open   smtp
80/tcp  open   http
443/tcp closed https
MAC Address: 08:00:27:DD:4E:9E (Cadmus Computer Systems)
Aggressive OS guesses: Netgear DG834G WAP or Western Digital WD TV media player (94%), Linux 2.6.32 (94%), Linux 2.6.32 - 3.9 (93%),
Crestron XPanel control system (93%), Linux 2.6.31 (92%), Linux 3.0 (92%), Linux 3.1 (90%), Linux 3.2 (90%), Linux 2.6.32 - 2.6.35
(90%), Linux 2.6.32 - 3.2 (90%)
No exact OS matches for host (test conditions non-ideal).
Network Distance: 1 hop

OS detection performed. Please report any incorrect results at http://nmap.org/submit/ .
Nmap done: 1 IP address (1 host up) scanned in 8.55 seconds
```

> The SELinux security framework may prevent global scripts from working.

Hooray, that worked! The nmap command took some time to run. When running global scripts on the agent, they obey the same timeout as the remote commands discussed earlier in this chapter. This script was run on the server. In this case, there's a 60-second timeout in the frontend.

Now on to examining other script options, and also configuring some scripts of our own. When there's a problem on a system, it might be resource starvation. We might want to find out which processes on a system are stressing the CPU the most. Navigate back to **Administration | Scripts** and click on **Create script**. For our first script, fill in the following:

* **Name**: Top CPU using processes
* **Commands**: top -n 1 -b | grep -A 10 "^[ ]*PID"

Name	Top CPU using processes
Type	Script
Execute on	Zabbix agent Zabbix server
Commands	top -n 1 -b	grep -A 10 "^[]*PID"

> Zabbix versions 3.0.0 and 3.0.1 have a bug—there's another **Command** field below the **Commands** field. Just ignore the second field. It is hoped that this bug will be fixed in later versions.

When done, click on **Add**. For the top command, we told it to only print the process list and do so once only. Then we grabbed the header line and the next 10 lines after it—assuming the header line starts with any amount of spaces and a string `PID`.

> We enabled remote commands on `Another host` earlier—if you skipped that, make sure to enable them before proceeding.

Navigate to **Monitoring | Events**, click on **Another host** in the **HOST** column, and choose **Top CPU using processes**.

You may use any other location where this context menu is available—we listed these locations earlier:

```
PID USER       PR  NI    VIRT    RES    SHR S  %CPU  %MEM    TIME+ COMMAND
  1 root       20   0  129216   3536   2076 S 0,000 1,444   0:04.24 systemd
  2 root       20   0       0      0      0 S 0,000 0,000   0:00.04 kthreadd
  3 root       20   0       0      0      0 S 0,000 0,000   0:03.39 ksoftirqd+
  5 root        0 -20       0      0      0 S 0,000 0,000   0:00.00 kworker/0+
  6 root       20   0       0      0      0 S 0,000 0,000   0:03.32 kworker/u+
  7 root       rt   0       0      0      0 S 0,000 0,000   0:00.00 migration+
  8 root       20   0       0      0      0 S 0,000 0,000   0:00.00 rcu_bh
  9 root       20   0       0      0      0 S 0,000 0,000   0:00.00 rcuob/0
 10 root       20   0       0      0      0 S 0,000 0,000   0:08.40 rcu_sched
 11 root       20   0       0      0      0 S 0,000 0,000   0:25.93 rcuos/0
```

In this specific case, the `systemd` process is using most of the CPU. The Zabbix agent, which is running on this system, is not even in the top 10 here. Well, to be fair, on this system nothing much is happening anyway—all of the processes are reported to use no CPU at all.

Other similar diagnostic commands might show some package details, **Media Access Control (MAC)** addresses, or any other information easily obtained from standard utilities. Note that getting a list of processes that use the most memory is not possible with `top` on most operating systems or distributions— the `ps` command will probably have to be used. The following code might provide a useful list of the top 10 memory-using processes:

```
ps auxw --sort -rss | head -n 11
```

We are grabbing the top 11 lines here because that also includes the header.

Now let's configure another script—one that would allow us to reboot the target system. Navigate to **Administration | Scripts** and click on **Create script**. Fill in the following:

- **Name**: Management/Reboot.

- **Commands**: reboot.

- **User group**: This command is a bit riskier, so we will limit its use to administrative users only—choose **Zabbix administrators**.

- **Host group**: As this would not work on SNMP devices, it would not make sense to make it show up for hosts other than Linux systems here—choose **Selected** and start typing Linux in the text field. Choose **Linux servers** in the dropdown.

- **Required host permissions**: We wouldn't want users with read-only access to be able to reboot hosts, so choose **Write**.

- **Enable confirmation**: This is a potentially destructive action, so mark this checkbox.

- **Confirmation text**: With the previous checkbox marked, we may fill in this field. Type Reboot this system?

> Even though the group selection field might look similar to other places where multiple groups can be selected, here only one host group may be selected.

We may also test what this confirmation message would look like—click on **Test confirmation**:

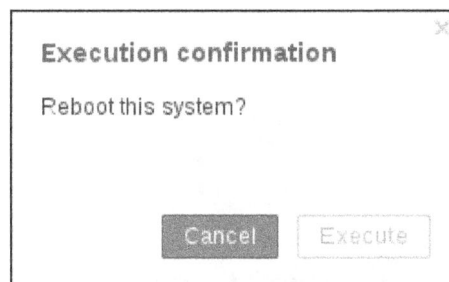

Execution confirmation

Reboot this system?

Cancel Execute

While the **Execute** button is disabled right now, we can see that this would look fairly understandable. Click on **Cancel** in the confirmation dialog. The final result should look like this—if it does, click on the **Add** button at the bottom:

Name	Management/Reboot
Type	Script ▼
Execute on	Zabbix agent Zabbix server
Commands	reboot
Command	
Description	
User group	Zabbix administrators ▼
Host group	Selected ▼
	Linux servers ✕ Select
Required host permissions	Write ▼
Enable confirmation	▣
Confirmation text	Reboot this system? Test confirmation
	Add Cancel

Now let's see what this script would look like in the menu—navigate to **Monitoring | Events** and click on **Another host** in the **HOST** column. In the pop-up menu, move the mouse cursor over the entry **Management**:

Notice how the syntax we used created a submenu — the slash is used as a separator. We could group **Ping**, **Traceroute**, and **Top CPU using processes** as **Diagnostics**, add more entries in the **Management** section, and create a useful toolset. Note that we can also use zabbix_get on the server here and poll individual items that we might not want to monitor constantly. Entries can be nested this way as many times as needed, but beware of creating too many levels. Such mouseover menus are hard to use beyond the first few levels, as it is too easy to make a wrong move and suddenly all submenus are closed.

Regarding the **Reboot** entry, if it seemed a bit risky to add, fear not — it does not work anyway. First, we had to use sudo for it in the command. Second, we had to configure sudoers to actually allow the running of that command by the zabbix user.

Reusing global scripts in actions

Some of the global scripts added this way only make sense when used interactively — most of the data gathering or diagnostic ones would probably fall under this category. But our **Reboot** entry might be reused in action operations, too. Instead of configuring such commands individually in global scripts and each action, we would have a single place to control how the rebooting happens. Maybe we want to change the reboot command to issue a pending reboot in 10 minutes. That way a system administrator who might be working on the system has some time to cancel the reboot and investigate the problem in more detail.

We already have the global script for rebooting created. If we had a trigger that warranted rebooting the whole system, we would create an action with appropriate conditions. In the action properties, global scripts may be reused by choosing **Remote command** in the **Operation type** dropdown when editing an operation. Then, in the **Type** dropdown, **Global script** must be selected and a specific script chosen:

Operation type	Remote command ▾	
	TARGET	ACTION
	New	
Target list		
Type	Global script ▾	
Script name	Management/Reboot	Select

As these scripts can be used both from the frontend and in actions, they're not called just **frontend scripts** — they are **global scripts**.

Summary

We started this chapter by discussing actions. Actions are the things controlling what is performed when a trigger fires, and they have a very wide range of things to configure at various levels, including conditions of various precision, message contents, and actual operations performed — starting with simple e-mail sending and using custom scripts, and ending with the powerful remote command execution. We also learned about other things affecting actions, such as user media configuration and user permissions.

Let's refresh our memory on what alerting-related concepts there are:

- **Trigger** is a problem definition including a severity level, with the trigger expression containing information on calculations and thresholds
- **Event** is something happening — that is, a trigger changing state from **PROBLEM** to **OK** and so on
- **Action** is a configuration entity, with specific sets of conditions that determine when it is invoked and the operations to be performed
- **Operation** is an action property that defined what to do if this action is invoked, and escalations were configured with the help of operations
- **Alert** or notification is the actual thing sent out — e-mail, SMS, or any other message

In addition to simple one-time messages, we also figured out how the built-in escalations work in Zabbix, and escalated a few problems. While escalations allow us to produce fairly complex response scenarios, it is important to pay attention when configuring them. Once enabled, they allow us to perform different operations, based on how much time has passed since the problem occurred, and other factors. We discussed common issues with notifications, including the fact that users must have permission to view a host to receive notifications about it, and recovery messages only being sent to the users that got the original problem message.

By now we have learned of three ways to avoid trigger flapping, resulting in excessive notifications:

- By using trigger expression functions such as min(), max(), and avg() to fire a trigger only if the values have been within a specific range for a defined period of time

- By using hysteresis and only returning to the **OK** state if the current value is some comfort distance below (or above) the threshold

- By creating escalations that skip the first few steps, thus only sending out messages if a problem has not been resolved for some time

The first two methods are different from the last one. Using different trigger functions and hysteresis changes the way the trigger works, impacting how soon it fires and how soon it turns off again. With escalations, we do not affect the trigger's behavior (thus they will still show up in **Monitoring | Triggers** and other locations), but we introduce delayed notification whenever a trigger fires.

And finally, we figured out what global scripts are and tried manually pinging a host and obtaining a list of the top CPU-using processes on it. As for action operations, we discussed several ways to react to a problem:

- Sending an e-mail
- Running a command (executed either on the Zabbix agent or server)
- Running an IPMI command
- Running a command over SSH or telnet
- Reusing a global script

The last one allowed us to configure a script once and potentially reconfigure it for all systems in a single location.

When configuring triggers and actions, there are several little things that can both make life easier and introduce hard-to-spot problems. Hopefully, the coverage of the basics here will help you to leverage the former and avoid the latter.

In the next chapter, we will see how to avoid configuring some of the things we already know, including items and triggers, on each host individually. We will use templates to manage such configurations on multiple hosts easily.

8
Simplifying Complex Configurations with Templates

Our current setup has two hosts with similar enough environments, so we copied items from one over to another. But what do we do when there are a lot of hosts with similar parameters to monitor? Copying items manually is quite tedious. It's even worse when something has to be changed for all the hosts, such as an item interval or a process name. Luckily, Zabbix provides a means to configure these things in a unified fashion with the templating system.

Identifying template candidates

Templates allow a Zabbix administrator to reduce their workload and streamline the configuration. But to deploy the templates properly we have to first identify use cases that require or benefit from them. Or, to put it short—we have to identify what templates in Zabbix actually are.

When we created the second monitored Linux host, we manually copied items from the first host. If we wish, we can also copy over triggers. Such copying around isn't the best job ever, so instead we can create items and triggers for a template, which are then linked to the host in question. As a result of the linkage, the host immediately gets all the items and triggers defined in the template. Later, when we want to change some item parameters for all the hosts, we only have to do it once. Changes made to the template propagate to the linked hosts. So templates make the most sense for items and triggers that you want to have on multiple hosts, such as those Linux machines. Even if you have only a single device of a certain class, it might be worth creating a template for it in case new devices appear that could benefit from the same configuration.

For example, if we had **Apache httpd** and **MySQL** running on a host, we could split all items and triggers that are relevant for each of these services in to separate templates:

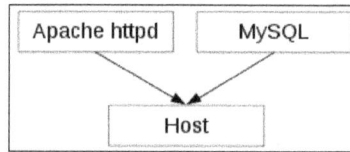

Modifying an item in the **MySQL** template would propagate those changes downstream in the **Host**. Adding more hosts would be simple — we would just link them to the appropriate templates. Making a change in the template would apply that change to all the downstream hosts.

While the snmptraps host we created seems like a good candidate for directly created objects, we could have a situation where SNMP agents send in traps that are properly distributed between configured hosts in Zabbix, but every now and then a device would send in a trap that wouldn't have a host or corresponding SNMP item configured. If we still wanted traps like that to get sorted in corresponding items in our generic trap host, we would again use templates to create such items for corresponding hosts and our generic host.

Templates are a valuable tool in Zabbix configuration. That all sounds a bit dry, though, so let's set up some actual templates.

Creating a template

Open **Configuration | Templates**. As we can see, there are already 38 predefined templates. We will create our own specialized one though; click on **Create template**. This opens a simple form that we have to fill in:

- **Template name**: C_Template_Linux
- **New group**: Custom templates

| Template name | C_Template_Linux |
| Visible name | |

Groups In groups   Other groups

	Discovered hosts
	Hypervisors
	Important SNMP hosts
◄	Linux servers
	SNMP devices
	Templates
►	Test group
	Virtual machines
	Zabbix servers

New group   Custom templates

The c_ at the front of the name stand for "**Custom**". We are also creating a new group to hold our templates in, and instead of going through the group configuration we use the shortcut for group creation on this form. When you are done, click on **Add**.

We now have the template, but it has no use—there are no items or triggers in it. Go to **Configuration | Hosts**, where we will use a lazy and quick solution—we will copy existing items and triggers into the new template. Select **Linux servers** in the **Group** dropdown, then click on **Items** next to **Another host**. Mark all items by clicking in the checkbox in the header and click on the **Copy** button at the bottom.

> Remember, to select a sequential subset of checkboxes you can use range selection—select the first checkbox for the range, hold down *Shift* and click on the last checkbox for the range.

In the next screen, choose **Templates** in the **Target type** dropdown and **Custom templates** in the **Group** dropdown. That leaves us with single entry, so mark the checkbox next to **C_Template_Linux** in the **Target** section:

Target type	Templates ▼
Group	Custom templates ▼
Target	☐ C_Template_Linux
	Copy Cancel

When you are done, click on **Copy**. All items should be successfully copied.

> In this case, the destination template did not have any items configured. As it is not possible to have two items for a single host with the same key, attempting to copy over an already existing item would fail.

In the upper left corner, click on the **Details** link. That expands the messages, and we can see that all of these items were added to the target template:

Details	Items copied
— Created: Item "Web server status" on "C_Template_Linux".	
— Created: Item "SSH server status" on "C_Template_Linux".	

Now we have to do the same with triggers, so click on **Triggers** in the navigation bar above the item list, then click the checkbox in the header. This time uncheck the **One SSH service is down**, because this trigger spans both hosts. If we copied this trigger to the template, that would create all kinds of weird effects.

> The sequence here, copying items first, then triggers, was important. A trigger cannot be created if an item it references is missing, so attempting to copy triggers first would have failed. Copying a trigger will not attempt to copy the items the trigger is referencing.

Again, click on the **Copy** button at the bottom. In the next screen, choose **Templates** in the **Target type** dropdown and **Custom templates** in the **Group** dropdown. Mark the checkbox next to **C_Template_Linux** in the **Target** section, then click on **Copy**. All triggers should be successfully copied. Of course, we don't have to create a host first, create entities on it, then copy them to a template — when creating a fresh template, you'll want to create entities on the template directly. If you have been less careful and haven't thought about templating beforehand, copying like this is a nice way to create the template more quickly.

Linking templates to hosts

Now we'd like to link this template to our very first host, "A test host". First, let's compare item lists between the freshly created template and that host. Open **Configuration | Hosts** in one browser window or tab and **Configuration | Templates** in another. In the first, choose **Linux servers** in the **Group** dropdown, then click on **Items** next to **A test host**. In the other one, select **Custom templates** in the **Group** dropdown, then click on **Items** next to **C_Template_Linux**. Place the windows next to each other and compare the listings:

NAME ▲	TRIGGERS	KEY	NAME ▲	TRIGGERS	KEY
CPU load	Triggers 1	system.cpu.load	CPU load		system.cpu.load
Full OS name		system.uname	Experimental SNMP trap		netSnmpExperimental2
ICMP ping performance		icmppingsec	ICMP ping performance		icmppingsec
Incoming traffic on interface lo		net.if.in[lo]	Incoming traffic on interface enp0s8		net.if.in[enp0s8]
Incoming traffic on interface enp0s8		net.if.in[enp0s8]	Incoming traffic on interface lo		net.if.in[lo]
SMTP server status	Triggers 1	net.tcp.service[smtp]	Local time	Triggers 1	system.localtime
SNMP trap fallback	Triggers 1	snmptrap.fallback	SMTP server status	Triggers 1	net.tcp.service[smtp]
SNMP trap tests		snmptrap[test]	SNMP trap fallback		snmptrap.fallback
SSH server status	Triggers 1	net.tcp.service[ssh]	snmptraps	Triggers 1	snmptraps2
Web server status	Triggers 1	net.tcp.service[http,,80]	SNMP trap tests		snmptrap[test]
Zabbix agent version		agent.version	SSH server status		net.tcp.service[ssh]
			Testfile exists	Triggers 1	vfs.file.exists[/tmp/testfile]
			Web server status	Triggers 1	net.tcp.service[http,,80]
			Zabbix agent version		agent.version

We can see here that the template has three more items than the host. Looking at the lists, we can see that the items available on the template but not the host, are both SNMP related items that we added later — **Experimental SNMP trap** and **snmptraps**, the time item **Local time**, and also the check for a file, **Testfile exists**. If the template has four items the host is missing, but in total it only has three items more, that means the host should have one item that the template doesn't — that's right, the **Full OS name** exists for the host but is missing in the template. Keeping that in mind, and return to **Configuration | Hosts**.

Make sure the **Group** dropdown says either **all** or **Linux servers** and click on **A test host** in the **NAME** column. We finally get to use the **Templates** tab—switch to it. Start typing c in the **Link new templates input** field. In the dropdown, our new template, **C_Template_Linux**, should be the very first one—click on it. Even though it might seem that this template is now added, it actually is not—if we would update the host now, it would not be linked:

Link new templates		
C_Template_Linux ✕		Select
type here to search		
Add		

Click on the **Add** control just below the template name. This form can be highly confusing, so try to remember that you have to do that extra click here. With the template added to the list, notice that it's actually a link. Clicking it will open template properties in a new window. When looking at host properties, this offers quick access to template properties. Such convenient links are available in many places in the Zabbix frontend:

Linked templates	NAME	ACTION
	C_Template_Linux	Unlink

In the end, click on the **Update** button at the bottom. Let's find out what this operation did—click on the **Details** link in the upper-left corner. In the expanded **Details** panel, we can see the operations that took place. In this case, some items were created and some were updated:

Details	Host updated
— Created: Item "Experimental SNMP trap" on "A test host".	
— Created: Item "snmptraps" on "A test host".	
— Created: Item "Local time" on "A test host".	
— Created: Item "Testfile exists" on "A test host".	
— Updated: Item "CPU load" on "A test host".	
— Updated: Item "Web server status" on "A test host".	

> When a template is linked to a host, identical entities that already exist on the host are linked against the template, but no historical data is lost. Entities that exist on the template only are added to the host and linked to the template.

Scrolling down a bit further, you'll be able to see that, same thing happened with triggers:

```
– Updated: Trigger "Web service is down" on "A test host".
– Updated: Trigger "SMTP service is down" on "A test host".
– Created: Trigger "SNMP trap has arrived on {HOST.NAME}" on "A test host".
```

Now this all seems like quite a lot of work for nothing, but if we had to add more hosts with the same items and triggers, without templates each host would require tedious manual copying, which is quite error-prone. With templates all we have to do is link the template to the freshly added host and all the entities are there automatically.

> Do not confuse templates for host groups. They are completely different things. Groups serve for a logical host grouping (and permission assigning), but templates define what is monitored on a host, what graphs it has, and so on. What's more, a single host group can contain both ordinary hosts and templates. Adding a template to a group will not affect hosts in that group in any way, only linking that template will. Think of groups as a way to organize the templates the same way as hosts are organized.

Now we could check out how linked items appear in the configuration. Open **Configuration | Hosts,** click on **Items** next to **A test host:**

NAME ▲	TRIGGERS	KEY
C_Template_Linux: CPU load	Triggers 1	system.cpu.load
C_Template_Linux: Experimental SNMP trap		netSnmpExperimental2
Full OS name		system.uname
C_Template_Linux: ICMP ping performance		icmppingsec

There are two observations we can make right away. First, almost all items are prefixed with a template name (**C_Template_Linux** in this case), in grey text. Obviously, this indicates items that are linked from the template. Clicking on the template name would open an item listing for that template.

Second, a single item is not prefixed like that—**Full OS name**. Remember, that was the only item existing for the host, but not for the template? If entities exist on the host only, linking does not do anything to them—they are left intact and attached to the host directly.

Let's see what a linked item looks like—click on **SMTP server status** in the **NAME** column:

Parent items	C_Template_Linux
Name	SMTP server status
Type	Simple check
Key	net.tcp.service[smtp]
Host interface	127.0.0.1 : 10050 ▼
User name	
Password	
Type of information	Numeric (unsigned)
Data type	Decimal
Units	

Hey, what happened? Why are most fields grayed out and can't be edited? Well, that's what a template is about. Most of the entity (in this case, item) parameters are configured in the template. As we can see, some fields are still editable. This means that we still can disable or enable items per individual host even when they are linked in from a template. The same goes for the update interval, history length, and a few other parameters.

We now want to make this particular item for this host slightly different from all other hosts that the template will be linked to, so let's change these things:

- **Update interval**: 360
- **History storage period**: 60

When you are done, click on **Update**. Now this host will have two parameters for a single item customized, while all other hosts that will get linked against the template will receive values from the template. Let's link one more host to our template now. Navigate to **Configuration | Templates**. Here we can see a full list of templates along with the hosts linked to them. The linkage area in this screen shows various entries and listed entities there have different color:

TEMPLATES ▲	APPLICATIONS	ITEMS	TRIGGERS	GRAPHS	SCREENS	DISCOVERY	WEB	LINKED TEMPLATES	LINKED TO
C_Template_Linux	Applications	Items 14	Triggers 5	Graphs	Screens	Discovery	Web		A test host
Template App LDAP Service	Applications 1	Items 1	Triggers 1	Graphs	Screens	Discovery	Web		
Template App MySQL	Applications 1	Items 14	Triggers 1	Graphs 2	Screens 1	Discovery	Web		Zabbix server

- **Gray**: Templates
- **Blue**: Enabled hosts
- **Red**: Disabled hosts

Click on **C_Template_Linux** in the **TEMPLATES** column. That provides us with a form where multiple hosts can be easily linked against the current template or unlinked from it. In this case we want to link a single host. In the **Hosts | Templates** section, choose **Linux servers** in the **Other | Group** dropdown, mark **Another host** in that box and click on the ◄ button:

In	Other	group	Linux servers ▼
A test host Another host			

Multi-select in the **Hosts | Templates** section now has two hosts that will be linked against the current template. Click on **Update**. You can expand the **Details** section to see what exactly was done. As we already copied all elements from **Another host** to the template beforehand, linking this host against the template did not create new items or triggers, it only updated them all. Looking at the template list, we can see two hosts linked against our template.

Move your mouse cursor over the hostnames in the template table—notice how they are actually links. Clicking them would open host properties to verify or change something, such as quickly disabling a host or updating its IP address:

TEMPLATES ▲	APPLICATIONS	ITEMS	TRIGGERS	GRAPHS	SCREENS	DISCOVERY	WEB	LINKED TEMPLATES	LINKED TO
C_Template_Linux	Applications	Items 14	Triggers 5	Graphs	Screens	Discovery	Web		Another host, A test host

Handling default templates

In the list, you can see many predefined templates. Should you use them as-is? Should you modify them? Or just use them as a reference?

It depends. Carefully evaluate the default templates and decide whether you really want to use them as-is—maybe item intervals are too low or the history storage period is too high? If there's anything you would like to change, the suggested approach is to clone those templates and leave the defaults as-is. That will allow you to update the official templates later and always have the latest version for reference.

Regarding keeping them in sync, the easiest way is XML import and we will discuss that in *Chapter 21, Working Closely with Data*.

And talking about community supplied templates—for many of those you will want to improve them. The user who supplied the template might have had completely different requirements, they might have misunderstood some aspect of Zabbix configuration or handled an older device that does not expose as much data as the one you are monitoring. Always evaluate such templates very carefully and don't hesitate to improve them.

Changing the configuration in a template

Now we could try changing an item that is attached to the template. Open
Configuration | Templates, select **Custom templates** from the **Group** dropdown
and click on **Items** next to **C_Template_Linux**, then click on **SMTP server status**
in the **NAME** column. As we can see, all fields are editable when we edit a directly
attached instance of an item. Change the **History storage period** field to read 14,
then click on **Update**. Expand the **Details** area at the top of the page to see what
got changed:

Details   Item updated

 - Updated: Item "SMTP server status" on "C_Template_Linux".

 - Updated: Item "SMTP server status" on "Another host".

 - Updated: Item "SMTP server status" on "A test host".

This reinforces the principle one more time—when an item is updated in a template,
the change is propagated to all linked hosts. This means that with a single action
both linked hosts have their history keeping period set to 14 days now. But we
changed two item properties for one downstream host before, and we just changed
one of those for the upstream template. What about down-streaming the host's other
item? Let's find out. Go to **Configuration | Hosts**, choose **Linux servers** in the **Group**
dropdown and click on **Items** next to **A test host**. In the **NAME** column, click on
SMTP server status:

Update interval (in sec)	360			
Custom intervals	TYPE	INTERVAL	PERIOD	ACTION
	Flexible Scheduling	50	1-7,00:00-24:00	Remove
	Add			
History storage period (in days)	14			

We can see that our downstream change for **Update interval** has been preserved,
but the **History storage period** value has been overwritten with the one set for
the template. That's because only changed properties are set to downstream when
editing template attached items. Now click on **Cancel**.

Macro usage

We previously added triggers from **Another host** to our template, but we didn't do that for A test host. Let's find out whether it has some triggers we could use in the template. Click on **Triggers** in the **Navigation** bar above the **Items** list. From the directly attached triggers in the list (the ones not prefixed with a template name), one is a trigger that takes into account items from two different hosts and we avoided copying it over before. The other directly attached triggers are the ones that we are interested in. Mark the checkboxes next to the **CPU load too high on A test host for last 3 minutes** and **Critical error from SNMP trap** triggers in the **NAME** column, then click on the **Copy** button at the bottom. In the next window, choose **Templates** in the **Target type** dropdown, **Custom templates** in the **Group** dropdown, then mark the checkbox next to the only remaining target (**C_Template_Linux**) and click on **Copy**. This time our copying had a bit more interesting effect, so let's expand the **Details** box again:

Details	Trigger added
— Created: Trigger "CPU load too high on A test host for last 3 minutes" on "C_Template_Linux".	
— Updated: Trigger "CPU load too high on A test host for last 3 minutes" on "A test host".	
— Created: Trigger "CPU load too high on A test host for last 3 minutes" on "Another host".	
— Created: Trigger "Critical error from SNMP trap" on "C_Template_Linux".	
— Updated: Trigger "Critical error from SNMP trap" on "A test host".	
— Created: Trigger "Critical error from SNMP trap" on "Another host".	

Two triggers we copied are added to the template. This causes the following:

- As A test host is linked to the modified template and it already has such triggers, these two triggers for that host are updated to reflect the linkage

- Another host does not have such triggers, so the triggers are created and linked to the template

While we are still in the trigger list, select **Another host** in the **Host** dropdown. Look carefully at the CPU load trigger that was added to this host in the previous operation:

NAME ▲
C_Template_Linux: CPU load too high on A test host for last 3 minutes

Wait, that's definitely incorrect. The trigger refers to A test host, while this is Another host. The trigger name was correct when we first added it, but now the same trigger is applied to multiple hosts. In turn, the reference is incorrect for all the hosts except one. Let's try to fix this. Select **Custom templates** in the **Group** dropdown, then click on the **CPU load too high on A test host for last 3 minutes** trigger in the **NAME** column. Change the **Name** field to CPU load too high on {HOST.NAME} for last 3 minutes.

Yes, that's right, macros to the rescue again.

> The use of the word macros can be confusing here—Zabbix calls them macros, although they might be more correctly considered to be variables. In this book, we will follow Zabbix terminology, but feel free to read macro as variable.

Now click on **Update**. In the trigger list for the template, the trigger name has now changed to **CPU load too high on {HOST.NAME} for last 3 minutes**. That's not very descriptive, but you can expect to see such a situation in the configuration section fairly often—Zabbix does not expand most macros in configuration. To verify that it is resolving as expected, navigate to **Monitoring | Triggers** and expand the filter. Set the **Triggers status** dropdown to **Any** and enter CPU in the **Filter by name** field, then click on the **Filter** button below the filter:

HOST	NAME
A test host	CPU load too high on A test host for last 3 minutes
Another host	CPU load too high on Another host for last 3 minutes

Notice how the trigger name includes the correct hostname now. In most cases, it is suggested to include a macro such as this in trigger names to easily identify the affected host.

The macro we used here, {HOST.NAME}, resolves to the host's visible name. We had no visible name specified and the hostname was used. If a host had the visible name defined, we could also choose to use the hostname with a macro {HOST.HOST}.

User macros

The macros we used before are built-in. Zabbix also allows users to define macros and use them later. In this case it might be even more important to call them variables instead, so consider using that term in parallel. Let's start with a practical application of a user macro and discuss the details a bit later.

Go to **Configuration | Templates** and click on **C_Template_Linux** in the **TEMPLATES** column. Switch to the **Macros** tab and add one new macro:

- **MACRO**: {$CPU_LOAD_THRESHOLD}
- **VALUE**: 1

Template	Linked templates	Macros		
	Template macros	Inherited and template macros		
MACRO			VALUE	
{$CPU_LOAD_THRESHOLD}		⇒	1	Remove
Add				
Update	Clone	Full clone	Delete	Delete and clear	Cancel

When done, click on **Update**. We have defined one macro on the template, but it is not used at this time. Click on **Triggers** next to **C_Template_Linux**, then click on **CPU load too high on {HOST.NAME} for last 3 minutes** in the **NAME** column. Change the trigger properties:

- **Name**: CPU load too high on {HOST.NAME} for last 3 minutes (over {$CPU_LOAD_THRESHOLD})
- **Expression**: {C_Template_Linux:system.cpu.load.avg(180)}>{$CPU_LOAD_THRESHOLD}

Notice how we used the same user macro name both in the trigger name and expression as in the template properties. When done, click on **Update**. The changes we just did had no functional impact—this trigger still works exactly the same as before, except having a bit more of an explanatory name. What we did was to replace the trigger threshold with the macro, parametrizing it instead of having a hardcoded value. Now we can try overriding this value for a single host—navigate to **Configuration | Hosts** and click on **A test host** in the **NAME** column. Switch to the **Macros** tab and switch to the **Inherited and host macros** mode:

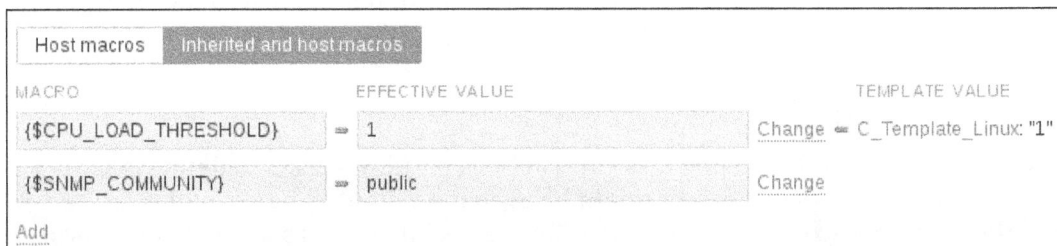

Host macros	Inherited and host macros			
MACRO		EFFECTIVE VALUE		TEMPLATE VALUE
{$CPU_LOAD_THRESHOLD}	⇒	1		Change ⇐ C_Template_Linux: "1"
{$SNMP_COMMUNITY}	⇒	public		Change
Add				

Notice how in this form we can see the macro we just created on the template. There's also a {$SNMP_COMMUNITY} macro—we will discuss where that one comes from a bit later. We can also see which exact template is providing the macro that we created. Although we remember that in this case, in real-world setups it is an extremely helpful feature when many templates are linked to a host. To customize this value on this host, click on the **Change** control next to {$CPU_LOAD_THRESHOLD}. The **EFFECTIVE VALUE** column input field becomes editable—change it to 0.9.

> Zabbix 3.0 is the first version that allows resolving macros like this. In previous versions, we would have to know the exact macro name to be able to override it. There was also no reasonable way to identify the template supplying the macro.

When done, click on **Update**. Now we finally have some use for the macro—by using the same name on the host level we were able to override the macro value for this single host. To double check this change, go to **Monitoring | Triggers** and expand the filter. Set the **Triggers status** dropdown to **Any** and enter CPU in the **Filter by name** field, then click on **Filter**:

HOST	NAME
A test host	CPU load too high on A test host for last 3 minutes (over 0.9)
Another host	CPU load too high on Another host for last 3 minutes (over 1)

This list confirms that **Another host** is getting the macro value 1 from the template, but **A test host** has it changed to 0.9. We are still using the same template and the same trigger, but we changed the trigger threshold for this single host. Feel free to test trigger firing, too. On **A test host**, this trigger should now fire at the new threshold, 0.9.

Remember the {$SNMP_COMMUNITY} macro we saw in the **Inherited and host macros** section? So far we have covered two locations where user macros may be defined — the template and host level. There's actually another location available. Go to **Administration | General** and select **Macros** in the dropdown in the upper right corner. This form looks the same as the template and host macro properties, and there's one macro already defined here.

Macros		
MACRO	VALUE	
{$SNMP_COMMUNITY}	⇒ public	Remove
Add		
Update		

We'll talk more about this macro in a moment, but first let's figure out how these three levels interact. As an example, we can look at a hypothetical use of the macro we just defined:

Global
{$CPU_LOAD_THRESHOLD} = 2

▼

Template
{$CPU_LOAD_THRESHOLD} = 1

▼

Host
{$CPU_LOAD_THRESHOLD} = 0.9

In addition to our template and host level definitions, we could define this macro on the global level with yet another value, in this example — 2. Now all other templates and hosts that would not have this macro defined would use the global value of 2. This change would not affect our template and host, as they have a macro with the same name already defined. In general, the macro definition that's closest to the host "wins". Zabbix first looks for a macro on the host, then the template, then the global level.

> The macro's name is up to us as long as we are using the allowed symbols — uppercase letters, numbers, underscores and, a dot.

But what happens if two templates define the same macro and are linked directly to a host? One of the macro values will be used, and the choice will depend on Zabbix's internal IDs — do not rely on such a configuration. One way to explicitly override the macro value would be introducing yet another template that would be linked directly to the host and would pull in the two original templates.

We used a user macro in the trigger name and expression as a threshold. Where else can they be used?

- **Item key parameters and item name**: One might run SSH on the default port 22, but override it for some hosts. Note that user macros cannot be used in the key itself, only in the parameters that are enclosed by square brackets.

- **Trigger function parameters**: We might change the trigger to {C_Template_ Linux:system.cpu.load.avg({$CPU_LOAD_TIME})}>{$CPU_LOAD_ THRESHOLD} and then use the {$CPU_LOAD_TIME} to change the averaging time for some hosts.

- **SNMP community**: That is where the default macro {$SNMP_COMMUNITY} we saw in the global configuration is used. If that macro had been used in SNMP item properties, we could use the same template on various SNMP devices and change the SNMP community as needed.

> If you are designing templates that use user macros, it is suggested to define such macros on the template level in addition to or instead of the global macro. Exporting such a template will not include global macros, only the macros that are defined on the template level.

Entities such as items and triggers are configured once in the template. When the template is applied to many hosts, macros provide a way to create personalized configuration for linked hosts.

Using multiple templates

There are two monitored hosts now, both having some services monitored and linked to the same template. Suddenly the situation changes and one of the hosts gets the responsibility of being an e-mail server removed. Our options from the Zabbix viewpoint include simply disabling e-mail related items for that host or creating a separate template for it and removing e-mail server related entities from the main template, instead leaving them on the other server. There's a better approach, though — splitting e-mail server related entities into a separate template.

Navigate to **Configuration | Templates**, then click on the **Create template** button. Enter C_Template_Email in the **Template name** field, mark **Custom templates** in the **Other groups** box, click on the ◄ button, then click on **Add**:

Template name	C_Template_Email
Visible name	
Groups	In groups
	Custom templates

Now let's populate this template—select **Custom templates** in the **Group** dropdown and click on **Items** next to **C_Template_Linux**. Mark the checkboxes next to **SMTP server status** and **Testfile** in the **NAME** column, then click on the **Copy** button at the bottom. In the next screen, select **Templates** in the **Target type** dropdown, and **Custom templates** in the **Group** dropdown, mark the checkbox next to **C_Template_Email**, then click on **Copy**.

That deals with the items, but there's still the triggers left. Click on **Triggers** in the navigation bar above the **Items** list, mark the checkboxes next to **SMTP service is down** and **Testfile is missing** in the **NAME** column, then click on the **Copy** button. In the next screen, again select **Templates** in the **Target type** dropdown, **Custom templates** in the **Group** dropdown and mark the checkbox next to **C_Template_Email**, then click on **Copy**.

> We also have to pull in our test file item and trigger, as the SMTP trigger depends on the test file trigger. We could not copy the SMTP trigger as that would leave an unsatisfied dependency.

We now have a simple dedicated e-mail server template that we can link to the hosts. It has the same item and trigger regarding the SMTP service as our custom Linux template. There's a problem though—as they both have an item with the same key, we cannot link these templates to the same host, it would fail. Attempting to do so would probably result in a message like this:

Details	Cannot update host
Template "C_Template_Linux" with item key "net.tcp.service[smtp]" already linked to host.	

We will perform some steps to change the template linkage:

- Unlink C_Template_Linux from "A test host" and "Another host"
- Remove SMTP related items and triggers from C_Template_Linux
- Link C_Template_Email to them both
- Link C_Template_Linux back to both hosts

This way SMTP related items and triggers will become templated from the e-mail template, while preserving all collected data. If we deleted those items from the Linux template and then linked in the e-mail template, we would also remove all collected values for those items.

Go to **Configuration | Hosts,** mark the checkboxes next to **A test host** and **Another host**, then click on **Mass update**. Switch to the **Templates** tab and mark the **Link templates** checkbox and the **Replace** checkbox. This will unlink the linked templates, but keep the previously templated entities as directly attached ones:

> We will discuss host mass update in more detail later in this chapter.

Click on **Update**. Now we will modify the Linux template to remove SMTP related items and triggers. Navigate to **Configuration | Templates**, click on **Items** for **C_Template_Linux** and mark the checkboxes next to **SMTP server status** and **Testfile exists** in the **NAME** column. At the bottom, click on the **Delete** button and confirm the popup. If you expand the details, you will see that the triggers that were depending on these items got deleted, too—we did not have to delete them manually:

Now we are ready to link in our new e-mail template, and link back the modified Linux template. We can even do that in one step and we will again use the mass update function to do that. Go to **Configuration | Hosts**, mark the checkboxes next to **A test host** and **Another host**, then click on **Mass update**. Switch to the **Templates** tab, mark the **Link templates** checkbox, and type "c_" in the input field. Both of our templates will show up—click on one of them, then type "c_" again and click on the other template:

Host	Templates	IPMI	Inventory	Encryption

Link templates ☐

C_Template_Linux ✕ C_Template_Email ✕   Select
type here to search

☐ Replace
☐ Clear when unlinking

Update   Cancel

Click on the **Update** button. Take a look at the template linkage list in **Configuration | Templates** after this operation. Each of the custom templates now has two hosts linked:

TEMPLATES ▲	APPLICATIONS	ITEMS	TRIGGERS	GRAPHS	SCREENS	DISCOVERY	WEB	LINKED TEMPLATES	LINKED TO
C_Template_Email	Applications	Items 2	Triggers 2	Graphs	Screens	Discovery	Web		Another host, A test host
C_Template_Linux	Applications	Items 12	Triggers 5	Graphs	Screens	Discovery	Web		Another host, A test host

A single host can be linked against multiple templates. This allows for a modular configuration where each template only provides a subset of entities, thus a server can be configured to have any combination of basic Linux, e-mail server, web server, file server, and any other templates.

Of course, with a single item and trigger this process seems too complex, but usually the e-mail server would have more parameters, such as mail server process counts, SMTP, IMAP, POP3 service status, spam and virus filter status, queue length, and many others. At that point the ability to quickly make a collection of metrics monitored on a machine with a couple of clicks is more than welcome.

> The method with unlinking, redesigning and linking back is a common and suggested approach to changing template configuration. Just be careful not to change item keys while templates are unlinked or deleting items while they are linked.

Unlinking templates from hosts

But we talked about one server losing the e-mail server duties, and linking both templates to both hosts was not the correct operation, actually. Let's deal with that now. Open **Configuration | Hosts** and choose **Linux servers** in the **Group** dropdown. Our first test host will not be serving SMTP any more, so click on **A test host** in the **NAME** column and switch to the **Templates** tab:

Host	Templates	IPMI	Macros	Host inventory	Encryption

Linked templates	NAME	ACTION
	C_Template_Email	Unlink Unlink and clear
	C_Template_Linux	Unlink Unlink and clear

Link new templates

type here to search	Select

Add

[Update] [Clone] [Full clone] [Delete] [Cancel]

This section properly lists two linked templates. We now want to unlink **C_Template_Email**, but there are two possible actions — **Unlink** and **Unlink and clear**. What's the difference then? Let's try it out and start with the one that looks safer — click on **Unlink** next to **C_Template_Email**, then click on **Update**. Expand the **Details** link to see what happened:

Details	Host updated

– Unlinked: Trigger "SMTP service is down" on "A test host".

– Unlinked: Trigger "Testfile is missing" on "A test host".

– Unlinked: Item "SMTP server status" on "A test host".

– Unlinked: Item "Testfile exists" on "A test host".

– Templates "C_Template_Email" unlinked from hosts "A test host".

Both item and trigger got unlinked, so it seems. Was that what we wanted? Let's see. Click on **Items** next to **A test host**:

SMTP server status
C_Template_Linux: SNMP trap fallback
C_Template_Linux: snmptraps
C_Template_Linux: SNMP trap tests
C_Template_Linux: SSH server status
Testfile exists

Well, not quite—SMTP related items are still there. So a simple unlink does unlinking only, and leaves a copy of the items on the previously linked host. That is handy if we want to create a different item or leave an item on the host to keep data for historical reasons, but not this time. To solve the current situation, we can manually delete both triggers and items, but that wouldn't be so easy if the host additionally had a bunch of directly attached entities. In that case, one would have to manually hunt them down and remove, which allows for mistakes to be made. Instead, let's try a different route—relink this template, then remove it without a trace.

Click on **A test host** in the navigation header and switch to the **Templates** tab. Start typing "C_" in the **Link new templates** field, then click on **C_Template_Email**. Carefully click on the small **Add** control just below it and click on **Update**. Expanding the details will show the SMTP item and trigger getting linked to the template again. We are now back at our starting point with two templates linked— time to unlink again. Click on **A test host** in the **NAME** column and switch to the **Templates** tab. Click on **Unlink and clear** next to **C_Template_Email** in the **Linked templates** block and click on **Update**, then expand **Details**:

Details	Host updated
— Deleted: Trigger "SMTP service is down" on "A test host".	
— Deleted: Trigger "Testfile is missing" on "A test host".	
— Deleted: Item "SMTP server status" on "A test host".	
— Deleted: Item "Testfile exists" on "A test host".	
— Templates "C_Template_Email" unlinked from hosts "A test host".	

And now it's done. Both items and triggers are actually deleted. Look at the host list; notice how the **TEMPLATES** column again offers a quick overview — that comes in handy when you might want to quickly verify a template linkage for all the hosts in a particular group:

NAME ▲	APPLICATIONS	ITEMS	TRIGGERS	GRAPHS	DISCOVERY	WEB	INTERFACE	TEMPLATES
Another host	Applications	Items 14	Triggers 9	Graphs	Discovery	Web	192.168.56.11: 10050	C_Template_Email, C_Template_Linux
A test host	Applications	Items 13	Triggers 6	Graphs	Discovery	Web	127.0.0.1: 10050	C_Template_Linux

Using mass update

Similar to items, mass update can also be used for hosts and we already used it a couple of times. Let's explore in more detail what functionality mass update might offer here — go to **Configuration | Hosts**. In the host list, mark the checkboxes next to **A test host** and **Another host** and click on the **Mass update** button at the bottom. Then switch to the **Templates** tab and mark the **Link templates** checkbox.

Selecting a template is done the same way as in the host properties — we can either type and search by that substring, or click on the **Select** button to choose from a list. We may specify multiple templates in that field, and there is no extra control to click like in the host properties — we had to click on **Add** there. In this form, it is enough to have the template listed in the first field. Switching between mass update and updating an individual host can be quite challenging as these forms work differently — be very, very careful.

There are also two checkboxes — before we discuss what they do, let's figure out what happens by default. If we list a template or several and then update the configuration, that template is linked to all selected hosts in addition to the existing templates — the existing ones are not touched in any way. The checkboxes modify this behavior:

Link templates ■		
	type here to search	Select
	☐ Replace	
	☐ Clear when unlinking	

- **Replace**: Existing templates are unlinked. Same as before, any entities coming from those templates are not touched. Items, triggers, and everything else that was controlled by that template stays on the host. If the templates we had specified in this form would have items with the same keys, such items would be linked to the new templates.

- **Clear when unlinking**: Existing templates are unlinked and cleared — that is, anything coming from them is deleted. It's almost like clearing the host, except that directly attached entities would not be touched, only templated entities are affected.

Of course, if there are any conflicts, such as the same item key being present in two templates, such a linkage would fail.

We will not modify the template linkage at this time, so click on the **Cancel** button here.

Nested templates

The one host still serving e-mails — **Another host** — now has two templates assigned. But what if we separated out in individual templates all services, applications, and other data that can be logically grouped? That would result in a bunch of templates that we would need to link to a single host. This is not tragic, but what if we had two servers like that? Or three? Or 20? At some point, even a configuration with templates can become hard to manage — each host can easily have a template count of a dozen in large and complicated environments.

This is where the simplicity is coupled with powerful functionality. Behind the scenes, templates aren't that different from hosts. Actually, they are hosts, just somewhat special ones. This means that a template can be linked to another template, thus creating a nested configuration.

How does that apply to our situation? Let's create a simple configuration that would allow the easy addition of more hosts of the same setup. In **Configuration | Templates**, click on the **Create template** button. In the **Template name** field enter C_Template_Email_Server, mark **Custom templates** in the **Other groups** box, and click the ◄ button.

Switch to the **Linked templates** tab. Here, we can link other templates to this one. Click on the **Select** button and in the pop-up window mark the checkboxes next to **C_Template_Email** and **C_Template_Linux**:

Click on **Select**. Click on the small **Add** link in the **Link new templates** section—not on the button yet. Both templates are added to the linkage section:

When you are done, click on the **Add** button at the bottom. We now have a template that encompasses a basic Linux system configuration with an e-mail server installed and running, so we still have to properly link it to a host that will serve this role.

Open **Configuration | Hosts**, click on **Another host** in the **NAME** column and switch to the **Templates** tab. In the **Linked templates** section, click on both **Unlink** links. In the **Link new templates input** field, type email and click on **C_Template_Email_Server**. Click on the small **Add** control, then click on **Update** at the bottom of the form. The action successfully completes, so expand the **Details** link. As we can see here, all elements were unlinked first and updated later. Essentially, the previous templates were unlinked, but the items and triggers were left in place and then they got relinked to the new template. The biggest benefit from such a sequence was keeping all item historical data.

But the biggest thing we did here was create a nested template. Such a template is linked against other templates, thus it inherits all the items, triggers, and other characteristics, while usually making some modifications to the original template conditions. In this case, our nested template contains entities from two other templates like this:

While that seems to be only a little gain from the previous situation, two templates linked to a single host, it is a very valid approach when your monitored environment is slightly larger. If there's a single host requiring a specific combination of multiple templates, it is fine to link those templates directly to the host. As soon as the count increases, it is more convenient to set up template nesting, creating a single template to link for these hosts. When you have done that, adding a new host of the same class requires linking against a single template only, which greatly simplifies configuration and minimizes the chance of mistakes.

Looking at the host list, we can see all templates that affect this host in the **TEMPLATES** column:

Notice how the new **C_Template_Email_Server** template is listed first, and the two other templates are listed in parentheses. Templates that are linked directly to the host are listed first, and second level templates that are pulled in by the first level are listed in parentheses. Only the first two levels are shown here — if we had more levels of nesting, we would not see them in the host list.

Let's review a templated item now. From the host list, click on **Items** next to **Another host**. Click on **SMTP server status** in the **NAME** column. This time we are interested in the very first row here, **Parent items**:

Parent items C_Template_Email ⇒ C_Template_Email_Server

This is something that shows up in templated items. Higher level items can be seen and accessed here, and for this item there are two levels displayed. Templates that are closer to the host are listed last and the very first template is the one the item originates from. If we had more than two levels, they would be shown as well. This line works as a quick information on where a particular item originates from and what could modify it, as well as a convenience access upstream. If we spot a simple mistake in some templated item, we can go to higher level items with one click, instead of going to **Configuration | Templates**, finding the correct page and/or template, then repeating that for the item. The same parent entity convenience access line is available for triggers and other entities, too.

When using a nested template setup, the inherited macro resolution helper is even more helpful. If we had a single host and a single template, without the helper, we would first check the macro on the host, if not defined there—on the template, and if not defined there either, on the global level. With nested templates we would have to check all the templates individually. With the helper, we can see the outcome and which exact template is providing the value from that same macro tab in the host properties.

Template nesting is a convenient way to group templates and apply a single template to the target hosts while still having different functionality properly split up and reused in multiple lower level templates. Nevertheless, care should be taken not to create excessive nesting. Two levels of nesting are quite common, but one advanced Zabbix user admitted that designing a templating system with five levels of nesting was a bit excessive and they would restrict themselves to a maximum of four levels next time.

Summary

In Zabbix, templates play a major role in simplifying the configuration and allowing large scale changes. If you are a proficient user of word processors, you probably use styles. The same concept is used in TeX, CSS styles for the Web, and elsewhere—separating content from the presentation helps to reduce the amount of work required when changes have to be made.

While the comparison to styles might seem far-fetched at first, it actually is similar enough. Just like styles, you can separate a host from the services you provide, and you can define these services in a centralized fashion. In the same way as a word processor document having a heading style that allows changing font size for all headings of that level with one action, templates in Zabbix allow changing some parameter for all linked hosts, direct or nested.

We used several locations that allow modifying template linkage in Zabbix:

- **Host properties**: This allow to link, unlink, and unlink and clear multiple templates to a single host
- **Host mass update**: This allows to link multiple templates to multiple hosts, as well as unlinking or unlinking and clearing all the previously linked templates (but not unlinking or unlinking and clearing a specific template)
- **Template properties**: This allows to link and unlink multiple hosts from a single template (but not unlink and clear)

In the preceding list, we could also talk about templates where we talk about hosts. That would be used when managing nested template configuration.

Macros in Zabbix are like variables—they provide a generic placeholder that is later replaced with a host-specific value. We looked at some built-in macros and also user macros that allow us to define our own variables to have customized items, triggers, and other entities on the host level.

As we saw with all the rearrangement of items and triggers in templates, it is easier to plan a sane template policy before getting to the actual configuration. It is strongly suggested that you sit down and draw at least a very basic hierarchy of monitored things before rushing into the configuration—that will make things easier in the long run.

In the next chapter, we will look at the ways data can be visualized in Zabbix. We'll start with graphs and network maps, and see how various runtime information can be displayed. We will discuss graph customization and usage in great detail.

Visualizing Data with Graphs and Maps

9

So far we have only briefly looked at some basic available data visualization options, mostly simple graphs that show us how an item has changed over time. That's not all Zabbix provides—there are more options, which we will explore now. The visualization options of Zabbix that we will look at in this chapter include the following:

- Graphs, including simple, ad hoc, and custom ones
- Maps that can show information laid out in different ways—for example, geographically

Visualize what?

We have set up actions that send us information when we want to be informed, we have remote commands that can even restart services as needed and do many other things. So why visualize anything?

While for most this question will seem silly because we know quite well what data we would like to visualize, not all functionality will be obvious.

Of course, it can be easier to assess the problem when looking at graphs, as this allows us to easily spot the time when a problem started, correlate various parameters easily, and spot recurring anomalies. Things such as graphs can also be used as a simple representation to answer questions such as so what does that Zabbix system do?" That does come in handy when trying to show results and benefits to non-technical management.

Another useful area is displaying data on a large screen. That usually is a high-level overview of the system state, and is placed in the system operators' or helpdesk location. Imagine a large plasma TV, showing the helpdesk map of the country, listing various company locations and any problems in any of those.

There surely are many more scenarios you can come up with when having a nice graph or otherwise visually laid out information can be very helpful. We'll now look at the options that are already shipped with Zabbix.

Individual elements

We can distinguish between individual and combined visual elements. With individual we will refer to elements showing certain information in one container, such as a graph or a network map. While individual elements can contain information from many items and hosts, in general they cannot include other Zabbix frontend elements.

Graphs

While the previous definition might sound confusing, it's quite simple—an example of an individual visual element is a graph. A graph can contain information on one or more items, but it cannot contain other Zabbix visual elements, such as other graphs. Thus a graph can be considered an individual element.

Graphs are hard to beat for capacity planning when trying to convince the management of a new database server purchase. If you can show an increase in visitors to your website and that with the current growth it will hit current limits in a couple of months, that is so much more convincing.

Simple graphs

We already looked at the first visual element in this list: so-called **simple graphs**. They are somewhat special: because there is no configuration required, you don't have to create them—simple graphs are available for every item. Right? Not quite. They are only available for numeric items, as it wouldn't make much sense to graph textual items. To refresh our memory, let's look at the items in **Monitoring | Latest data**:

NAME ▲	LAST CHECK	LAST VALUE	CHANGE
- other - (13 Items)			
CPU load	2016-04-27 15:15:25	0	Graph
Experimental SNMP trap			History
Full OS name	2016-04-27 15:15:22	Linux testhost 3.12.53-40-defa...	History
ICMP ping performance	2016-04-27 15:15:32	0.04 ms	Graph

For anything other than numeric items the links on the right-hand side show **History**. For numeric items, we have **Graph** links. This depends only on how the data is stored — things such as units or value mapping do not influence the availability of graphs. If you want to refresh information on basic graph controls such as zooming, please refer to *Chapter 2*, *Getting Your First Notification*.

While no configuration is required for simple graphs, they also provide no configuration capabilities. They are easily available, but quite limited. Thus, being useful for single items, there is no way to graph several items or change the visual style. Of course, it would be a huge limitation if there was no other way, but luckily there are two additional graph types — **ad hoc** graphs and **custom** graphs.

Ad hoc graphs

Simple graphs are easy to access, but they display a single item only. A very easy way to quickly see multiple items on a single graph exists — in Zabbix, these are called **ad hoc** graphs. Ad hoc graphs are accessible from the **Latest data** page, the same as the simple graphs. Let's view an ad hoc graph — navigate to **Monitoring | Latest data** and take a look at the left-hand side. Similar to many pages in the configuration section, there are checkboxes. Mark the checkboxes next to the CPU load and network traffic items for **A test host**:

▼	A test host	- **other** - (13 Items)
☑		CPU load
☐		Experimental SNMP trap
☐		Full OS name
☐		ICMP ping performance
☑		Incoming traffic on interface enp0s8
☑		Incoming traffic on interface lo

Checkboxes next to non-numeric items are disabled.

At the bottom of the page, click on the **Display graph** button. A graph with all selected items is displayed:

		last	min	avg	max
CPU load	[avg]	1.04	0	0.143	1.15
Incoming traffic on interface enp0s8	[avg]	183 Bps	0 Bps	227.53 Bps	390 Bps
Incoming traffic on interface lo	[avg]	257 Bps	225 Bps	164.89 KBps	3.22 MBps

Now take a look at the top of the graph—there's a new control there, **Graph type**:

It allows us to quickly switch between normal and stacked graphs. Click on **Stacked**:

		last	min	avg	max
Incoming traffic on interface lo	[avg]	246 Bps	225 Bps	161.23 KBps	3.22 MBps
Incoming traffic on interface enp0s8	[avg]	149 Bps	0 Bps	224.82 Bps	390 Bps
CPU load	[avg]	1.01	0	0.1714	1.15

With this graph, stacked mode does not make much sense as CPU load and network traffic have quite different scales and meaning, but at least there's a quick way to switch between the modes. Return to **Monitoring | Latest data** and this time mark the checkboxes next to the network traffic items only. At the bottom of the list, click on **Display stacked graph**. An ad hoc graph will be displayed again, this time defaulting to stacked mode. Thus the button at the bottom of the **Latest data** page controls the initial mode, but switching the mode is easy once the graph is opened.

> At the time of writing this in Zabbix version 3.0.2, the time period can be changed in ad hoc graphs, but refreshing the ad hoc graph page will reset the graph period to 1 hour.

Unfortunately, there is no way to save an ad hoc graph as a custom graph or in your dashboard favorites at this time. If you would like to revisit a specific ad hoc graph later, you can copy its URL.

Custom graphs

These have to be created manually, but they allow a great deal of customizability. To create a custom graph, open **Configuration | Templates** and click on **Graphs** next to **C_Template_Linux**, then click on the **Create graph** button. Let's start with a recreation of a simple graph, so enter CPU load in the **Name** field, then click on the **Add** control in the **Items** section. In the popup, click on **CPU load** in the **NAME** column. The item is added to the list in the graph properties. While we can change some other parameters for this item, for now let's change the color only. Color values can be entered manually, but that's not too convenient, so just click on the colored rectangle in the **COLOUR** column. That opens a color chooser. Pick one of the middle range red colors—notice that holding your mouse cursor over a cell for a few seconds will open a tooltip with a color value:

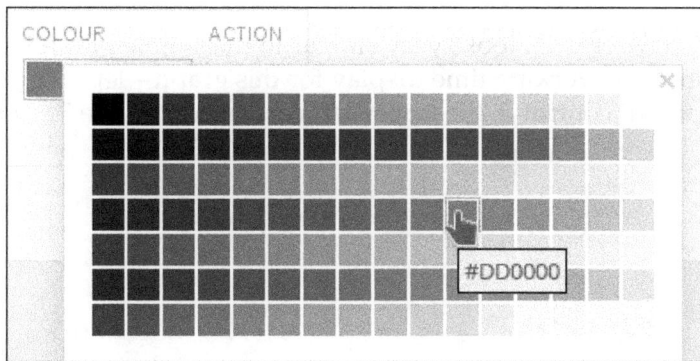

We might want to see what this will look like—switch over to the **Preview** tab. Unfortunately, the graph there doesn't help us much currently, as we chose an item from a template, which does not have any data itself.

> The Zabbix color chooser provides a table to choose from the available colors, but it still is missing some colors, such as orange, for example. You can enter an RGB color code directly in hex form (for example, orange would be similar to FFAA00). To find other useful values, you can either experiment, or use an online color calculator. Or, if you are using KDE, just launch the **KColorChooser** application.

Working time and trigger line

We already saw one simple customization option—changing the line color. Switch back to the **Graph** tab and note the checkboxes **Show legend, Show working time**, and **Show triggers**. We will leave those three enabled, so click on the **Add** button at the bottom.

Our custom graph is now saved, but where do we find it? While simple graphs are available from the **Monitoring | Latest data** section, custom graphs have their own section. Go to **Monitoring | Graphs**, select **Linux servers** in the **Group** dropdown, **A test host** in the **Host** dropdown, and in the **Graph** dropdown, select **CPU load**.

> There's an interesting thing we did here, that you probably already noticed. While the item was added from a template, the graph is available for the host, with all the data correctly displayed for that host. That means an important concept, templating, works here as well. Graphs can be attached to templates in Zabbix, and afterwards are available for each host that is linked to such a template.

The custom graph we created looks very similar to the simple graph. We saw earlier that we can control the working time display for this graph—let's see what that is about. Click on the **7d** control in the upper-left corner, next to the **Zoom caption**:

A test host: CPU load (7d)

	last	min	avg	max
■ CPU load [avg]	0.0539	0	0.0948	1.19

○ Trigger: CPU load too high on A test host for last 3 minutes (over 0.9)   [> 0.9]

> If you created the CPU load item recently, longer time periods might not be available here yet. Choose the longest available in that case.

We can see that there are gray and white areas on the graph. The white area is considered *working time*, the gray one — *non-working time*.

By the way, that's the same with the simple graphs, except that you have no way to disable the working time display for them. What is considered a working time is not hardcoded — we can change that. Open **Administration | General**, choose **Working time** from the dropdown in the upper right corner.

This option uses the same syntax as When active for user media, discussed in *Chapter 7, Acting upon Monitored Conditions and Item Flexible Intervals*, and *Chapter 3, Monitoring with Zabbix Agents and Basic Protocols*. Monday-Sunday is represented by 1-7 and a 24-hour clock is used to configure time. Currently, this field reads 1-5,09:00-18:00;, which means Monday-Friday, 9 hours each day. Let's modify this somewhat to read 1-3,09:00-17:00;4-5,09:00-15:00,

Working time	1-3,09:00-17:00;4-5,09:00-15:00
	Update

> This setting is global; there is no way to set it per user at this time.

That would change to 09-17 for Monday-Wednesday, but for Thursday and Friday it's shorter hours of 09-15. Click on **Update** to accept the changes. Navigate back to **Monitoring | Graphs**, and make sure **CPU load** is selected in the **Graph** dropdown.

The gray and white areas should now show fewer hours to be worked on Thursday and Friday than on the first three weekdays.

Note that these times do not affect data gathering or alerting in any way — the only functionality that is affected by the working time period is graphs.

But what about that trigger option in the graph properties? Taking a second look at our graph, we can see both a dotted line and a legend entry, which explains that it depicts the trigger threshold. The trigger line is displayed for simple expressions only.

> If the load on your machine has been low during the displayed period, you won't see the trigger line displayed on a graph. The y axis auto-scaling will exclude the range where the trigger would be displayed.

Same as working time, the trigger line is displayed in simple graphs with no way to disable it.

There was another checkbox that could make this graph different from a simple graph — **Show legend**. Let's see what a graph would look like with these three options disabled. In the graph configuration, unmark **Show legend**, **Show working time**, and **Show triggers**, then click on **Update**.

> When reconfiguring graphs, it is suggested to use two browser tabs or windows, keeping **Monitoring | Graphs** open in one, and the graph details in the **Configuration** section in the other. This way, you will be able to refresh the monitoring section after making configuration changes, saving a few clicks back and forth.

Open this graph in the monitoring section again:

Sometimes, all that extra information can take up too much space, especially the legend if you have lots of items on a graph. For custom graphs, we may hide it. Re-enable these checkboxes in the graph configuration and save the changes by clicking on the same **Update** button.

Graph item function

What we have now is quite similar to the simple graphs, though there's one notable difference when the displayed period is longer — simple graphs show three different lines, with the area between them filled, while our graph has single line only (the difference is easier to spot when the displayed period approaches 3 days). Can we duplicate that behavior? Go to **Configuration | Templates** and click on **Graphs** next to **C_Template_Linux**, then click on **CPU load** in the **NAME** column to open the editing form. Take a closer look at, **FUNCTION** dropdown in the Items section:

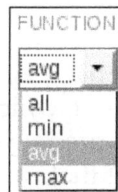

Currently, we have **avg** selected, which simply draws average values. The other choices are quite obvious, **min** and **max**, except the one that looks suspicious, **all**. Select **all**, then click on **Update**. Again, open **Monitoring | Graphs**, and make sure **CPU load** is selected in the **Graph** dropdown:

The graph now has three lines, representing minimum, maximum, and average values for each point in time, although in this example the lower line is always at zero.

The default is average, as showing three lines with the colored area when there are many items on a graph would surely make the graph unreadable. On the other hand, even when **average** is chosen, the graph legend shows minimum and maximum values from the raw data, used to calculate the average line. That can result in a situation where the line does not go above 1, but the legend says that the maximum is 5. In such a case, almost always the raw values could be seen by zooming in on the area which has them, but such a situation can still be confusing.

Two y axes

We have now faithfully replicated a simple graph (well, the simple graph uses green for average values, while we use red, which is a minor difference). While such an experience should make you appreciate the availability of simple graphs, custom graphs would be quite useless if that was all we could achieve with them. Customizations such as color, function, and working time displaying can be useful, but they are minor ones. Let's see what else can we throw at the graph. Before we improve the graph, let's add one more item. We monitored the incoming traffic, but not the outgoing traffic. Go to **Configuration | Templates**, click on **Items** next to **C_Template_Linux**, and click on **Incoming traffic on interface eth0** in the **NAME** column. Click the **Clone** button at the bottom and change the following fields:

- **Name:** Incoming traffic on interface $1
- **Key:** net.if.out[enp0s8]

When done, click on the **Add** button at the bottom.

Now we are ready to improve our graph.

Open **Configuration | Templates**, select **Custom templates** in the **Group** dropdown and click on **Graphs** next to **C_Template_Linux**, then click on **CPU load** in the **NAME** column.

Click on **Add** in the **Items** section. Notice how the dropdown in the upper right corner is disabled. Moving the mouse cursor over it might display a tooltip:

This tooltip might not be visible in some browsers.

We cannot choose any other host or template now. The reason is that a graph can contain either items from a single template, or from one or more hosts. If a graph has an item from a host added, then no templated items may be added to it anymore. If a graph has one or more items added from some template, additional items may only be added from the same template.

Graphs are also similar to triggers — they do not really belong to a specific host, they reference items and then are associated with hosts they reference items from. Adding an item to a graph will make that graph appear for the host to which the added item belongs. But for now, let's continue with configuring our graph on the template.

Mark the checkboxes next to **Incoming traffic on interface eth0** and **Outgoing traffic on interface eth0** in the **NAME** column, then click on **Select**. The items will be added to the list of graph items:

Items	NAME	FUNCTION	DRAW STYLE	Y AXIS SIDE	COLOUR	ACTION
	1: C_Template_Linux: CPU load	all ▼	Line ▼	Left ▼	DD0000	Remove
	2: C_Template_Linux: Incoming traffic on interface enp0s8	avg ▼	Line ▼	Left ▼	F63100	Remove
	3: C_Template_Linux: Outgoing traffic on interface enp0s8	avg ▼	Line ▼	Left ▼	2774A4	Remove
Add						

Notice how the colors were automatically assigned. When multiple items are added to a custom graph in one go, Zabbix chooses colors from a predefined list. In this case the CPU load and the incoming traffic got very similar colors. Click on the colored rectangle in the **COLOR** column next to the incoming traffic item and choose some shade of green.

As our graph now has more than just the CPU load, change the **Name** field to CPU load & traffic. While we're still in the graph editing form, select the **Filled region** in the **Draw style** dropdown for both network traffic items, then click on **Update**. Check the graph in the **Monitoring | Graphs** section:

Hey, that's quite ugly. Network traffic values are much larger than system load ones, thus even the system load trigger line can be barely seen at the very bottom of the graph. The y axis labels are not clear either—they're just some "к". Let's try to fix this back in the graph configuration. For the CPU load item, change the **Y AXIS SIDE** dropdown to **Right**, then click on **Update**:

> We could have changed the network traffic items, too. In this case, that would have been two extra clicks, though.

Take a look at **Monitoring | Graphs** to see what this change did:

That's way better; now each of the different scale values is mapped against an appropriate y axis. Notice how the y axis labels on the left hand side now show network traffic information, while the right-hand side is properly scaled for the CPU load. Placing things like the system load and web server connection count on a single graph would be quite useless without using two y axes, and there are lots of other things we might want to compare that have a different scale.

Notice how the filled area is slightly transparent where it overlaps with another area. This allows us to see values even if they are behind a larger area, but it's suggested to avoid placing many elements with the filled region draw style on the same graph, as the graph can become quite unreadable in that case. We'll make this graph a bit more readable in a moment, too.

In some cases, the automatic y axis scaling on the right-hand axis might seem a bit strange—it could have a slightly bigger range than needed. For example, with values ranging from 0 to 0.25 the y axis might scale to 0.9. This is caused by an attempt to match horizontal leader lines on both axes. The left side y axis is taken as a more important one, and the right-hand side is adjusted to it.

One might notice that there is no indication in the legend about the item placement on the y axis. With our graph, it is trivial to figure out that network traffic items go on the left side and **CPU load** on the right, but with other values that could be complicated. Unfortunately, there is no nice solution at this time. Item names could be hacked to include "L" or "R", but that would have to be synchronized to the graph configuration manually.

Item sort order

Getting back to our graph, the CPU load line can be seen at times when it's above the network traffic areas, but it can hardly be seen when the traffic area covers the CPU load line. We might want to place the line on top of those two areas in this case.

Back in the graph configuration, take a look at the item list. Items are placed on the Zabbix graph in the order in which they appear in the graph configuration. The first item is placed, then the second one on top of the first one, and so on. Eventually the item that is listed the first in the configuration is in the background. For us that is the **CPU load** item, the one we want to have on top of everything else. To achieve that, we must make sure it is listed last. Item ordering can be changed by dragging those handles to the left of them. Grab the handle next to the CPU load item and drag it to be the last entry in the list:

Items	NAME	FUNCTION	DRAW STYLE	Y AXIS SIDE	COLOUR	ACTION
	2: C_Template_Linux: Incoming traffic on interface enp0s8	avg ▾	Filled region ▾	Left ▾	00CC00	Remove
	3: C_Template_Linux: Outgoing traffic on interface enp0s8	avg ▾	Filled region ▾	Left ▾	2774A4	Remove
	1: C_Template_Linux: CPU load	all ▾	Line ▾	Right ▾	DD0000	Remove
Add						

Items will be renumbered. Click on **Update**. Let's check how the graph looks now in **Monitoring | Graphs**:

That's better. The **CPU load** line is drawn on top of both network traffic areas.

> Quite often, one might want to include a graph in an e-mail or use it in a document. With Zabbix graphs, usually it is not a good idea to create a screenshot—that would require manually cutting off the area that's not needed. But all graphs in Zabbix are PNG images, thus you can easily use graphs right from the frontend by right clicking and saving or copying them. There's one little trick, though—in most browsers, you have to click outside of the area that accepts dragging actions for zooming. Try the legend area, for example. This works for simple, ad hoc, and custom graphs in the same way.

Gradient line and other draw styles

Our graph is getting more and more useful, but the network traffic items cover each other. We could change their sort order, but that will not work that well when traffic patterns change. Let's edit the configuration of this graph again. This time, we'll change the draw style for both network traffic items. Set it to **Gradient line**:

	NAME	FUNCTION	DRAW STYLE
1:	C_Template_Linux: Incoming traffic on interface enp0s8	avg ▼	Gradient line ▼
2:	C_Template_Linux: Outgoing traffic on interface enp0s8	avg ▼	Gradient line ▼

Click on **Update** and check the graph in the monitoring section:

A test host: CPU load & traffic (1h)

		last	min	avg	max
Incoming traffic on interface enp0s8	[avg]	549 Bps	0 Bps	299.48 Bps	549 Bps
Outgoing traffic on interface enp0s8	[avg]	1.92 KBps	0 Bps	2.5 KBps	5.44 KBps
CPU load	[all]	0	0	0.108	0.7
○ Trigger: CPU load too high on A test host for last 3 minutes (over 0.9)	[> 0.9]				

Selecting the gradient option made the area much more transparent, and now it's easy to see both traffic lines even when they would have been covering each other previously.

We have already used line, filled region, and gradient line draw styles. There are some more options available:

- Line
- Filled region
- Bold line
- Dot
- Dashed line
- Gradient line

The way the filled region and gradient line options look was visible in our tests. Let's compare the remaining options:

This example uses a line, bold line, dots, and a dashed line on the same graph.

Note that dot mode makes Zabbix plot the values without connecting them with lines. If there are a lot of values to be plotted, the outcome will look like a line because there will be so many dots to plot.

> We have left the **FUNCTION** value for the CPU load item at **all**. At longer time periods this can make the graph hard to read. When configuring Zabbix graphs, check how well they work for different period lengths.

Custom y axis scale

As you have probably noticed, the y axis scale is automatically adjusted to make all values fit nicely in the chosen range. Sometimes you might want to customize that, though. Let's prepare a quick and simple dataset for that.

Go to **Configuration | Templates** and click on **Items** next to **C_Template_Linux**, then click on the **Create item** button. Fill in these values:

- **Name**: Diskspace on $1 ($2)
- **Key**: vfs.fs.size[/,total]
- **Units**: B
- **Update interval**: 120

When you are done, click on the **Add** button at the bottom.

Now, click on **Diskspace on / (total)** in the **NAME** column and click on the **Clone** button at the bottom. Make only a single change, replace total in the **Key** field with used, so that the key now reads vfs.fs.size[/,used], then click on the **Add** button at the bottom.

> Usually it is suggested to use bigger intervals for the total diskspace item—at least 1 hour, maybe more. Unfortunately, there's no way to force item polling in Zabbix, thus we would have to wait for up to an hour before we would have any data. We're just testing things, so an interval of 120 seconds or 2 minutes should allow to see the results sooner.

Click on **Graphs** in the navigation header above the item list and click on **Create graph**. In the **Name** field, enter Used diskspace. Click on the **Add** control in the **Items** section, then click on **Diskspace on / (used)** in the **NAME** column. In the **DRAW STYLE** dropdown, choose **Filled region**. Feel free to change the color, then click on the **Add** button at the bottom.

Take a look at what the graph looks like in the **Monitoring | Graphs** section for
`A test host:`

So this particular host has a bit more than two and a half gigabytes used on the
root file system. But the graph is quite hard to read—it does not show how full the
partition relatively is. The y axis starts a bit below our values and ends a bit above
them. Regarding the desired upper range limit on the y axis, we can figure out the
total disk space on root file system in **Monitoring | Latest data**:

So there's a total of almost 60 GB of space, which also is not reflected on the graph.
Let's try to make the graph slightly more readable. In the configuration of the **Used
diskspace** graph in the template, take a look at two options—**Y axis MIN value** and
Y axis MAX value. They are both set to **Calculated** currently, but that doesn't seem
to work too well for our current scenario. First, we want to make sure graph starts at
zero, so change the **Y axis MIN value** to **Fixed**. This allows us to enter any arbitrary
value, but a default of zero is what we want.

For the upper limit, we could calculate what 58.93 GB is in bytes and insert that
value, but what if the available disk space changes? Often enough filesystems
increase either by adding physical hardware, using **Logical Volume Management
(LVM)** or other means.

Does this mean we will have to update the Zabbix configuration each time this could happen? Luckily, no. There's a nice solution for situations just like this. In the **Y axis MAX value** dropdown, select **Item**. That adds another field and a button, so click on **Select**. In the popup, click on **Diskspace on / (total)** in the **NAME** column. The final y axis configuration should look like this:

Y axis MIN value	Fixed	▼	0.0000	
Y axis MAX value	Item	▼	C_Template_Linux: Diskspace on / (total)	Select

If it does, click on **Update**. Now is the time to check out the effect on the graph — see the **Used diskspace** graph in **Monitoring | Graphs**:

> If the y axis maximum is set to the amount of used diskspace, the total diskspace item has not received a value yet. In such a case, you can either wait for the item to get updated or temporarily decrease its interval.

Now the graph allows to easily identify how full the disk is. Notice how we used a graph like this on the template. All hosts would have used and total diskspace items, and the graph would automatically scale to whatever amount of total diskspace that host has. This approach can also be used for used memory or any other item where you want to see the full scale of possible values. A potentially negative side-effect could appear when monitoring large values such as petabyte-size filesystems. With the y axis range spanning several petabytes, we wouldn't really see any normal changes in the data, as a single pixel on the y axis would be many gigabytes.

> At this time it is not possible to set y axis minimum and maximum separately for left and right y axes.

Percentile line

A percentile is the threshold below which a given percentage of values fall. For example, if we have network traffic measurements, we could calculate that 95% of values are lower than 103 Mbps, while 5% of values are higher. This allows us to filter out peaks while still having a fairly precise measurement of the bandwidth used. Actually, billing by used bandwidth most often happens by a percentile. As such, it can be useful to plot a percentile on a network traffic graph, and luckily Zabbix offers a way to do that. To see how this works, let's create a new graph. Navigate to **Configuration | Templates**, click on **Graphs** next to **C_Template_ Linux**, then click on the **Create graph** button. In the **Name** field, enter Incoming traffic on eth0 with percentile. Click on **Add** in the **Items** section and in the popup, click on **Incoming traffic on interface eth0** in the **NAME** column. For this item, change the color to red. In the graph properties, mark the checkbox next to **Percentile line (left)** and enter 95 in that field. When done, click on the **Add** button at the bottom. Check this graph in the monitoring section:

When the percentile line is configured, it is drawn in the graph in green color (although this is different in the dark theme). Additionally, percentile information is shown in the legend. In this example, the percentile line nicely evens out a few peaks to show average bandwidth usage. With 95% of the values being above the percentile line, only 5% of them are above 2.24 KBps.

> We changed the default item color from green so that the percentile line had a different color and it would be easier to distinguish it. Green is always used for the left side y axis percentile line; the right side y axis percentile line would always be red.

We only used a single item on this graph. When there are multiple items on the same axis, Zabbix adds up all the values and computes the percentile based on that result. At this time there is no way to specify the percentile for individual items in the graph.

> To alert on the percentile value, the trigger function percentile() can be used. To store this value as an item, see calculated items in *Chapter 11, Advanced Item Monitoring*.

Stacked graphs

Our previous graph that contained multiple items, network traffic and CPU load, placed the items on the y axis independently. But sometimes we might want to place them one on top of another on the same axis — stack them. Possible uses could be memory usage, where we could stack buffers, cached and other used memory types (and link the y axis maximum value to the total amount of memory), stacked network traffic over several interfaces to see total network load, or any other situation where we would want to see both total and value distribution. Let's try to create a stacked graph. Open **Configuration | Templates**, click on **Graphs** next to **C_Template_Linux**, then click on the **Create graph** button. In the **Name** field, enter Stacked network traffic and change the **Graph type** dropdown to **Stacked**. Click on **Add** in the **Items** section and in the popup, mark the checkboxes next to **Incoming traffic on interface eth0** and **Outgoing traffic on interface eth0** in the **NAME** column, then click on **Select**. When done, click on the **Add** button at the bottom.

Notice how we did not have a choice of draw style when using a stacked graph — all items will have the *Filled region* style.

If we had several active interfaces on the test machine, it might be interesting to stack incoming traffic over all the interfaces, but in this case we will see both incoming and outgoing traffic on the same interface.

Check out **Monitoring | Graphs** to see the new graph, make sure to select **Stacked network traffic** from the dropdown:

With stacked graphs we can see both the total amount (indicated by the top of the data area) and the individual amounts that items contribute to the total.

Pie graphs

The graphs we have created so far offer a wide range of possible customizations, but sometimes we might be more interested in proportions of the values. For those situations, it is possible to create pie graphs. Go to **Configuration | Templates**, click on **Graphs** next to **C_Template_Linux** and click on the **Create graph** button. In the **Name** field, enter Used diskspace (pie). In the **Graph** type dropdown, choose **Pie**. Click on **Add** in the **Items** section and mark the checkboxes next to **Diskspace on / (total)** and **Diskspace on / (used)** items in the **NAME** column, then click on **Select**.

Graph item configuration is a bit different for pie graphs. Instead of a draw style, we can choose a type. We can choose between **Simple** and **Graph sum**:

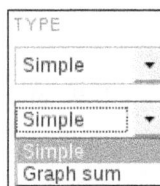

The proportion of some values can be displayed on a pie graph, but to know how large that proportion is, an item must be assigned to be the "total" of the pie graph. In our case, that would be the total diskspace. For **Diskspace on / (total)**, set select **Graph sum** in the **TYPE** dropdown:

NAME	TYPE
C_Template_Linux: Diskspace on / (total)	Graph sum ▾
C_Template_Linux: Diskspace on / (used)	Simple ▾

When done, click on the **Add** button at the bottom:

> Luckily, the total diskspace got the green color and the used diskspace got red assigned. For more items we might want to adjust the colors.

Back in **Monitoring | Graphs**, select **Used diskspace (pie)**:

Great, it looks about right, except for the large, empty area on the right side. How can we get rid of that? Go back to the configuration of this graph. This time, width and height controls will be useful. Change the **Width** field to 430 and the **Height** field to 300 and click on **Update**. Let's check out whether it's any better in **Monitoring | Graphs** again:

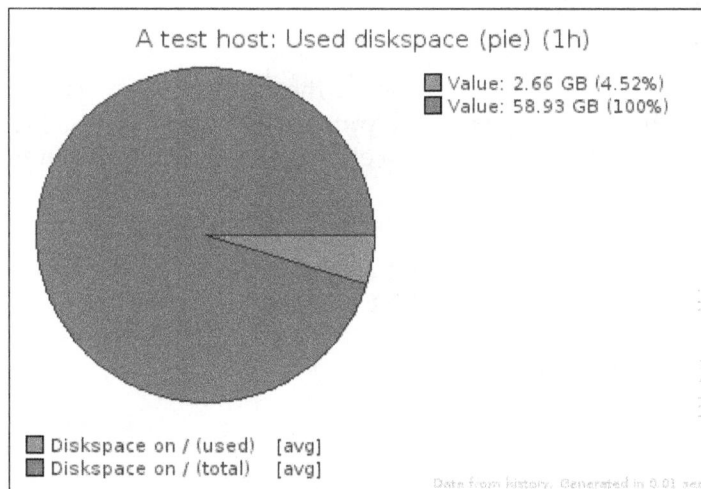

[💡 Preview is of a limited use here as we wouldn't see actual values on the template level, including name and value length.]

It really is better, we got rid of the huge empty area. Pie graphs could also be useful for displaying memory information—the whole pie could be split into buffers, cached, and actual used memory, laid on top of the total amount of memory. In such a case, total memory would get a type set to **Graph sum**, but for all other items, **TYPE** would be set to **Simple**.

Let's try another change. Edit the **Used diskspace (pie)** graph again. Select **Exploded** in the **Graph type** dropdown and mark the checkbox next to **3D view**. Save these changes and refresh the graph view in **Monitoring | Graphs**:

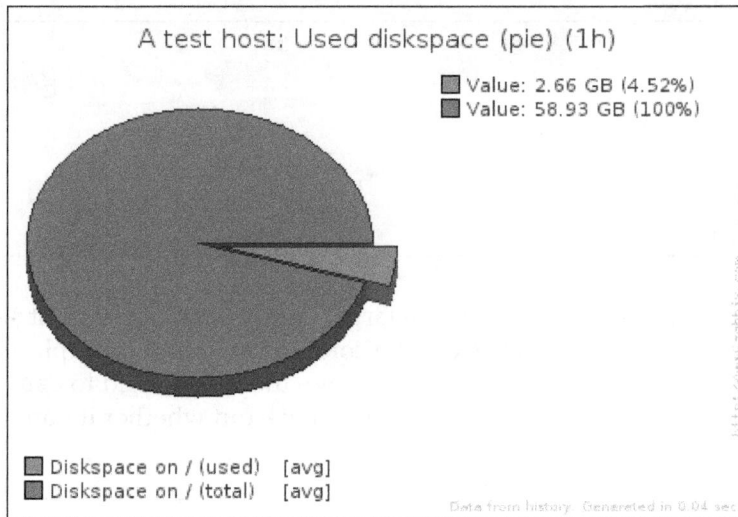

Remember the "function" we were setting for the normal graph? We changed between **avg** and **all**, and there were also **min** and **max** options available. Such a parameter is available for pie graphs as well, but it has slightly different values:

For pie graphs, **all** is replaced by **last**. While the pie graph itself doesn't have a time series, we can still select the time period for it. The function determines how the values from this period will be picked up. For example, if we are displaying a pie graph with the time period set to 1 hour and during this hour we received free diskspace values of 60, 40 and 20 GB, **max**, **avg** and **min** would return one of those values, respectively. If the function is set to **last**, no matter what the time period length, the most recent value of 20 GB will be always shown.

> When monitoring a value in percentages, it would be desirable to set graph sum to a manual value of 100, similar to the y axis maximum value. Unfortunately, it is not supported at this time, thus a fake item that only receives values of "100" would have to be used. A calculated item with a formula of "100" is one easy way to do that. We will discuss calculated items in *Chapter 11, Advanced Item Monitoring*.

Maps

We have covered several types of data visualization, which allow quite a wide range of views. While the ability to place different things on a single graph allows us to look at data and events in more context, sometimes you might want to have a broader view of things and how they are connected. Or maybe you need something shiny to show off.

There's a functionality in Zabbix that allows one to create maps. While sometimes referred to as network maps, nothing prevents you from using these to map out anything you like. Before we start, make sure there are no active triggers for both servers—check that under **Monitoring | Triggers** and fix any problems you see.

Creating a map

Let's try to create a simple map now—navigate to **Monitoring | Maps** and click on **Create map**. Enter "First map" in the **Name** field and mark the **Expand single problem** checkbox.

> Previous Zabbix versions allowed us to configure the maps in the configuration section and view them in the monitoring section. Zabbix 3.0 has moved both operations to the monitoring section.

When done, click on the **Add** button at the bottom. Hey, was that all? Where can we actually configure the map? In the **ACTIONS** column, click on **Constructor**. Yes, now that's more of an editing interface. First we have to add something, so click on **Add** next to the **Icon** label at the top of the map. This adds an element at the upper-left corner of the map. The location isn't exactly great, though. To solve this, click and drag the icon elsewhere, somewhere around the cell at 50x50:

> Notice how it snaps to the grid. We will discuss this functionality a bit later.

The map still doesn't look too useful, so what to do with it now? Simply click once on the element we just added—this opens up the element properties form. Notice how the element itself is highlighted as well now. By default, an added map element is an image, which does not show anything regarding the monitored systems. For a simple start, we'll use hosts, so choose **Host** in the **Type** dropdown—notice how this changes the form slightly. Enter "A test host" in the **Label** text area, then type "test" in the **Host** field and click on **A test host** in the dropdown. The default icon is **Server_(96)**—let's reduce that a bit. Select **Server_(64)** in the **Default** dropdown in the **Icons** section. The properties should look like this:

Map element

Type	Host ▾
Label	A test host
Label location	Default ▾
Host	A test host ✕ Select
Application	Select
Automatic icon selection	☐

Icons		
	Default	Server_(64) ▾
	Problem	Default ▾
	Maintenance	Default ▾
	Disabled	Default ▾

Coordinates	X 39 Y 27

URLs	NAME	URL	ACTION
			Remove
	Add		

Apply   Remove   Close

For a simple host that should be enough, so click on **Apply**, then **Close** to remove the property popup. The map is regenerated to display the changes we made:

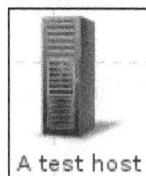

A test host

A map with a single element isn't that exciting, so click on **Add** next to the **Icon** label again, then drag the new element around the cell at 450x50. Click it once and change its properties. Start by choosing **Host** in the **Type** dropdown, then enter Another host for the **Label** and start typing "another" in the **Host** field. In the dropdown, choose **Another host**. Change the default icon to **Server_(64)**, then click on **Apply**. Notice how the elements are not aligned to the grid anymore — we changed the icon size and that resulted in them being a bit off the centers of the grid cells. This is because of the alignment happening by the icon center, but icon positioning — the upper left corner of the icon. As we changed the icon size, its upper left corner was fixed, while the center changed as it was not aligned anymore. We can drag the icons a little distance and the icons will snap to the grid, or we can click on the **Align icons** control at the top. Click on **Align icons** now. Also notice other **Grid controls** above the map — clicking on **Shown** will hide the grid (and change that label to **Hidden**). Clicking on **On** will stop icons from being aligned to the grid when we move them (and change that label to **Off**).

A map is not saved automatically — to do that, click on the **Update** button in the upper-right corner. The popup that appears can be quite confusing — it is not asking whether we want to save the map. Actually, as the message says, the map is already saved at that point. Clicking on **OK** would return to the list of the maps, clicking on **Cancel** would keep the map editing form open. Usually it does not matter much whether you click on **OK** or **Cancel** here.

> It is a good idea to save a map every now and then, especially when making a large amount of changes.

Now is a good time to check what the map looks like, so go to **Monitoring | Maps** and click on **First map** in the **NAME** column. It should look quite nice, with the grid guidance lines removed, except for the large white area, like we had with the pie graph. That calls for a fix, so click on **All maps** above the map itself and click on **Properties** next to **First map**. Enter "600" in the **Width** field and "225" in the **Height** field, then click on **Update**. Click on **Constructor** in the **ACTIONS** column next to the **First map** again.

Both displaying and aligning to the grid are controllable separately — we can have grid displayed, but no automatic alignment to it, or no grid displayed, but still used for alignment:

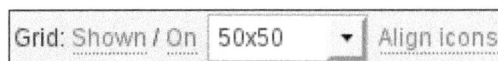

Grid: Shown / On   50x50 ▼   Align icons

By default, a grid of 50x50 pixels is used, and there are predefined rectangular grids of 20, 40, 50, 75 and 100 available. These sizes are hardcoded and can not be customized:

Grid: Shown / On	50x50 ▾
	20x20
	40x40
	50x50
	75x75
	100x100

For our map, change the grid size to 75x75 and with alignment to grid enabled, position the icons so that they are at the opposing ends of the map, one cell away from the borders. Click on the **Update** button to save the changes.

> Always click on **Update** when making changes to a map.

Go to **Monitoring | Maps** and click on **First map** in the **NAME** column:

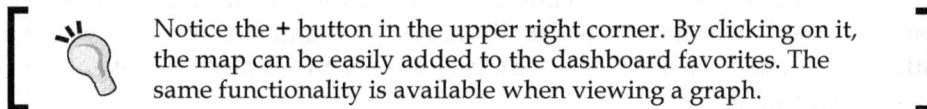

> Notice the + button in the upper right corner. By clicking on it, the map can be easily added to the dashboard favorites. The same functionality is available when viewing a graph.

That looks much better, and we verified that we can easily change map dimensions in case we need to add more elements to the map.

[🔍 Zabbix maps do not auto-scale like the width of normal and stacked graphs does—the configured dimensions are fixed.]

What else does this display provide besides a nice view? Click on the **Another host** icon:

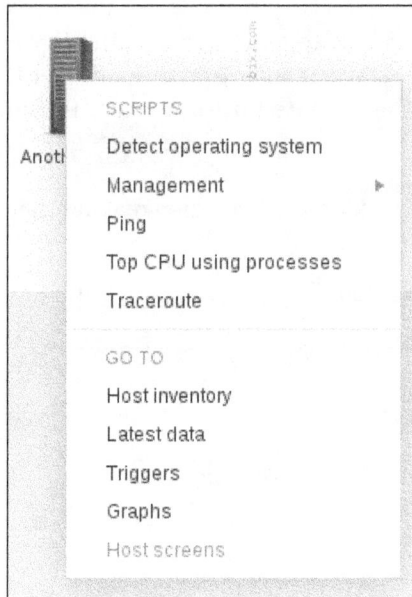

Here we have access to some global scripts, including the default ones and a couple we configured in *Chapter 7, Acting upon Monitored Conditions*. There are also quick links to the host inventory, discussed in *Chapter 5, Managing Hosts, Users, and Permissions*, and to the latest data, trigger, and graph pages for this host. When we use these links, the corresponding view would be filtered to show information about the host we clicked on initially. The last link in this section, **Host screens**, is disabled currently. We will discuss host (or templated) screens in *Chapter 10, Visualizing Data with Screens and Slideshows*.

We talked about using maps to see how things are connected. Before we explore that further, let's create a basic testing infrastructure—we will create a set of three items and three triggers that will denote network availability. To have something easy to control, we will check whether some files exist, and then just create and remove those files as needed. On both "A test host" and "Another host" execute the following:

```
$ touch /tmp/severity{1,2,3}
```

In the frontend, navigate to **Configuration | Templates** and click on **Items** next to **C_Template_Linux**, then click on **Create item** button. Enter "Link $1" in the **Name** field and vfs.file.exists[/tmp/severity1] in the **Key** field, then click on the **Add** button at the bottom. Now clone this item (by clicking on it, then clicking on the **Clone** button) and create two more, changing the trailing number for the filename to "2" and "3" accordingly.

> Do not forget to click on **Clone** after opening item details, otherwise you will simply edit the existing item.

Verify that you have those three items set up correctly:

NAME ▼	TRIGGERS	KEY
Link /tmp/severity1		vfs.file.exists[/tmp/severity1]
Link /tmp/severity2		vfs.file.exists[/tmp/severity2]
Link /tmp/severity3		vfs.file.exists[/tmp/severity3]

And now for the triggers—in the navigation bar click on **Triggers** and click on the **Create trigger** button. Enter "Latency too high on {HOST.NAME}" in the **Name** field and {C_Template_Linux:vfs.file.exists[/tmp/severity1].last()}=0 in the **Expression** field. Select **Warning** in the **Severity** section, then click on the **Add** button at the bottom. Same as with items, clone this trigger twice and change the severity number in the **Expression** field. As for the names and severities, let's use these:

- Second trigger for the **severity2** file: Name "**Link down for 5 minutes on {HOST.NAME}**" and severity **Average**

- Third trigger for the **severity3** file: Name "**Link down for 10 minutes on {HOST.NAME}**" and severity **High**

The final three triggers should look like this:

Warning	Latency too high on {HOST.NAME}	{C_Template_Linux:vfs.file.exists[/tmp/severity1].**last()**}=0
Average	Link down for 5 minutes on {HOST.NAME}	{C_Template_Linux:vfs.file.exists[/tmp/severity2].**last()**}=0
High	Link down for 10 minutes on {HOST.NAME}	{C_Template_Linux:vfs.file.exists[/tmp/severity3].**last()**}=0

> While cloning items and triggers brings over all their detail, cloning a map only includes map properties—actual map contents with icons, labels, and other information are not cloned. A relatively easy way to duplicate a map would be exporting it to XML, changing the map name in the XML file and then importing it back. We discuss XML export and import functionality in *Chapter 21, Working Closely with Data*.

Linking map elements

We now have our testing environment in place. Zabbix allows us to connect map elements with lines called **links**—let's see what functionality we can get from the map links. Go to **Monitoring | Maps** and click on **All maps** above the displayed map and then click on **Constructor** in the **ACTIONS** column next to **First map**.

The triplet of items and triggers we created before can be used as network link problem indicators now. You can add links in maps connecting two elements. Additionally, it is possible to change connector properties depending on the trigger state. Let's say you have a network link between two server rooms. You want the displayed link on the network map to change appearance depending on the connection state like this:

- **No problems**: Green line
- **High latency**: Yellow line
- **Connection problems for 5 minutes**: Orange, dashed line
- **Connection problems for 10 minutes**: Red, bold line

The good news is, Zabbix supports such a configuration. We will use our three items and triggers to simulate each of these states. Let's try to add a link—click on **Add** next to the **Link** label at the top of the map. Now that didn't work. A popup informs us that *Two elements should be selected*. How can we do that?

Click once on **A test host**, then hold down *Ctrl* and click on **Another host**. This selects both hosts. The property popup changed as well to show properties that can be mass-changed for both elements in one go. Apple system users might have to hold down *Command* instead.

> If the popup covers some element you wanted to select, do not close the popup, just drag the popup so that the covered element can be accessed. While it is not obvious in the default theme, the popup can be dragged by the upper area of it.

Another way to select multiple elements is to drag a rectangle around them in the map configuration area:

> Even though multiple elements can be drag-selected like this, currently there is no way to move multiple elements — even when multiple elements are selected, only the element that we would drag would be moved.

Whichever way you used to select both hosts, now click on **Add** next to the **Link** label again. The map will now show the new link between both hosts, which by default is green. Notice how at the bottom of the property editor the **Links** section has appeared:

Links	FROM	TO	LINK INDICATORS	ACTION
	A test host	Another host		Edit

> The way elements are put in the **FROM** and **TO** columns doesn't really matter — there is no direction concept for map links in Zabbix.

This is where we can edit the properties of the link itself — click on **Edit** in the **ACTION** column.

Let's define conditions and their effect on the link. Click on **Add** in the **Link** indicators section. In the resulting popup, select **Linux servers** in the **Group** field and **A test host** in the **Host** dropdown, then mark the checkboxes next to those three triggers we just created, then click on **Select**:

Latency too high on A test host	Warning
Link down for 5 minutes on A test host	Average
Link down for 10 minutes on A test host	High

Now we have to configure what effect these triggers will have when they will be active. For the high latency trigger, change the color to yellow in the color picker. For the 5 minute connection loss trigger, we might want to configure an orange dashed line. Select **Dashed line** in the **TYPE** dropdown for it, then choose orange in the color picker. Or maybe not. The color picker is a bit limited, and there is no orange. But luckily, the hex RGB input field allows us to specify any color. Enter FFAA00 there for the second trigger. For the 10-minute connection loss trigger, select **Bold line** in the **TYPE** dropdown and leave the color as red.

The final link configuration should look similar to this:

Links	FROM	TO	LINK INDICATORS	ACTION
	A test host	Another host		Edit

Label	

Type (OK)	Line ▾

Colour (OK)	▨ 00CC00

Link indicators	TRIGGER	TYPE	COLOUR	ACTION
	A test host: Latency too high on A test host	Line ▾	EEEE00	Remove
	A test host: Link down for 5 minutes on A test host	Dashed line ▾	FFAA00	Remove
	A test host: Link down for 10 minutes on A test host	Bold line ▾	DD0000	Remove
	Add			

Apply   Remove   Close

When you are done, click on **Apply** in the connector area, then close the map element properties and click on the **Update** button above the map and click on **OK** in the popup. Click on **First map** in the **NAME** column. Everything looks fine, both hosts show **OK**, and the link is green. Execute on "A test host":

```
$ rm /tmp/severity2
```

We just broke our connection to the remote datacenter for 5 minutes. Check the map again. You might have to wait for up to 30 seconds for the changes to show:

First map

A test host
Link down for 5 minutes on A test host

Another host
OK

2016-04-29 15:17:20

That's great, in a way. The link is shown as being down and one host has the active trigger listed. Notice how the label text is close to the map edge. With a slightly longer trigger or hostname it would be cut off. When creating maps, keep in mind the possibility of trigger names being long. Alternatively, trigger name expanding can be disabled. Let's check what this would look like — click on **All maps** and click on **Properties** next to **First map**. In the properties, clear the **Expand single problem** checkbox, click on **Update**, and then click on **First map** in the **NAME** column:

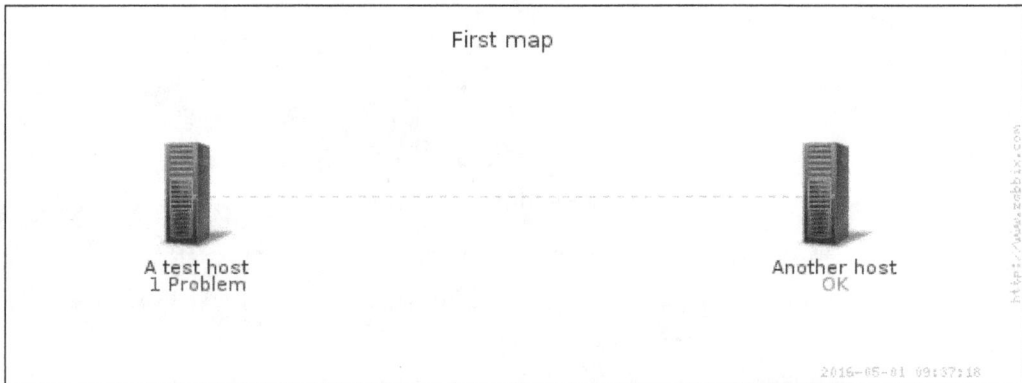

Instead of the full trigger name, just **1 Problem** is shown. Even though showing the trigger name is more user friendly, it doesn't work well when long trigger names are cut at the map border or overlap with other elements or their labels.

Our network was down for 5 minutes previously. By now, some more time has passed, so let's see what happens when our link has been down for 10 minutes. On "A test host", execute the following:

```
$ rm /tmp/severity3
```

Wait for 30 seconds and, check the map again:

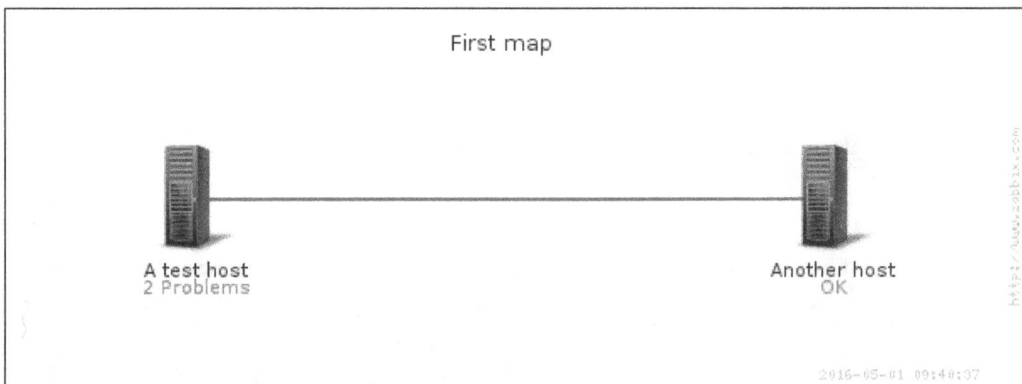

[☞ In Zabbix version 3.0.0, there is a bug—maps are not automatically refreshed. It is expected to be fixed in version 3.0.3.]

To attract more attention from an operator, the line is now red and bold. As opposed to a host having a single problem and the ability to show either the trigger name or the string **1 Problem**, when there are multiple triggers active, the problem count is always listed. Now, let's say our latency trigger checks a longer period of time, and it fires only now. On "A test host", execute the following:

```
$ rm /tmp/severity1
```

Wait for 30 seconds, then refresh the map. We should now see a yellow line not. Actually, the bold red line is still there, even though it has correctly spotted that there are three problems active now. Why so? The thing is, the order in which triggers fire does not matter—trigger severity determines which style takes precedence. We carefully set three different severities for our triggers, so there's no ambiguity when triggers fire. What happens if you add multiple triggers as status indicators that have the same severity but different styles and they all fire? Well, don't. While you can technically create such a situation, that would make no sense. If you have multiple triggers of the same severity, just use identical styles for them. Let's fix the connection, while still having a high latency:

```
$ touch /tmp/severity{2,3}
```

Only one problem should be left, and the link between the elements should be yellow finally—higher severity triggers are not overriding the one that provides the yellow color anymore.

Feel free to experiment with removing and adding test files; the link should always be styled like specified for the attached active trigger with the highest severity.

There's no practical limit on the amount of status indicators, so you can easily add more levels of visual difference.

We used triggers from one of the hosts that are connected with the link, but there is no requirement for the associated trigger to be on a host that's connected to the link—it could even not be on the map at all. If you decided to draw a link between two hosts, the trigger could come from a completely different host. In that case both elements would show status as "**OK**", but the link would change its properties.

Selecting links

Our map currently has one link only. To access **Link** properties, we may select one of the elements this link is connecting, and a link section will appear at the bottom of the element properties popup. In a more complicated map, it might be hard to select the correct link if an element has lots of links. Luckily, the Zabbix map editing interface follows a couple of rules that make it easier:

- If only one element is selected, all links from it are displayed
- If more than one element is selected, only links between any two of the selected elements are displayed

A few examples to illustrate these rules:

Selecting one or both elements will show one link:

- Selecting **Element 1** will show the link between **Element 1** and **Element 2**
- Selecting **Element 3** will show the link between **Element 2** and **Element 3**
- Selecting **Element 2** will show both links
- Selecting **Element 2** and either **Element 1** or **Element 3** will show the link between the selected elements
- Selecting **Element 1** and **Element 3** will show no links at all
- Selecting all three elements will show both links

Most importantly, even if we had 20 links going out of **Element 2**, we could select a specific one by selecting **Element 2** and the element at the other end of that link.

> For named elements such as hosts, the name is displayed in the list of the links. For images, only the icon name would be shown. If all images use the same icon, the names would be the same in the list.

Routed and invisible links

Links in Zabbix are simply straight lines from the center of one element to the center of another. What if there's another element between two connected elements? Well, the link will just go under the "obstructing" element. There is no built-in way to "route" a link in some other way, but there's a hackish workaround. We may upload a transparent PNG image to be used as a custom icon (we discuss uploading additional images later in this chapter), then use it to route the link:

> Notice the informative labels on the hosts and on the link—we will discuss such functionality later in this chapter.

Note that we would have to configure link indicators, if used, on all such links—otherwise, some segments would change their color and style according to the trigger state, some would not.

This approach could be also used to have a link that starts as a single line out of some system, and only splits in to multiple lines later. That could reduce clutter in some maps.

Another issue could be that in some maps there are lots and lots of links. Displaying them could result in a map that is hard to read. Here, a trick could be to have the link default color as the map background color, only making such links show up when there's some problem with the help of link indicators.

Further map customization

Let's find out some other things that can add nice touches to the map configuration.

Macros in labels

Map elements that we have used so far had their name hardcoded in the label, and the status was added to them automatically. We can automatically use the name from the host properties and display some additional information. In **Monitoring | Maps**, click on **All maps** if a map is displayed, then click on the **First map** in the **NAME** column.

> Notice how the grid settings have been kept. Grid settings, including snapping to the grid, displaying the grid, and grid size, are saved for each map separately.

Click on the **A test host** icon. In the **Label** field, enter "{HOST.NAME} - {HOST.IP}" and select **Top** in the **Label location** dropdown. Click on **Apply**:

> The {HOST.IP} macro always picks up the interface address sequentially, starting with the agent interfaces. If a host has multiple interface types, there is no way to specify how to, for example, prefer the SNMP interface over the agent interface.

Strange... the value we entered is not resolved, the actual macros are shown. By default, macros are not resolved in map configuration for performance reasons. Take a look at the top bar above the map; there's an **Expand macros** control that by default is set to **Off**:

Click on it to toggle it to **On** and observe the label we changed earlier. It should show the hostname and IP address now:

The macros for the hostname and IP address are useful when either could change and we would not want to check every map and then manually update those values. Additionally, when a larger amount of hosts is added to a map, we could do a mass update on them and enter "{HOST.NAME}" instead of setting the name individually for each of them.

> It's a good idea to save the map every now and then by clicking on the **Update** button—for example, now might be a good time to do so. Dismiss the strange popup by clicking on **Cancel**; the map was saved anyway.

Notice how we could also change the label position. By default, whatever is set in the map properties is used, but that can be overridden for individual elements.

There are more macros that work in element labels, and the Zabbix manual has a full list of those. Of special interest might be the ability to show the actual data from items; let's try that one out. In the label for **A test host**, add another line that says "{A test host:system.cpu.load.last()}" and observe the label:

```
A test host - 127.0.0.1
           0
```

> There is no helper like in triggers—we always have to enter the macro data manually.
>
> If the label does not show the **CPU load** value but an *UNKNOWN* string, there might be a typo in the hostname or item key. It could also be displayed if there's no data to show for that item with the chosen function. If it shows the entered macro but not the value, there might be a typo in the syntax or trigger function name. Note that the hostname, item key, and function name all are case sensitive. Attempting to apply a numeric function such as avg() to a string or text item will also show the entered macro.

Real-time monitoring data is now shown for this host. The syntax is pretty much the same as in the triggers, except that map labels support only a subset of trigger functions, and even for the supported functions only a subset of parameters is supported. We may only use the trigger functions last(), min(), max(), and avg(). In the parameters, only a time period may be used, specified either in seconds, or in the user friendly format. For example, both avg(300) and avg(5m) would work in map labels.

It's not very clear to an observer what that value is, though. An improvement would be prefixing that line with `"CPU load:"`, which would make the label much more clear:

```
A test host - 127.0.0.1
      CPU load: 0.03
```

This way, as much information as needed (or as much as fits) can be added to a map element—multiple lines are supported. One might notice the hardcoded hostname here. When updating a larger amount of map elements, that can be cumbersome, but luckily we can use a macro here again—change that line to read `"CPU load: {{HOST.HOST}:system.cpu.load.last()}"`. Actual functionality in the map should not change, as this element should now pick up the hostname from the macro. Notice the nested use here.

> Macro `{HOST.NAME}` would not work here. That macro resolves to the visible name of a host, but to identify a host we must reference its hostname or so-called **"host technical name"**. Yes, the macro naming can be a bit confusing.

What could element labels display? CPU load, memory or disk usage, number of connected users to a wireless access point—whatever is useful enough to see right away in a map.

We can also see that this host still has one problem, caused by our simulated latency trigger. Execute on `"A test host"`:

```
$ touch /tmp/severity1
```

Link labels

As mentioned before, we can also put labels on links. Back in the constructor of the **First map**, click on the **A test host** icon. Click on **Edit** in the **Links** section to open the link properties, then enter `"Slow link"` in the Label area, and click on **Apply** in the link properties. Observe the change in the map:

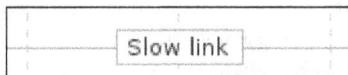

```
        Slow link
```

On the links, the label is always a rectangular box that has the same color as the link itself. It is centered on the link—there is no way to specify offset.

Having hardcoded text can be useful, but showing monitoring data, like we did for a host, would be even better. Luckily, that is possible, and we could display network traffic data on this link. Change the link label to the following:

```
Incoming traffic: {A test host:net.if.in[eth0].last()}
Outgoing traffic: {A test host:net.if.out[eth0].last()}
```

> We cannot use automatic references such as {HOST.HOST} here. The link is not associated with any host and such a reference would fail.

We are mixing here both freeform text (you could label some link "Slow link", for example), and macros (in this case, referring to specific traffic items). Click on **Apply** for the link properties. This might also be a good moment to save the changes by clicking on **Update** in the upper right corner:

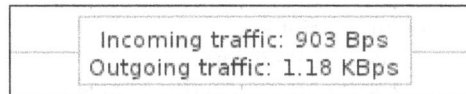

```
Incoming traffic: 903 Bps
Outgoing traffic: 1.18 KBps
```

Both macros we used and multiline layout work nicely.

> We can reference any item type—agent, SNMP, and others. As long as it's gathering data, values can be shown on a map.

For a full list of supported macros in map element labels, see the Zabbix manual.

Reflecting problems on map elements

Having the problem count listed in the label is useful, but it's not that easy to see from a distance on a wall-mounted display. We also might want to have a slightly nicer looking map that would make problems stand out more for our users. Zabbix offers two methods to achieve this:

- Custom icons
- Icon highlighting

In the **First map** constructor, click on **A test host**. In the **Icons** section, choose a different icon in the **Problem** dropdown—for the testing purposes, we'll go with the **Crypto-router_(24)** icon, but any could be used. Click on **Apply**, then **Update** for the map. Additionally, run on "A test host":

```
$ rm /tmp/severity1
```

After some 30 seconds check the map in the monitoring view—status icons are not displayed in the configuration section:

As soon as a problem appeared on a host, the icon was automatically changed. In the configuration, there were two additional states that could have their own icons – when a host is *disabled* and when it is in *maintenance*. Of course, a server should not turn into a router or some other unexpected device. The usual approach is to have a normal icon and then an icon that has a red cross over it, or maybe a small colored circle next to it to denote the status.

> Notice how the link is not horizontally aligned anymore. As the icons are positioned by their top-left corner, a smaller icon had its center moved. The link is attached to the center of the icon.

Manually specifying different icons is fine, but doing that on a larger scale could be cumbersome. Another feature to identify problematic elements is called **icon highlighting**. As opposed to selecting icons per state, here a generic highlighting is used. This is a map-level option, there is no way to customize it per map element. Let's test it. In the list of all the maps, click on **Properties** next to **First map** and mark the checkbox **Icon highlight**. This setting determines whether map elements receive additional visualization depending on their status. Click on **Update**, then open **Configuration | Hosts**. Click on **Enabled** next to **Another host** to toggle its status and acknowledge the popup to disable this host. Check the map in the monitoring view:

Both hosts now have some sort of background. What does this mean?

- The round background denotes the trigger status. If any trigger is not in the **OK** state, the trigger with the highest priority determines the color of the circle

- The square background denotes the host status. Disabled hosts receive gray highlighting. Hosts that are in maintenance receive an orange background

Click on **A test host**, then click on **Triggers**. In the trigger list, click on **No** in the **ACK** column, enter some message and click on **Acknowledge**. Check the map in the monitoring view again:

The colored circle now has a thick, green border. This border denotes the acknowledgment status—if it's there, the problem is acknowledged.

Zabbix default icons currently are not well centered. This is most obvious when icon highlighting is used—notice how **Another host** is misaligned because of that shadow. For this icon, it's even more obvious in the problem highlighting. In the constructor of the **First map**, click on **A test host** and choose **Default** in the **Problem** dropdown in the **Icons** section. Click on **Apply** and then on **Update** for the map, then check the map in the monitoring section view:

In such a configuration, another icon set might have to be used for a more eye-pleasing look.

> The Zabbix source archive has older icons, used before Zabbix 2.0, in the `misc/images/png_classic` directory.

To return things to normal state, open **Configuration | Hosts,** click on **Disabled** next to **Another host** and confirm the popup, then execute on "A test host":

```
$ touch /tmp/severity1
```

Available map elements

Hosts are not the only element type we could add to the map. In the constructor for the **First map,** click on `Another host` and expand the **Type** dropdown in the element properties. We won't use additional types right now, but let's look at what's available:

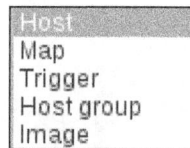

```
Host
Map
Trigger
Host group
Image
```

- **Host**: We already covered what a host is. A host displays information on all associated triggers.

- **Map**: You can actually insert a link to another map. It will have an icon like all elements, and clicking it would offer a menu to open that map. This allows us to create interesting drilldown configurations. We could have a world map, then linked in continental maps, followed by country-level maps, city-level maps, data center-level maps, rack-level maps, system-level maps, and at the other end we could actually expand to have a map with different planets and galaxies! Well, we got carried away. Of course, each level would have an appropriate map or schematic set as a background image.

- **Trigger**: This works very similar to a host, except only information about a single trigger is included. This way you can place a single trigger on the map that is not affected by other triggers on the host. In our nested maps scenario we could use triggers in the last display, placing a core router schematic in the background and adding individual triggers for specific ports.

- **Host group**: This works like a host, except information about all hosts in a group is gathered. In the simple mode, a single icon is displayed to represent all hosts in the selected group. This can be handy for a higher-level overview, but it's especially nice in the preceding nested scenario in which we could group all hosts by continent, country, and city, thus placing some icons on an upper-level map. For example, we could have per country host group elements placed on the global map, if we have enough room, that is. A host group element on a map can also display all hosts individually — we will cover that functionality a bit later.

- **Image**: This allows us to place an image on the map. The image could be something visual only, such as the location of a conditioner in a server room, but it could also have an URL assigned; thus, you can link to arbitrary objects.

Talking about **URLs**, take a look at the bottom of the element properties popup:

URLs	NAME	URL	ACTION
			Remove
	Add		

Here, multiple URLs can be added and each can have a name. When a map is viewed in the monitoring section, clicking on an element will include the **URL** names in the menu. They could provide quick access to a web management page for a switch or a UPS device, or a page in an internal wiki, describing troubleshooting steps with this specific device. Additionally, the following macros are supported in the **URL** field:

- {TRIGGER.ID}
- {HOST.ID}
- {HOSTGROUP.ID}
- {MAP.ID}

This allows us to add links that lead to a Zabbix frontend section, while specifying the ID of the entity we clicked on in the opened URL.

Map filtering

Map elements "host", "host group", and "map" aggregate the information about all the relevant problems. Often that will be exactly what is needed, but Zabbix maps also allow filtering the displayed problems. The available conditions are as follows:

- **Acknowledgment status**: This can be set for the whole map
- **Trigger severity**: This can be set for the whole map
- **Application**: This can be set for individual hosts

In the map properties, the **Problem display** dropdown controls what and how problems are displayed based on their acknowledgment status. This is a configuration-time only option and cannot be changed in the monitoring section. The available choices are as follows:

- **All**
- **Separated**
- **Unacknowledged only**

The **All** option is what we have selected currently and the acknowledgment status will not affect the problem displaying there. The **Separated** option would show two lines—one, displaying the total amount of problems and another displaying the amount of unacknowledged problems:

Notice the total and unacknowledged lines having different colors. The option **Unacknowledged only**, as one might expect, shows only the problems that are not acknowledged at this time.

Another way to filter the information that is displayed on a map is by trigger severity. In the map properties, the **Minimum trigger severity** option allows us to choose the severity to filter on:

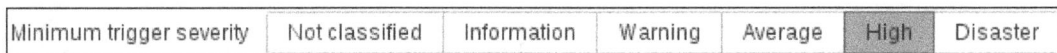

Minimum trigger severity	Not classified	Information	Warning	Average	High	Disaster

If we choose **High,** like in the preceding screenshot, opening the map in the monitoring section would ignore anything but the two highest levels of severity. By default, **Not classified** is selected and that shows all problems. Even better, when we are looking at a map in the monitoring section, in the upper right corner we may change the severity, no matter which level is selected in the map configuration:

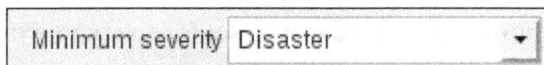

Minimum severity	Disaster ▼

> At this time, link indicators ignore the severity filter. That is likely a bug, but at the time of this writing it is not known when it will be fixed.

Yet another way to filter what is shown on a map is by application (which are just groups of items) on the host level. When editing a map element that is showing host data, there is an **Application** field:

Map element	
Type	Host ▾
Label	{HOST.NAME} - {HOST.IP} CPU load: {{HOST.HOST}:system.cpu.load.last()}
Label location	Top ▾
Host	A test host ✕ Select
Application	Select

Choosing an application here will only take into account triggers that reference items from this application. This is a freeform field – if entering the application name manually, make sure that it matches the application used in the items exactly. Only one application may be specified here. This is a `configuration-time only` option and can not be changed in the monitoring section.

Custom icons and background images

Zabbix comes with icons to be used in the maps. Quite often one will want to use icons from another source, and it is possible to do so by uploading them to Zabbix first. To upload an image to be used as an icon, navigate to **Administration | General** and choose **Images** in the dropdown. Click on the **Create icon** button and choose a name for your new icon, then select an image file – preferably not too large:

Name	Zabbix logo
Upload	Browse... zabbix_logo_100x27.png
	Add Cancel

> Even though the button label says **create** we are just uploading an image.

Click on **Add**. Somewhere in the following images, the one we just uploaded should appear. In addition to custom icons, we can also upload background images to be used in maps. In the **Type** dropdown, switch to **Background** and click on the **Create background** button. Note that this dropdown, different from all the other pages, is located on the left hand side in 3.0.0. Again, enter a name for the background and choose an image—preferably, one sized 600x225 as that was the size of our map. Smaller images will leave empty space at the edges and larger images will be cut:

For the background images, it is suggested to have simple PNG images as they will provide less distraction from the actual monitoring data and will be smaller to download whenever the map is viewed.

Click on **Add**. As Zabbix comes with no background images by default, the one we added should be the only one displayed now. With the images uploaded, let's try to use them in our map. Go to **Monitoring | Maps** and click on **All maps** if a map is shown. Click on **Constructor** next to **First map** and click on **Add** next to the **Icon** label, then click on the newly added icon. In the **Icons** section, change the **Default** dropdown to display whatever name you chose for the uploaded icon, then click on **Apply**. Position this new icon wherever it would look best (remember about the ability to disable snapping to the grid). You might want to clear out the **Label** field, too. Remember to click on **Apply** to see the changes on the map:

[🔆 In this screenshot, the border around the Zabbix logo is the selection border in the editing interface. Grid lines have been hidden here.]

When you are satisfied with the image placement, click on **Update** in the upper right corner to save the map. This time we might click on **OK** in the popup to return to the list of the maps. Let's set up the background now — click on **Properties** next to **First map**. In the configuration form, the **Background image** dropdown has **No image** selected currently. The background we uploaded should be available there — select it:

Background image | No image ▾
No image
Map

Click on **Update**, then click on **Constructor** next to **First map** again. The editing interface should display the background image we chose and it should be possible to position the images to match the background now:

Map image courtesy of MapQuest and OpenStreetMap

Uploading a large amount of images can be little fun. A very easy way to automate that using XML import will be discussed in *Chapter 21, Working Closely with Data,* and we will also cover the possibility to use the Zabbix API for such tasks.

Here's an example of what a larger geographical map might look like:

Map image courtesy of Wikimedia and OpenStreetMap:

A geographical map is used as a background here, and different elements are interconnected.

Icon mapping

The images we used for the elements so far were either static, or changed depending on the host and trigger status. Zabbix can also automatically choose the correct icon based on host inventory contents. This functionality is called icon mapping. Before we can benefit from it, we must configure an icon map. Navigate to **Administration | General** and choose **Icon mapping** in the dropdown, then click on the **Create icon map** button in the upper right corner. The icon map entries allow us to specify a regular expression, and an inventory field to match this expression against and an icon to be used if a match is found. All the entries are matched in sequential order, and the first one that matches determines which the icon will be used. If no match is found, the fallback icon, specified in the **Default** dropdown, will be used.

Let's try this out. Enter "Zabbix 3.0" in the **Name** field. In the **Inventory** field dropdown, choose **Software application A** and in the **Expression** field enter "^3.0".

In *Chapter 5*, *Managing Hosts, Users, and Permissions*, we set the agent version item on "A test host" to populate the "**Software application A**" field. Let's check whether that is still the case. Go to **Configuration | Hosts** and click on **Items** next to A test host. In the item list, click on the Zabbix agent version (Zabbix 3.0) in the **NAME** column. The **Populates host inventory** field option is set to **-None-**. How so? In *Chapter 8*, *Simplifying Complex Configuration with Templates*, this item was changed to be controlled by the template, but it was copied from "Another host", which did not have the inventory option set. When we linked our new template to "A test host", this option was overwritten. The last collected value was left in the inventory field, thus currently "A test host" has the agent version number in that inventory field, but "Another host" does not. To make this item populate the inventory for both hosts, click on **C_Template_Linux** next to **Parent** items and choose **Software application A** in the **Populates host inventory** field dropdown. When done, click on **Update**.

We populated the **Software application A** field automatically with the Zabbix agent version, and in the icon map we are now checking whether it begins with "3.0". In the **ICON** dropdown for the first line, choose an icon — in this example, the Zabbix logo that was uploaded earlier is used. For the **Default** dropdown, select a different icon — here we are using **Hub_(48)**:

Name	Zabbix 3.0			
Mappings	INVENTORY FIELD	EXPRESSION	ICON	ACTION
	1: Software application A ▼	^3.0	Zabbix logo ▼	Remove
	Add			
	Default		Hub_(48) ▼	
	Add Cancel			

> Images on the right can be clicked to see them full size.

We have only used one check here. If we wanted to match other inventory fields, we'd click on the **Add** control in the **Mappings** section. Individual entries could be reordered by grabbing the handle to the left of them and dragging them to the desired position, same as the custom graph items in the graph configuration. Remember that the first match would determine the icon used.

When done, click on the **Add** button at the bottom. Now navigate to **Monitoring | Maps** and if a map is shown, click on **All maps**. Click on **Properties** next to **First map** and in the **Automatic icon mapping** dropdown, choose the icon mapping we just created — it should be the only choice besides the **<manual>** entry. Click on the **Update** button at the bottom. If we check this map in the monitoring view now, we would see no difference, actually. To see why, let's go to the list of maps and click on **Constructor** next to **First map**. In the map editing view, click on **A test host**. The **Automatic icon selection** is not enabled. If we add a new element to this map, the automatic icon selection would be enabled for it because the map now has an icon map assigned. The existing elements keep their configuration when the icon map is assigned to the map — those elements were added when there was no icon map assigned. Holding down *Ctrl*, click on **Another host**. In the mass update form, first mark the checkbox to the left of **Automatic icon selection**, then — to the right. The first checkbox instructs Zabbix to overwrite this option for all selected elements, the second checkbox specifies that the option should be enabled for those elements:

Mass update elements

Selected elements	TYPE	NAME
	Host	A test host
	Host	Another host

Label

Label location   Default

Automatic icon selection

Icon (default)   Cloud_(24)

Icon (problem)   Default

Icon (maintenance)   Default

Icon (disabled)   Default

Apply   Remove   Close

> Marking the **Automatic icon selection** checkbox disables the manual icon selection dropdowns — these features cannot be used at the same time for the same icon.

Click on **Apply** and notice how both hosts change their icon to the default one from the icon map properties. This seems incorrect, at least "A test host" had the 3.0 version number in that field the reason is performance related again—in the configuration, icon mapping does not apply and the default icon is always used. Make sure to save our changes by clicking on **Update**, then open this map in the monitoring view:

Here, **A test host** got the icon that was supposed to be used for Zabbix agent 3.0 (assuming you have Zabbix agent 3.0 on that host). **Another host** did not match that check and got the default icon, because the item has not yet updated the inventory field. A bit later, once the agent version item has received the data for "Another host", it should change the icon, too.

Icon mapping could be used to display different icons depending on the operating system the host is running. For network devices, we could show a generic device icon with a vendor logo in one corner, if we base icon mapping on the sysDescr OID. For a UPS device, the icon could change based on the device state—one icon when it's charging, one when it's discharging, and another when it tells to change the battery.

Other global map options

While working with this map we have discussed quite a few global map options already, but some we have not mentioned yet. Let's review the remaining ones. They are global in the sense that they affect the whole map (but not all maps). Go to the list of maps, then click on **Properties** next to **First map**:

Owner	Admin (Zabbix Administrator) ✕ Select
Name	First map
Width	600
Height	225
Background image	Map ▾
Automatic icon mapping	Zabbix 3.0 ▾ show icon mappings
Icon highlight	▣
Mark elements on trigger status change	
Expand single problem	
Advanced labels	
Icon label type	Label ▾
Icon label location	Bottom ▾
Problem display	Separated ▾
Minimum trigger severity	Not classified Information Warning Average High Disaster
URLs	NAME URL ELEMENT ACTION
	Host ▾ Remove
	Add

Skipping the options we already know about, the remaining ones are as follows:

- **Owner**: This is the user who created the map and has control over it. We will discuss it in more detail later in this chapter.

- **Mark elements on trigger status change**: This will mark elements that have recently changed their state. By default, the elements will be marked for 30 minutes and we discussed the possibility to customize this in *Chapter 6, Detecting Problems with Triggers*. The elements are marked by adding three small triangles on all the sides of an element, except where the label is located:

- **Icon label type**: This sets whatever is used for labels. By default it's set to **Label**, like we used. Other options are **IP address**, **Element name**, **Status only**, and **Nothing**, all of which are self-explanatory. If a host has multiple interfaces, we cannot choose which **IP address** should be displayed—same as with the {HOST.IP} macro, Zabbix automatically picks an IP address, starting with the agent interface. Some of these only make sense for some element types—for example, IP address only makes sense for host elements. Just above this, **Advanced labels** allow us to set the label type for each element type separately:

- **Icon label location**: This allows us to specify the default label location. For all elements that use the default location, this option will control where the label goes.

> Zabbix 3.0.0 has a bug—enabling **Advanced labels** will show an extra text field below each dropdown. At the time of this writing, it is not yet known which version will fix this issue.

Displaying host group elements

When we discussed the available map elements earlier, it was mentioned that we can automatically show all hosts in a **Host group**. To see how that works, navigate to the map list and click on **Create map**. Enter "Host group elements" in the **Name** field, then click on the **Add** button at the bottom. Now click on **Constructor** next to **Host group elements map** and click on **Add** next to the **Icon** label. Click on the new element to open its properties and select **Host group** in the **Type** dropdown. In the **Host group** field, start typing "linux" and click on **Linux servers** in the dropdown. In the **Show** option, select **Host group elements**. That results in several additional options appearing, but for now, we won't change them. One last thing—change the **Label** to "{HOST.NAME}":

Map element		
Type	Host group ▾	
Show	Host group	Host group elements
Area type	Fit to map	Custom size
Placing algorithm	Grid	
Label	{HOST.NAME}	
Label location	Default ▾	
Host group	Linux servers ✕	Select

> Zabbix 3.0.0 has a bug—for a new host group icon, the **Show** selector does not show which choice is selected at first. At the time of writing this, it is not yet known which version will fix this issue.

When done, click on **Apply**. Notice how the element was positioned in the middle of the map and the rest of the map area was shaded. This indicates that the host group element will utilize all of the map area. Click on **Update** in the upper right corner to save this map and then check it out in the monitoring view. All hosts (in our case—two) from the selected **Host group** are positioned near the top of the map:

Let's try some changes now. Return to the constructor of this map and click on the icon that represents our **Host group**. In the properties, switch **Area type** to **Custom size** and for the **Area size** fields, change **Width** to 400 and **Height** to 550. In the **Label** field, add CPU load {{HOST.HOST}:system.cpu.load.last()}:

> The **Placing algorithm** option has only one choice—**Grid**. When this feature was developed, it was expected that additional algorithms would appear later, but that has not happened so far.

When done, click on **Apply**. The grayed out area shrunk and got a selection border. Drag it to the bottom-right corner by grabbing the icon. That does not seem to work that well—the center of the area snaps to the grid and we are prevented from positioning it nicely. Disable snapping to the grid by clicking on next to the **Grid** label above the map and try positioning the area again—it should work better now. Click on **Update** to save the map and check the map in the monitoring view:

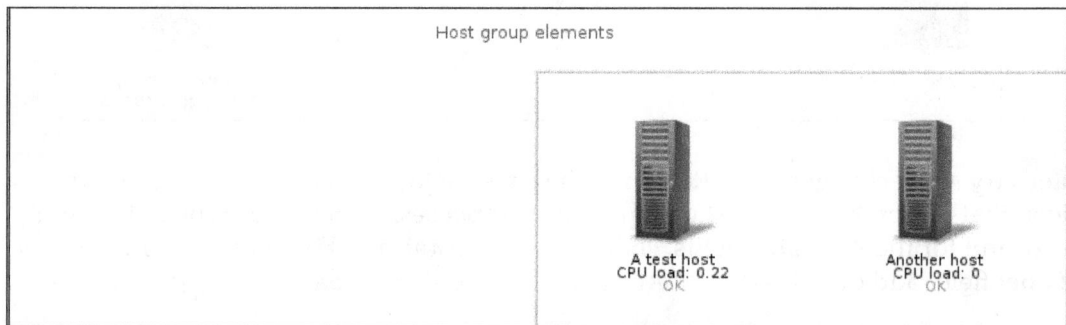

The hosts are now positioned in a column that is denoted with a gray border—that's our **Host group** area. The macros we used in the label are applied to each element and in this case each host has its CPU load displayed below the icon. The nested macro syntax that automatically picked item values from the host it is added to is even of more use now. If hosts are added to the **Host group** or removed from it, this map would automatically update to reflect that. The placement algorithm might not work perfectly in all cases, though—it might be a good idea to test how well the expected amount of hosts fits in the chosen area.

The ability to use a specific area only allows the placement of other elements to the left in this map—maybe some switches, routers, or firewalls that are relevant for the servers, displayed on the right-hand side.

Numbers as icons

When looking at a map from a large distance, small label text might be hard to read. We can zoom in using the browser functionality, but that would make the icons large—and if the systems that we display on some map are all the same, there would be no need to use a visual icon at all. What we could try, though, is displaying a large number for each system. Zabbix maps do not allow changing font size, but we could work around this limitation by generating images that are just numbers and using them as icons in the map. One way to do so would be using the `ImageMagick` suite. To generate numbers from `01` to `50`, we could run a script such as this on Linux:

```
for imagenum in {01..50}; do
    convert -font DejaVu-Sans-Mono-Bold -gravity center -size
    52x24 -background transparent -pointsize 32 label:
    "$imagenum"      "$imagenum".png
done
```

It loops from `01` to `50` and runs the `convert` utility, generating an image with a number, using `DejaVu` font. We are prefixing single-digit numbers with a zero—using 01 instead of just 1, for example. If you do not want the leading zero, just replace 01 with 1. Later we would upload these images as icons and use them in our maps, and a smaller version of our map could look like this:

If we have lots of systems and there is no way to fit them all in one map, we could have a map for a subset of systems and then automatically loop through all the maps on some wall-mounted display—we will discuss later in this chapter a way to do that using the built-in slideshow feature in Zabbix.

You should be able to create good-looking and functional maps now. Before you start working on a larger map, it is recommended that you plan it out—doing large-scale changes later in the process can be time consuming.

Creating a large amount of complicated maps manually is not feasible—we will cover several options for generating them in an automated fashion in *Chapter 21, Working Closely with Data*.

Sharing the maps

When creating the maps, we ignored the very first field—**Owner**. The map ownership concept is new in Zabbix 3.0. In previous versions, only administrators were able to create maps. Now any user may create a map and even share it with other users. Another change is that maps are by default created in **Private** mode—they are not visible for other users. The maps we created are not visible to our monitoring and advanced users, covered in *Chapter 5, Managing Hosts, Users, and Permissions*. Let's share our maps.

In another browser, log in as "monitoring_user" and visit **Monitoring | Maps**. Notice how no maps are available currently. Back in the first browser, where we are logged in as the "Admin" user, go to the list of maps. Click on **Properties** next to **First map** and switch to the **Sharing** tab. In the **Type** selection, switch to **Public** and click on **Update**:

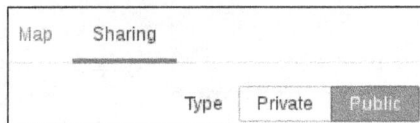

Map	Sharing
	Type Private Public

Refresh the map list as the "monitoring_user"—**First map** appears in the list. The **ACTIONS** column is empty, as this user may not perform any changes to the map currently. Setting a map to public makes it visible to all users—this is the same how network maps operated before Zabbix 3.0.

Back in the first browser, let's go to the **Sharing** tab in the properties of **First map** again. This time, click on **Add** in the **List of user shares** section and click on monitoring_user in the popup. Make sure **PERMISSIONS** are set to **Read-write**. When a map is public, adding read-only permission is possible, but it makes no difference, so let's switch the **Type** back to **Private**. We had another user—click on **Add** in the **List of user shares** section again and this time click on advanced_user. For this user, set **PERMISSIONS** to **Read-only**:

Type	Private Public		
List of user group shares	USER GROUPS PERMISSIONS ACTION		
	Add		
List of user shares	USERS	PERMISSIONS	ACTION
	monitoring_user (monitoring user)	Read-only Read-write	Remove
	advanced_user (advanced user)	Read-only Read-write	Remove
	Add		

> Maps may also be shared with all users in a group by using the **List of user group shares** section.

When done, click on **Update**. Refresh the map list as "monitoring_user" and notice how the **ACTIONS** column now contains the **Properties** and **Constructor** links. Check out the **Sharing** tab in **Properties** — this user now can see the existing sharing configuration and share this map with other users both in **Read-only** and in **Read-write** mode. Note that the normal users may only share with user groups they are in themselves, and with users from those groups. Switch back to the **Map** tab and check the **Owner** field:

Owner	Admin (Zabbix Administrator) x	Select

Even though this user has **Read-write** permissions, they cannot change the ownership — only super admin and admin users may do that.

Let's log in as "advanced_user" in the second browser now and check the map list:

NAME ▲	WIDTH	HEIGHT	ACTIONS
First map	600	225	Properties Constructor
Host group elements	800	600	Properties Constructor

We only shared one map with this user, and only in **Read-only** mode — how come they can see both maps and also have write permissions on them? Sharing only affects Zabbix users, not admins or super admins. Super admins, as always, have full control over everything. Zabbix admins can see and edit all maps as long as they have write permission on all the objects, included in those maps. And if we share a map in **Read-write** mode with a Zabbix user that does not have permission to see at least one object, included in that map, the user would not even see the map. It is not possible to use map sharing as a way around the permission model in Zabbix — which is: the user must have permission to see all the included objects to see the map. If we include aggregating objects such as hosts, host groups, or even sub-maps, the user must have permission to see all of the objects down to the last trigger in the last sub-map to even see the top level map.

Probably the biggest benefit from the sharing functionality would be the ability for users to create their own maps and share them with other users — something that was not possible before.

Summary

We have learned to create graphs of different types and how to customize them. This allows us to place multiple items in a single graph, change their visual characteristics, choose different graph types, modify y axis scaling, and several other parameters. We were able to show basic trigger information and a percentile line on a graph.

We discovered simple, ad hoc, and custom graphs, with each category fitting a different need.

Simple graphs show data for a single item. Ad hoc graphs allow us to quickly graph multiple items from the latest data, although there's no way to save them. Custom graphs can have several items, all kinds of customization, and are similar to triggers — they are associated with all the hosts that they reference items from.

The creation of network maps also should not be a problem any more. We will be able to create nice-looking network maps, whether they show a single data center, or lots of locations spread out all over the world. Our maps will be able to show real-time data from items, network link status, and use nice background images.

In the next chapter we will look at additional ways to visualize data. Zabbix screens will allow us to combine graphs, maps, and many other elements on a single page. We will also discover how a single screen could be easily adapted to change the displayed information to a specific host. Combining the screens, slide shows will be able to show one screen for some period of time, then another, and cycle through all the selected screens that way.

10
Visualizing Data with Screens and Slideshows

Having become familiar with simple, ad hoc, and custom graphs as well as network maps, we will explore a few more visualization options in this chapter. We will cover the following topics:

- Screens that can include other entities, including global and templated or host screens
- Slideshows that change displayed information on a periodic basis automatically

We looked at the individual visualization elements before; now is the time to move forward. Compound elements (which have nothing to do with map elements) allow us to combine individual elements and other sources to provide a more informative or good-looking overview. We might want to see a map of our network together with a graph of main outbound links, and perhaps also a list of current problems.

Screens

The graphs and maps we are familiar with cannot be combined in a single page on their own—for that, we may use an entity called a **screen**. Let's proceed with creating one together: navigate to **Monitoring | Screens**, and click on the **Create screen** button. Enter **Local servers** in the **Name** field and 2 in the **Columns** field. We will be able to add more later, if needed:

Owner	Admin (Zabbix Administrator) ✕ Select
Name	Local servers
Columns	2
Rows	1
	Add Cancel

> The same as with network maps, the way screens are configured has changed in Zabbix 3.0—it's now done in the monitoring section. Screens may also be created and shared by users.

Click on **Add**, and then click on **Constructor** next to **Local servers**. We are presented with a fairly unimpressive view:

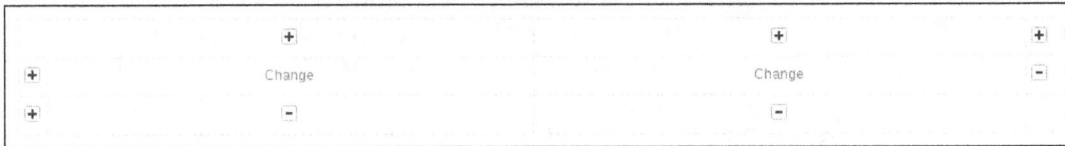

+	+	+
+ Change	Change	−
+ −	−	

So it's up to us to spice it up. Click on the left-hand **Change** link, and we have an editing form replacing the previous cell contents. The default resource type is graph, and we created some graphs earlier: click on **Select** next to the **Graph** field. In the upcoming window, make sure **A test host** is selected in the **Host** dropdown, and then click on **CPU load & traffic**. That's all we want to configure here for now, so click on **Add**.

> It is not required to save a screen explicitly, unlike most other configuration sections. All changes made are immediately saved.

Now, click on the right-hand **Change** link and then on **Select** next to the **Graph** field. In the upcoming window, click on **Used diskspace (pie)**. Remember how we tuned the pie-chart dimensions before? When inserting elements for screens, we override their configured dimensions. This time, our pie chart has to share space with the other graph, so enter 390 in the **Width** field and 290 in the **Height** field, and then click on **Add**. While we can immediately see the result of our work here, let's look at it in all its glory — go to **Monitoring | Screens** and click on **Local servers** in the **NAME** column:

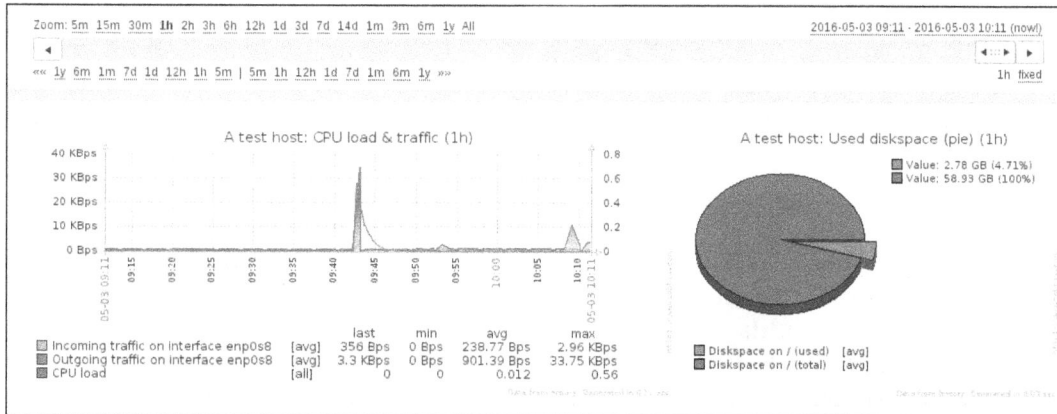

We now have both graphs displayed on a single page. But hey, take a look above the screen: the controls there look very much like the ones we used for graphs. And they are: using these controls, it is possible to do the same things as with graphs, only for all the screen elements. We can make all screen elements display data for a longer period of time or see what the situation was at some point in the past.

Two graphs are nice, but earlier, we talked about having a map and a graph on the same page. Let's see how we can make that happen. Click on **All screens** above the currently displayed screen, and click on **Constructor** next to **Local servers**. We want to add our map at the top of this screen, but we can see here that we created our screen with two columns and single row, so we have to add more. Couldn't we do that in the general screen properties, using the same fields we used when we created the screen? Of course we could, but with one limitation: increasing the column and row count there will only add new columns and rows to the right or at the bottom, respectively. There is no way to insert rows and columns at arbitrary positions using that form. That's why we will use a different approach.

> Reducing the column and row count is only possible from the right-hand side and bottom when using the generic screen properties form. Any elements that have been configured in the removed fields will also be removed.

Look at those **+** and **–** buttons around the screen. They allow you to insert or remove columns and rows at arbitrary positions. While the layout might seem confusing at first, understanding a few basic principles should allow you to use them efficiently:

- Buttons at the top and bottom operate on columns
- Buttons on the left and right operate on rows
- **+** buttons add a column or row before the column or row they are positioned at
- **–** buttons remove the column or the row where they are positioned

In this case, we want to add another row at the top, so click on the upper-left **+** icon in the first column—the column that has **+** and **–** controls only, not the one that has a graph already. This adds a row above our graphs with two columns, both having a **Change** link, just like before. Click on the first **Change** link. It's not a graph we want to add, so choose **Map** from the **Resource** dropdown. Click on **Select** next to the **Map** field, and then click on **First map**. If we leave other parameters as they are, the map will appear on top of the left-hand column. Having it centered above both columns would look better. That's what the **Column** span option is: enter 2 in that field, and then click on **Add**. As can be immediately seen, this screen element now spans two columns. This capability is not limited to maps; any element can span multiple columns or rows.

Dynamic screens

We now have a screen containing a network map and two graphs, showing data about **A test host**. Now, we should create a screen showing data for **Another host**. We'll probably have to repeat all the steps we performed for this one as well. That would be quite bad, especially for many hosts, wouldn't it? That's why there is a different, much easier approach.

Click on the **Change** link below the **CPU load & traffic** graph in the screen configuration, and look at the last parameter in there:

Dynamic item

Let's find out what a dynamic item means—mark this option and click on **Update**. While that seemingly did nothing, edit the other graph, mark the **Dynamic item** checkbox, and click on **Update**. It's now time to check out the result—go to **Monitoring | Screens**, and click on **Local servers** in the **NAME** column. Look at the available dropdowns at the top of the screen:

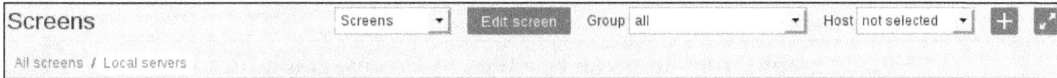

As soon as we marked some elements as dynamic, we got given the choice of other hosts. Let's check out how well this works. Select **Linux servers** from the **Group** dropdown and **Another host** from the **Host** dropdown:

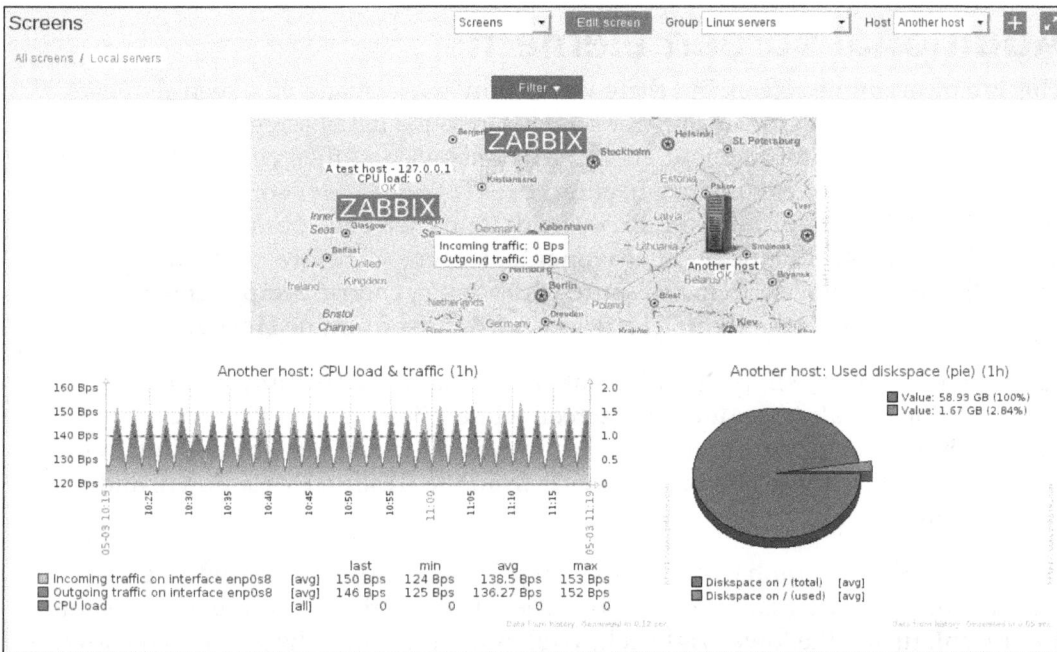

Wonderful! Elements marked as dynamic now show data from the selected host, while non-dynamic elements show the same data no matter which host is selected. The static elements could be maps like in our screen, but they could also be graphs if the **Dynamic item** option hasn't been checked for them. That would allow us to switch a screen to show server information in some graphs, but other graphs could keep on showing general network information.

> Only graphs from hosts can be added to screens; graphs from templates cannot. For a dynamic screen item, there is a risk that the host from which the graph was initially selected gets deleted, thus breaking the screen. Old versions of Zabbix allowed us to include graphs from templates here, and that functionality might return later.

Additional screen elements

This is a nice, simple screen, but there were many more available screen elements to choose from, so let's create another screen. Go to the list of screens — if a screen is shown in the monitoring view, click on **All screens**, and then click on the **Create screen** button. In the resulting form, enter "Experimental screen" in the **Name** field, enter 2 for both the **Columns** and **Rows** fields, and then click on **Add**. In the screen list, click on **Constructor** next to **Experimental screen**. As before, click on the **Change** link in the upper-left cell. In the **Resource** dropdown, choose **Simple graph**, and then click on **Select** next to the **Item** field. Select **A test host** from the **Host** dropdown.

As we can see, all the simple graphs that are available without any manual configuration can also be added to a screen. Here, click on the **CPU load** entry. In the **Width** field, enter 600, and then click on **Add**. Click on the **Change** link in the upper-right cell. Choose **History of events** from the **Resource** dropdown, and then click on **Add**.

Well, suddenly our graph doesn't look that great any more — it should be taller to fit this layout. We could place it below the events list, but that would require deleting it and reconfiguring the lower-right cell. Well, not quite. Drag the graph to the lower-right cell and release the mouse button:

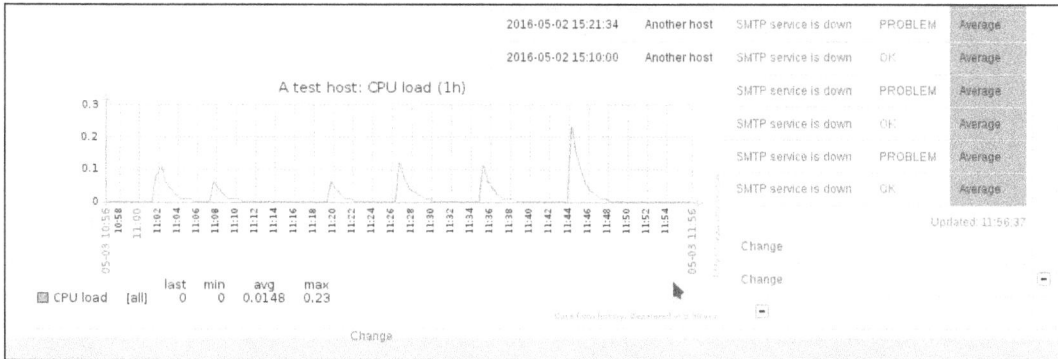

> Previous Zabbix versions highlighted the target cell to inform the user that the object would be placed there. This functionality has been lost in Zabbix 3.0.0. At the time of writing, it is not known which version will fix this issue.

The element (in this case, a graph) is moved from one cell to another, requiring no reconfiguration of individual cells.

The upper-left cell is now empty, so click on **Change** there. Select **Triggers info** from the **Resource** dropdown, select **Vertical** in the **Style** option, and then click on **Add**. This screen element provides us with high-level information on trigger distribution by severity. Let's populate this screen even more now. Click on the **Change** link in the lower-left corner. In the screen element configuration, select **Triggers overview** from the **Resource** dropdown, and start typing linux in the **Group** field. Click on **Linux servers** from the dropdown. We have more triggers than hosts in this group—select **Top** for the **Hosts location** option, and click on **Add**. The elements are misaligned again, right?

We'll try out some alignment work now. Click on the second **+** button from the top in the first column (next to the overview element we just added). This inserts a row before the second row. Drag the **Triggers overview** element (the one we added last) up one row, to the first cell in the row we just added. Click on the **Change** link for the **History of events** element (upper-right cell), enter 20 in the **Show lines** field and 2 in the **Row span** field, and click on **Update**.

Our screen now looks quite nice, except that the lower-left corner is empty. Click on **Change** in that cell, select **Server info** from the **Resource** dropdown, and then click on **Add**. The screen looks fairly well laid out now. Let's look at it in the monitoring view by going to **Monitoring | Screens** and clicking on **Experimental screen** in the **NAME** column:

Triggers info

20 Ok	
0 Not classified	
0 Information	
0 Warning	
0 Average	
0 High	
0 Disaster	

Updated 12:28:31

Triggers overview   Group: Linux servers

TRIGGERS	ANOTHER HOST	A TEST HOST
CPU load too high on {HOST.NAME} for last 3 minutes (over {$CPU_LOAD_THRESHOLD})		
Critical error from SNMP trap		
Incorrect clock on {HOST.NAME}		
Latency too high on {HOST.NAME}		
Link down for 10 minutes on {HOST.NAME}		
Link down for 5 minutes on {HOST.NAME}		
One SSH service is down		
SMTP service is down		
SNMP trap has arrived on {HOST.NAME}		
Testfile is missing		
Web service is down		

Updated 12:28:31

History of events

TIME	HOST	DESCRIPTION	VALUE	SEVERITY
2016-05-03 09:43:00	Another host	SMTP service is down	OK	Average
2016-05-03 09:42:34	Another host	SMTP service is down	PROBLEM	Average
2016-05-03 01:57:00	Another host	SMTP service is down	OK	Average
2016-05-03 01:05:04	Another host	SMTP service is down	PROBLEM	Average
2016-05-02 22:48:00	Another host	SMTP service is down	OK	Average
2016-05-02 22:47:34	Another host	SMTP service is down	PROBLEM	Average
2016-05-02 22:14:00	Another host	SMTP service is down	OK	Average
2016-05-02 22:13:34	Another host	SMTP service is down	PROBLEM	Average
2016-05-02 20:30:00	Another host	SMTP service is down	OK	Average
2016-05-02 20:29:34	Another host	SMTP service is down	PROBLEM	Average
2016-05-02 19:50:30	Another host	SMTP service is down	OK	Average
2016-05-02 19:50:04	Another host	SMTP service is down	PROBLEM	Average
2016-05-02 18:14:30	Another host	SMTP service is down	OK	Average
2016-05-02 18:14:04	Another host	SMTP service is down	PROBLEM	Average
2016-05-02 16:36:00	Another host	SMTP service is down	OK	Average
2016-05-02 16:35:34	Another host	SMTP service is down	PROBLEM	Average
2016-05-02 16:14:00	Another host	SMTP service is down	OK	Average
2016-05-02 16:13:34	Another host	SMTP service is down	PROBLEM	Average
2016-05-02 15:22:00	Another host	SMTP service is down	OK	Average
2016-05-02 15:21:34	Another host	SMTP service is down	PROBLEM	Average

Updated: 12:28:31

Zabbix server info

Users (online): 4(1)

Logged in as Admin

Zabbix server is running

Hosts (m/n/t): 47(5/31/11)

Items (m/d/n): 47(36/9/2)

Triggers (e/d)[p/o]: 20(20/0)[0/20]

Updated: 12:28:31

A test host: CPU load (1h)

	last	min	avg	max
CPU load [all]	0.02	0	0.0197	0.27

It was mentioned earlier that all graphs show the same time period in a screen. That is true if the graphs are added as normal screen elements. It is possible to add graphs that show a static period of time using the URL screen element, which allows including any page in a screen. In that case, the URL should point back to the Zabbix frontend instance. For example, showing a simple graph could be achieved using a URL such as this: `http://zabbix.frontend/zabbix/chart.php?period=3600&itemids[0]=23704&width=600`. You can find out the item ID by opening the simple graph of that item and looking at the URL. Note that the width of the graph image should be manually adjusted to match the screen cell width and avoid scrollbars in the screen cell. This way, we could configure a screen that shows hourly, daily, weekly, monthly, and yearly graphs of the same item.

As we discovered, screens in Zabbix allow very flexible visual layouts. You can choose to have a map, followed by more detailed graphs. Or you can have graphs of the most important information for a group of servers, and a trigger summary at the top. Or any other combination—there are many more possible screen elements to be added. It might be a good idea to try out all of the available screen elements and see what information they provide.

> As screens can contain lots of information, they can be performance intensive, especially if many users look at them at the same time.

Templated screens

The screens we have configured so far are global screens—they can contain lots of different elements, are available in the **Monitoring | Screens** section, and, if some elements are set to be dynamic, we can choose any other host in the dropdown to see its data. Zabbix also offers another way to configure and use screens: templated screens, also known as **host screens**. These are configured on a template and are then available for all the hosts that are linked to that template. Let's create a simple screen: navigate to **Configuration | Templates** and click on **Screens** next to **C_Template_ Linux**. Then, click on the **Create screen** button. In the **Name** field, enter `Templated screen` and click on **Add**. The same as with **global screens**, click on **Constructor** in the **ACTIONS** column. So far, the configuration has been pretty much the same. Now, click on the **Change** link in the only cell, and expand the **Resource** dropdown. The list of available resources is much smaller than it was in the global screens. Let's compare those lists:

Global screen resources	Templated screen resources
Action log	Clock
Clock	Graph
Data overview	Graph prototype
Graph	Plain text
Graph prototype	Simple graph
History of events	Simple graph prototype
Host group issues	URL
Host issues	
Hosts info	
Map	
Plain text	
Screen	
Server info	
Simple graph	
Simple graph prototype	
System status	
Triggers info	
Triggers overview	
URL	

As can be seen, global screens offer 19 different types of elements, while templated screens offer only seven.

For our screen right now, leave the **Resource** dropdown at **Graph** and click on **Select** next to the **Graph** field. Notice how the current template is selected and cannot be changed—all elements added to a templated screen must come from the same template. In the popup, click on **CPU load & traffic** in the **NAME** column, and then click on **Add**. Click on the **+** icon in the upper-right corner to add another column, and click on the **Change** link in the rightmost cell. In the **Resource** dropdown, choose **Simple graph**, click on **Select** next to the **Item** field, and then click on **CPU load** in the **NAME** column. Click on the **Add** button. Now, navigate to **Configuration | Hosts** and take a look at the available columns for each host. There is no column for screens. Templated or host screens are only configured on the template level; they do not get a copy on the host like items, triggers, and other entities do.

Let's go to **Monitoring | Screens**. If we look at the screen list there, the screen we just configured cannot be found. Templated or host screens can only be accessed from the host pop-up menu in the following locations:

- **Monitoring | Dashboard** (in the **Last 20 issues** widget)
- **Monitoring | Overview** (if hosts are located on the left-hand side)
- **Monitoring | Latest data** (if filtering by the **Host** field isn't done)
- **Monitoring | Triggers**
- **Monitoring | Events**
- **Monitoring | Maps**

They are also available from these two pages:

- Global search results
- The host inventory page

Let's move on to **Monitoring | Maps**: click on **Host group elements** in the **NAME** column. In the map, click on either **A test host** or **Another host**. This time, the **Host screens** entry in the menu is enabled — click on that one:

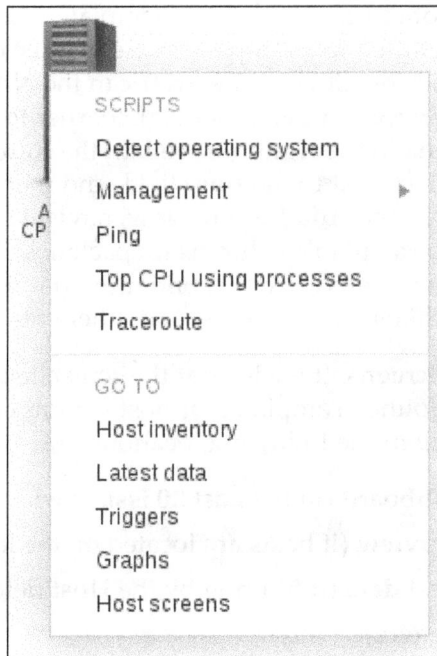

The screen we configured earlier opens, showing the data from this specific host:

If we had multiple screens configured in this template, they would be available in the dropdown in the upper-right corner. Remember that these screens will only be available for hosts that are linked to this template.

One thing to notice on this screen is the difference in height for both graphs. When configuring the screen, we did not change the height value, and it was the same for both graphs, `100`. Unfortunately, that's not the height of the whole graph, but only of the graph wall area. As a result, if having different item counts, a trigger or a percentile line will result in a different graph height. For a screen, this means a quite tedious configuration to get the dimensions to match. The same also applies to width—there, having one or two Y-axis values will result in a different graph width.

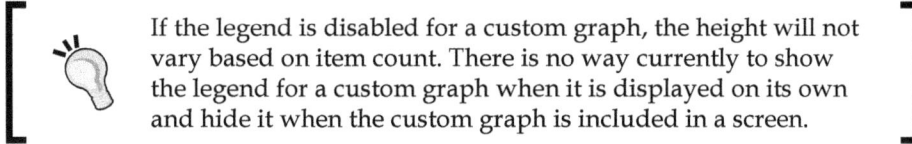

> If the legend is disabled for a custom graph, the height will not vary based on item count. There is no way currently to show the legend for a custom graph when it is displayed on its own and hide it when the custom graph is included in a screen.

Should one use a templated or global screen? Several factors will affect that decision:

*   The availability of the elements (global screens have many more)
*   Navigation (**Monitoring | Screens** versus the popup menus)
*   Which and how many hosts need such a screen

Slide shows

We now have a couple of screens, but to switch between them, a manual interaction is required. While that's mostly acceptable for casual use, it would be hard to do if you wanted to display them on a large display for a helpdesk. Manual switching would soon get annoying even if you simply had Zabbix open on a secondary monitor all the time.

Another functionality comes to the rescue—slide shows. Slide shows in Zabbix are simple to set up, so go to **Monitoring | Screens**. Why a screen page? Zabbix 3.0 changed the slide show operations to be the same way as maps and screens by moving both viewing and configuration to the monitoring section. Slide shows didn't get their own section, though; to access them, choose **Slide shows** from the dropdown in the upper-right corner. Click on the **Create slide show** button. Enter `First slide show` in the **Name** field, and click on the **Add** control in the **Slides** section. **Slides** are essentially screens, which is what we can see in the popup. Click on **Local servers**. We do not change the default value in the **Delay** field for this slide or screen. Leaving it empty will use the value of `30` from the **Default delay** field above.

Again, click on **Add** in the **Slides** section, and then click on **Experimental screen**. This time, enter 5 in the **DELAY** field for this screen:

Owner	Admin (Zabbix Administrator) ✕		Select
Name	First slide show		
Default delay (in seconds)	30		
Slides	SCREEN	DELAY	ACTION
	⠿ 1 Local servers	default	Remove
	⠿ 2 Experimental screen	5	Remove
	Add		
	Add Cancel		

Notice the handles on the left-hand side — the same as in graphs and icon mapping, we can reorder the slides here. We won't do that now; just click on the **Add** button at the bottom.

> If you want to add a single element to a slide show, such as a map or graph, you will have to create a screen containing this element only.

Now, click on **First slide show** in the **NAME** column. It starts plain, showing a single screen, and it then switches to the other screen after 30 seconds, then back after 5 seconds, and so the cycle continues. As we have dynamic screen items included in the slideshow, we can also choose the host in the upper-right corner — that will affect the dynamic screen items only.

We could show more screens, for example, a large high-level overview for 30 seconds, and then cycle through the server group screens, showing each one for 5 seconds.

Take a look at the buttons in the upper-right corner:

| Slide shows ▼ | Edit slide show | Group Linux servers ▼ | Host Another host ▼ | ➕ 🔧 ⤢ |

The first button allows us to add this slideshow to the dashboard favorites, the same as with graphs and screens. The third button is the full-screen one again. But the middle button allows us to slow down or speed up the slideshow—click on it:

```
REFRESH TIME MULTIPLIER

    x0.25

    x0.5

✓   x1

    x1.5

    x2

    x3

    x4

    x5
```

Instead of setting a specific time, we can make the slideshow faster or slower by applying a multiplier, thus maintaining the relative time for which each slide should be displayed.

There's also another reason to choose global screens over templated or host screens: only global screens can be included in slideshows.

Old versions of Zabbix had a memory leak in the slide show functionality. There have also been several cases of memory leaks in browsers. If you see browser memory usage consistently increasing while using Zabbix slide shows, consider upgrading. If that is not possible, one of the slides could reload the page using a URL element and JavaScript, which, in most cases, should reduce memory usage. `http://www.phpied.com/files/location-location/location-location.html` suggests 535 different ways of doing this.

Both screens and slide shows can also be created by normal users and then shared since Zabbix 3.0, the same way we shared maps in *Chapter 9, Visualizing the Data with Graphs and Maps*. The same as with maps, other users will need access to all the elements and subelements included in such screens and slide shows to be able to access them.

Showing data on a big display

While visualization on an individual level is important, the real challenge emerges when there's a need to create views for a large display, usually placed for helpdesk or technical operators to quickly identify problems. This poses several challenges.

Challenges

Displaying Zabbix on a large screen for many people requires taking into account the display location, the experience level of the people who will be expected to look at it, and other factors that can shape your decisions on how to configure this aspect of information displaying.

Non-interactive display

In the majority of cases, data displayed on such a screen will be non-interactive — people are expected to view it, but not click around. Such a requirement is posed because drilldown usually happens on individual workstations, leaving the main display accessible for others. Additionally, somebody could easily leave the main display in an unusable state, so no direct access is usually provided. This means that data placed on the display must not rely on the ability to view problem details. It should be enough for the level of technical support to gather the required knowledge.

Information overload

Having to place all information regarding the well-being of the infrastructure of an organization can result in a cluttered display, where too many details in a font that's way too small are crammed on the screen. This is the opposite of the previous challenge — you would have to decide which services are important and how to define each of them. This will require you to be working closely with the people responsible for those services so that correct dependency chains can be built. This is the method used most often to simplify and reduce displayed data while still keeping it useful.

> Both of these challenges can be solved with careful usage of screens and slide shows that display properly dependent statuses. Do not rely on slide shows too much — it can become annoying to wait for that slide to come by again because it was up for a few seconds only and there are now 10 more slides to cycle through.

Displaying a specific section automatically

There are some more requirements for a central display. It should open automatically upon boot and display the desired information, for example, a nice geographical map. While this might be achieved with some client-side scripting, there's a much easier solution, which we have already explored.

As a reminder, go to **Administration | Users**, click on **monitoring_user** in the **ALIAS** column, and look at two of the options, **Auto-login** and **URL (after login)**:

Auto-login	
Auto-logout (min 90 seconds)	900
Refresh (in seconds)	60
Rows per page	50
URL (after login)	tr_status.php

If we marked the **Auto-login** option for a user that is used by such a display station, it would be enough to log in once, and that user would be logged in automatically upon each page access. This feature relies on browser cookies, so the browser used should support and store cookies. The **URL (after login)** option allows the user to immediately navigate to a specified page. All that's left is that the display box launch a browser upon bootup and point to the Zabbix frontend URL, which should be simple to set up. When the box starts up, it will, without any manual intervention, open the specified page (which will usually be a screen or slide show). For example, to open a screen with an ID of 21 whenever that user accesses the Zabbix frontend, a URL like this could be used: http://zabbix.frontend/zabbix/screens. php?elementid=21. To open that screen in Zabbix's fullscreen mode, a fullscreen parameter has to be appended: http://zabbix.frontend/zabbix/screens. php?elementid=21&fullscreen=1.

When displaying data on such large screens, explore the available options and functionality carefully — perhaps the latest data display is the most appropriate in some cases. When using trigger overviews, evaluate the host/trigger relationship and choose which should be displayed on which axis.

Summary

In this chapter, we learned to combine graphs, maps, and other data on a single page by using screens. Screens are able to hold a lot of different elements, including the statistics of currently active triggers and even history and any custom page by using the URL element. The URL element also allows us to create a screen that contains graphs, showing different time periods. The screens are available either on the global or template levels.

Especially useful for unattended displays, slide shows allow cycling through screens. We can set the default delay and override it for individual screens. To include a single map or graph in a slide show, we still have to create a screen containing that map or graph.

In the next chapter, we will try to gather data using more advanced methods. We'll look at reusing already collected data with calculated and aggregate items, running custom scripts with external checks, and monitoring log files. We will also try out the two most popular ways to get custom data in Zabbix: user parameters on the agent side and the great `zabbix_sender` utility.

11
Advanced Item Monitoring

Having set up passive and active Zabbix agent items, simple checks such as ICMP ping or TCP service checks, or SNMP and IPMI checks, can we go further? Of course we can. Zabbix provides several more item types that are useful in different situations — let's try them out.

In this chapter, we will explore log file monitoring, computing values on the server from the already collected data, running custom scripts on the Zabbix server or agents, sending in complete custom data using a wonderful utility, `zabbix_sender`, and running commands over SSH and Telnet. Among these methods, we should be able to implement monitoring of any custom data source that is not supported by Zabbix out of the box.

Log file monitoring

Log files can be a valuable source of information. Zabbix provides a way to monitor log files using the Zabbix agent. For that, two special keys are provided:

- `log`: Allows us to monitor a single file
- `logrt`: Allows us to monitor multiple, rotated files

Both of the log monitoring item keys only work as active items. To see how this functions, let's try out the Zabbix log file monitoring by actually monitoring some files.

Monitoring a single file

Let's start with the simpler case, monitoring a single file. To do so, we could create a couple of test files. To keep things a bit organized, let's create a directory /tmp/ zabbix_logmon/ on A test host and create two files in there, logfile1 and logfile2. For both files, use the same content as this:

```
2016-08-13 13:01:03 a log entry
2016-08-13 13:02:04 second log entry
2016-08-13 13:03:05 third log entry
```

> Active items must be properly configured for log monitoring to work — we did that in *Chapter 3, Monitoring with Zabbix Agents and Basic Protocols*.

With the files in place, let's proceed to creating items. Navigate to **Configuration | Hosts**, click on **Items** next to **A test host**, then click on **Create item**. Fill in the following:

- **Name**: First logfile
- **Type: Zabbix agent (active)**
- **Key**: log[/tmp/zabbix_logmon/logfile1]
- **Type of information**: Log
- **Update interval**: 1

Name	First logfile
Type	Zabbix agent (active) ▾
Key	log[/tmp/zabbix_logmon/logfile1] Select
Type of information	Log ▾
Update interval (in sec)	1

When done, click on the **Add** button at the bottom. As mentioned earlier, log monitoring only works as an active item, so we used that item type. For the key, the first parameter is required — it's the full path to the file we want to monitor. We also used a special type of information here, **Log**. But what about the update interval, why did we use such a small interval of 1 second? For log items, this interval is not about making an actual connection between the agent and the server, it's only about the agent checking whether the file has changed — it does a stat() call, similar to what tail -f does on some platforms/filesystems. Connection to the server is only made when the agent has anything to send in.

> With active items, log monitoring is both quick to react, as it is checking the file locally, and also avoids excessive connections. It could be implemented as a somewhat less efficient passive item, but that's not supported yet as of Zabbix 3.0.0.

With the item in place, it should not take longer than 3 minutes for the data to arrive—if everything works as expected, of course. Up to 1 minute could be required for the server to update the configuration cache, and up to 2 minutes could be required for the active agent to update its list of items. Let's verify this—navigate to **Monitoring | Latest data** and filter by host A test host. Our **First logfile** item should be there, and it should have some value as well:

First logfile	2016-05-09 10:01:05	2016-08-13 13:03:05 third log …

> Even short values are excessively trimmed here. It is hoped that this will be improved in further releases.
>
> If the item is unsupported and the configuration section complains about permissions, make sure permissions actually allow the Zabbix user to access that file. If the permissions on the file itself look correct, check the execute permission on all the upstream directories, too. Here and later, keep in mind that unsupported items will take up to 10 minutes to update after the issue has been resolved.

As with other non-numeric items, Zabbix knows that it cannot graph logs, thus there's a **History** link on the right-hand side—let's click on it:

TIMESTAMP	LOCAL TIME	VALUE
2016-05-09 10:01:05		2016-08-13 13:03:05 third log entry
2016-05-09 10:01:05		2016-08-13 13:02:04 second log entry
2016-05-09 10:01:05		2016-08-13 13:01:03 a log entry

> If you see no values in the **History** mode, it might be caused by a bug in the Zabbix time scroll bar. Try selecting the 500 latest values in the dropdown in the upper-right corner.

All the lines from our log file are here. By default, Zabbix log monitoring parses whole files from the very beginning. That is good in this case, but what if we wanted to start monitoring some huge existing log file? Not only would that parsing be wasteful, we would also likely send lots of useless old information to the Zabbix server. Luckily, there's a way to tell Zabbix to only parse new data since the monitoring of that log file started. We could try that out with our second file, and to keep things simple, we could also clone our first item. Let's return to **Configuration | Hosts**, click on **Items** next to **A test host**, then click on **First logfile** in the **NAME** column. At the bottom of the item configuration form, click on **Clone** and make the following changes:

- **Name:** `Second logfile`
- **Key:** `log[/tmp/zabbix_logmon/logfile2,,,,skip]`

> There are four commas in the item key—this way we are skipping some parameters and only specifying the first and fifth parameters.

When done, click on the **Add** button at the bottom. Same as before, it might take up to 3 minutes for this item to start working. Even when it starts working, there will be nothing to see in the latest data page—we specified the skip parameter and thus only any new lines would be considered.

> Allow at least 3 minutes to pass after adding the item before executing the following command below. Otherwise, the agent won't have the new item definition yet.

To test this, we could add some lines to **Second logfile**. On "A test host", execute:

```
$ echo "2016-08-13 13:04:05 fourth log entry" >> /tmp/zabbix_logmon/
logfile2
```

> This and further fake log entries increase the timestamp in the line itself—this is not required, but looks a bit better. For now, Zabbix would ignore that timestamp anyway.

A moment later, this entry should appear in the latest data page:

Second logfile	2016-05-09 11:42:15	2016-08-13 13:04:05 fourth log...

If we check the item history, it is the only entry, as Zabbix only cares about new lines now.

> The skip parameter only affects behavior when a new log file is monitored. While monitoring a log file with and without that parameter, the Zabbix agent does not re-read the file, it only reads the added data.

Filtering for specific strings

Sending everything is acceptable with smaller files, but what if a file has lots of information and we are only interested in error messages? The Zabbix agent may also locally filter the lines and only send to the server the ones we instruct it to. For example, we could grab only lines that contain the string error in them. Modify the **Second logfile** item and change its key to:

```
log[/tmp/zabbix_logmon/logfile2,error,,,skip]
```

That is, add an error after the path to the log file. Note that now there are three commas between error and skip—we populated the second item key parameter. Click on **Update**. Same as before, it may take up to 3 minutes for this change to propagate to the Zabbix agent, so it is suggested to let some time pass before continuing. After making a tea, execute the following on "A test host":

```
$ echo "2016-08-13 13:05:05 fifth log entry" >> /tmp/zabbix_logmon/
logfile2
```

This time, nothing new would appear in the **Latest data** page—we filtered for the error string, but this line had no such string in it. Let's add another line:

```
$ echo "2016-08-13 13:06:05 sixth log entry - now with an error" >> /tmp/
zabbix_logmon/logfile2
```

Checking the history for the logfile2 logfile item, we should only see the latest entry.

How about some more complicated conditions? Let's say we would like to filter for all error and warning string occurrences, but for warnings only if they are followed by a numeric code that starts with numbers 60-66. Luckily, the filter parameter is actually a regular expression—let's modify the second log monitoring item and change its key to:

```
log[/tmp/zabbix_logmon/logfile2,"error|warning 6[0-6]",,,skip]
```

We changed the second key parameter to "error|warning 6[0-6]", including the double quotes. This regular expression should match all errors and warnings that start with numbers 60-66. We had to double quote it, because the regexp contained square brackets, which are also used to enclose key parameters. To test this out, let's insert in our log file several test lines:

```
$ echo "2016-08-13 13:07:05 seventh log entry - all good" >> /tmp/zabbix_
logmon/logfile2
$ echo "2016-08-13 13:08:05 eighth log entry - just an error" >> /tmp/
zabbix_logmon/logfile2
$ echo "2016-08-13 13:09:05 ninth log entry - some warning" >> /tmp/
zabbix_logmon/logfile2
$ echo "2016-08-13 13:10:05 tenth log entry - warning 13" >> /tmp/zabbix_
logmon/logfile2
$ echo "2016-08-13 13:11:05 eleventh log entry - warning 613" >> /tmp/
zabbix_logmon/logfile2
```

Based on our regular expression, the log monitoring item should:

- Ignore the seventh entry, as it contains no error or warning at all
- Catch the eighth entry, as it contains an error
- Ignore the ninth entry — it has a warning, but no number following it
- Ignore the tenth entry — it has a warning, but the number following it does not start within range of 60-66
- Catch the eleventh entry — it has a warning, the number starts with 61, and that is in our required range, 60-66

Eventually, only the eighth and eleventh entries should be collected. Verify that in the latest data page only the entries that matched our regexp should have been collected.

The regexp we used was not very complicated. What if we would like to exclude multiple strings or do some other, more complicated filtering? With the POSIX EXTENDED regular expressions that could be somewhere between very complicated and impossible. There is a feature in Zabbix, called **global regular expressions**, which allows us to define regexps in an easier way. If we had a global regexp named Filter logs, we could reuse it in our item like this:

```
log[/tmp/zabbix_logmon/logfile2,@Filter logs,,,skip]
```

Global regular expressions are covered in more detail in *Chapter 12, Automating Configuration*.

Monitoring rotated files

Monitoring a single file was not terribly hard, but there's a lot of software that uses multiple log files. For example, the Apache HTTP server is often configured to log to a new file every day, with the date included in the filename. Zabbix supports monitoring such a log rotation scheme with a separate item key, logrt. To try it out, navigate to **Configuration** | **Hosts**, click on **Items** next to **A test host**, then click on **Create item**. Fill in the following:

- **Name**: Rotated logfiles
- **Type: Zabbix agent (active)**
- **Key**: logrt["/tmp/zabbix_logmon/access_[0-9]{4}-[0-9]{2}-[0-9]{2}.log"]
- **Type of information: Log**
- **Update interval**: 2

When done, click on the **Add** button at the bottom. But the key and its first parameter changed a bit from what we used before. The key now is logrt, and the first parameter is a regular expression, describing the files that should be matched. Note that the regular expression here is supported for the file part only, the path part must describe a specific directory. We also double quoted it because of the square brackets that were used in the regexp. The regexp should match filenames that start with access_, followed by four digits, a dash, two digits, a dash, two more digits, and ending with .log. For example, a filename such as access_2015-12-31.log would be matched. One thing we did slightly differently – the update interval was set to 2 seconds instead of 1. The reason is that the logrt key is periodically re-reading directory contents, and this could be a bit more resource intensive than just checking a single file. That is also the reason why it's a separate item key, otherwise we could have used the regular expression for the file in the log item.

> The Zabbix agent does not re-read directory contents every 2 seconds if a monitored file still has lines to parse – it only looks at the directory again when the already known files have been fully parsed.

With the item in place, let's proceed by creating and populating some files that should be matched by our regexp. On "A test host", execute:

```
$ echo "2016-08-30 03:00:00 rotated first" > /tmp/zabbix_logmon/
access_2015-12-30.log
```

Checking the latest data page, the rotated log files item should get this value. Let's say that's it for this day and we will now log something the next day:

```
$ echo "2015-12-31 03:00:00 rotated second" > /tmp/zabbix_logmon/
access_2015-12-31.log
```

Checking the history for our item, it should have successfully picked up the new file:

TIMESTAMP	LOCAL TIME	VALUE
2016-05-09 13:56:55		2015-12-31 03:00:00 rotated second
2016-05-09 13:56:25		2016-08-30 03:00:00 rotated first

As more files with a different date appear, Zabbix will finish the current file and then start on the next one.

Alerting on log data

With the data coming in, let's talk about alerting on it with triggers. There are a few things somewhat different than the thresholds and similar numeric comparisons that we have used in triggers so far.

If we have a log item which is collecting all lines and we want to alert on the lines containing some specific string, there are several trigger functions of potential use:

- str(): Checks for a substring; for example, if we are collecting all values, this function could be used to alert on errors: str(error)

- regexp: Similar to the str() function, allows us to specify a regular expression to match

- iregexp: Case-insensitive version of regexp()

> These functions only work on a single line; it is not possible to match multiline log entries.

For these three functions, a second parameter is supported as well — in that case, it's either the number of seconds or the number of values to check. For example, str(error,600) would fire if there's an error substring in any of the values over last 10 minutes.

That seems fine, but there's an issue if we only send error lines to the server by filtering on the agent side. To see what the problem is, let's consider a "normal" trigger, like the one checking for **CPU load** exceeding some threshold. Assuming we have a threshold of 5, the trigger currently in the **OK** state and values such as 0, 1, 2 arriving, nothing happens, no events are generated. When the first value above 5 arrives, a **PROBLEM** event is generated and the trigger switches to the **PROBLEM** state. All other values above 5 would not generate any events, nothing would happen.

And the problem would be that it would work this way for log monitoring as well. We would generate a **PROBLEM** event for the first error line, and then nothing. The trigger would stay in the **PROBLEM** state and nothing else would happen. The solution is somewhat simple — there's a checkbox in the trigger properties, **Multiple PROBLEM events generation**:

| Multiple PROBLEM events generation |

Marking this checkbox would make the mentioned **CPU load** trigger generate a new **PROBLEM** event for every value above the threshold of 5. Well, that would not be very useful in most cases, but it would be useful for the log monitoring trigger. It's all good if we only receive error lines; a new **PROBLEM** event would be generated for each of them.

Note that even if we send both errors and good lines, errors after good lines would be picked up, but subsequent errors would be ignored, which could be a problem as well.

With this problem solved, we arrive at another one — once a trigger fires against an item that only receives error lines, this trigger never resolves — it always stays in the **PROBLEM** state. While that's not an issue in some cases, in others it is not desirable. There's an easy way to make such triggers time out by using a trigger function we are already familiar with, `nodata()`. If the item receives both error and `normal` lines, and we want it to time out 10 minutes after the last error arrived even if no "normal" lines arrive, the trigger expression could be constructed like this:

```
{host.item.str(error)}=1 and {host.item.nodata(10m)}=0
```

Here, we are using the `nodata()` function the other way around — even if the last entry contains errors, the trigger would switch to the **OK** state if there were no other values in the last 10 minutes.

> We also discussed triggers that time out in *Chapter 6, Detecting Problems with Triggers*, in the *Triggers that time out* section.

If the item receives error lines only, we could use an expression like the one above, but we could also simplify it. In this case, just having any value is a problem situation, so we would use the reversed `nodata()` function again and alert on values being present:

```
{host.item.nodata(10m)}=0
```

Here, if we have any values in the last 10 minutes, that's it—it's a **PROBLEM**. No values, the trigger switches to **OK**. This is somewhat less resource intensive as Zabbix doesn't have to evaluate the actual item value.

Yet another trigger function that we could use here is `count()`. It would allow us to fire an alert when there's a certain number of interesting strings—such as errors—during some period of time. For example, the following will alert if there are more than 10 errors in the last 10 minutes:

```
{host.item.count(10m,error,like)}>10
```

Extracting part of the line

Sometimes we only want to know that an error was logged. In those cases, grabbing the whole line is good enough. But sometimes the log line might contain an interesting substring, maybe a number of messages in some queue. A log line might look like this:

```
2015-12-20 18:15:22 Number of messages in the queue: 445
```

Theoretically, we could write triggers against the whole line. For example, the following `regexp` should match when there are 10,000 or more messages:

```
messages in the queue: [1-9][0-9]{4}
```

But what if we want to have a different trigger when the message count exceeds 15,000? That trigger would have a `regexp` like this:

```
messages in the queue: (1[5-9]|[2-9].)[0-9]{3}
```

And if we want to exclude values above 15,000 from our first `regexp`, it would become the following:

```
messages in the queue: 1[0-4][0-9]{3}
```

That is definitely not easy to maintain. And that's with just two thresholds. But there's an easier way to do this, if all we need is that number. Zabbix log monitoring allows us to extract values by regular expressions. To try this out, let's create a file with some values to extract. Still on "A test host", create the file /tmp/zabbix_logmon/queue_log with the following content:

```
2016-12-21 18:01:13 Number of messages in the queue: 445
2016-12-21 18:02:14 Number of messages in the queue: 5445
2016-12-21 18:03:15 Number of messages in the queue: 15445
```

Now on to the item — go to **Configuration | Hosts,** click on **Items** next to **A test host,** then click on **Create item**. Fill in the following:

- **Name:** Extracting log contents
- **Type: Zabbix agent (active)**
- **Key:** log[/tmp/zabbix_logmon/queue_log,"messages in the queue: ([0-9]+)",,,,\1]
- **Type of information: Log**
- **Update interval:** 1

We quoted the regexp because it contained square brackets again. The regexp itself extracts the text "messages in the queue", followed by a colon, space, and a number. The number is included in a capture group — this becomes important in the last parameter to the key we added, \1 — that references the capture group contents. This parameter, "output", tells Zabbix not to return the whole line, but only whatever is referenced in that parameter. In this case — the number.

> We may also add extra text in the output parameter — for example, a key such as log[/tmp/zabbix_logmon/queue_log, messages in the queue: "([0-9]+)",,,,Extra \1 things] would return "Extra 445 things" for the first line in our log file. Multiple capture groups may be used as well, referenced in the output parameter as \2, \3, and so on.

When done, click on the **Add** button at the bottom. Some 3 minutes later, we could check the history for this item in the latest data page:

TIMESTAMP	LOCAL TIME	VALUE
2016-05-09 14:25:01		15445
2016-05-09 14:25:01		5445
2016-05-09 14:25:01		445

Hooray, extracting the values is working as expected. Writing triggers against them should be much, much easier as well. But one thing to note — for this item we were unable to see the graphs. The reason is the **Type of information** property in our log item — we had it set to **Log**, but that type is not considered suitable for graphing. Let's change it now. Go to **Configuration | Hosts**, click on **Items** next to **A test host**, and click on **Extracting log contents** in the **NAME** column. Change **Type of information** to **Numeric (unsigned)**, then click on the **Update** button at the bottom.

> If the extracted numbers have the decimal part, use **Numeric (float)** for such items.

Check this item in the latest data section — it should have a **Graph** link now. But checking that reveals that it has no data. How so? Internally, Zabbix stores values for each type of information separately. Changing that does not remove the values, but Zabbix only checks the currently configured type. Make sure to set the correct type of information from the start. To verify that this works as expected, run the following on "A test host":

```
$ echo "2016-12-21 18:16:13 Number of messages in the queue: 113" >> /
tmp/zabbix_logmon/queue_log
$ echo "2016-12-21 18:17:14 Number of messages in the queue: 213" >> /
tmp/zabbix_logmon/queue_log
$ echo "2016-12-21 18:18:15 Number of messages in the queue: 150" >> /
tmp/zabbix_logmon/queue_log
```

Checking out this item in the **Latest data** section, the values should be there and the graph should be available, too. Note that the date and time in our log file entries still doesn't matter — the values will get the current timestamp assigned.

> Value extracting works the same with the `logrt` item key.

Parsing timestamps

Talking about the timestamps on the lines we pushed in Zabbix, the date and time in the file did not match the date and time displayed in Zabbix. Zabbix marked the entries with the time it collected them. This is fine in most cases when we are doing constant monitoring—content is checked every second or so, gathered, timestamped and pushed to the server. When parsing some older data, the timestamps can be way off, though. Zabbix does offer a way to parse timestamps out of the log entries. Let's use our very first log file monitoring item for this. Navigate to **Configuration | Hosts**, click on **Items** next to **A test host**, and click on **First logfile** in the **NAME** column. Notice the **Log time format** field—that's what we will use now. It allows us to use special characters to extract the date and time. The supported characters are:

- y: Year
- M: Month
- d: Day
- h: Hour
- m: Minute
- s: Second

In our test log files, we used the time format like this:

```
2015-12-13 13:01:03
```

The time format string to parse out date and time would look like this:

```
yyyy-MM-dd hh:mm:ss
```

Note that only the supported characters matter—the other ones are just ignored and can be anything. For example, the following would work exactly the same:

```
yyyyPMMPddPhhPmmPss
```

You can choose any characters outside of the special ones. Which ones would be best? Well, it's probably best to aim for readability. Enter one of the examples here in the **Log time format** field:

Log time format	yyyy-MM-dd hh:mm:ss

> When specifying the log time format, all date and time components must be present—for example, it is not possible to extract the time if seconds are missing.

When done, click on the **Update** button at the bottom. Allow for a few minutes to pass, then proceed with adding entries to the monitored file. Choose the date and time during the last hour for your current time, and run on "A test host":

```
$ echo "2016-05-09 15:30:13 a timestamped log entry" >> /tmp/zabbix_
logmon/logfile1
```

Now check the history for the **First logfile** item in the latest data page:

TIMESTAMP	LOCAL TIME	VALUE
2016-05-09 15:31:52	2016-05-09 15:30:13	2016-05-09 15:30:13 a timestamped log entry

There's one difference from the previous cases. The **LOCAL TIME** column is populated now, and it contains the time we specified in our log line. The **TIMESTAMP** column still holds the time when Zabbix collected the line.

Note that only numeric data is supported for date and time extraction. The standard syslog format uses short textual month names such as Jan, Feb, and so on—such a date/time format is not supported for extraction at this time.

Viewing log data

With all the log monitoring items collecting data, let's take a quick look at the displaying options. Navigate to **Monitoring | Latest data** and click on **History** for **Second logfile**. Expand the **Filter**. There are a few very simple log viewing options here:

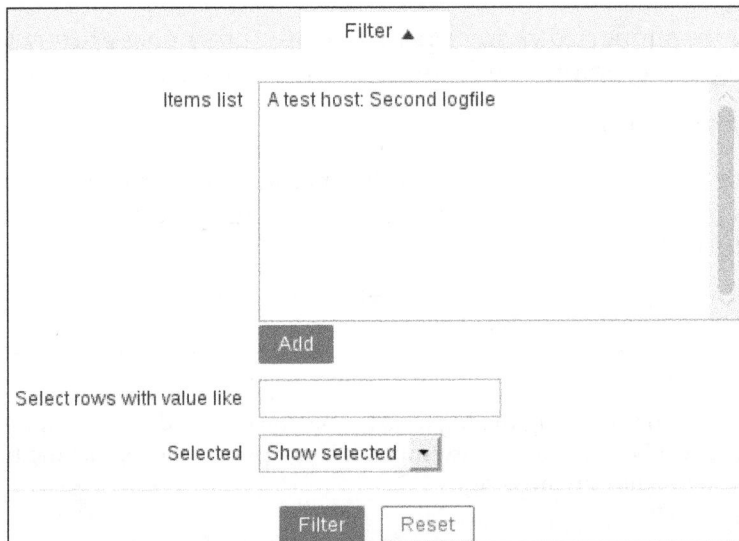

- **Items list**: We may add multiple items and view log entries from them all at the same time. The entries will be sorted by their timestamp, allowing us to determine the sequence of events from different log files or even different systems.

- **Select rows with value like** and **Selected**: Based on a substring, entries can be shown, hidden, or colored.

As a quick test, enter "error" in the **Select rows with value like** field and click on **Filter**. Only the entries that contain this string will remain. In the **Selected** dropdown, choose **Hide selected**—and now only the entries that do not have this string are shown. Now choose **Mark selected** in the **Selected** dropdown and notice how the entries containing the "error" string are highlighted in red. In the additional dropdown that appeared, we may choose red, green, or blue for highlighting:

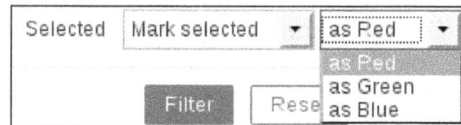

Let's add another item here—click on **Add** below the **Items** list entry. In the popup, choose **Linux servers** in the **Group** dropdown and **A test host** in the **Host** dropdown, then click on **First logfile** in the **NAME** column. Notice how the entries from both files are shown, and the coloring option is applied on top of that.

That's pretty much it regarding log viewing options in the Zabbix frontend. Note that this is a very limited functionality and for a centralized syslog server with full log analysis options on top of that, a specialized solution should be used—there are quite a lot of free software products available.

Reusing data on the server

The items we have used so far were collecting data from some Zabbix agent or SNMP device. It is also possible to reuse this data in some calculation, store the result and treat it as a normal item to be used for graphs, triggers, and other purposes. Zabbix offers two types of such items:

- **Calculated** items require writing exact formulas and referencing each individual item. They are more flexible than the aggregate items, but are not feasible over a large number of items and have to be manually adjusted if the items to be included in the calculation change.

- **Aggregate** items operate on items that share the same key across a host group. Minimum, maximum, sum, or average can be computed. They cannot be used on multiple items on the same host, but if hosts are added to the group or removed from it, no adjustments are required for the aggregate item.

Calculated items

We will start with calculated items that require typing in a formula. We are already monitoring total and used disk space. If we additionally wanted to monitor free disk space, we could query the agent for this information. This is where calculated items come in — if the agent or device does not expose a specific view of the data, or if we would like to avoid querying monitored hosts, we can do the calculation from the already retrieved values. To create a calculated item that would compute the free disk space, navigate to **Configuration | Hosts**, click on **Items** next to **A test host**, and then click on **Create item**. Fill in the following information:

- **Name:** `Diskspace on / (free)`
- **Type: Calculated**
- **Key:** `calc.vfs.fs.size[/,free]`
- **Formula:** `last("vfs.fs.size[/,total]")-last("vfs.fs.size[/,used]")`
- **Units:** `B`
- **Update interval:** `1800`

When done, click on the **Add** button at the bottom.

> We chose a key that would not clash with the native key in case somebody decides to use that later, but we are free to use any key for calculated items.

All the referenced items must exist. We cannot enter keys here and have them gather data by extension from the calculated item. Values to compute the calculated item are retrieved from the Zabbix server caches or the database; no connections are made to the monitored devices.

With this item added, let's go to the **Latest data** page. As the interval was set to 1,800 seconds, we might have to wait a bit longer to see the value, but eventually it should appear:

Diskspace on / (free)	2016-05-09 17:40:05	56.16 GB

> If the item turns unsupported, check the error message and make sure the formula you typed in is correct.

The interval we used, 1,800 seconds, was not matched to the intervals of both referenced items. Total and used disk space items were collecting data every 3,600 seconds, but calculated items are not connected to the data collection of the referenced items in any way. A calculated item is not evaluated when the referenced items get values—it follows its own scheduling, which is completely independent from the schedules of the referenced items, and is semi-random. If the referenced items stopped collecting data, our calculated item would keep on using the latest value for the calculation, as we used the `last()` function. If one of them stopped collecting data, we would base our calculation on one recent and one outdated value. And if our calculated item could get very incorrect results if called at the wrong time because one of the referenced items has significantly changed but the other has not received a new value yet, there is no easy solution to that, unfortunately. The custom scheduling, discussed in *Chapter 3, Monitoring with Zabbix Agents and Basic Protocols*, could help here, but it could also introduce performance issues by polling values in uneven batches—and it would also be more complicated to manage. It is suggested to be used only as an exception.

> The free disk space that we calculated might not match the "available" diskspace reported by system tools. Many filesystems and operating systems reserve some space which does not count as used, but counts against the available disk space.

We might also want to compute the total of incoming and outgoing traffic on an interface, and a calculated item would work well here. The formula would be like this:

```
last(net.if.it[enp0s8])+last(net.if.out[enp0s8])
```

> Did you spot how we quoted item keys in the first example, but not here? The reason is that calculated item formula entries follow a syntax of `function(key,function_parameter_1,function_parameter_2...)`. The item keys we referenced for the disk space item had commas in them like this— `vfs.fs.size[/,total]`. If we did not quote the keys, Zabbix would interpret them as the key being `vfs.fs.size[/` with a function parameter of `total]`. That would not work.

Quoting in calculated items

The items we referenced had relatively simple keys—one or two parameters, no quoting. When the referenced items get more complicated, it is a common mistake to get quoting wrong. That in turn makes the item not work properly or at all. Let's look at the formula that we used to calculate free disk space:

```
last("vfs.fs.size[/,total]")-last("vfs.fs.size[/,used]")
```

The referenced item keys had no quoting. But what if the keys have the filesystem parameter quoted like this:

```
vfs.fs.size["/",total]
```

We would have to escape the inner quotes with backslashes:

```
last("vfs.fs.size[\"/\",total]")-last("vfs.fs.size[\"/\",used]")
```

The more quoting the referenced items have, the more complicated the calculated item formula gets. If such a calculated item does not seem to work properly for you, check the escaping very, very carefully. Quite often users have even reported some behavior as a bug which turns out to be a misunderstanding about the quoting.

Referencing items from multiple hosts

The calculated items we have created so far referenced items on a single host or template. We just supplied item keys to the functions. We may also reference items from multiple hosts in a calculated item—in that case, the formula syntax changes slightly. The only thing we have to do is prefix the item key with the hostname, separated by a colon— the same as in the trigger expressions:

```
function(host:item_key)
```

Let's configure an item that would compute the average CPU load on both of our hosts. Navigate to **Configuration | Hosts**, click on **Items** next to **A test host**, and click on **Create item**. Fill in the following:

- **Name**: Average system load for both servers
- **Type: Calculated**
- **Key**: calc.system.cpu.load.avg
- **Formula**: (last(A test host:system.cpu.load)+last(Another host:system.cpu.load))/2
- **Type of information**: **Numeric (float)**

When done, click on the **Add** button at the bottom.

For triggers, when we referenced items, those triggers were associated with the hosts which the items came from. Calculated items also reference items, but they are always created on a single, specific host. The item we created will reside on A test host only. This means that such an item could also reside on a host which is not included in the formula—for example, some calculation across a cluster could be done on a meta-host which holds cluster-wide items but is not directly monitored itself.

Let's see whether this item works in **Monitoring | Latest data**. Make sure both of our hosts are shown and expand all entries. Look for three values—**CPU load** both for **A test host** and **Another host**, as well as **Average system load for both servers**:

HOST	NAME ▲	LAST CHECK	LAST VALUE
Another host	**- other -** (1 Item)		
	CPU load	2016-05-09 21:06:34	0.94
A test host	**- other -** (2 Items)		
	Average system load for both servers	2016-05-09 21:06:06	0.46
	CPU load	2016-05-09 21:06:25	0.01

> You can filter by "load" in the item names to see only relevant entries.

The value seems to be properly calculated. It could now be used like any normal item, maybe by including it and individual **CPU load** items from both hosts in a single graph. But if we look at the values, the system loads for individual hosts are 0.94 and 0.01, but the average is calculated as 0.46. If we calculate it manually, it should be 0.475—or 0.48, if rounding to two decimal places. Why such a difference? Data for both items that the calculated item depends on comes in at different intervals, and the calculated value also is computed at a slightly different time, thus, while the value itself is correct, it might not match the exact average of values seen at any given time. Here, both **CPU load** items had some values, the calculated average was correctly computed. Then, one or both of the **CPU load** items got new values, but the calculated item has not been updated with them yet.

> We discuss a few additional aspects regarding calculated items in *Chapter 12, Automating Configuration*.

Aggregate items

The calculated items allowed us to write a specific formula, referencing exact individual items. This worked well for small-scale calculations, but the **CPU load** item we created last would be very hard to create and maintain for dozens of hosts—and impossible for hundreds. If we want to calculate something for the same item key across many hosts, we would probably opt for *aggregate items*. They would allow us to find out the average load on a cluster, or the total available disk space for a group of file servers, without naming each item individually. Same as the calculated items, the result would be a normal item that could be used in triggers or graphs.

To find out what we can use in such a situation, go to **Configuration | Hosts**, select **Linux servers** in the **Group** dropdown and click on **Items** next to **A test host**, then click on **Create item**. Now we have to figure out what item type to use. Expand the **Type** dropdown and look for an entry named **Zabbix aggregate**. That's the one we need, so choose it and click on **Select** next to the **Key** field. Currently, the key is listed as grpfunc, but that's just a placeholder—click on it. We have to replace it with the actual group key—one of grpsum, grpmin, grpmax, or grpavg. We'll calculate the average for several hosts, so change it to grpavg. This key, or group function, takes several parameters:

- group: As the name suggests, the host group name goes here. Enter Linux servers for this parameter.

- key: The key for the item to be used in calculations. Enter system.cpu.load here.

- func: A function used to retrieve data from individual items on hosts. While multiple functions are available, in this case, we'll want to find out what the latest load is. Enter last for this field.

- param: A parameter for the function above, following the same rules as normal function parameters (specifying either seconds or value count, prefixed with #). The function we used, last(), can be used without a parameter, thus simply remove the last comma and the placeholder that follows it.

For individual item data, the following functions are supported:

Function	Details
avg	Average value
count	Number of values
last	Last value
max	Maximum value

Function	Details
min	Minimum value
sum	Sum of values

For aggregate items, two levels of functions are available. They are nested—first, the function specified as the `func` parameter gathers the required data from all hosts in the group. Then, `grpfunc` (`grpavg` in our case) calculates the final result from all the intermediate results retrieved by `func`.

> All the referenced items must exist. We cannot enter keys here and have them gather data by extension from the aggregate item. Values to compute the calculated item are retrieved from the Zabbix server caches or the database; no connections are made to the monitored devices.

The final item key should be `grpavg[Linux servers,system.cpu.load,last]`.

> If the referenced item key had parameters, we would have to quote it.

To finish the item configuration, fill in the following:

- **Name**: `Average system load for Linux servers`
- **Type of information**: **Numeric (float)**

The final item configuration should look like this:

Name	Average system load for Linux servers
Type	Zabbix aggregate ▾
Key	grpavg[Linux servers,system.cpu.load,last] Select
Type of information	Numeric (float) ▾

When done, click on the **Add** button at the bottom. Go to **Monitoring | Latest data**, make sure all hosts are shown and look for the three values again—**CPU load** both for **A test host** and **Another host**, as well as **Average system load for Linux servers**:

HOST	NAME ▲	LAST CHECK	LAST VALUE
Another host	**- other -** (1 Item)		
	CPU load	2016-05-09 21:16:34	1.06
A test host	**- other -** (3 Items)		
	Average system load for both servers	2016-05-09 21:16:36	0.54
	Average system load for Linux servers	2016-05-09 21:16:37	0.54
	CPU load	2016-05-09 21:16:55	0

> You can filter by "load" in the item names again.

Same as before, the computed average across both hosts does not match our result if we look at the values on individual hosts—and the reason is exactly the same as with the calculated items.

> As the key parameters indicate, an aggregate item can be calculated for a host group—there is no way to pick individual hosts. Creating a new group is required if arbitrary hosts must have an aggregate item calculated for them. We discussed other benefits from careful host group planning in *Chapter 5, Managing Hosts, Users, and Permissions*.

We used the grpavg aggregate function to find out the average load for a group of servers, but there are other functions:

Function	Details
grpmax	Maximum value is reported. One could find out what the maximum SQL queries per second are across a group of database servers.
grpmin	Minimum value is reported. The minimum free space for a group of file servers could be determined.
grpsum	Values for the whole group are summed. Total number of HTTP sessions could be calculated for a group of web servers.

This way, a limited set of functions can be applied across a large number of hosts. While less flexible than calculated items, it is much more practical in case we want to do such a calculation for a group that includes hundreds of hosts. Additionally, a calculated item has to be updated whenever a host or item is to be added or removed from the calculations. An aggregate item will automatically find all the relevant hosts and items. Note that *only enabled items on enabled hosts will be considered*.

Nothing limits the usage of aggregate items by servers. They can also be used on any other class of devices, such as calculating average **CPU load** for a group of switches, monitored over SNMP.

Aggregating across multiple groups

The basic syntax allows us to specify one host group. Although we mentioned earlier that aggregating across arbitrary hosts would require creating a new group, there is one more possibility—an aggregate item may reference several host groups. If we modified our aggregate item key to also include hosts in a "Solaris servers" group, it would look like this:

```
grpavg[[Linux servers,Solaris servers],system.cpu.load,last]
```

That is, multiple groups can be specified as comma-delimited entries in square brackets. If any host appears in several of those groups, the item from that host would be included only once in the calculation. There is no strict limit on the host group count here, although both readability and overall item key length limit—2,048 characters—should be taken into account.

> Both calculated and aggregate items can reuse values from any other item, including calculated and aggregate items. They can also be used in triggers, graphs, network map labels, and anywhere else where other items can be used.

User parameters

The items we have looked at so far allowed us to query the built-in capabilities of a Zabbix agent, query SNMP devices, and reuse data on the Zabbix server. Every now and then, a need arises to monitor something that is not supported by Zabbix out of the box. The easiest and most popular method to extend Zabbix data collection is user parameters. They are commands that are run by the Zabbix agent and the result is returned as an item value. Let's try to set up some user parameters and see what things we should pay extra attention to.

Just getting it to work

First, we'll make sure that we can get the agent to return any value at all. User parameters are configured on the agent side—the agent daemon contains the key specification, which includes references to commands. On "A test host", edit zabbix_agentd.conf and look near the end of the file. An explanation of the syntax is available here:

```
UserParameter=<key>,<shell command>
```

This means that we can freely choose the key name and command to be executed. It is suggested that you keep key names to lowercase alphanumeric characters and dots. For starters, add a very simple line like this:

```
UserParameter=quick.test,echo 1
```

Just return 1, always. Save the configuration file and restart the Zabbix agent daemon. While it might be tempting to add an item like this in the frontend, it is highly recommended to test all user parameters before configuring them in the frontend. That will provide the results faster and overall make your life simpler. The easiest way to test an item is with zabbix_get—we discussed this small utility in *Chapter 3, Monitoring with Zabbix Agents and Basic Protocols*. Run on "A test host":

```
$ zabbix_get -s 127.0.0.1 -k quick.test
```

> If testing user parameters on a different host, run zabbix_get from the Zabbix server or make sure the agent allows connections from the localhost—that is configured with the server parameter in zabbix_agentd.conf.

That should return just "1". If it does, great—your first user parameter is working. If not, well, there's not much that could go wrong. Make sure the correct file was being edited and the agent daemon was really restarted. And that the correct host was queried.

> This trivial user parameter actually illustrates a troubleshooting suggestion. Whenever a user parameter fails and you can't figure out why, simplify it and test every iteration with zabbix_get. Eventually, you will get to the part that is responsible for the failure.

We won't actually add this item in the frontend as it won't provide much value. Instead, let's re-implement an item that is already available in the Zabbix agent—counting the number of logged-in users. Edit `zabbix_agentd.conf` again and add the following near our previous modification:

```
UserParameter=system.test,who | wc -l
```

Notice how we can chain multiple commands. In general, anything the underlying shell would accept would be good. Save the file and restart the Zabbix agent daemon. Now to the quick test again:

$ zabbix_get -s 127.0.0.1 -k system.test

That should return a number—as you are probably running `zabbix_get` from the same system, it should be at least `1`. Let's create an item to receive this data in the frontend. Open **Configuration | Hosts**, make sure **Linux servers** is selected in the **Group** dropdown and click on **Items** next to **A test host**, then click on **Create item**. Fill in these values:

- **Name:** `Users logged in`
- **Type: Zabbix agent (active)**
- **Key:** `system.test`

We are using the active item type with our user parameter. User parameters are suggested to be used as active items as they can tie up server connections if they do not return very quickly. Notice how we used exactly the same key name as specified in the agent daemon configuration file. When you are done, click on **Add**.

Now check **Monitoring | Latest data**. As this is an active item, we might have to wait for the agent to request the item list from the server, then return the data, which can take up to 2 minutes in addition to the server updating its cache in 1 minute. Sooner or later, the data will appear.

The great thing is that it is all completely transparent from the server side—the item looks and works as if it was built in.

We have gotten a basic user parameter to work, but this one replicates the existing Zabbix agent item, thus it still isn't that useful. The biggest benefit provided by user parameters is the ability to monitor virtually anything, even things that are not natively supported by the Zabbix agent, so let's try some slightly more advanced metrics.

Querying data that the Zabbix agent does not support

One thing we might be interested in is the number of open TCP connections. We can get this data using the `netstat` command. Execute the following on the Zabbix server:

```
$ netstat -t
```

The `-t` switch tells `netstat` to list TCP connections only. As a result, we get a list of connections (trimmed here):

```
Active Internet connections (w/o servers)
Proto Recv-Q Send-Q Local Address          Foreign Address       State
tcp      0       0 localhost:zabbix-trapper localhost:52932
TIME_WAIT
tcp      0       0 localhost:zabbix-agent   localhost:59779       TIME_
WAIT
tcp      0       0 localhost:zabbix-agent   localhost:59792       TIME_
WAIT
```

> On modern distributions, the `ss` utility might be a better option. It will also perform better, especially when there are many connections. An alternative command for `ss`, matching the aforementioned `netstat` command, would be `ss -t state connect`.

To get the number of connections, we'll use the following command:

```
netstat -nt | grep -c ^tcp
```

Here, `grep` first filters out connection lines and then just counts them. We could have used many other approaches, but this one is simple enough. Additionally, the `-n` flag is passed to `netstat`, which instructs it to perform no resolving on hosts, thus giving a performance boost.

Edit `zabbix_agentd.conf` and add the following line near the other user parameters:

```
UserParameter=net.tcp.conn,netstat -nt | grep -c ^tcp
```

In the frontend, go to **Configuration | Hosts**, click on **Items** next to **A test host**, then click on **Create item** and fill in the following values:

- **Name**: Open connections
- **Type**: **Zabbix agent (active)**
- **Key**: net.tcp.conn

When you are done, click on the **Add** button at the bottom. Did you notice that we did not restart the agent daemon after modifying its configuration file? Do that now. Using such an ordering of events will give us values faster, because the agent queries the active items list immediately after startup, and this way the server already has the item configured when the agent is restarted. Feel free to check **Monitoring | Latest values**:

Open connections	2016-05-09 21:55:55	33

Flexible user parameters

We are now gathering data on all open connections. But looking at the `netstat` output, we can see connections in different states, such as TIME_WAIT and ESTABLISHED:

```
tcp         0      0 127.0.0.1:10050          127.0.0.1:60774          TIME_
WAIT
tcp         0      0 192.168.56.10:22         192.168.56.1:51187
ESTABLISHED
```

If we want to monitor connections in different states, would we have to create a new user parameter for each? Fortunately, no. Zabbix supports the so-called flexible user parameters, which allow us to pass parameters to the command executed.

Again, edit `zabbix_agentd.conf` and modify the user parameter line we added before to read as follows:

```
UserParameter=net.tcp.conn[*],netstat -nt | grep ^tcp | grep -c "$1"
```

> The ss utility again might be better in modern distributions. For example, filtering for established connections could be easily done by the established `ss -t state`.

We have made several changes here. First, the addition of `[*]` indicates that this user parameter itself accepts parameters. Second, adding the second `grep` statement allows us to use such passed parameters in the command. We also moved the `-c` flag to the last `grep` statement to do the counting.

> Was it mentioned that it might be easier with `ss`?

All parameters we would use now for this key will be passed to the script—$1 substituted for the first parameter, $2 for the second, and so on. Note the use of double quotes around $1. This way, if no parameter is passed, the result would be the same as without using grep at all.

Restart the agent to make it pick up the modified user parameter.

Back in the frontend **Configuration | Hosts**, click on **Items** next to **A test host**, and click on **Open connections** in the **NAME** column, then click on the **Clone** button at the bottom of the editing form. Change the following fields:

- **Name**: Open connections in $1 state
- **Key**: net.conn[TIME_WAIT]

Click on the **Add** button at the bottom. Now click on **Open connections in the TIME_WAIT** state in the **NAME** column, click on **Clone** and modify the **Key** field to read net.conn[ESTABLISHED], then click on the **Add** button at the bottom.

> See man page for netstat for a full list of possible connection states.

Take a look at **Monitoring | Latest data**:

Open connections	2016-05-10 05:14:53	48
Open connections in ESTABLISHED state	2016-05-10 05:14:23	2
Open connections in TIME_WAIT state	2016-05-10 05:14:23	45

It is possible that the values don't match—summing open connections in all states might not give the same number as all open connections. First, remember that there are more connection states, so you'd have to add them all to get a complete picture. Second, as we saw before, all of these values are not retrieved simultaneously, thus one item grabs data, and a moment later another comes in, but the data has already changed slightly.

> We are also counting all the connections that we create either by remotely connecting to the server, just running the Zabbix server, or by other means.

We are now receiving values for various items, but we only had to add a single user parameter. Flexible user parameters allow us to return data based on many parameters. For example, we could provide additional functionality to our user parameter if we make a simple modification like this:

```
UserParameter=net.conn[*],netstat -nt | grep ^tcp | grep "$1" | grep -c "$2"
```

We added another `grep` command on the second parameter, again using double quotes to make sure the missing parameter won't break anything. Now we can use the IP address as a second parameter to figure out the number of connections in a specific state to a specific host. In this case, the item key might be `net.conn[TIME_WAIT,127.0.0.1]`.

Note that the item parameter ordering (passing state first, IP second) in this case is completely arbitrary. We could swap them and get the same result, as we are just filtering the output by two strings with `grep`. If we were to swap them, the description would be slightly incorrect, as we are using positional item key parameter references in it.

Level of the details monitored

There are almost unlimited combinations of what details one can monitor on some target. It is possible to monitor every single detailed parameter of a process, such as detailed memory usage, the existence of PID files, and many more things, and it is also possible to simply check whether a process is running.

Sometimes a single service can require multiple processes to be running, and it might be enough to monitor whether a certain category of processes is running as expected, trusting some other component to figure that out. One example could be Postfix, the e-mail server. Postfix runs several different processes, including `master`, `pickup`, `anvil`, `smtpd`, and others. While checks could be created against every individual process, often it would be enough to check whether the `init` script thinks that everything is fine.

We would need an `init` script that has the `status` command support. As init scripts usually output a textual strings `Checking for service Postfix: running`, it would be better to return only a numeric value to Zabbix that would indicate the service state. Common exit codes are "0" for success and nonzero if there is a problem. That means we could do something like the following:

```
/etc/init.d/postfix status > /dev/null 2>&1 || echo 1
```

That would call the init script, discard all stdin and stderr output (because we only want to return a single number to Zabbix), and return "1" upon a non-successful exit code. That should work, right? There's only one huge problem — parameters should never return an empty string, which is what would happen with such a check if Postfix was running. If the Zabbix server were to check such an item, it would assume the parameter is unsupported and deactivate it as a consequence. We could modify this string so that it becomes the following:

```
/etc/init.d/postfix status > /dev/null 2>&1 && echo 0 || echo 1
```

This would work very nicely, as now a Boolean is returned and Zabbix always gets valid data. But there's a possibly better way. As the exit code is 0 for success and nonzero for problems, we could simply return that. While this would mean that we won't get nice Boolean values only, we could still check for nonzero values in a trigger expression like this:

```
{hostname:item.last()}>0
```

As an added benefit, we might get a more detailed return message if the init script returns a more detailed status with nonzero exit codes. As defined by the **Linux Standard Base**, the exit codes for the status commands are the following:

Code	Meaning
0	Program is running or service is OK
1	Program is dead and /var/run pid file exists
2	Program is dead and /var/lock lock file exists
3	Program is not running
4	Program or service status is unknown

There are several reserved ranges that might contain other codes, used by a specific application or distribution — those should be looked up in the corresponding documentation.

For such a case, our user parameter command becomes even simpler, with the full string being the following:

```
UserParameter=service.status[*],/etc/init.d/"$1" status > /dev/null
2>&1; echo $?
```

We are simply returning the exit code to Zabbix. To make the output more user friendly, we'd definitely want to use value mapping. That way, each return code would be accompanied on the frontend with an explanatory message like the above. Notice the use of $1. This way, we can create a single user parameter and use it for any service we desire. For an item like that, the appropriate key would be `service.status[postfix]` or `service.status[nfs]`. If such a check does not work for the non-root user, `sudo` would have to be used.

In open source land, multiple processes per single service are less common, but they are quite popular in proprietary software, in which case a trick like this greatly simplifies monitoring such services.

> Some distributions have recently moved to `systemd`. In that case, the user parameter line would be `UserParameter=service.status[*],systemctl status "$1" > /dev/null 2>&1; echo $?.`

Environment trap

Let's try to find out what other interesting statistics we can gather this way. A common need is to monitor some statistics about databases. We could attempt to gather some MySQL query data; for example, how many queries per second are there? MySQL has a built-in query per second measurement, but that isn't quite what most users would expect. That particular value is calculated for the whole uptime MySQL has, which means it's quite useful, though only for the first few minutes. Longer-running MySQL instances have this number approaching the average value and only slightly fluctuating. When graphed, the queries per second graph gets more and more flat as time passes.

The flexibility of Zabbix allows us to use a different metric. Let's try to create a slightly more meaningful MySQL query items. We can get some data on the **SELECT** statements with a query like this:

```
mysql> show global status like 'Com_select';
```

That is something we should try to get working as a user parameter now. A test command to parse out only the number we are interested in would be as follows:

```
$ mysql -N -e "show global status like 'Com_select';" | awk '{print $2}'
```

We are using `awk` to print the second field. The `-N` flag for `mysql` tells it to omit column headers. Now on to the agent daemon configuration — add the following near our other user parameters:

```
UserParameter=mysql.queries[*],mysql -u zabbix -N -e "show global
status like 'Com_$1';" | awk '{print $$2}'
```

It's basically the user parameter definition with the command appended, but we have made a few changes here. Notice how we used `[*]` after the key, and replaced `"select"` in `Com_select` with `$1` — this way, we will be able to use query type as an item key parameter. This also required adding the second dollar sign in the `awk` statement. If a literal dollar sign placeholder has to be used with a flexible user parameter, such dollar signs must be prefixed with another dollar sign. And the last thing we changed was adding `-u zabbix` to the `mysql` command. Of course, it is best not to use `root` or a similar access for database statistics, if possible — but if this command is supposed to be run by the Zabbix agent, why specify the username again? Mostly because of an old and weird bug where MySQL would sometimes attempt to connect with the wrong user. If you'd like to see the current status of that issue, see `https://bugs.mysql.com/bug.php?id=64522`. With the changes in place, save and close the file, then restart the agent daemon.

> You might want to create a completely separate database user that has no actual write permissions for monitoring.

Now, same as before, let's do a quick `zabbix_get` test:

```
$ zabbix_get -s 127.0.0.1 -k mysql.queries[select]
```

Well, you might have seen this one coming:

```
ERROR 1045 (28000): Access denied for user 'zabbix'@'localhost' (using
password: NO)
```

Our database user did require a password, but we specified none. How could we do that? The `mysql` utility allows us to specify a password on the command line with the `-p` flag, but it is best to avoid it. Placing passwords on the command line might allow other users to see this data in the process list, so it's a good idea to develop a habit — no secret information on the command line, ever.

> On some platforms, some versions of the MySQL client will mask the passed password. While that is a nice gesture from MySQL's developers, it won't work on all platforms and with all software, so such an approach should be avoided just to make it a habit. The password in such a case is likely to be written to the shell history file, making it available to attackers even after the process is no longer running.

How could we pass the password in a secure manner then? Fortunately, MySQL can read the password from a file which we could secure with permissions. A file .my. cnf is searched in several directories, and in our case the best option might be placing it in the user's home directory. On the Zabbix server, execute the following as the zabbix user:

```
$ touch ~zabbix/.my.cnf
$ chmod 600 ~zabbix/.my.cnf
$ echo -e "[client]\npassword=<password>" > ~zabbix/.my.cnf
```

> If your password contains the hash mark #, enclose it in double quotes in this file.
>
> You can change to the zabbix user with su - zabbix, or use sudo.

Use the password that the Zabbix database user has. You can remind yourself what it was by taking a look at zabbix_server.conf. If running the above commands as root, also run chown -R zabbix.zabbix ~zabbix after creating the file. Note that we first create and secure the file, and only then place the password in it. Before we proceed with the agent side, let's test whether MySQL utilities pick up the password file. As the zabbix user, run:

```
$ mysqladmin -u zabbix status
```

> Run the above either in the same su session or as sudo -u zabbix mysqladmin -u zabbix status.

If everything went well with the file we put the password in, it should return some data:

```
Uptime: 10218  Threads: 23  Questions: 34045  Slow queries: 0  Opens: 114
Flush tables: 2  Open tables: 140  Queries per second avg: 3.331
```

If that does not work, double-check the password, path, and permissions to the file. We use mysqladmin for this test, but both mysql and mysqladmin should use the same procedure for finding the .my.cnf file and reading the password from it. Now that we know it's working, let's turn to zabbix_get again (no agent restart is needed as we did not modify the agent configuration file this time):

```
$ zabbix_get -s 127.0.0.1 -k mysql.queries[select]
```

But the result seems weird:

```
ERROR 1045 (28000): Access denied for user 'zabbix'@'localhost' (using
password: NO)
```

> In some cases, when using systemd, the home directory might be set—if so, skip the next change, but keep in mind this potential pitfall.

It's failing still. And with the same error message. If we carefully read the full error, we'll see that the password is still not used. How could that be?

> It does not matter which user account we run zabbix_get as—it connects to the running agent daemon over a TCP port, thus when the user parameter command is run, information about the user running zabbix_get has no impact at all.

The environment is not initialized for user parameter commands. This includes several common variables, and one we are quite interested in—HOME. This variable is used by the MySQL client to determine where to look for the .my.cnf file. If the variable is missing, this file (and in turn, the password) can't be found. Does that mean we're doomed? Of course not, we wouldn't let such a minor problem stop us. We simply have to tell MySQL where to look for this file, and we can use a very simple method to do that. Edit zabbix_agentd.conf again and change our user parameter line to read as follows:

```
UserParameter=mysql.queries[*],HOME=/home/zabbix mysql -u zabbix -N -e
"show global status like 'Com_$1';" | awk '{print $$2}'
```

> If you installed from packages, use the directory which is set as the home directory for the zabbix user.

This sets the HOME variable for the mysql utility and that should allow the MySQL client to find the configuration file which specifies the password. Again, restart the Zabbix agent and then run the following:

```
$ zabbix_get -s 127.0.0.1 -k mysql.queries[select]
229420
```

You'll see a different value, and finally we can see the item is working. But what is that number? If you repeatedly run zabbix_get, you will see that the number is increasing. That looks a lot like another counter — and indeed, that is the number of SELECT queries since the database engine startup. We know how to deal with this. Back to the frontend, let's add an item to monitor the SELECT queries per second. Navigate to **Configuration | Hosts**, click on **Items** next to **A test host**, then click on the **Create item** button. Fill in these values:

- **Name**: MySQL $1 queries per second
- **Type: Zabbix agent (active)**
- **Key**: mysql.queries[select]
- **Type of information: Numeric (float)**
- **Units**: qps
- **Store value: Delta (speed per second)**
- **New application**: MySQL

When you are done, click on the **Add** button at the bottom. Notice how we used **Delta (speed per second)** together with **Numeric (float)** here. For the network traffic items, we chose **Numeric (unsigned)** instead, as there the value could overflow the float. For this query item, that is somewhere between highly unlikely and impossible, and we will actually benefit a lot from increased precision here. The unit qps is just that — a string. It does not impact the displaying of data in any way besides appearing next to it.

Again, we might have to wait for a few minutes for any data to arrive. If you are impatient, feel free to restart the Zabbix agent daemon, then check the **Latest data** page:

NAME ▲	LAST CHECK	LAST VALUE
MySQL (1 Item)		
MySQL select queries per second	2016-05-09 23:36:52	2.96 qps

The data is coming in nicely and we can see that our test server isn't too overloaded. Let's benefit from making that user parameter flexible now. Navigate back to **Configuration | Hosts,** click on **Items** next to **A test host,** then click on **MySQL select queries per second** in the **NAME** column. At the bottom of the form, click on the **Clone** button and change select in the key to update, then click on the **Add** button at the bottom. Clone this item two more times, changing the key parameter to insert and delete. Eventually, there should be four items:

NAME ▲	TRIGGERS	KEY
MySQL delete queries per second		mysql.queries[delete]
MySQL insert queries per second		mysql.queries[insert]
MySQL update queries per second		mysql.queries[update]
MySQL select queries per second		mysql.queries[select]

The items should start gathering the data soon; let's try to see how they look all together. Click on **Graphs** in the navigation header above the item list, then click on **Create graph.** Enter "MySQL queries" in the **Name** field and click on **Add** in the **Items** section. Mark the checkboxes next to the four MySQL items we created and click on **Select** at the bottom, then click on the **Add** button at the bottom. Now let's go to **Monitoring | Graphs,** select **A test host** in the **Host** dropdown and **MySQL queries** in the **Graph** dropdown. The graph, after some time, might look like this:

		last	min	avg	max
■ MySQL delete queries per second	[avg]	0 qps	0 qps	0.0009 qps	0.0665 qps
■ MySQL insert queries per second	[avg]	0.7313 qps	0.6315 qps	0.7403 qps	1.23 qps
■ MySQL select queries per second	[avg]	5.88 qps	2.79 qps	5.92 qps	12.07 qps
■ MySQL update queries per second	[avg]	0.5651 qps	0.133 qps	0.2954 qps	0.7647 qps

As we can see, the SELECT queries are at the top here, the DELETE ones are almost non-existent. There are other query types, but this should be enough for our user parameter implementation.

Things to remember about user parameters

We saw that the flexibility of user parameters is basically unlimited. Still, there might be cases when additional measures have to be applied.

Wrapper scripts

Commands to be executed can be specified in the Zabbix agent daemon configuration file on a single line only. Pushing whole scripts there can be very messy and sometimes it can be hard to figure out the quotation. In such cases, a wrapper script has to be written. Such a script can be useful if parsing data requires more complex actions or if parsing out multiple different values cannot be easily done with flexible user parameters.

It is important to remember that using user parameters and custom scripts requires these to be distributed on all monitored hosts—that involves the scripts themselves and changes to the Zabbix agent daemon's configuration file.

This can soon become hard to manage. Various systems will require different user parameters, thus you'll either end up with a messy agent configuration file containing all of them, or a myriad of different combinations. There's a quite widespread feature to help with this problem—configuration file inclusion. You can specify the inclusion of individual files by adding to zabbix_agentd.conf entries like these:

```
Include=/etc/zabbix/userparameters/zabbix_lm_sensors.conf
Include=/etc/zabbix/userparameters/zabbix_md_raid.conf
```

If such a file is missing, Zabbix will complain, but will still start up. Inclusions can be nested—you can include one file which in turn includes several others, and so on.

It's also possible to include whole directories—in that case, all files placed there will be used. This method allows other packages to place, for example, user parameter configuration in a specific directory, which will then be automatically used by Zabbix:

```
Include=/etc/zabbix/userparameters/
```

Or, to be sure that only files ending with "conf" are included:

```
Include=/etc/zabbix/userparameters/*.conf
```

Then other packages would only need to place files such as `zabbix_lm_sensors.conf` or `zabbix_md_raid.conf` in the directory `/etc/zabbix/userparameters` and they would be used without any additional changes to the agent daemon configuration file. Installing the Apache web server would add one file, installing Postfix another, and so on.

When not to use user parameters

There are also cases when user parameters are best replaced with a different solution. Usually, that will be when:

- The script takes a long time
- The script returns many values

In the first case, the script could simply time out. The default timeout on the agent side is 3 seconds, and it is not suggested to increase it in most cases.

In the second case, we might be interested in 100 values that a script could return in a single invocation, but Zabbix does not allow several values to be obtained from a single key or from a single invocation, thus we would have to run the script 100 times — not very efficient.

> If a script supplies values for multiple trapper items, it might be worth adding a `nodata()` trigger for some of them — that way, any issues with the script and missing data would be discovered quickly.

There are several potential solutions, with some drawbacks and benefits for each case:

- A special item (usually an external check, discussed below, or another user parameter) that could send the data right away using `zabbix_sender` if the data collection script is quick. If not, it could write data to temporary files or invoke another script with `nohup`.
- `crontab`: A classic solution that can help both when the script takes a long time and when it returns many values. It does have the drawback of having interval management outside Zabbix. Values are usually sent right away using `zabbix_sender` (discussed later in this chapter), although they could also be written to temporary files and read by other items using the `vfs.file.contents` or `vfs.file.regexp` key.

- A special item (usually another user parameter) that adds an `atd` job. This solution is a bit more complicated, but allows us to keep interval management in Zabbix while still allowing the use of long-running scripts for data collection. See `http://zabbix.org/wiki/Escaping_timeouts_with_atd` for more detail.

> There are reports that `atd` can be crashed in RHEL 5 and 6, and possibly other distributions. If using this method, monitor `atd` as well.

External checks

All the check categories we explored before cover a very wide range of possible devices, but there's always that one which doesn't play well with standard monitoring protocols, can't have the agent installed, and is buggy in general. A real-life example would be a UPS that provides temperature information on the web interface, but does not provide this data over SNMP. Or maybe we would like to collect some information remotely that Zabbix does not support yet—for example, monitoring how much time an SSL certificate has until it expires.

In Zabbix, such information can be collected with external checks or external scripts. While user parameters are scripts run by the Zabbix agent, external check scripts are run directly by the Zabbix server.

First, we should figure out the command to find out the remaining certificate validity period. We have at least two options here:

- Return the time when the certificate expires
- Return 0 or 1 to identify that the certificate expires in some period of time

Let's try out both options.

Finding a certificate expiry time

We could find out the certificate expiry time with an OpenSSL command like this:

```
$ echo | openssl s_client -connect www.zabbix.com:443 2>/dev/null |
openssl x509 -noout -enddate
```

> Feel free to use any other domain for testing here and later.

We are closing the `stdin` for the `openssl` command with `echo` and passing the retrieved certificate information to another `openssl` command, `x509`, to return the date and time when the certificate will expire:

```
notAfter=Jan  2 10:35:38 2019 GMT
```

The resulting string is not something we could easily parse in Zabbix, though. We could convert it to a UNIX timestamp like this:

```
$ date -d "$(echo | openssl s_client -connect www.zabbix.com:443 2>/dev/
null | openssl x509 -noout -enddate | sed 's/^notAfter=//')" "+%s"
```

We're stripping the non-date part with `sed` and then formatting the date and time as a UNIX timestamp with the date utility:

```
1546425338
```

Looks like we have the command ready, but where would we place it? For external checks, a special directory is used. Open `zabbix_server.conf` and look for the option `ExternalScripts`. You might see either a specific path, or a placeholder:

```
# ExternalScripts=${datadir}/zabbix/externalscripts
```

If it's a specific path, that's easy. If it's a placeholder like above, it references the compile-time data directory. Note that it is not a variable. When compiling from the sources, the `${datadir}` path defaults to `/usr/local/share/`. If you installed from packages, it is likely to be `/usr/share/`. In any case, there should be a `zabbix/externalscripts/` subdirectory in there. This is where our external check script will have to go. Create a script `zbx_certificate_expiry_time.sh` there with the following contents:

```
#!/bin/bash
date -d "$(echo | openssl s_client -connect "$1":443 2>/dev/null |
openssl x509 -noout -enddate | sed 's/^notAfter=//')" "+%s"
```

Notice how we replaced the actual website address with a `$1` placeholder—this allows us to specify the domain to check as a parameter to this script. Make that file executable:

```
$ chmod 755 zbx_certificate_expiry_time.sh
```

And now for a quick test:

```
$ ./zbx_certificate_expiry_time.sh www.zabbix.com
1451727126
```

Great, we can pass the domain name to the script and get back the time when the certificate for that domain expires. Now, on to placing this information in Zabbix. In the frontend, go to **Configuration | Hosts**, click on **Items** next to **A test host**, and click on **Create item**. Fill in the following:

- **Name**: `Certificate expiry time on $1`
- **Type**: **External check**
- **Key**: `zbx_certificate_expiry_time.sh[www.zabbix.com]`
- **Units**: `unixtime`

We specified the domain to check as a key parameter, and it will be passed to the script as the first positional parameter, which we then use in the script as `$1`. If more than one parameter is needed, we would comma-delimit them, the same as for any other item type. The parameters would be properly passed to the script as `$1`, `$2`, and so on. If we need no parameters, we would use empty square brackets `[]`, or just leave them off completely. If we wanted to act upon the host information instead of hardcoding the value like we did, we could use some macro—for example, `{HOST.HOST}`, `{HOST.IP}`, and `{HOST.DNS}` are common values. Another useful macro here would be `{HOST.CONN}`, which would resolve either to the IP or DNS, depending on which one is selected in the interface properties.

When done, click on the **Add** button at the bottom. Now check this item in the **Latest data** page:

Certificate expiry time on www.zabbix.com	2016-05-09 23:59:21	2019-01-02 12:35:38

The expiry time seems to be collected correctly and the `unixtime` unit converted the value in a human-readable version. What about a trigger on this item? The easiest solution might be with the `fuzzytime()` function again. Let's say we want to detect a certificate that will expire in 7 days or less. The trigger expression would be as follows:

```
{A test host:zbx_certificate_expiry_time.sh[www.zabbix.com].
fuzzytime(604800)}=0
```

The huge value in the trigger function parameters, `604800`, is 7 days in seconds. Can we make it more readable? Sure we can, this would be exactly the same:

```
{A test host:zbx_certificate_expiry_time.sh[www.zabbix.com].
fuzzytime(7d)}=0
```

The trigger would alert with 1 week left, and from the item values we could see how much time exactly is left. We discussed triggers in more detail in *Chapter 6, Detecting Problems with Triggers*.

> We are conveniently ignoring the fact that the certificate might not be valid yet. While our trigger would fire if the certificate was not valid for a week or more, it would ignore certificates that would only become valid in less than a week.

Determining certificate validity

A simpler approach might be passing the threshold to the OpenSSL utilities and let them determine whether the certificate will be good after that many seconds. A command to check whether the certificate is good for 7 days would be as follows:

```
$ echo | openssl s_client -connect www.zabbix.com:443 2>/dev/null |
openssl x509 -checkend 604800
Certificate will not expire
```

That looks simple enough. If the certificate expires in the given time, the message would say "Certificate will expire". The great thing is that the exit code also differs based on the expiry status, thus we could return 1 when the certificate is still good and 0 when it expires.

> This approach returns 1 upon success, similar to many built-in items. One could also follow the openssl command with "echo $?" that would return 0 upon success.

```
$ echo | openssl s_client -connect www.zabbix.com:443 2>/dev/null
| openssl x509 -checkend 604800 -noout && echo 1 || echo 0
```

> In this version, values such as 7d are not supported, although they are accepted. Be very careful to use only values in seconds.

In the same directory as before, create a script zbx_certificate_expires_in.sh with the following contents:

```
#!/bin/bash
echo | openssl s_client -connect "$1":443 2>/dev/null | openssl x509
-checkend "$2" -noout && echo 1 || echo 0
```

This time, in addition to the domain being replaced with $1, we also replaced the time period to check with a $2 placeholder. Make that file executable:

```
$ chmod 755 zbx_certificate_expires_in.sh
```

And now for a quick test:

```
$ ./zbx_certificate_expires_in.sh www.zabbix.com 604800
1
```

Looks good. Now, on to creating the item—in the frontend, let's go to **Configuration | Hosts**, click on **Items** next to **A test host**, and click on **Create item**. Start by clicking on **Show value mappings** next to the **Show value** dropdown. In the resulting popup, click on the **Create value** map. Enter "Certificate expiry status" in the **Name** field, then click on the **Add** link in the **Mappings** section. Fill in the following:

- 0: Expires soon
- 1: Does not expire yet

Name	Certificate expiry status		
Mappings	VALUE	MAPPED TO	ACTION
	0	⇒ Expires soon	Remove
	1	⇒ Does not expire yet	Remove
	Add		

We're not specifying the time period here as that could be customized per item. When done, click on the **Add** button at the bottom and close the popup. Refresh the item configuration form to get our new value map and fill in the following:

- **Name**: Certificate expiry status for $1
- **Type: External check**
- **Key**: zbx_certificate_expires_in.sh[www.zabbix.com,604800]
- **Show value: Certificate expiry status**

When done, click on the **Add** button at the bottom. And again, check this item in the **Latest data** page:

Certificate expiry status for www.zabbix.com	2016-05-10 00:31:22	Does not expire yet (1)

Seems to work properly. It does not expire yet, so we're all good. One benefit over the previous approach could be that it is more obvious which certificates are going to expire soon when looking at a list.

It is important to remember that external checks could take quite a long time. With the default timeout being 3 or 4 seconds (we will discuss the details in *Chapter 22, Zabbix Maintenance*), anything longer than a second or two is already too risky. Also, keep in mind that a server poller process is always busy while running the script; we cannot offload external checks to an agent like we did with the user parameters being active items. It is suggested to use external checks only as a last resort when all other options to gather the information have failed. In general, external checks should be kept lightweight and fast. If a script is too slow, it will time out and the item will become unsupported.

Sending in the data

In some cases, there might be custom data sources where none of the previously discussed methods would work sufficiently well. A script could run for a very long time, or we could have a system without the Zabbix agent but with a capability to push data. Zabbix offers a way to send data to a special item type, Zabbix trapper, using a command line utility, Zabbix sender. The easiest way to explain how it works might be to set up a working item like that—let's navigate to **Configuration | Hosts**, click on **Items** next to **A test host**, and click on **Create item**, then fill in the following:

- **Name:** Amount of persons in the room
- **Type:** **Zabbix trapper**
- **Key:** room.persons

When you are done, click on the **Add** button at the bottom. We now have to determine how data can be passed into this item, and this is where zabbix_sender comes in. On the Zabbix server, execute the following:

```
$ zabbix_sender --help
```

We won't reproduce the output here, as it's somewhat lengthy. Instead, let's see which parameters are required for the most simple operation, sending a single value from the command line:

- -z to specify the Zabbix server
- -s to specify the hostname, as configured in Zabbix
- -k for the key name
- -o for the value to send

Note that the hostname is the hostname in the Zabbix host properties—not the IP, not the DNS, not the visible name. Let's try to send a value then:

```
$ zabbix_sender -z 127.0.0.1 -s "A test host" -k room.persons -o 1
```

> As usual, the hostname is case sensitive. The same applies to the item key.

This command should succeed and show the following output:

```
info from server: "processed: 1; failed: 0; total: 1; seconds spent: 0.000046"

sent: 1; skipped: 0; total: 1
```

> If you are very quick with running this command after adding the item, the trapper item might not be in the Zabbix server configuration cache. Make sure to wait at least 1 minute after adding the item.

Let's send another value—again, using `zabbix_sender`:

```
$ zabbix_sender -z 127.0.0.1 -s "A test host" -k room.persons -o 2
```

This one should also succeed, and now we should take a look at **Monitoring | Latest data** over at the frontend. We can see that the data has successfully arrived and the change is properly recorded:

NAME ▲	LAST CHECK	LAST VALUE	CHANGE
- **other** - (1 Item)			
Amount of persons in the room	2016-05-10 00:35:18	2	+1

Now we could try being smart. Let's pass a different data type to Zabbix:

```
$ zabbix_sender -z 127.0.0.1 -s "A test host" -k room.persons -o nobody
```

We are now trying to pass a string to the Zabbix item even though in the frontend, its data type is set to an integer:

```
info from server: "processed: 0; failed: 1; total: 1; seconds spent: 0.000074"

sent: 1; skipped: 0; total: 1
```

Zabbix didn't like that, though. The data we provided was rejected because of the data type mismatch, thus it is clear that any process that is passing the data is responsible for the data contents and formatting.

Now, security-concerned people would probably ask—who can send data to items of the trapper type? A zabbix_sender can be run on any host by anybody, and it is enough to know the hostname and item key. It is possible to restrict this in a couple of ways—for one of them, see **Configuration | Hosts**, click on **Items** next to **A test host** and click on **Amount of persons in the room** in the **NAME** column. Look at one of the last few properties, **Allowed hosts**. We can specify an IP address or DNS name here, and any data for this item will be allowed from the specified host only:

Allowed hosts	127.0.0.1

Several addresses can be supplied by separating them with commas. In this field, user macros are supported as well. We discussed user macros in *Chapter 8, Simplifying Complex Configuration with Templates*.

Another option to restrict who can send the data to trapper items is by using the authentication feature with PSK or SSL certificates. That is discussed in *Chapter 20, Encrypting Zabbix Traffic*.

Using an agent daemon configuration file

So far, we specified all the information that zabbix_sender needs on the command line. It is also possible to automatically retrieve some of that information from the agent daemon configuration file. Let's try this (use the correct path to your agent daemon configuration file):

```
$ zabbix_sender -c /usr/local/etc/zabbix_agentd.conf -k room.persons -o 3
```

This succeeds, because we specified the configuration file instead of the Zabbix server address and the hostname—these were picked up from the configuration file. If you are running zabbix_sender on many hosts where the Zabbix agent also resides, this should be easier and safer than parsing the configuration file manually. We could also use a special configuration file for zabbix_sender that only contains the parameters it needs.

> If the ServerActive parameter contains several entries, values are sent only to the first one. The HostnameItem parameter is not supported by zabbix_sender.

Sending values from a file

The approach we used allows us to send one value every time we run `zabbix_sender`. If we had a script that returned a large number of values, that would be highly inefficient. We can also send multiple values from a file with `zabbix_sender`. Create a file like this anywhere—for example, in `/tmp/`:

```
"A test host" room.persons 4
"A test host" room.persons 5
"A test host" room.persons 6
```

Each line contains the hostname, item key, and value. This means that any number of hosts and keys can be supplied from a single file.

> Notice how values that contain spaces are double quoted—the input file is whitespace (spaces and tabs) separated.

The flag for supplying the file is `-i`. Assuming a filename of `sender_input.txt`, we can run the following:

```
$ zabbix_sender -z 127.0.0.1 -i /tmp/sender_input.txt
```

That should send all three values successfully:

```
info from server: "processed: 3; failed: 0; total: 3; seconds spent:
0.000087"
```

```
sent: 3; skipped: 0; total: 3
```

When sending values from a file, we could still benefit from the agent daemon configuration file:

```
$ zabbix_sender -c /usr/local/etc/zabbix_agentd.conf -i /tmp/sender_
input.txt
```

In this case, the server address would be taken from the configuration file, while hostnames would still be supplied from the input file. Can we avoid that and get the hostname from the agent daemon configuration file? Yes, that is possible by replacing the hostname in the input file with a dash like this:

```
- room.persons 4
"A test host" room.persons 5
- room.persons 6
```

In this case, the hostname would be taken from the configuration file for the first and the third entry, while still overriding that for the second entry.

> If the input file contains many entries, zabbix_sender sends them in batches of 250 values per connection.

When there's a need to send lots of values constantly, one might wish to avoid repeatedly running the zabbix_sender binary. Instead, we could have a process write to a file new entries without closing the file, and then have zabbix_sender read from that file. Unfortunately, by default, values would be sent to the server only when the file is closed — or every 250 values received. Fortunately, there's also a command line flag to affect this behavior. Flag -r enables a so-called **real-time mode**. In this mode, zabbix_sender reads new values from the file and waits for 0.2 seconds. If no new values come in, the obtained values are sent. If more values come in, it waits for 0.2 seconds more, and so on up to 1 second. If there's a host that's constantly streaming values to the Zabbix server, zabbix_sender would connect to the server once per second at most and send all the values received in that second in one connection. Yes, in some weird cases, there could be more connections — for example, if we supplied one value every 0.3 seconds exactly.

If sending a huge number of values and using a file could became a performance issue, we could even consider a named pipe in place of the file — although that would be a quite rare occurrence.

Sending timestamped values

The data that we sent so far was considered to be received at that exact moment — the values had the timestamp assigned by the server when it got them. Every now and then, there's a need to send values in batches for a longer period of time, or import a backlog of older values. This can be easily achieved with zabbix_sender — when sending values from a file, it supports supplying a timestamp. When doing so, the value field in the input file is shifted to the right and the timestamp is inserted as the third field. For a quick test, we could generate timestamps 1, 2, and 3 days ago:

```
$ for i in 1 2 3; do date -d "-$i day" "+%s"; done
```

Take the resulting timestamps and use them in a new input file:

```
- room.persons 1462745422 11
"A test host" room.persons 1462659022 12
- room.persons 1462572622 13
```

With a file named `sender_input_timestamps.txt`, we would additionally use the `-T` flag to tell `zabbix sender` that it should expect the timestamps in there:

```
$ zabbix_sender -c /usr/local/etc/zabbix_agentd.conf -T -i /tmp/sender_
input_timestamps.txt
```

All three values should be sent successfully.

> When sending in values for a longer period of time, make sure the history and trend retention periods for that item match your needs. Otherwise, the housekeeper process could delete the older values soon after they are sent in.

Looking at the graph or latest values for this item, it is probably slightly messed up. The timestamped values we just sent in are likely to be overlapping in time with the previous values. In most cases, sending in values normally and with timestamps for the same item is not suggested.

> If the Zabbix trapper items have triggers configured against them, timestamped values should only be sent with increasing timestamps. If values are sent in a reversed or chaotic older-newer-older order, the generated events will not make sense.
>
> If data is sent in for a host which is in a no-data maintenance, the values are also discarded if the value timestamp is outside the current maintenance window. Maintenance was discussed in *Chapter 5, Managing Hosts, Users, and Permissions*.

SSH and Telnet items

We have looked at quite a lot of fairly custom and customizable ways to get data into Zabbix. Although external checks should allow us to grab data by any means whatsoever, in some cases we might need to collect data from some system that is reachable over SSH or even Telnet, but there is no way to install an agent on it. In that case, a more efficient way to retrieve the values would be to use the built-in SSH or Telnet support.

SSH items

Let's look at the SSH items first. As a simple test, we could re-implement the same Zabbix agent parameter we did as our first user parameter, determining the number of the currently logged-in users by running who | wc -l. To try this out, we need a user account we could use to run that command, and it is probably best to create a separate account on "A test host". Creating one could be as simple as the following:

```
# useradd -m -s /bin/bash zabbixtest
# passwd zabbixtest
```

> Do not create unauthorized user accounts in production systems. For remote systems, verify that the user is allowed to log in from the Zabbix server.

With the user account in place, let's create the SSH item. In the frontend, go to **Configuration | Hosts**, click on **Items** next to **A test host**, and click on **Create item**. Fill in the following:

- **Name**: Users logged in (SSH)
- **Type**: **SSH agent**
- **Key**: ssh.run[system.users]
- **User name**: zabbixtest (or whatever was the username for your test account)
- **Password**: fill in the password, used for that account
- **Executed script**: who | wc -l

Name	Users logged in (SSH)
Type	SSH agent
Key	ssh.run[system.users]
Host interface	127.0.0.1 : 10050
Authentication method	Password
User name	zabbixtest
Password	zabbixtest
Executed script	who	wc -l

> The username and password will be kept in plain text in the Zabbix database.

When done, click on the **Add** button at the bottom. For the key, we could customize the IP address and port as the second and third parameter respectively. Omitting them uses the default port of 22 and the host interface address. The first parameter for the item key is just a unique identifier. For SSH items, the key itself must be ssh. run, but the first parameter works in a similar fashion to the whole key for user parameters. In the **Latest data** page, our first SSH item should be working just fine and returning values as expected. This way, we could run any command and grab the return value.

> In most cases, it is suggested to use user parameters instead of SSH checks — one should resort to direct SSH checks only when it is not possible to install the Zabbix agent on the monitored system.

The item we just created uses a directly supplied password. We could also use key-based authentication. To do so, in the item properties, choose **Public key** for the **Authentication method** dropdown and fill in the name of the file that holds the private key in the **Private key file** field. Although the underlying library allows skipping the public key when compiled with OpenSSL, Zabbix currently requires specifying the public key filename in the **Public key file** field. If the key is passphrase-protected, the passphrase should be supplied in the **Key passphrase** field. But where should that file be located? Check the Zabbix server configuration file and look for the SSHKeyLocation parameter. It is not set by default, so set it to some directory and place the private and public key files there. Make sure the directory and all key files are only accessible for the Zabbix user.

> Encrypted or passphrase-protected keys are not supported by default on several distributions, including Debian. Dependency libssh2 might have to be compiled with OpenSSL to allow encrypted keys. See https://www.zabbix.com/documentation/3.0/manual/installation/known_issues#ssh_checks for more detail.

Telnet items

In case of a device that can have neither the Zabbix agent installed, nor supports SSH, Zabbix also has a built-in method to obtain values over Telnet. With Telnet being a really old and insecure protocol, that is probably one of the least suggested methods for data gathering.

Telnet items are similar to SSH items. The simplest item key syntax is the following:

```
telnet.run[<unique_identifier>]
```

The key itself is a fixed string, while the first parameter is a unique identifier, the same as for the SSH items. Also the second and third parameter are IP address and port, if they are different from the host interface IP and the default Telnet port, 23. The commands to run will go in the **Executed script** field, and the username and password should be supplied as well.

> The username and password are transmitted in plain text with Telnet. Avoid it if possible.

For the login prompt, Zabbix looks for a string that ends with : (colon). For the command prompt, the following are supported:

- $
- #
- >
- %

When the command returns, at the beginning of the string, up to one of these symbols is trimmed.

Custom modules

Besides all of the already covered methods, Zabbix also offers a way to write loadable modules. These modules have to be written in C and can be loaded in the Zabbix agent, server, and proxy daemons. When included in the Zabbix agent, from the server perspective, they act the same as the built-in items or user parameters. When included in the Zabbix server or proxy, they appear as simple checks.

Modules have to be explicitly loaded using the LoadModulePath and LoadModule parameters. We won't be looking at the modules in much detail here, but information about the module API and other details are available at https://www.zabbix.com/documentation/3.0/manual/config/items/loadablemodules.

Summary

In this chapter, we looked at more advanced ways to gather data.

We explored **log monitoring** and either tracking a single file or multiple files, matching a regular expression. We filtered the results and parsed some values out of them.

Calculated items gave us a field to type any custom formula and the results were computed from the data the server already had without querying the monitored devices again. Any trigger function could be used, providing great flexibility.

Aggregate items allowed us to calculate particular values, such as minimum, maximum, and average for items over a host group. This method is mostly useful for cluster or cluster-like systems, where hosts in the group are working to provide a common service.

External checks and **user parameters** provided a way to retrieve nearly any value — at least any that can be obtained on the command line. While very similar conceptually, they also have some differences that we'll try to summarize now:

External checks	User parameters
Are executed by the Zabbix server process	Are executed by the Zabbix agent daemon
Are executed on the Zabbix server	Are executed on the monitored hosts
Can be attached to any host	Can only be attached to the host where the Zabbix agent daemon runs
Can reduce server performance	Have no notable impact on server performance if set up as active items

As can be seen from this comparison, external checks should be mostly used with remote systems where the Zabbix agent cannot be installed, because they can be attached to any host in the Zabbix configuration. Given the possible negative performance impact, it is suggested to use user parameters in most situations.

Note that it is suggested for user parameters to have an active Zabbix agent type. That way, a server connection is not tied up in case the executed command fails to return in a timely manner. We also learned that we should take note of the environment the agent daemon runs in, as it is not initialized.

For scripts that return a large number of values or for scripts that take a long time to run, it was suggested to use the command line utility `zabbix_sender` with a corresponding Zabbix trapper item. This not only allowed us to send in anything at our preferred rate, it also allowed us to specify the timestamp for each value.

And for those cases where we have to execute a command on a remote host to get the value, the built-in support of SSH or even Telnet items could come in handy.

Armed with this knowledge, we should be able to gather any value that traditional methods such as Zabbix agents, SNMP, IPMI, and other built-in checks can't retrieve.

In the next chapter, we will cover several ways to automate the configuration in Zabbix. That will include network discovery, low-level discovery, and active agent autoregistration.

12

Automating Configuration

So far, we have mostly done manual configuration of Zabbix by adding hosts, items, triggers, and other entities. With the exception of templates, discussed in *Chapter 8, Simplifying Complex Configuration with Templates*, we haven't looked at ways to accommodate larger and more dynamic environments. In this chapter, we will discover ways to automatically find out about resources such as network interfaces or filesystems on hosts by using low-level discovery, scanning a subnet using network discovery, and allowing hosts to register themselves using active agent autoregistration.

While learning about these methods, we will also explore related features, such as global regular expressions, and find out more details about the features we already know of—including context for user macros.

As Zabbix has several ways to manage automatic entity configuration and they all operate in a different fashion, it is highly suggested to never use the term **auto-discovery** when talking about Zabbix—nobody would know for sure which functionality is meant. Instead, it is suggested to always specify whether it's low-level discovery, network discovery, or active agent autoregistration.

Low-level discovery

Currently, we are monitoring several parameters on our hosts, including network traffic. We configured those items by finding out the interface name and then manually specifying it for all of the relevant items. Interface names could be different from system to system, and there could be a different number of interfaces on each system. The same could happen with filesystems, CPUs, and other entities. They could also change—a filesystem could get mounted or unmounted. Zabbix offers a way to deal with such different and potentially dynamic configurations with a feature called **low-level discovery**. In the Zabbix documentation and community, it it usually known as LLD, and that is how we will refer to it in this book, too.

Low-level discovery normally enables us to discover entities on existing hosts (we will discuss more advanced functionality related to discovering hosts with LLD in *Chapter 18, Monitoring VMware*). LLD is an extremely widely used feature, and there are few Zabbix users who do not benefit from it. There are several LLD methods that are built in, and it is fairly easy to create new ones, too. The available LLD methods are:

- Network interfaces (Zabbix agent)
- Filesystems (Zabbix agent)
- CPUs (Zabbix agent)
- SNMP tables
- ODBC queries
- Custom LLD

We'll discuss Windows service discovery in *Chapter 14, Monitoring Windows*. ODBC monitoring can be a bit cumbersome in the case of many databases being monitored, so we won't spend much time on it and won't be covering ODBC LLD in this book. See the official documentation on it at `https://www.zabbix.com/documentation/3.0/manual/discovery/low_level_discovery#discovery_using_odbc_sql_queries`.

Network interface discovery

Network interfaces on servers seem simple to monitor, but they tend to get more complicated as the environment size increases and time goes by. Back in the day, we had `eth0` and everybody was happy. Well, not everybody — people needed more interfaces, so it was `eth1`, `eth2`, and so on. It would already be a challenge to manually match the existing interfaces to Zabbix items so that all interfaces are properly monitored. Then Linux-based systems changed the interface naming scheme, and now, one could have `enp0s25` or something similar, or a totally different interface name. That would not be easy to manage on a large number of different systems. Interface names on Windows are even more fun — they could include the name of the vendor, driver, antivirus software, firewall software, and a bunch of other things. In the past, people have even written VB scripts to sort of create fake `eth0` interfaces on Windows systems.

Luckily, LLD should solve all that by providing a built-in way to automatically discover all the interfaces and monitor the desired items on each interface. This is supported on the majority of the platforms that the Zabbix agent runs on, including Linux, Windows, FreeBSD, OpenBSD, NetBSD, Solaris, AIX, and HP-UX. Let's see how we can discover all the interfaces automatically on our monitored systems. Navigate to **Configuration | Templates** and click on **Discovery** next to **C_Template_ Linux**. This is the section that lists the LLD rules—currently, we have none. Before we create a rule, it might be helpful to understand what an LLD rule is and what other entities supplement it.

A **Discovery** rule is a configuration entity that tells Zabbix what it should discover. In the case of network interfaces, an LLD rule would return a list of all interfaces. Assuming our system has interfaces called eth0 and eth1, the LLD rule would just return a list of them:

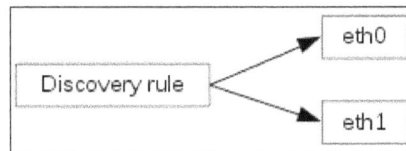

Then, the LLD rule contains prototypes. In the first place, prototypes for items would be required, although LLD allows us to add trigger and custom graph prototypes as well. What actually are prototypes? We discussed templates in *Chapter 8, Simplifying Complex Configuration with Templates*. You can think of LLD prototypes as mini-templates. Instead of affecting the whole host, they affect items or triggers, or custom graphs on a host. For example, an item prototype for network interface discovery could tell Zabbix to monitor incoming network traffic on all discovered interfaces the same way.

Getting back to creating an LLD rule, in the empty list of LLD rules, click on **Create discovery rule** in the upper-right corner. Fill in the following:

- **Name**: Interface discovery
- **Key**: net.if.discovery
- **Update interval**: 120

When done, click on **Add**. The **Discovery** rule is added, although it won't do much useful work for now. The key we used, `net.if.discovery`, is supposed to return all the interfaces on the system. As you probably spotted, the properties of an LLD rule look quite similar to item properties: there's an update interval, and there are flexible intervals. Overall, the built-in agent LLD rules actually are items. We will later look at the details of how they operate.

A discovery rule returns macros. The same as before, it might be safer to think about them as variables, although we will refer to them as macros again. These macros return various properties of the discovered entities. In the case of the network interface discovery by the Zabbix agent, these macros return interface names. LLD macros always use the syntax of `{#NAME}`, that is, the name wrapped in curly braces and prefixed with a hash mark. The macros can be later used in prototypes to create items for each discovered interface. The built-in LLD rule keys return a fixed set of such macros, and we will discuss each set whenever we look at the specific discovery method, such as network interfaces first, filesystems and others later. We have an LLD rule now, but it just discovers the interfaces. Nothing is done about them without the prototypes. To have any benefit from the previous step, let's create some prototypes. Still in the LLD rule list, click on **Item prototypes** in the **ITEMS** column next to **Interface discovery**. Then, click on the **Create item prototype** button, and fill in the following:

- **Name**: `Incoming traffic on $1`
- **Key**: `net.if.in[{#IFNAME}]`
- **Units**: `Bps`
- **Store value**: **Delta (speed per second)**

Our prototype here uses a discovery macro in the item key parameters. Actually, this is required. These macros will be replaced with different values when creating the final items, so the resulting item keys will be different. We could create item prototypes without using LLD macros in the key parameters, but the resulting discovery would fail as it would attempt to create one item per LLD macro.

When done with the configuration, click on the **Add** button at the bottom. Let's see whether this item prototype now works as intended. We set the interval in our LLD rule to a low value—120 seconds. As we cannot force items and discovery rules to run manually, this will allow us to play with various configuration changes and see the results much sooner. Wait for a few minutes, and go to **Configuration | Hosts**. Then, click on **Discovery** next to **A test host**. Something's not right—in the **INFO** column, there's a red error icon. Move your mouse cursor over it to see what the error message is:

KEY	INTERVAL	TYPE	STATUS	INFO
net.if.discovery	2m	Zabbix agent	Enabled	⊠

> Cannot create item: item with the same key "net.if.in[enp0s8]" already exists.
> Cannot create item: item with the same key "net.if.in[lo]" already exists.

It's complaining that an item that would have to be created based on the LLD item prototype already exists. That is correct; we created an item exactly like that earlier, when we manually added items for interface monitoring.

> If an LLD rule attempts to create items that have already been created, the discovery fails and no items will be created.

The same as always, item uniqueness is determined by the item key, including all the parameters. Unfortunately, there is no way to merge manually configured items with LLD-generated ones. There is also no easy way to keep the collected history. We could change the item key either for the existing item or for the item prototype slightly and keep the manually added item for historic purposes and then remove it later when the new, LLD-generated item has collected enough historical data. In this case, we could apply a small hack to the existing item key. Navigate to **Configuration | Templates**, and click on **Items** next to **C_Template_Linux**. Click on **Incoming traffic on interface eth0** in the **NAME** column. In the properties, make these changes:

- **Name**: Incoming traffic on interface $1 (manual)
- **Key**: net.if.in[enp0s8,]

Name	Incoming traffic on interface $1 (manual)
Type	Zabbix agent (active) ▾
Key	net.if.in[enp0s8,] Select

That is, add (manual) to the name and a trailing comma inside the square brackets. The first change was not strictly required, but it will allow us to identify these items. The second change does not change anything functionally — the item will still collect exactly the same information. We changed the item key, though. Even a small change like this results in the key being different, and the discovery rule should be able to create those items now. When done, click on **Update**. Now, make the same changes to the outgoing network traffic item and the loopback interface item.

> This trick works because the item key accepts parameters. For item keys that accept no parameters, it is not possible to add empty square brackets to indicate no parameters.

With the item keys changed, we could also monitor outgoing traffic automatically. Let's go to **Configuration | Templates**, click on **Discovery** next to **C_Template_Linux**, and then **Item prototypes** next to **Interface discovery**. Click on **Incoming traffic on {#IFNAME}** and then on the **Clone** button. Change Incoming to Outgoing in the **Name** field, and change the **Key** field to read net.if.out[{#IFNAME}]. When done, click on the **Add** button at the bottom.

Let a few minutes pass, and head back to **Configuration | Hosts**. Click on **Discovery** next to **A test host**. The error icon should be gone — if not, track down any other items mentioned here and make the same changes to them. Once there are no errors listed in this section, navigate to **Configuration | Hosts** and click on **Items** next to **A test host**. There should be several new items, and they should all be prefixed with the LLD rule name — **Interface discovery**:

Interface discovery: Incoming traffic on lo

Interface discovery: Incoming traffic on enp0s8

Interface discovery: Incoming traffic on enp0s3

Clicking on the discovery rule name will open the list of prototypes in the LLD rule.

> The number of items created depends on the number of interfaces on the system — for each interface, two items should be created.

Our first discovery rule seems to be working nicely now; all interfaces on the system have been discovered and network traffic is being monitored on them. If we wanted to monitor other parameters on each interface, we would add more prototypes, using the discovery macro in the item key parameters so that the created items have unique keys.

Automatically creating calculated items

For our manually created network traffic items, we created calculated items to collect the total incoming and outgoing traffic in *Chapter 11, Advanced Item Monitoring*. While we could go ahead and create such calculated items manually for all LLD-created items, too, that would be a huge amount of manual work.

Let's try to create a calculated item per interface by the LLD rule instead — go to **Configuration | Templates**, click on **Discovery** next to **C_Template_Linux**, and click on **Item prototypes** next to **Interface discovery**. Then, click on **Create item prototype**. Fill in the following values:

- **Name**: Total traffic on $1
- **Type**: **Calculated**
- **Key**: calc.net.if.total[{#IFNAME}]
- **Formula**: last(net.if.in[{#IFNAME}])+last(net.if.out[{#IFNAME}])
- **Units**: B

> We did not change **Type of information** as we intentionally left it at **Numeric (unsigned)** for the network traffic items we referenced here. To remind yourself why, refer to *Chapter 3, Monitoring with Zabbix Agents and Basic Protocols*.

When done, click on the **Add** button at the bottom. If you check the latest data page, this item should start gathering data in a couple of minutes.

> The item key for calculated items is for our own convenience. The key does not affect the data collection in any way — that is completely determined by the formula.

But let's say we're not that interested in very detailed statistics on the total traffic, but more in a longer-term trend. We could modify the item we just created to collect the sum of average incoming and outgoing traffic over the past 10 minutes and do so every 10 minutes. Let's go back to **Configuration | Templates**, click on **Discovery** next to **C_Template_Linux**, and click on **Item prototypes** next to **Interface discovery**. Then, click on **Total traffic on {#IFNAME}**. Change these four fields:

- **Name**: Total traffic on $1 over last 10 minutes
- **Key**: calc.net.if.total.10m[{#IFNAME}]
- **Formula**: avg(net.if.in[{#IFNAME}],10m)+avg(net.if.out[{#IFNAME}],10m)
- **Update interval**: 600

> In the formula, we could also have used 600 instead of 10m.

When done, click on the **Update** button at the bottom. We now have to allow a couple of minutes for the discovery rule to run again and then up to 10 minutes for this item to get the new value.

Let's discuss the changes we made. The most important one was the **Formula** update. We changed the last() function for both item references to avg(). We can use any trigger function in calculated items. We also supplied a parameter for this function after a comma, and that was the reason we had to double-quote item keys in the disk space item. The referenced keys contained a comma, and that comma would be misunderstood by Zabbix to separate the item key from the function parameters.

> Additional parameters can be specified by adding more commas. For example, in avg(net.if.in[{#IFNAME}],10m,1d),1d would be a time shift as that's the second parameter for the avg() trigger function. See more on trigger functions in *Chapter 6, Detecting Problems with Triggers*.
>
> If we only want to display the total on a graph, there is no need to create an item—stacked graphs allow us to do that. We discussed stacked graphs in *Chapter 9, Visualizing the Data with Graphs and Maps*.

The total traffic item (or items) should be updated in the latest data to display the average total traffic over the past 10 minutes. Normally, we would probably use an even longer interval for these averages, such as an hour, but 10 minutes are a bit faster in supplying us with the data. This approach could also be used to configure a floating average for some item. For example, a formula like this would calculate the floating average for 6 hours for the CPU load:

```
avg(system.cpu.load,6h)
```

Calculated items do not have to reference multiple items; they can also reference a single item to perform some calculation on it. Such a floating average could be used for better trend prediction or writing relative triggers by comparing current CPU load values to the floating average.

Automatically creating triggers

Creating items for all discovered entities is useful, but even looking through them would be quite a task. Luckily, LLD allows us to create triggers automatically as well. The same as with items, this is done by creating prototypes first; actual triggers will be created by the discovery process later.

To create the prototypes, navigate to **Configuration | Templates**, click on **Discovery** next to **C_Template_Linux**, and then click on **Trigger prototypes**. In the upper-right corner, click on **Create trigger prototype**, and configure it like this:

* **Name**: Incoming traffic too high for {#IFNAME} on {HOST.NAME}.

* **Expression**: Click on **Add** next to this field. In the popup, click on **Select prototype**, and then click on **Incoming traffic on {#IFNAME}** in the **NAME** column. Click on Insert and modify the generated expression. Change =0 to >5K. This would alert you whenever the incoming traffic exceeded 5,000 bytes per second, as the item is collecting in bytes per second.

* **Severity**: Select **Warning**.

When done, click on the **Add** button at the bottom. That was for incoming traffic; now, let's create a prototype for outgoing traffic. Click on the name of the prototype we just created, and then click on **Clone**. In the new form, change Incoming in the **NAME** field to Outgoing and net.if.in in the **Expression** field to net.if.out, and then click on the **Add** button at the bottom. With both prototypes in place, let's go to **Configuration | Hosts** and click on **Triggers** next to **A test host**. It is likely that there are several new triggers here already, for the incoming traffic — we created that prototype first, so discovery might have had a chance to process it already. Nevertheless, it should not take longer than a few minutes for all of the LLD-created triggers to show up. Make sure to refresh the page manually to see any changes — configuration pages do not get automatically refreshed like monitoring ones do:

Warning	Interface discovery: Incoming traffic too high for enp0s3 on {HOST.NAME}	{A test host:net.if.in[enp0s3].**last()**}>5K
Warning	Interface discovery: Incoming traffic too high for enp0s8 on {HOST.NAME}	{A test host:net.if.in[enp0s8].**last()**}>5K
Warning	Interface discovery: Incoming traffic too high for lo on {HOST.NAME}	{A test host:net.if.in[lo].**last()**}>5K

The same as with items, triggers are prefixed with the LLD rule name. Notice how we got one trigger from each prototype for each interface, the same as with the items. The {#IFNAME} LLD macro was replaced by the interface name as well. Note that we did not have to worry about making the created triggers unique — we must reference an item key in a trigger, and that already includes the appropriate LLD macros in item key parameters.

The threshold we chose here is very low — it is likely to fire even on our small test systems. What if we had various systems and we wanted to have a different threshold on each of them? The concept we discussed earlier, user macros, would help here. Instead of a hardcoded value, we would use a user macro in the trigger expression and override it on specific hosts as needed. We discussed user macros in *Chapter 8, Simplifying Complex Configuration with Templates*.

Automatically creating graphs

We have items and triggers automatically created for all interfaces, and we could also have a graph created for each interface, combining incoming and outgoing traffic. The same as before, this is done with the help of prototypes. Go to **Configuration | Templates**, click on **Discovery** next to **C_Template_Linux**, and then click on **Graph prototypes**. Click on **Create graph prototype**, and enter `Traffic on {#IFNAME}` in the **Name** field.

Click on **Add prototype** in the **Items** section, and mark the checkboxes next to the incoming and outgoing network traffic items. Then, click on **Select**. Choose **Gradient line** for both items in the **DRAW STYLE** dropdown:

Items	NAME	FUNCTION	DRAW STYLE	Y AXIS SIDE	COLOUR	ACTION
	1: C_Template_Linux: Incoming traffic on {#IFNAME}	avg ▾	Gradient line ▾	Left ▾	▊ 1A7C11	Remove
	2: C_Template_Linux: Outgoing traffic on {#IFNAME}	avg ▾	Gradient line ▾	Left ▾	▊ F63100	Remove
	Add Add prototype					

When done, click on the **Add** button at the bottom. Note that we had to specify the LLD macro in the graph name—otherwise, Zabbix would be unable to create graphs, as they would have had the same name. With the prototype in place, let's go to **Configuration | Hosts** and click on **Graphs** next to **A test host**. If you see no graphs, wait a couple of minutes and refresh the page—the graphs should show up, one for each interface, again prefixed with the LLD rule name:

Interface discovery: Traffic on enp0s3

Interface discovery: Traffic on enp0s8

Interface discovery: Traffic on lo

Navigating to **Monitoring | Graphs** and selecting **A test host** in the **Host** dropdown will show all of these graphs in the **Graph** dropdown. This way, traffic on a specific interface can be easily reviewed by selecting the appropriate graph—and without configuring those graphs manually first.

> There is no way to automatically create a graph with all the discovered items in it at this time.

Filtering discovery results

Looking at the items, triggers, and graphs that were created, besides real interfaces, the loopback interface also got discovered, and all of those entities got created for it. In some cases, it would be useful to monitor that interface as well, but for most systems, such data would not be useful.

If we look at the list of items in the configuration, the LLD-generated items have the checkbox next to them disabled, and we can't click on them to edit properties directly either. The controls in the **STATUS** column allow us to enable or disable them individually, though. LLD-generated items on a host cannot be edited, except for being disabled or enabled. Note that in the frontend, this can only be done one by one for each item — we cannot use mass update as the checkboxes are disabled.

Disabling an LLD-generated item on many hosts could be a massive manual task. We could think about disabling the prototype, but that would not work for two reasons. Firstly, we only want to disable items for the loopback interface, but the same prototype is used for items on all interfaces. Secondly, state changes in the prototype are not propagated to the generated items. The initial state in which these items are created — enabled or disabled — will be kept for them.

What about other changes to these items, such as changing the item key or some other property? Those would get propagated downstream, but only when the discovery itself was run by the Zabbix server, not when we made the changes to the prototype in the frontend. In practice, this means that we would have to wait for up to the LLD rule interval to see these changes applied downstream.

Luckily, there's a way to easily avoid creating items for some of the discovered entities, such as in our case: not creating items for the loopback interface. This is possible by filtering the entities' LLD returns on the LLD rule level. Let's change our existing rule to ignore interfaces with the name `lo`.

> If we wanted to keep LLD-generated items but disable or enable several of them, in some cases, that might be worth doing via the Zabbix API — we will have a brief introduction to the API in *Chapter 21, Working Closely with Data*.

Navigate to **Configuration | Templates**, and click on **Discovery** next to
C_Template_Linux. Then, click on **Interface discovery** in the **NAME** column.
Notice how there's another tab here: **Filters**. Switch to that tab, and in the first and
only **Filters** entry, fill in the following:

- **MACRO**: {#IFNAME}
- **REGULAR EXPRESSION**: ^([^l].*|l[^o]|lo.+)$

When done, click on **Update**. LLD filters work by only returning matching entries.
In this case, we wanted to exclude the entry lo and keep everything
else. Unfortunately, Zabbix daemons only support POSIX extended regular
expressions—in this flavor, negating a string is fairly complicated. The filter we used
will exclude lo but match everything else—including eth0, enp0s8, and loop.

> We will explore a way to negate strings in an easier way later in
> this chapter.

To see whether this worked, navigate to **Configuration | Hosts** and click on **Items**
next to **A test host**. In the list, notice how both lo interface items have an orange icon
with an exclamation mark in the **INFO** column. If you move the mouse cursor over
it, a message explains that this item is not discovered anymore and will be deleted at
some later time:

> The item is not discovered anymore and will be deleted in 29d 23h 57m (on 2016-06-10 at 05:54).

In this case, the item is not discovered because it got excluded by the filter, but the reason does not matter that much—it could be an interface being removed or having its name changed as well. But why will it be removed after that specific amount of time, a bit more than 29 days? If we look at the properties of our LLD rule again, there's a field called **Keep lost resources period**:

Keep lost resources period (in days)	30

Here, we may specify how long items will be kept for when they are not discovered again, and the default is 30 days. The tooltip helpfully told us how much time we have left before the item will be deleted and at what time exactly it will be deleted. Other entities, including triggers and custom graphs, are kept as long as the underlying items are kept.

> An LLD rule is only evaluated when it gets new data. If the rule stops getting data, items would tell you that they are supposed to be deleted, but they won't be deleted until the rule gets new data and is evaluated.

Now, navigate to **Monitoring | Latest data**, and click on **Graph** for **Incoming traffic on lo**. Let some time pass, and notice that items that are scheduled for deletion still continue collecting data. This might be undesirable, when we had initially been monitoring a lot of things on a device, overloaded it, and then applied filtering, hoping to remedy the situation. There is no way to directly control this, but we may temporarily set the resource-keeping to 0, which would remove the items that are not discovered anymore next time the LLD rule runs. In the LLD rule properties, set the value of this field to 0 and click on **Update**. After a couple of minutes, check the item list for A test host in the configuration—both of the automatic lo interface items should be gone now.

What if we would like to have a different set of items for different discovered entities, for example, monitoring more things on interfaces with a specific name? That is not easily possible, unfortunately. One way would be by creating two different LLD rules with different item prototypes, then filtering for one set of entities in one LLD rule, and another set in the other LLD rule. Still, that is more complicated than one might expect. LLD rules have the same uniqueness criteria as items: the key. With some items, we can use a little trick and have an item with a key called key and another with key[]. Specifying empty square brackets will denote empty parameters, but functionally, the item will be exactly the same. Unfortunately, the agent LLD keys do not accept parameters, so this trick won't work. One workaround would be specifying an alias on an item key—we will discuss how that can be done in *Chapter 22, Zabbix Maintenance*.

Filesystem discovery

We have found out that a Zabbix agent has built-in support for discovering network interfaces. It can also discover other things, one of the most popular being filesystems. Before we configure that, let's find out what we can expect from such a feature.

Introducing the LLD JSON format

The discovery does not just look a bit like an item in the frontend; it also operates in the same way underneath. The magic happens based on the contents of a specific item value. All the found things are encoded in a JSON structure. The easiest way to see what's returned is to use `zabbix_get` and query a Zabbix agent. On A test host, run this command:

```
$ zabbix_get -s 127.0.0.1 -k net.if.discovery
```

Here, `net.if.discovery` is just an item key, not different from other item keys. This will return a small string, similar to the following:

```
{data:[{{#IFNAME}:enp0s3},{{#IFNAME}:enp0s8},{{#IFNAME}:lo}]}
```

While it's mostly understandable, it would be even better with some formatting. The easiest way is to use Perl or Python tools. The Python method would be this:

```
$ zabbix_get -s 127.0.0.1 -k net.if.discovery | python -mjson.tool
```

The Perl method would be one of these:

```
$ zabbix_get -s 127.0.0.1 -k net.if.discovery | json_pp
$ zabbix_get -s 127.0.0.1 -k net.if.discovery | json_xs
```

The latter method should be faster but requires the `JSON::XS` Perl module. For our purposes, performance should not be a concern, so choose whichever method works for you. The output will be similar to this:

```
{
    data : [
        {
            {#IFNAME} : enp0s3
        },
        {
            {#IFNAME} : enp0s8
        },
        {
            {#IFNAME} : lo
        }
    ]
}
```

The number of interfaces and their names might differ, but we can see that for each found interface, we are returning one macro: the interface name. The key for filesystem discovery is similar: `vfs.fs.discovery`. We can now run this:

```
$ zabbix_get -s 127.0.0.1 -k vfs.fs.discovery | json_pp
```

This would most likely return lots and lots of entries. Here's a snippet:

```
{
    data : [
        {
            {#FSNAME} : /dev/pts,
            {#FSTYPE} : devpts
        },
        {
            {#FSNAME} : /,
            {#FSTYPE} : ext3
        },
        {
            {#FSNAME} : /proc,
            {#FSTYPE} : proc
        },
        {
            {#FSNAME} : /sys,
            {#FSTYPE} : sysfs
    . . .
```

Two things can be seen here: one, it definitely returns way more than we would want to monitor. Two, it returns two values for each filesystem: name and type. While we could filter by the filesystem name, some monitored systems could have the root filesystem only, some could have separate /home, and so on. The best way would be to filter by filesystem type. In this example, we only want to monitor filesystems of type ext3. With this knowledge in hand, let's navigate to **Configuration | Templates**, click on **Discovery** next to **C_Template_Linux**, and then click on **Create discovery rule**. Fill in these values:

- **Name:** Filesystem discovery
- **Key:** vfs.fs.discovery
- **Update interval:** 120

The same as with network interface discovery, we set the update interval to 120. The default in the form, 30 seconds, is very low and should not be used. Discovery can be resource intensive, and, if possible, should be run hourly or so. Now, switch to the **Filters** tab, and fill in these values:

- **Macro**: {#FSTYPE}
- **Regular expression**: ^ext3$

> Replace the filesystem type with the one used on your system.
> Multiple filesystem types can be accepted, like this: ^ext3|ext4$.

When done, click on the **Add** button at the bottom. We have the discovery now, but no prototypes. Click on **Item prototypes** next to **Filesystem discovery**, and click on **Create item prototype**. Fill in the following:

- **Name**: Free space on {#FSNAME}
- **Key**: vfs.fs.size[{#FSNAME},free]

When done, click on the **Add** button at the bottom. We now expect the discovery to get the list of all filesystems, discard most of those except the ones with the type exactly ext3, and then create a free disk space item for each of them. We filter by one LLD macro, {#FSTYPE}, but use another — {#FSNAME} — in the actual item configuration. After a couple of minutes have passed, navigate to **Configuration | Hosts** and click on **Items** next to **A test host**. For each filesystem of type ext3, there should be a free disk space item:

| Filesystem discovery: Free space on / | vfs.fs.size[/,free] |

With more prototypes, we could also monitor total space, inode statistics, and other data. We could have triggers as needed on all of these filesystems.

As this discovery returns multiple macros, it might be desirable to filter by multiple macros at the same time. For example, we might want to exclude the /boot filesystem from monitoring. Similar to the type of calculation in action conditions, discussed in *Chapter 7, Acting upon Monitored Conditions*, we can choose between the automatic options of **And**, **Or**, and **And/Or**—and there's also the **Custom expression** option. This should allow us to create discovery logic of varying complexity.

Including discovered graphs in screens

When we configure screens with normal graphs, we just choose the graph that should be included in the screen. With LLD-generated graphs, it becomes more complicated—we never know for sure how many graphs could be there for each host. Luckily, Zabbix allows us to include LLD-generated graphs in a way that automatically figures out the number of the discovered entities. To try this feature out, let's go to **Monitoring | Screens**, go to the list of screens, and click on **Constructor** next to **Local servers**. Click on the **+** icon in the lower-left corner to add another row here, and then click on **Change** in the lower-left cell. In the **Resource** dropdown, select **Graph prototype**. Click on **Select** next to the **Graph prototype** field. In the popup, choose **Linux servers** in the **Group** dropdown and **A test host** in the **Host** dropdown, and then click on **Traffic on {#IFNAME}** in the NAME column. In the **Width** field, enter 400.

Resource	Graph prototype ▼	
Graph prototype	A test host: Traffic on {#IFNAME}	Select
Max columns	3	
Width	400	

Click on **Add**. Notice how this cell does not seem that useful in the screen configuration—no data is displayed, and the title just says **Traffic on {#IFNAME}**. Let's check this screen in the monitoring view and see whether it's any better.

Depending on the number of network interfaces your system had, the lower-left corner of the screen will have a different number of graphs. If there's only one interface (excluding `lo`), the screen will look decent. If there are more, all of them will be displayed, but they will be stuffed in a single cell, making the screen layout less pleasing:

> We did not set **Dynamic item** for this screen element. When the host selection is changed in the monitoring section, these graphs always show data for `A test host`. We discussed screen configuration in more detail in *Chapter 10, Visualizing the Data with Screens and Slideshows*.

To improve this, return to the constructor of the **Local servers** screen and click on the **Change** link in the lower-left corner. Change **Column span** to 2. Our screen has two columns, so the network interface graphs will now use full screen width. Additionally, take a look at the **Max columns** field: by default, it is set to 3. If your system had three or more network interfaces discovered, the graphs would take the width of three columns, not two, breaking the screen layout again. Let's set it to 2. When done, click on **Update**, and then check the screen in the monitoring view again:

This looks better now; the network traffic graphs take full screen width, and any further traffic graphs will be placed below in two columns. This was a custom graph prototype that we added—let's see how it works for simple graphs now. Open the constructor of the **Local servers** screen again, and click on the **+** icon in the lower-left corner. Click on the **Change** link in the lower-left table cell, and select **Simple graph prototype** in the **Resource** dropdown. Then, click on **Select** next to the **Item prototype** field. Choose **Linux servers** in the **Group** dropdown and **A test host** in the **Host** dropdown, and then click on **Free space on {#FSNAME}** in the **NAME** column. Set both **Max columns** and **Column span** to 2 again, and click on **Add**. Check this screen in the monitoring view. All of the discovered filesystems should be shown in this screen, below the network traffic graphs.

It works the same way in templated screens (also known as host screens), except that we may only select item and graph prototypes from a single template:

Custom thresholds with user macro context

The triggers we created from the network interface LLD prototypes always used the same threshold. We could use a user macro and customize the threshold for an individual host, but all interfaces would get the same threshold on that host. With filesystem monitoring, it could be desirable to have different thresholds on different filesystems. For example, we could use 80% warning on the root filesystem, 60% on the /boot filesystem, and 95% on the /home filesystem. This is possible using the user macro context.

> Refer to *Chapter 8, Simplifying Complex Configuration with Templates,* for more details on user macros.

The normal syntax for user macros is {$MACRO}. The context is specified inside the curly braces, separated with a colon—{$MACRO:context}. A trigger prototype to check for the filesystem being 80% full in our LLD rule could have an expression like this:

```
{C_Template_Linux:vfs.fs.size[{#FSNAME},free].last()}<20
```

> It might be a good idea to use trigger functions such as `avg()` or `max()` to avoid trigger flapping, as discussed in *Chapter 6, Detecting Problems with Triggers*.

This would alert on any filesystem having less than 20% free disk space or being above 80% utilization. We could rewrite it to use the user macro as the threshold value:

```
{C_Template_Linux:vfs.fs.size[{#FSNAME},free].last()}<{$FS_FREE_
THRESHOLD}
```

This would allow us to customize the threshold per host but not per filesystem. Expanding on this, we would instruct the LLD rule to put the discovered filesystem as the macro context, like this:

```
{C_Template_Linux:vfs.fs.size[{#FSNAME},free].last()}<{$FS_FREE_
THRESHOLD:{#FSNAME}}
```

As the LLD prototypes are processed, the LLD macros are replaced with the discovered values in created items. The trigger for the root filesystem that would be created on the host would look like this:

```
{A test host:vfs.fs.size[{#FSNAME},free].last()}<{$FS_FREE_
THRESHOLD:/}
```

The trigger for the `/home` filesystem would look like this:

```
{A test host:vfs.fs.size[{#FSNAME},free].last()}<{$FS_FREE_THRESHOLD:/
home}
```

When Zabbix evaluates this trigger, it will first look for a macro with this context value on the host. If that is not found, it will look for this macro with this context in the linked templates. If it's not found there, it will look for a global macro with such a context. If it's still not found, it will revert to the macro without the context and evaluate that as a normal user macro. This means that we don't have to define user macros with all possible context values — only the ones where we want to modify the behavior. If there's a filesystem for which a specific user macro is not available, there's always the host, template, or global macro to fall back to.

This feature is really nice, but properly explaining it seems to be complicated, so here's a schematic. Without context, user macros were evaluated as in the right-hand column — that is, the host level was checked first, then template, and then global. With context, it is the same — just that the macro name with context is looked up in all three levels first, then we fall back to the macro name without context on all three levels. The first place where there's a match will determine the value for that macro.

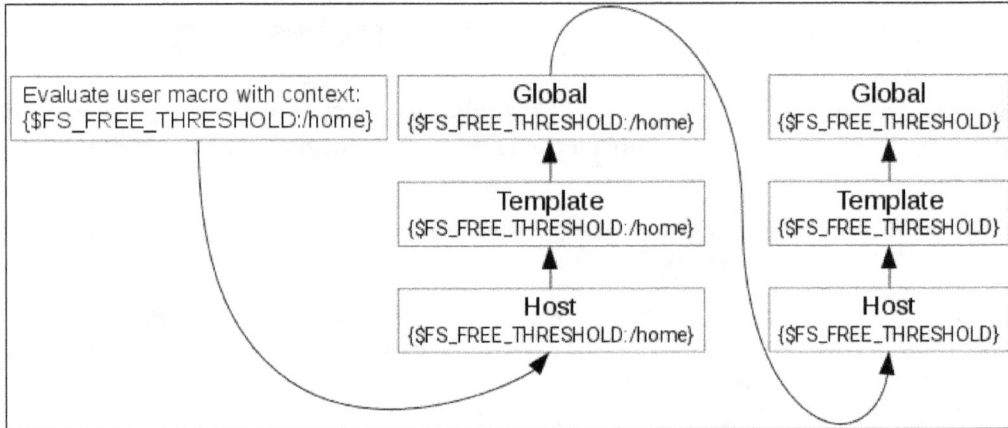

When used in triggers like this, this feature allows us to have different thresholds for different filesystems — and that can also be customized per host. We could have a user macro `{$FS_FREE_THRESHOLD:/home}` set to 20 on one host, 30 on another, and so on.

Of course, this is not limited to triggers — it is supported in all the locations where user macros are supported, including item-key parameters and trigger-function parameters. A trigger could check the average temperature for 5 minutes on one system and 15 minutes on another.

CPU discovery

Yet another discovery method supported by the Zabbix agent is **CPU discovery**. It returns all CPUs (or cores) present on a system. Now that we know how to get the LLD JSON, we only need to know which item key is used to return CPU information — that's `system.cpu.discovery`. Run this on A test host:

```
$ zabbix_get -s 127.0.0.1 -k system.cpu.discovery | json_pp
```

For a single-core system, it will return this:

```
{
    data : [
        {
            {#CPU.NUMBER} : 0,
            {#CPU.STATUS} : online
        }
    ]
}
```

The CPU discovery returns two macros for each discovered CPU:

* {#CPU.NUMBER} is a CPU number, as assigned by the system
* {#CPU.STATUS} tells us the CPU's status — again, according to the host system

This can be used to monitor various states on individual CPUs and cores. If our application is supposed to utilize all cores evenly, it might be useful to know when the utilization is not even. Simple CPU utilization monitoring will return the average result across all CPUs, so a runaway process that consumes 100% of a single CPU on a quad-core system would only register as having 25% utilization. We might also want to know when a CPU is not online for some reason.

SNMP discovery

The discovery methods we examined before were all Zabbix-agent based. Zabbix also supports discovering entities over SNMP. This is different from the dynamic SNMP index support we discussed in *Chapter 4, Monitoring SNMP Devices*. The dynamic SNMP index allows us to monitor a specific entity by name — for example, a network interface by its name. SNMP support in LLD allows us to discover all entities and monitor them. Let's see how we could use it to discover all network interfaces.

Navigate to **Configuration | Hosts,** click on **Discovery** next to the host for which you created SNMP items before, and click on **Create discovery rule.** Populate these fields:

- **Name**: SNMP interface discovery
- **Type**: **SNMPv2 agent** (or choose another, supported SNMP version)
- **Key**: snmp.interface.discovery
- **SNMP OID**: discovery[{#IFDESCR}, IF-MIB::ifDescr]
- **Update interval**: 120

Name	SNMP interface discovery
Type	SNMPv2 agent ▾
Key	snmp.interface.discovery
Host interface	127.0.0.1 : 161 ▾
SNMP OID	discovery[{#IFDESCR}, IF-MIB::ifDescr]
SNMP community	public
Port	
Update interval (in sec)	120

> Zabbix versions before 2.4 used a different SNMP OID syntax for LLD rules. While upgrading Zabbix would change the syntax to the current one, importing an older template would use the old syntax, which would fail in Zabbix 2.4 and later. At this time, it is not known which Zabbix version could fix this.

When done, click on the **Add** button at the bottom. The discovery itself was very similar to what we have created so far, with one exception: the SNMP OID value. For the SNMP LLD, we define the macro name and the OID table to be discovered. In this case, Zabbix would look at all the individual values in the IF-MIB::ifDescr table and assign them to the {#IFDESCR} macro, which is the name we just specified in the SNMP OID field. In addition to the macro we specified, Zabbix will also add one extra macro for each found entity: {#SNMPINDEX}. That, as we will see in a moment, will be useful when creating item prototypes.

To create some prototypes, next to the new discovery rule, click on **Item prototypes**, and then click on **Create item prototype**. Fill in the following:

- **Name**: `Incoming traffic on interface $1 (SNMP LLD)`
- **Type**: **SNMPv2 agent**
- **Key**: `lld.ifInOctets[{#IFDESCR}]`
- **SNMP OID**: `IF-MIB::ifInOctets.{#SNMPINDEX}`
- **Units**: `Bps`
- **Store value**: **Delta (speed per second)**

When done, click on the **Add** button at the bottom.

Notice how we prefixed `lld` to the item key — that way there is no chance it could clash with the items we created manually earlier. As for the SNMP OID, we used the built-in `{#SNMPINDEX}` macro, which should uniquely identify values in the SNMP table. If we add such an item manually, we would find out which is the correct index for the desired interface and use that number directly. That's for the incoming traffic — to make this more complete, click on **Incoming traffic on interface {#IFDESCR} (SNMP LLD)** in the **NAME** column, then click on the **Clone** button at the bottom. In the **Name** field, change `Incoming` to `Outgoing`. In both of the **Key** and **SNMP OID** fields, change `In` to `Out` so that the **OID** has `ifOutOctets`. When done, click on the **Add** button at the bottom. Navigate to **Configuration | Hosts** and click on **Items** next to the host we just worked on. After a couple of minutes, there should be new items here, according to those two prototypes. As this is a configuration page, make sure to refresh it every now and then, otherwise the changes will not be visible.

> If the items don't show up after a longer period of time, go to the discovery list for that host and check the **INFO** column — there could be an error listed there.

Most likely, the loopback interface will be in the list as well — we did not apply any filtering for this LLD rule:

SNMP interface discovery: Incoming traffic on interface enp0s3 (SNMP LLD)	lld.ifInOctets[enp0s3]
SNMP interface discovery: Incoming traffic on interface lo (SNMP LLD)	lld.ifInOctets[lo]
SNMP interface discovery: Incoming traffic on interface enp0s8 (SNMP LLD)	lld.ifInOctets[enp0s8]

Like before, let's create a graph prototype for these items. Click on **Discovery rules** in the navigation header above the item list, click on **Graph** prototypes next to **SNMP interface discovery**, and click on the **Create graph prototype** button. In the **Name** field, enter Traffic on {#IFDESCR} (SNMP). Click on **Add prototype** in the **Items** section, mark the checkboxes next to both of the prototypes, and click on **Select**. Click on the **Add** button at the bottom. If you look at the list of graphs in the configuration section for this host after a few minutes, a new graph should appear for each interface there.

The ifDescr OID usually is the interface name. It is quite common to use the ifAlias OID for a more user-friendly description. We could change our discovery to ifAlias instead of ifDescr, but not all systems will have a useful ifAlias value on all interfaces, and we might want to know the ifDescr value anyway. Zabbix can discover multiple OIDs in one LLD rule as well. Let's go back to the discovery rule configuration for this host and click on **SNMP interface discovery** in the **NAME** column. Modify the **SNMP OID** field to read:

```
discovery[{#IFDESCR}, IF-MIB::ifDescr, {#IFALIAS}, IF-MIB::ifAlias]
```

Further OIDs are added as extra parameters, where the macro name is always followed by the OID. We could also add more OIDs, if needed:

```
key[{#MACRO1}, MIB::OID1, {#MACRO2}, MIB::OID2, {#MACROn}, MIB::OIDn]
```

In this case, though, ifAlias should be enough. Click on the **Update** button at the bottom, and then click on **Graph prototypes** next to the **SNMP interface discovery** entry. Click on **Traffic on {#IFDESCR} (SNMP)** in the **NAME** column, and change the name for this graph prototype:

```
Traffic on {#IFDESCR} ({#IFALIAS}) (SNMP)
```

This way, if an interface has ifAlias set, it will be included in the graph name. We still keep the ifDescr value, as that is a unique interface identifier, and some interfaces might have nothing to return for the ifAlias OID. Let's go to the graph configuration for this host. After a few minutes have passed, the graph names should be updated, with ifAlias included in the parentheses.

> If you are monitoring a Linux system that's running the Net-SNMP daemon, ifAlias will most likely be empty.

This approach also provides an easy way to monitor selected interfaces only. If you have a large number of network devices and only a few selected ports are to be monitored, the description for those ports could be changed on the device—for example, they could all be prefixed with zbx. This will show up in the ifAlias OID, and we would filter by the {#IFALIAS} macro in the LLD rule properties.

> The macro names are user configurable and could be different on a different Zabbix installation. Only the built-in {#SNMPINDEX} macro will always have the same name.

Creating custom LLD rules

The built-in low-level discovery support is great for discovering filesystems, network interfaces, CPUs, and other entities. But what if we have some custom software that we would like to discover components with or perhaps are running an older Zabbix agent on some system that does not support a particular type of discovery yet? The great thing about LLD is that it is very easy to extend with our own discovery rules. Let's take a look at two examples:

- Re-implementing CPU discovery on Linux
- Discovering MySQL databases

> An LLD rule never returns item values. It discovers entities that allow creating items from prototypes. Items receive values from agents, SNMP devices, using zabbix_sender, or any of the other data-collection methods.

Re-implementing CPU discovery

First, let's try to do something that is already available in recent Zabbix agents— discovering CPUs. We do this both because it could be useful if you have some system running an old agent and because it shows how simple LLD can be sometimes. To do this, let's consider the following script:

```
for cpu in $(ls -d /sys/devices/system/cpu/cpu[0-9]*/); do
    cpui=${cpu#/sys/devices/system/cpu/cpu}
    [[ $(cat ${cpu}/online 2>/dev/null) ==
    1 || ! -f ${cpu}/online]] &&
    status=online || status=offline;
    cpulist=$cpulist,'{{#CPU.NUMBER}:'${cpui%/}',
    {#CPU.STATUS}:'$status'}'
done
echo '{data:['${cpulist#,}']}'
```

It relies on /sys/devices/system/cpu/ holding a directory for each CPU, named cpu, followed by the CPU number. In each of those directories, we look for the online file — if that file is there, we check the contents. If the contents are 1, the CPU is considered to be online; if something else — offline. In some cases, changing the online state for CPU0 will not be allowed — this file would then be missing, and we would interpret that as the CPU being online. We then append {#CPU.NUMBER} and {#CPU.STATUS} macros with proper values and eventually print it all out, wrapped in the LLD data array. Let's use this as a user parameter now.

> We explored user parameters in *Chapter 11, Advanced Item Monitoring*.

We will concatenate it all in a single line, as we don't need a wrapper script for this command. In the Zabbix agent daemon configuration file on A test host, add the following:

```
UserParameter=reimplementing.cpu.discovery,for cpu in $(ls -d /sys/
devices/system/cpu/cpu[0-9]*/); do cpui=${cpu#/sys/devices/system/cpu/
cpu}; [[ $(cat ${cpu}/online 2>/dev/null) == 1 || ! -f ${cpu}/online
]] && status=online || status=offline; cpulist=$cpulist,'{{#CPU.
NUMBER}:'${cpui%/}',{#CPU.STATUS}:'$status'}'; done; echo
'{data:['${cpulist#,}']}'
```

> For more complicated cases or production implementation, consider a proper JSON implementation, such as the JSON::XS Perl module.

Restart the agent daemon, and on the same system, run this:

```
$ zabbix_get -s 127.0.0.1 -k reimplementing.cpu.discovery
```

On a quad-core system, it would return something similar to this:

```
{data:[{{#CPU.NUMBER}:0,{#CPU.STATUS}:online},{{#CPU.NUMBER}:1,{#CPU.
STATUS}:online},{{#CPU.NUMBER}:2,{#CPU.STATUS}:offline},{{#CPU.
NUMBER}:3,{#CPU.STATUS}:online}]}
```

> You can reformat JSON for better readability using Perl or Python — we did that earlier in this chapter.

We can now use this item key for an LLD rule the same way as with the built-in item. The item prototypes would work exactly the same way, and we wouldn't even need to use different LLD macros.

On most Linux systems, you can test this by bringing some CPUs or cores offline—for example, the following will bring the second CPU offline:

```
# echo 0 > /sys/devices/system/cpu/cpu1/online
```

Discovering MySQL databases

With the CPU discovery re-implemented, let's try to discover MySQL databases. Instead of user parameters, let's use a Zabbix trapper item, which we will populate with Zabbix Sender.

> We explored Zabbix Sender in *Chapter 11*, *Advanced Item Monitoring*.

We will use a different item type now. This is completely normal—the item type used for LLD does not matter as long as we can get the correct JSON into the Zabbix server. Let's start by creating the LLD rule with some item prototypes and proceed with generating JSON after that. With this rule, we could discover all MySQL databases and monitor their sizes using a user parameter. The following assumes that your Zabbix database is on A test host. Navigate to **Configuration | Hosts**, click on **Discovery** next to **A test host**, and click on **Create discovery rule**. Fill in the following:

- **Name:** MySQL database discovery
- **Type: Zabbix trapper**
- **Key:** mysql.db.discovery

When done, click on **Add**. Now, click on **Item prototypes** next to **MySQL database discovery**, and click on **Create item prototype**. Here, fill in the following:

- **Name:** Database $1 size
- **Type: Zabbix agent (active)**
- **Key:** mysql.db.size[{#MYSQL.DBNAME}]
- **Units:** B
- **Update interval:** 300
- **Applications: MySQL**

When done, click on the **Add** button at the bottom. For this item, we used an active agent as this is suggested for user parameters, and we also set the update interval to 5 minutes—usually, the database size won't change that quickly, and we will be interested in more long-term trends. We now have the item, which will be a UserParameter variable, and that item in turn will be created by an LLD rule that is populated by Zabbix sender. Let's set up the UserParameter variable now. In the Zabbix agent daemon configuration file for A test host, add the following:

```
UserParameter=mysql.db.size[*],HOME=/home/zabbix mysql -Ne select
sum(data_length+index_length) from information_schema.tables where
table_schema='$1';
```

This UserParameter variable will query the total database size, including both actual data and all indexes. Notice how we are setting the HOME variable again. Don't forget to save the file and restart the agent daemon afterwards. It's also a good idea to test it right away:

```
$ zabbix_get -s 127.0.0.1 -k mysql.db.size[zabbix]
```

This will most likely return some number:

```
147865600
```

If it fails, double-check the MySQL parameter configuration we used in *Chapter 11, Advanced Item Monitoring*.

> Notice how it takes some time for this value to be returned. For large databases, it might be a better to idea to use Zabbix Sender for such an item as well.

With the LLD rule and item prototype in place, let's get to sending the JSON for discovery. The following should discover all databases that are accessible to the current user and generate the LLD JSON for Zabbix:

```
for db in $(mysql -u zabbix -Ne show databases;); do
    dblist=$dblist,'{{#MYSQL.DBNAME}:'$db'}'
done
echo '{data:['${dblist#,}']}'
```

> We are removing the trailing comma in the JSON database list—JSON does not allow a trailing comma, and including it will make the discovery fail. Zabbix will complain that the incoming data is not valid JSON.

The principle here is similar to the CPU discovery reimplementation from earlier: we find all the databases and list them in the JSON after the proper macro name. It should return a line similar to this:

```
{data:[{{#MYSQL.DBNAME}:information_schema},{{#MYSQL.DBNAME}:zabbix}]}
```

And now on to actually sending this to our LLD rule—we will use Zabbix Sender for that.

If you tested this and thus modified the `dblist` variable, run `unset dblist` before running the following command:

```
$ zabbix_sender -z 127.0.0.1 -s A test host -k mysql.db.discovery
-o $(for db in $(mysql -u zabbix -Ne show databases;);
do dblist=$dblist,'{{#MYSQL.DBNAME}:'$db'}'; done; echo
'{data:['${dblist#,}']}')
```

> This command should be run as the user the Zabbix agent daemon runs as; otherwise, it might include databases that the Zabbix user has no permission for, and such items would become unsupported.

Visiting the item list for `A test host` in the configuration should reveal one item created for each database:

MySQL database discovery: Database information_schema size	mysql.db.size[information_schema]
MySQL database discovery: Database zabbix size	mysql.db.size[zabbix]

It might take up to 3 minutes for the first value to appear in the **Latest data** page—first, up to a minute for the configuration cache to refresh and then, up to 2 minutes for the active agent to update its configuration from the server.

> Also remember that the rule is only evaluated when it gets new data. If a database were removed and scheduled for deletion, it would never get deleted if the trapper item got no more data.

After some time, the values should be visible in the **Monitoring | Latest data** page:

NAME ▲	LAST CHECK	LAST VALUE
MySQL (6 Items)		
Database information_schema size	2016-05-11 10:45:42	144 KB
Database zabbix size	2016-05-11 10:45:42	77.89 MB

LLD rules cannot be nested—for example, we cannot discover tables in the databases we discovered. If the tables had to be discovered, it would required a separate, independent LLD rule.

Global regular expressions

Now that we know about some of the automation features, let's take a look at a feature in Zabbix that allows us to define regular expressions in an easier—and sometimes more powerful—way. This feature can be used in low-level discovery, discussed here, and other locations.

There are quite a lot of places in Zabbix where regular expressions can be used—we already looked at icon mapping in *Chapter 9*, *Visualizing the Data with Graphs and Maps*, and log filtering in *Chapter 11*, *Advanced Item Monitoring*. In all these places, we defined the regular expression directly. But sometimes, we might want to have a single expression that we could reuse, or the expression could be overly complicated when typed in directly. For example, our filtering of loopback interfaces earlier was not the most readable thing. This is where global regular expressions can help. Let's see how we could have used this feature to simplify that filtering. Navigate to **Administration | General**, choose **Regular expressions** from the dropdown, and click on **New regular expression**. To see what we could potentially do here, expand the **EXPRESSION TYPE** dropdown:

Character string included
Any character string included
Character string not included
Result is TRUE
Result is FALSE

Character string included and **Character string not included** both seem pretty simple. This expression would match or negate the matching of a single string. **Any character string included** is a bit more complicated — according to the **DELIMITER** dropdown (which appears when we choose **Any character string**), we could enter multiple values and if any of those were found, it would be a match:

For example, leaving the **Delimiter** dropdown at the default setting, comma, and entering ERROR, WARNING in the **Expression** field would match either the ERROR or WARNING string.

The two remaining options, **Result is TRUE** and **Result is FALSE**, are the powerful ones. Here, we could enter ^[0-9] in the **Expression** field and match when the string either starts or does not start with a number. Actually, only these last two work with regular expressions; the first three are string-matching options. They do not even offer any extra functionality besides making things a bit simpler — technically, they are not regular expressions, but are supported here for convenience.

Previously, when we wanted to filter out an interface with the name lo, we used the following regular expression for that:

```
^([^l].*|l[^o]|lo.+)$
```

It's fairly complicated. Let's create a global regular expression that would do the same. Enter **Name** as Exclude loopback.

In the **Expressions** block, fill in:

- **EXPRESSION TYPE: Result is FALSE**
- **EXPRESSION:** ^lo$

Click on the **Add** button at the very bottom.

> Using lo with **Character string not included** would exclude anything containing lo, not just the exact string lo.

But once something like that has been configured here, how would we use it in the LLD rule filter? Global regular expressions can be used in place of a normal regular expression by prefixing its name with the at (@) sign. To do so, go to **Configuration | Templates**, click on **Discovery** next to **C_Template_Linux**, and click on **Interface discovery** in the **NAME** column. Switch to the **Filters** tab, and replace the only value in the **REGULAR EXPRESSION** column with @Exclude loopback.

> Here, no quoting should be used — just the at sign and then the global regular expression name, exactly as configured in the administration section.

When done, click on **Update**. The new configuration should work exactly the same, but it seems to be much easier to understand.

> There is no check done when a global regular expression gets its name changed — this way, one could break configuration elsewhere, so it should be done with great care, if at all.

Another place where global regular expressions come in handy is log monitoring. Similar to LLD rule filters, we just use an @-prefixed expression name instead of typing the regexp in directly. For example, we could define a regular expression like this:

```
(ERROR|WARNING) 13[0-9]{3}
```

It would catch any errors and warnings with the error code in the 13,000 range — because that might be defined to be of concern to us. Assuming we named our global "regexp errors and warnings 13k", the log monitoring key would look like this:

```
log[/path/to/the/file,@errors and warnings 13k]
```

Testing global regexps

Let's return to **Administration | General**, choose **Regular expressions** in the dropdown, and click on **New regular expression**. Add three expressions here as follows:

- First expression:
    - ◦ **EXPRESSION TYPE: Character string included**
    - ◦ **EXPRESSION**: A
    - ◦ **CASE SENSITIVE**: yes

- Second expression:
    - ◦ **Expression type: Result is TRUE**
    - ◦ **Expression:** ^[0-9]

- Third expression:
    - ◦ **Expression type: Result is FALSE**
    - ◦ **Expression:** [0-9]$

This should match a string that contains an uppercase A, starts with a number, and does not end with a number. Now, switch to the **Test** tab and enter 1A2 in the **Test string** field; then, click on **Test expressions**. In the following screenshot of the result area, it shows that a string starting with a number and containing an uppercase A matches, but then, the string ends with a number, which we negated. As a result, the final test fails.

Expressions	Test		

Test string	1A2		

Test expressions

Result	EXPRESSION TYPE	EXPRESSION	RESULT
	Character string included	A	TRUE
	Result is TRUE	^[0-9]	TRUE
	Result is FALSE	[0-9]$	FALSE
	Combined result		FALSE

Add   Cancel

> Zabbix frontend uses PCRE but Zabbix daemons use POSIX EXTENDED. Do not use PCRE character classes, lookarounds or any other features supported by PCRE but not by POSIX ERE — they will seem to work in the frontend testing but then fail when interpreted by the Zabbix daemons.

Usage in the default templates

As we created our own global regexp, you probably noticed that there were a few already existing there. Let's navigate to **Administration | General** and choose **Regular expressions** in the dropdown again. Besides the one we created for the loopback interface filtering, there are three existing expressions:

File systems for discovery	1 » ^(btrfs|ext2|ext3|ext4|jfs|reiser|xfs|ffs|ufs|jfs|jfs2|vxfs|hfs|ntfs|fat32|zfs)$	[Result is TRUE]
Network interfaces for discovery	1 » ^lo$	[Result is FALSE]
	2 » ^Software Loopback Interface	[Result is FALSE]
Storage devices for SNMP discovery	1 » ^(Physical memory|Virtual memory|Memory buffers|Cached memory|Swap space)$	[Result is FALSE]

One of them, **Network interfaces for discovery**, actually does almost the same thing as ours did, except that it also excludes interfaces whose names start with **Software Loopback Interface** — that's for MS Windows monitoring. The **File systems for discovery** one can be used to limit the types of filesystems to monitor — besides ext3, which we filtered for, it includes a whole bunch of other filesystem types. The **Storage devices for SNMP discovery** one excludes memory statistics from storage devices when monitoring over SNMP. While the filesystem type regexp could be typed in directly, the others would be nearly impossible — POSIX EXTENDED does not really support negating multiple strings in a reasonable way.

Network discovery

LLD is concerned with discovering entities on an individual host. Zabbix also supports a way to scan a network address range and perform some operation based on what has been discovered there — that's called **network discovery**.

Configuring a discovery rule

To see how this could work, let's have a simple discovery rule. We can discover our test systems, or we can point the discovery at some other network range that is accessible to the Zabbix server.

To create a network discovery rule, navigate to **Configuration | Discovery** and click on **Create discovery rule**. Fill in the name and IP range as desired, and then click on **New** in the **Checks** block. Choose **ICMP ping** in the **Check type** dropdown, and click on **Add** in this block. Additionally, change **Delay** to 120 so that we can more easily see the effects of any changes:

Name	A test discovery
Discovery by proxy	No proxy ▾
IP range	192.168.56.10-20
Delay (in sec)	120
Checks	ICMP ping Edit Remove
	New
Device uniqueness criteria	⦿ IP address
Enabled	▣
	Add Cancel

> Make sure `fping` is properly configured — we did that in *Chapter 3, Monitoring with Zabbix Agents and Basic Protocols*.

When done, click on the **Add** button at the bottom.

Viewing the results

After a few minutes have passed, check the **Monitoring | Discovery** section:

DISCOVERED DEVICE ▲	MONITORED HOST	UPTIME/DOWNTIME	ICMP PING
A test discovery (2 devices)			
192.168.56.10 (testhost)		00:23:22	
192.168.56.11	Another host	00:23:20	

All the devices that respond to the ping in the configured range will be listed here. If a device is already monitored as a host in Zabbix, it will be listed in the **MONITORED HOST** column. We will also see for how long the host is known to be up, and the **ICMP PING** column will list this specific service in green for all hosts. But why is only one host listed as already monitored here? Hosts are recognized here by their IP addresses, and for A test host, we used 127.0.0.1. The address by which it was discovered differs, so it's not really considered to be the same host or device.

> Hosts are not clickable here at this time — probably the easiest way to get to the host properties is copying and pasting the hostname in the global search field.

Now, navigate back to **Configuration | Discovery** and click on **A test discovery** in the **NAME** column. Click on **New** in the **Checks** block and choose a service that is accessible and would be easy to control on these hosts — perhaps **SMTP** again. Click on **Add** in the **Checks** section, and then click on **New** there again. This time, choose a service that is not present on any host in the configured range — **FTP** might be a good choice. Then, click on **Add** in this block again:

Checks		
	ICMP ping	Edit Remove
	SMTP	Edit Remove
	FTP	Edit Remove

Finally, click on **Update**. After a couple of minutes, visit **Monitoring | Discovery**:

DISCOVERED DEVICE ▲	MONITORED HOST	UPTIME/DOWNTIME	ICMP PING	SMTP
A test discovery (2 devices)				
192.168.56.10 (testhost)		02:07:13		
192.168.56.11	Another host	02:07:11		

SMTP has appeared, which is great. But why is there no **FTP** column? Could this view be limited to two services? It's not limited to a specific number of services, but a service that is not discovered on any of the hosts does not show up at all at this time. If a service were initially discovered on some systems but not on others, the column would be shown and the systems where the service was not discovered would get a Grey cell.

If we move the cursor over the green cells, we will be able to see for how long this service has been up (or discovered):

Let's break something now—bring down the SMTP service on one of the hosts, and wait for a couple of minutes. The **SMTP** cell for that host should turn red, and the popup should start tracking downtime for that service now. If all services on a host went down, the host itself would be considered as down, and that would be reflected in the **UPTIME/DOWNTIME** column.

Reacting to the discovery results

The discovery monitoring page is interesting at first but not that useful in the long term. Luckily, we can make Zabbix perform operations in response, and the configuration is somewhat similar to how we reacted to triggers firing. To see how this is configured, navigate to **Configuration | Actions**, and switch to **Discovery** in the **Event source** dropdown in the upper-right corner. Then, click on **Create action**. One thing to notice right away is that this action still has the default subject and message filled in, but the contents are different: the macros used here are specific to network discovery. Fill in the name of Network discovery test, and let's switch to the **Conditions** tab and expand the first dropdown in the **New condition** section:

```
Discovery check
Discovery object
Discovery rule
Discovery status
Host IP
Proxy
Received value
Service port
Service type
Uptime/Downtime
```

The available conditions are completely different from what was available for trigger actions. Let's review them:

- **Discovery check**: A specific check in a specific discovery rule must be chosen here.

- **Discovery object**: Either a device or service can be chosen here. In our example, the discovered host would be a device object and SMTP would be a service object.

- **Discovery rule**: A specific network discovery rule must be chosen here.

- **Discovery status**: This condition has possible values of **Up**, **Down**, **Discovered**, and **Lost**. For devices, they are considered to be discovered or up if at least one service on them can be reached. Here is what the values mean:
  - **Discovered**: This device or service is being seen for the first time or after it was detected to be down
  - **Lost**: This device or service has been seen before, but it has just disappeared

- ○ **Up**: The device or service has been discovered — no matter how many times it might have happened already

- ○ **Down**: The device or service has been discovered at some point, but right now, it is not reachable — no matter how many times that has happened already

- **Host IP**: Individual addresses or ranges may be specified here.

- **Proxy**: Action may be limited to a specific Zabbix proxy. We will discuss proxies in *Chapter 19, Using Proxies to Monitor Remote Locations*.

- **Received value**: If we are polling a Zabbix agent item or an SNMP OID, we may react to a specific value — for example, if discovering by the `system.uname` item key, we could link all hosts that have `Linux` in the returned string to the Linux template.

- **Service port**: Action may be limited to a specific port or port range on which the discovery has happened.

- **Service type**: Action may be restricted to a service type. This is similar to the **Discovery check** condition, except that choosing SMTP here would match all SMTP checks from all network discovery rules, not just a specific one.

- **Uptime/Downtime**: Time in seconds may be entered here to limit the action only after the device or service has been up or down for some period of time.

Most of these are pretty self-explanatory, but let's take a closer look at two of them. The **Discovery status** condition allows us to differentiate between the initial check or being discovered after downtime and periodic checks. As an example, if we matched the **Up** status and added the host to a **Host group**, this addition would be checked and performed every time the host can be reached. If somebody removed that host from that host group, it would be re-added during every discovery cycle. If we matched the **Discovered** status, it would only happen when the host is first discovered and when it goes down and then up again. Automatic re-adding to the group is most likely to happen later in this case.

The **Uptime/Downtime** condition allows us to react with some delay, not immediately. For example, we might want to have an uptime of a few hours before monitoring some device as it might be a temporary troubleshooting laptop that is attached to the network. Probably even more importantly, we might not want to delete a host with all its history if that host is down for 5 minutes. Checking for a week-long downtime might be reasonable — if nobody bothered with that host for a week, it's safe to delete.

For now, let's leave the conditions empty and switch to the **Operations** tab. Adding a new operation and expanding the **Operation type** dropdown will reveal all the available operations. We will discuss them in more detail a bit later, but for now, let's choose **Add to host groups**. In the input field, start typing `linux`, and choose **Linux servers** from the dropdown. Then, click on the small **Add** control in the **Operation details** block. Be very careful here, as it is easy to lose some configuration. When done, click on the **Add** button at the bottom:

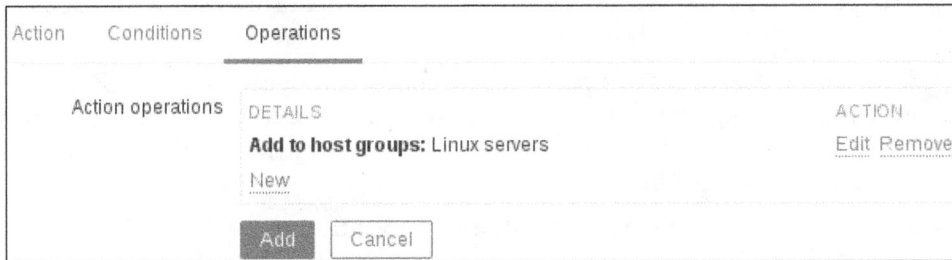

Action	Conditions	Operations	
Action operations	DETAILS		ACTION
	Add to host groups: Linux servers		Edit Remove
	New		
	Add Cancel		

After a couple of minutes, go to **Configuration | Hosts** to observe the results. If discovering our test systems, we should see one new host added.

> Even though we did not tell the action to add the host itself, it still happened. If the operation implies that there's a host — for example, adding it to a host group or linking to a template — the host will be automatically added.

Why only one host? The other host already existed as per **Monitoring | Discovery** earlier. For this host, you will see either its hostname or the IP address used as the hostname in Zabbix. If the Zabbix server was able to perform a reverse lookup on the IP address, the result will be used as the hostname. If not, the IP address will be used as the hostname.

> If multiple addresses reverse-resolved to the same name, others would be added as name_2 and so on.

Click on **New host** in the **NAME** column. In the **Groups** section, this host is in the **Linux servers** group, as expected. But it is also in some other group, **Discovered hosts**. Where did that come from?

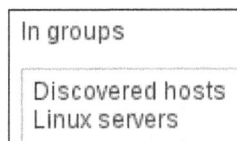

In groups
Discovered hosts
Linux servers

By default, all hosts discovered by network discovery are added to a specific group. Which group? That's a global setting. Navigate to **Administration | General**, then choose **Other** in the dropdown. The **Group for discovered hosts** setting allows us to choose which group that is. What if you don't want the discovered hosts to end up in that group? In the action operations, we could add another operation, **Remove from host group**, and specify the **Discovered hosts** group.

Let's review all available discovery operations now:

```
Send message
Remote command
Add host
Remove host
Add to host group
Remove from host group
Link to template
Unlink from template
Enable host
Disable host
Set host inventory mode
```

- **Send message**: The same as for trigger actions, we may send a message to users and user groups. This could be used both to supplement an action that adds devices ("Hey, take a look at this new server we just started monitoring") or as a simple notification that a new device has appeared on the network ("This new IP started responding, but I won't automatically monitor it").

- **Remote command**: Zabbix can attempt to run a remote command on a passive Zabbix agent or Zabbix server, a command using IPMI, SSH, or Telnet, and even a global script. This would only succeed if remote commands are enabled on the Zabbix agent side. We discussed remote commands in *Chapter 7, Acting upon Monitored Conditions*.

- **Add host**: A host will be added and only included in the **Discovered hosts** group.

- **Remove host**: A host will be removed. This probably makes most sense to perform when a host has not been discovered, and to be safe, only do so when the downtime exceeds some period of time.

- **Add to host group**: A host will be added to a host group. If there is no such host, one will be added first.

- **Remove from host group**: A host will be removed from a host group.

- **Link to template**: A host will be linked to a template. If there is no such host, one will be added first.

- **Unlink from template**: A host will be unlinked from a template.

- **Enable host**: A host will be enabled. If there is no such host, one will be added first.

- **Disable host**: A host will be disabled. This could be used as a safer alternative to removing hosts, or we could disable a host first and remove it later. If there is no such host, one will be added first.

When linking to a template, the host still needs all the proper interfaces as required by the items in that template. During discovery, only successful discovery checks result in the adding of interfaces of a corresponding type. For example, if we only found SNMP on a host, only an SNMP interface would be added. If both SNMP and Zabbix agent discovery checks succeeded on a host, both interfaces would be added. If some checks succeed later, additional interfaces are created.

Uniqueness criteria

But what about multi-homed hosts that have multiple interfaces exposed to Zabbix network discovery? Let's return to **Configuration | Discovery** and click on **A test discovery**. Look at the **Device uniqueness criteria** option—the only setting there is **IP address**. In the **Checks** block, click on **New** and choose **Zabbix agent** in the **Check type** dropdown. In the **Key** field, enter system.uname, and then click on **Add** in the **Checks** block. Notice how the **Device uniqueness criteria** got a new option—**Zabbix agent "system.uname"**:

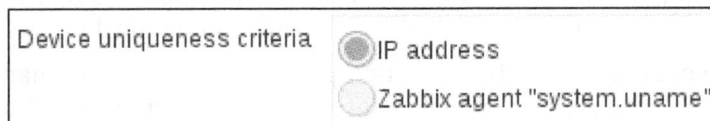

Device uniqueness criteria	◉ IP address
	◯ Zabbix agent "system.uname"

By default, with the uniqueness criteria set to **IP address**, Zabbix will create a new host for each discovered IP address. If there's a system with multiple addresses, a new host will be created for each address. If the uniqueness criteria is set to a Zabbix agent item, it will look at all the IP addresses it has seen before and the values it got back for that item key. If the new value matches some previous value, it will add a new interface to the existing host instead of creating a new host. It works the same way with SNMP—adding an SNMP check will add another uniqueness criteria option, and Zabbix will compare values received for that specific OID. It is common to discover SNMP devices by the SNMPv2-MIB::sysDescr.0 OID.

[🔆 Both a Zabbix agent and SNMP must be preconfigured to accept connections from the Zabbix server.]

Now that we have discussed network discovery, I'll give you one short suggestion about it—don't use it. Well, maybe not that harsh, but do not cling to it too much. There are use cases for network discovery, but quite often, there's a decent list of devices that should be monitored coming either from a **configuration management database (CMDB)** or some other source. In that case, it is better to integrate and automatically update your Zabbix configuration based on that authoritative source. If your answer to "What's your most definitive list of hosts in your environment?" is "Zabbix", then network discovery is for you.

Active agent autoregistration

We just explored network discovery—it scanned a network range. Zabbix also supports a feature that goes the other way around, where Zabbix agents can chime in and Zabbix server can automatically start monitoring them. This is called active agent autoregistration.

Whenever a Zabbix agent connects to the Zabbix server, the server compares the incoming agent hostname with the existing hosts. If a host with the same name exists, it proceeds with the normal active item monitoring sequence. This includes both enabled and disabled hosts. If the host does not exist, the autoregistration sequence kicks in, that is, an event is generated.

The fact that an event is generated every time an unknown agent connects to the Zabbix server is important. If you do not use active items or autoregistration, switch off active checks on the agent side. Otherwise, each such check results in a network connection, log entry on the agent and server side, and an event in the Zabbix database. There have been cases where that increases the database size and results in significantly reduced performance. In some instances, there are millions of such completely useless autoregistration events, up to 90% of the total event count. It is suggested to check the server log for entries such as this:

```
cannot send list of active checks to [127.0.0.1]: host [Register me]
not found
```

If found, they should all be solved. The first pair of square brackets tells us where the connection came from, and second, what host the agent claimed to be.

Similar to trigger and network-discovery events, we may react to that event with an action. Let's configure an autoregistration action now — head to **Configuration | Actions** and switch to **Auto registration** in the **Event source** dropdown. Then, click on **Create action**. Enter `Testing registration` in the **Name** field, and then switch to the **Operations** tab. Click on **New** in the **Action operations** block. The **Operation type** dropdown reveals a subset of operations that are available for network discovery. Most notably, we cannot remove hosts, remove hosts from host groups, and unlink hosts from templates. The operations are functionally the same as for network discovery, so we won't look into them much — just choose **Add host** this time, and click on the small **Add** control in the **Operation details** block. Then, click on the **Add** button at the bottom. With the action in place, probably the easiest way to test this is to fake a new agent. Edit the agent daemon configuration file on A `test host` and change the **Hostname** parameter to `Register me`. Then, restart the agent daemon. Go to **Configuration | Hosts** — there's a new host again. If you check the host properties, it is included in the **Discovered hosts** group — the same group is used here as in the network discovery. Let's change the **Hostname** parameter back to the previous value in the agent daemon configuration file and restart the agent.

We haven't looked at the conditions for autoregistration yet — let's return to **Configuration | Actions**, click on **Testing registration**, and switch to the **Conditions** tab. The dropdown next to the **New condition** section reveals the available conditions:

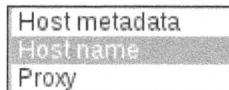

```
Host metadata
Host name
Proxy
```

As we can see, the list of available conditions is much shorter here. We can filter by hostname — for example, if all our **Linux hosts** have `'linux'` in the name, we could detect them that way. We can also filter by proxy if we use Zabbix proxies for the autoregistration. There's also an entry called **Host metadata** — what's that?

Auto-registration metadata

When a Zabbix agent connects to the server, it sends its hostname. But it may additionally send some custom string to the server. What exactly it sends is controlled by a configuration parameter called `HostMetadata` in the agent daemon configuration file. This could be used to define which type the host is: database or application. Or it could list individual services running on a host. As we can match against received metadata in the autoregistration action, we could list all the running services, delimited with pipes. In the action conditions, we could look for |MySQL| and link the new host to the appropriate templates.

> Metadata is limited to 255 characters.

Controlling the metadata parameter directly in the configuration file is possible, but it could be cumbersome. There's a way to make an agent dynamically obtain that value. Instead of `HostMetadata`, we would define `HostMetadataItem` and specify an item key. We could use one of the built-in item keys or configure a user parameter and run a script. Note that we can also use the `system.run` item key here and specify any command directly in the `HostMetadataItem` parameter even if remote commands are not enabled — as it is not arriving from the network, it is not considered to be a remote command. For example, the following is a valid `HostMetadataItem` line:

```
HostMetadataItem=system.run[rpm -qa mariadb]
```

If the package `mariadb` is present on an RPM-based system, the agent would send that in the metadata; we could match it in the action conditions and link that host to the MariaDB/MySQL template.

There's also another use case for this parameter. You might have noticed that as long as there's an autoregistration action, somebody could maliciously or accidentally create lots and lots of hosts, potentially slowing down Zabbix a lot. There is no secret challenge mechanism to prevent that, but we can use metadata here. Action conditions could check for a specific secret string to be included in the metadata — if it's there, create the host. If not, send an e-mail for somebody to investigate. Note that the key can't be too long, as the 255-character length limit still applies.

Summary

In this chapter, we learned about several features in Zabbix that allow automatically creating and maintaining configuration:

- Low-level discovery or LLD
- Network discovery
- Active agent autoregistration

LLD allows discovering entities using Zabbix agents — it has built-in support for network interfaces, filesystems, and CPUs. We talked about customizing thresholds and other values per discovered entity with user macro context support. Zabbix can also discover SNMP tables like network interfaces, but it is not limited to that — any SNMP table can be discovered. We also looked at creating custom discoveries, including MySQL database discovery.

LLD offers a way to filter results by regular expressions, and we checked out how global regular expressions can make that easier here and also in other places, such as log monitoring.

After that, we explored network discovery, which is all about scanning an address range and automatically adding hosts, potentially linking them to proper templates and adding to host groups.

In the other direction, there's active agent autoregistration, where active agents can chime in and the server starts monitoring them automatically. Metadata support for this feature allows quite fine-grained rules on what templates to link in or what host groups the hosts should belong to. We noted that, if not used, active checks should be disabled on agents; otherwise, unnecessary load would be put on the whole Zabbix infrastructure.

In the next chapter, we will explore the built-in web-monitoring feature. It allows us to define scenarios that consist of steps. Steps check a page and may look for a specific HTTP response code or string in the returned page. We will also try out logging in to applications and extracting data from one page and then passing it to another.

13
Monitoring Web Pages

In this chapter we will look at the built-in capability of Zabbix to monitor web pages. We will check different sections of a web page and monitor it for failures as well as monitoring download speed and response time. We'll also find out how Zabbix can extract a value from some page and then reuse that value. Besides the more advanced scenarios and step-based solution, we will also explore web monitoring-related items that are available for the Zabbix agent.

Monitoring a simple web page

The Internet is important in every aspect of modern life: socializing, business, entertainment, and everything else happens over the wire. With all the resources devoted to this network, many are tasked with maintaining websites—no matter whether it's an internally hosted site or one trusted to an external hosting provider, we will want to know at least its basic health status. We could start by monitoring a few simple things on a real-life website.

Creating a web-monitoring scenario

Web monitoring in Zabbix happens through scenarios that in turn have steps. Each step consists of a URL and things to check on it. This allows both checking a single page and verifying that several pages work properly in a succession. The web-monitoring scenarios in Zabbix are still assigned to hosts, and they can also be templated. To see how this works, we could monitor a couple of pages from the open mapping project OpenStreetMap.

While we could attach a web-monitoring scenario to any of the existing hosts, that wouldn't correctly depict what the scenario is monitoring, so we will create a dedicated host. As there's only one OpenStreetMap website, we won't use templates for this. Navigate to **Configuration | Hosts**, click on **Create host**, and fill in these values:

- **Name:** OpenStreetMap
- **Groups**: If there are any groups in the **In Groups** box, mark them and click on the ▸ button
- **New group**: Web pages

We don't have to change any other values here, so click on the **Add** button at the bottom. We're now ready to create the scenario itself—in the list of hosts, click on **Web** next to OpenStreetMap and click on **Create web scenario**. In the scenario properties, enter these values:

- **Name:** Main page
- **New application**: Webpage
- **Update interval**: 300

Now on to the individual steps. Steps for web monitoring are the actual queries performed on the web server; each step has a URL. Switch to the **Steps** tab and click on **Add** in the **Steps** section. Fill in these values in the new popup:

- **Name:** First page
- **URL**: http://www.openstreetmap.org/
- **Required string**: Enter OpenStreetMap is a map of the world, created by people like you. This field will search for a particular string in the returned page, and this step will fail if such a string is not found. We can use POSIX regular expressions here, but not global regular expressions, as discussed in *Chapter 12, Automating Configuration*.
- **Required status codes**: Enter 200. Here, acceptable HTTP return codes can be specified, separated with commas. Again, if the return code doesn't match, this step will be considered a failure. A status code of 200 means **OK**.

> The required string is checked only against the page source, not against the HTTP headers. The scenario only downloads the content the step URL points at; other elements of the web page are never downloaded.

This form should look like this:

Name	First page
URL	http://www.openstreetmap.org/
Post	
Variables	
Headers	
Follow redirects	▓
Retrieve only headers	
Timeout	15
Required string	OpenStreetMap is a map of the world, created by peo
Required status codes	200
	Add Cancel

If it does, click on the **Add** button. Let's also check whether the **GPS traces** page can be accessed. Again, click on **Add** in the **Steps** section, and enter these values:

- **Name**: Traces
- **URL**: http://www.openstreetmap.org/traces/
- **Required string**: Public GPS traces
- **Required status codes**: 200

In the **Required string** field, we entered the text that should be present on the traces page. When done, click on **Add**.

The final step of the configuration should look like this:

Steps		NAME	TIMEOUT	URL	REQUIRED	STATUS CODES	ACTION
	1:	First page	15 sec	http://www.openstreetmap.org/	OpenStreetMap is a map of the world, created by people like you	200	Remove
	2:	Traces	15 sec	http://www.openstreetmap.org/traces/	Public GPS traces	200	Remove
Add							

If everything looks fine, click on the **Add** button at the bottom. Let's see what web monitoring visually looks like. Open **Monitoring | Web** and click on **Main page** next to **OpenStreetMap**. It looks as if all the steps were completed successfully, so we can consider the monitored website to be operating correctly as the **STATUS** column happily says **OK**—or at least the parts that we are monitoring. As with plain items, we can see when the last check was performed:

HOST	NAME ▲	NUMBER OF STEPS	LAST CHECK	STATUS
OpenStreetMap	Main page	2	2016-05-13 00:46:22	OK

We also have an overview of how many steps each scenario contains, but that's all very vague. Click on **Main page** in the **NAME** column—maybe there's more information. Indeed, there is! Here, we can see statistics for each step, such as **SPEED, RESPONSE TIME**, and **RESPONSE CODE**. And, if that's not enough, there are nice predefined and pretty graphs for **SPEED** and **RESPONSE TIME**. Note that these are stacked graphs, so we can identify moments when all steps together take more time. Above the graphs, we can notice those familiar timescale controls— the scrollbar, zoom, and calendar controls—so these graphs provide the same functionality as anywhere else, including clicking and dragging to zoom in:

Details of web scenario: Main page

STEP	SPEED	RESPONSE TIME	RESPONSE CODE	STATUS	
First page	31.29 KBps	429.7ms	200	OK	
Traces	80.01 KBps	302.5ms	200	OK	Debug
TOTAL		**732.2ms**		OK	

Filter ▲

Zoom: 5m 15m 30m 1h All   2016-05-13 00:31 - 2016-05-13 01:06 (now!)

◄   ◄   :::   ► ►

«« 1h 5m | 5m 1h »»   35m fixed

Main page: Speed (1h)

		last	min	avg	max
▣ Download speed for step "First page" of scenario "Main page".	[avg]	31.29 KBps	3.09 KBps	29.39 KBps	53.07 KBps
▣ Download speed for step "Traces" of scenario "Main page".	[avg]	80.01 KBps	61.4 KBps	73.68 KBps	80.01 KBps

Main page: Response time (1h)

		last	min	avg	max
▣ Response time for step "First page" of scenario "Main page".	[avg]	429.7ms	253.4ms	1s 120.01ms	4s 348.1ms
▣ Response time for step "Traces" of scenario "Main page".	[avg]	302.5ms	302.5ms	338.64ms	409.5ms

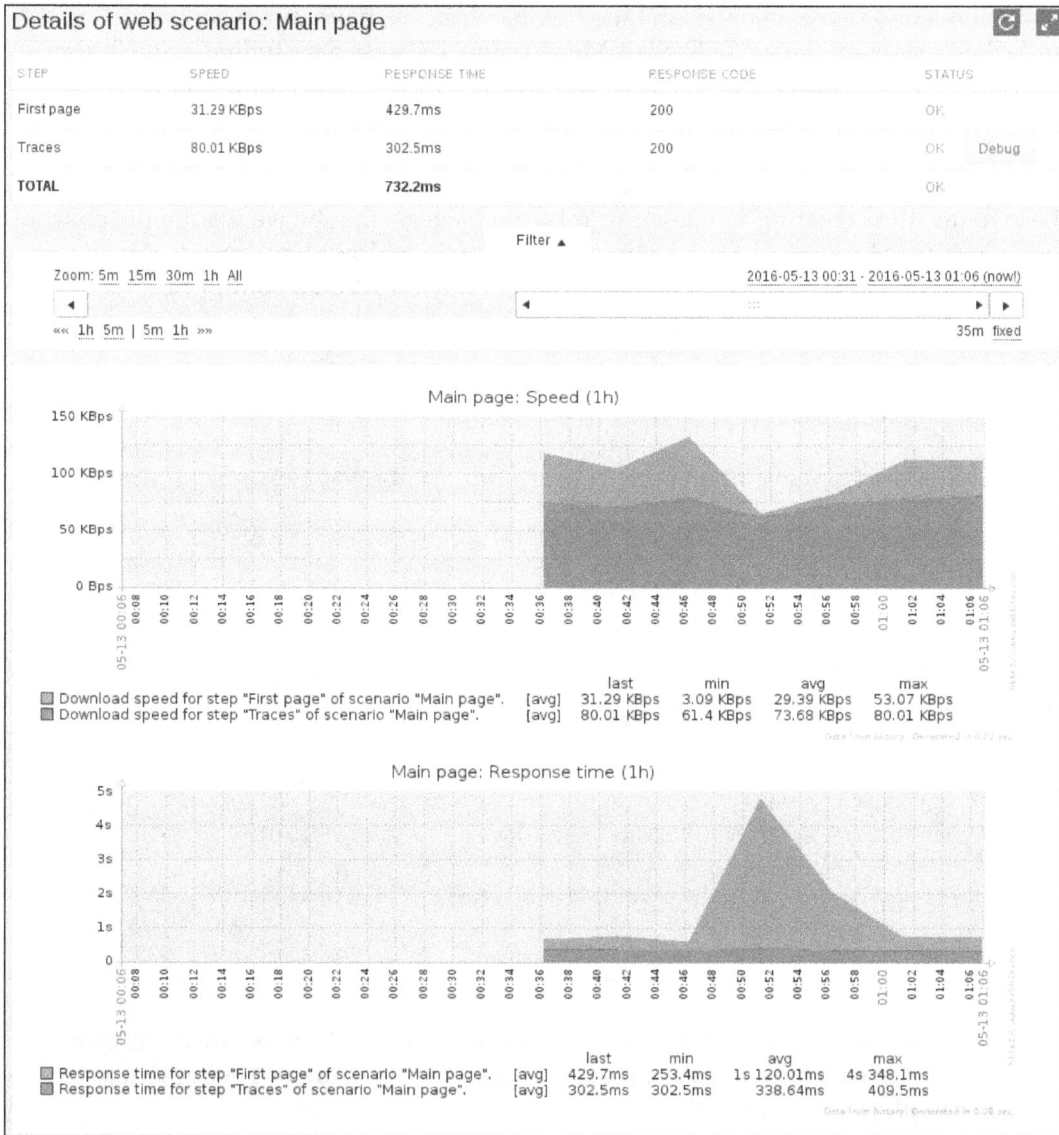

We can see the relative time each step took and how fast it was compared to the others. In this case, both operations together on average take slightly less than a second, although there has been a spike of almost 5 seconds.

While this view is very nice, it isn't too flexible. Can we have direct access to underlying data, perhaps? Let's visit **Monitoring | Latest data** to find out. Choose **Webpages** in the **Host groups** field, and click on **Filter**. Items within the **Webpage** application will show up. Take a look at the data—all of the collected values are accessible as individual items, including download **SPEED, RESPONSE TIME, RESPONSE CODE**, and even the last error message per scenario. We may reuse these items, thus creating whatever graphs we please—maybe we want a pie chart of response times for each step or a non-stacked graph of download speeds. Of course, as with all items, we get simple graphs without any additional configuration.

NAME ▲	LAST CHECK	LAST VALUE
Webpage (9 Items)		
Download speed for scenario "Main page".	2016-05-13 01:16:37	28.78 KBps
Download speed for step "First page" of scenario "Main page".	2016-05-13 01:16:37	3.16 KBps
Download speed for step "Traces" of scenario "Main page".	2016-05-13 01:16:37	54.41 KBps
Failed step of scenario "Main page".	2016-05-13 01:16:37	0
Last error message of scenario "Main page".		
Response code for step "First page" of scenario "Main page".	2016-05-13 01:16:37	200
Response code for step "Traces" of scenario "Main page".	2016-05-13 01:16:37	200
Response time for step "First page" of scenario "Main page".	2016-05-13 01:16:37	4s 257.7ms
Response time for step "Traces" of scenario "Main page".	2016-05-13 01:16:37	439.2ms

There's also a failed step item, which returns 0 if none of the steps failed. As that value is 0 when everything is fine, we can check for this value not being 0 in a trigger, and alert based on that.

> While we could use value mapping to show **Success** when the failed step is 0, we would have to add a value map entry for every step number—value mapping does not support ranges or default values yet.

Other scenarios and step properties

Before we continue with alerting, let's review the other options on the scenario level:

- **Attempts**: Web pages are funny beasts. They mostly work, but that single time when the monitoring system checks it, it fails. Or is it just that users reload a page that fails to load once and never complain? No matter what, this field allows us to specify how many times Zabbix tries to download a web page. For pages that experience an occasional hiccup, a value of 2 or 3 could be appropriate.

- **Agent**: When a web browser connects to a web server, it usually sends along a string identifying itself. This string includes the browser name, version, operating system, and often other information. This information is used for purposes such as gathering statistics, making a specific portion of a site work better in some browser, denying access, or limiting experience on the site. Zabbix web monitoring checks also send user agent strings to web servers. By default, it identifies as zabbix, but one may also choose from a list of predefined browser strings or enter a completely custom string by choosing **other...**:

- **HTTP proxy**: If needed, an HTTP proxy can be set per scenario. A username, password, and port may be specified as well:

> The default HTTP proxy can be set with the `http_proxy` and `https_proxy` environment variables for the Zabbix Server process—these variables would be picked up by `libcurl`, which is used underneath for the web monitoring. If a proxy is specified on the scenario level, it overrides such a default proxy setting. There is no way to set a proxy on the step level.

We'll discuss the remaining fields, **Variables** and **Headers**, a bit later.

> Web monitoring in Zabbix does not support JavaScript at all.

Alerting on web scenarios

Let's create a trigger that warns us when any one of the steps in the scenario fails. As discovered previously, the failed step item holds 0 when all is good. Anything else is a sequential number of the step that failed. As a web scenario stops at any failure, a failed step number of 3 means that the first two steps were executed successfully, and then the third step failed. If there are any further steps, we don't know about their state—they were not processed.

To create a trigger, we always need an item key. We could try to find it in the item list. Go to **Configuration | Hosts** and click on **Items** next to **OpenStreetMap** host—no items. The reason is that these items are special—they are items that are internal to Zabbix web scenarios (not to be confused with the internal monitoring items, discussed in *Chapter 22, Zabbix Maintenance*), and thus are not available for manual configuration. We should be able to select them when creating a trigger, though. Click on **Triggers** in the navigation header, and then click on **Create trigger**. In the trigger-editing form, enter these values:

- **Name**: {HOST.NAME} website problem
- **Expression**: Click on **Add**, and then click on **Select** next to the **Item** field in the resulting pop up. Select **Web pages** in the **Group** dropdown and **OpenStreetMap** in the **Host** dropdown, and then click on **Failed step of scenario Main page** in the **NAME** column. We have to find out when this item is not returning zero. In the **Function** dropdown, choose **Last (most recent) T value is NOT N** and click on **Insert**. The final trigger expression should be like this:

```
{OpenStreetMap:web.test.fail[Main page].last()}<>0
```

When you are done, click on the **Add** button at the bottom. We can see how the item key `web.test.fail[Main page]` was used; thus, web scenario items are very much like normal items. They have names and keys, even though they can't be seen in the item configuration view. This way, we can create triggers for all web scenario items, such as response time and download speed, to also spot performance issues or for return codes to spot exact steps that fail. The same items are available for custom graphs, too.

The trigger we created would alert upon the first failure in this web scenario. One might want to make this monitoring less sensitive, and there are at least two ways to achieve that:

- Set **Attempts** in the scenario properties to some larger value.
- Check item values over a longer period of time. We discussed such a strategy in *Chapter 6*, *Detecting Problems with Triggers*.

If a web-monitoring step fails, Zabbix stops and does not proceed to the next step. If the website you are monitoring has multiple sections that can work independently of one another, you should create a separate scenario for each.

> When web monitoring fails, it could be very useful to know what exactly we received from the web server. Unfortunately, Zabbix does not store retrieved content anywhere by default. We'll discuss a way to temporarily view all the retrieved web pages in the *Controlling running daemons* section of *Appendix A, Troubleshooting*.

Logging in to the Zabbix interface

Our first steps in website testing were fairly simple. Let's do something more fancy now. We will attempt to log in to the Zabbix frontend, check whether that succeeds, and then log out. We should also verify that the logout operation was successful, by the way.

> We will use the default `Admin` user account for these tests. Note that this will pollute the audit log with login/logout entries for this user.

We will do this with a larger number of individual steps for greater clarity:

- Step 1: Check the first page
- Step 2: Log in
- Step 3: Check login
- Step 4: Log out
- Step 5: Check logout

We will set up this scenario on A test host. Go to **Configuration | Hosts**, click on **Web** next to **A test host**, and click on **Create web scenario**. Fill in these values:

- **Name**: Zabbix frontend
- **New application**: Zabbix frontend
- **Variables**: Enter the following lines here:
  ```
  {user}=Admin
  {password}=zabbix
  ```

> Remember that the host we assign the web scenario to does not matter much—actual checks are still performed from the Zabbix server.

The variables we filled in use a different syntax than other macros/variables in Zabbix. We will be able to use them in the scenario steps, and we'll see how exactly that is done in a moment. And now, on to the steps—switch to the **Steps** tab. For each of the steps, first click on the **Add** link in the **Steps** section. In the end, click on the **Add** button in the step properties, and proceed to the next step. For all the steps, adapt the URL as needed—the IP address or hostname and the actual location of the Zabbix frontend.

Step 1: check the first page

On the first page, fill in the following details:

- **Name**: First page
- **URL**: http://127.0.0.1/zabbix/index.php
- **Required string**: Zabbix SIA
- **Required status codes**: 200

In the URL, we also appended index.php to reduce the amount of redirects required. **Required string** will be checked against the page contents. That also includes all the HTML tags, so make sure to list them if your desired string has any included. We also chose a text that appears at the bottom of the page to ensure that the page is likely to have loaded completely. And the status code: the HTTP response code of 200 is ok; we require that specific code to be returned.

Step 2: log in

And now, on to logging in:

- **Name**: Log in
- **URL**: http://127.0.0.1/zabbix/index.php
- **Post**: name={user}&password={password}&enter=Sign in
- **Required status codes**: 200

Most of the things in this step should be clear, except maybe the new **Post** string. It follows the standard syntax of specifying multiple values, concatenated with an ampersand. We are finally using the variables we specified earlier, and we pass them according to the input field names in the login form. The last variable, enter, is a hidden input in the Zabbix frontend login page, and we must pass a hardcoded value of Sign in to it. To find out these values for other pages, check the page source, use browser debugging features, or sniff the network traffic.

Step 3: check login

We could assume that the logging in succeeded. But it is always best to check such things. We could have missed some hidden variable, or we could have made a mistake in the password. So, we'll use a separate step to be sure that logging in really succeeded. Note that all further steps in this scenario will act as a logged-in user until we log out. Zabbix keeps all received cookies for latter steps during the whole scenario. When logged in, one distinguishing factor is the profile link, which uses the top-nav-profile class—and that would be the string we would check for:

- **Name**: Check login
- **URL**: http://127.0.0.1/zabbix/index.php
- **Required string**: top-nav-profile
- **Required status codes**: 200

Don't add this step yet. Before continuing with the next step—logging out—we should discuss what will we need for it. Logging out is considered an action that modifies something, so we actually have to pass a session ID as an sid variable. We must obtain it somehow now, and that can be done by extracting the ID from the page source here. Values can be extracted from the web page, assigned to variables, and reused in subsequent steps. Let's also fill in the following:

```
Variables: {sid}=regex:sid=([0-9a-z]{16})
```

Now, the step can be added. The syntax here deserves to be discussed in more detail. While the first part of the variable assignment is the same as assigning some value manually, the second part, after the equals sign, starts with the keyword `regex`. Then, separated by a colon, a regular expression follows. It is matched against the page source. In our case, we start by looking for the `sid=` string, followed by `16` alphanumeric characters. These alphanumeric characters are the session ID, and we have included them in a capture group. Note that this is not Zabbix-specific but a standard regular expression functionality. The contents of the matched capture group will be assigned to the variable. Extracting and reusing the session ID is the most common use of this functionality, but anything one might want to reuse in subsequent steps can be extracted from the page and assigned to a variable if we can come up with a regex for that.

> Newline matching is not supported, so the matched content must be on a single line.

Step 4: log out

Now that we have the session ID, we are ready to log out. We have to use a different URL, though. If you look at the page source, the logout control uses JavaScript to redirect to a relative URL, like this:

```
index.php?reconnect=1&sid=b208d0664fa8df35
```

The two important variables here are `reconnect` and `sid`. The `reconnect` one has to be simply set to `1`. As for `sid`, we luckily extracted that value in the previous step, so we have all the components to log out:

- **Name:** `Log out`
- **URL:** `http://127.0.0.1/zabbix/index.php?reconnect=1&sid={sid}`
- **Required status codes:** `200`

> Logging out is important. Otherwise, the sessions won't be removed for a year by default, and every frontend check will add one session. A large number of sessions will slow down the Zabbix frontend. We'll discuss session maintenance in *Chapter 22, Zabbix Maintenance*.

Step 5: check logout

We will check whether there's a string we only expect to see on the login page. Logging out could have invisibly failed otherwise:

- **Name:** Check logout
- **URL:** http://127.0.0.1/zabbix/index.php
- **Required string:** Sign in
- **Required status codes:** 200

The final steps should look like this:

Steps		NAME	TIMEOUT	URL	REQUIRED	STATUS CODES	ACTION
	1:	First page	15 sec	http://127.0.0.1/zabbix/index.php	Zabbix SIA	200	Remove
	2:	Log in	15 sec	http://127.0.0.1/zabbix/index.php		200	Remove
	3:	Check login	15 sec	http://127.0.0.1/zabbix/index.php	top-nav-profile	200	Remove
	4:	Log out	15 sec	http://127.0.0.1/zabbix/index.php?reconnect=1&sid={sid}		200	Remove
	5:	Check logout	15 sec	http://127.0.0.1/zabbix/index.php	Sign in	200	Remove
Add							

If everything looks good, click on the **Add** button at the bottom of the page to finally save this scenario. We could let the scenario run for a while now and discuss some step parameters we didn't use:

- **Follow redirects:** This specifies whether Zabbix should follow redirects. If enabled, it follows up to 10 hardcoded redirects, so there is no way to check whether there's been a specific number of redirects. If disabled, we can check for the HTTP response code to be 301 or some other valid redirect code.

- **Retrieve only headers:** If the page is huge, we may opt to retrieve headers only. In this case, the **Required string** option will be disabled as Zabbix does not support matching strings in the headers yet.

- **Timeout:** This specifies the timeout for this specific step. It is applied both to connecting and performing the HTTP request, separately. Note that the default timeout is rather large at 15 seconds, which can lead to Zabbix spending up to 30 seconds on a page.

> We could have used a user macro for a part or all of the URL — that way, we would only define it once and then reference it in each step. We discussed user macros in *Chapter 8, Simplifying Complex Configuration with Templates*.

After the scenario has had some time to run, let's go to **Monitoring | Web page**. Choose **Linux servers** in the **Group** dropdown and click on **Zabbix frontend** in the **NAME** column:

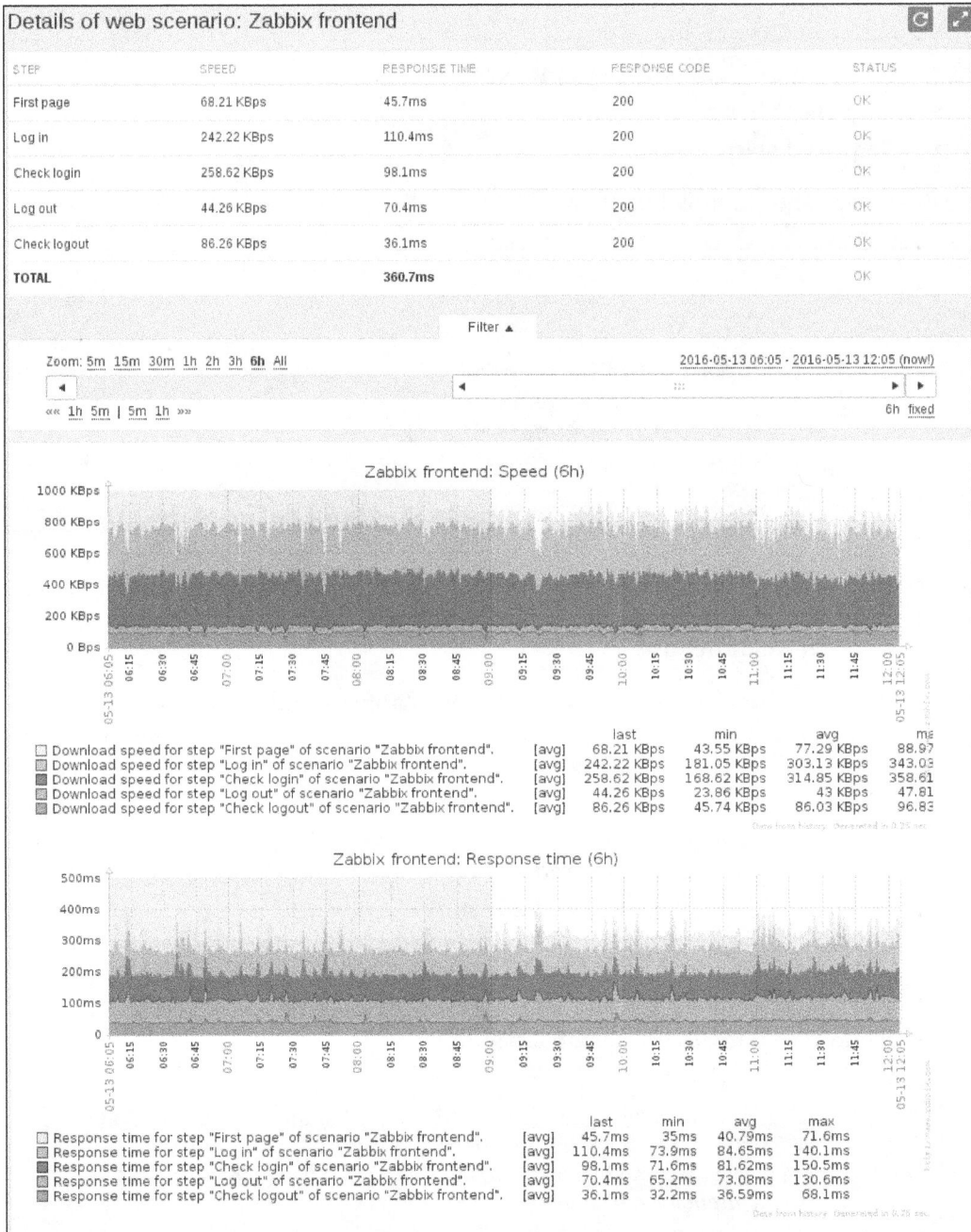

Details of web scenario: Zabbix frontend

STEP	SPEED	RESPONSE TIME	RESPONSE CODE	STATUS
First page	68.21 KBps	45.7ms	200	OK
Log in	242.22 KBps	110.4ms	200	OK
Check login	258.62 KBps	98.1ms	200	OK
Log out	44.26 KBps	70.4ms	200	OK
Check logout	86.26 KBps	36.1ms	200	OK
TOTAL		**360.7ms**		OK

Filter ▲

Zoom: 5m 15m 30m 1h 2h 3h 6h All   2016-05-13 06:05 - 2016-05-13 12:05 (now!)

◄   ◄   :::   ► ►

«« 1h 5m | 5m 1h »»   6h fixed

Zabbix frontend: Speed (6h)

		last	min	avg	ma
☐ Download speed for step "First page" of scenario "Zabbix frontend".	[avg]	68.21 KBps	43.55 KBps	77.29 KBps	88.97
☐ Download speed for step "Log in" of scenario "Zabbix frontend".	[avg]	242.22 KBps	181.05 KBps	303.13 KBps	343.03
☐ Download speed for step "Check login" of scenario "Zabbix frontend".	[avg]	258.62 KBps	168.62 KBps	314.85 KBps	358.61
☐ Download speed for step "Log out" of scenario "Zabbix frontend".	[avg]	44.26 KBps	23.86 KBps	43 KBps	47.81
☐ Download speed for step "Check logout" of scenario "Zabbix frontend".	[avg]	86.26 KBps	45.74 KBps	86.03 KBps	96.83

Zabbix frontend: Response time (6h)

		last	min	avg	max
☐ Response time for step "First page" of scenario "Zabbix frontend".	[avg]	45.7ms	35ms	40.79ms	71.6ms
☐ Response time for step "Log in" of scenario "Zabbix frontend".	[avg]	110.4ms	73.9ms	84.65ms	140.1ms
☐ Response time for step "Check login" of scenario "Zabbix frontend".	[avg]	98.1ms	71.6ms	81.62ms	150.5ms
☐ Response time for step "Log out" of scenario "Zabbix frontend".	[avg]	70.4ms	65.2ms	73.08ms	130.6ms
☐ Response time for step "Check logout" of scenario "Zabbix frontend".	[avg]	36.1ms	32.2ms	36.59ms	68.1ms

The scenario seems to be running correctly: log in and log out seem to work properly. Note that if it fails for you, the failure could actually be in the previous step. For example, if it fails on *Step 3: Check login*, the actual fault is likely in *Step 2: Log in* — that is, the login failed.

The approach we took with five steps was not the most simple one. While it allowed us to split out each action in its own step (and provided nice graphs with five values), we could have used a much more simple approach. To check login and logout, the simplest approach and the minimum number of steps would have been these:

- Log in and check whether that is successful
- Log out and check whether that is successful

As an extra exercise, consider creating a new scenario and achieving the same goal in two steps.

Authentication options

In the scenario properties, there was also a tab that we didn't use — **Authentication**:

For **HTTP authentication**, Zabbix currently supports two options — **Basic** and **NTLM**. Digest authentication is not supported at this time.

Choosing one of the **HTTP authentication** methods will provide input fields for a username and password.

All the other options are SSL/TLS related. The checkboxes allow us to validate the server certificate—the **SSL verify peer** option checks the certificate validity, and **SSL verify host** additionally checks that the server hostname matches the **Common Name** or the **Subject Alternate Name** in the certificate. The certificate authority is validated against the system default. The location of the CA certificates can also be overridden by the SSLCALocation parameter in the server configuration file.

The last three fields enable us to set up client authentication using a certificate. Zabbix supports all possible combinations of certificate, key, and key password: single unencrypted file, completely separate certificate, key and key password, and so on. The client certificate files must be placed in the directory specified by the SSLCertLocation parameter in the server configuration file. Key files, if any, must be placed in the directory specified by the SSLKeyLocation parameter in the server configuration file.

Using agent items

The web scenario-based monitoring we just set up is quite powerful, but there might be cases when a more simple approach would be enough. On the agent level, there are some interesting item keys that allow retrieving web pages and performing simple verification. An additional benefit is the ability to do that from any agent, so it is very easy to check web page availability from multiple geographically distributed locations. There are three web page-related item keys:

- web.page.get
- web.page.perf
- web.page.regexp

> Also keep in mind the more simple item keys such as net.tcp.service, discussed in *Chapter 3, Monitoring with Zabbix Agents and Basic Protocols*.

Getting the page

The most simple web page-related agent item key, web.page.get, allows us to retrieve page content. The same as scenario-based web monitoring, it does not retrieve any included content, such as images. Let's create a simple item with this key. Navigate to **Configuration | Hosts**, and select **Web pages** in the **Group** dropdown. Click on **Items** next to **OpenStreetMap**, and click on **Create item**. Fill in the following:

- **Name:** OpenStreetMap main page
- **Key:** web.page.get[www.openstreetmap.org,/]

- **Type of information: Text**
- **New application:** OSM

> We are creating an agent item for our Zabbix server. This means that this web item will be checked by the local agent.

When done, click on the **Add** button at the bottom. In this item, we specified / as the second parameter, but that is optional—by default, root on the web server is requested. If a custom port has to be used, it can be specified as the third parameter, like this:

```
web.page.get[www.site.lan,/,8080]
```

Instead of checking the results of each of the items we are creating individually, let's create all three items first and then verify the results.

Checking page performance

Another web page-related agent item is web.page.perf. It returns the loading time of the page in seconds. While still in the item list, click on **Create item**, and fill in the following:

- **Name:** OpenStreetMap main page load time
- **Key:** web.page.perf[www.openstreetmap.org,/]
- **Type of information: Numeric (float)**
- **Units:** s
- **Applications: OSM**

When done, click on the **Add** button at the bottom. We changed **Type of information** as this item key returns the time it took to load the page in seconds, and that value usually will have a decimal part.

Extracting content from web pages

When creating the web monitoring scenario earlier, we used the ability to extract content from a page and reuse it later. With the more simple agent monitoring, it is still possible to extract some content from a page. As a test, we could try to extract the text after OpenStreetMap is and up to the first comma. Click on **Create item** again, and fill in the following:

- **Name:** OpenStreetMap is
- **Key:** web.page.regexp[www.openstreetmap.org,,,OpenStreetMap is ([a-z]*),,,\1]

- **Type of information**: **Character**
- **Applications**: **OSM**

> The inner square brackets contain a-z — there is a space after z.

When done, click on the **Add** button at the bottom.

> The item key works with **OpenStreetMap** page contents at the time of writing this. If the web page gets redesigned, consider it an extra challenge to adapt the regular expression.

For this item, we are extracting search results from the page directly. The important parameter here is the fourth one — it is a regular expression that would be matched in the page source. In this case, we are looking for the OpenStreetMap is string and including everything after it up to the first comma in a capture group. We included the regular expression in double quotes because it contains a comma. A comma is the **item key parameter separator**, so it could be misinterpreted. Then, in the last parameter, we request only the contents of the first capture group to be included. By default, the whole matched string is returned. For more detail on value extraction with this method, refer to *Log file monitoring* in *Chapter 11, Advanced Item Monitoring*. We also chose **Type of information** to be **Character** — that will limit the values to 255 symbols, just in case it matches a huge string.

> For this key, the fifth parameter allows us to limit the length of the returned key. If you want to extract a number and send it over SMS, limiting the length of the extracted string to 50 characters would reduce the possibility of the message being too long.

A practical application of this item would be extracting statistics from an Apache web server when using mod_status or similar functionality with other server software.

> None of the three web.page.* items support HTTPS, authentication, or redirects at this time.

With the items configured, let's check their returned values — head to **Monitoring | Latest data**, clear out the **Host groups** field, select **OpenStreetMap** in the **Hosts** field, and then click on **Filter**. Look for items in the OSM application:

NAME ▲	LAST CHECK	LAST VALUE
OSM (3 Items)		
OpenStreetMap is	2016-05-13 13:41:21	a map of the world
OpenStreetMap main page	2016-05-13 13:41:20	HTTP/1.1 200 OK Date: Fri, 13 May 2016 10:41:20 GMT …
OpenStreetMap main page load time	2016-05-13 13:41:21	604.8ms

> Each item requests the page separately.

The items should be returning full page contents, the time it took to load the page, and the result of our regular expression. The web.page.get item always includes headers, too. If you see empty values appearing every now and then in the web.page.get and web.page.regexp items, it probably happens because of the request timing out. While web scenarios had their own timeout setting, the agent items obey the agent timeout of 3 seconds by default. The web.page.perf item returns 0 upon a timeout.

> The Zabbix web.page.get item currently does not work properly with chunked transfer encoding, which is widely used. Extra data is inserted in the page contents. This was expected to be fixed in Zabbix 3.0 by using libcurl for these agent items as well, but that development was not finished. At the time of writing this, it is not known when this could be fixed.

Using these items, we could trigger when a page takes long to load or does not work at all or when a specific string cannot be found on the page – using str() and similar trigger expressions either on the whole page item or on the content extraction item.

> Web scenarios are executed on the Zabbix server, agent items on the agent. We will discuss the ability of running web scenarios on remote systems in *Chapter 19, Using Proxies to Monitor Remote Locations*.

The items we created all went to the same Zabbix agent. We can also create a host with multiple interfaces and assign items to each interface. This allows us to check a web page from multiple locations but keep the results in a single host. We still have to make the item keys unique – if needed, either use the trick with empty key parameters, extra commas in key parameters, or key aliasing, discussed in *Chapter 22, Zabbix Maintenance*. Note that templates can't be used in such a setup.

Summary

First, we learned to monitor web pages based on various parameters, including response time, transfer speed, HTTP return code, and text, contained in the page itself. We also found out about how to set up multiple scenarios and steps in them as well as setting up variables to be used in all steps. As a more advanced example, we logged in to the Zabbix frontend and logged out of it. For that to work, we extracted the session ID and reused it in subsequent steps. With this knowledge, it should be possible to monitor most of the functionality web pages have.

For production systems, there usually will be way more applications, scenarios, and steps. Web monitoring can be used for many different purposes, the most popular being site availability and performance, but there are many different cases one could monitor, including things such as watching the Slashdot front page for a company name and replacing the usual first web page with a more simple one to withstand the coming load—slashdotting—easier.

As a simpler alternative, we also explored web page items on the agent side. They have three features:

- Retrieving full page contents
- Finding out page load time
- Extracting a string from the page using regular expressions

Web scenarios are only available on the server side, while the simpler items are only available on the agent side.

Having mostly concentrated on Linux system monitoring so far, we'll depart from that in the next chapter and look at *Chapter 14, Monitoring Windows*. We'll look at the native agent for Windows, performance counter and **Windows Management Instrumentation (WMI)** monitoring, and service discovery and Windows Event Log monitoring.

Monitoring Windows

14

Up to now, we have explored the monitoring of various services and Linux systems. While monitoring Microsoft Windows is very similar in many aspects, some Windows-specific support is available in Zabbix. Most of the things we learned about the Zabbix agent, using items and even user parameters, are still relevant on Windows. In this chapter we will explore installing the Zabbix agent on Windows, monitoring Windows performance counters, and using the built-in **Windows Management Instrumentation (WMI)** support. We will also try out Windows service monitoring, including the ability to discover them automatically, and the event log system support in the Zabbix agent. For this section you will need a Windows machine that is accessible from the Zabbix server.

Installing the Zabbix agent for Windows

To install the agent, it first has to be obtained. On Windows, compiling software is less common and most users get binary distributions, which is exactly what we will do now.

The Windows build of the Zabbix agent can be obtained from two official locations—either from the download page at http://www.zabbix.com/download.php, or from the source archive. While the practice of keeping binaries in the sources is not suggested, that's how Zabbix does it and sometimes, we can use it to our advantage. If you installed from source, it might be a good idea to use the Windows agent binary from the same archive so that the versions match. The agent executable is located in the subdirectory bin/win32 or bin/win64—choose the one that is appropriate for your architecture. If you installed from the packages, visit the download page and grab the Windows agent archive—but make sure to use the same or older major version of the Zabbix server. With the agent at hand one way or another, place it in the same directory on the Windows machine. For simplicity, we'll use C:\zabbix this time, but you are free to use any other directory. We will also need the configuration file, so grab the example provided at conf/zabbix_agentd.win.conf if you used the binary from the sources, or from the conf/ directory inside the archive if you downloaded the binaries from the Zabbix website. Place the configuration file in the same directory—there should be two files now. Before we continue with the agent itself, let's figure out whether we need to alter the configuration in any way. Open C:\zabbix\zabbix_agentd.win.conf in your favorite text editor and look for any parameters we might want to change. First, the log file location isn't quite right—it's set to C:\zabbix_agentd.log, so let's change it to read:

```
LogFile=c:\zabbix\zabbix_agentd.log
```

> You can use both forward and back slashes on the Windows Zabbix agent daemon command line and in the configuration file.

We have already learned that the server line, which currently reads Server=127.0.0.1, will have to be changed. Replace the 127.0.0.1 part with the IP address of your Zabbix server. And to be sure that active items will work as expected, let's check the Hostname directive—it is set to the Windows host by default and we could leave it like that. Another parameter for active checks was ServerActive. Replace 127.0.0.1 here with the Zabbix server IP address as well and save the file.

If we were to start our agent now, it would automatically register on the Zabbix server, based on the configuration we created in *Chapter 12*, *Automating Configuration*. While it would be convenient, we want to test things in a stricter fashion this time—go to **Configuration | Actions**, switch to **Auto registration** in the **Event source** dropdown, and click on **Enabled** next to **Testing registration**—that should disable the autoregistration we set up earlier.

Now let's try to start the agent up. Start the Windows `cmd.exe` and execute:

```
C:\zabbix>zabbix_agentd.exe -c c:/zabbix/zabbix_agentd.win.conf
```

> You might have to prefix the commands with `.\` on some versions of Windows.
>
> If you see no output or another window appears very briefly, you should start the command prompt as the admin user. In recent versions of Windows, the menu entry is called **Command Prompt (Admin)**.

The agent daemon refuses to start up:

```
zabbix_agentd.exe [6348]: use foreground option to run Zabbix agent as
console application
```

Let's find out how we can supply the foreground option, then. The agent daemon executable on Windows has additional options that can be passed to it, so execute it in the command prompt (when located in the directory where `zabbix_agentd.exe` resides):

```
C:\zabbix>zabbix_agentd.exe --help
```

Looking at the **Options** section, the foreground parameter is listed there:

```
   -f --foreground              Run Zabbix agent in foreground
```

Let's try to use that option:

```
C:\zabbix>zabbix_agentd.exe --foreground -c c:/zabbix/zabbix_agentd.win.
conf
Starting Zabbix Agent [Windows host]. Zabbix 3.0.0 (revision 58455).
Press Ctrl+C to exit.
```

Looks like the agent is started up. For a quick test, try running the following from the Zabbix server. On the Zabbix server, execute:

```
$ zabbix_get -s <Windows host IP> -k system.cpu.load
0.316667
```

The agent is running and we can query values from it—looks great. There's one issue, though—we are currently running it in our terminal. If we were to close the terminal, the agent wouldn't run anymore. If the system was rebooted, the agent would not be started automatically. Running the agent in the foreground is nice, but we can also run it as a Windows service. How, exactly? First, stop it by pressing *Ctrl* + *C*, then look at the --help output again. Among all the parameters, we are interested in the **Functions** section this time:

```
Functions:
-i --install     Install Zabbix agent as service
-d --uninstall      Uninstall Zabbix agent from service
-s --start     Start Zabbix agent service
-x --stop     Stop Zabbix agent service
```

> The --multiple-agents in the Options section is intended to run multiple agents on the same system as separate Windows services. If used, the service name will include the Hostname parameter value from the specified configuration file in the service name.

The Zabbix agent daemon for Windows includes the functionality to install it as a standard Windows service, which is controlled by the options in this section. Unless you are simply doing some testing, you'll want to properly install it, so let's do that now:

```
C:\zabbix>zabbix_agentd.exe -c c:/zabbix/zabbix_agentd.win.conf -i
```

A confirmation dialog might come up at this time. Click on **Yes**. If you were running the command prompt as an administrative user, installing the service should succeed:

```
zabbix_agentd.exe [6248]: service [Zabbix Agent] installed successfully
```

```
zabbix_agentd.exe [6248]: event source [Zabbix Agent] installed
successfully
```

If not, this command might fail with the following:

```
zabbix_agentd.exe [3464]: ERROR: cannot connect to Service Manager:
[0x00000005] Access is denied.
```

In this case, you should either run the command prompt as an administrative user, or allow the program to run as the administrative user. To do the second, right-click on `zabbix_agentd.exe`, and choose **Troubleshoot compatibility**. In the resulting window, click on **Troubleshoot program** and mark **The program requires additional permissions**:

Click on **Next**, then **Test the program**, and **Next** again. In the final window, choose **Yes**, save these settings for this program, then click on **Close**.

> If running the agent daemon seems to have no input or shows a window very briefly, use the administrative command prompt as suggested earlier.

If everything was successful, the Zabbix agent daemon will have been installed as a Windows service using the configuration file, specified by the -c flag. You can verify, in the **Windows Control Panel**, **Services** section, that the Zabbix service has indeed been installed:

Name ▼	Description	Status	Startup Type	Log On As
Zabbix Agent	Provides system monitoring		Automatic	Local System

While it has been set to start up automatically, it is stopped now. We can start it by either right-clicking on the **Zabbix Agent** service entry and choosing **Start**, or by using the command line switch to zabbix_agentd.exe. Let's try the latter method now:

```
C:\zabbix>zabbix_agentd.exe --start
```

You might have to answer another security prompt here, but the service should start up successfully. We can verify in the services list that the Zabbix service has started up:

Name ▼	Description	Status	Startup Type	Log On As
Zabbix Agent	Provides system monitoring	Running	Automatic	Local System

> If you opened the service list earlier, refresh the contents by pressing *F5*.

It looks like everything is fine on the monitored host, which we will now have to configure in the frontend. Open **Configuration | Hosts** and click on **Create host**, then fill in the following values:

- **Host name**: Windows host
- **Groups**: If there's any group in the **In groups** box, remove it
- **New group**: Windows servers
- **Agent interfaces, IP ADDRESS**: Enter the IP address of that host

When done, click on the **Add** button at the bottom. Now select **Windows servers** in the **Group** dropdown, click on **Items** next to **Windows host**, then click on **Create item**. Enter these values:

- **Name**: CPU load
- **Key**: system.cpu.load
- **Type of information: Numeric (float)**

When done, click on the **Add** button at the bottom. We can now check out incoming data at **Monitoring | Latest data** — clear out the other filter fields, select **Windows host** in the **Host group** field, and then click on **Filter**:

HOST	NAME ▲	LAST CHECK	LAST VALUE
Windows host	- **other** - (1 Item)		
	CPU load	2016-05-14 17:15:52	0.07

> CPU load on Windows works in a similar manner as on Unix systems, although Windows administrators are less familiar with it. CPU utilization is more often used on Windows.

We have now successfully retrieved data on the CPU load for this Windows machine. Notice how the key syntax is the same as for Linux. This is true for several other keys, and you can check out the Zabbix documentation to determine which keys are supported on which platform.

Querying performance counters

While many keys match between platforms, there's a whole category that is specific to Windows. Zabbix supports Windows' built-in metrics-gathering system, performance counters. People who are familiar with Windows probably know that these can be found at **Control Panel | Administrative Tools | Performance** in older versions of Windows and **Administrative Tools | Performance Monitor** in more recent versions, with a lot of counters to add. How exactly it operates depends on the Windows version again—in older versions we can click on the + icon in the child toolbar, or press *Ctrl + I* to see available counters:

In this dialog, we can gather the information required to construct a performance counter string. First, the string has to start with a backslash, \. The **Performance object** follows, in this case, **Processor**. Then we have to include the desired instance in parentheses, which makes our string so far \Processor(_Total) (notice the leading underscore before Total). The counter string is finished by adding an individual counter string from the **Select counters from list** list box, again separated by a backslash. So the final performance counter string looks like this:

```
\Processor(_Total)\% Idle Time
```

In recent Windows versions we expand **Data Collector Sets**, right-click on **User Defined**, and choose **New | Data Collector Set**:

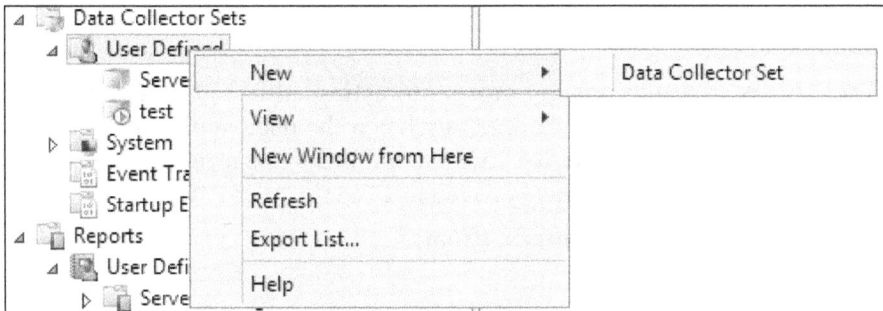

In the resulting window, enter a name for the data collector set, choose **Create manually**, and click on **Next**. Choose **Performance Counter Alert**, and click on **Next** again, then click on **Add**. Here we finally get to the performance counters—expand **Processor** and click on **% Idle Time**, then click on **Add >>**. Now click on **OK** to see the constructed performance counter string:

Now that we have constructed it, what do we do with it? Create an item, of course. Back in the frontend, navigate to **Configuration | Hosts**, click on **Items** next to the **Windows host**, and click on **Create item**. Fill in these values:

- **Name**: CPU idle time, %
- **Key**: This is where things get more interesting, although the principle is quite simple — the perf_counter key has to be used with the performance counter string like the one we constructed before as a parameter; thus, enter perf_counter[\Processor(_Total)\% Idle Time] here
- **Type of information**: **Numeric (float)**
- **Units**: %

When you are done, click on the **Add** button at the bottom. This item should show us the total time all CPUs spend idling on the machine, so let's look at **Monitoring | Latest data**. We can see that the data is directly fetched from the built-in performance counter:

CPU idle time, %	2016-05-14 17:20:24	97.42 %

Looking at the list of available performance objects and corresponding counters in Windows, we can see many different metrics. Navigating this window is cumbersome at best, thanks to small widgets, no proper filtering or searching capabilities, and the fact that constructing the required string to be used as a key is a manual typing job, as entries can't be copied. Luckily there's a solution available — the command line utility typeperf.exe. To see how it can help us, execute:

```
C:\zabbix>typeperf -qx > performance_counters.txt
```

This will direct all output of this command to be saved in the file performance_counters.txt. Open that file with a text editor and observe the contents. You'll see lots and lots of performance counter strings, covering various software and hardware information. There is no need to struggle with that clumsy dialog anymore; we can easily search for and copy these strings.

Using numeric references to performance counters

If you have a localized Windows installation, you have probably noticed by now that all performance counters are in the localized language, not in English. This becomes especially cumbersome to handle if you have to monitor several Windows machines with different locales configured for them. For example, a counter that on an English Windows installation is \System\Processes would be \Système\Processes in a French one. Would it be possible to use some other, more universal method to refer to the performance counters? Indeed, it would; we can use numeric references, but first we have to find out what they are.

Launch regedit and look for the key HKEY_LOCAL_MACHINE\SOFTWARE\Microsoft\ Windows NT\CurrentVersion\Perflib. Under this key, you'll see one or more entries, with one being 009, which is the entry for the English language. Select this entry and pay attention to the **Counter** key, which has suspiciously similar contents to performance counter names. Expect to see something like this in an older version of Windows:

You would see something like this in a recent version:

Double-click this value to see its contents in a somewhat more manageable form:

Each performance counter string can be translated to a number. But figuring out exact conversions in this tiny window is awfully hard, so let's copy all the contents and save them to a file, which we'll then be able to search—name it `numeric.txt`. To see how this works, let's translate the performance counter string we used before: \ `Processor(_Total)\% Idle Time`.

First we have to translate the performance object, `Processor`. While it is possible to search these contents in any text editor, it soon becomes cumbersome, especially if we have to translate lots of values. In that case we can turn to the basic GNU tools, such as `grep`, which you might have installed on the Windows machine—if not, copy this file over to the Zabbix server:

```
$ grep -B 1 "^Processor$" numeric.txt
```

This command will search for a line containing the string `Processor` exactly and will also output the line immediately before it, which contains the numeric ID of this performance object:

```
238
Processor
```

> Numeric values might differ between Windows versions, so make sure to use the values found in your file.

If you are using `grep` on the Zabbix server, the saved file might contain Windows-style newlines and you might get no output. In that case, convert the newlines by executing:

```
$ sed -i 's/\r//' numeric.txt
```

Now that we have the numeric value for the first part, do the same for the second part of the performance counter:

```
$ grep -B 1 "^% Idle Time$" numeric.txt
1482

% Idle Time
```

We now have numeric values for all parts of the performance counter except the `_Total`. How can we translate that? We don't have to—this string is used as is on all locales. Our resulting performance counter would then look like this:

```
\238(_Total)\1482
```

As we already have an item gathering this information, we won't add another one. Instead, let's test it with the `zabbix_get` utility. On the Zabbix server, execute:

```
$ zabbix_get -s <Windows host IP> -k "perf_counter[\238(_Total)\1482]"
```

This should return the same data as the `\Processor(_Total)\% Idle Time` key does:

```
99.577165
```

> Additional software can add additional performance counters, and numeric values for such counters can differ between systems. In some cases, software modifies existing performance counters; for example, adding the firewall software vendor's name to a network interface.

Using aliases for performance counters

Another method to unify item keys that are using Zabbix configurations (so that a single template could be used for all hosts) is to specify performance counter aliases. To do that, add an `Alias` directive to the Zabbix agent configuration file.

For example, if we wanted to refer to the performance counter we used, `\Processor(_Total)\% Idle Time`, as `cpu.idle_time`, we would add the following:

```
Alias = cpu.idle_time:perf_counter[\Processor(_Total)\% Idle Time]
```

> Do not forget to restart the agent after making the changes.

On systems with a different locale the `Alias` entry would use a different performance counter, but from now on we can use the same item key for all systems: `cpu.idle_time`.

Averaging performance counters over time

The Zabbix agent has another Windows-specific feature. It can gather performance counter values and return the average. This way, we can smooth out counters that return data for the last second and reduce the chance of missing abnormal data. For example, we could add a line like this in the agent demon configuration file:

```
PerfCounter = disk.writes,"\PhysicalDisk(_Total)\Disk Writes/sec",300
```

Based on this, the agent will collect the values from that performance counter every second and compute the average over five minutes. We could then query the agent once every five minutes and get an accurate idea of what the average writes per second were. If we didn't use the averaging, we would only get the data for the last second once every five minutes.

Querying WMI

Besides built-in support for performance counters, the Zabbix agent also supports WMI queries.

> Zabbix supports WMI through the Zabbix agent — remote WMI is not supported at this time.

To extract some useful information, we need a WMI query, and we might want to test the queries quickly — that can be done in Windows or by using the Zabbix agent. On the Windows side, the `wbemtest.exe` utility can be used. When launching it, click on **Connect**, accept the default namespace of `root\cimv2`, and click on **Connect** again. Then, in a dialog like this, click on **Query**:

You can enter complete queries here. For example, we could ask for the current time zone with a query:

```
SELECT StandardName FROM Win32_TimeZone
```

An alternative way to test such queries through the Zabbix agent would be with the `zabbix_get` utility, discussed in *Chapter 3, Monitoring with Zabbix Agents and Basic Protocols*.

With the query available, we can proceed with creating an item. Navigate to **Configuration | Hosts**, click on **Items** next to **Windows host**, and click on **Create item**. Fill in the following:

- **Name:** Time zone
- **Key:** wmi.get[root\cimv2,SELECT StandardName FROM Win32_TimeZone]
- **Type of information: Character**
- **Update interval:** 300

The key here was `wmi.get`, the first parameter was namespace, and the second parameter was the query itself. We don't expect the time zone to change that often, so we increased the update interval a bit—normally one would use an even larger interval, but we will want the first value to come in soon enough. When done, click on the **Add** button at the bottom. Check **Monitoring | Latest data**—in some five minutes the value should be there:

Time zone	2016-05-14 18:06:54	FLE Standard Time

This way one can monitor any output from the WMI queries—but note that a single value should be returned; multiple values are not supported. If multiple values are returned, only the first value will be processed.

Monitoring Windows services

There's yet another item category that is Windows-specific: a dedicated key for Windows service state monitoring. Let's try to monitor a service now. First we have to figure out how to refer to this service. For that, open the services list and then open up the details of a service—let's choose **DNS Client**:

Look at the top of this tab. **Service name** is the name we will have to use, and we can see that it differs noticeably from the display name—instead of using **DNS Client**, the name is **Dnscache**. Let's create the item now. Navigate to **Configuration | Hosts**, click on **Items** next to the **Windows host**, then click on **Create item**. Enter these values:

- **Name:** DNS client service state
- **Key:** service.info[Dnscache]

> Service names are case insensitive.
>
> The key used here, service.info, is new in Zabbix 3.0. Older versions of Zabbix used service_state key. This key is deprecated but still supported, and you are likely to see it in older Zabbix installations and templates. The service.info key has more parameters—for the complete documentation, consult the Zabbix manual.

When done, click on the **Add** button at the bottom, open **Monitoring | Latest data**, and look for our newly added item:

DNS client service state	2016-05-14 18:20:25	0

So data is gathered, and the state is "0". That's probably normal, but how can we know what the state number means? Back in **Configuration | Hosts**, click on **Items** next to **Windows host** and click on **DNS client service state** in the **NAME** column. Look at our old friend, the **Show value property**. Click on the **Show value mappings** link and examine the mapping near the bottom of the list:

Windows service state	0 ⇒ Running 1 ⇒ Paused 2 ⇒ Start pending 3 ⇒ Pause pending 4 ⇒ Continue pending 5 ⇒ Stop pending 6 ⇒ Stopped 7 ⇒ Unknown 255 ⇒ No such service

It turns out there's already a predefined mapping for Windows service states available. Close this window and choose **Windows service state** in the **Show value** dropdown, then click on **Update**. Back in **Monitoring | Latest data**, verify that the service state is now displayed in a much more user-friendly way:

NS client service state	2016-05-14 18:23:55	Running (0)

Now we will be able to easily identify different service states in the frontend. With the item in place, let's also create a trigger that will alert us when this service has stopped. Go to **Configuration | Hosts**, click on **Triggers** next to **Windows host**, and click on **Create trigger**. Enter DNS client service down on {HOST.NAME} in the **Name** field, then click on **Add** next to the **Expression** field. Click on **Select** next to the **Item** field, choose **DNS client service state**, and click on **Insert**. But wait, the value of 0 was for when the service was running; we should actually test for the value not being 0. We just avoided using the dropdown function that changes the insert expression:

```
{Windows host:service.info[Dnscache].last()}<>0
```

Change the severity to **Warning** and click on the **Add** button at the bottom. Unless this is a production system, it should be pretty safe to stop this service—do so, and observe **Monitoring | Triggers**; select **Windows servers** in the **Group** dropdown. Zabbix should now warn you that this service is down:

SEVERITY	STATUS	INFO	LAST CHANGE ▼	AGE	ACK	HOST	NAME
Warning	PROBLEM		2016-05-14 19:09:25	20s	No 1	Windows host	DNS client service down on Windows host

Checking automatic services

Sometimes we are not interested in the exact details of every service, and we might have to configure an item and trigger for each of them manually. Instead, we might want to see a high-level overview; for example, whether any of the services that are started automatically have stopped. Zabbix provides an item that allows you to make such a comparison very easily: services. It allows us to retrieve lists of services based on different parameters, including ones that should be started automatically and are stopped. How can we use this?

An item should be added with the following key:

```
services[automatic,stopped]
```

> For a list of all supported services key parameters, consult the Zabbix manual.

This will take care of getting the required data. Whenever a service that is set to start automatically is stopped, it will be listed in the data from this item.

It is also possible that on some Windows versions there will be services that are supposed to start up automatically and shut down later. In this case, they would appear in the listing and break our monitoring. Luckily, Zabbix has a solution for such a problem, too—we can add third parameter to this key and list services to be excluded from this check. For example, to exclude the `RemoteRegistry` and `sppsvc` services, the key would be:

```
services[automatic,stopped,"RemoteRegistry,sppsvc"]
```

Notice how the services to be excluded are comma-delimited, and the whole list is included in double quotes.

> If the list of such services is different between hosts, consider using a user macro to hold the service list. We discussed user macros in *Chapter 8, Simplifying Complex Configuration with Templates*.

But how do we check that everything is good in a trigger? If the list is empty, the Zabbix agent returns 0. As a result, by simply checking whether the last value was zero, we can trigger when an automatically started service is stopped. A trigger expression for such a check would be:

```
{Windows host:services[automatic,stopped].last()}<>0
```

Of course, you can apply a method—such as using the `count()` function—to only fire the trigger after it has been non-zero for more than a single check:

```
{Windows host:services[automatic,stopped].count(#3,0)}=0
```

Such a trigger expression will only fire if there has been at least one such stopped service in all of the last three checks.

Service discovery

The preceding method just tells you that some service that was supposed to be running has stopped. To see which service that is, we'd have to look at the item values. We can actually monitor all services individually, as Zabbix has supports **Windows service discovery** since version 3.0. Let's discover all Windows services and monitor some parameter on all of them—we can choose the service description here.

Navigate to **Configuration | Hosts,** click on **Discovery** next to **Windows host,** and click on **Create discovery rule**. Fill in the following:

- **Name:** Windows service discovery
- **Key:** service.discovery
- **Update interval:** 300

We used a built-in agent key and increased the update interval. In production, it is probably a good idea to increase the interval even more; an average default interval for discovery rules of one hour is likely a good idea. When done, click on the **Add** button at the bottom. We have the rule itself; now we need some prototypes—click on **Item prototypes,** then click on **Create item prototype**. Before we fill in the data, it would be useful to know what this discovery item returns—an example for one service is as follows:

```
{
    "{#SERVICE.STARTUP}" : 0,
    "{#SERVICE.DISPLAYNAME}" : "Zabbix Agent",
    "{#SERVICE.DESCRIPTION}" : "Provides system monitoring",
    "{#SERVICE.STATENAME}" : "running",
    "{#SERVICE.STARTUPNAME}" : "automatic",
    "{#SERVICE.USER}" : "LocalSystem",
    "{#SERVICE.PATH}" : "\"C:\\zabbix\\zabbix_agentd.exe\" --config
\"c:\\zabbix\\zabbix_agentd.win.conf\"",
    "{#SERVICE.STATE}" : 0,
    "{#SERVICE.NAME}" : "Zabbix Agent"
}
```

> The Zabbix agent can be queried for the raw LLD data using zabbix_get. We discussed low-level discovery in more detail in *Chapter 12, Automating Configuration.*

This snippet also shows what other things we could monitor for each service. For now, we want to extract descriptions for all services, but to add the items we need the actual service names. Although the description is available here, we will query it in the item, so for item prototypes it will actually be the macro {#SERVICE.NAME}. With this knowledge, we are ready to fill in the item prototype form:

- **Name:** Service $1 description
- **Key:** service.info[{#SERVICE.NAME},description]
- **Type of information: Character**
- **Update interval:** 300

When done, click on the **Add** button at the bottom. With our discovery running every five minutes, it might take up to five minutes for this prototype to generate actual items, and then it would take up to six minutes for these items to get their first value—the added time of configuration cache update and item interval. First, go to item configuration for the Windows host. After a while, our discovery rule should add the items:

Windows service discovery: Service SysMain description	service.info[SysMain,description]
Windows service discovery: Service swprv description	service.info[swprv,description]
Windows service discovery: Service TabletInputService description	service.info[TabletInputService,description]
Windows service discovery: Service svsvc description	service.info[svsvc,description]
Windows service discovery: Service SystemEventsBroker description	service.info[SystemEventsBroker,description]
Windows service discovery: Service SSDPSRV description	service.info[SSDPSRV,description]

There will likely be a fairly large number of such items. Visiting **Monitoring | Latest data,** after a few more minutes we should see descriptions for all services:

Service ADWS description	2016-05-14 19:21:58	This service provides a Web Service interface to instances of the directory ser…
Service AeLookupSvc description	2016-05-14 19:21:59	Processes application compatibility cache requests for applications as they a…
Service ALG description	2016-05-14 19:22:00	Provides support for 3rd party protocol plug-ins for Internet Connection Sharing
Service AppHostSvc description	2016-05-14 19:22:01	Provides administrative services for IIS, for example configuration history and …
Service AppIDSvc description	2016-05-14 19:22:02	Determines and verifies the identity of an application. Disabling this service w…

A more common approach would be to monitor the current service state or its startup configuration—anything the service.info key supports should be possible.

> We can also use any of the LLD macros to filter the discovered services. For example, via filtering for the {#SERVICE.STARTUP}, we could discover only the services that are configured to start up automatically (value 0), or start automatically with a delay (value 1).

Windows event log monitoring

Zabbix supports log file monitoring on Windows as well—the topics we discussed in *Chapter 11, Advanced Item Monitoring* still apply. But on Windows there is also a specialized logging subsystem, and Zabbix does offer built-in event log system support. Windows has various event log categories, and we could monitor the Security event log. Other common logs are System and Application, and there will be more logs in recent versions of Windows. For now, let's head to **Configuration | Hosts**, click on **Items** next to **Windows host**, and click on **Create item**. Fill in the following:

- **Name**: Windows $1 log
- **Type**: **Zabbix agent (active)**
- **Key**: eventlog[Security,,,,,,skip]
- **Type of information**: **Log**
- **Update interval**: 1

> Event log monitoring on Windows works as an active item, same as normal log file monitoring.

That's six commas in the item key. When done, click on the **Add** button at the bottom. The last parameter we specified here, skip, will prevent the agent from reading all of the security log—a pretty good idea for systems that have been around for some time. Visit **Monitoring | Latest data** and click on **History** for the **Windows Security log** item:

TIMESTAMP	LOCAL TIME	SOURCE	SEVERITY	EVENT ID	VALUE
					An account was logged off.
					Subject:
					Security ID:
					Account Name:
2016-05-14 19:34:38	2016-05-14 19:34:37	Microsoft-Windows-Security-Auditing	Success Audit	4634	Account Domain:
					Logon ID:
					Logon Type:
					This event is generated when ID value. Logon IDs are only

> [💡 If no values appear, sign in into the Windows system — that should generate some entries in this log.]

A few notable differences, compared to normal log file monitoring, include automatic data population in the **LOCAL TIME** column, as well as source, severity, and the event ID being stored. Actually, we can filter by some of these already at the agent level; we don't have to send all entries to the server. Let's discuss some of the item key parameters in a bit more detail. The general key syntax is this:

```
eventlog[name,<regexp>,<severity>,<source>,<eventid>,<maxlines>,<mo
de>]
```

The second parameter, `regexp`, operates the same as in normal log file monitoring — it matches a regular expression against the log entry. The `maxlines` and `mode` parameters work the same as they do for `log` and `logrt` item keys. The severity, `source`, and `eventid` parameters are specific to the `eventlog` key, and they are all regular expressions to be matched against the corresponding field. This way, we can filter the `eventlog` quite extensively on the agent side, but people make a somewhat common mistake sometimes — they forget that these are regular expressions, not exact match strings. What does that mean? Well, the following item key would not only match events with the ID of `13`, as follows:

```
eventlog[Security,,,,13]
```

It would also match events with IDs of `133`, `1333`, and `913`. To match `13`, and `13` only, we'd have to anchor the regular expression:

```
eventlog[Security,,,,^13$]
```

> [💡 Remember that it is true for the `severity` and `source` parameters as well — while they are less likely to match unintended value, one should always make sure the expression is anchored if an exact match is desired.]

Summary

In this chapter, we explored various things that were either different on Windows, or things that Zabbix explicitly supports on Windows.

We installed the Zabbix agent as a Windows service and verified that, in many ways, it works exactly the same as the Linux agent. Then we moved to Windows-specific feature support:

- Performance counters
- WMI using the Zabbix agent
- Windows services, including the ability to automatically discover them
- Event log system

Not only did we discuss details and potential issues for all of these, we also monitored some data using each of these features. Coupled with the generic monitoring and reporting knowledge we have now, this should allow us to efficiently monitor Windows installations as well.

Having explored quite a lot of lower-level configuration, in the next chapter we will look at a more business-oriented aspect—SLA monitoring. Zabbix allows us to create an IT service tree, assign triggers that depict service availability, and calculate how much of an adherence to the SLA that is.

15
High-Level Business Service Monitoring

Monitoring IT systems usually involves poking at lots of small details — CPU, disk, memory statistics, process states, and a myriad other parameters. All of these are very important, and every detail should be available to technical people. But in the end, the goal of these systems is not to have enough disk space — the goal is to serve a specific need. If one only looks at the low-level detail, it can be very hard to figure out what impact the current problem might have on users. Zabbix offers a way to have a higher-level view, called **IT services**. Relationships between individual systems can be configured to see how they build up to deliver services, and **Service Level Agreement (SLA)** calculation can be enabled for any part of the resulting tree.

Deciding on the service tree

Before configuring things, it is useful to think through the setup, and doubly so with IT services. A large service tree might look impressive, but it might not represent the actual functionality well, and might even obscure the real system state. Disk space being low is important, but it does not actually bring the system down — it does not affect the SLA. The best approach likely would be to only include specific checks that identify a service being available or operating in an acceptable manner — for example, SLA might require some performance level to be maintained. Unless we want to have a large, complicated IT service tree, we should identify key factors in delivering the service and monitor those.

What are the key factors? If the service is simple enough and can be tested easily, we could have a direct test. Maybe the SLA requires that a website is available—in that case, a simple `web.page.get` item would suffice. If it is a web page-based system, we might want to check the page itself, log in, and perform some operation as a logged-in user—this is possible with web scenarios.

> We discussed web monitoring in more detail in *Chapter 13, Monitoring Web Pages*.

Sometimes, it might not be possible to use the interface directly—maybe it is not possible to have a special user for monitoring purposes, or we are not allowed to connect to the actual interface. In that case we should use lower-level monitoring, concentrating on the main pieces of the system that must be available. We should still attempt to have the highest-level checks possible. For example, we could check whether web server software is running, whether we can connect to a TCP port, and whether we can connect to the backend database from the frontend system. Memory or disk usage on the database system, and database low-level health, do not matter from the high-level monitoring point of view. It should all be monitored, of course, but having the delete query rate too high usually does not affect the top-level service. On the other hand, if a service goes down, we might be unable to see, in the same tree, that it happened because a disk filled up—but that is an operational failure, and we can expect that the responsible personnel are using such low-level triggers with proper dependencies to resolve the issue.

Setting up IT services

The best way to learn about a feature is to use it. We don't have any business services in our environment, thus we could use a similar approach as with the network map link indicator feature, where we created "fake" items and triggers to simulate network issues. We'll create items and triggers that will act as high-level service monitors.

We will invent two companies, called "Banana" and "Pineapple". Our company would be hosting various services for these two companies:

- A code repository system for "Banana"
- A warehouse analytics system for "Pineapple"
- A ticketing system for "Banana" and "Pineapple"

Our service tree could look like this:

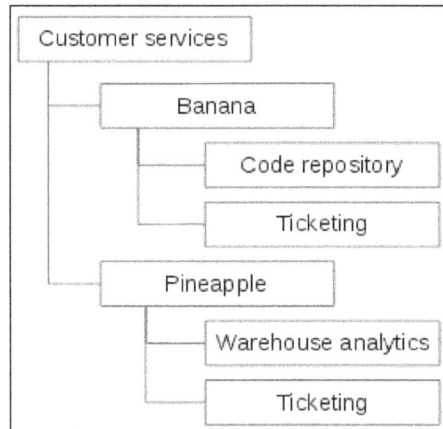

If everything is green at the top level, we know that all our customers are happy. If not, we see which customer is having an issue with a system, and we could see which system is affected. The ticketing system going down would affect both customers. And anything below these services — well, that's operational monitoring.

Unfortunately, IT services functionality is not that easy to evaluate without collecting data for a longer period of time; SLA graphs are more interesting when we have data for a few weeks or more. Maybe if we could send in data and pretend it's past data. Actually, we can do that. The small but great tool zabbix_sender, which we discussed in *Chapter 11, Advanced Item Monitoring*, allows us to specify a timestamp for each value. This means that we will create Zabbix trapper items and push values in those.

Creating test items and triggers

Proceed to **Configuration | Hosts** and click on **Create host**. Normally, items such as these would reside in different hosts, but for our test setup a single host will be best. Enter "IT services" in the **Host name** and **New group** fields and make sure no groups are in the **In groups** selectbox, then click on the **Add** button at the bottom. Switch to **IT services** in the **Group** drop-down, click on **Items** next to **IT services**, then click on **Create item**. This way, we create three different items with these settings:

- **Name**: Code repository service
- **Type**: **Zabbix trapper**
- **Key**: code_repo
- **New application**: IT services

You can use the item cloning feature to create the remaining two items more rapidly. Use the **Applications** field instead of the **New application** field for the remaining items:

- **Name**: `Warehouse analytics service`
- **Type**: **Zabbix trapper**
- **Key**: `warehouse_analytics`
- **Application**: **IT services**

And for the last item:

- **Name**: `Ticketing service`
- **Type**: **Zabbix trapper**
- **Key**: `ticketing`
- **Application**: **IT services**

The final list of items should look like this:

NAME ▲	TRIGGERS	KEY	INTERVAL	HISTORY	TRENDS	TYPE	APPLICATIONS
Code repository service		code_repo		90d	365d	Zabbix trapper	IT services
Ticketing service		ticketing		90d	365d	Zabbix trapper	IT services
Warehouse analytics service		warehouse_analytics		90d	365d	Zabbix trapper	IT services

Now click on **Triggers** in the navigation bar above the item list, then click on **Create trigger**. Create three triggers with settings as follows. For the first trigger:

- **Name**: `Code repository down`
- **Expression**: `{IT services:code_repo.last()}=0`
- **Severity**: **High**

For the second trigger:

- **Name**: `Warehouse analytics down`
- **Expression**: `{IT services:warehouse_analytics.last()}=0`
- **Severity**: **High**

And for the third trigger:

- **Name**: `Ticketing down`
- **Expression**: `{IT services:ticketing.last()}=0`
- **Severity**: **High**

SEVERITY	NAME ▲	EXPRESSION
High	Code repository down	{IT services:code_repo.**last()**}=0
High	Ticketing down	{IT services:ticketing.**last()**}=0
High	Warehouse analytics down	{IT services:warehouse_analytics.**last()**}=0

> We did not include the host name in the trigger name here to keep them shorter—you will likely want to do that for production systems.

In these triggers, the severity setting was very important. By default, triggers in Zabbix have the lowest severity, "**Not classified**". SLA calculation in IT services ignores the two lowest severities, "**Not classified**" and "**Information**". There does not seem to be a functional benefit from that, and the reasons are most likely historic. It is somewhat common for users to create quick testing triggers only to see that the SLA calculation does not work. When creating the trigger, the severity setting was not changed as a relatively unimportant one for a quick test. Luckily, we knew about it and created triggers that will work in the SLA calculation.

Configuring IT services

We are getting closer to sending in our slightly fake data, but we must configure IT services before the data comes in. In Zabbix, SLA results cannot be calculated retroactively. IT services must be configured at the beginning of the period for which we want to collect the SLA. SLA state is stored separately from trigger and event information and is calculated at runtime by the Zabbix server.

Let's go to **Configuration | IT services**. The interface for managing **IT services** is different from most other places in Zabbix. We have **root**, which is an immutable entry. All other service entries must be added as children to it. Click on **Add child** next to the root entry.

We will start by grouping all customer services in an entry—we might have internal services later. In the **Name** field, enter "Customer services" and click on the **Add** button at the bottom.

We have two customers—click on **Add** child next to **Customer services**. Enter "Banana" in the **Name** field, enable the **Calculate SLA** checkbox, then click on **Add**.

> The default acceptable SLA level when adding a new service entry is 99.05, and we will leave it at this level for all services. When editing an existing service entry, the default is 99.9 instead. At the time of writing, it is not yet known when this might be fixed.

Click on **Add child** next to **Customer services** again. Enter "Pineapple" in the **Name** field, enable the **Calculate SLA** checkbox, then click on **Add**. Notice how the **Customer services** entry can be expanded now. Expand it and observe the result, which should be like this:

```
root

   ▼ Customer services

      Banana

      Pineapple
```

The customers are in place; let's add their services now. Click on **Add child** next to **Banana**. Enter "Code repository" in the **Name** field and enable the **Calculate SLA** checkbox. This will be our "leaf" or lower-level service, and we will now link it to a trigger. The trigger state will affect the SLA state for this service and for all upper-level services with SLA calculation enabled. Click on **Select** next to the **Trigger** field, then click on **Code repository down** in the **NAME** column. The final configuration for this service should look like this:

Service	Dependencies	Time

Name	Code repository
Parent service	Banana	Change
Status calculation algorithm	Problem, if at least one child has a problem ▾
Calculate SLA, acceptable SLA (in %)	99.05
Trigger	IT services: Code repository down	Select
Sort order (0->999)	0
	Add Cancel

When done, click on **Add**. Then click on **Add child** next to **Banana** again. Enter "Ticketing" in the **Name** field, enable the **Calculate SLA** checkbox and click on **Select** next to the **Trigger** field, then click on **Ticketing down** in the **NAME** column. Click on the **Add** button to add the second child service for this customer.

Our first customer is configured; now click on **Add** child next to **Pineapple**. Enter "Warehouse analytics" in the **Name** field, enable the **Calculate SLA** checkbox, and click on **Select** next to the **Trigger** field. Click on **Warehouse analytics down** in the **NAME** column then click on the **Add** button.

We can add the ticketing service as another child service for "**Pineapple**", but services here can also be defined once, then added at multiple places in the service tree. This is done by making parent services depend on additional services. Click on **Pineapple** and switch to the **Dependencies** tab. Notice how its only child service, **Warehouse analytics**, is already listed here. Click on the **Add** link and click on **Ticketing entry**. Click on the **Update** button:

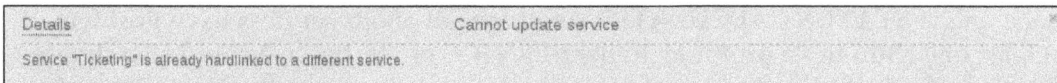

Details	Cannot update service	
Service "Ticketing" is already hardlinked to a different service.		

That didn't work well. If one is familiar with filesystem concepts, the error message might be a bit helpful; otherwise, it is probably a very confusing one. IT services in Zabbix have one "hard link" — they are attached to a parent service. To attach them to another service, we add them as a dependency, but we have to add them as a "soft link", as only one "hard link" is allowed per service. Mark the **SOFT** checkbox next to **Ticketing** and click on **Update** again. This time the operation should be successful and the **Ticketing entry** should now be visible for both companies.

> When deleting either a hard- or soft-linked entry, all occurrences of that service will be deleted.

If the entries are collapsed for you, expand them all and observe the final tree:

SERVICE	ACTION	STATUS CALCULATION	TRIGGER
root	Add child		
▼ Customer services	Add child	Problem, if at least one child has a problem	
▼ Banana	Add child	Problem, if at least one child has a problem	
Code repository	Add child Delete	Problem, if at least one child has a problem	Code repository down
Ticketing	Add child Delete	Problem, if at least one child has a problem	Ticketing down
▼ Pineapple	Add child	Problem, if at least one child has a problem	
Ticketing	Add child Delete	Problem, if at least one child has a problem	Ticketing down
Warehouse analytics	Add child Delete	Problem, if at least one child has a problem	Warehouse analytics down

Note that we enabled SLA calculation starting from the company level. Computing total SLA across all customers is probably not a common need, although it could be done. In the **STATUS CALCULATION** column, all of our services have **Problem, if at least one child has a problem**. In the **SERVICE** properties, we could also choose **Problem, if all children have problems**. At this time, those are the only options for problem state propagation; setting the percentage or amount of child services is not possible (it could be useful for a cluster solution, for example).

Sending in the data

Now is the time to send in our data, which will be a bit fake. As mentioned, IT services/SLA functionality is more interesting when we have data for a longer period of time, and we could try to send in data for a year. Of course, we won't create it manually — we will generate it. Create a script like this on the Zabbix server:

```
#!/bin/bash
hostname="IT services"
time_period=$[3600*24*365] # 365 days
interval=3600 # one hour
probability=100
current_time=$(date "+%s")
for item_key in code_repo warehouse_analytics ticketing; do
        [[ -f $item_key.txt ]] && {
                echo "file $item_key.txt already exists"
                exit
        }
        for ((value_timestamp=$current_time-$time_period;
            value_timestamp<$current_time;
            value_timestamp=value_timestamp+$interval)); do
```

```
        echo "\"$hostname\" $item_key $value_timestamp
        $([[ $(($RANDOM%$probability)) < 1 ]] && echo 0 ||
        echo 1)" >> $item_key.txt
    done
done
```

This script will generate values for each of our three item keys every hour, for one year in the past, starting at the current time. For each entry, there is a small chance of getting a value of 0, which is failure. The result will be random, but it should fluctuate around our acceptable SLA level, so hopefully we will get some services that do meet the SLA level and some that do not. As all of the values are sent in with a one-hour interval and it is quite unlikely that two failures would follow one another, no downtime should be longer than one hour. Assuming the script was saved as generate_values.sh, you just have to run it once:

```
$ ./generate_values.sh
```

Three files should be generated:

- code_repo.txt
- ticketing.txt
- warehouse_analytics.txt

> The following could generate quite a lot of alert e-mails. If you would like to avoid that, disable the actions we added earlier.

Now run zabbix_sender for each of these files:

```
$ zabbix_sender -z 127.0.0.1 -T -i code_repo.txt
$ zabbix_sender -z 127.0.0.1 -T -i ticketing.txt
$ zabbix_sender -z 127.0.0.1 -T -i warehouse_analytics.txt
```

The output on each invocation should be similar to this:

```
info from server: "processed: 250; failed: 0; total: 250; seconds spent:
0.001747"

...

info from server: "processed: 10; failed: 0; total: 10; seconds spent:
0.000063"

sent: 8760; skipped: 0; total: 8760
```

> Zabbix sender processes up to 250 values per connection – refer to *Chapter 11, Advanced Item Monitoring,* for more details about this small, but great, utility.

If all of the above succeeded, great; we now have a year's worth of data.

Viewing reports

Finally, we are ready to see the results of all the work done previously. Navigate to **Monitoring | IT services** and you should see a report like this:

SERVICE	STATUS	REASON	PROBLEM TIME		SLA / ACCEPTABLE SLA
root					
▼ Customer services	OK				
▼ Banana	OK			2.3810	97.6190 / 99.0500
Code repository - Code repository down	OK			0.5952	99.4048 / 99.0500
Ticketing - Ticketing down	OK			1.7857	98.2143 / 99.0500
▼ Pineapple	OK			1.7857	98.2143 / 99.0500
Ticketing - Ticketing down	OK			1.7857	98.2143 / 99.0500
Warehouse analytics - Warehouse analytics down	OK			0.0000	100.0000 / 99.0500

It shows the current state of each service, the calculated SLA value, and whether it meets the projected value. In this example, out of three services, only one has met the SLA level: the **Warehouse analytics** service. You are most likely seeing a different result.

The bar does not actually represent **100%** – if you compare the value with how much of the bar is colored red, it does not seem to match. Move the mouse cursor over any of the bars to see why:

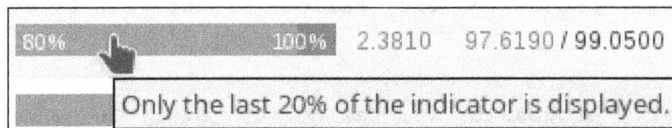

80%	100%	2.3810	97.6190 / 99.0500
Only the last 20% of the indicator is displayed.			

This bar only displays the last **20%** – for the SLA monitoring, we don't expect anything much below **80%** available, and showing a smaller part of a full bar allows us to see the impact more.

What we are looking at right now is the report for **Last 7 days**, as can be seen in the upper right corner. Expand the dropdown there and check the available options:

```
Today
This week
This month
This year
Last 24 hours
Last 7 days
Last 30 days
Last 365 days
```

Play with the choices there and see how our random data either met or did not meet the expected SLA level. Unfortunately, at this time it is not possible to generate such a report for an arbitrary period of time—if you want to see the SLA values for a specific week two months ago, you are out of luck.

There are several other reports slightly hidden on this page. Clicking on these options will give the following results:

- **Service name** will open the availability report for that service
- **Trigger name** (if linked to the service) will open the event history for that trigger
- **SLA** bar will open a yearly availability graph for that service

Let's click on **Banana** for now—this will open the availability report.

By default, it shows a weekly report for the current year. Let's switch to **Yearly** in the **Period** dropdown:

YEAR	OK	PROBLEMS	DOWNTIME	SLA	ACCEPTABLE SLA
2016	134d 0h 4m	2d 7h 0m		98.3186	99.0500
2015	360d 18h 0m	4d 6h 0m		98.8356	99.0500
2014	365d 0h 0m			100.0000	99.0500
2013	365d 0h 0m			100.0000	99.0500
2012	366d 0h 0m			100.0000	99.0500
2011	365d 0h 0m			100.0000	99.0500

This shows a report for the last five years, and that will almost always span six calendar years—which is why we get six entries. Here and elsewhere, Zabbix SLA calculation assumes that we will get information about problems—if there is no information about any problem, Zabbix assumes that services were available for that period. In this page, we may also choose **Monthly**, **Weekly**, and **Daily** periods—for all of these, a year can be selected and data for all months, weeks, or days in that year will be displayed. When looking at the year list, one can observe that the years available are the same as in the yearly report—five years that span six calendar years:

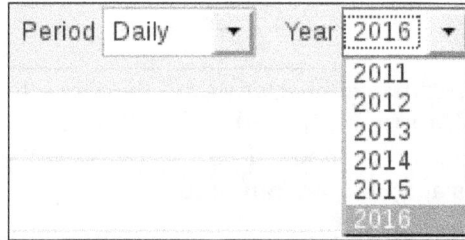

Clicking on the trigger name, if a trigger is linked to the service, will show the event history for that trigger. We looked at the event view in *Chapter 6, Detecting Problems with Triggers*, so we won't spend more time on it here.

Now let's return to **Monitoring | IT services** and click on one of the bars in the **PROBLEM TIME** column. A yearly **SLA** graph is displayed:

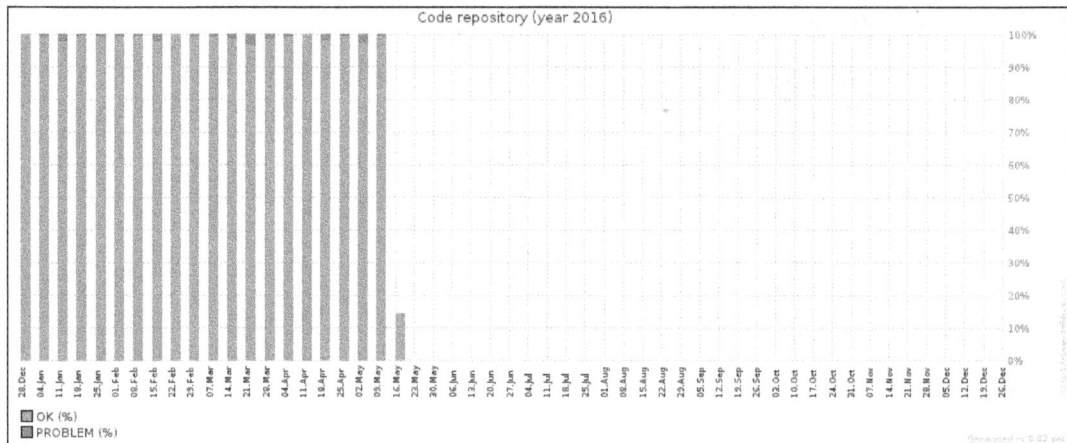

Each column represents one week. The time this service was down is displayed at the top, in red. Our service was mostly up, but we can see that there was a bit of downtime on most of the weeks.

Both for the availability reports and the yearly graph, there's nothing to configure, and the time period cannot be set to a custom time — we only have the predefined periods available here, and we cannot customize SLA graph size or other parameters. For the yearly graph, we can only see the current year.

> There is no way to restrict access to IT service monitoring and reports — they are available for all users and normal permissions are not taken into account here.

Specifying uptime and downtime

With SLA monitoring configured, we can happily proceed with making sure our systems run smoothly; we do some maintenance during a properly-scheduled maintenance period, only to discover that our SLA level has dropped. Was sure downtime during maintenance periods would not be counted against the SLA monitoring? Wrong. Zabbix host and host group-level maintenance does not affect SLA monitoring. If something is down during such a maintenance, Zabbix still considers that as an unacceptable unavailability of the service.

> Host and host group-level maintenance was discussed in *Chapter 5, Managing Hosts, Users, and Permissions.*

There is a way to avoid calculating SLA data for a specific period, though. Let's go to **Configuration | IT services** and click on **Code repository**. In the service properties, switch to the **Time** tab. Here we may add three types of time periods:

* **Uptime**
* **Downtime**
* **One-time downtime**

Let's start with the simplest one—the **One-time downtime**. When adding a time period like that, we may enter a short description in the **Note** field, and we choose **From-Till** dates and times:

Period type	One-time downtime ▾
Note	short description
From	2016 - 05 - 16 00 : 00
Till	2016 - 05 - 17 00 : 00
Add	

The note is not used for much, though—it is only displayed in the list of configured times, as shown in the preceding screenshot.

The **Downtime** option allows us to define times that will be excluded from the SLA calculation:

Period type	Downtime ▾
From	Sunday ▾ Time hh : mm
Till	Sunday ▾ Time hh : mm
Add	

This is done on a weekly basis, where we may choose the weekday and time with minute precision. Unfortunately, here is the only place in Zabbix where a week sort of starts with **Sunday**. The biggest issue is that these periods cannot cross the week border, thus it is actually impossible to add SLA calculation downtime for the weekend in one go—we would have to add one entry for **Saturday** and one for **Sunday**.

But what about the **Uptime** option? That one works in the reverse way. If an uptime entry is added, SLA calculation only happens during that time period; all other time is considered to be "downtime".

Of course, when adding time periods here, one should obey the clauses from the actual agreement, not use this to hide problems from the SLA calculation, right?

Summary

In this chapter, we departed a bit from the low-level monitoring of CPU, disks, and memory. We discussed a higher level of monitoring, one that looked at business services, called "**IT services**" in Zabbix. We were able to configure a service tree to represent real life dependencies and structure, link individual entries against triggers to propagate problem states to services, and configure SLA calculation for those services. We did not have a large IT system to test against, so we sent in fake data and observed the resulting reports, including a service availability report and yearly SLA graph.

We noted two important facts about IT service functionality in Zabbix:

- Triggers with severity of "**Not classified**" or "**Information**" are ignored when calculating the SLA
- SLA information cannot be calculated at a later time — the IT services must be configured in advance

For those cases when a service does not have full-time SLA coverage, we learned about a way to specify when the SLA calculation should take place based on weekly time periods — but we also noted that host and host group-level maintenance does not affect the SLA calculation and the uptime/downtime configuration has to be done for the IT services themselves.

In the next chapter, we'll go back to lower-level monitoring — even lower than before. We will cover monitoring hardware directly using the **Intelligent Platform Management Interface (IPMI)**. Zabbix supports monitoring both "normal" or analog IPMI sensors and discrete IPMI sensors. There is even a special trigger function for discrete sensors. What is it? See the next chapter for details.

Monitoring IPMI Devices 16

By now, we are familiar with monitoring using Zabbix agents, SNMP, and several other methods. While SNMP is very popular and available on the majority of network-attached devices, there's another protocol that is aimed at system management and monitoring: **Intelligent Platform Management Interface (IPMI)**. IPMI is usually implemented as a separate management and monitoring module independent of the host operating system that can also provide information when the machine is powered down. IPMI is becoming more and more popular, and Zabbix has direct IPMI support. IPMI is especially popular on so-called **lights-out** or **out-of-band** management cards, available for most server hardware today. As such, it might be desirable to monitor hardware status directly from these cards, as that does not depend on the operating system type or even whether it's running at all.

Getting an IPMI device

For this section, you will need an IPMI-enabled device, usually a server with a remote management card. The examples here will use real hardware that could have vendor-specific quirks, but it should be possible to apply the general principles to any product from any vendor.

Preparing for IPMI monitoring

To gather data using IPMI, Zabbix must be configured accordingly, and the device must accept connections from Zabbix. If you installed Zabbix from packages, IPMI support should be available. If you compiled Zabbix Server from source, OpenIPMI library support should be included as well. To be sure, check the startup messages in the server log file. Make sure the line about IPMI says YES:

```
IPMI monitoring:          YES
```

That is not enough yet—by default, Zabbix Server is configured to not start any IPMI pollers; thus, any added IPMI items won't work. To change this, open `zabbix_server.conf` and look for the following line:

```
# StartIPMIPollers=0
```

Uncomment it and set the poller count to 3, so that it reads as this:

```
StartIPMIPollers=3
```

Save the file and restart `zabbix_server`.

On the monitored device side, add a user that Zabbix would use. The IPMI standard specifies various privilege levels, and for monitoring, the user level might be the most appropriate. The configuration of IPMI users could be done using the vendor-supplied command line tools, web interface, or some other method. Consult the vendor-specific documentation for the details on this step.

Setting up IPMI items

Before we can add IPMI items to Zabbix, we should test IPMI access. By default, IPMI uses UDP port 623, so make sure it is not blocked by a firewall. Check whether your Zabbix server has the `ipmitool` package installed—if not, install it, and then execute the following:

```
$ ipmitool -U zabbix -H <IP address of the IPMI host> -I lanplus -L user
sdr
Password:
```

Provide the password that you have set in the IPMI configuration. We are using user-level access, as specified by the `-L user` flag, so that administrative privileges should not be required for the Zabbix IPMI user. The `-I lanplus` flag instructs `ipmitool` to use the IPMI v2.0 LAN interface, and the `sensor` command queries the host for the available sensors. If your device has IPMI running on a non-default port, you can specify the port with the `-p` flag.

> Zabbix does not use `ipmitool` to query IPMI devices; it uses the OpenIPMI library instead. This library historically has had a few bugs, and a working `ipmitool` instance does not guarantee that IPMI monitoring will work with Zabbix Server. When in doubt, test with the latest version of OpenIPMI.

The output will contain a bunch of sensors, possibly including some such as these:

```
BB +5.0V          | 4.97 Volts     | ok
Baseboard Temp    | 23 degrees C   | ok
System Fan 2      | 3267 RPM       | ok
Power Unit Stat   | 0x00           | ok
```

That looks like useful data, so let's try to monitor fan RPM in Zabbix. In the frontend, navigate to **Configuration | Hosts**. To keep things organized, let's create a new host for our IPMI monitoring—click on **Create host**. Then, enter the following values:

- **Name:** IPMI host

- **Groups**: Click on **Linux servers** in the **Other groups** box, then click on the ◄ button, and make sure no other groups are in the **In groups** listbox

- **IPMI interfaces**: Click on the **Add** control and enter the IPMI address, and then click on **Remove** next to **Agent interfaces**

> Some IPMI solutions work on the primary network interface, intercepting IPMI requests. In such a case, simply set the same IP address to be used for IPMI.

Switch to the **IPMI** tab, and enter the following values:

- **IPMI username**: Enter the username used for IPMI access

- **IPMI password**: Enter the password you have set for IPMI access

> If you have set a long IPMI password and revisit the host editing screen, you'll see it being trimmed. This is normal, as the maximum password length for IPMI v2.0 is 20 characters.

If you have a different configuration for IPMI, such as a different privilege level, port, or other parameters, set them appropriately. When done, click on the **Add** button at the bottom.

> For this host, we reused the **Linux servers** group—feel free to add it in a separate group.

Creating an IPMI item

Now that we have the host part of IPMI connectivity sorted out, it's time to create actual items. Make sure **Linux servers** is selected in the **Group** dropdown, then click on **Items** next to the **IPMI host**, and then click on **Create item**. Enter these values:

- **Name**: Enter System Fan 2 (or, if your IPMI-capable device does not provide such a sensor, choose another useful sensor)

- **Type**: **IPMI agent**

- **Key**: System_Fan_2

- **IPMI sensor**: System Fan 2

- **Units**: RPM

When done, click on the **Add** button at the bottom.

> For this item type, the item key is only used as an item identifier, and we could enter any string in there. We opted to use the sensor name with spaces replaced with underscores to make it easier to identify the item in trigger expressions and other places. The IPMI sensor name will determine what data will be collected.

On some devices, the sensor name could have a trailing space. This is not obvious from the default sensor output in ipmitool. If the sensor name seems correct but querying it from Zabbix fails, try to retrieve data for a single sensor from the Zabbix server:

```
$ ipmitool -U zabbix -H <IP address of the IPMI host> -I lanplus -L user
sensor get "System Fan 2"
```

This will print detailed information for that sensor. If it fails, the sensor name is probably incorrect.

Let's check out the results of our work; open **Monitoring | Latest data**, and then select **IPMI host** in the filter:

NAME ▲	LAST CHECK	LAST VALUE
- other - (1 Item)		
System Fan 2	2016-05-18 12:26:49	3348 RPM

> Notice how the value is displayed fully and is not shortened to 3.3K. The RPM unit is included in a hardcoded unit blacklist, and items that use such units do not get the unit multiplier prefix added. We will discuss the unit blacklist in more detail in *Chapter 22, Zabbix Maintenance*.

Great, the hardware state information is being gathered correctly. What's even better, this information is retrieved independently of the installed operating system or specific agents and is retrieved even if there is no operating system running or even installed.

> There is no built-in low-level discovery support at this time. If you would like to discover available sensors, it might be best done with an external check or Zabbix trapper item type for the low-level discovery rule itself.

Monitoring discrete sensors

The sensor list shows some sensors where the value is quite clear: temperatures, fan RPMs, and so on. Some of these can be a bit more tricky, though. For example, your sensor listing could have a sensor called Power Unit Stat or similar. These are discrete sensors. One might hopefully think that they could return 0 for an **OK** state and 1 for **Failure**, but they're usually more complicated. For example, the power unit sensor can actually return information about eight different states in one retrieved value. Let's try to monitor it and see what value we can get in Zabbix for such a system. Navigate to **Configuration | Hosts**, click on **Items** next to **IPMI host**, and click on **Create item**. Fill in the following:

- **Name**: Enter Power Unit Stat (or, if your IPMI-capable device does not provide such a sensor, choose another useful sensor)
- **Type: IPMI agent**
- **Key**: Power_Unit_Stat
- **IPMI sensor**: Power Unit Stat

When done, click on the **Add** button at the bottom.

> If normal sensors work but discrete ones do not, make sure you try with the latest version of the OpenIPMI library — older versions add an extra .0 to discrete sensor names.

Check this item in the **Latest data** section—it likely returns 0. But what could it return? It is actually a decimal representation of a binary value, where each bit could identify a specific state, most often a failure. For this sensor, the possible states are listed in *Intelligent Platform Management Interface Specification Second Generation v2.0.*

> The latest version of this specification can be reached at http://www.intel.com/content/www/us/en/servers/ipmi/ipmi-home.html.

According to it, the individual hex values have the following meaning:

00h	Power Off/Power Down
01h	Power Cycle
02h	240 VA Power Down
03h	Interlock Power Down
04h	AC lost/Power input lost (the power source for the power unit was lost)
05h	Soft Power Control Failure (the unit did not respond to a request to turn on)
06h	Power Unit Failure detected
07h	Predictive Failure

Looking at the description of the first bit, a binary value of 0 means that the unit is running and reports no problems. A binary value of 1 means that the unit is powered down. We could compare the returned value to 0, and that would indicate that everything is fine with the unit, but what if we would like to check some other bit—for example, the "**Predictive failure**" one? If only that bit were set, the item would return 128. As mentioned before, discrete items return a decimal representation of the binary value. The original binary value is 10000000 (or 07h in the previous table), where the eighth bit, counting from the least significant, is set. By the way, this is also the reason why we left the **Type of information** field as **Numeric (unsigned)** and **Data type** as **Decimal** for this item—although the actual meaning is encoded in a binary representation, the value is transmitted as a decimal integer.

Thus, to check for a predictive failure, we could compare the value to 128, couldn't we? No, not really. If the system is down and reports a predictive value, the original binary value would be 10000001, and the decimal value would be 129. It gets even messier when we start to include other bits in there. This is also the reason it is not possible to use value mapping for such items at this time—in some cases, a value could mean all bits are set, and there would have to be a value-mapping entry for every possible bit combination. Oh, and we cannot detect a system being down just by checking for the value to be 1—a value of 129 and a whole bunch of other values would also mean that.

If we can't compare the last value in a simple way, can we reasonably check such discrete sensor values at all? Luckily, yes; Zabbix provides a bitwise trigger function called `band()`, which was originally implemented specifically for discrete IPMI sensor monitoring.

Using the bitwise trigger function

The special function `band()` is somewhat similar to the simple function `last()`, but instead of just returning the last value, it applies a bitmask with bitwise AND to the value and returns the result of this operation. If we wanted to check for the least significant bit, the one that lets us know whether the unit is powered on, we would use a bitmask of 1. Assuming some other bits have been set, we could receive a value of 170 from the monitored system. In binary, that would be 10101010. Bitwise AND would multiply each bit down:

	Decimal value	Binary value
Value	170	10101010
Bitwise AND (multiplied down)		
Mask	1	00000001
Result	0	00000000

The general syntax for the `band()` trigger function is as follows:

```
band(#number|seconds,mask)
```

> It also supports a third parameter, `time shift` — we discussed time shifts in *Chapter 6, Detecting Problems with Triggers*.

While thinking about the binary representation, we have to use decimal numbers in Zabbix. In this case, it is simple — the trigger expression would be as follows:

```
{host:item.band(#1,1)}=1
```

We are checking the last value received with #1, applying a decimal mask of 1, and verifying whether the last bit is set.

As a more complicated example, let's say we wanted to check for bits (starting from the least significant) 3 and 5, and we received a value of 110 (in decimal):

	Decimal value	Binary value
Value	110	01101110
Bitwise AND (multiplied down)		
Mask	20	00010100
Result	4	00000100

A simple way to think about the operation of the mask would be that all the bits that match a 0 in the mask are set to 0, and all other bits pass through it as is. In this case, we are interested in whether both bits 3 and 5 are set, so the expression would be this:

```
{host:item.band(#1,20)}=20
```

In our value, only bit 3 was set, the resulting value from the function was 4, and that does not match 20 — both bits are not set, so the trigger expression evaluates to FALSE. If we wanted to check for bit number 3 being set and bit 5 being not, we would compare the result to 4. And if we wanted to check for bit number 3 not being set and bit 5 being set, we would compare it to 16 — because in binary, that is 00010000.

And now, let's get back to checking for the predictive failure bit being set — it was the eighth bit, so, our mask should be 10000000, and we should compare the result to 10000000. But both of these should be in decimal format, so we should set both the mask and comparison values to 128. Let's create a trigger in the frontend with this knowledge. Go to **Configuration | Hosts**, click on **Triggers** next to **IPMI host**, and click on **Create trigger**. Enter Power unit predictive failure on {HOST.NAME} in the **Name** field, and then click on **Add** next to the **Expression** field. Click on **Select** next to the **Item** field, and then choose **Power Unit Stat**. Set the **Function** dropdown to **Bitwise AND of last (most recent) T value and mask = N**, enter 128 in both the **Mask** and **N** fields, and then click on **Insert**. The resulting trigger expression should be this:

```
{IPMI host:Power_Unit_Stat.band(,128)}=128
```

Notice how the first function parameter is missing? As with the last() function, omitting this parameter is equal to setting it to #1, like in the earlier examples. This trigger expression will ignore the 7 least significant bits and check whether the result is set to 10000000 in binary, or 128 in decimal.

Bitwise comparison is possible with the count() function, too. Here, the syntax is potentially more confusing: both the pattern and mask are to be specified as the second parameter, separated with a slash. If the pattern and mask are equal, the mask can be omitted. Let's try to look at some examples to clear this up.

For example, to count how many values had the eighth bit set during the previous 10 minutes, the function part of the expression would be as follows:

```
count(10m,128,band)
```

Our pattern and mask were the same, so we could omit the mask part. The previous expression is equivalent to this:

```
count(10m,128/128,band)
```

If we would like to count how many values had bit 5 set and bit 3 not set during the previous 10 minutes, the function part of the expression would be this:

```
count(10,16/20,band)
```

Here, the pattern is 16 or 10000, and the mask is 20 or 10100.

Beware of adding too many IPMI items against a single system — it is very easy to overload the IPMI controller.

Summary

IPMI, while not yet as widespread as SNMP, can provide software-independent hardware monitoring for some devices, usually servers. It is becoming more and more popular as the out-of-band monitoring and management solution that should help us watch over hardware states for compliant devices.

Zabbix supports monitoring normal sensors such as voltage, RPM, or temperature, as well as discrete sensors that can pack a lot of information in to a single integer. To decrypt the information hidden in that integer, Zabbix offers a special trigger function called band(), which enables us to do bitwise masking and matching specific bits.

IPMI, covered in this chapter, is at a fairly low level in the system stack. In the next chapter, we will go notably higher: we will discuss ways to monitor Java applications using the JMX protocol. Zabbix supports JMX via a dedicated process called the Zabbix Java gateway, which we will set up.

17

Monitoring Java Applications

Among all the other features that Zabbix can query directly is monitoring Java application servers using the **Java Management Extensions (JMX)** protocol. Actually, it's not just application servers—other server software written in Java can be monitored as well. Even standalone Java applications can be monitored, as the JMX framework does not have to be implemented by application developers—it is provided with Java. The main Zabbix daemons are written in C, but the JMX protocol is somewhat complicated, especially all the authorization and encryption methods. Thus, a separate component is used for JMX monitoring: the Zabbix Java gateway. This gateway runs as a separate process and queries JMX interfaces on behalf of Zabbix Server. In this chapter, we will set up the Java gateway and monitor a simple property on it.

Setting up the Zabbix Java gateway

Let's start by getting the gateway up and running. If you installed from packages, there likely is a Java gateway package available—just install that one. If you installed from source, the Java gateway can be compiled and installed by running the following from the Zabbix source directory:

```
$ ./configure --enable-java && make install
```

> If the compilation fails because it is unable to find `javac`, you might be missing Java development packages. The package name could be similar to `java-1_7_0-openjdk-devel`. Consult your distribution's documentation for the exact package name.

By default, when compiling from source, the Zabbix Java gateway files are placed in the `/usr/local/sbin/zabbix_java` directory. From here on, we will use files found in that directory. If you installed from packages, consult the package configuration information to locate those files.

Let's try something simple: just starting up the gateway. Go to the Java gateway directory and run this:

```
# ./startup.sh
```

The Zabbix Java gateway comes with a convenient startup script, which we used here. If all went well, you should see no output, and a Java process should appear in the process list. Additionally, the gateway should listen on port 10052. While this port is not an officially registered port for the Zabbix Java gateway, it's just one port above the Zabbix trapper port, and there does not seem to be any other application using that port. With the gateway running, we still have to tell Zabbix Server where the gateway is to be found. Open zabbix_server.conf and look for the JavaGateway parameter. By default, it is not set, and we have to configure the gateway IP or hostname here. As we can point the server at a remote system, we are not required to run the Java gateway on the same system where Zabbix Server is located — in some cases, we might want to place the gateway closer to the Java application server, for example. Set this parameter to the localhost IP address:

```
JavaGateway=127.0.0.1
```

Right below is a parameter called JavaGatewayPort. By default, it is set to 10052 — the same unregistered port as our running gateway already listens on — so we won't change that. The next parameter is StartJavaPollers. The same as with IPMI pollers, no Java pollers are started by default. We won't hammer our Java gateway much, so enable a single Java poller:

```
StartJavaPollers=1
```

With this, Zabbix Server should be sufficiently configured. Restart it to apply the Java gateway configuration changes. Great, we have the gateway running, and Zabbix Server knows where it is. Now, we just need something to monitor. If you have a Java application server that you can use for testing, try monitoring it. If not, or for something more simple to start with, you could monitor the gateway itself. It is a Java application, and thus, the JMX infrastructure is available. There's one thing we should change before enabling JMX for the gateway. Java is quite picky about DNS and name resolution in general. If JMX functionality is enabled and the local system hostname does not resolve, Java applications are likely to fail to start up. For a local Java gateway, check the /etc/hosts file. If there is no entry for the current hostname, add a line like this:

```
127.0.0.1 testhost
```

We're ready to enable JMX functionality for the gateway now; it is not enabled by default. To enable JMX on the Zabbix Java gateway, edit the `startup.sh` script we used earlier, and look for this line:

```
# uncomment to enable remote monitoring of the standard JMX objects on
the Zabbix Java Gateway itself
```

As the first line says, uncomment the two lines following it.

> A single variable is assigned across two lines there.

One parameter in there is worth paying extra attention to:

```
-Dcom.sun.management.jmxremote.port=12345
```

This sets the JMX port—the one that the gateway itself will query. Yes, in this case, we will start a process that will connect to itself on that port to query JMX data. The port is definitely not a standard one—as you might guess, it's just a sequence of 1-2-3-4-5. Other Java applications will most likely use a different port, which you will have to find out.

If you installed from packages, a recent package should include the same lines in the init script. If not, consider reporting that to the package maintainers, and use the following parameters in addition to the `port` parameter, listed in the previous code:

```
-Dcom.sun.management.jmxremote
-Dcom.sun.management.jmxremote.authenticate=false
-Dcom.sun.management.jmxremote.ssl=false
```

The first parameter tells Java to enable JMX, and the last two parameters instruct Java not use any authentication or encryption.

> At the time of writing this book, JMX functionality in the Zabbix gateway does not work with Java 1.9. The solution is to downgrade to Java 1.8.

With this change done, run the shutdown and startup scripts:

```
# ./shutdown.sh
```

```
# ./startup.sh
```

We are finally ready for adding actual hosts and JMX items.

> Currently, Zabbix only supports a hardcoded **Remote Method Invocation** (**RMI**) endpoint for JMX monitoring. Java application servers that use other protocols are not supported — that includes JBoss 6 and later. Do not use RMI parameters to enable JMX on JBoss — they can prevent JBoss from starting.

Monitoring JMX items

Let's create a separate host for JMX monitoring. Navigate to **Configuration | Hosts**, and click on **Create host**. Enter Zabbix Java gateway in the **Host name** field, clear everything in the **In groups** listbox, and enter Java in the **New group** field. We will need JMX items on this host: remove the default agent interface and click on **Add** next to **JMX interfaces**. In our case, the gateway is running on the local host, so we can leave the IP address at the default, 127.0.0.1. But what about the port? We had the Java gateway listen on 10052, but then there was also that 12345 port in the startup.sh script. If a confusion arises, we should think about which functionality is available on each of these ports. On port 10052, we had the gateway itself, which was the port Zabbix server connects to. We already saw this port set in the server configuration file. Normally, the gateway would then connect to some other Java application to query JMX information.

JMX interfaces	127.0.0.1		IP	DNS	12345	⦿ Remove
	Add					

The 12345 port was in the lines we uncommented in the gateway's startup. sh script, and that was the JMX interface for the gateway. That was also what we wanted to monitor: our Java application. After Zabbix server connects to the Java gateway on port **10052**, we expect the gateway to connect to itself, on port **12345**:

Thus, in the host interface, we would want to use port 12345 — and surprise surprise, that is also the default:

JMX interfaces							
	127.0.0.1			IP	DNS	12345	Remove
	Add						

> The JMX system can actually return a different IP address and port that the JMX querying client should connect to. Zabbix uses Java functionality that automatically obeys this information, but in some cases, it can be wrong. If you see error messages and the Zabbix Java gateway seems to connect to a different address or port than the one configured in the host properties, check the configuration of the target Java application, specifically the Djava.rmi.server.hostname and Dcom.sun.management.jmxremote.rmi.port parameters.

The rest of the host configuration should be sufficient for our needs — click on the **Add** button at the bottom. Now, make sure **Java** is selected in the **Group** dropdown, click on **Items** next to **Zabbix Java gateway**, and click on **Create item**. Enter the following data:

- **Name:** Used heap memory
- **Type:** JMX agent
- **Key:** jmx[java.lang:type=Memory,HeapMemoryUsage.used]
- **Units:** B

When done, click on the **Add** button at the bottom. Check this item in the latest data section after a few minutes — it should be collecting values successfully.

Querying JMX items manually

Creating items on the server and then waiting for them to be updated through the gateway can be quite cumbersome if we don't know the exact parameters beforehand. We could query the gateway manually using netcat and similar tools, but that's not that easy either. There is an easier method with zabbix_get, courtesy of the Zabbix community member Bunjiboys. The following simple script acts as a wrapper:

```
#!/bin/bash
ZBXGET="/usr/bin/zabbix_get"
# accepts positional parameters:
# 1 - JAVA_GW_HOST
# 2 - JAVA_GW_PORT
# 3 - JMX_SERVER
```

```
# 4 - JMX_PORT
# 5 - ITEM_KEY
# 6 - USERNAME
# 7 - PASSWORD
QUERY="{\"request\": \"java gateway jmx\",\"conn\": \"$3\",\"port\":
$4,\"username\": \"$6\",\"password\": \"$7\", \"keys\": [\"$5\"]}"
$ZBXGET -s $1 -p $2 -k "$QUERY"
```

If you save this as `zabbix_get_jmx` and make it executable, querying an item key through the gateway can be done like this:

```
$ ./zabbix_get_jmx localhost 10052 java-application-server.local.net 9999
'jmx[\"java.lang:type=Threading\",\"PeakThreadCount\"]'
```

In this example, the JMX instance is listening on port `9999`. Notice the escaping of double quotes in the item key. The result will be raw JSON from the Zabbix Java gateway protocol:

```
{"response":"success","data":[{"value":"745"}]}
```

When Zabbix server queries the gateway, it will parse the numeric value out of that JSON — `745` in this case.

> This example script doesn't do any error checking — check out
> `https://www.zabbix.org/wiki/Docs/howto/zabbix_`
> `get_jmx` for any potential future improvements.

What to monitor?

With a Java application server, monitoring is not initiated by the actual Java application developers often enough, and it is quite often that it's not clear what would be a good set of things to monitor first. In general, the same advice applies as with any other system — somebody who knows the monitored application should determine what is monitored. It's even better if the available Java developers are reasonable and actually implement additional JMX items to monitor application-specific logic. If that is not easy to achieve, one can always start with a basic set of memory usage, thread count, garbage collector, and other generic metrics. A few potentially useful parameters are as follows:

- `jmx["java.lang:type=ClassLoading","LoadedClassCount"]`: How many classes have been loaded

- `jmx["java.lang:type=Memory",NonHeapMemoryUsage.used]`: We already monitored the heap memory usage on the gateway; this will monitor the non-heap memory usage

In general, it's fairly hard to suggest a static list of things to monitor for JMX—there are several garbage collectors, and exact keys for garbage collection monitoring will differ depending on which one is in use. Zabbix also provides a couple of templates out of the box for generic and Tomcat-specific JMX monitoring, which could be a good start.

What if we would like to use multiple Java gateways—maybe one at each datacenter, or even one on each Java application server so that JMX connections do not happen over the network? Zabbix server only supports a single Zabbix gateway. Attaching multiple Java gateways to a single server is actually possible using Zabbix proxies, but we will discuss that in *Chapter 19, Using Proxies to Monitor Remote Locations*.

Summary

Java is sometimes called the "king of the enterprise." It is so incredibly popular in large systems despite often-cited drawbacks such as memory usage that one might wonder what makes it so attractive. One reason could be that it lowers maintenance costs—at least that is claimed sometimes, and it would make a lot of sense in large, long-living systems. Developing a system is usually cheap compared to maintaining it over a long period of time. Given the widespread usage of Java-based systems, the built-in JMX support is very handy—except maybe the limiting endpoint support. In this chapter, we looked at setting up a separate daemon called the Zabbix Java gateway and performing the initial configuration to make it work with a Zabbix server. We also monitored heap memory usage on the gateway itself, and that should be a good start for JMX monitoring. For easier debugging, we used a simple wrapper around `zabbix_get` to query JMX through the gateway manually.

Lately, we have been discussing the monitoring of somewhat niche products and protocols. The next chapter will continue that trend—we will discuss the built-in VMware monitoring that enables us to discover and monitor all the virtual machines from a hypervisor or a vCenter.

18
Monitoring VMware

There are a lot of virtualization solutions available today. Their target markets and popularity differ, but for enterprise shops that can afford it, VMware solutions are quite widespread. Zabbix offers built-in support for monitoring VMware. This support includes:

- Monitoring vSphere and/or vCenter
- Automatically discovering all hypervisors
- Automatically discovering all virtual machines

Monitoring VMware does not involve any custom layers — Zabbix accesses the VMware API directly, and the monitoring of such an environment is very easy to set up. For this chapter, you will need access to a VMware instance API, including a username and password. It might be a good idea to try this on a smaller or non-production environment first.

> If discovering a large environment from a vCenter, the vCenter API endpoint could get overloaded, as Zabbix would connect to it and request data for all the vSphere instances and virtual machines that have been discovered. It might make sense to split the monitoring over individual vSphere instances instead.

Preparing for VMware monitoring

To try out VMware support, we will need:

- The IP address or hostname on which we have access to the VMware API
- The username for an account with permissions to retrieve the information
- The password for that account

First, the server must be compiled with VMware support. If you have installed from packages, the support most likely is included. If you installed from source, check whether the Zabbix server log file lists VMware monitoring as enabled:

```
VMware monitoring: YES
```

When compiling from source, the following options are needed for VMware support:

* `--with-libcurl`
* `--with-libxml2`

As with several other features we have explored so far, the Zabbix server doesn't start any VMware-specific processes by default. Edit `zabbix_server.conf` and look for the `StartVMwareCollectors` parameter. Add a new line and tell Zabbix to start two VMware collectors:

```
StartVMwareCollectors=2
```

Restart the server. Why two collectors? Zabbix developers recommend the number of the collectors to be based on the number of monitored VMware instances. For the best performance, it is suggested to start more collectors than the monitored instance count, but less than double the monitored instance count. Or, if we put that in an equation, `instances < StartVMwareCollectors < ( instances * 2 )`. We start small and monitor a single instance for now, so we'll have `1 < StartVMwareCollectors < 2`. It is also recommended to always start at least two VMware collectors, so the choice is obvious here. If we had two VMware instances to monitor, it would be three collectors: `2 < StartVMwareCollectors < 4`.

> A VMware instance is a vSphere or vCenter instance, not an individual virtual machine. That is, the number of collectors depends on the endpoints Zabbix actually connects to for data collection.

We will start by unleashing Zabbix at the VMware API and allowing it to automatically discover everything using the templates that are shipped with Zabbix. Once we see that it works as expected, we will discover how we can customize and expand this monitoring, as well as looking under the hood a bit at the mechanics of VMware monitoring.

Automatic discovery

We will create a separate host, which will be the starting point for the discovery. This host won't do anything else for us besides monitoring generic VMware parameters and discovering all other entities. Go to **Configuration | Hosts** and click on **Create host**. Enter VMware in the **Host name** field, clear out existing groups in the **In groups** block, and enter VMware in the **New group** field. Switch to the **Macros** tab, and fill in values for these three macros:

- {$URL}: The VMware API/SDK URL in the form https://server/sdk
- {$USERNAME}: The VMware account username
- {$PASSWORD}: The VMware account password

> The API or SDK is available on vSphere or vCenter systems.

Now, switch to the **Templates** tab, start typing vmware, choose **Template Virt VMware**, and click on the **Add** control in the **Link new templates** section. When done, click on the **Add** button at the bottom.

What's next? Well, nothing. If everything has been done right, everything should be monitored automatically. Hypervisors should be discovered and monitored, and virtual machines discovered and placed in groups based on hypervisors and monitored as well. It might not happen immediately, though. Like other LLD rules in default templates, VMware discovery also has a 1-hour interval—wait, LLD rules? Yes, VMware discovery also uses LLD functionality. We discussed it in detail in *Chapter 12, Automating Configuration*. VMware support takes it a step further, though: besides item, trigger, and graph prototypes, it also uses host prototypes. We will cover host prototypes a bit later. For now, we can either leave the discovery to happen, or we can go to **Configuration | Templates**, click on **Discovery** next to **Template Virt VMware**, and reduce the update interval for all three discovery rules. Just make sure to set it it back later.

After waiting for a while—or after reducing the intervals—check **Configuration | Host groups**. You should see several new host groups, prefixed with **Discover VMware VMs**. Depending on how large the monitored VMware instance is, the new group count could be from two up to many. There will be a group called **Hypervisors** and a group for virtual machines per cluster. If there are clusters, there will also be a group for hypervisors per cluster.

> If there are no clusters configured, the group for virtual machines will just be called (vm).

Available metrics

With some groups and hosts automatically created, let's see what data they are collecting. Navigate to **Monitoring | Latest data** and select **Hypervisors** in the **Host groups** field. Then, click on **Filter**:

NAME ▲	LAST CHECK	LAST VALUE
CPU (5 Items)		
CPU cores	2015-11-02 10:49:58	4
CPU frequency	2015-11-02 10:49:56	2.53 GHz
CPU model	2015-11-02 10:49:57	Intel(R) Xeon(R) CPU
CPU threads	2015-11-02 10:49:59	8
CPU usage	2015-11-02 10:59:51	61 MHz
Datastore (2 Items)		
Average read latency of the datastore datastore1	2015-11-02 10:59:44	0
Average write latency of the datastore datastore1	2015-11-02 10:59:45	0

There will be more items for each hypervisor. Some of them might not have data yet, but a bit of patience should reveal all the details.

> Datastore items might appear later — they are discovered by the datastore discovery LLD rule in **Template Virt VMware Hypervisor** with a default interval of 1 hour.

Now, filter for a hypervisor virtual machine group in the **Host groups** field, or by a single discovered virtual machine in the **Hosts** field:

NAME ▲	LAST CHECK	LAST VALUE
CPU (2 Items)		
CPU usage	2015-11-02 11:17:14	10 MHz
Number of virtual CPUs	2015-11-02 11:17:13	1
Disks (4 Items)		
Average number of kilobytes read from the disk Hard disk 1	2015-11-02 11:16:50	0 Bps
Average number of kilobytes written to the disk Hard disk 1	2015-11-02 11:16:52	1 KBps
Average number of reads from the disk Hard disk 1	2015-11-02 11:16:51	0
Average number of writes to the disk Hard disk 1	2015-11-02 11:16:53	0
Filesystems (4 Items)		
Free disk space on /	2015-11-02 11:16:54	2.64 GB
Free disk space on / (percentage)	2015-11-02 11:16:55	68.03 %
Total disk space on /		
Used disk space on /	2015-11-02 11:16:57	1.24 GB

Again, there should be more items, and some could still be missing values. They all should eventually get populated, though.

> Disks, filesystems, and interface items might appear later — they are discovered by the **disk device discovery**, **mounted filesystem discovery**, and **network device discovery** LLD rules in the **Template Virt VMware Guest** template, with a default interval of 1 hour.

Once all the LLD rules on the host level have run, we'll see quite a lot of items being covered by the default templates. In many cases, these templates might even be enough. Sometimes, you might want to extend them, though. The same as with other default templates, it is strongly suggested you clone the template first and then make the modifications to the new template.

But what other things could be supported besides the already included items? To see the full list of supported VMware item keys, visit the item type section in the Zabbix manual. VMware items are listed below simple checks, and at the time of writing this, the full URL is `https://www.zabbix.com/documentation/3.0/manual/config/items/itemtypes/simple_checks/vmware_keys`. Why below simple checks? That is the item type for all VMware keys. When adding new items, the type must be set to simple check. The same as other simple checks, these items are processed by the Zabbix server directly.

> Currently, discovered VMware hosts cannot have other templates linked in, or other item types added. It is not possible to merge VMware monitoring and other monitoring — such as a Zabbix agent — on the same host. If both virtualization and OS-level statistics are to be monitored, separate hosts must be used for that.

The underlying operation

While automatic discovery and monitoring works great, it is useful to understand how exactly it works, both to be able to extend it and to solve problems as they arise. We'll look at two areas in more detail:

- LLD configuration in the default templates and host prototypes
- Server operation and configuration details

VMware LLD configuration

Let's dissect the default templates and how they operate. We only linked a single template, and it ended up discovering all hypervisors and virtual machines — it's time to find out how that happened. The top-level template, **Template Virt VMware**, also does some direct monitoring, although not much — it has items for VMware **Event log**, **Full name**, and **Version**:

NAME ▲	TRIGGERS	KEY
Event log		vmware.eventlog[{$URL}]
Full name		vmware.fullname[{$URL}]
Version		vmware.version[{$URL}]

These would be collected on the vCenter or vSphere level. It all grows more interesting and complicated when we look at the LLD rules on this template. It discovers VMware clusters, hypervisors, and individual virtual machines. Admittedly, cluster discovery isn't that complicated — it only has a single item prototype to monitor cluster status. Hypervisor discovery uses an LLD feature we haven't looked at yet — **host prototypes**.

Host prototypes

If we go to **Configuration | Templates** and click on **Discovery** next to **Template Virt VMware**, we'll see that there is a single host prototype in the **Discover VMware hypervisors** LLD rule. Click on **Host prototypes**, and then click on **{#HV.NAME}** in the **NAME** column:

Host name	{#HV.UUID}
Visible name	{#HV.NAME}

Here, LLD macros are used again. We looked at their use in item and trigger prototypes, but here, they are used for the **Host name** and **Visible name** in the host prototype. The interesting part is the usage of different macros in these fields. **Host name**, the one used to identify the host, is not the hypervisor name, but its UUID. The human-friendly name goes in the **Visible name** field. When a hypervisor is referenced, it must be done by the UUID, and it will also be referenced by that UUID in the server log messages.

The **Templates** tab does not hold many surprises — it instructs Zabbix to link any discovered hypervisors to **Template Virt VMware Hypervisor**. Let's switch to the **Groups** tab now:

Groups	Hypervisors ✕	Select
	type here to search	
Group prototypes	{#CLUSTER.NAME}	Remove
	Add	

This is a bit more interesting. Host prototypes can instruct created hosts to be placed in existing host groups, listed in the **Groups** field. Additionally, they can instruct new groups to be created based on **Group prototypes** and created hosts to be included in those groups. Group prototypes are similar to other prototypes — the resulting names must be unique, and that means we should use some LLD macro in the group name.

[💡 If there are no clusters configured, there will be no per-cluster groups created.]

The **Discover VMware VMs** LLD rule in this template is similar: it holds a single host prototype to be used for all discovered virtual machines. Just as with hypervisors, the UUID is used for the hostname, and that would also be the one appearing in the server log file:

Host name	{#VM.UUID}
Visible name	{#VM.NAME}

In the frontend, we may search both by the **Host name** and **Visible name**. If searching by the hostname — and this might be common as we will see it in log files — the visible name will be shown as usual, with the hostname displayed below it and made bold to indicate that it matched the search:

HOST

A test vitual machine
(ca2642f7-345c-40ee-b8f6-75341cc8c84c)

In the **Templates** tab, we can see that the created hosts will be linked to **Template Virt VMware Guest**. It's worth looking at the **Groups** tab for this host prototype. Besides adding all discovered virtual machines to an existing group, **Virtual machines**, two group prototypes are used here:

Groups	Virtual machines ✕	Select
	type here to search	
Group prototypes	{#HV.NAME}	Remove
	{#CLUSTER.NAME} (vm)	Remove
	Add	

As seen in the host-group page earlier, a group would be created per hypervisor and per cluster, holding all virtual machines on that hypervisor or in that cluster.

Summarizing default template interaction

We have looked at what the default set of VMware templates does, but it can be a bit confusing to understand how they interact and what configuration entity creates what. Let's try to summarize their interaction and purpose in a schematic. Here, hosts that receive the listed template are represented with a thick border, while various LLD rules with a thin border:

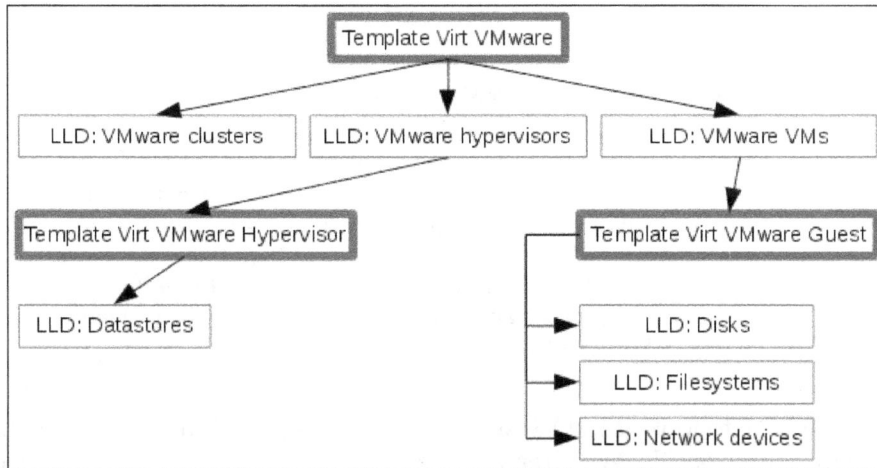

If a template has host prototypes, thus resulting in more hosts being created, it points to another thick-bordered host box, which in turn is linked to another template.

But remember that for this tree to start working, we only had to create a single host and link it to a single template, **Template Virt VMware**.

Server operation and configuration details

We know how Zabbix deals with information once that information has been received, but there is a whole process to get it. That process is interesting on its own, but there are also parameters to tune in addition to `StartVMwareCollectors`, which we discussed earlier. First, let's examine how the values end up in items. The following schematic shows data flow starting with VMware and ending with the Zabbix history cache:

Here, the steps happening inside the Zabbix server are grouped, and arrows indicate the data flow direction — connections are actually made from the VMware collectors to the VMware SDK interface. The collectors start by grabbing data and placing it in a special cache — caches are indicated with a dashed border here. Then pollers, the same processes that are responsible for passive Zabbix agents, SNMP, and other item types, grab some values from that cache and place them in the Zabbix history cache. For now, ignore the details in the history cache — we will discuss that more in *Chapter 22, Zabbix Maintenance*.

> **Why the intermediate VMware cache?**
>
> When VMware items are added, there are quite a lot of them, with various intervals. If Zabbix were to make a connection to VMware for every value, it would be a performance disaster. Instead, VMware collectors grab everything from the VMware SDK interface, place that in the cache, and then the pollers pick the required values from that cache. This way, a lot of items can get their values grabbed from the VMware cache instead of having to bother VMware every single time.

Now is a good time to look at the VMware-related configuration parameters in the server configuration file. We already covered StartVMwareCollectors, the processes that connected to the VMware interface and placed information in a special VMware cache. This cache by default is set to 8 MB, and this size can be controlled with the VMwareCacheSize parameter. How would one know when that should be changed? The best way is to monitor the usage and adjust accordingly. We will discuss the monitoring of internal caches in *Chapter 22, Zabbix Maintenance*.

Sometimes, connections to the VMware interface could get stuck. It could either be a single slow instance that slows down the monitoring of other instances, or it could be a single request going bad. In any case, connections to VMware instances will time out after 10 seconds by default. This time can be controlled with the VMwareTimeout parameter.

We just have two VMware-specific parameters left: VMwareFrequency and VMwarePerfFrequency. Zabbix queries some of the information using the VMware internal performance counters. At the time of writing this, the following item keys on the hypervisor level are extracted from the performance counters:

- vmware.hv.network.in
- vmware.hv.network.out
- vmware.hv.datastore.read
- vmware.hv.datastore.write
- vmware.hv.perfcounter

On the virtual machine level, the following keys are extracted from the performance counters:

- vmware.vm.cpu.ready
- vmware.vm.net.if.in
- vmware.vm.net.if.out
- vmware.vm.perfcounter
- vmware.vm.vfs.dev.read
- vmware.vm.vfs.dev.write

What does this actually mean? The item keys, listed previously, get new information as often as VMwarePerfFrequency is set to. To put it differently, it does not make sense to set the frequency of any items listed here lower than VMwarePerfFrequency. All other items, including low-level discoveries, get their information as often as VMwareFrequency is set to, and it does not make sense to set the frequency of other items and LLD rules lower than VMwareFrequency.

We could also say that both of these parameters should be set to match the lowest frequency for their corresponding items, but we have to be careful—setting these too low could overload VMware instances. By default, both of these parameters are set to 60 seconds. This is fine for small and average environments, but on a large VMware instance, we might want to increase them both, while potentially increasing VMwareTimeout as well.

Summary

To monitor VMware, just a single template is all we need. Well, that's not entirely true; the other two templates for hypervisors and virtual machines must be present, too, but besides that, Zabbix can automatically discover all hypervisors and virtual machines, just like we did in the beginning of this chapter.

We looked in detail at the default templates—how they work and interact and what each provides. The main template discovered everything and then created hosts and linked in hypervisor and virtual machine templates as needed.

In the end, we looked at lower-level details, including how data is passed through the VMware cache, how often that happens, and how we can tune all of that.

In the next chapter, we will discuss a new Zabbix process: Zabbix proxy. Zabbix proxies are remote data collectors that are really great. Similar to agents, they can operate in passive or active mode, and they support almost everything Zabbix server supports, including monitoring Zabbix agents, SNMP devices, VMware, and much more. We'll set up both active and passive proxies and discuss the best way to handle a proxy becoming unavailable.

19

Using Proxies to Monitor Remote Locations

The Zabbix server can do monitoring using lots of different methods—it can communicate with Zabbix agents, SNMP devices, and IPMI devices; run commands; and a whole lot of other things. A problem arises when the number of devices to be monitored increases—a single endpoint (our Zabbix server) is supposed to communicate with lots of others, and a large number of connections can cause problems both on the Zabbix server and in the network components between the Zabbix server and monitored devices.

It gets worse if we have to monitor remote environments—be it a branch office, another data center, or a customer site. Zabbix agents? Port 10050 must be open to all servers. SNMP? Port 161 must be open to all devices. It becomes unmanageable real quick.

A solution is to use Zabbix proxies. A Zabbix proxy is a remote data collector process that is capable of collecting data using all the methods the Zabbix server supports. In this chapter, we will set up a Zabbix proxy, use it for data gathering, and discuss the best methods to determine whether the proxy itself is available.

[Zabbix proxies are not available for Windows.]

Active proxy, passive proxy

The Zabbix proxy first appeared in Zabbix version 1.6, back in 2008. Since then, it has proven to be a very good solution. When the Zabbix proxy first appeared, it supported connecting to the Zabbix server only, similarly to active agent. Zabbix version 1.8.3 introduced a capability of the server to connect to the proxy, and now active proxies and passive proxies are available. While the Zabbix agent can communicate with the server in both ways at the same time by having active and passive items on the same host, the Zabbix proxy communicates with the server only in one way at a time – the whole proxy is designated active or passive.

The proxy mode does not change the direction of connections to or from the monitored devices. If using active items through a proxy, the agent will still be the one making the connections, and if using passive items, the agent will be accepting connections. It's just that instead of the server, the agent will now communicate with the proxy.

In both active and passive mode, server-proxy communication requires a single TCP port, to a single address only, to be open. That is much easier to handle on the firewall level than allowing connections to and from all of the monitored devices. There are more benefits a proxy may provide – but let's discuss those once we have a proxy running.

Setting up an active proxy

We'll start with an active proxy – one that connects to the Zabbix server.

> When setting up the proxy for this exercise, it is suggested to use a separate machine. If that is not possible, you can choose to run the proxy on the Zabbix server system.

If installing the proxy from packages, we will have to choose a database – Zabbix proxy uses its own database. If compiling the proxy from the sources, use the parameter `--enable-proxy` and the corresponding database parameter. Additionally, the proxy must have support compiled in for all features it should monitor, including SNMP, IPMI, web monitoring, and VMware support. See *Chapter 1, Getting Started with Zabbix*, for compilation options.

> If a proxy is compiled from the same source directory the server was compiled from, and the compilation fails, try running `make clean` first.

Which database to choose for the Zabbix proxy? If the proxy will be monitoring a small environment, SQLite might be a good choice. Using SQLite for the Zabbix server backend is not supported, as it is likely to have locking and performance issues. On a Zabbix proxy it should be much less of a problem. If setting up a large proxy, MySQL or PostgreSQL would be a better choice. During this chapter we will use the proxy with a SQLite database, as that is very easy to set up.

> If compiling from the sources, SQLite development headers will be needed. In most distributions, they will be provided in a package named `sqlite-devel` or similar.

Edit `zabbix_proxy.conf`. We will change three parameters:

* `DBName`
* `Hostname`
* `Server`

Change them to read:

```
DBName=/tmp/zabbix_proxy.db
Hostname=First proxy
Server=<Zabbix server IP address>
```

The first parameter, `DBName`, is the same as for the Zabbix server, except we do not just specify the database name here. For SQLite, the path to database file is specified here. While a relative path may be used, in most situations it will be much more complicated to start the proxy, thus an absolute path is highly suggested. We used a file in `/tmp` to make the setup of our first proxy simpler—no need to worry about filesystem permissions. What about the database username and password? As the comments in the configuration file indicate, they are both ignored when SQLite is used.

> On a production system, it is suggested to place the database file in a location other than `/tmp`. In some distributions `/tmp` might be cleared upon reboot. On the other hand, for performance reasons one might choose to place the database in a `tmpfs` volume, gaining some performance but losing the proxy database upon every system restart.

The second parameter, `Hostname`, will be used by the proxy to identify itself to the Zabbix server. The principle is the same as with the active agent—the value, specified here, must match the proxy name as configured on the server side (we will set that up in a moment), and it is case-sensitive.

The third parameter, `Server`, acts the same way as it did with active agents again. The active proxy connects to the Zabbix server and we specify the server IP address here.

> If you are running the proxy on the same machine as the Zabbix server, also change the port the proxy listens on — set `ListenPort=11051`. The default port would conflict with the Zabbix server.
>
> As with the Zabbix server, you must ensure that the appropriate pollers are configured to start. For example, if you want to monitor IPMI devices through a proxy, make sure to set the `StartIPMIPollers` parameter in the proxy configuration file to a value other than the default `0`.

Start the Zabbix proxy now. Wait, we did not create the database for the proxy. What will it do? Let's look at the proxy log file — check `/tmp/zabbix_proxy.log`, or the location set in the proxy configuration file. Paying close attention, we can find some interesting log records:

```
20988:20151120:064740.867 cannot open database file "/tmp/zabbix_
proxy.db": [2] No such file or directory
20988:20151120:064740.867 creating database ...
```

It first failed to open an existing database file, then proceeded to create the database. The Zabbix proxy can automatically create the required SQLite database and populate it. Note that this is true for SQLite only — if using any other database, we would have to create the database manually and insert `schema`. This is also possible for SQLite — using the `sqlite3` utility, we would do it like this:

```
$ sqlite3 /tmp/zabbix_proxy.db < schema.sql
```

But schema only! Not just for SQLite — for all databases — the proxy needs `schema` only. No data, and no image SQL files should be used. If the Zabbix proxy detects some extra data in the database, it exits, complaining that it cannot use the server database. Older proxy versions could crash or even corrupt the server database in such a case.

> Do not create an empty file. Either allow the proxy to create the database file, or create it yourself and populate it using the `sqlite3` utility. An empty file will be perceived as an empty database and the proxy will fail to start up.
>
> If a proxy complains that it cannot work with a server database, it will have found entries in the `users` table.

We could also verify that the Zabbix proxy is listening on the port it should be by running the following:

```
$ ss -ntl | grep 10051
```

The output should confirm that everything is correct:

```
LISTEN     0      128           *:10051            *:*
```

> If installing on the same machine, check for port `11051`, or whichever other port you chose.

There are probably a few log entries that indicate something is not working properly:

```
cannot send heartbeat message to server at "192.168.56.10": proxy
"First proxy" not found
cannot obtain configuration data from server at "192.168.56.10": proxy
"First proxy" not found
```

> Zabbix 3.0 introduced the IP address in these messages. If you struggled with figuring out which proxy is the issue in a larger environment before, it should not be a problem anymore.

We only configured and started the proxy daemon, but we did not configure anything about proxies on the server side. Let's monitor a host through our new proxy.

Monitoring a host through a proxy

Now that we have the proxy configured and running, we have to inform Zabbix about it somehow. To do this, open **Administration | Proxies** in the frontend, then click on the **Create proxy** button. Enter `First proxy` in the **Proxy name** field.

> The proxy name we enter here must match the one configured in the `zabbix_proxy.conf` file—and it's case-sensitive.

In the following section, **Hosts** allows us to specify which hosts will be monitored by this proxy. To make one host monitored by the proxy, select **Another host** in the **Other hosts** list box and click on the ◂ button:

Proxy name	First proxy

Proxy mode Active ▾

Hosts Proxy hosts   Other hosts

Another host		A test host
		discovered !
		IPMI host
	◂	IT services
		OpenStreetMap
	▸	Register me
		SNMP device
		snmptraps
		VMware
		Windows host

Description

[Add] [Cancel]

When done, click on **Add**. Next time the proxy connects to the server, the names should match and the proxy should get the information on what it is supposed to monitor. But when will that next time be? By default, the Zabbix proxy connects to the Zabbix server once per hour. The first connection attempt happens upon proxy startup, and at one-hour intervals from then on. If you configured the frontend part soon after the proxy was started, it could take up to an hour for the proxy to get the configuration data and start working. There are two ways to force re-reading of the configuration data from the Zabbix server:

- Restart the proxy
- Force reloading of its configuration cache

The first one would be acceptable on our test proxy, but it would not be that nice on a larger production proxy that is actively collecting data already. Let's see how we can force reloading of the configuration cache. First run:

```
# zabbix_proxy --help
```

In the output, pay attention to the runtime control section and the first parameter in it:

```
-R --runtime-control runtime-option    Perform administrative functions
  Runtime control options:
    config_cache_reload         Reload configuration cache
```

When an active proxy is told to reload its configuration cache, it connects to the server, gets the new configuration data, and then updates the local cache. Let's issue that command now:

```
# zabbix_proxy --runtime-control config_cache_reload
```

> Runtime commands depend on the PID file being properly configured. When you run the previous command, it looks for the `PidFile` option in the default proxy configuration file, looks up the PID from the PID file, and sends the signal to that process. If multiple active proxies are running on the system, a signal can be sent to a specific proxy by specifying its configuration file with the `-c` option.

The `reload` command should be processed successfully:

```
zabbix_proxy [19293]: command sent successfully
```

Check the proxy logfile now:

```
forced reloading of the configuration cache
received configuration data from server at "192.168.56.10", datalen
6545
```

First, the proxy logs that it has received an order to reload the configuration cache. Then it connects to the server and successfully retrieves the configuration data from the server.

> We will discuss reloading of the configuration cache in somewhat greater detail in *Appendix A, Troubleshooting*.

You can verify whether the proxy can successfully connect to the server by opening **Administration | Proxies** again. Look at the **LAST SEEN (AGE)** column for the new proxy. Instead of saying **never**, it should show some time period. If it does not, check that both the Zabbix server and proxy are running, and that you can open a connection from the proxy host to the Zabbix server, port `10051`.

But if you look at the **HOSTS** column, you'll see that it is empty now. What happened here? We clearly added **Another host** to be monitored by this proxy — why did it disappear? This could be a challenging task to figure out, and a situation like that could easily arise in a production environment, too. The reason for the host disappearing from the proxy configuration is `active-agent auto-registration`. We configured it in *Chapter 12, Automating Configuration*, and the agent has been sort of repeatedly auto-registering ever since. But why does that affect the host assignment to proxy? When an active agent connects and `auto-registration` is active, it matters where it connects to. Instead of creating a new host, the Zabbix server reassigns that host to the Zabbix server or some proxy, whichever received the agent connection. It considers that agent as having migrated from the server to some proxy or vice versa, or from one proxy to another. We assigned a host to our new proxy, the agent kept on connecting to the server, and the server reassigned that host back to be monitored directly by the server. How could we solve it? We have two options:

- Disable the active agent `auto-registration` action and reconfigure the host manually

- Configure the agent to connect to the proxy instead

Let's try the second, fancier approach. On **Another host**, edit `zabbix_agentd.conf` and change `ServerActive` to the proxy IP address, then restart the agent.

> If you installed the Zabbix proxy on the same system as the Zabbix server, make sure to specify the proxy port in this parameter, too.
>
> Do not set the proxy address in addition to the server address — in that case the agent will try to work with both the server and proxy in parallel. See *Chapter 3, Monitoring with Zabbix Agents and Basic Protocols* for more detail on pointing the agent at several servers or proxies.

Check the proxy list again. There should be **Another host** in the **HOSTS** column now, and it should not disappear anymore. Let's check data for this host in **Monitoring | Latest data**. Unfortunately, it looks like most items have stopped working. While we changed the active server parameter in the agent daemon configuration file and active agent items work now, there are more item categories that could have failed:

- Passive agent items do not work because the agent does not accept connections from the proxy

- ICMP items likely do not work as `fping` is either missing or does not have proper permissions

- While **Another host** does not have items of SNMP, IPMI, and other types, those could have started to fail because appropriate support was not compiled into the proxy, or respective pollers were not started
- If you configured the proxy on the Zabbix server system, passive items will work, as the IP address the agent gets the connections from will stay the same

Let's fix at least the passive agent items. Edit `zabbix_agentd.conf` on **Another host** and change the `Server` parameter. Either replace the IP address in there with the proxy address, or add the proxy address to it, then restart the agent. In a few minutes, most of the passive agent items should start receiving data again.

As for the ICMP items, refer to *Chapter 3, Monitoring with Zabbix Agents and Basic Protocols* for `fping` configuration. It's the same as on the server side; it's just that the changes have to be performed on the proxy system now.

In general, when a host is monitored by proxy, all connections to and from that host must and will be performed by the proxy. The agent must allow connections from the proxy for passive items and connect to the proxy for active items. Even the Zabbix sender must send data to the proxy for Zabbix trapper items, not the Zabbix server anymore.

With the host monitored by the proxy, let's check whether there is any indication of that in the frontend. Open **Configuration | Hosts**, make sure **Linux servers** is selected in the **Group** dropdown, and take a look at the **NAME** column. As can be seen, **Another host** is now prefixed by the proxy name and reads **First proxy:Another host**:

NAME ▲
First proxy: Another host
A test host
IPMI host

> When having multiple proxies, it is a common practice to name them by location name—for example, `proxy-London` or `Paris-proxy`.

But do we always have to go to **Administration | Proxies** whenever we want to have a host monitored by proxy? Click on **Another host** in the **NAME** column, and observe the available properties. There's a dropdown available, **Monitored by proxy**. Using this dropdown, we can easily assign a host to be monitored by the chosen proxy (remembering to change the server IP address in the agent daemon configuration file):

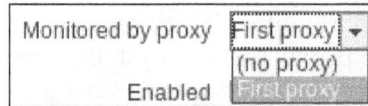

Monitored by proxy	First proxy ▾
	(no proxy)
Enabled	First proxy

> If you decide to monitor **A test host** through the proxy, be very careful with its address. If the address is left at 127.0.0.1, the proxy will connect to the local agent for passive items and then report that data to the server, claiming it came from **A test host**. That would also be not that easy to spot, as the data would come in just fine; only it would be wrong data.

Proxy benefits

With our first proxy configured, let's discuss in more detail its operation and the benefits it provides. Let's start with the main benefits:

- A proxy collects data when the server is not available
- A proxy reduces the number of connections to and from remote environments
- A proxy allows us to use incoming connections for polled items

We talked about the proxy retrieving configuration data from the server, and we talked about it having a local database. The Zabbix proxy always needs a local database, and this database holds information on the hosts the proxy is supposed to monitor. The same database also holds all the data the proxy has collected, and if the server cannot be reached, that data is not lost. For how long? By default, data is kept for one hour. This can be configured in the zabbix_proxy.conf file, the ProxyOfflineBuffer parameter. It can be set up to 30 days, but beware of running out of disk space, as well as of the potential to overload the Zabbix server when connectivity is back — we will discuss that risk in more detail later:

> There are more proxy-specific configuration parameters available; they are listed later in this chapter.

Fewer connections to remote environments can be very important, too. Monitoring using passive items means one connection for each value. With active items it's a bit better; multiple values will be sent in a single connection often. But the proxy pools up to 1000 values in a single connection. That is done even when they are of different types, such as agent, SNMP, IPMI, and SSH items. Fewer connections means healthier firewalls and other network devices, and much better performance from smaller total latency and less work for the Zabbix server to handle the incoming connections:

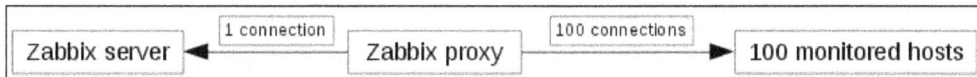

The third main benefit is the ability to receive incoming connections on the server side and still gather data by polling devices. For example, when monitoring a customer environment, the Zabbix server might have no access to the network devices. The Zabbix proxy could connect to them, collect data using SNMP, and then connect to the server to send the data. Also, keep in mind that only a single port for a single address would have to be opened in firewalls, as opposed to a lot of ports for all of the monitored devices when a proxy is not used:

There are a few more benefits Zabbix proxies provide:

- Single point of control for all proxies on the Zabbix server
- Ability to use multiple Java gateways

As proxies grab the configuration data from the Zabbix server, configuration of all proxies is done on a single system. This also allows us to ship out small, preconfigured devices that are plugged into a remote environment. As long as they get network connectivity and can connect to the Zabbix server, all configuration regarding what should be monitored can be changed at will from the Zabbix server.

As for Java gateways, we discussed them in *Chapter 17, Monitoring Java Applications*. Only a single Java gateway could be configured for the Zabbix server, but a gateway may also be configured for each proxy. With proxies being simple to set up, it's fairly easy to have lots of Java gateways working on behalf of a single Zabbix server. Additionally, the Java gateway only supports connections from the server to the gateway. Using an active proxy in front of the gateway allows JMX monitoring using incoming connections to the Zabbix server:

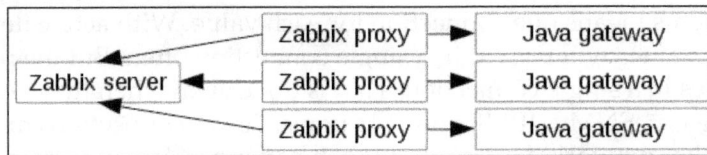

Proxy limitations

While proxies have many benefits, they do have some limitations, too. Well, pretty much one main limitation—they are only data collectors. If the server cannot be reached, the proxy cannot do independent notifications. They can't even generate events; all logic regarding triggers is processed on the server only. Remember, proxies do not process events, send out alerts, or execute remote commands. Remote commands, discussed in *Chapter 7, Acting upon Monitored Conditions*, are currently scheduled for Zabbix 3.2—but one would have to see that version released to be sure about such a feature being implemented.

Proxy operation

Let's talk about how proxies operate a bit. We'll cover three things here:

- Synchronization of the configuration
- Synchronization of the collected data
- Operation during maintenance

By default, proxies synchronize the configuration once per hour, and this period can be set in the `zabbix_proxy.conf` configuration file. Look for the parameter named `ConfigFrequency`, which by default will look like this:

ConfigFrequency=3600

This means that a Zabbix proxy can lag in configuration up to an hour, which might sound scary, but once a production installation settles, the configuration usually doesn't change that often. While testing, you might wish to decrease this period, but in a stable production setup it is actually suggested to increase this value.

> If you must have configuration changes pushed to a proxy immediately, force the configuration to be reloaded.

The collected data is sent to the server every second by default. That can be customized in the `zabbix_proxy.conf` file with the `DataSenderFrequency` parameter.

> The active proxy won't connect to the server every second if it has no values to send — a 1-second interval will be used only if it has data to send. On the other hand, if it has lots of values to send and cannot push them all in a single connection (which means 1000 values), the next connection will be performed as soon as possible without waiting that one second.

Regarding host and host group maintenance, when a host is in maintenance without data collection, data is still sent by proxy, but the server discards it. This way, changes in the maintenance status do not suffer from the default one-hour delay for configuration sync.

Proxies and availability monitoring

With all the benefits that a proxy brings, one would be tempted to use them a lot — and a good idea that would be, too. Proxies are really great. There's still the issue of monitoring availability for hosts behind proxies. If a proxy goes down or cannot communicate with the Zabbix server, we would be missing data for all the hosts behind that proxy. If we used the `nodata()` trigger function to detect unavailable hosts (we could call such triggers **availability triggers**), that could mean thousands of hosts declared unavailable. Not a desirable situation. There is no built-in dependency for hosts behind a proxy, but we can monitor proxy availability and set trigger dependencies for all hosts behind that proxy. But what should we set those dependencies to? Let's discuss the available ways to monitor proxy availability and their potential shortcomings.

Method 1 – Last access item

There was the last access column in **Administration | Proxies**. Of course, looking at it all the time is not feasible, thus it can also be added as an internal item. To create such an item, let's go to **Configuration | Hosts**, click on **Items** next to the host that runs your proxy, and click on **Create item**. Fill in the following values:

- **Name:** $2: last access
- **Type: Zabbix internal**
- **Key:** zabbix[proxy,First proxy,lastaccess]
- **Units:** unixtime

> This item can be created on any host, but it is common to create it either on the Zabbix proxy host, or on the Zabbix server host.

In the key here, the second parameter is the proxy name. Thus, if your proxy was named kermit, the key would become zabbix[proxy,kermit,lastaccess].

> If items like these are created on hosts that represent the proxy system and have the same name as the proxy, a template could use the {HOST.HOST} macro as the second parameter in this item key. We discussed templates in *Chapter 8, Simplifying Complex Configuration with Templates*.

When done, click on the **Add** button at the bottom. Notice how we used a special unit here—unixtime. Now what would it do? To find out, navigate to **Monitoring | Latest data**, expand the **Filter**, select the host you created the last item on and enter proxy in the **Name** field, then click on the **Filter** button. Look at the way data is presented here—we can see very nicely, in a human-readable form, when the proxy last contacted the Zabbix server:

NAME ▲	LAST CHECK	LAST VALUE
- other - (1 Item)		
First proxy: last access	2015-11-24 17:14:59	2015-11-20 17:27:53

So this item will be recording the time when the proxy last contacted the Zabbix server. That's great, but hardly enough to notice problems in an everyday routine—we already know quite well that a trigger is absolutely needed. Here, the already familiar `fuzzytime()` function comes to the rescue. Navigate to **Configuration | Hosts**, click on **Triggers** next to the host you created the proxy last access item on, then click on the **Create trigger** button.

Let's say we have a fairly loaded and critical proxy—we would like to know when three minutes have passed without the proxy reporting back. In such a case, a trigger expression like this could be used:

```
{host:zabbix[proxy,proxy name,lastaccess].fuzzytime(180)}=0
```

> One could consider using the delta **Store value** for the last access item, which would return 0 when the proxy was not communicating. The trigger for such an item is more obscure, thus `fuzzytime()` is the most common trigger function for this purpose.

As we might recall, the proxy connected to the server in two cases—it either synchronized the configuration, or sent the collected data. What if, for some reason, all occurrences of both of these events are further apart than three minutes? Luckily, the Zabbix proxy has a heartbeat process, which reports back to the server at regular intervals. Even better, this timing is configurable. Again, take a look at `zabbix_proxy.conf`, this time looking for the `HeartbeatFrequency` variable, which by default looks like this:

 # HeartbeatFrequency=60

Specified in seconds, this value means that every minute the proxy will report back to the server, even if there are no new values to send. The `lastaccess` item is quite a reliable way to figure out when a proxy is most likely down or at least inaccessible, even if it would not be sending data for a longer period of time.

For our trigger, fill in the following values:

- **Name:** `Proxy "First proxy" not connected for 3 minutes`
- **Expression:** `{Another host:zabbix[proxy,First proxy,lastaccess].fuzzytime(3m)}=0`
- **Severity: High**

> Replace the proxy name with the host name on which the proxy last access item was created. If the last access item used the `{HOST.HOST}` macro, use the same macro in the trigger name and expression, too.

We could have used 180 in place of 3m, but the time suffix version is a bit easier to read. Time suffixes were discussed in *Chapter 6, Detecting Problems with Triggers*. When done, click on the **Add** button at the bottom.

This combination of an item and a trigger will nicely alert us when the proxy will be unavailable. Now we just have to set up trigger dependencies for all availability triggers behind this proxy on this proxy last access trigger.

Unfortunately, there's a common problem situation. When proxy-server communication is interrupted, the proxy last access trigger fires and masks all other triggers because of the dependency. While the proxy is unable to connect to the server for some time, it still collects the values. Once the communication is restored, the proxy sends all the values to the server, *older values first*. The moment the first value is sent, the last access item is updated and the trigger resolves. Unfortunately, at this point the proxy is still sending values that were collected 5, 30, or 60 minutes ago. Any nodata() triggers that check a shorter period will fire. This makes the proxy trigger dependency work only until the proxy comes back, and results in a huge event storm when it does come back. How can we solve it? We could try to find out how many unsent values the proxy has, and if there are too many, ignore all the triggers behind the proxy—essentially, treating a proxy with a large value buffer the same as an unreachable proxy.

Method 2 – Internal proxy buffer item

We can turn to Zabbix internal items to figure out how large the proxy buffer is—that is, how many values it has to send to the Zabbix server. Let's go to **Configuration | Hosts**, click on **Items** next to **Another host**, and click on **Create item**. Fill in the following values:

- **Name**: First proxy: buffer size
- **Type**: **Zabbix internal**
- **Key**: zabbix[proxy_history]

> This item must be created on a host, monitored through the proxy for which the buffer size should be monitored. If assigned to a host and monitored by the Zabbix server, this item will become unsupported.

When done, click on the **Add** button at the bottom. With the default proxy configuration update interval of one hour, it might take quite some time before we can see the result of this item. To speed up configuration update, run the following on the proxy host:

```
# zabbix_proxy --runtime-control config_cache_reload
```

The proxy will request item configuration from the server and update its own cache. After a short while, we should be able to see the result in the latest data page:

NAME ▲	LAST CHECK	LAST VALUE
- other - (1 Item)		
First proxy: buffer size	2015-11-26 14:44:59	0

What is that value, though? It's quite simply the number of values that are still in the proxy buffer and must be sent to the server. This might allow us to create a trigger against this item. Whenever the buffer is bigger than a hundred, two hundred, or a thousand values, we would consider the proxy data not up-to-date and make all host triggers depend on the buffer size. Except that there's still a significant problem. Values for this item are kept in the same proxy buffer it monitors and are subject to the same sequential sending, older values being sent first. With this item, we would still suffer from the same problem as before—while the proxy was unavailable, the proxy buffer item would hold 0 or some other small value. As values start we to flow in, individual host triggers would fire, and only after some time would we see that the buffer was actually really large. It would be useful for some debugging later, but would not help with masking the hosts behind the proxy. Is there a solution then?

Method 3 – Custom proxy buffer item

A solution could be some method that would send us the proxy buffer size, bypassing the buffer itself. Zabbix does not offer such a method, thus we will have to implement it ourselves. Before we do that, let's figure out how we could obtain information on the buffer size. For that, we will delve into the proxy database.

> You might have to install the SQLite 3 package to get the `sqlite3` utility.

On the proxy host, run:

```
$ sqlite3 /tmp/zabbix_proxy.db
```

The proxy keeps all of the collected values in a single table, `proxy_history`. Let's grab the last three collected values:

```
sqlite> select * from proxy_history order by id desc limit 3;
1850|24659|1448547689|0||0|0|0|749846420|0|0|0|0
1849|23872|1448547664|0||0|0.000050|0|655990544|0|0|0|0
1848|24659|1448547659|0||0|0|0|744712272|0|0|0|0
```

We will discuss other fields in a bit more detail in *Chapter 21, Working Closely with Data*, but for now it is enough to know that the first field is a sequential ID. Still, how does the proxy know which values it has sent to the server already? Let's look at the IDs table:

```
sqlite> select * from ids where table_name='proxy_history';
proxy_history|history_lastid|1850
```

The `history_lastid` value here is the last ID that has been synchronized to the server. On a busy proxy, you might have to run these statements really quickly to see the real situation, as new values will be constantly added and sent to the server. We can get the current buffer (unsent values) size with this:

```
sqlite> select (select max(proxy_history.id) from proxy_history)-nextid
from ids where field_name='history_lastid';
```

It will calculate the difference between the biggest ID and the `history_lastid` value. On our proxy, this will likely return 0 all the time.

> Try stopping the Zabbix server and see how this value increases. Don't forget to start the Zabbix server again.

Now we should put this in an item. The most important thing is to make sure this item is processed directly by the server, without involving the Zabbix proxy. We have several options:

- Passive agent item
- Active agent item
- Zabbix trapper item that is populated by `zabbix_sender`

For a passive agent, the server should query it directly. For an active agent, it should point at the Zabbix server. For the trapper item, `zabbix_sender` should be used to connect to the Zabbix server. In all three cases, the host should be assigned to be monitored by the Zabbix server. If we are using internal monitoring to collect proxy values in a dedicated host, a separate host will be needed to collect the buffer data. This way, we will avoid these values getting stuck in the proxy buffer.

For the agent items, we could use a `UserParameter` like this:

```
UserParameter=proxy.buffer,sqlite3 /tmp/zabbix_proxy.db "select
(select max(proxy_history.id) from proxy_history)-nextid from ids
where field_name='history_lastid';"
```

> You might have to use the full path to the `sqlite3` binary.

As for the Zabbix trapper approach, it could be run from `crontab` or using any other method. The command would be similar to this:

```
zabbix_sender -z zabbix_server -s target_host -k item_key -o $(sqlite3
/tmp/zabbix_proxy.db "select (select max(proxy_history.id) from proxy_
history)-nextid from ids where field_name='history_lastid';")
```

Here we use the basic `zabbix_sender` syntax, but the value is obtained from the SQLite query. See *Chapter 11, Advanced Item Monitoring* for more information on `UserParameters` and `zabbix_sender`. The Zabbix trapper item would receive the same data as the internal buffer monitoring — the buffer size. The trigger would check for this buffer exceeding some threshold.

Note that all three methods are likely to result in some missing values for the buffer item — the values would not be available while the connection between server and proxy is down. The active agent item approach would suffer less as it has in-memory buffer, but it there might still be missing values. If it would be valuable to know how the buffer changed during the communication breakdown; this item could be used for the trigger and an internal item, as discussed earlier, for more complete buffer statistics.

Regarding triggers and dependencies, it is suggested to make the buffer trigger depend on the last access trigger. This way, hosts behind the proxy will be silenced if the proxy disappears completely, and when the proxy comes back with a large buffer, the buffer trigger will keep those hosts silent.

Setting up a passive proxy

So far, we configured and discussed only one way a proxy can work, an active proxy. A proxy may also be configured to accept incoming connections from the server, and similar to the agent; it is called a passive proxy in that case:

As opposed to the Zabbix agent, where this mode was set on the item level and a single agent could work in both active and passive mode, a Zabbix proxy can only work in one mode at a time.

Let's switch our active proxy to the passive mode. First, edit `zabbix_proxy.conf` and set the `ProxyMode` parameter to `1`. That's all that is required to switch the proxy to the passive mode—now restart the proxy process.

> As opposed to the passive agent, the `Server` parameter is currently ignored by the passive proxy.

In the frontend, navigate to **Administration | Proxies** and click on **First proxy** in the **NAME** column. Choose **Passive** in the **Proxy mode** dropdown, and notice how an **Interface** section appears. In there, set the IP address and port of your proxy:

Proxy name	First proxy				
Proxy mode	Passive ▼				
Interface	IP ADDRESS	DNS NAME		CONNECT TO	PORT
	192.168.56.11			IP DNS	10051

When done, click on **Update**. Now, when will the server send configuration information to the passive proxy? By default, the interval is one hour. Unfortunately, scheduling of configuration data sending is done the same way as the polling of passive items — it's distributed in time and could happen any time from now until one hour has passed. Well, let's try to force reloading of the configuration cache on the proxy:

```
# zabbix_proxy --runtime-control config_cache_reload
zabbix_proxy [3587]: command sent successfully
```

That seemed promising. Let's check the proxy logfile:

```
forced reloading of the configuration cache cannot be performed for a
passive proxy
```

Well, not that good. The configuration cache reloading command is ignored by passive proxies.

There is no way to force sending of that data from the server side either, currently. Restarting the server won't help — it could make things worse, if the sending was scheduled while the server was not running. What we could do in our small installation is reduce that interval. Edit zabbix_server.conf and look for the ProxyConfigFrequency option. Set it to 180, or some similarly small value, and restart the server. After a few minutes, check the server logfile:

```
    sending configuration data to proxy "First proxy" at "192.168.56.11",
    datalen 6363
```

Such a line indicates successful sending of the configuration data to the passive proxy. Note that ProxyConfigFrequency affects communication with all passive proxies; we cannot set this interval to a different value for different proxies.

When would one choose an active or passive proxy? In most cases, an active proxy would be preferred, as it can result in a smaller number of connections and we may force it to reload its configuration from the server. If the proxy cannot or should not connect to the server, a passive proxy could be used. A common situation when a passive proxy is used is when the Zabbix server is located in the internal network, and the proxy is monitoring a DMZ. We wouldn't want to have connections from the DMZ to the internal network, thus the choice of a passive proxy.

Tweaking the proxy configuration

While many configuration parameters for a proxy are the same as for the server (the pollers to start, port to listen on, and so on), and some are the same as for the agent daemon (hostname), there are some proxy-specific parameters. Knowing about these can be helpful when diagnosing a proxy-related problem, or when the proxy must be deployed in a specific environment. For an active proxy, the following parameters affect it:

Option	Description
ProxyLocalBuffer	Proxy will keep data in the local database for this many hours. By default, all data that is synchronized to the Zabbix server is removed. This could be useful if we would like to extract some data that is not stored permanently on the Zabbix server, such as network discovery values.
ProxyOfflineBuffer	Proxy will keep data for this many hours if the Zabbix server is unavailable. By default, data older than one hour is discarded.
HeartbeatFrequency	By default, the Zabbix proxy sends a heartbeat message to the Zabbix server every minute. This parameter allows us to customize that.
ConfigFrequency	By default, the Zabbix proxy retrieves a new configuration from the server once per hour. You might want to increase this for large, fairly static setups, or maybe decrease it for smaller, more dynamic installations. Configuration data retrieval can be forced by reloading the active proxy configuration cache.
DataSenderFrequency	This parameter specifies how often the proxy pushes collected data to the Zabbix server. By default, it's one second. As all the trigger and alert processing is done by the server, it is suggested to keep this value low. If there are no values to send, an active proxy will not connect to the server except for heartbeat connections.

For a passive proxy, `ProxyMode` allows us to switch to the passive mode. Now the communication is controlled by parameters in the server configuration file:

Option	Description
StartProxyPollers	The number of processes that will be started and will connect to passive proxies to send configuration data and poll collected values. By default, one such process is started, and more might be needed if there are several passive proxies.
ProxyConfigFrequency	By default, Zabbix servers send configuration data to passive proxies once per hour. There is no way to force sending of configuration data to passive proxies. This parameter affects connections to all passive proxies.
ProxyDataFrequency	This parameter specifies how often the proxy pushes collected data to the Zabbix server. By default, it's one second. The Zabbix server will connect to passive proxies even if they have no values to provide. This parameter affects connections to all passive proxies.

Summary

In this chapter, we covered a great and easily maintainable solution for larger-scale data collection—Zabbix proxies. Zabbix proxies are also very desirable for remote environments. Similar to Zabbix agents, Zabbix proxies can operate either in active or in passive mode, reducing the hassle with firewall configuration.

Let's recap the main benefits of Zabbix proxies:

- Connections between the Zabbix proxy and the Zabbix server are done on a single TCP port, thus allowing us to monitor devices behind a firewall or devices that are inaccessible because of network configuration

- The Zabbix server is freed up from keeping track of checks and actually performing them, thus increasing performance

- Local buffering on the proxy allows it to continue gathering data while the Zabbix server is unavailable, transmitting it all when connectivity problems are resolved

Remember that active agents must point to the proxy if a host is monitored through that proxy. Passive agents must allow incoming connections from the proxy by specifying the proxy IP address in the `Server` parameter. The `zabbix_sender` utility must also send data to the proper proxy; sending data to the Zabbix server is not supported for hosts that are monitored through a proxy.

It is important to remember that proxies do not process events, do not generate trends, and do not send out alerts—they are remote data-gatherers, and alerting can happen only when the data is delivered to the Zabbix server. Additionally, proxies do not support remote commands. While scheduled for implementation in Zabbix 3.2, we will have to wait for that version to be released to know whether the development was successful.

With proxies taking over the monitoring of hosts, it is important to know that they are available, and it is also important to be silent about hosts behind a proxy if the proxy itself is not available. We discussed several ways that could be done, including proxy buffer monitoring to avoid alerting if the proxy has collected a lot of data during connectivity problems and value sending is behind.

Zabbix proxies are easy to set up, easy to maintain, and offer many benefits, thus they are highly recommended for larger environments.

In the next chapter, we will finally discuss that green **NONE** you might have noticed next to all hosts and proxies in the configuration section. It refers to encryption configuration—a new feature in Zabbix 3.0. Zabbix supports pre-shared key and certificate- (TLS-) based authentication and encryption. Encryption is supported for all components—server, proxy, agent, zabbix_get, and zabbix_sender. We will set up both pre-shared key and TLS-based encryption.

20
Encrypting Zabbix Traffic

Communication between Zabbix components is done in plaintext by default. In many environments, that is not a significant problem, but monitoring over the Internet in plaintext is likely not a good approach—transferred data could be read or manipulated by malicious parties. In previous Zabbix versions, there was no built-in solution, and various VPN, stunnel, and SSH port-forwarding solutions were being used. Such solutions can still be used, but 3.0 is the first Zabbix version to provide built-in encryption. In this chapter, we will set up several of the components to use different types of encryption.

Overview

For Zabbix communication encryption, two types are supported:

- Pre-shared key
- Certificate-based encryption

The **pre-shared key** (**PSK**) type is very easy to set up but is likely harder to scale. Certificate-based encryption can be more complicated to set up but easier to manage on a larger scale and potentially more secure.

This encryption is supported between all Zabbix components—server, proxy, agent, and even `zabbix_sender` and `zabbix_get`.

For outgoing connections (such as server-to-agent or proxy-to-server), only one type may be used (no encryption, and PSK or certificate-based). For incoming connections, multiple types may be accepted. This way, an agent could work with encryption by default for active or passive items from the server and then work without encryption with `zabbix_get` for debugging.

Backend libraries

Behind the scenes, Zabbix encryption can use one of three different libraries: OpenSSL, GnuTLS, or mbedTLS. Which one to choose? If using packages, the easiest and safest is to start with whichever the packages are compiled with. If compiling from source, choose the one that is easiest to compile with. In both cases, that is likely to be the library that is endorsed by the packagers and maintained well. The Zabbix team has made a significant effort to implement support for all three libraries in as similar a way as possible from the user perspective. There could be differences regarding support for some specific features, but those are likely to be more obscure ones — if such problems do come up later, switching from one library to another should be as easy as recompiling the daemons. While in most cases it would likely not matter much which library you are using, it's a good idea to know that — one good reason for supporting these three different libraries is also the ability to switch to a different library if the currently used one has a security vulnerability.

> These libraries are used in a generic manner, and there is no requirement to use the same library for different Zabbix components — it's totally fine to use one library on the Zabbix server, another on the Zabbix proxy, and yet another with zabbix_sender.

In this chapter, we will try out encryption with Zabbix server and zabbix_sender first and then move on to encrypting agent traffic using both PSK and certificate-based encryption. If you have installed from packages, your server most likely already supports encryption. Verify that by looking at the server and agent startup messages:

```
TLS support:            YES
```

> One way to find out which library the binary has been compiled against would be to run ldd zabbix_server | egrep -i "ssl|tls" — replace the binary name as needed.

If you compiled from source and TLS support is not present, recompile the server and agent by adding one of these parameters: --with-openssl, --with-gnutls, or --with-mbedtls.

Pre-shared key encryption

Let's start with a simple situation—a single new host for which the Zabbix server will accept PSK-encrypted incoming connections only for the ones we will send some values to using `zabbix_sender`. For that to work, both Zabbix server and `zabbix_sender` must be compiled with TLS support. The PSK configuration consists of a PSK identity and key. The identity is some string that is not considered to be secret—it is not encrypted during the communication; do not put sensitive information in the identity string. The key is a hex string.

> Zabbix requires the key to be at least 32 characters (hexadecimal digits) long. The maximum in Zabbix is 512 characters, but it might depend on the specific version of the backend library you are using.

We could just type the key in manually, but a slightly easier method might be using the `openssl` command:

```
$ openssl rand -hex 64
```

This will generate a 512-bit key, which we will use in a moment. Navigate to **Configuration | Hosts**, click on **Create host**, and fill in these values:

- **Hostname:** `Encrypted host`
- **Groups:** Have only **Linux servers** in the **In groups** block

Switch to the **Encryption** tab, and in the **Connections from host** section, leave only **PSK** marked. In the **PSK identity** field, enter `secret` and paste the key we generated earlier in the **PSK** field:

Host	Templates	IPMI	Macros	Host inventory	Encryption

Connections to host	No encryption PSK Certificate
Connections from host	☐ No encryption ☑ PSK ☐ Certificate
PSK identity	secret
PSK	f94c55ab57671af3de922f383ddbad5861ed79ff10222bd2b6a9cba11fa26fda22c80b1e742d9
	Add Cancel

When done, click on the **Add** button at the bottom. Take a look at the **AGENT ENCRYPTION** column for this host:

The first block has only one field and currently says **NONE**. For connections to the agent, only one type was possible, so this column must be showing the currently selected types for outgoing connections from the server perspective. The second block has three fields. We could choose a combination of the acceptable incoming connection types, so this column must be showing what types of incoming connections from the server perspective are accepted for this host.

Now, click on **Items** next to **Encrypted host**, and click on **Create item**. Fill in these values:

- **Name**: Beers in the fridge
- **Type**: **Zabbix trapper**
- **Key**: fridge.beers

Click on the **Add** button at the bottom. Let's try to send a value now, like we did in *Chapter 11, Advanced Item Monitoring*:

```
$ zabbix_sender -z 127.0.0.1 -s "Encrypted host" -k fridge.beers -o 1
```

That should fail:

```
info from server: "processed: 0; failed: 1; total: 1; seconds spent:
0.000193"
```

Notice how the processed count is 0 and the failed count is 1. Let's check the Zabbix server log file:

```
12254:20160122:231030.702 connection of type "unencrypted" is not
allowed for host "Encrypted host" item "fridge.beers" (not every
rejected item might be reported)
```

Now that's actually quite a helpful message—we did not specify any encryption for zabbix_sender, but we did require an encrypted connection for our host. Notice the text in parentheses—if multiple items on the same host fail because of this reason, we might only see some of them, and searching the log file only by item key might not reveal the reason.

Now is the time to get the PSK working for `zabbix_sender`. Run it with the `--help` parameter, and look at the TLS connection options section. Oh yes, there are quite a lot of those. Luckily, for PSK encryption, we only need three of them: `--tls-connect`, `--tls-psk-identity`, and `--tls-psk-file`. Before running the command, create a file in the current directory called `zabbix_encrypted_host_psk.txt`, and paste the hex key we generated earlier in it.

> It is more secure to create an empty file first, change its permissions to `400` or `600`, and paste the key in the file afterwards—that way, another user won't have a chance to snatch the key from the file. If a specific user is supposed to invoke `zabbix_sender`, make sure to set that user as the owner of the file.

Run `zabbix_sender` again, but with the three additional encryption parameters:

```
$ zabbix_sender -z 127.0.0.1 -s "Encrypted host" -k fridge.beers -o
1 --tls-connect psk --tls-psk-identity secret --tls-psk-file zabbix_
encrypted_host_psk.txt
```

We set the connection type to `psk` with the `--tls-connect` flag and specified the PSK identity and key file now.

> Zabbix does not support specifying the PSK key on the command line for security reasons—it must be passed in from a file.

This time, the value should be sent successfully:

```
info from server: "processed: 1; failed: 0; total: 1; seconds spent:
0.000070"
```

To be sure, verify that this item now has data in the frontend.

Certificate-based encryption

With PSK-based encryption protecting our sensitive Zabbix trapper item, let's move to certificates. We will generate certificates for the Zabbix server and agent and require encrypted connections on the Zabbix agent side for passive items. Certificate authorities sign certificates, and Zabbix components can trust one or more authorities. By extension, they trust the certificates signed by those authorities.

You might have a certificate infrastructure in your organization, but for our first test, we will generate all required certificates ourselves. We will need a new **certificate authority** (**CA**) that will sign our certificate. Zabbix does not support self-signed certificates.

> It is strongly recommended to use intermediate certificate authorities to sign client and server certificates — we will not use them in the following simple example.

Being our own authority

We'll start by creating the certificates in a separate directory. For simplicity's sake, let's do this on A test host — choose any directory where our certificate signing will happen.

The following is not intended to be a good practice. It is actually doing quite a few bad and insecure things to get the certificates faster. Do not follow these steps for any production setup.

```
$ mkdir zabbix_ca
$ chmod 700 zabbix_ca
$ cd zabbix_ca
```

Generate the root CA key:

```
$ openssl genrsa -aes256 -out zabbix_ca.key 4096
```

When prompted, enter a password twice to protect the key. Generate and self-sign the root certificate:

```
$ openssl req -x509 -new -key zabbix_ca.key -sha256 -days 3560 -out zabbix_ca.crt
```

When prompted, enter the password you used for the key before. Fill in the values as prompted — the easiest might be supplying empty values for most except the country code and common name. The common name does not have to be anything too meaningful for our test, so using a simple string like zabbix_ca will suffice.

Now, on to creating a certificate we will use for the Zabbix server — first, let's generate a server key and **certificate signing request** (**CSR**):

```
$ openssl genrsa -out zabbix_server.key 2048
$ openssl req -new -key zabbix_server.key -out zabbix_server.csr
```

When prompted, enter the country code and common name strings as before. The common name does not have to match the server or agent name or anything else, so using a simple string such as `zabbix_server` will suffice. Let's sign this request now:

```
$ openssl x509 -req -in zabbix_server.csr -CA zabbix_ca.crt -CAkey
zabbix_ca.key -CAcreateserial -out zabbix_server.crt -days 1460 -sha256
```

When prompted, enter the CA passphrase. Let's continue with the certificate we will use for the Zabbix agent. Generate an agent key and certificate signing request:

```
$ openssl genrsa -out zabbix_agent.key 2048
```

```
$ openssl req -new -key zabbix_agent.key -out zabbix_agent.csr
```

When prompted, enter the country code and common name strings as before. The common name does not have to match the server or agent name or anything else, so using a simple string such as `zabbix_agent` will suffice. Now, let's sign this request:

```
$ openssl x509 -req -in zabbix_agent.csr -CA zabbix_ca.crt -CAkey zabbix_
ca.key -CAcreateserial -out zabbix_agent.crt -days 1460 -sha256
```

When prompted, enter the CA passphrase.

We're done with creating our test certificates. Both keys were created unencrypted—Zabbix does not support prompting for the key password at this time.

Setting up Zabbix with certificates

Now on to making the passive items on **A test host** use the certificates we just generated. We must provide the certificates to the Zabbix agent. In the directory where the Zabbix agent configuration file is located, create a new directory called `zabbix_agent_certs`. Restrict access to it, like this:

```
# chown zabbix zabbix_agent_certs
```

```
# chmod 500 zabbix_agent_certs
```

From the directory where we generated the certificates, copy the relevant certificate files over to the new directory:

```
# cp zabbix_ca.crt /path/to/zabbix_agent_certs/
```

```
# cp zabbix_agent.crt /path/to/zabbix_agent_certs/
```

```
# cp zabbix_agent.key /path/to/zabbix_agent_certs/
```

Edit `zabbix_agentd.conf`, and modify these parameters:

```
TLSAccept=cert
TLSConnect=unencrypted
TLSCAFile=/path/to/zabbix_agent_certs/zabbix_ca.crt
TLSCertFile=/path/to/zabbix_agent_certs/zabbix_agent.crt
TLSKeyFile=/path/to/zabbix_agent_certs/zabbix_agent.key
```

This will make the agent only accept connections when they are encrypted and use a certificate signed by that CA, either directly or through intermediates. We'll still use an unencrypted connection for active items. A user could supply certificates and expect all communication to be encrypted now, which would not be the case unless either of the `TLSAccept` or `TLSConnect` parameters required encryption. To prevent silently ignoring certificate files, Zabbix enforces one of `TLSAccept` or `TLSConnect` when certificates are supplied. Restart the Zabbix agent.

> If a certificate becomes compromised, the certificate authority can revoke it by listing the certificate in a **Certificate Revocation List** (**CRL**). Zabbix supports CRLs with the `TLSCRLFile` parameter.

Let's take a look at the host configuration list in the Zabbix frontend:

INTERFACE	TEMPLATES	STATUS	AVAILABILITY	AGENT ENCRYPTION	INFO
127.0.0.1: 10050	C_Template_Linux	Enabled	ZBX SNMP JMX IPMI	NONE	
Received empty response from Zabbix Agent at [127.0.0.1]. Assuming that agent dropped connection because of access permissions.					

Looks like connections to **A test host** do not work anymore. Let's check the agent log file:

```
failed to accept an incoming connection: from 127.0.0.1: unencrypted
connections are not allowed
```

Looks like we broke it. We did set up encryption on the agent but did not get around to configuring the server side. What if we would like to roll out encryption to all the agents and deal with the server later? In that case, it would be best to set `TLSAccept=cert,unencrypted` – then, agents would still accept unencrypted connections from our server. Once the certificates are deployed and configured on the Zabbix server, we only have to remove `unencrypted` from that parameter and restart the Zabbix agents. Let's try this out – change `zabbix_agentd.conf` again:

```
TLSAccept=cert,unencrypted
```

Restart the agent daemon and observe monitoring resuming from the Zabbix server. Now, let's make the server uses its certificate. We'll place the certificate in a place where the Zabbix server can use it. In the directory where the Zabbix server configuration file is located, create a new directory called `zabbix_server_certs`. Restrict access to it, like this:

```
# chown zabbix zabbix_server_certs
# chmod 500 zabbix_server_certs
```

> If using packages that run Zabbix server with a different username such as `zabbixs` or `zabbixsrv`, replace the username with the proper one in the two commands.

From the directory where we generated the certificates, copy the certificates over to the new directory:

```
# cp zabbix_ca.crt /path/to/zabbix_server_certs/
# cp zabbix_server.crt /path/to/zabbix_server_certs/
# cp zabbix_server.key /path/to/zabbix_server_certs/
```

Edit `zabbix_server.conf`, and modify these parameters:

```
TLSCAFile=/path/to/zabbix_server_certs/zabbix_ca.crt
TLSCertFile=/path/to/zabbix_server_certs/zabbix_server.crt
TLSKeyFile=/path/to/zabbix_server_certs/zabbix_server.key
```

Now, restart Zabbix server. Although we have specified the certificates on both agents and the server, passive items still work in unencrypted mode. Let's proceed with making them encrypted. In the Zabbix frontend, navigate to **Configuration | Hosts**, click on **A test host**, and switch to the **Encryption** tab. In the **Connections to host** selection, choose **Certificate**, and then click on the **Update** button. After the server configuration cache has been updated, it will switch to using certificate-based encryption for this host.

> We are changing the configuration for **A test host**, not **Encrypted host**.

Going back to our scenario where we slowly rolled out certificate-based configuration to our agents and added it to the server later, we can now disable unencrypted connections on the agent side. Change `zabbix_agentd.conf`:

```
TLSAccept=cert
```

Restart the agent. If we had followed this process from the very beginning, monitoring would have continued uninterrupted. Let's try to use `zabbix_get`:

```
$ zabbix_get -s 127.0.0.1 -k system.cpu.load

zabbix_get [5746]: Check access restrictions in Zabbix agent
configuration
```

That fails because the agent only accepts encrypted connections now. As we did for `zabbix_sender`, we can specify the certificate — but we must use the Zabbix server certificate now.

Access to the Zabbix server certificate is required for this command:

```
$ zabbix_get -s 127.0.0.1 -k system.cpu.load --tls-connect cert --tls-ca-
file /path/to/zabbix_server_certs/zabbix_ca.crt --tls-cert-file /path/to/
zabbix_server
_certs/zabbix_server.crt --tls-key-file /path/to/zabbix_server_certs/
zabbix_server.key

0.030000
```

Certainly, this results in a more secure environment. It is not enough to spoof the IP address to access this agent. It is not enough to have an account on the Zabbix server to have access to all agents — access to the server certificate is needed, too. On the other hand, it makes debugging a bit more complicated, as we can't query the agent that easily, and sniffing the traffic is much harder, too.

We used PSK and certificate-based encryption with `zabbix_sender`, `zabbix_get`, and a passive agent, but the same principles apply for active agents. As an exercise, try to get the active agent items working with encryption, too.

Concerns and further reading

At this time, encryption is a very new feature in Zabbix. While it has been developed and tested extremely carefully and pedantically, it is likely to receive further improvements. Make sure to read through the official documentation on encryption for more details and in case changes are made. Right now, let's touch on basic concerns and features that are missing.

So far in this chapter, we've covered Zabbix server, agents, `zabbix_get`, and `zabbix_sender` — what about Zabbix proxies? Zabbix proxies fully support encryption. Configuration on the proxy side is very similar to agent configuration, and configuration in the frontend side is done in a similar way to agent encryption configuration, too. Keep in mind that all involved components must be compiled with TLS support — any proxies you have might have to be recompiled. When considering encryption, think about the areas where it's needed most — maybe you have the Zabbix server and proxy communicating over the Internet while all other connections are in local networks. In that case, it might make sense to set up encryption only for server-proxy communication at first. Note that encryption is not supported when communicating with the Zabbix Java gateway, but one could easily have the gateway communicate with a Zabbix proxy on the localhost, which in turn provides encryption for the channel to the Zabbix server.

We've already figured out how the upgrading and transitioning to encryption can happen seamlessly without interrupting data collection — the ability for all components to accept various connection types allows us to roll the changes out sequentially.

An important reason why one might want to implement encryption only partially is performance. Currently, Zabbix does not reuse connections, implement a TLS session cache, or use any other mechanism that would avoid setting up an encrypted connection from scratch every time. This can be especially devastating if you have lots of passive agent items. Make sure to understand the potential impact before reconfiguring it all.

Encryption isn't currently supported for authentication purposes. That is, we cannot omit active agent hostnames and figure out which host it is based on the certificate alone. Similarly, we cannot use encrypted connections for active agent autoregistration.

For certificate-based encryption, we only specified the certificates and the CA information. If the CA used is large enough, that would not be very secure — any certificate signed by that CA would be accepted. Zabbix also allows verifying both the issuer and subject of the remote certificate. Unless you are using an internal CA that is used for Zabbix only, it is highly recommended to limit the issuer and subject. This can be done on the host or proxy properties in the frontend and by using the `TLSServerCertIssuer` and `TLSServerCertSubject` parameters in the agent or proxy configuration file.

Summary

In this chapter, we explored the built-in Zabbix encryption that is supported between all components — server, proxy, agent, zabbix_sender, and zabbix_get. While not supported for the Java gateway, a Zabbix proxy could easily be put in front of the gateway to provide encryption back to the Zabbix server.

Zabbix supports pre-shared key and TLS certificate-based encryption and can use one of three different backend libraries — OpenSSL, GnuTLS, or mbedTLS. In case of security or other issues with one library, users have an option to switch to another library.

The upgrade and encryption deployment can be done in steps. All Zabbix components can accept multiple connection types at the same time. In our example, the agent would be set up to accept both encrypted and unencrypted connections, and when we would be done with configuring all agents for encryption, we would switch to encrypted connections on the server side. Once that would be verified to work as expected, unencrypted connections could be disabled on the agents.

With the encryption being built in and easy to set up, it is worth remembering that encrypted connections will need more resources and that Zabbix does not support connection pooling or other methods that could decrease load. It might be worth securing the most important channels first, leaving endpoints for later. For example, encrypting the communication between the Zabbix server and proxies would likely be a priority over connections to individual agents.

In the next chapter, we will work more closely with Zabbix data. That will include retrieving monitoring data directly from the database and modifying the database in an emergency case, such as losing all administrative passwords. We will also discuss the XML export and import functionality and the Zabbix API.

21
Working Closely with Data

Using a web frontend and built-in graphing is nice and easy, but sometimes, you might want to perform some nifty graphing in an external spreadsheet application or maybe feed data into another system. Sometimes, you might want to make some configuration change that is not possible or is cumbersome to perform using the web interface. While that's not the first thing most Zabbix users would need, it is handy to know when the need arises. Thus, in this chapter, we will find out how to:

- Get raw monitored metric data from the web frontend or database
- Perform some simple, direct database modifications
- Use XML export and import to implement more complex configuration
- Get started with the Zabbix API

Getting raw data

Raw data is data as it's stored in the Zabbix database, with minor, if any, conversion performed. Retrieving such data is mostly useful for analysis in other applications.

Extracting from the frontend

In some situations, it might be a simple need to quickly graph some data together with another data that is not monitored by Zabbix (yet you plan to add it soon, of course), in which case a quick hack job of spreadsheet magic might be the solution. The easiest way to get data to be used outside of the frontend is actually the frontend itself.

Let's find out how we can easily get historical data for some item. Go to **Monitoring | Latest data** and select **A test host** from the **Hosts filter** field, and then click on **Filter**. Click on **Graph** next to **CPU load**. That gives us the standard Zabbix graph. That wasn't what we wanted, now, was it? But this interface allows us to access raw data easily using the dropdown in the top-right corner—choose **Values** in there.

If the item has stopped collecting data some time ago and you just want to quickly look at the latest values, choose `500` latest values instead. It will get you the data with fewer clicks.

One thing worth paying attention to is the time period controls at the top, which are the same as the ones available for graphs, screens, and elsewhere. Using the scrollbar, zoom, move, and calendar controls, we can display data for any arbitrary period. For this item, the default period of 1 hour is fine. For some items that are polled less frequently, we will often want to use a much longer period:

TIMESTAMP	VALUE
Zoom: 5m 15m 30m **1h** 2h 3h 6h 12h 1d 3d 7d 14d 1m 3m All	
◄	
«« 1m 7d 1d 12h 1h 5m	5m 1h 12h 1d 7d 1m »»	
2016-06-03 19:19:55	0.02
2016-06-03 19:19:25	0.03
2016-06-03 19:18:55	0.05

While we could copy data out of this table with a browser that supports HTML copying, then paste it into some receiving software that can parse HTML, that is not always feasible. A quick and easy solution is in the upper-right corner — just click on the **As plain text** button.

This gives us the very same dataset, just without all the HTML-ish surroundings, such as the Zabbix frontend parts and the table. We can easily save this representation as a file or copy data from it and reuse it in a spreadsheet software or any other application. An additional benefit this data provides — all entries have the corresponding Unix timestamps listed as well.

> Technically, this page is still an HTML page. Zabbix users have asked to provide a proper plaintext version instead.

Querying the database

Grabbing data from the frontend is quick and simple, but this method is unsuitable for large volumes of data and hard to automate—parsing the frontend pages can be done, but isn't the most efficient way of obtaining data. Another way to get to the data would be directly querying the database.

> We'll look at the Zabbix API a bit later. It is suggested to use the API unless there are performance issues.

Let's find out how historical data is stored. Launch the MySQL command line client (simply called `mysql`, usually available in the `path` variable), and connect to the `zabbix` database as user `zabbix`:

```
$ mysql -u zabbix -p zabbix
```

When prompted, enter the `zabbix` user's password (which you can remind yourself of by looking at the contents of `zabbix_server.conf`) and execute the following command in the MySQL client:

```
mysql> show tables;
```

This will list all the tables in the `zabbix` database—exactly `113` in Zabbix 3.0. That's a lot of tables to figure out, but for our current need (getting some historical data out), we will only need a few. First, the most interesting ones—tables that contain gathered data. All historical data is stored in tables whose names start with `history`. As you can see, there are many of those with different suffixes—why is that? Zabbix stores retrieved data in different tables depending on the data type. The relationship between types in the Zabbix frontend and database is as follows:

- `history`: **Numeric (float)**
- `history_log`: **Log**
- `history_str`: **Character**
- `history_text`: **Text**
- `history_uint`: **Numeric (unsigned)**

To grab the data, we first have to find out the data type for that particular item. The easiest way to do that is to open item properties and observe the **Type of information** field. We can try taking a look at the contents of the history table by retrieving all fields for three records:

```
mysql> select * from history limit 3;
```

The output will show us that each record in this table contains four fields (your output will have different values):

```
+--------+------------+--------+-----------+
| itemid | clock      | value  | ns        |
+--------+------------+--------+-----------+
|  23668 | 1430700808 | 0.0000 | 644043321 |
|  23669 | 1430700809 | 0.0000 | 644477514 |
|  23668 | 1430700838 | 0.0000 | 651484815 |
+--------+------------+--------+-----------+
```

The next-to-last field, `value`, is quite straightforward — it contains the gathered value. The `clock` field contains the timestamp in Unix time — the number of seconds since the so-called Unix epoch, 00:00:00 UTC on January 1, 1970. The `ns` column contains nanoseconds inside that particular second.

> An easy way to convert the Unix timestamp to a human-readable form that does not require an Internet connection is using the GNU `date` command: `date -d@<timestamp>`. For example, `date -d@1234567890` will return `Sat Feb 14 01:31:30 EET 2009`.

The first field, `itemid`, is the most mysterious one. How can we determine which ID corresponds to which item? Again, the easiest way is to use the frontend. You should still have the item properties page open in your browser, so take a look at the address bar. Along with other variables, you'll see part of the string that reads like `itemid=23668`. Great, so we already have the `itemid` value on hand. Let's try to grab some values for this item from the database:

```
mysql> select * from history where itemid=23668 limit 3;
```

Use the `itemid` value that you obtained from the page URL:

```
+--------+------------+--------+-----------+
| itemid | clock      | value  | ns        |
+--------+------------+--------+-----------+
|  23668 | 1430700808 | 0.0000 | 644043321 |
|  23668 | 1430700838 | 0.0000 | 651484815 |
|  23668 | 1430700868 | 0.0000 | 657907318 |
+--------+------------+--------+-----------+
```

The resulting set contains only values from that item, as evidenced by the `itemid` field in the output.

One usually will want to retrieve values from a specific period. Guessing Unix timestamps isn't entertaining, so we can again use the date command to figure out the opposite—a Unix timestamp from a date in human-readable form:

```
$ date -d "2016-01-13 13:13:13" "+%s"
1452683593
```

The -d flag tells the date command to show the specified time instead of the current time, and the %s format sequence instructs it to output in Unix timestamp format. This fancy little command also accepts more freeform input, such as last Sunday or next Monday.

As an exercise, figure out two recent timestamps half an hour apart, then retrieve values for this item from the database. Hint—the SQL query will look similar to this:

```
mysql> select * from history where itemid=23668 and clock >= 1250158393
and clock < 1250159593;
```

You should get back some values. To verify the period, convert the returned clock values back to a human-readable format. The obtained information can be now passed to any external applications for analyzing, graphing, or comparing.

With history* tables containing the raw data, we can get a lot of information out of them. But sometimes, we might want to get a bigger picture only, and that's when table trends can help. Let's find out what exactly this table holds. In the MySQL client, execute this:

```
mysql> select * from trends limit 2;
```

We are now selecting two records from the trends table:

```
+--------+------------+-----+-----------+-----------+-----------+
| itemid | clock      | num | value_min | value_avg | value_max |
+--------+------------+-----+-----------+-----------+-----------+
|  23668 | 1422871200 |  63 |    0.0000 |    1.0192 |    1.4300 |
|  23668 | 1422874800 | 120 |    1.0000 |    1.0660 |    1.6300 |
+--------+------------+-----+-----------+-----------+-----------+
```

> Like the history tables had history and history_uint, there are trends and trends_uint tables for **Numeric (float)** and **Numeric (unsigned)** type of information. There are no corresponding _log, _str, or _text tables as trend information can be calculated for numeric data only.

Here, we find two familiar friends, itemid and clock, whose purpose and usage we just discussed. The last three values are quite self-explanatory — value_min, value_ avg, and value_max contain the minimal, average, and maximal values of the data. But for what period? The trends table contains information on hourly periods. So if we would like to plot the minimal, average, or maximal values per hour for 1 day in some external application, instead of recalculating this information, we can grab data for this precalculated data directly from the database. But there's one field we have missed: num. This field stores the number of values there were in the hour that is covered in this record. It is useful if you have hundreds of records each hour in a day that are all more or less in line but data is missing for 1 hour, except a single extremely high or low value. Instead of giving the same weight to the values for every hour when calculating daily, weekly, monthly, or yearly data, we can more correctly calculate the final value.

If you want to access data from the database to reuse in external applications, beware of the retention periods — data is removed from the history* and trends* tables after the number of days specified in the History storage period and Trend storage period fields for the specific items.

Using data in a remote site

We covered data retrieval on the Zabbix server. But what if we have a remote site, a Zabbix proxy, a powerful proxy machine, and a slow link? In situations like this, we might be tempted to extract proxy data to reuse it. However, the proxy stores data in a different way than the Zabbix server.

Just like in the previous chapter, run the following command:

```
$ sqlite3 /tmp/zabbix_proxy.db
```

This opens the specified database. We can look at which tables are present by using the .tables command:

```
sqlite> .tables
```

Notice how there still are all the history* tables, although we already know that the proxy does not use them, opting for proxy_history instead. The database schema is the same on the server and proxy, even though the proxy does not use most of those tables at all. Let's look at the fields of the proxy_history table.

> To check the table definition in SQLite, you can use the .schema proxy_history command.

The following table illustrates the item fields and their usage:

Field	Usage
id	The record ID, used to determine which records have been synchronized back to the server
itemid	The item ID as it appears on the Zabbix server
clock	The Unix time of the record, using proxy host time
timestamp	Relevant for time, parsed through the log file time format field, or for Windows event log monitoring — the timestamp as it appears on the monitored machine
source	Relevant for Windows event log monitoring only — event log source
severity	Relevant for Windows event log monitoring only — event log severity
value	The actual value of the monitored item
logeventid	Relevant for Windows event log monitoring only — event ID
ns	Nanoseconds for this entry
state	Whether this item is working normally or it is in the unsupported state
lastlogsize	The size of the log file that has been parsed already
mtime	The modification time of rotated log files that have been parsed already
meta	If set to 1, it indicates that this entry contains no actual log data, only lastlogsize and mtime

> The proxy doesn't have much information on item configuration; you'll need to snatch that from the Zabbix server if you are doing remote processing. For example, the proxy has item keys and intervals, but item names are not available in the proxy database.

As can be seen, several fields will be used for log file monitoring, and some other only for Windows event log monitoring.

Diving further into the database

With some knowledge on how to extract historical and trend data from tables, we might as well continue looking at other interesting, and relatively simple, things that we can find and perhaps even change directly in the database.

Managing users

We saw how managing users was an easy task using the frontend. But what if you have forgotten the password? What if some remote installation of Zabbix is administered by local staff, and the only Zabbix super admin has left for a month-long trip without a phone and nobody else knows the password? If you have access to the database, you can try to solve such problems. Let's find out what exactly Zabbix stores about users and how. In the MySQL console, execute this:

```
mysql> select * from users limit 2;
```

This way, we are listing all data for two users at the most:

```
MariaDB [zabbix]> select * from users limit 2;
+--------+-------+---------+---------------+----------------------------------+-
| userid | alias | name    | surname       | passwd                           |
+--------+-------+---------+---------------+----------------------------------+-
|      1 | Admin | Zabbix  | Administrator | 5fce1b3e34b520afeffb37ce08c7cd66 |
|      2 | guest |         |               | d41d8cd98f00b204e9800998ecf8427e |
+--------+-------+---------+---------------+----------------------------------+-
2 rows in set (0.00 sec)
```

> The example output is trimmed on the right-hand side and fewer than half of the original columns are shown here. You can also replace the trailing semicolon in the SQL query with \G to obtain vertical output, like this: `select * from users limit 2 \G`.

That's a lot of fields. We'd better find out what each of them means:

Field	Usage
userid	Quite simple, it's a unique, numeric ID.
alias	More commonly known as a username or login name.
name	User's name, usually their given name.
surname	This surely can't be anything else but the surname.
passwd	The password hash is stored here. Zabbix stores MD5 hashes for authentication.
url	The after-login URL is stored in this field.
autologout	Whether auto-logout for this user is enabled. Non-zero values indicate timeout.
lang	The language for the frontend.
refresh	The page refresh in seconds. If zero, page refresh is disabled.
theme	The frontend theme to use.
attempt_failed	How many consecutive failed login attempts there have been.

Field	Usage
attempt_ip	The IP of the last failed login attempt.
attempt_clock	The time of the last failed login attempt.
rows_per_page	How many rows per page are displayed in long lists.

As we can see, many of the fields are options that are accessible from the user profile or properties page, although some of these are not directly available. We mentioned password resetting before; let's look at a simple method to do that. If passwords are stored as MD5 hashes, we must obtain those first. A common method is the command line utility md5sum. Passing some string to it will output the desired result, so we can try executing this:

```
$ echo "somepassword" | md5sum
531cee37d369e8db7b054040e7a943d3  -
```

The MD5 hash is printed, along with a minus sign, which denotes standard input. If we had run md5sum on a file, the filename would have been printed there instead.

> The command line utility provides a nice way to check various sequences. For example, try to figure out what the default guest password hash, d41d8cd98f00b204e9800998ecf8427e, represents.

Now, the problem is that if we try to use this string as a password hash, it will fail. In this case, the hash is calculated on the passed string, including the newline at the end. For the correct version, we have to pass the -n flag to echo, which suppresses the trailing newline:

```
$ echo -n "somepassword" | md5sum
9c42a1346e333a770904b2a2b37fa7d3  -
```

Notice the huge difference in the resulting string. Great, now we only have to reset the password.

The following statement changes the Zabbix administrative user password. Do not perform this on a production system, except in an emergency situation:

```
mysql> update users set passwd='9c42a1346e333a770904b2a2b37fa7d3' where userid=1;
Query OK, 1 row affected (0.01 sec)
Rows matched: 1  Changed: 1  Warnings: 0
```

From here on, you should be able to log in to the Zabbix frontend as `Admin`/`somepassword`—try it out. Feel free to change the password back after that.

There's actually an easier method available. MySQL has a built-in function for calculating MD5 hashes, so all this trickery could be replaced with a simpler approach:

```
mysql> update users set passwd=MD5('somepassword') where alias='Admin';
```

> At this time, Zabbix does not use password salting. While making it simpler to reset the password, it also makes it easier to find the actual password in MD5 tables.

We also mentioned making some user a Zabbix super admin. This change is fairly simple—all we have to do is change a single number:

```
mysql> update users set type=3 where alias='wannabe_admin';
```

And that's it, the user `wannabe_admin` will become a Zabbix super admin.

Changing existing data

While once the monitoring data has been gathered you usually won't have a need to change it, there might be some rare cases when that might be required. Back in *Chapter 3, Monitoring with Zabbix Agents and Basic Protocols*, we created items for network traffic monitoring, and we gathered data in bytes, but in network management, usually bits per second are used instead. While it would often be possible for you to simply reconfigure the items and clear the old data, what if you need to preserve already gathered values? Directly editing the database might be the only solution.

Before doing that, you would have to modify the item in question. If data is coming in bytes but we want bits, what do we do? Right, we configure the multiplier for that item and set the multiplier to be 8. Additionally, change `units` to b (bits) while performing the change.

When performing the change to the item, take a quick look at a clock.

While this will deal with all future incoming values, it will leave us with inconsistent data before that moment. As we do not want to delete it, we must find some way to fix it. Our problem is twofold:

- We have incorrect data in the database
- We have both incorrect and correct data in the database (old and new values)

This means that we can't simply convert all values, as that would break the new, correct ones.

[🔅 If you have set any triggers based on traffic amount, do not forget to change those as well.]

Finding out when

Figuring out the moment when correct information started flowing in can be most easily done by looking at the frontend. Navigate to **Monitoring | Latest data**, click on **History** for that item, and then select **Values** or **500 latest values**. Look around the time you changed the item multiplier plus a minute or so, and check for a notable change in the scale. While it might be hard to pinpoint the exact interval between two checks (network traffic can easily fluctuate over eight times in value between two checks), there should be a pretty constant increase in values. Look at the times to the left of the values and choose a moment between the first good value and the last bad value.

The when in computer language

But as we now know, all time-related information in the Zabbix database is stored as Unix timestamps. For that, the GNU `date` command can help again. Execute on the Zabbix server the following, by replacing the exact time with what you deduced from the latest values:

```
$ date -d "2016-03-13 13:13:13" "+%s"
```

That will output the Unix timestamp of that moment, which in the case of this example would be `1457867593`.

Beware of the difference in time zones, though—values, displayed in the frontend, usually will have the local time zone applied. Check that the value for the timestamp you obtained matches the value in the database for that same timestamp. There is actually an easier and safer way to obtain the value timestamp. While still looking at the value history for the item in the frontend, click the **As plain text** button in the upper-right corner:

```
A test host: Incoming traffic on enp0s8
2015-11-29 06:43:49 1448772229 175
2015-11-29 06:43:19 1448772199 169
```

Notice how the third column is exactly what we wanted: the Unix timestamp. In this case, we don't have to worry about the time zone, either.

Finding out what

Now that we know the exact time that limits the change, we must also know which item we must modify for it. Wait, but we do know that already, don't we? Almost. What we need is the item ID to make changes to the database. The easiest way to find that out is by opening the item properties in the configuration section and copying the ID from the URL, like we did before.

Performing the change

By now, we should have two cryptic-looking values:

- The time in Unix timestamp format
- The item ID

What do we have to do now? Multiply by eight all the values for the item ID before that timestamp. With the data we have, it is actually quite simple — in the MySQL console, we would have to execute this:

```
mysql> update history_uint set value=value*8 where
itemid=<our ID>   and clock<'<our timestamp>';
```

> To be safe, you might want to perform the modifications in a transaction and check the results while the transaction is still open. If the results are satisfactory, commit the changes. If not, roll them back.

We are updating `history_uint`, because even though the data for the network traffic is a decimal number because of the **Store as item** option, we dropped the decimal part by storing the data as an integer. See *Chapter 3, Monitoring with Zabbix Agents and Basic Protocols*, to remind yourself why we did so. This single query should be enough to convert all the old data to bits.

> If you have lots of historical data in total and for this item, such a query can take quite some time to complete. When running such commands on a remote system, use a tool such as `screen`.

> We are only modifying the `history` table here. If the item has been collecting data for a longer period of time, we would also have to modify the corresponding `trends` or `trends_uint` table.

Using XML import/export for configuration

The web frontend is an acceptable tool for making configuration changes to a Zabbix server, unless you have to make lots of modifications, which are not made easier in the frontend with methods such as mass update. One simple method is exporting configuration to an XML file, making some changes, and importing it back in.

XML import/export is very often used to share templates—you can find a large number of those on `https://zabbix.org` and `http://share.zabbix.com`.

> We'll look at the Zabbix API a bit later. It is suggested to use the API to modify Zabbix configuration, as it also offers much more complete functionality than XML import/export—although the XML approach might be simpler in some cases.

Let's look at how a simple roundtrip would work.

Exporting the initial configuration

In the frontend, open **Configuration** | **Templates** and select **Custom Templates** in the **Group** dropdown. Mark the checkbox next to **C_Template_Email** and click on the **Export** button at the bottom. Your browser will offer to save a file called `zbx_export_templates.xml`—save it somewhere on your local machine.

Modifying the configuration

Now, with the file in hand, we can modify the configuration. This method gives us free rein on host and host-attached information, so modifications are limited only by Zabbix's functionality and our imagination. At this time, the following entities are available for XML export and import:

- Hosts
- Templates
- Host groups
- Network maps
- Map images (icons and backgrounds)
- Screens
- Value maps

Out of these, host groups and images are only exported indirectly. For hosts, all of their properties and sub-entities are exported and imported, except the web scenarios (this functionality might be available in Zabbix 3.2). Host groups are exported together with hosts or templates, and when exporting a map, the images used in it are exported in the same file. It is possible to import both a single type of entity and any number and combination of them in the same XML file.

The XML export format

Open the saved XML export in your favorite editor. In this file, you'll see all the data that this host has, and the file will start like this:

```
<?xml version="1.0" encoding="UTF-8"?>
<zabbix_export>
    <version>3.0</version>
    <date>2015-11-29T05:08:14Z</date>
    <groups>
        <group>
            <name>Custom templates</name>
        </group>
    </groups>
    <templates>
        <template>
            <template>C_Template_Email</template>
```

In this case, each template is contained in a `<template>` block, which in turn has blocks for all the things attached to that template. The format is simple, and most things should be obvious simply from taking a glance at the XML and maybe sometimes by comparing values in XML with values in the frontend configuration section. An exception might be the values available for each field. Those can often be gleaned from the API documentation, which we will cover in a moment.

While we look at the exported template, we can see the same information that an exported host would have, including template linkage—that's what the second nested `<templates>` block denotes.

Scripting around the export

While manually making a single change to an exported file can be handy, it's the large changes that expose the benefit of this approach best. As the most simple approach to creating an XML file, we can use shell scripts.

For example, if we had to add a lot of similar items, we could script an XML file with them all and import them in one go. The easiest approach would be to create some items in the frontend, export that host, and write a quick script that loops over these item definitions and creates the remaining items. The same can be done for triggers and custom graphs as well. Again, it's best to create all data for a single element, export it, and examine it to find out how it should be put back together.

> Unless individual entities are to be modifiable, consider using a custom LLD rule, as covered in *Chapter 12, Automating Configuration*.

Other larger-scale problems that can be solved by an XML roundtrip are:

- **Adding lots of devices**: If you are given a large list of switches with IP addresses, adding them all through the interface is a monstrous task. With XML, it becomes a very easy and quick one instead. To do that, simply create a single host, linked against the previously created template or several ones, and then export it to get some sort of a template. In this export, you'll basically have to change a couple of values only—notably, the connection details in the `<interfaces>` element. Then, just proceed to create a loop that creates new `<host>` entries with the corresponding IP and hostname data. Note that it is enough to only specify host information in this file—all items, triggers, graphs, and other entities will be attached based on the information that is contained in the template or templates specified in the `<templates>` block.

- **Creating many graphs with lots of arbitrary items**: Sometimes, it might be required to create not only one graph per port, but also graphs grouping items from several devices and other arbitrary collections. Export an example host and script graph items in a loop—these are located in the `<graph_elements>` block.

> A graph with a huge number of items can soon become unreadable. Don't overdo items on a single graph.

Importing modified configuration

For our first XML export/import, we won't do large-scale scripting. Instead, let's make a simple modification. In the saved `zbx_export_templates.xml` file, find the item block with the key `net.tcp.service[smtp]`. An item block starts with an `<item>` tag and ends with an `</item>` tag. Copy this item block and insert it below the existing block, and then change the item name to `POP3 server status` and key to `net.tcp.service[pop3]`.

Save this as a new file. Now on to the actual import process. Back in the frontend, in the **Configuration | Templates** section, click on **Import** in the upper right-hand corner. In this form, click on the **Choose** next to the **Import file** field and choose the saved file. Feel free to explore the **Rules** section, although the defaults will do for us. The only type of entities we are interested in are missing items, and the respective checkbox in the **CREATE NEW** column next to **Items** is already marked.

Click on **Import** to proceed. This should complete successfully, so click on **Details** in the upper-left corner. While all other records will be about updating, there should be two entries about an item being created. These will be the only ones that make any changes, as all the updates do nothing—the data in the XML file is the same as in the database. As we are adding this item for a template, it also gets added to all other hosts and templates that are linked against this one:

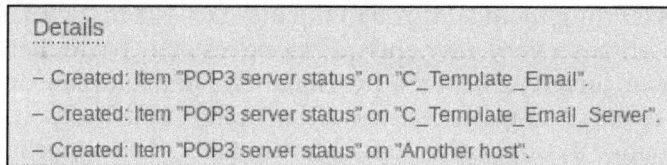

Details

– Created: Item "POP3 server status" on "C_Template_Email".

– Created: Item "POP3 server status" on "C_Template_Email_Server".

– Created: Item "POP3 server status" on "Another host".

Let's verify that this item was added with the key we used in the XML file. Navigate to **Configuration | Hosts**, make sure **Linux servers** is selected in the **Group** dropdown, and click on the **Items** link next to the **Another host** entry. Our new item should be visible in the item list, showing that it has been correctly added to the linked host. Remember that we only added it to the upstream template in our import process:

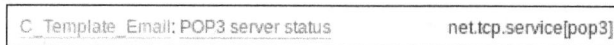

C_Template_Email: POP3 server status   net.tcp.service[pop3]

Generating hosts

One of the possible problems to solve using XML importing is creating a larger number of hosts. We could use a hackish script like this to generate a Zabbix host XML out of a CSV file:

```bash
#!/bin/bash

split="%"
agent_port=10050
useip=1

[[ -s "$1" ]] || {
        echo "Usage: pass an input CSV file as the first parameter
```

```
File should contain data in the following format: hostname,dns,ip,host
group,linked_template,agent_port
agent_port is optional
For groups and templates multiple entries are separated with %
First line is ignored (assuming a header)"
        exit 1
}

echo "<?xml version=\"1.0\" encoding=\"UTF-8\"?>
<zabbix_export>
    <version>3.0</version>
    <date>$(date "+%Y-%m-%dT%H:%M:%SZ")</date>
    <hosts>"
while read line; do
        hostname=$(echo $line | cut -d, -f1)
        dns=$(echo $line | cut -d, -f2)
        ip=$(echo $line | cut -d, -f3)
        group=$(echo $line | cut -d, -f4)
        template=$(echo $line | cut -d, -f5)
        port=$(echo $line | cut -d, -f6)

        hostname1=${hostname%\"}
        dns1=${dns%\"}
        ip1=${ip%\"}
        group1=${group%\"}
        template1=${template%\"}
        port1=${port%\"}

        hostgroups=$(echo $group1 | tr "$split" "\n")
        templates=$(echo $template1 | tr "$split" "\n")

        echo "          <host>
            <host>$(echo ${hostname1#\"})</host>
            <name>$(echo ${hostname1#\"})</name>
            <status>0</status>
            <description/>
            <proxy/>
            <ipmi_authtype>-1</ipmi_authtype>
            <ipmi_privilege>2</ipmi_privilege>
            <ipmi_username/>
            <ipmi_password/>
            <tls_connect>1</tls_connect>
            <tls_accept>1</tls_accept>
            <tls_issuer/>
```

```
                        <tls_subject/>
                        <tls_psk_identity/>
                        <tls_psk/>
                        <interfaces>
                            <interface>
                                <default>1</default>
                                <type>1</type>
                                <useip>$useip</useip>
                                <ip>${ip1#\"}</ip>
                                <dns>${dns1#\"}</dns>
                                <port>${port1:-$agent_port}</port>
                                <bulk>1</bulk>
                                <interface_ref>if1</interface_ref>
                            </interface>
                        </interfaces>"
            echo "               <groups>"
            while read hostgroup; do
                    echo "                   <group>
                        <name>${hostgroup#\"}</name>
                    </group>"
            done < <(echo "$hostgroups")
            echo "              </groups>
                <templates>"
            while read hosttemplate; do
                    echo "                  <template>
                        <name>${hosttemplate#\"}</name>
                    </template>"
            done < <(echo "$templates")
            echo "               </templates>"
            echo "           </host>"
    done < <(tail -n +2 $1)

    echo "     </hosts>
    </zabbix_export>"
```

Save this script as `csv_to_zabbix_xml.sh` and make it executable:

```
$ chmod 755 csv_to_zabbix_xml.sh
```

> Some people say that the shell is not an appropriate tool to handle XML files. The shell is a great tool for anything and perfectly fine for our simple, quick host generation.

This script takes a CSV file as the input, ignores the first line, and uses all other lines as host entries. We must specify the hostname, DNS, IP, and agent port. Additionally, for each host, we may specify multiple host groups and templates the host should be linked to by delimiting multiple entries with a percent sign. The useip parameter defaults to 1; setting it to 0 will use DNS instead. Notice how we are generating all kind of fields we are not interested in at this time — all the IPMI and TLS fields, setting the bulk parameter for the agent interface. Unfortunately, Zabbix XML exports are unnecessarily verbose, and it expects the same verbosity back. For a larger number of hosts, this will significantly increase the size of the XML file.

> Quoting in the CSV file allows us to use commas in host group names.

To use this file, let's create a simple CSV file called test.csv:

```
"Host name","Host DNS","Host IP","Host groups","Templates","port"
"test-xml-import","dns.name","1.2.3.4","Linux servers%Zabbix
servers","Template ICMP Ping"
```

We used a header line here, as the first line is always excluded — a single line in a file would not do anything at all. Now, let's run our script:

```
$ ./csv_to_zabbix_xml.sh test.csv > zabbix_generated_hosts.xml
```

In the frontend, navigate to **Configuration | Hosts**, click on **Import** in the upper-right corner, choose the zabbix_generated_hosts.xml file in the **Import file** field, and click on **Import**. The import should be successful — verify that back in **Configuration | Hosts**. As this host is not very useful right now, feel free to delete it.

Importing images

When configuring network maps, we had a chance to upload our own icons. It is highly inefficient to upload a lot of images one by one. One could script the process using a utility such as curl, but that requires a new connection to the frontend for every image and could break if the Zabbix interface is changed in future versions. Images are supported in XML import, though, and we may also have a file with just the images. We could write our own script for this, but there is already a script shipped with Zabbix — look for the png_to_xml.sh script in the misc/images directory. This script accepts two parameters: the directory where the images are found and the output filename. For example, if we had images in a directory called map_icons, we would run the script as follows:

```
./png_to_xml.sh map_icons zabbix_images.xml
```

To import the images, we would go to any page that has the **Import** button, such as **Configuration | Maps**, click the **Import** button, and mark the checkboxes next to the **Images** row. Only super admins may import images. Images are exported and imported in base64 format, so there is no binary data in the XML file. An example of an exported image is this:

```
<encodedImage>iVBORw0KGgoAAAANSUhEUgAAADAAAAAwCAYAAABXAvmHAAAABm
JLR0QA/wD/AP+gvaeTAAAM70lEQVR42u2ZeXBV133HP+cub9NDSGGG5hyR
...
</encodedImage>
```

This output is significantly cut—the real base64 value would take a few pages here.

Starting with the Zabbix API

The approaches we looked at earlier—direct database edits and XML import/export—were either risky or limited. Editing the database is risky because there is very little validation, and upgrading to a newer version of Zabbix can change the database schema, making our tools and approaches invalid. XML import/export was nice, but very limited—it did not allow modifying users, network discovery rules, actions lots, and lots of things in the Zabbix configuration.

This is where the Zabbix API could help. It is a JSON-based interface to Zabbix configuration and data. It offers way more functionality than XML import/export does, although there are still bits and pieces of configuration that cannot be controlled using it.

The Zabbix API currently is frontend based: it is implemented in PHP. To use it, we connect to the web server running the frontend and issue our requests. There are a lot of ways to do this, but here, we will try to do things in a manner that is language independent—we will use curl and issue the requests from the shell.

Simple operations

The Zabbix API is request-response based. We send a request and get a response—either the data we requested or a success/failure indicator. Let's look at some simple, practical examples of what one can do with the API. We will use simple curl requests to the API. Let's try this on the Zabbix server:

```
$ curl -s -X POST -H 'Content-Type: application/json-rpc' -d ''
http://127.0.0.1/zabbix/api_jsonrpc.php
```

In this request, we use the POST method and send the JSON string with the -d parameter—empty for now. We also specify the -s parameter, which enables silent or quiet mode and suppresses progress and error messages. The URL is the Zabbix API endpoint, api_jsonrpc.php. This will be the same for all API requests. Additionally, we specify the content type to be application/json-rpc. This is required. If omitted, the Zabbix API will return an empty response, which does not help much. The request we issued should return a response like this:

```
{"jsonrpc":"2.0","error":{"code":-32600,"message":"Invalid
Request.","data":"JSON-rpc version is not specified."},"id":null}
```

That did not work, but at least there's an error message. Let's proceed with more valid requests now.

Obtaining the API version

One of the simplest things we can do is query the API for the Zabbix version. This will return the frontend version, which is considered to be the same as the API version. This is the only request that does not require being logged in, besides the login request itself.

To make it easier to edit and issue the requests, let's assign the JSON to a variable, which we will then use in the curl command.

> Alternatively, you can put the JSON string in a file and pass the file contents to curl as -d @file_name.

```
$ json='{"jsonrpc":"2.0","method":"apiinfo.version","id":1}'
```

We are using a method called apiinfo.version. How to know which methods are available and what their names are? That information can be found in the Zabbix manual, and we will explore it a bit later. Let's send this request to the API now. API responses lack a trailing newline, and that might make them harder to read—let's also add a newline in the curl command:

```
$ curl -s -w '\n' -X POST -H 'Content-Type: application/json-rpc' -d
"$json" http://localhost/zabbix/api_jsonrpc.php
```

Notice the use of the $json variable in double quotes for the -d parameter and the -w parameter to add the newline. This command should return the API version:

```
{"jsonrpc":"2.0","result":"3.0.0","id":1}
```

The version of this instance is 3.0.0. What about the `jsonrpc` and `id` values? The `jsonrpc` value specifies the JSON-RPC version itself. The Zabbix API uses version 2.0, so this will be the same in all requests and all responses. The `id` value was specified by us in the request, and the response had the same value. It could be useful if we used a framework that allowed asynchronous requests and responses — that way, we could correlate the responses to requests. JSON also supports batching, where multiple requests can be sent in a single connection and responses can be matched by the ID, but this feature is currently broken in Zabbix 3.0.

Logging in

Before one can perform any useful operations via the API, they must log in. Our JSON string would be as follows:

```
$ json='{"jsonrpc":"2.0","method":"user.login","id":2,"params":
{"user":"Admin","password":"zabbix"}}'
```

Now, run the same `curl` command we used to get the API version. In all further API requests, we will only change the `json` variable and then reuse the same `curl` command. In this case, assuming a correct username and password, it should return the following:

```
{"jsonrpc":"2.0","result":"df83119ab78bbeb2065049412309f9b4","id":2}
```

> We increased the request ID to 2. That was not really required — we could have used 3, 5, or 1013. We could have used 1 again — the way we use the API, all requests have a very obvious response, so we do not care about the ID at all. The response still did have the same ID as our request, 2.

This response also has an alphanumeric string in the `result` property, which is very important for all further work with the API. This is an authentication token or session ID that we will have to submit with all subsequent requests. For our tests, just copy that string and use it in the `json` variable later.

Enabling and disabling hosts

Hosts may be enabled or disabled by setting a single value. Let's disable our IPMI host and re-enable it a moment later. To do this, we will need the host ID. Usually, when using the API, we'd query the API itself for the ID. In this case, let's keep things simple and look up the ID in the host properties — as with the item before, open the host properties and copy the value for the `hostid` parameter from the URL. With that number available, let's set our JSON variable:

```
$ json='{"jsonrpc":"2.0","method":"host.update","params":
{"hostid":"10132","status":1},"auth":"df83119ab78bbeb2065049412309f9b4","
id":1}'
```

> We got back to using an ID of 1. It really does not matter when using `curl` like this.

Run the `curl` command:

```
{"jsonrpc":"2.0","result":{"hostids":["10132"]},"id":1}
```

This should indicate success, and the host should be disabled — check the host state in the frontend. Enabling it again is easy, too:

```
$ json='{"jsonrpc":"2.0","method":"host.update","params":
{"hostid":"10132","status":0},"auth":"df83119ab78bbeb2065049412309f9b4","
id":1}'
```

Run the `curl` command again to re-enable this host.

Creating a host

Now on to creating a host using the API. Let's set our JSON variable:

```
$ json='{"jsonrpc":"2.0","method":"host.create","params":{"host":"API
created host","interfaces":[{"type":1,"main":1,"useip":1,
"ip":"127.0.0.2","dns":"","port":"10050"}],"groups":[{"groupid":"2"}],"te
mplates":[{"templateid":"10104"}]},"auth": "df83119ab78bbeb2065049412309f
9b4","id":1}'
```

In the default Zabbix database, the group ID of 2 should correspond to the Linux servers group, and the template ID of `10104` should correspond to the **Template ICMP Ping** template. If the IDs are different on your system, change them in this JSON string. Run the `curl` command now, and the host should be created successfully:

```
{"jsonrpc":"2.0","result":{"hostids":["10148"]},"id":1}
```

As part of the response, we also got the ID of the new host. Feel free to verify in the frontend that this host has been created.

Deleting a host

And the returned ID will be useful now. Let's delete the host we just created:

```
$ json='{"jsonrpc":"2.0","method":"host.delete","params"
:["10148"],"auth":"df83119ab78bbeb2065049412309f9b4","id":1}'
```

> Make sure the host ID in this request is the same as was returned in the previous request; otherwise, a different host could be deleted.

Run the `curl` command again. The host should be successfully deleted.

```
{"jsonrpc":"2.0","result":{"hostids":["10148"]},"id":1}
```

Creating a value map

Value maps could not be controlled via the API before Zabbix 3.0. They were needed for many templates, though, and people resorted to SQL scripts or even manually creating value maps with hundreds of entries. That's dedication. In Zabbix 3.0, things are much easier, and now, value maps are supported both in the API and XML import/export. Let's create a small value map:

```
$ json='{"jsonrpc":"2.0","method":"valuemap.create","params":
{"name":"Mapping things","mappings":[{"value":"this",
"newvalue":"that"},{"value":"foo","newvalue":"bar"}]},
"auth":"df83119ab78bbeb2065049412309f9b4","id":1}'
```

Run the `curl` command:

```
{"jsonrpc":"2.0","result":{"valuemapids":["16"]},"id":1}
```

If you check the new value map in the frontend, it is a bit easier to read than in that JSON:

| Mapping things | foo ⇒ bar |
| | this ⇒ that |

> We covered value maps in *Chapter 3, Monitoring with Zabbix Agents and Basic Protocols*.

Obtaining history and trends

The methods we have discussed so far mostly dealt with configuration. We may also query some historical data. For example, to grab item history data, we would need to know several things:

- **Item ID**
- The **Type of information** setting for that item

Both of these can be found out by opening the item properties in the configuration section—the ID will be in the URL, and the type of information will be in that dropdown. Why do we have to specify the type of information? Unfortunately, the Zabbix API does not look it up for us but tries to find the values only in a specific table. By default, the `history_uint` (integer values) table is queried. To get the values for the CPU load item on **A test host**, the JSON string would look like this:

```
$ json='{"jsonrpc":"2.0","method":"history.get","params":
{"history":0,"itemids":"23668","limit":3},
"auth":"df83119ab78bbeb2065049412309f9b4","id":1}'
```

> Remember to replace both `auth` and `itemid` for this query.

Here are a couple extra parameters worth discussing here:

- The `history` parameter tells the API which table to query. With 0, the `history` table is queried. With 1, the `history_str` table is queried. With 2, the `history_log` table is queried. With 3, `history_int` is queried (which was the default). With 4, the `history_text` table is queried. We must manually match this value to the setting in the item properties.

- The `limit` parameter limits the number of entries returned. This is quite useful here, as an item could have lots and lots of values. By the way, `limit` is supported for all other methods as well—we can limit the number of entries when retrieving hosts, items, and all other entities.

Now, run the `curl` command:

```
{"jsonrpc":"2.0","result":[{"itemid":"23668","clock":"1430988898","val
ue":"0.0000","ns":"215287328"},{"itemid":"23668","clock":"1430988928",
"value":"0.0000","ns":"221534597"},{"itemid":"23668"
,"clock":"1430988958","value":"0.0000","ns":"229668635"}],"id":1}
```

We got our three values, but the output is a bit hard to read. There are many ways to format JSON strings, but in the shell, the easiest would be using Perl or Python commands. Rerun the `curl` command and append to it `| json_pp`:

```
$ curl ... | json_pp
```

> You might also have `json_xs`, which will have better performance, but performance should be no concern at all for us at this time.

This will invoke the Perl JSON tool, where **pp** stands for **pure Perl**, and the output will be a bit more readable:

```
{
   "jsonrpc" : "2.0",
   "id" : 1,
   "result" : [
      {
         "clock" : "1430988898",
         "itemid" : "23668",
         "value" : "0.0000",
         "ns" : "215287328"
      },
      {
         "ns" : "221534597",
         "value" : "0.0000",
         "itemid" : "23668",
         "clock" : "1430988928"
      },
      {
         "value" : "0.0000",
         "ns" : "229668635",
         "clock" : "1430988958",
         "itemid" : "23668"
      }
   ]
}
```

> Notice how the output isn't really sorted. Ordering does not mean anything with JSON data, so tools do not normally sort the output.

Alternatively, use `python -mjsontool`, which will invoke Python's JSON tool module. That's a bit more typing, though.

In the output from the `history.get` method, each value is accompanied with an item ID, UNIX timestamp, and nanosecond information, the same as the history tables we looked at earlier. That's not very surprising, as the API output comes from those tables. If we convert these values to human-readable format as discussed before by running `date -d@<UNIX timestamp>`, we will see that they are not recent—actually, they are the oldest values. We can get the most recent values by adding the `sortfield` and `sortorder` parameters:

```
$ json='{"jsonrpc":"2.0","method":"history.get","params":
{"history":0,"itemids":"23668","limit":3,"sortfield":"clock","sortorder":
"DESC"},"auth":"df83119ab78bbeb2065049412309f9b4","id":1}'
```

These will sort the output by the clock value in descending order and then grab the three most recent values—check the returned Unix timestamps to make sure of that. If there are multiple values with the same clock value, other fields will not be used for secondary sorting.

We can also retrieve trend data—a new feature in Zabbix 3.0:

```
$ json='{"jsonrpc":"2.0","method":"trend.get","params":
{"itemids":"23668","limit":3},"auth":"df83119ab78bbeb2065049412309f9b4","
id":1}'
```

> The Zabbix API does not allow submitting historical data—all item values have to go through the Zabbix server using the `zabbix_sender` utility, which we discussed in *Chapter 11, Advanced Item Monitoring*. There are rumors that the API might be moved to the server side, which might allow merging data-submitting in the main API.

Issues with the Zabbix API

The Zabbix API is really great, but there are a few issues with it worth knowing about:

- **Audit**: Many Zabbix API operations are not registered in the Zabbix audit log, which can be accessed by going to **Administration** | **Audit**. That can make it really complicated to find out who made a particular change and when.

- **Validation**: Unfortunately, the API validation leaves a lot to be desired. For example, using the API, one could change a host to a proxy or vice versa, or even set the `host status` value to a completely bogus value, making that host disappear from the frontend, although no new host with that name could be created. Be very, very careful with the possibility of sending incorrect data to the Zabbix API. It might complain about that data, or it might just silently accept it and make some silly changes.

- **Error messages**: Similarly, even when validating input data, the error messages are not always that helpful. Sometimes, they will tell you exactly what is wrong, but you may also get `incorrect parameters` for a long JSON input string.

- **Performance**: The Zabbix API's performance can be extremely bad for some operations. For example, modifying items for a template that is linked to a large number of hosts or linking many hosts to a template might be impossible to perform. While some of these operations could be split up, for example, linking the template to a few hundred hosts at a time, in some cases, one would have to fall back to doing direct SQL queries.

- **Missing functionality**: Although the Zabbix API allows us to control most of the Zabbix configuration, there are still some missing areas. By now, that mostly concerns things found in the **Administration | General** section. Once such functionality is implemented, it will be finally possible for the Zabbix frontend to stop performing direct database queries, and the API will allow writing custom frontends without ever resorting to direct database access.

Using API libraries

While we looked at a low-level API example, you are not likely to use shell scripts to work with the Zabbix API. The shell is not that well suited for working with JSON data even with extra tools, so another programming or scripting language might be a better choice. For many of those languages, one would not have to implement full raw JSON handling, as there are libraries available. At the time of writing this, a list of available libraries is maintained at `http://zabbix.org/wiki/Docs/api/libraries`. Alternatively, just go to `http://zabbix.org` and look for the **Zabbix API libraries** link.

All of these libraries are community supplied. There are no quality guarantees, and any bugs should be reported to the library maintainers, not to Zabbix.

For example, a Perl library called `Zabbix::Tiny` aims to be a very simple abstraction layer for the Zabbix API, solving the authentication and request ID issues and other repetitive tasks when working with the API. It can be easily installed from the **Comprehensive Perl Archive Network (CPAN)**:

```
# cpan Zabbix::Tiny
```

To create a new user, we would save the following in a file:

```perl
use strict;
use warnings;
use Zabbix::Tiny;
my $zabbix = Zabbix::Tiny->new(
    server => http://localhost/zabbix/api_jsonrpc.php,
    password => 'zabbix',
    user => 'Admin',
);
$zabbix->do(
    'user.create',
    alias   => 'new_user',
    passwd => 'secure_password',
    usrgrps => [ '13' ],
    name => 'New',
    surname => 'User',
    type => 3,
);
```

This would create a new user. While most parameters are self-explanatory, the type parameter tells the API whether this is a user, admin, or super admin. A value of 3 denotes the super admin user type. The group ID is hardcoded to 13 — that is something to customize. If the file we saved this in were called zabbix_tiny-add_user.pl, we would call it like this:

$ perl   zabbix_tiny-add_user.pl

While this might seem longer than our raw JSON string, it also deals with logging in, and it is easier to write than raw JSON. For more information on this particular Zabbix API library, refer to http://zabbix.org/wiki/Docs/howto/Perl_Zabbix::Tiny_API.

There are a lot of different Zabbix API libraries for various languages — Python alone has seven different libraries at the time of writing this. It can be a bit of a challenge to choose the best one.

If programming around a library is not your thing, there is also a Python-based project to create command line tools for API operations, called **Zabbix Gnomes**. It can be found at https://github.com/q1x/zabbix-gnomes.

Further reading

We only covered a small portion of the Zabbix API in this chapter; there's lots and lots more. If you plan to use it, consult the official Zabbix manual for information on all the methods, their parameters, and object properties. At the time of this writing, the Zabbix API manual can be found at `https://www.zabbix.com/documentation/3.0/manual/api` — but even if that changes, just visit `https://www.zabbix.com`, and look for the documentation.

Summary

In this chapter, we dived deeper into the internal data structures Zabbix uses. While that's still just a small part of a large amount of database, XML import/export, API, and other information, it should help with some of the common problems users encounter at first.

We figured out how to get raw data from the frontend, which is the easiest method for small datasets. For bigger amounts of data, we learned to grab data from different history tables depending on data type. We also found out how Zabbix proxies keep data in their local databases. For situations where less precision is needed, we learned about the `trends` table and the calculation of the hourly minimal, maximal, and average values that are stored there. We also covered resetting user passwords directly in the database and fixing item history values if the item configuration was incorrect initially.

We explored the Zabbix XML import/export functionality, which allowed us to add and partially update hosts, templates, network maps, screens, host groups, images, and value maps. We looked at the XML format in brief and created a simple script to generate hosts from a CSV file.

And in the end, we looked at the Zabbix API, which allows us to control almost all of the Zabbix configuration. We logged in, controlled the host status, added and deleted a host, created a value map and retrieved some historical item values, and formatted the output a bit with the `json_pp` tool. Although the API was really great, we also discussed various issues with it, including the lack of auditing, proper validation, and error messages. While we could only cover a small part of the Zabbix API here, we figured out how to find out further information in the Zabbix manual and step up the API usage by using a Perl library. We also discovered the list of API libraries for various languages at `http://zabbix.org/wiki/Docs/api/libraries`.

We will continue diving into Zabbix in the next chapter. Various maintenance-related topics will be covered, including internal monitoring to find out cache usage and process busy rates, backing up our Zabbix configuration, and upgrading Zabbix when new versions come out. We will also explore all the parameters in the daemon configuration files.

22
Zabbix Maintenance

It's great when Zabbix runs smoothly — we get all the data, nice graphs, and alerts. To keep it running like that, we should follow the health of Zabbix itself, be ready to recover from disastrous events, and upgrade to the latest version every now and then. In this chapter, we will cover the following topics:

- **Monitoring the internals of Zabbix**: Caches, busy rates, performance items, and other data that reveals how well Zabbix is feeling

- **Making backups**: Suggestions on how to perform backups and potential restore strategies

- **Upgrading Zabbix**: How to know what changes to expect from new versions, which components are compatible with others in different versions, and how to perform the upgrade itself

We will also review generic suggestions regarding Zabbix setup to reduce performance issues and take a look at the audit log — a way to see who made changes to the Zabbix configuration and when, although this feature has some problems that we will make sure to find out. We'll finish this chapter with a look at all the configuration parameters in the server, proxy, and agent configuration files, concentrating on the ones we haven't discussed so far.

Internal monitoring

Zabbix can monitor a lot of things about other systems, but what do we know about Zabbix itself? We can see a few basic indicators in the Zabbix frontend right away. In the frontend, go to **Reports** | **Status of Zabbix**. Here, we can observe high-level information, such as whether the Zabbix server is running, and values, such as the number of hosts, items, triggers, and users online.

This information is also visible as a widget in the dashboard. Both the widget and the report are available to super admin users only.

Let's look at the value next to **Required server performance, new values per second**. It is the main value when determining how large a Zabbix installation is:

Status of Zabbix

PARAMETER	VALUE	DETAILS
Zabbix server is running	Yes	localhost:10051
Number of hosts (enabled/disabled/templates)	59	16 / 2 / 41
Number of items (enabled/disabled/not supported)	318	250 / 1 / 67
Number of triggers (enabled/disabled [problem/ok])	36	36 / 0 [13 / 23]
Number of users (online)	4	2
Required server performance, new values per second	8.1	

New values per second

Why is the new values per second setting so important? While knowing how many hosts or even items a system has is important, the underlying load could vary a lot. For example, we could have a system with 1,000 hosts, 100 items each, but the items would be polled once every 15 minutes. In this case, the approximate expected **New Values Per Second** (**NVPS**) would be 111. Or we could have only 10 hosts with 100 items per host, but if the interval were 10 seconds (that is a very low interval; if possible, never use such a low interval), the total expected NVPS would be 100. As we can see, host and item count have an impact, but so does the average interval. NVPS is a generic value that can be compared to other systems more easily. In our installation, the expected NVPS, based on our current host and item configuration, is likely to be somewhere between 7 and 9. This means that every second, the Zabbix server is expected to receive and process that many historical values—this also includes calculating any trigger expressions, calculating trend information for numeric items, and storing any resulting events and these historical values in the database. It's quite a lot of seemingly invisible work for each value.

We can see the value for the current configuration in the Zabbix status report, but how can we calculate the expected NVPS for a larger system we are building, without adding all the hosts and items? If we had 60 items on a single host each polled once per minute, the NVPS could be calculated like this:

```
<item count> / <item interval>
```

So, 60 items per minute would result in 1 NVPS. By the way, one item per minute would be `1/60` or `0.01557`. To get the total NVPS in the projected environment, we would simply multiply it all by the amount of hosts:

```
<average item count per host> / <average item interval> * <total host
count>
```

Plug in various values and see how the expected NVPS changes as one of these values is changed. The more hosts you have, the more impact the average interval and average item count per host will have.

The value that the frontend gives us is a nice way to determine the expected NVPS right now, but it is not that easy to see how it has changed over time and how configuration changes have impacted it. We can add an internal item that will store this value so that we can see long-term changes and graph them. Navigate to **Configuration | Hosts**, click on **Items** for **A test host**, and then click on the **Create item** button. In this form, start by clicking on **Select** next to the **Key** field, and change the **Type** dropdown to **Zabbix internal** in the item helper. This presents us with a nice list of the available internal items. We will set up a few of these, but won't discuss every single item in there. If you are curious about some after we are done with this topic, consult the Zabbix manual for detailed information on each internal item. Remember how we created an item to monitor the time when the proxy last contacted the server? That also was an internal item.

In this list, click on `zabbix[requiredperformance]`. Fill in the following:

- **Name**: Expected NVPS
- **Type**: **Zabbix internal**
- **Type of information**: **Numeric (float)**
- **Units**: NVPS
- **New application**: Zabbix performance

When done, click on the **Add** button at the bottom. Check this item in the **Latest data** page. After a short while, it should have the value, somewhat similar to what we saw in the Zabbix status report:

Zabbix performance (1 Item)		
Expected NVPS	2015-12-09 11:36:46	8.13 NVPS

This value is likely to be different than the one we saw in the report. We just added an item to monitor the expected NVPS, which provides values of its own, so this action has affected the NVPS already.

With this item configured, let's talk about what it actually is. You might have noticed how it was stressed many times before that this is the expected NVPS. It is based on our host and item configuration and does not actually reflect how many values we are receiving. If we had all the items of the active agent type and all agents were stopped, the expected NVPS would not change, even though we would receive no information at all. Barring such technical issues, this number could differ from the values we normally process because of other reasons. Log-monitoring items are always counted according to their interval. If we have a log item with an interval of 1 second, it is included as 1 NVPS even if the log file itself gets no values—or if it gets 10 values every second. Flexible intervals and item scheduling are ignored, and trapper items are not included in the expected NVPS estimate at all. If we send a lot of values to trapper items, our real, processed NVPS will be higher than the expected NVPS, sometimes several times higher.

As the expected or estimated NVPS can be inaccurate, we also have a way to figure out the real NVPS value—there is another internal item for that purpose. Let's go back to **Configuration | Hosts** and then **Items** for **A test host** again and click on **Create item**. Fill in the following values:

- **Name:** Real NVPS
- **Type: Zabbix internal**
- **Key:** zabbix[wcache,values]
- **Type of information: Numeric (float)**
- **Units:** NVPS
- **Store value: Delta (speed per second)**
- **Applications: Zabbix performance**

When done, click on the **Add** button at the bottom. In the key, we used the keywords wcache and values. The first one is supposed to stand for **write cache**, or we can think of it as a cache of the values to be written to the database. The values parameter tells it to **report the number of values passing through that cache**. We will look at other possible parameters a bit later.

> We could also obtain the number of processed values per type by specifying the third parameter as float, uint, str, log, or text. The third parameter defaults to all, reporting all value types.

Another thing worth noting is the **Store value** — this internal item reports a counter of all values, and this way, we are getting the number of values per second. We both obtain a value, easily comparable with the expected NVPS, and avoid a hill graph. How would one know which internal items return a final value and which ones are counter items? Consult the Zabbix manual, as usual.

With the item in place, let's compare the expected and real values in the latest data page:

Zabbix performance (2 Items)		
Expected NVPS	2015-12-09 13:17:46	8.17 NVPS
Real NVPS	2015-12-09 13:17:47	1.29 NVPS

Notice how the expected NVPS value increased again after adding another item.

On this system, parts of the monitoring infrastructure are down, so the real NVPS value is significantly lower than the expected one. You might want to mark the checkboxes next to both of these items and display an ad-hoc graph to visually compare the values and see how they change over time. The expected NVPS is likely to be pretty stable, only changing when the configuration is changed. The real NVPS is likely to go up and down as the value retrieval and processing changes over time.

Zabbix server uptime

Let's try to monitor another Zabbix internal item. Go to **Configuration | Hosts**, click on **Items** next to **A test host**, and then click on **Create item**. Let's monitor the uptime of the Zabbix server — not the whole system, but the Zabbix server daemon. Fill in these values:

- **Name**: Zabbix server uptime
- **Type**: **Zabbix internal**
- **Key**: zabbix[uptime]
- **Units**: uptime

When done, click on **Add** at the bottom, and then check this item in the **Latest data** page. Notice how our use of the uptime unit resulted in the raw uptime value in seconds being converted to a human-readable format that shows how long the Zabbix server process has been running for:

NAME ▲	LAST CHECK	LAST VALUE
- other - (1 Item)		
Zabbix server uptime	2015-12-09 20:04:49	00:34:27

We could display this item in a screen and have a trigger on it to let us know when the Zabbix server was restarted.

Cache usage

We have already discussed several caches in Zabbix and what they are used for. As these caches fill up, it can have different effects on Zabbix. Let's take a look at how we can monitor how much of some of those caches is free or used. We could monitor the free space in the first cache we found out about: the configuration cache. Let's go to **Configuration | Hosts**, then click on **Items** next to **A test host**, and click on **Create item**. Fill in the following values:

- **Name**: `Zabbix configuration cache, % free`
- **Type**: **Zabbix internal**
- **Key**: `zabbix[rcache,buffer,pfree]`
- **Type of information**: **Numeric (float)**
- **Units**: `%`

When done, click on the **Add** button at the bottom. For this item key, we used the `rcache` keyword, which stands for **read cache**. Coupled with `buffer`, it refers to the configuration cache. With `pfree`, we are requesting free space in this cache as a percentage. Notice how we're setting **Type of information** to **Numeric (float)** — we could have left it at **Numeric (unsigned)**, in which case Zabbix would cut off the decimal part, which is not suggested in this case. Check this item in the **Latest data** page:

NAME ▲	LAST CHECK	LAST VALUE
- other - (1 Item)		
Zabbix configuration cache, % free	2015-12-09 20:45:20	95.92 %

On our system, it is highly unlikely to see the free configuration cache size drop below 90% with the default settings.

There are other internal caches on the server we can monitor. We will discuss what they hold in more detail and the suggested sizes when we look at the daemon configuration parameters a bit later, but let's have a quick list for now:

- **Configuration cache**: We are monitoring it already. It holds host, item, trigger, and other configuration information
- **Value cache**: This holds historical values to speed up triggers, calculated items, aggregate items, and other things
- **VMware cache**: This holds fairly raw VMware data
- **History cache and history cache index**: These two hold historical values before they are processed for triggers and written to the database
- **Trend cache**: This holds trend information for the current hour for all items that are receiving values

> It is a very, very good idea to monitor all of these parameters.

Note that most of the caches can be monitored for Zabbix proxies, too. This can be done by assigning the host with those items to be monitored by a specific Zabbix proxy. At that point, these internal items will return information about that proxy. Only relevant items will work — for example, monitoring the trend cache on a proxy is not possible simply because there is no trend cache on a proxy. The same approach with having such a host assigned to a proxy works also for the items under the internal process busy rate, which we will discuss next.

Internal process busy rate

Zabbix has a bunch of processes internally, and we have already covered a few — we enabled IPMI and VMware pollers as well as SNMP trappers. For several of these, we were also able to configure how many processes to start. How can we know whether one process is enough or maybe we should have a hundred of them? We will discuss general guidelines per type a bit later, but a very important thing to know is how busy the currently running processes are. There are internal items for this purpose as well. For these items, the general syntax is as follows:

```
zabbix[process,<type>,<mode>,<state>]
```

Here, process is a fixed keyword. The second parameter, type, is the process type, as in poller, trapper, and so on. The third parameter, mode, could be one of these:

- avg: The average rate across all processes of the specified type.
- count: The number of processes of the specified type.
- max: The maximum rate across the processes of the specified type.
- min: The minimum rate across the processes of the specified type.
- A number: The rate for an individual process of the specified type. For example, there are five pollers running by default. With a process number specified here, we could monitor poller 1 or poller 3. Note that this is the internal process number, not the system PID.

We talked about rate here — this is the amount of time a target process or processes spent in a state, specified by the fourth parameter. It could either be busy or idle.

Should we monitor the busy rate or the idle one? In most cases, the average busy time for all processes of a specific type is monitored. Why busy? Just by convention, when this monitoring got implemented, the first templates monitored the busy rate. Additionally, when debugging a specific issue, it could be helpful to monitor the busy rate for individual processes. Unfortunately, there is no way to query such values directly from the server — we would have to add an item in the frontend and then wait for it to start working. There is no built-in LLD for process types or the number of them — we would have to create such items manually or automate them using XML importing or the Zabbix API.

To see how this works, let's monitor the average busy rate for all poller processes. Go to **Configuration | Hosts**, click on **Items** next to **A test host**, and then on **Create item**. Fill in these values:

- **Name**: Zabbix $4 process $2 rate
- **Type**: **Zabbix internal**
- **Key**: zabbix[process,poller,avg,busy]
- **Type of information**: **Numeric (float)**
- **Units**: %
- **New application**: Zabbix process busy rates

> Creating such an item on a host that is monitored through a Zabbix proxy will report data about that proxy, not the Zabbix server.

We used positional variables in the item name again—if we wanted to monitor another process, it would be easy to clone this item and change the process name in the item key only.

When done, click on the **Add** button at the bottom. Check this item in the **Latest data** page:

NAME ▲	LAST CHECK	LAST VALUE
Zabbix process busy rates (1 Item)		
Zabbix busy process poller rate	2015-12-11 08:52:51	0.69 %

Most likely, our small Zabbix instance is not very busy polling values. By default, there are 5 pollers started, and they are dealing with the current load without any issues.

As an exercise, monitor a few more process types—maybe trapper and unreachable pollers. Check the Zabbix manual section on internal items for the exact process names to be used in this item.

After adding a few more items, you will probably observe that there are a lot of internal processes. We discussed creating such items automatically using XML importing or the API, but then there were also all the caches we could and should monitor. Zabbix tries to help here a bit and ships with default internal monitoring templates. In the search box in the upper-right corner, enter app zabbix and hit the *Enter* key. Look at the **Templates** block:

Templates							⌃
TEMPLATE	APPLICATIONS	ITEMS	TRIGGERS	GRAPHS	SCREENS	DISCOVERY	WEB
Template **App Zabbix** Agent	Applications 1	Items 3	Triggers 3	Graphs	Screens	Discovery	Web
Template **App Zabbix** Proxy	Applications 1	Items 21	Triggers 19	Graphs 4	Screens 1	Discovery	Web
Template **App Zabbix** Server	Applications 1	Items 30	Triggers 26	Graphs 5	Screens 1	Discovery	Web
							Displaying 3 of 3 found

While the agent template is quite simple and not of much interest at this time, the server and proxy templates cover quite a lot, with 31 and 21 items respectively. These templates will allow out-of-the-box monitoring of internal process busy rates, cache usage, queue, values processed, and a few other things. It is highly recommended to use these templates in all Zabbix installations.

These templates might still be missing a few interesting items, such as the expected NVPS item we created earlier. It is suggested to create a separate template with such missing things instead of modifying the default template. Such an approach will allow easier upgrades, as new versions could add more processes, caches, and have other improvements to the default templates. If we leave the default templates intact, we can import a new XML file, tell Zabbix to add all missing things, update existing things, and remove whatever is not in the XML, and we will have an up-to-date default template. If we had it modified...it could be a lot of manual work to update it.

Unsupported items and more problems

We now know quite a bit about the internal monitoring of Zabbix, but there are still more possibilities. Unsupported items are no good, so let's discuss the ways we could monitor the situation with them.

Counting unsupported items

Similar to cache usage and process busy rates, we may also monitor the count of unsupported items with an internal item. To create such an item, let's go to **Configuration | Hosts**, click on **Items** next to **A test host**, and then click on **Create item**. Fill in these values:

- **Name:** Amount of unsupported items
- **Type: Zabbix internal**
- **Key:** zabbix[items_unsupported]

When done, click on the **Add** button at the bottom. After a short while, check this item on the **Latest data** page:

Amount of unsupported items	2015-12-11 17:02:52 58

58? That is an extremely high value for such a small installation, although in this case it is caused by the VMware monitoring being down. At this time, a VMware timeout results in all VMware items becoming unsupported. In a perfect environment, there would be no unsupported items, so we could create a trigger to alert us whenever this item receives a value larger than 0. That wouldn't be too useful anywhere but in really small environments, though—usually, a thing becomes broken here or there, and the unsupported item count is never 0. A more useful trigger would thus be one that alerts about a larger increase in the number of unsupported items. The change() trigger function could help here:

```
{A test host:zabbix[items_unsupported].change()}>5
```

Whenever the unsupported item count increases by more than 5 in 30 seconds, which is the default item interval, this trigger will fire. The threshold should be tuned to work best for a particular environment.

Such a global alert will be useful, but in larger environments with more distributed responsibilities, we might want to alert the responsible parties only. One way to do that would be monitoring the unsupported item count per host. With this item, it probably makes most sense to create it in some base template so that it is applied to all the hosts it is needed on. Let's create such an item: navigate to **Configuration | Templates**, click on **Items** next to **C_Template_Linux**, and then click on **Create item**. Fill in these values:

- **Name**: Unsupported item count
- **Type**: **Zabbix internal**
- **Key**: zabbix[host,,items_unsupported]

When done, click on the **Add** button at the bottom. Check this item on the **Latest data** page:

A test host	- **other** - (1 Item)		
	Unsupported item count	2015-12-13 09:06:24	2

Apparently, the test host has two unsupported items in this installation. We would now create a trigger on the same template, alerting whenever a host has a non-zero count of unsupported items. Such a combination would work fairly well, although in larger installations, it could result in a large number of triggers firing if an item got misconfigured in the template or if a broken userparameter script were distributed. Unfortunately, there is no built-in item to determine the unsupported item count per host group. One workaround would be to use aggregate items, as discussed in *Chapter 11*, *Advanced Item Monitoring*. For example, to obtain the unsupported item count for a group called **Linux servers**, the aggregate item key could look like this:

```
grpsum[Linux servers,"zabbix[host,,items_unsupported]",last]
```

We should probably avoid creating a trigger for the unsupported item count on individual hosts, creating one on the aggregate item instead. While the individual items would keep collecting data, which is a bit of a load on the Zabbix server and increases database size, at least the alert count would be reasonable.

> If an item turns unsupported, all triggers that reference it stop working, even if they are looking for missing data using the nodata() function. That makes it very hard to alert somebody of such issues unless an internal item such as this is used — it is highly unlikely to become unsupported itself.

There are still more internal items. It is a good idea to look at the full list of available items for the latest version of Zabbix in the online manual.

Reviewing unsupported items

The items that tell us about the number of unsupported items either for the whole Zabbix installation or for a specific host are useful and tell us when things are not good. But what exactly is not good? There is a very easy way to review the unsupported item list in the frontend. Navigate to **Configuration | Hosts**, click on any of the **Items** links, and expand the item filter. Clear out any host, host group, or other filter option that is there, and look at the right-hand side of the filter. In the **State** dropdown, choose **Not supported**, and click on **Filter**. This will display all the unsupported items in this Zabbix instance. Note that we may not display all items in all states like this — the filter will require at least one condition to be set, and the state condition counts.

It is highly recommended to visit this view every now and then and try to fix as many unsupported items as possible. Unsupported items are bad. Note that by default, up to 1,000 entries will be shown. If you have more than 1,000 unsupported items, that's a pretty bad situation and should be fixed.

> In you see unsupported items in templates, it is most likely a Zabbix instance that has been upgraded from an older version. The broken item state was a bug in older versions of Zabbix. To fix this issue, the state for these items should be manually changed in the database. Look up the item ID and set the **State** value for it to 0. As usual, be very careful with direct database updates.

Internal events and unknown triggers

Alerting on unsupported items, which we covered a moment ago, is likely the best approach, as it allows us to have a small number of triggers and a relatively easy way to split up alerting about them. There's another built-in approach that allows us to alert about unsupported items and triggers in an unknown state—Zabbix has the concept of internal events. To configure an alert based on those internal events, go to **Configuration | Actions**, choose **Internal** in the **Event source** dropdown, and click on **Create action**. In the **Action** tab, mark the **Recovery message** checkbox, and enter these values:

- **Name**: A trigger changed state to `unknown`
- **Default subject**: {TRIGGER.STATE}: {TRIGGER.NAME}
- **Recovery subject**: {TRIGGER.STATE}: {TRIGGER.NAME}

Switch to the **Conditions** tab; in the **New condition** block, select **Event type** in the first dropdown, and choose **Trigger in "unknown" state** in the last dropdown:

New condition				
	Event type ▼	= ▼	Trigger in "unknown" state	▼
	Add			

Click on the small **Add** link in the **New condition** block and switch to the **Operations** tab. Click on **New** in the **Action operations** block, and then click on **New** in the **Send to Users** section.

> We set up e-mail for `monitoring_user` in *Chapter 2, Getting Your First Notification*—if another user has e-mail properly set up in your Zabbix instance, choose that user instead.

Click on `monitoring_user` in the popup, and then click on the small **Add** link in the **Operation details** block—the last one, just above the buttons at the very bottom. Be careful; this form is very confusing. When done, click on the **Add** button at the bottom.

We discussed actions in more detail in *Chapter 7, Acting upon Monitored Conditions*.

Now, whenever a trigger becomes `unknown`, an alert will be sent.

While we can limit these actions by application, host, template, or host group, we cannot react to internal events in the same actions we use for trigger events. If we already have a lot of actions carefully splitting up notification per host groups, applications, and other conditions, we would have to replicate all of them for internal events to get the same granularity. That is highly impractical, so at this time, it might be best to have a few generic actions, such as ones that inform key responsible persons, who would investigate and pass the issue to the team assigned to that host group, application, or other unit.

Backing things up

It is a good feeling to have a backup when things go wrong. When setting up a monitoring system, it is a good idea to spend some time to figure out how backups could be made so that the good feeling is not replaced by a bad feeling. With Zabbix, there are components and data to be considered:

- **Zabbix binaries**: Such as the server and proxy agent: They're probably not worth backing up. Hopefully, they're easily available from packages or by recompiling.

- **Zabbix frontend files**: Hopefully, they're easily available as well. If any changes have been made, they're presumably stored as a patch in a version control system.

- **Zabbix configuration files**: Hopefully, these are stored in a version control system or a system configuration tool.

- **Zabbix server database**: This contains all the monitoring-related configuration data, such as hosts and items, and it also holds all the collected values. Now that is worth backing up!

Backing up the database

Several different databases could be used for the Zabbix backend. We won't spend much time on database-specific information, besides a brief look at a simple possible way to create backups with the most widely used backend—MySQL—or one of its forks. A very simple way to back up a database with MySQL, compressing it on the way, would be this:

```
$ mysqldump zabbix --add-drop-table --add-locks --extended-insert
--single-transaction --quick -u zabbix -p | bzip2 > zabbix_database_
backup.db.bz2
```

Here, we are allowing the backup to drop existing tables in the target database and telling it to lock each table when restoring, which is supposed to offer better restore performance. We're also using **extended insert**, which uses one insert for many values instead of one per value—a much smaller backup and much faster restore. Performing the backup in a single transaction should ensure a consistent state across all the tables being backed up. And finally, the `--quick` option should instruct MySQL to dump large tables partially instead of buffering all of their contents in memory.

We also used `bzip2` to compress the data before writing it to the disk. You can choose other compression software such as `gzip` or `xz` or change the compression level, depending on what you need more—disk space savings or a less-taxed CPU during the backup and restore. Memory usage can also be quite high with some compression utilities. The great thing is you can run this backup process without stopping the MySQL server (actually, it has to run) and even the Zabbix server.

Now, you can let your usual backup software grab this created file and store it on a disk array, tape, or some other, more exotic media.

Restoring from a backup

Restoring such a backup is simple as well. We pass the saved statements to the MySQL client, uncompressing them first, if necessary:

```
$ bzcat zabbix_database_backup.db.bz2 | mysql zabbix -u zabbix -p
```

> Use `zcat` or `xzcat` as appropriate if you have chosen a different compression utility.

> The Zabbix server must be stopped during the restore process.

Of course, backups are useful only if it is possible to restore them. As required by any backup policy, the ability to restore from backups should be tested. This includes restoring the database dump, but it is also suggested to compare the schema of the restored database and the default schema as well as running a copy of Zabbix Server on a test system. Make sure to disallow any outgoing network connections by the test server, though; otherwise, it might overload the network or send false alerts.

Separating configuration and data backups

While we can dump a whole database in a single file, it is not always the best solution. There might be cases when restoring only the configuration data would be useful:

- When testing a Zabbix upgrade on a less powerful system than the Zabbix server.

- When attempting to recover from a disastrous event, it would be useful to restore configuration only and resume monitoring as quickly as possible. If needed, history and trend data can be restored later in small portions to avoid overloading the database.

Usually, data tables, such as the ones holding history, trend, and event information, will be much bigger than the configuration tables. Restoring the data tables would take much longer or even be impossible on a test system. We could split all the tables into configuration and data ones, but it is likely even more simple to back each table up separately and deal with the desired tables when restoring. An example command to do so is as follows:

```
$ for table in $(mysql -N -e "show tables;" zabbix); do mysqldump --add-
locks --extended-insert --single-transaction --quick zabbix $table |
bzip2 > zabbix_database_backup_$table.bz2; done
```

Note that in this case, we are not performing the backup for the whole database in a single transaction, and changes to the configuration could lead to inconsistencies across the tables. It is a good idea to schedule such a backup at a time when configuration changes would be unlikely.

If the consistency of the configuration tables is a likely problem, we could instead back up the configuration tables in a single transaction, and the tables that hold collected and recorded information separately:

```
$ mysqldump --add-locks --extended-insert --single-transaction zabbix
--ignore-table=zabbix.history --ignore-table=zabbix.history_uint
--ignore-table=zabbix.history_text --ignore-table=zabbix.history_
str --ignore-table=zabbix.history_log --ignore-table=zabbix.trends
--ignore-table=zabbix.trends_uint --ignore-table=zabbix.events --ignore-
table=zabbix.alerts --ignore-table=zabbix.auditlog --ignore-table=zabbix.
auditlog_details --ignore-table=zabbix.acknowledges | bzip2 > zabbix_
database_backup_config_tables.bz2

$ mysqldump --add-locks --extended-insert --single-transaction zabbix
history history_uint history_text history_str history_log trends trends_
uint events alerts auditlog auditlog_details acknowledges | bzip2 >
zabbix_database_backup_data_tables.bz2
```

Note that the configuration and data table distinction is a bit fuzzy in Zabbix, and several configuration tables still hold runtime information.

Upgrading Zabbix

Even though Zabbix is a mature product with more than 15 years behind it, it is still very actively developed. Bugs are fixed and new features are added. At some point, accumulated improvements make it worth upgrading. In this section, we will look at the following:

- **General version policy**: Which versions are stable and which ones are supported for longer periods of time

- **The upgrade process**: What can be upgraded to what and how it should be done

- **Compatibility between Zabbix components**: Which versions of the server can be used with which versions of the agent and so on

General version policy

The Zabbix versioning scheme has changed a few times over the years. In general, the first two numbers have denoted a major version, such as 2.4 and 3.0, while the third number has denoted a minor version number. Previously, an even second number denoted a stable branch, while an odd second number denoted a development branch. Thus, 2.3 was a development branch for 2.4, while 2.4 was the resulting stable branch. This has slightly changed with 3.0. The development releases have moved away from the odd numbering, that is, the 2.5 number. They are now called `3.0.0alpha1`, `3.0.0beta2`, and so on. This is deemed to be more user friendly, although the internal numbering is still based on 2.5 in several places — the database version, for example, which we will explore in more detail a bit later.

The new version numbering since Zabbix 3.0 could be summed up as follows:

- A version number with just digits (and dots) in it denotes a stable release

- A version number with the `alpha`, `beta`, or `rc` (release candidate) keywords added is not a stable release

Long-term support and short-term support

For stable branches, there are even more differences. The release and support policy has changed as well, and the current policy states that there are two types of stable branches:

- **Long-term support or LTS branches**: These branches are supported for 3 years for general bug fixes and 2 more years for only critical and security fixes

- **Short-term support branches**: These are supported for roughly 1 month after the first release in the next stable branch, LTS or non-LTS

Historically, the 2.2 branch was designated as an LTS branch, with plans to release 2.4 and 2.6 as short-term support branches. Plans tend to change, and the 2.6 branch was canceled. 3.0 is the current LTS branch, with 3.2 and 3.4 planned as short term support branches, 4.0 following as the next LTS branch, and all further LTS branches aligning to N.0 versioning. Will this hold? That is very hard to predict, so you might want to check the current policy at http://www.zabbix.com/life_cycle_and_release_policy.php.

> This support mostly references commercial services, although it strongly affects all users. We will discuss support options in *Appendix B, Being Part of the Community*.

How to decide which branch to use? Consider the available features and how quickly you would be able to upgrade. Does the latest LTS version satisfy you and you don't plan to upgrade for years? Stick with it. Really desire a feature in a non-LTS branch and plan to upgrade when the next stable branch comes out? Go with the non-LTS branch. Anything in-between, and you'll have to make a decision based on the support policy that's in effect at that time. Here's a quick lookup table to help you decide:

Use a non-LTS branch when...	Use an LTS branch when...
You need a new feature in the non-LTS branch	The LTS-branch features satisfy you
You plan to upgrade to every new version quickly	You prefer to stay with one version as long as possible
You can tolerate slight instability	You prefer a more stable version

Note that the **slight instability** mentioned in the table does not mean that there are serious issues with the non-LTS versions. In some cases, **more stable** might mean this bug is pretty stable, but has not been fixed for a long time.

The upgrade process

Read the upgrade notes.

What was that? Yes, before performing any upgrades, take a little time, go to the Zabbix manual, and read the upgrade notes. If you are jumping over a few major versions, do read all the upgrade notes in between. Even if you have followed Zabbix development a bit, you might have missed some change that could cause problems — removed or added configuration parameters, memory requirement changes, API changes...upgrade notes should list all significant changes.

It is also highly suggested to read the pages on new features and improvements, called **What's new**. While it's much less risky to miss some of those changes, knowing about them could help you use Zabbix in a more efficient way.

Let's talk about the upgrade process itself now. This process and compatibility will differ depending on the version change you are performing:

- A minor version upgrade inside the same major version is simple and easy to undo
- A major version upgrade is more complicated and hard or impossible to undo

Minor version upgrade

This is the simplest case. For example, upgrading from 3.0.0 to 3.0.1 or from 3.0.1 to 3.0.5 would be considered a minor version upgrade.

Zabbix uses the third number to denote a minor version.

When performing a minor version upgrade, we may upgrade any combination of components — server, agents, proxies, Java gateway, and so on. While it is suggested to keep the main components of the same version to reduce confusion, a 3.0.0 server will happily work with a 3.0.1 frontend, 3.0.2 proxies, and 3.0.3 agents. Inside one major version, all components are compatible with each other.

It is also perfectly fine to skip minor versions when upgrading — as mentioned, going from 3.0.1 directly to 3.0.5 is perfectly fine.

While minor versions won't have upgrade notes often, do make sure to check for them. And read those **What's new** pages.

Upgrading binaries

Zabbix Server, agents, and potentially proxy binaries have to be updated. The exact process will depend on how you installed them in the first place. Compiled from the source? Perform the same steps as during the installation. Installed from packages? Use the distribution package-management tools to perform the upgrade. This process should be fairly simple, and we discussed the details back in *Chapter 1, Getting Started with Zabbix*.

After starting the upgraded Zabbix server, in some rare cases, you might see a log entry like this:

```
10852:20151231:094918.820 starting automatic database upgrade
```

For a minor version upgrade, that could be a change to the database indexes to improve performance, but we will discuss that in more detail when we get to the major version upgrades.

Upgrading the frontend

Upgrading the Zabbix frontend from one minor to another minor version should be simple as well. If installed from the sources, copy over the new frontend files. Instead of overwriting the frontend, it might be a good idea to copy the frontend to a separate directory first, verify that it works as intended, and then move over your users.

For example, if your original installation had the Zabbix frontend in the relative path zabbix/, place the new frontend files in zabbix-<new_version>/, rename the zabbix/ directory to zabbix-<old_version>/, and create a symlink called zabbix that points at the new version so that you don't have to use a different URL whenever you upgrade. To skip the configuration wizard, copy over the configuration file:

```
# cp zabbix-<old_version>/conf/zabbix.conf.php zabbix/conf/
```

That should be enough. Now, you can refresh the Zabbix frontend in the browser and check the page footer—the new version number should be visible there.

This approach with keeping the old frontend versions is useful if a new version turns out to have a problem and you would like to test whether the old version also had the same problem—just load up a URL in your browser that points to the old frontend directory. If the problem indeed turns out to be a regression, simply change the symlink to point to the old directory, and revert to the old version.

> If you modified the defines.inc.php file, make sure to perform the same modifications in the new version of the file.

You may keep and use multiple versions of the Zabbix frontend in parallel, as long as they all are of the same major version. While normally not needed, it can be very helpful when some debugging or comparison has to be performed.

Major-level upgrades

A major-level upgrade is slightly different from a minor version upgrade. As a quick reminder, definitely go and read the upgrade notes—major versions will always have some. Remember about the What's new pages, too.

Back to the major version upgrade itself, the most significant differences from a minor version upgrade are as follows:

- Database schema changes
- Compatibility
- Reading the upgrade notes

> When performing major-level upgrades from source, it is suggested to avoid copying the new frontend files over the old files. Leftover files from the old version might cause problems.

Let' talk about database schema changes right now, let's discuss compatibility in detail a bit later, and let's always remember to read our upgrade notes.

While the Zabbix team works hard to keep minor version upgrades without database changes, for major releases, it's open season. Changes to the database schema and its contents are made to accommodate new features, improve performance, and increase flexibility. Users wouldn't appreciate it if they couldn't keep gathered data and created configuration in the name of new greatness, so with each new version, a database upgrade patch is provided. This may include adding new tables and columns, removing tables and columns, and changing the data layout.

Given that a major version upgrade changes the database, make sure you have a recent backup. While upgrades are extensively tested, it is not possible for the developers to test all scenarios. What has worked for a thousand people might break in some obscure way for you. Additionally, interrupting the upgrade process because of a hardware or electricity failure is likely to leave your database in a broken state. You have been warned, so get that backup ready.

You are strongly encouraged to test the upgrade on a test installation, preferably using a production dataset (maybe with trimmed history and trend data, if the available hardware does not permit testing with a full copy).

With a fresh backup created, we are ready to engage the major version upgrade. The database upgrade process significantly changed for Zabbix version 2.2. In older versions, we had to apply the database patch manually. If you happen to have an old Zabbix installation—old being pre-2.0—you will have to patch it up to the 2.0 database schema manually. For your reference, the database patches are located in the `upgrades/dbpatches` directory in the source tree, but if you really want to follow that path, make sure to consult with the Zabbix community via the channels discussed in *Appendix B, Being Part of the Community*.

For upgrading to Zabbix 2.0 or more recent versions, no manual patching is required. Starting up the new server will automatically upgrade the database schema. Note that this database upgrading happens without a confirmation. Be careful not to start a more recent server binary against an older database version if you do not intend to change the database.

One last note regarding the upgrade notes: promise. While the latest Zabbix upgrades are really quick even in large installations, older versions sometimes upgraded historical data tables, and that took a long time—like, really, a long time. In some reported cases, it was days. If such a change is required in any of the future versions, it will be mentioned in the upgrade notes, and you'll be glad you read them.

Database versioning

With all this talk about the database version and schema changes, let's take a closer look at how version information is stored and how we can check the upgrade status. Examine the `dbversion` table in your Zabbix database:

```
mysql> select * from dbversion;

+-----------+-----------+
| mandatory | optional  |
+-----------+-----------+
|   3000000 |   3000000 |
+-----------+-----------+
1 row in set (0.00 sec)
```

This table is the way Zabbix components determine which version of the database schema they are dealing with. There are two numbers in there: the mandatory and optional version. The following rules are important regarding version numbers:

- Inside one major version, the mandatory version number is always the same
- If a more recent server is started, it upgrades the database to the latest mandatory and optional version

- The server and frontend can work with a database as long as its mandatory version matches their mandatory version exactly — the optional version does not affect compatibility

The mandatory version encodes things such as table changes, column changes, and otherwise significant changes that break compatibility. The optional version would usually denote an index change — something that is helpful but does not prohibit older versions from working with a more recent database.

> Zabbix server can upgrade to the latest database schema version on all versions from 2.0 onwards. To upgrade the database from version 2.0 to 3.2, it is not required to use server versions in succession — it is enough to start server version 3.2.

When a new major version of Zabbix Server is started, it is possible to observe the current status and database upgrade progress in the server log file:

```
10852:20151209:094918.686 Starting Zabbix Server. Zabbix 3.0.0
(revision {ZABBIX_REVISION}).
10852:20151209:094918.729 ****** Enabled features ******
...
10852:20151209:094918.730 TLS support:               NO
10852:20151209:094918.730 *****************************
10852:20151209:094918.730 using configuration file: /usr/local/etc/
zabbix_server.conf
10852:20151209:094918.820 current database version (mandatory/
optional): 3000000/ 3000000
10852:20151209:094918.820 required mandatory version:  3000000
10852:20151209:094918.820 starting automatic database upgrade
...
10852:20151209:094918.866 completed 20% of database upgrade
...
10852:20151209:094918.937 completed 100% of database upgrade
10852:20151209:094918.937 database upgrade fully completed
```

Notice how it prints out the current mandatory and optional database versions we just examined in the database and the required mandatory version. If the mandatory or optional database version numbers are lower than the required version, the server will upgrade the database. If the database mandatory version is higher than the server version, the server will refuse to start up. During the database schema upgrade, no monitoring happens. Monitoring restarts once the database upgrade is complete.

What happens if you upgrade the fronted before upgrading and starting the server to take care of the database upgrade? You are likely to see a message like this in the frontend:

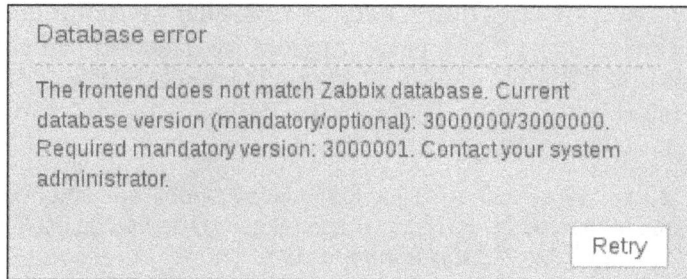

```
Database error

The frontend does not match Zabbix database. Current
database version (mandatory/optional): 3000000/3000000.
Required mandatory version: 3000001. Contact your system
administrator.

                                              Retry
```

If you see such a message when upgrading, start the new server and ensure the database upgrade is successful. If that doesn't help, make sure you are not starting some older Zabbix server binary or pointing Zabbix server at a different database. If you see a message like that when not upgrading Zabbix, you likely have a quite significant misconfiguration. Such a situation should never happen during the normal operation of Zabbix or minor version upgrades. Note that the Zabbix frontend stores the major version it is compatible with in the `defines.inc.php` file in the `ZABBIX_DB_VERSION` constant.

Gathering data during the upgrade

The database upgrade process can be very quick, but in some cases, it can also take quite some time. It might be required to keep gathering data even during the Zabbix upgrade, but how can we achieve that if the monitoring does not resume until the upgrade is finished?

Remember the additional Zabbix process, the proxy? It was able to gather data and buffer it for sending to the Zabbix server, so no data was lost even if the server was down for some time, which sounds pretty much like our situation. If all your actual monitoring is already done by Zabbix proxies, you are already on the right track.

If you have items that are polled directly by server, you might want to set up a temporary proxy installation, maybe even on the same server, that would be running during the Zabbix server upgrade and removed later. To do this easily, use the mass update functionality in the **Configuration | Hosts** section in the frontend and set the **Monitored by proxy** option. Make sure the proxy can actually gather data by testing it first with a single host.

> Setting up a temporary proxy installation will be notably harder if you are using active items. It would be required to reconfigure all Zabbix agents as they connect to the address, specified in the `ServerActive` parameter. On the other hand, active agents do buffer data for a short while themselves, so a quick server upgrade might not miss that data anyway.

The proxy method sounds great, but it is a bit more complicated than just upgrading the server. Officially, only the same major version is supported for server-proxy compatibility. This means that we should not use proxies of the previous version with our upgraded server. Proxies, if used with a MySQL or PostgreSQL backend, can upgrade their database as well. The suggested path for using proxies to continue data collection through the major version upgrade would be like this:

1. Block all proxy-server communication (possibly using a local firewall such as `iptables`).
2. Stop the old Zabbix server, upgrade it, and start the new server.
3. Stop one of the old Zabbix proxies, upgrade it, and start the new version to upgrade the local database.
4. Restore the communication between the proxy and the new server.
5. Proceed the same way with all the remaining proxies.

This should ensure minimum data loss through the upgrade, especially if the steps for an individual proxy upgrade are scripted and happen with no delays.

> Proxy database upgrade is not supported if using SQLite. In that case, the previous method would not work, and the proxy database file should simply be removed when upgrading.

The frontend configuration file

While the database upgrade is the most important step when moving from one major version to another, it's worth paying a moment of attention to the Zabbix frontend configuration file. It is suggested to compare the old configuration file with the new one and see whether there are any new parameters or significant changes to the existing parameters. The easiest way might be comparing with the `zabbix.conf.php.example` file in the `conf/` subdirectory. This configuration file is pretty small, so spotting the differences should be easy.

> When installing from packages, the frontend configuration file could also be placed in /etc/zabbix/, /etc/zabbix/web/ or /etc/zabbix/frontend/.

Compatibility

We have discussed upgrading the Zabbix server. But there are quite a lot of components, and the compatibility between each of them differs slightly. Actually, the official compatibility rule list is very short:

- All older versions of Zabbix agents are supported
- Zabbix server, proxies, and Java gateways must be of the same major version

Regarding the agents, it really is as great as it sounds. All the old agent versions will work with the latest version of the Zabbix server or proxy, even down to 1.0 from 2001. If you upgrade Zabbix server, you can keep your agents as-is — although you would not benefit from new features, performance, or even security improvements.

Technically, combinations outside of the support rules might work. For example, a more recent agent might work with an older server in some cases, and the Zabbix Java gateway protocol has not changed much, so it is likely to work with different major versions of Zabbix server, too. Such combinations are not tested by Zabbix developers, are not supported, and should be avoided in general.

Performance considerations

Zabbix tends to perform nicely for small installations, but as the monitored environment grows, one might run into performance problems. A full Zabbix performance discussion is out of scope here, but let's discuss the starting points to having a healthy configuration and the directions for further research:

- Monitor only what you really need, as rarely as possible, and keep the data only for as long as really needed. It is common to new users of Zabbix to use default templates as-is, add a lot of new items with low intervals...and never look at the data. It is suggested to clone the default templates, eliminate all that is not needed, and increase the intervals as much as possible. This involves trimming item lists, increasing intervals, and reducing history and trend-retention periods. There are also events, alerts, and other data — we will discuss their storage settings a bit later.

- When using Zabbix agents, use active items. Active items will result in a smaller number of network connections and reduce the load on the Zabbix server. There are some features not supported with active items, so sometimes, you will have to use passive items. We discussed what can and cannot be done with active items in *Chapter 3, Monitoring with Zabbix Agents and Basic Protocols*.

- Use Zabbix proxies. They will provide bulk data to Zabbix Server, reducing the work the server has to do even further. We discussed proxies in *Chapter 19, Using Proxies to Monitor Remote Locations*.

We already know about the history and trend-retention periods for items — but for how long does Zabbix store events, alerts, acknowledgment messages, and other data? This is configurable by going to **Administration | General** and choosing **Housekeeping** in the dropdown in the upper-right corner:

	Events and alerts
Enable internal housekeeping	▓
Trigger data storage period (in days)	365
Internal data storage period (in days)	365
Network discovery data storage period (in days)	365
Auto-registration data storage period (in days)	365

> This page is excessively long, so the preceding screenshot only shows a small section from the top.

Here, we may configure for how long to keep the following data:

- **Events**: We may choose separate storage periods for trigger, internal, network discovery, and active agent autoregistration events. Note that removing an event will also remove all associated alerts and acknowledgment messages.

- **IT service data**: The IT service up and down state is recorded separately from trigger events, and its retention period can be configured separately as well.

- **Audit data**: This specifies how long to store the audit data for. We will discuss what that actually is in a moment.

- **User sessions**: User sessions that have been closed will be removed more frequently, but active user sessions will be removed after 1 year by default. This means that one may not be logged in longer than a year

These values should be kept reasonably low. Keeping data for a long period of time will increase the database size, and that can impact the performance a lot.

What about the history and trend settings in here? While they're configurable per item normally, we may override those here. Also, for each of the entries, internal housekeeping may be disabled. These options are aimed at users who have to manage large Zabbix installations. When the database grows really large, its performance significantly degrades, and can be improved by partitioning the biggest tables — splitting them up by some criteria. With Zabbix, it is common to partition the history and trends tables, sometimes adding events and alerts tables. If partitioning is used, parts of tables (partitions) are removed, and the internal housekeeping for those tables should be disabled. A lot of people in the Zabbix community will eagerly suggest partitioning at the first opportunity. Unless you plan to have a really large installation or know database partitioning really well, it might be better to hold off. There is no officially supported or built-in partitioning scheme yet, and one might appear in the future. If it does and your partition scheme is different, it will be up to you to synchronize it with the official one.

Who did that?

"Now who did that?" — a question occasionally heard in many places, IT workplaces included. Weird configuration changes, unsolicited reboots — accountability and a trace of actions help a lot to determine whether the questioner was the one who made the change and then forgot about it. For Zabbix configuration changes, an internal audit log is available. Just like most functionality, it is conveniently accessible from the web frontend. During our configuration quest, we made quite a lot of changes — let's see what footprints we left. Navigate to **Reports | Audit**, and set the filter time bar to a period that approximately matches the initial installation of this Zabbix instance. We are presented with a list of the things we did, although you can also only see logging in and out in the first page of the audit records:

TIME	USER	IP	RESOURCE	ACTION	ID	DESCRIPTION	DETAILS
2015-12-12 14:06:12	Admin	127.0.0.1	User	Login	1		
2015-12-12 14:06:12	Admin	127.0.0.1	User	Logout	1		Manual Logout
2015-12-12 14:05:11	Admin	127.0.0.1	User	Login	1		
2015-12-12 14:05:11	Admin	127.0.0.1	User	Logout	1		Manual Logout
2015-12-12 14:04:10	Admin	127.0.0.1	User	Login	1		
2015-12-12 14:04:10	Admin	127.0.0.1	User	Logout	1		Manual Logout

And what if you set up Zabbix frontend monitoring, like we did in *Chapter 13, Monitoring Web Pages*? You are likely to see only such records, as our web scenario logs in and out every minute. But notice the filter—we may also filter by user, action, and resource:

Expand the **Action** and **Resource** dropdowns—notice that they are quite fine grained, especially the **Resource** dropdown.

In the Zabbix 1.8 version of this book, it said:

> *In the first Zabbix 1.8 releases some actions are not registered in the audit log. Such issues are expected to be fixed in near future.*

Oh well. Unfortunately, it did not get fixed in further 1.8 releases, 2.0, 2.2, or 2.4. Nor in 3.0. The Zabbix audit log is still missing lots of operations performed, especially when the API is used. While the audit log can be extremely useful, it can easily miss the specific operation you are interested in. Perform a test with the version you are interested in to be sure—the list of operations that are not logged can easily change in a minor version.

Moving forward from the sad fact of the broken audit log, as an exercise, try to find out at what time you added the **Restart Apache** action.

While looking at this section, let's remind ourselves of another logging area—the action log that we briefly looked at before. Go to **Reports | Action log**. Here, all actions performed by the Zabbix server are recorded. This includes sending e-mails, executing remote commands, sending SMS messages, and executing custom scripts. This view provides information on what content was sent to whom, whether it was successful, and error messages, if any. It is useful for verifying whether Zabbix has or has not sent a particular message as well as figuring out whether the configured actions are working as expected.

Together, the action and log audit sections provide a good overview of internal Zabbix configuration changes as well as debugging help to determine what action operations have been performed.

Exploring configuration file parameters

Let's conclude this chapter by digging into the configuration files of the Zabbix agent and server and examining each parameter in them. We'll start with the agent configuration file and discuss the ways in which common parameters apply to other daemons. We will skip the proxy configuration file, as the common parameters will be discussed by then, and the proxy-specific parameters were discussed in *Chapter 19, Using Proxies to Monitor Remote Locations*. We will also skip all the parameters that start with TLS, as those are related to Zabbix daemon traffic encryption, and we discussed that in *Chapter 20, Encrypting Daemon Traffic*.

We will look at the parameters in the order they appear in in the default example configuration files—no other meaning should be derived from the ordering here.

While reading the following descriptions, it is suggested to have the corresponding configuration file open. It will allow you to verify that the parameters are the same in your version of Zabbix. Make sure to read the comments next to each parameter— they might show that some parameters have changed since the time of writing this. In general, when in doubt, read the comments in the configuration files. The Zabbix team tries really hard to make them both short and maximally relevant and helpful.

Zabbix agent daemon and common parameters

Let's start with the agent daemon parameters. For the parameters that are also available for other daemons, we'll discuss their relevance to all the daemons here:

- `PidFile`: This is common to all daemons. They write the PID of the main process in this file. The default configuration files use `/tmp` for simplicity's sake. In production systems, this should be set to the distribution recommended location.

- `LogType`: This is common to all daemons and can be one of file, syslog, or console. The default is file, and in that case, the `LogFile` parameter determines where the logs are written. The syslog value directs the daemon to log to syslog, and the console parameter tells it to log the messages to `stdout`.

- `LogFile`: This is common to all daemons. Log data is written to this file when `LogType` is set to file. The default configuration files use `/tmp` for simplicity's sake. In production systems, this should be set to the distribution-recommended location.

- LogFileSize: This is common to all daemons. When logging to a file, if the file size exceeds this number of megabytes, move it to file.0 (for example, zabbix_agentd.log.0) and log to a new file. Only one such move is performed (that is, there is never zabbix_agentd.log.1).

- DebugLevel: This is common to all daemons and specifies how much logging information to provide, starting with 0 (nearly nothing) and ending with 5 (a lot). It is probably best to run at DebugLevel 3 normally, and use something higher for debugging. For example, starting with DebugLevel 4, all server and proxy database queries are logged. At DebugLevel 5, two extra things are currently logged:

    ◦ Received pages for web monitoring
    ◦ Received raw data for VMware monitoring

> We will look at changing the log level for a running daemon in *Appendix A, Troubleshooting*.

- SourceIP: This is common to all daemons. If the system has multiple interfaces, outgoing connections will use the specified address. Note that not all connections will obey this parameter — for example, the backend database connections on the server or proxy won't.

- EnableRemoteCommands: This determines whether the system.run item should allow running commands. Disabled by default.

- LogRemoteCommands: If EnableRemoteCommands is enabled, this parameter allows us to log all the received commands. Unless system.run is used to retrieve data, it's probably a good idea to enable logging of the remote commands.

- Server: This is also available for the Zabbix proxy, but not for the Zabbix server. It's a comma-delimited list of IP addresses or host names the agent should accept connections from. It's only relevant for passive items, zabbix_get, and other incoming connections.

- ListenPort: This is common to all daemons and specifies the port to listen on.

- ListenIP: This is common to all daemons and specifies the IP address to listen on — could also be a comma-delimited list of addresses.

- StartAgents: This is the number of processes to start that are responsible for incoming connection handling. If it's a very resource-starved system, it might be a good idea to reduce this. If this agent is expected to get lots of queries for passive items, increase this number. Note that it has nothing to do with the collector or active check processes; their numbers cannot be directly changed. If set to 0, the agent will stop listening to incoming connections. This could be better security-wise, but could also make debugging much harder.

- ServerActive: This is the list of servers and ports to connect to for active checks. It follows the syntax of server:port, with multiple entries delimited by commas. If not set, no active checks are processed. We discussed this functionality in *Chapter 3, Monitoring with Zabbix Agents and Basic Protocols*.

- Hostname: This is also available for the Zabbix proxy, but not for the Zabbix server. If specified, the exact string will be sent to the Zabbix server as the host name for this system.

- HostnameItem: If Hostname is not specified but HostnameItem is, the value in this parameter will be interpreted as an item key and the result of the evaluation will be sent to the server as the host name for this system.

- HostMetadata: This is an exact string to be sent to the server — used in active agent autoregistration.

- HostMetadataItem: If HostMetadata is not specified but HostMetadataItem is, the value in this parameter will be interpreted as an item key and the result of the evaluation will be sent to the server as the host metadata to be used in active agent autoregistration.

- RefreshActiveChecks: This specifies how often the agent should connect to the server and ask for active items. It's set to 2 minutes by default. If active checks are not used at all, it means a useless connection every 2 minutes from each agent — it's best not to set ServerActive at all in such a case.

- BufferSend: Active agents will send values every BufferSend seconds — by default, every 5 seconds. This allows us to reduce the number of network connections if multiple values are collected within a 5-second window.

- BufferSize: This is a buffer to hold the values for active items. By default, it's set to 100 values. This is an in-memory buffer — do not set it too large if memory usage is a concern. The buffer is actually split in half if there is at least one log-monitoring item — one half is used for "normal" values, the other for log entries. If the buffer is full, new "normal" values will result in the dropping of older "normal" values, but it won't affect log entries. If the log entry half of the buffer is full, log file processing stops, but no entries are dropped there. If there are log items only and no "normal" items, half of the buffer is still reserved for "normal" entries. If there are only "normal" items, the whole buffer is used for them until at least one log item is added.

- `MaxLinesPerSecond`: This is the default maximum number of lines of log items that should be sent to the server. We discussed this in *Chapter 11, Advanced Item Monitoring*.

- `Alias`: This is a way to set an alias for an item key. While usable on all platforms, we discussed it in *Chapter 14, Monitoring Windows*. This parameter can also be used to create two LLD rules with the same key, even if the key itself does not accept parameters. One rule could use the original key, another the key that is aliased.

- `Timeout`: This is common to all daemons. It specifies the timeout for running commands, making connections, and so on. Since Zabbix 3.0, it has a default of 3 on agents and 4 on the server and proxy. This could affect `userparameters`, for example—a script that takes more than a few seconds would time out. It is highly suggested not to increase the timeout on the server side—if we have to handle many values every second, it's not good to have a server process wait on a single script that long. If you have such a script that takes a long time to return the value, consider using `zabbix_sender` instead, as discussed in *Chapter 11, Advanced Item Monitoring*.

- `AllowRoot`: By default, Zabbix daemons, if started as root, try to drop the privileges to a user specified in the User parameter (refer to the next point). If the User parameter is not specified, the outcome depends on this parameter. If it's set to 0, startup fails. If it's set to 1, the daemon starts as the root user.

- `User`: This is common to all daemons. If daemons are started as the `root` user and `AllowRoot` is set to `0`, try to change to the user specified in this parameter. This is set to `zabbix` by default.

- `Include`: This is common to all daemons. It allows you to include individual or multiple configuration files. We discussed this feature in *Chapter 11, Advanced Item Monitoring*. Note that files are included sequentially as if literally "included" in the location where the `Include` directive appeared. Also keep in mind that if specified more than once, most parameters will override all previous occurrences—that is, the last option with the same name wins.

- `UnsafeUserParameters`: By default, a subset of characters is disallowed to be passed as parameters to `userparameter` keys. If enabled, this option will allow anything to be passed and is essentially equivalent to `EnableRemoteCommands`—the originally prohibited symbols make it simple to gain shell access. See the default configuration file for a full list of symbols this parameter would allow.

- `UserParameter`: This allows us to extend agents by adding custom item keys to it. We discussed this in quite a lot of detail and configured some userparameters in *Chapter 11, Advanced Item Monitoring*. This parameter may be specified multiple times as long the item key is unique — that is a way to add multiple userparameters.

- `LoadModulePath`: This is common to all daemons. It specifies a path to load modules, written in the C language. This is an advanced way to extend Zabbix daemons that's a bit out of scope for this book. Refer to the Zabbix manual for more details.

- `LoadModule`: This is common to all daemons. Multiple entries of this parameter may be specified for individual .so files to load inside the `LoadModulePath` directory.

Zabbix server daemon parameters

We will now skip the common parameters we already discussed when looking at the agent daemon configuration file. The remaining ones are as follows:

- `DBHost`: This is useful if the backend database is on a different system. Using an IP address is highly recommended here.

- `DBName`: This is the database name; we set it in *Chapter 1, Getting Started with Zabbix*. As the comment explains, it should be set to the database file path when the SQLite backend is used for a proxy.

- `DBSchema`: This is the database schema, only useful with PostgreSQL and IBM DB2.

- `DBUser` and `DBPassword`: These are database access credentials. As the comment explains, they're ignored when the SQLite backend is used for a proxy.

- `DBSocket`: This is the path to the database socket, if needed. Unless the Zabbix server or proxy is compiled against a different database library than the one available at runtime, you'll likely never need this parameter.

- `DBPort`: If connecting to a local or remote database on a nonstandard port, specify it here.

- `StartPollers`: Pollers are internal processes that collect data in various ways. By default, five pollers are started, and this is plenty for tiny installations such as our test setup. In larger installations, it is common to have hundreds of pollers. Notice that there are no separate SNMP pollers—the same processes are responsible for passive agent and SNMP device polling. How to know whether you have enough? Using the internal monitoring, find out the average busy rate. If it's above some 70%, just add more pollers. Pollers are responsible for:

    ○ Connecting to passive agents

    ○ Connecting to SNMP devices

    ○ Performing simple checks, such as service/port checks

    ○ Retrieving internal monitoring data

    ○ Retrieving VMware data from the VMware cache

    ○ Running external check scripts

- `StartIPMIPollers`: This specifies how many processes should be started that poll IPMI devices. We configured this parameter in *Chapter 16, Monitoring IPMI devices.*

- `StartPollersUnreachable`: If a host is not reachable, it is not polled by normal pollers anymore—special types called **unreachable pollers** now deal with that host, including IPMI items. This is done to avoid a situation where a few hosts that time out take up most of the poller time. If there aren't enough unreachable pollers, the worst thing that happens is that hosts, declared unreachable, are not noticed as being back up as quickly. By default, only one unreachable poller is started. To know whether that is enough, observe their busy rate, especially when there are systems down in the monitored environment.

- `StartTrappers`: By default, there are five trappers. As with pollers, monitor their busy rate and add more as needed. Trappers are responsible for receiving incoming connections from:

    ○ Active agents

    ○ Active proxies

    ○ `zabbix_sender`

    ○ The Zabbix frontend, including server availability check, global scripts, and queue data

- `StartPingers`: These processes create temporary files and then call `fping` against those files to perform ICMP ping checks. If there are lots of ICMP ping items; make sure to check the busy rate of these processes and add more as needed.

- `StartDiscoverers`: Discoverers perform network discovery. Discovery happens sequentially for each rule. Even if there are lots of available discoverers, only one at a time works on a single discovery rule. Note that discoverers split up the rules they will serve—for example, if there are two discovery rules and two discoverers, one discoverer will always work with a particular rule. We discussed network discovery in *Chapter 12, Automating Configuration.*

- `StartHTTPPollers`: These processes are responsible for processing web scenarios. Like discoverers, HTTP pollers split up the web scenarios they will serve. We discussed web monitoring in *Chapter 13, Monitoring Web Pages.*

- `StartTimers`: Timer processes can be quite resource intensive, especially if lots of triggers use time-based functions such as `now()`. We discussed time-based trigger functions in *Chapter 6, Detecting Problems with Triggers.* These processes are responsible for:
  - Placing hosts in and out of maintenance at second 0 of every minute—this is only done by the first timer process if more than one is started
  - Evaluating all triggers that include at least one time-based trigger function at second 0 and second 30 every minute

- `StartEscalators`: These processes move escalations forward in steps, as discussed in *Chapter 7, Acting upon Monitored Conditions.* They also run remote commands, if instructed so by action operations.

- `JavaGateway`, `JavaGatewayPort`, and `StartJavaPollers`: These parameters point at the Java gateway and its port and tell the server or proxy how many processes should connect to that gateway. Note that they all connect to the same gateway, so the gateway should be able to handle the load if the number of Java pollers is increased. We discussed Java monitoring in *Chapter 17, Monitoring Java Applications.*

- `StartVMwareCollectors`, `VMwareFrequency`, `VMwarePerfFrequency`, `VMwareCacheSize`, and `VMwareTimeout`: These control the way VMware monitoring works. We discussed these parameters in detail in *Chapter 18, Monitoring VMware.*

- `SNMPTrapperFile` and `StartSNMPTrapper`: When receiving SNMP traps, we must specify the temporary trap file and whether the SNMP trapper should be started. Note that only one SNMP trapper process may be started. We configured these parameters in *Chapter 4, Monitoring SNMP Devices*.

- `HousekeepingFrequency`: This specifies how often the internal housekeeper process runs — or, to be more specific, how long after the previous run finished the next run should start. It is not suggested to change the default interval of one hour — the housekeeper may be disabled as needed for specific data in **Administration | General**, as discussed earlier in this chapter. The first run of the housekeeper happens 30 minutes after the server or proxy starts. The housekeeper may be manually invoked using the runtime control option.

- `MaxHousekeeperDelete`: For deleted items, this specifies how many values per item should be deleted in a single run, with the default being 5,000. For example, if we had deleted 10 items with 10,000 values each, it would take two housekeeper runs to get rid of all of the values for all items. If an item had a huge number of values, deleting them all in one go could cause database performance issues. Note that this parameter does not affect value cleanup for existing items.

- `SenderFrequency`: This specifies how often unsent alerts are sent out. Note that changing this value will affect both the time from the trigger to the first message and retries. With the default of 30 seconds, it may take up to 30 seconds to send out a message after a trigger fires. It also means that there will be 30 seconds between attempts — Zabbix tries to send a message 3 times before declaring it as failed. If this parameter is reduced to result in the faster sending of the first message, it will also decrease the time between repeated attempts. With the default value of 30 seconds, an e-mail server being down for a bit more than one minute would still result in the message being sent on the third attempt. If this parameter is reduced to 10 seconds, a 30-second email-server downtime would be enough to potentially miss a message.

- `CacheSize`: This is the size of the main configuration cache that holds hosts, items, triggers, and lots of other information. Usage of this cache depends on the size of the configuration data — which is influenced by the number of hosts, items, and other entities. Be very proactive with this parameter — if cache usage significantly increases or you plan to add monitoring for lots of new hosts, increase the configuration cache. If the configuration cache is full, the Zabbix server stops.

- `CacheUpdateFrequency`: This specifies how often the configuration cache is updated. The default of 1 minute is quite fine for most installations, although in large environments, it might be a good idea to increase this parameter, as a configuration cache update itself can increase database load.

- `StartDBSyncers`: This specifies how many database or history syncers should be started (both names are used interchangeably in various places in Zabbix). These processes are responsible for calculating triggers that reference items, receiving new values, and storing the resulting events and those history values in the database—probably the most database-taxing processes in Zabbix. The default of four database or history syncers should be enough for most environments, although it could be useful to increase for big installations. Be careful with increasing this number—having too many of these can have a negative effect on performance; although you might see that if their average busy rate decreases, the number of values processed could decrease.

- `HistoryCacheSize`: When values are collected, they are first stored in a history cache. History or database syncers take values from this cache, process triggers, and store the values in the database. The history cache getting full usually indicates performance issues—increasing the cache size is unlikely to help. If this cache is full, no new values are inserted in it, but the Zabbix server keeps running.

- `HistoryIndexSize`: This cache holds information about the most recent and oldest value for all items in the history cache. It is used to avoid scanning the history cache, which could get rather large. Usage of this cache depends on the number of items that collect data. As with the main configuration and trend cache, make sure to have enough room in this cache—if it's full, the Zabbix server will shut down.

- `TrendCacheSize`: This cache holds trend information for the current hour for each item—not the current hour per the clock, but the current hour based on the incoming values. That is, the last value that came in for an item determines the current hour value. For example, if values are sent in using `zabbix_sender` for the hour 09:00–10:00 yesterday, that is the current hour, and its trend data is in the trend cache. As soon as the first value for hour 10:00–11:00 arrives, the trend cache information for that item is written to the database and 10:00–11:00 becomes the new current hour. Usage of this cache depends on the amount of items that collect data. As with the main configuration cache, make sure to have enough room in this cache—if it's full, the Zabbix server will shut down.

- `ValueCacheSize`: This parameter controls the size of the cache that holds historical values — but as opposed to the history cache, it holds values that are expected to be useful in the future. The values in here are not meant to be written out to the database, but quite the opposite — values are often read into this cache from the database. The value cache is used when item values are needed for trigger calculation (for example, computing the average value for last 10 minutes), for calculated or aggregate items, for including in notifications, and other purposes. Value cache population can take a while when the server first starts up. If the value cache is full, the Zabbix server will keep running, but its performance will likely degrade. Monitor this cache and increase the size as needed.

- `TrapperTimeout`: This parameter controls how long trappers spend on communicating with active agents and proxies as well as `zabbix_sender`. Being set to the maximum value of 5 minutes by default, this timeout is highly unlikely to be reached.

- `UnreachablePeriod`, `UnavailableDelay`, and `UnreachableDelay`: These parameters work together to determine how value retrieval failures should be handled. If value retrieval fails with a network error, the host is considered to be unreachable and is checked every `UnreachableDelay` seconds (by default, 15). This goes on for `UnreachablePeriod` seconds (45 by default), and if all checks fail (with the default settings we end up with 4 checks), the host is marked unavailable and is checked every `UnavailableDelay` seconds. Note that since Zabbix 3.0, if an item fails twice in a row but another item of the same type on the same host succeeds, the failing item is marked unsupported instead. It is probably best to leave these values at the defaults, as changing them could lead to fairly confusing results.

- `AlertScriptsPath`: Custom scripts to be be called from actions must be placed in the directory specified by this parameter. We configured such a script in *Chapter 7, Acting upon Monitored Conditions*.

- `ExternalScripts`: Scripts that are to be used in external check items must be placed in the directory specified by this parameter. We configured such an item in *Chapter 11, Advanced Item Monitoring*.

- `FpingLocation` and `Fping6Location`: These parameters should point at the `fping` binaries for IPv4 and IPv6, if different. The `fping` utility is required for ICMP checks, which we configured in *Chapter 3, Monitoring with Zabbix Agents and Basic Protocols*.

- `SSHKeyLocation`: If using SSH items with keys, the keys must be placed in the directory specified by this parameter. We configured SSH items in *Chapter 11, Advanced Item Monitoring*.

- **LogSlowQueries**: Normally, SQL queries are not logged up to `DebugLevel` 4. This parameter allows us to log all queries that take longer than the number of milliseconds, specified here, at `DebugLevel` 3. By default, since Zabbix 3.0, any query that takes longer than 3 seconds is logged. They appear in the log file like this:

  ```
  13890:20151223:152504.421 slow query: 3.005859 sec, "commit;"
  ```

- **TmpDir**: This is a temporary directory for any files the Zabbix server or proxy need to store. Currently, only used for files that are passed to `fping`.

- **SSLCertLocation**, **SSLKeyLocation**, and **SSLCALocation**: These parameters specify where certificates, keys, and certificate authority files will be looked up when the SSL functionality is used with web monitoring.

Again, all the parameters starting with TLS are relevant for daemon traffic encryption and won't be discussed here.

The available parameters might be slightly different if you have a more recent version of Zabbix. To list the supported parameters in the configuration file you have, the following command could help:

```
$ grep "### Option" zabbix_agentd.conf
```

Now, if you get confused about some parameter, what's the first place you should check? If you said or thought "comments in the configuration files themselves, of course," great. If not, go take a look at those comments and remember that the Zabbix team really, really tries hard to make those comments useful and wants you to read them. You will save your own time that way.

Summary

After Zabbix is installed and configured, a moment comes when maintenance tasks become important. In this last chapter, we looked at three important tasks:

- **Monitoring Zabbix itself**: We covered internal items that allow figuring out how much data the Zabbix server or proxy is receiving, monitoring cache usage, verifying how busy the internal processes are, how many unsupported items we have, and a few other things.

- **Making backups**: We discussed the suggested and popular approaches to making backups (and restoring from them, too) of the most important thing in Zabbix—its database.

- **Upgrading Zabbix**: We found out the differences between minor and major version upgrades and how the database is automatically patched by the Zabbix server. We also learned about LTS versions, which are supported for 3 years, and for 2 extra years for critical and security fixes, while the other versions are supported for about 1 month from when the next version is released.

While talking about upgrades, we also figured out how the compatibility between different Zabbix components works. With minor-level upgrades, it was very easy — all components, including the server, proxy, and agent, are compatible with each other. Let's try to visualize the major upgrade level compatibility matrix:

Older \ Newer	Agent	Proxy	Server
Agent		Y	Y
Proxy	N		N
Server	N	N	

As a reminder, from the support perspective, the server and proxy should be of the same major version, and they support all older agent versions. Regarding the Zabbix Java gateway, it should to be from the same major version as the server or proxy — although the protocol has not changed, there are no official tests done and no support provided for different major versions.

> Before performing a major Zabbix version upgrade, make sure to have a database backup.

After dealing with these three major topics, we discussed general suggestions to keep Zabbix performance acceptable, paying extra attention to housekeeper configuration.

We also found out a way to see the changes made to the Zabbix configuration — the audit log. It allows us to see who made what changes to hosts, items, and other entities. We were a bit disappointed to find out this log does not actually record all operations, especially those performed through the API.

We concluded with quite a detailed look at the parameters in the server, proxy, and agent configuration files. Is it maybe worth reminding you to pay close attention to the comments in the configuration files themselves?

We will conclude the book with two appendices, where we'll discuss the steps and methods for Zabbix troubleshooting as well as ways to interact with and join the Zabbix community.

A
Troubleshooting

Installing and configuring Zabbix can happen without a hiccup for one user and with a constant stream of problems for another. The reasons for the problems can differ from user to user — buggy libraries, bad distribution packaging, unintuitive configuration in Zabbix, or maybe even an occasional bug in Zabbix itself. Here, we will look at common problems new users experience when performing various tasks:

- Setting up the initial Zabbix installation
- Working with the web frontend
- Monitoring different devices
- Configuring thresholds and alerting

If you face a case that is more complicated than that, we will continue with more detailed debugging instructions, including:

- The Zabbix log file format
- Reloading the server and proxy configuration cache
- Controlling running daemons
- Observing the work performed by individual daemon processes

Chapter introduction

This chapter caused a bit of mental agony. Having worked with Zabbix since 2001, there were quite a lot of potential problem cases to describe. I'd wake up in the middle of the night with an idea of a brilliant problem (and solution) to include, only to have forgotten it by the time morning came. But this would have been a never-ending chapter then. A compromise was needed, and reluctantly accepted. This chapter does not aim to help you with every single problem you will ever encounter in your life—or with Zabbix. It tries to help with more common issues and give you some hints and starting points for further debugging.

Common issues

Here are a few issues you might face:

Installation

There are several common stumbling blocks in the installation process, some caused by well-hidden factors.

Compilation

- **Q**: I am trying to compile Zabbix on a 64-bit system. I have the corresponding development packages installed, but Zabbix claims they are not present.

- **A**: Double-check that the 64-bit development packages are installed, not just the 32-bit ones.

- **Q**: I am trying to compile Zabbix from an SVN checkout, but the configuration script fails with this error:

  ```
  syntax error near unexpected token `IKSEMEL,iksemel,'
  ```

- **A**: Install the `pkg-config` package and rerun the commands to generate the configuration script.

- **Q**: I am trying to compile Zabbix, but it fails.

- **A**: It is useful to reduce the number of possible causes. Verify that you are not compiling with `--enable-static`, which is known to cause compilation problems. If compilation fails without that flag, check the `config.log` file contents in the source directory. It often contains exact error details.

Frontend

- **Q**: I have installed the Zabbix frontend. What's the default username and password?

- **A**: The username is `Admin`, and the password is `zabbix`.

- **Q**: I'm setting up Zabbix from an SVN checkout. When I switch languages in the frontend, nothing happens.

- **A**: In the frontend directory, in the `locale` subdirectory, there's a `make_mo.sh` script. It compiles the needed `mo` files out of the translation source `po` files — run it. Note that it will need `Gettext` tools, and the webserver might have to be restarted afterwards.

Backend

- **Q**: Zabbix is working correctly, but some/all graphs are not displayed.

- **A**: Refer to the Apache error log for more details. Usually, this is caused by the PHP script memory limit being too low — if that is the case, increase it by setting the `memory_limit` parameter to a higher value and restarting the webserver. Another possible cause is a broken `conf/zabbix.conf.php` file — verify that it does not have any weird characters, especially at the end of the file.

- **Q**: Complex views, such as screens with many elements, sometimes fail to load. What could be causing this?

- **A**: Like the previous problem, check that the PHP memory limit has not been exceeded. Additionally, check the PHP script timeout (`max_execution_time` parameter) and increase it if necessary.

- **Q**: My graphs have gaps.

- **A**: It's not only graphs — data is missing in the database as well. This problem should be resolved by finding out what causes the data loss. Common reasons for this are:

  - **Network problems**: If the network is unreliable, data will be missing.

  - **An overloaded monitored device**: For example, if you have added a switch with many ports and are monitoring several items on each port very often, try increasing the intervals and disabling unneeded items.

  - **An overloaded Zabbix server**: It's usually the database. Check the system load on the Zabbix database server, especially `iowait`.

- **Q**: I had Zabbix installed and running, but it is suddenly showing me the installation screen again.

- **A**: Check the accessibility of the `conf/zabbix.conf.php` file.

- **Q**: The `conf/zabbix.conf.php` file is there, but I still see the installation screen.

- **A**: In some distribution packages, the frontend might expect the frontend configuration file to be in `/etc/zabbix/web` or a similar location. Check the package documentation.

- **Q**: I am trying to open a large page with many elements, but refresh kicks in before the page even finishes loading. How can I solve this?

- **A**: Increase the refresh period in your user profile. While the page loading speed won't be improved by that, at least the page will get a chance to load completely.

- **Q**: The clock on my server is correct, but the frontend shows incorrect times.

- **A**: Check that the time zone is set correctly in the PHP configuration.

- **Q**: Zabbix server is running, but the frontend claims it is not.

- **A**: This could be caused by multiple factors:

    ° Check the `conf/zabbix.conf.php` file — the frontend uses the server address and port specified there to query the Zabbix server process.

    ° Make sure no firewall is blocking connections from the frontend to the Zabbix server.

    ° Make sure SELinux is not blocking connections from the frontend to the Zabbix server.

    ° Make sure you have at least one trapper process enabled — they accept frontend connections. It is also possible that there are not enough trappers to service all requests. This is especially likely if the message about the server being unavailable appears only every now and then. Monitor the busy rate of the trapper processes like we did in *Chapter 22, Zabbix Maintenance*.

- **Q**: I am having a problem with the frontend that is not listed here.

- **A**: Check the Apache error log and PHP log — these often offer an insight into the cause. Also go to **Administration | Users** or **User groups** and add your user to the **Enabled debug mode** group. Afterwards, all frontend pages will have a small **Debug** control in the lower-right corner. Clicking on it will show a lot of detail about that specific page, including the exact API and SQL queries that were performed. Debug mode can use more resources — if some frontend pages stop working after enabling debug mode, try disabling it.

Locked out of the frontend

A common mistake, performed by both new and seasoned users, is locking oneself out of the frontend. This can happen in several ways, but we're more interested here in how to get back in.

- **Q**: I forgot my password and tried to log in until the Zabbix frontend stopped responding.

- **A**: By default, Zabbix denies access for 30 seconds after five failed login attempts, so just wait for 30 seconds. You can customize these values in `includes/defines.inc.php`:

    ○ `ZBX_LOGIN_ATTEMPTS`: The number of unsuccessful attempts after which Zabbix denies access

    ○ `ZBX_LOGIN_BLOCK`: How long to deny access for, in seconds

- **Q**: I have forgotten my `Admin` user password, or I have been tasked with managing a Zabbix installation where the `Admin` user's password is not known.

- **A**: You can easily reset the `Admin` user password by directly modifying the database:

```
mysql> update zabbix.users set passwd=MD5('somepassword') where
alias='Admin';
```

> Of course, replace `somepassword` with some other string. Keep in mind that MySQL by default saves console commands in the `~/.mysql_history` file, so you might want to set the password to some temporary version and update it in the frontend later.

- **Q**: I changed the authentication method, but it didn't work as planned and now I can't log in anymore.

- **A**: You can restore Zabbix's internal authentication method by editing the database:

```
mysql> update zabbix.config set authentication_type='0' where
configid='1';
```

Authentication type `0` is the internal one. For the record, other types are `1` (LDAP) and `2` (HTTP). Zabbix expects only one `config` table entry with a `configid` value of `1`.

Monitoring

Sometimes monitoring something proceeds without a hitch; sometimes it just won't work.

General monitoring

- **Q**: I added a host or item, but I don't see it in **Monitoring | Latest data**.

- **A**: Check that the filter there includes the host or its group. Make sure that the **Show items without data** checkbox is marked and that other filter options do not exclude the item you are looking for.

- **Q**: I can see my host in **Latest data**, and new values are coming in—but it is missing in **Monitoring | Overview**.

- **A**: **Overview** is probably set to display triggers—verify that the host has triggers configured. Hosts without triggers are not displayed in trigger mode.

Monitoring with the Zabbix agent

- **Q**: I am trying to monitor a host using passive Zabbix agent checks, but it doesn't work.

- **A**: Common reasons why Zabbix agent items won't work include the following:

  - ° The Zabbix agent daemon is not running. Simple, right? Still, start by checking that it is actually running.

  - ° The Zabbix daemon is not listening on the correct port or interface. You can check which port and interface the Zabbix agent daemon is listening on by running `netstat -ntpl` on the monitored host. The default agent daemon port is `10050`.

  - ° The server IP address in the agent daemon configuration file is incorrect. Check the configuration file and make sure the server directive specifies the IP that the Zabbix server will be connecting from.

  - ° Network problems prevent the server from connecting to the agent daemon properly. This includes things such as local and network firewalls blocking connections, but also some network devices and setups actually changing the source IP address of the Zabbix server outgoing connections. Test connectivity by executing `telnet <monitored host IP> 10050` from the Zabbix server. If you have customized the agent listen port, use that port in this command. If the connection is not opened, debug it as a network problem. If the connection is immediately closed, the Zabbix agent daemon does not see the connection as coming from the IP address set in the configuration file. Note that, in some cases, you might have to actually use the IPv6 address, as the Zabbix agent is receiving that as one of the incoming connections.

- **Q**: I am trying to monitor a host using active Zabbix agent checks, but it does not work.

- **A**: Active items are a bit more tricky. Here are some things to verify:

    ° Check network connectivity as with normal items — from the monitored machine, execute `telnet <Zabbix server IP> 10051`. If you have customized the agent listen port, use that port in this command.

> The Zabbix proxy IP address and port should be used in almost all commands if the host is monitored by a proxy.

    ° Make sure to wait for the Zabbix server to refresh its configuration cache and that the time specified in the `RefreshActiveChecks` option in the agent daemon configuration file has passed before expecting results from the active items. If you want to force the agent to reload the list of items from the server, restart the agent.

    ° Check whether the host name specified in the agent daemon configuration file in the `Hostname` option matches the one configured for the host in the frontend. Note that this is not the IP address or DNS name; only the host name will work — it is also not the visible name, but the so-called **technical host name**. Like nearly everything else in Zabbix, it is case-sensitive.

    ° Make sure that the Zabbix server you want to send active checks to (or retrieve them from) is listed in the `ServerActive` option in the agent daemon configuration file.

- **Q**: I am verifying that I can get the value on the monitored host, but the Zabbix agent says it is not supported or gives me wrong data.

- **A**: There are several possible cases:

    ° You are checking things such as the process count or using the `zabbix_agentd -t` syntax as root, but various permission limitations, including `grsecurity` and `SELinux`, can prevent access for the Zabbix agent. This includes the Zabbix agent showing the number of unique running processes as 0 even when with root access you can see the actual number.

- ○ Another case when the local process count differs from what the Zabbix agent returns: various interpreted processes, such as Python or Perl ones, can appear to the agent as interpreter processes, only with user processes as a parameter. Processes known to display this problem include `amavisd` and `xend`. In those situations, you can use a different approach, for example with the `proc.num[python,,,xend]` item key. This will look for Python processes having the `xend` string in their parameters.

- ○ The monitored instance is missing. For example, if you are asking for a metric with the `net.if.in[eth0,bytes]` key and the Zabbix agent claims it is not supported, verify that the `eth0` interface actually exists.

- ○ Another server has an active Zabbix agent configured with the same host name and is also sending in data for this host.

- **Q**: I modified a parameter in the agent daemon configuration file, but it ignores my changes.

- **A**: Check several things:

  - ○ Verify that the modified line is not commented out.

  - ○ Make sure you are editing the file on the correct system.

  - ○ Check that the Zabbix agent daemon uses the modified configuration file. All Zabbix daemons log the configuration file they are using when starting up.

  - ○ Check for `Include` directives. Pay extra attention to ones that include all files in a directory, and nested includes.

  - ○ Make sure you properly restarted the daemon. Note that simply running `zabbix_daemon` or `zabbix_daemon restart` will not restart the daemon.

> Some distribution packages may provide a configuration file and a convenient symlink to that file. If you use `sed -i` on a `symlink`, it does not edit the target file—it replaces the `symlink` with a regular file instead. Some versions of `sed` may provide an option called `--follow-symlinks` to edit the target file.

- **Q**: I see the configuration file specifying one value for a parameter, but the Zabbix agent uses a different value.

- **A**: Refer to the answer to the previous question, especially the parts about making sure it's the correct file on the correct system and that `Include` directives do not override the first instance of the parameter.

- **Q**: I'm trying to use active items or autoregistration on a Windows system, but the automatically acquired hostname is all uppercase and cut at 15 characters.

- **A**: Set `HostnameItem=system.hostname[host]` in the agent daemon configuration file. We discussed this in *Chapter 14, Monitoring Windows*.

- **Q**: I verified that an item works as expected when running `zabbix_agentd -t` or `-p`, but it does not work when I check the values in the frontend.

- **A**: When manually running `zabbix_agentd`, the user and environment are likely different from a running daemon, so permissions and environment values differ. Check the detailed operations that that item is expected to perform and what could prevent it from succeeding with the Zabbix agent daemon permissions. Do not test `zabbix_agentd` directly as root. The best approach is testing against a running agent daemon with `zabbix_get`.

- **Q**: I can get item values in Zabbix Server or with `zabbix_get`, but when I test with `zabbix_agentd -t` or `-p`, I get an error `[m|ZBX_NOTSUPPORTED]` `[Collector is not started.]`.

- **A**: Some items, including `system.cpu.util` and `proc.cpu.util`, have their values calculated by a running agent, as they need multiple samples before providing a useful value. Such items only work when an agent daemon is queried by Zabbix Server or `zabbix_get`.

User parameters

The following list details queries related to user parameters:

- **Q**: My user parameter does not work.

- **A**: Common causes that break user parameters are as follows:

    ○ A missing environment is one of the biggest stumbling blocks when setting up user parameters. The Zabbix agent does not explicitly initialize environment details, such as the HOME variable or other information. This can lead to an inability to read the required configuration files and other issues. Make sure to set the environment as required either by setting variables in the user parameter directly or in a wrapper script.

    ○ Again, restricted permissions for the Zabbix user will be confusing to debug if you run commands for testing as root, so always test user parameters as the Zabbix user. If you need root access for some check, configure access via `sudo`.

- ° Returning unclean data can also easily break data retrieval. When retrieving data with user parameters, make sure it does not contain characters making it unsuitable for storage (such as returning `26.6 c` for a float datatype item) or has other weird characters (such as having a CR/LF newline at the end of the data string).

- ° By default, agent items will time out after three seconds. It is not suggested to increase this timeout in most cases, although it might be reasonably safe to do so if the `userparameter` variable is used as an active item. Remember that active items are not parallel — only one agent process works on them, one item at a time. Consider using `zabbix_sender` for such items instead.

SNMP devices

- **Q**: My SNMP items do not work.

- **A**: Double-check that the SNMP version and community string are set correctly. Specifying an incorrect SNMP version will often cause timeouts, making it harder to debug. Of course, check general connectivity and permissions by using the `snmpwalk` and `snmpget` commands from the Zabbix server.

> Additionally, make sure you are not overloading the monitored device by querying lots of values too frequently.

- **Q**: My SNMP items either do not work at all or fail frequently.

- **A**: Perhaps your device does not properly support `SNMP GETBULK` — try disabling `bulk get` support in the host properties for the SNMP interface.

- **Q**: I imported a template, but the LLD fails with `Invalid SNMP OID: pairs of macro and OID are expected`.

- **A**: The Zabbix SNMP LLD key syntax changed in Zabbix 2.4. Unfortunately, the XML import process was not updated accordingly, and the imported LLD rule uses the old syntax. Refer to *Chapter 12, Automating Configuration*, for details on the key syntax.

- **Q**: I added MIB files, and they work with the command line tools, but Zabbix Server seems to be ignoring the MIB files.

- **A**: Make sure to restart the server daemon — MIB definitions are loaded only upon startup.

- **Q**: My SNMP items work, but some OIDs on a specific device do not, even though data appears in `snmpwalk` output.

- **A**: Try `snmpget` with those OIDs. Some UPSes are known to have buggy firmware that prevents these metrics from working with GET requests, but they do work with the GETNEXT requests that `snmpwalk` uses. If this is the case, upgrade the firmware on the device.

- **Q**: I listed all SNMP MIBs I want to use in `/etc/snmp/snmp.conf`, but Net-SNMP utilities do not use them all properly.

- **A**: Some Net-SNMP versions silently trim lines in this file to 1024 symbols, including the newline character. Try splitting options on multiple lines so that a single line does not exceed 1023 printable characters.

- **Q**: I'm monitoring network traffic, but it returns incorrect data.

- **A**: If it's a high-speed interface; make sure to use 64-bit counter OIDs such as `ifHCInOctets` and `ifHCOutOctets`.

- **Q**: I'm adding SNMP devices to Zabbix, but adding new devices stops the monitoring of the previous devices. If I query each device with `snmpget`, they still respond as expected.

- **A**: If it's SNMPv3, make sure all devices have a unique `snmpEngineID` variable.

IPMI monitoring

- **Q**: I can't get the IPMI item to work.

- **A**: There are several things to verify when IPMI items do not work:

  - Make sure that the Zabbix server is configured with IPMI support. Simple, but easy to miss.

  - Check whether the `StartIPMIPollers` option in the server's configuration file is set to the default value, `0`. If it is, set it to `1` and restart Zabbix Server.

  - Make sure that the sensor names are correct. You can get the sensor names with `IPMItool`, and you have to use the name as it appears in the `IPMItool` output, with spaces and without quoting it.

  - Check using the latest OpenIPMI version. Older OpenIPMI versions are known to have various issues.

ICMP checks

- **Q**: All of my ICMP checks are failing.

- **A**: Here are a few possible reasons:

  Check that `fping` may be run `setuid` as `root` by the user runs on Zabbix Server.

  Make sure SELinux does not prevent Zabbix from running `fping`. The `grep fping /var/log/audit/audit.log` command might reveal more information.

Problems with simple checks

- **Q**: My service works, but the `net.tcp.service` or `net.udp.service` item says it does not.

- **A**: Besides verifying that the correct server is queried, check whether the service responds as Zabbix expects—simple checks are documented in detail at `https://www.zabbix.com/documentation/3.0/manual/appendix/items/service_check_details`.

Problems with zabbix_sender and trapper items

- **Q**: I send in values with a timestamp, but a different timestamp is entered in the server database.

- **A**: The Zabbix sender includes the current time on the host in a `clock` property for the whole request, and Zabbix server adjusts the timestamp for all values accordingly. It is not possible to tell the server not to do so or the sender not to send it. Either fix the time on the sending system or implement the basic protocol without sending the request timestamp.

General issues

- **Q**: I am monitoring network traffic, but the numbers are unrealistically huge.

- **A**: As the data is likely provided as a counter, make sure the result is stored as delta (speed per second) on Zabbix.

- **Q**: I'm monitoring a 10G interface speed in bytes per second, and when the interface is loaded, I lose values.

- **A**: Make sure **Type of information** is set to **Numeric (unsigned)**. This way, you'll lose the precision of a fraction of a bit, but keep all the values.

- **Q**: Zabbix does not like the formula for my calculated item.

- **A**: Make sure to use proper quoting, especially if the referenced item keys have quotes. For example, if the referenced item key is `key["parameter",param]`, in the calculated item formula, it can be used like this: `last("key[\"parameter\",param]")`. Notice the escaping of the inner double quotes with backslashes.

- **Q**: I'm trying to use an item key such as `proc.num['apache']`, but it does not work.

- **A**: Zabbix supports only double quotes; do not use single quotes for quoting.

- **Q**: I'm trying to use a trigger expression such as `{host:item.LAST()=13}`, but it does not work.

- **A**: Case sensitivity—almost everything is case-sensitive in Zabbix: item keys, their parameters, host names, trigger functions, and so on. If you come from Windows, keep reminding yourself that case matters.

Triggers

- **Q**: My trigger does not work, or Zabbix refuses to add my trigger.

- **A**: Check the trigger's syntax, paying close attention to parentheses—is the correct type used? Are they all properly closed? The same goes for quotes, and remember about case sensitivity. Try splitting up complex expressions to pinpoint the error.

Actions

- **Q**: My actions do not work.

- **A**: If the notifications do not appear in **Reports | Action log**, make sure the user you want to send notifications to has read permission to at least one of the hosts that participated in generating the event. Also check the action conditions, host maintenance settings, and action operations. Make sure your actions are not disabled—Zabbix can silently and automatically disable actions if the resources referenced in action conditions or operations are deleted. Also check the user media settings, such as severity and time filter, and whether the configured media type is enabled. If the messages do appear in the action log and there are error messages, hopefully the error is helpful. If the messages appear in the action log as successfully sent, check the logs on your MTA or other receiving system.

- **Q**: My e-mail notifications are not sent, and I can see error messages such as `[127.0.0.1] did not issue MAIL/EXPN/VRFY/ETRN during connection to MTA` in e-mail server log files.

- **A**: These messages are most likely caused by Zabbix monitoring the SMTP service, not by notification attempts. Check the permissions as mentioned in the previous question, and check the action log in **Reports | Action log** to find out why notifications are failing.

- **Q**: Something happened, and my Zabbix server is sending out a terrible number of messages. Can I quickly stop that?

- **A**: There exists a harsh method to stop runaway or excessive escalations—you can delete all the currently active escalations. Note that even when deleting the active escalations, Zabbix will create new ones—a good way to solve that is to have the action operation condition only send out messages when the trigger is not acknowledged, and acknowledge the problematic triggers. Beware: this will also remove correct escalations. In the correct database, execute this:

```
mysql> delete from escalations;
```

Discoveries and autoregistration

- **Q**: I remove a host from some host group, but it gets mysteriously re-added later.

- **A**: Check network discovery and active agent autoregistration actions—most likely, they re-add the host.

- **Q**: I move a host to be monitored by a specific proxy or Zabbix server instance, but it changes back to another proxy or Zabbix server instance later.

- **A**: Check active agent autoregistration actions and the `ServerActive` parameter on the agent. The created host will be assigned to the proxy or server that last received the autoregistration request.

- **Q**: I disable an LLD prototype, but the downstream items or triggers are not disabled.

- **A**: Unfortunately, that's by design and cannot be changed. You can disable individual items and triggers in the configuration list. For changing the state of many downstream items or triggers, try using the Zabbix API.

Troubleshooting Zabbix

All of the previous Q&As cover a few of the most common issues new users might encounter. There are a lot of other issues one might run into, and with new versions of Zabbix, new issues will appear. While it's good to have quick solutions to common problems, let's look at some details that could be helpful when debugging Zabbix problems.

The Zabbix log file format

One of the first places we should check when there's an unexplained issue is log files. This is not just a Zabbix-specific thing; log files are great. Sometimes. Other times, they do not help, but we will discuss some other options for when log files do not provide the answer. To be able to find the answer, though, it is helpful to know some basics about the log file format. The Zabbix log format is as follows:

```
PPPPPP:YYYYMMDD:HHMMSS.mmm
```

Here, PPPPPP is process ID, space-padded to 6 characters, YYYYMMDD is the current date, HHMMSS is the current time, and mmm is milliseconds for the timestamp. Colons and the dot are literal symbols. This prefix is followed by a space and then by the actual log message. Here's an example log entry:

```
10372:20151223:134406.865 database is down: reconnecting in 10 seconds
```

If there's a line in the log file without this prefix, it is most likely coming from an external source such as a script, or maybe from some library such as Net-SNMP.

During startup, output similar to the following will be logged:

```
12331:20151215:163629.968 Starting Zabbix Server. Zabbix 3.0.0
(revision {ZABBIX_REVISION}).
12331:20151215:163630.020 ****** Enabled features ******
12331:20151215:163630.020 SNMP monitoring:           YES
12331:20151215:163630.020 IPMI monitoring:           YES
12331:20151215:163630.020 Web monitoring:            YES
12331:20151215:163630.020 VMware monitoring:         YES
12331:20151215:163630.020 SMTP authentication:       YES
12331:20151215:163630.020 Jabber notifications:       NO
12331:20151215:163630.020 Ez Texting notifications:  YES
12331:20151215:163630.020 ODBC:                      YES
12331:20151215:163630.020 SSH2 support:              YES
12331:20151215:163630.020 IPv6 support:               NO
12331:20151215:163630.020 TLS support:                NO
12331:20151215:163630.020 ******************************
12331:20151215:163630.020 using configuration file: /usr/local/etc/
zabbix_server.conf
12331:20151215:163630.067 current database version (mandatory/
optional): 03000000/03000000
12331:20151215:163630.067 required mandatory version: 03000000
```

The first line prints out the daemon type and version. Depending on how it was compiled, it might also include the current SVN revision number. A list of the compiled-in features follows—very useful to know whether you should expect SNMP, IPMI, or VMware monitoring to work at all. Then, the path to the currently used configuration file is shown—helpful when we want to figure out whether the file we changed was the correct one. In the server and proxy log files, both the current and the required database versions are present—we discussed those in *Chapter 22, Zabbix Maintenance*.

After the database versions, the internal process startup messages can be found:

```
2583:20151231:155712.323 server #0 started [main process]
2592:20151231:155712.334 server #5 started [poller #3]
2591:20151231:155712.336 server #4 started [poller #2]
2590:20151231:155712.337 server #3 started [poller #1]
2593:20151231:155712.339 server #6 started [poller #4]
```

There will be many more lines like these; the output here is trimmed. This might help verify that the expected number of processes of some type has been started. When looking at log file contents, it is not always obvious which process logged a specific line—and this is where the startup messages can help. If we see a line such as the following, we can find out which process logged it:

```
21974:20151231:184520.117 Zabbix agent item "vfs.fs.size[/,free]" on
host "A test host" failed: another network error, wait for 15 seconds
```

We can do that by looking for the startup message with the same PID:

```
# grep 21974 zabbix_server.log | grep started
21974:20151231:184352.921 server #8 started [unreachable poller #1]
```

> If more than one line is returned, apply common sense to find out the startup message.

This demonstrates that hosts are deferred to the unreachable poller after the first network failure.

But what if the log file has been rotated and the original startup messages are lost? Besides more advanced detective work, there's a simple method, provided that the daemon is still running. We will look at that method a bit later in this chapter.

Reloading the configuration cache

We met the configuration cache in *Chapter 2, Getting Your First Notification*, and we discussed ways to monitor it in *Chapter 22, Zabbix Maintenance*. While it helps a lot performance-wise, it can be a bit of a problem if we are trying to quickly test something. It is possible to force Zabbix server to reload the configuration cache. Run the following to display Zabbix server options:

```
# zabbix_server --help
```

> We briefly discussed Zabbix proxy configuration cache reloading in *Chapter 19, Using Proxies to Monitor Remote Locations*.

In the output, look for the `runtime control` options section:

```
-R --runtime-control runtime-option  Perform administrative functions
Runtime control options:
  config_cache_reload  Reload configuration cache
```

Thus, reloading the server configuration cache can be initiated by the following:

```
# zabbix_server --runtime-control config_cache_reload
zabbix_server [2682]: command sent successfully
```

Examining the server log file will reveal that it has received the signal:

```
forced reloading of the configuration cache
```

In the background, the sending of the signal happens like this:

1. The server binary looks up the default configuration file.
2. It then looks for the file specified in the `PidFile` option.
3. It sends the signal to the process with that ID.

As discussed in *Chapter 19, Using Proxies to Monitor Remote Locations*, the great thing with this feature is that it's also supported for active Zabbix proxies. Even better, when an active proxy is instructed to reload its configuration cache, it connects to the Zabbix server, gets all the latest configuration, and then reloads the local configuration cache. If such a signal is sent to a passive proxy, it ignores the signal.

What if you have several proxies running on the same system—how can you tell the binary which exact instance should reload the configuration cache? Looking back at the steps that were taken to deliver the signal to the process, all that is needed is specifying the correct configuration file. If running several proxies on the same system, each must have its own configuration file already, specifying different PID files, log files, listening ports, and so on. Instructing a proxy that used a specific configuration file to reload the configuration cache would be this simple:

```
# zabbix_proxy -c /path/to/zabbix_proxy.conf --runtime-control config_
cache_reload
```

> The full or absolute path must be provided for the configuration file; a relative path is not supported.

> The same principle applies for servers and proxies, but it is even less common to run several Zabbix servers on the same system.

Manually reloading the configuration cache is useful if we have a large Zabbix server instance and have significantly increased the CacheUpdateFrequency parameter.

Controlling running daemons

A configuration cache reload was only one of the things available in the runtime section. Let's look at the remaining options in there:

```
housekeeper_execute          Execute the housekeeper
log_level_increase=target    Increase log level, affects all processes
if target is not specified
log_level_decrease=target    Decrease log level, affects all processes
if target is not specified
Log level control targets: pid
Process identifier process-type All processes of specified type (for
example, poller)
process-type,N               Process type and number (e.g., poller,3)
```

As discussed in *Chapter 22, Zabbix Maintenance*, the internal housekeeper is first run 30 minutes after the server or proxy startup. The housekeeper_execute runtime option allows us to run it at will:

```
# zabbix_server --runtime-control housekeeper_execute
```

Even more interesting is the ability to change the log level for a running process. This feature first appeared in Zabbix 2.4, and it made debugging much, much easier. Zabbix daemons are usually started and just work—until we have to change something. While we cannot tell any of the daemons to re-read their configuration file, there are a few more options that allow us to control some aspects of a running daemon. As briefly mentioned in *Chapter 22*, *Zabbix Maintenance*, the DebugLevel parameter allows us to set the log level when the daemon starts, with the default being 3. Log level 4 adds all the SQL queries, and log level 5 also adds the received content from web monitoring and VMware monitoring. For the uninitiated, anything above level 3 can be very surprising and intimidating. Even a very small Zabbix server can easily log tens of megabytes in a few minutes at log level 4. As some problem might not appear immediately, one might have to run it for hours or days at log level 4 or 5. Imagine dealing with gigabytes of logs you are not familiar with. The ability to set the log level for a running process allows us to increase the log level during a problem situation and lower it later, without requiring a daemon restart.

Even better, when using the runtime log level feature, we can select which exact components should have their log level changed. Individual processes can be identified by either their system PID or by the process number inside Zabbix. Specifying processes by the system PID could be done like this:

```
# zabbix_server --runtime-control log_level_increase=1313
```

Specifying an individual Zabbix process is done by choosing the process type and then passing the process number:

```
# zabbix_server --runtime-control log_level_increase=trapper,3
```

A fairly useful and common approach is changing the log level for all processes of a certain type—for example, we don't know which trapper will receive the connection that causes the problem, so we could easily increase the log level for all trappers by omitting the process number:

```
# zabbix_server --runtime-control log_level_increase=trapper
```

And if no parameter is passed to this runtime option, it will affect all Zabbix processes:

```
# zabbix_server --runtime-control log_level_increase
```

When processes are told to change their log level, they log an entry about it and then change the log level:

```
21975:20151231:190556.881 log level has been increased to 4 (debug)
```

Note that there is no way to query the current log level or set a specific level. If you are not sure about the current log level of all the processes, there are two ways to sort it out:

- Restart the daemon
- Decrease or increase the log level five times so that it's guaranteed to be at 0 or 5, then set the desired level

As a simple test of the options we just explored, increase the log level for all pollers:

```
# zabbix_server --runtime-control log_level_increase=poller
```

Follow the Zabbix server logfile:

```
# tail -f /tmp/zabbix_server.log
```

Notice the amount of data just 5 poller processes on a tiny Zabbix server can generate. Then decrease the log level:

```
# zabbix_server --runtime-control log_level_decrease=poller
```

Runtime process status

Zabbix has another small trick to help with debugging. Run `top` and see which mode gives you a more stable and longer list of Zabbix processes — one of sorting by processor usage (hitting *Shift + P*) or memory usage (hitting *Shift + M*) might.

> Alternatively, hit *o* and type COMMAND=zabbix_server.

Press *C* and notice how Zabbix processes have updated their command line to show which exact internal process it is and what is it doing:

```
zabbix_server: poller #1 [got 0 values in 0.000005 sec, idle 1 sec]
zabbix_server: poller #4 [got 1 values in 0.000089 sec, idle 1 sec]
zabbix_server: poller #5 [got 0 values in 0.000004 sec, idle 1 sec]
```

Follow their status and see how the task and the time it takes changes for some of the processes. We could also have output that could be redirected or filtered through other commands:

```
# top -c -b | grep zabbix_server
```

The -c option tells it to show the command line, the same thing we achieved by hitting C before. The -b option tells top to run in batch mode without accepting input and just outputting the results. We could also specify -n 1 to run it only once or specify any other number as needed.

It might be more convenient to use ps:

```
# ps -f -C zabbix_server
```

The -f flag enables full output, which includes the command line. The -c flag filters by the executable name:

```
zabbix    21969 21962   0 18:43 ?          00:00:00 zabbix_server: poller
#1 [got 0 values in 0.000006 sec, idle 1 sec]
zabbix    21970 21962   0 18:43 ?          00:00:00 zabbix_server: poller
#2 [got 0 values in 0.000008 sec, idle 1 sec]
zabbix    21971 21962   0 18:43 ?          00:00:00 zabbix_server: poller
#3 [got 0 values in 0.000004 sec, idle 1 sec]
```

The full format prints out some extra columns — if all we needed was the PID and the command line, we could limit columns in the output with the -o flag, like this:

```
# ps -o pid=,command= -C zabbix_server
```

```
21975 zabbix_server: trapper #1 [processed data in 0.000150 sec, waiting
for connection]
```

```
21976 zabbix_server: trapper #2 [processed data in 0.001312 sec, waiting
for connection]
```

> The equals sign after pid and command tells ps not to use any header for these columns.

And to see a dynamic list that shows the current status, we can use the watch command:

```
# watch -n 1 'ps -o pid=,command= -C zabbix_server'
```

This list will be updated every second. Note that the interval parameter -n also accepts decimals, so to update twice every second, we could use -n 0.5.

This is also the method to find out which PID corresponds to which process type if startup messages are not available in the log file — we can see the process type and PID in the output of top or ps.

Further debugging

There are a lot of things that could go wrong, and a lot of tools to help with finding out why. If you are familiar with the toolbox , including tools such as `tcpdump`, `strace`, `ltrace`, and `pmap`, you should be able to figure out most Zabbix problems.

> Some people claim that everything is a DNS problem. Often, they are right—if nothing else helps, check the DNS. Just in case.

We won't discuss them here, as it would be quite out of scope—that's general Linux or Unix debugging. Of course, there's still a lot of Zabbix-specific things that could go wrong. You might want to check out the Zabbix troubleshooting page on the wiki: `http://zabbix.org/wiki/Troubleshooting`. If that does not help, make sure to check the community and commercial support options, such as the Zabbix IRC channel we will discuss in *Appendix B*, *Being Part of the Community*.

Being Part of the Community

B

An important aspect of Zabbix is its open source nature. Zabbix is a true open source solution — it's not "open core", and it doesn't have an Enterprise version or some proprietary plugins. Such approaches could be labeled as "fake open source". All components of Zabbix are completely open source; there are no closed or hidden components. Its developers have undertaken to keep Zabbix that way — feel free to look this up in the Zabbix conference 2013 videos: see the opening speech by Zabbix creator Alexei Vladishev, around 27 minutes and 30 seconds in.

Besides being open source, a lot of Zabbix development happens out in the open, too. That makes it easy to closely follow the development and to get community support. But each open source project is different in how it is run and what guidelines it has, so let's look at what one can expect to find from this aspect of Zabbix:

- Community support can be a great way to solve a problem, by chatting on the IRC channel, looking at the wiki, discussing it on the official forum, or using the open bug tracker

- Following the development more closely by getting the latest source code can allow one to try out fixes for problems as soon as possible, provide early feedback, and get more familiar with the internals of Zabbix

- For product development, support contracts, or other services, commercial support might be handy

The development of Zabbix happens out in the open, but external contributions are usually not accepted, except in one area: translations. Contributors to all the translations Zabbix has are welcome, and we will also find out how to get involved in that area.

Community and support

There's a vibrant community of Zabbix users, who communicate and share using different means. You are free to choose the communication and information exchange method you prefer, but it is good to know how things are arranged.

You are welcome to ask questions and help others by answering theirs, but it is suggested to observe some basic rules, which will help you to get the answers:

- Be polite; remember that nobody is obliged to respond to you in IRC, on the forum, or elsewhere.

- If you get no response, perhaps nobody knows the answer right now — be patient. Remember that people live in different time zones, so what is the middle of the working day for you might be the middle of the night for somebody else.

- Use English, unless communicating in a dedicated native-language section. Avoid the use of single-letter substitutions for words. Keep in mind that for many participants, English is a second or third language, so pointing out mistakes should be polite. Perception of language also varies a lot — what is considered offensive in one region might be completely fine in another.

- Make sure to try to resolve the problem yourself first, consulting with the official documentation, wiki, and other sources. It is not polite to require volunteer community members to do your work for you. On the other hand, if you would prefer somebody to work on your Zabbix instance, a commercial support service, mentioned at the end of this chapter, might be more suitable for you.

- When asking for help, provide as much relevant information as possible. This usually includes your Zabbix version, a detailed problem description, and other things, depending on the problem you are having. That could be the database used, the operating system or distribution, and information about other dependencies. It is very helpful to note what steps you have already taken while trying to resolve the problem. Don't make others guess the details — if they have to ask for more information, it will delay the solution.

These and other guidelines are listed at `http://zabbix.org/wiki/Getting_help` — make sure to read through those as well.

Chatting on IRC

IRC, or **Internet Relay Chat**, is a fairly old communication method and is especially popular within open source project communities. Zabbix users also like to gather for Zabbix-related discussions on a dedicated channel. Located on the Freenode network at freenode.net, the channel #zabbix is where you can expect to get help from, and communicate with, fellow Zabbix users. The most advanced and knowledgeable community members are to be found here. You may use one of the many web-IRC gateways, such as http://webchat.freenode.net/, or connect to any Freenode IRC server with a dedicated program called an IRC client. There are many different options available for different operating systems, and you are free to choose any one — it won't impact your ability to communicate with people using a different one. In addition to general communication guidelines, there are some IRC-specific ones as well:

- Reiterating the basic suggestion — be patient. Too often, people come in, ask their question, and leave a few minutes later. Other members of the channel might be sleeping, eating, or otherwise away from their computer. So ask your question and stay around for a while. If it happens to be a weekend, a while might even be several days.

- Do not ask to ask. If your question is about Zabbix, and it is well thought out, then just go ahead and ask. Starting with "Hey, can I ask a question about Zabbix?" will require somebody to confirm with "Yes, you can," then you typing the question, and only then can the helping process start. In the end, it will take much longer.

- Do not repeat your question too often; it will only annoy others. While it might be tempting to ask again and again when new people join, they are unlikely to be the experts you are waiting for, so again, be patient. On the other hand, it usually is fine to repeat the question if no answer has appeared for a longer time — a day, for example.

- Do not type the names of people present, hoping it will net you help. That will needlessly distract them. Wait for somebody to respond instead.

Regarding politeness, remember that all communication is logged and publicly available. If you reveal yourself to be a person hard to communicate with, it will not only stay in people's memories, but also in the logs.

The Zabbix IRC channel also has a couple of automated helpers, called **bots**. All new bug reports and feature requests are announced in the channel by them, and they have other features as well. At this time, current bot features are described at http://zabbix.org/wiki/Getting_help#IRC_bots.

Not only the most knowledgeable users are available on the Zabbix IRC channel. This channel is also quite popular. At the time of writing this, the average number of participants is about 300. It is actually the most popular IRC channel about monitoring. The demo Zabbix instance at `http://zabbix.org/zabbix/` monitors the number of users on the channel, and a graph from 2006 until mid-2016 looks like this:

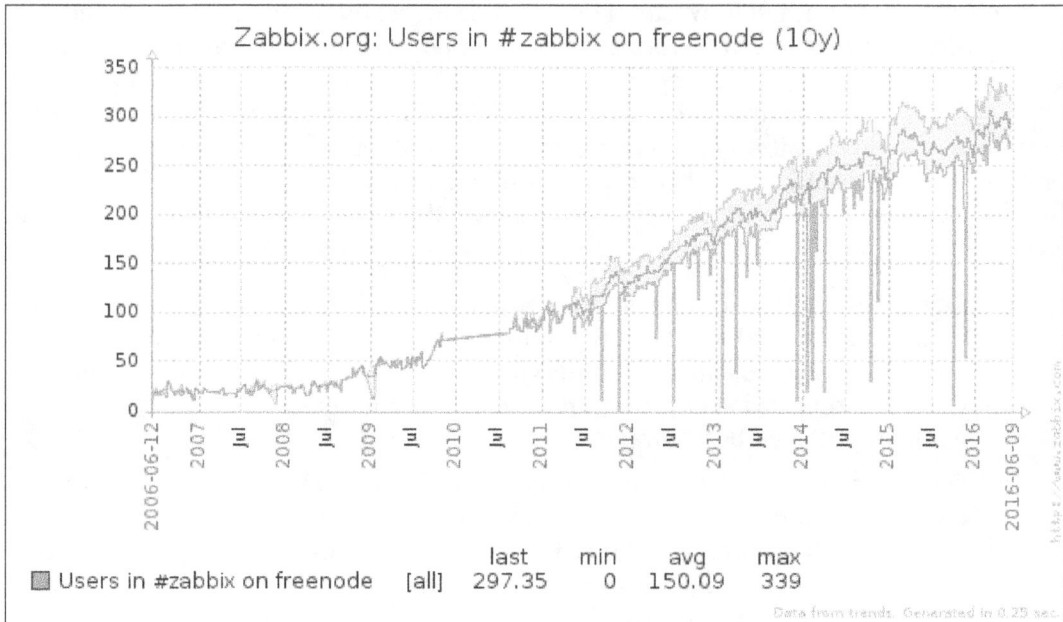

The number of participants on the channel has grown significantly since 2006. You can access the current version by going to `http://zabbix.org/zabbix/` and looking up the simple graph **Users in #zabbix on freenode** on host **Zabbix.org**.

Using the Zabbix wiki

The system that hosts the demo instance we discovered a moment ago also serves as a community platform. Primarily, it's a MediaWiki instance that has a large amount of useful information, and we have referred to it a few times before already. A few things of interest at this time are:

- Zabbix templates
- Zabbix technical documentation, including the Zabbix protocol documentation
- Various Zabbix guidelines, including bug-reporting guidelines and IRC etiquette

- A list of Zabbix API libraries
- Various how-tos, including instructions on high availability setups and the installation process

The content is flexible, and it is suggested to investigate what is available on `http://zabbix.org/wiki/Main_Page` every now and then.

> This book was also supposed to cover how great it is to have new feature specifications available on the Zabbix website, but unfortunately, the Zabbix team has decided to withdraw them. One can still find old specifications at `http://zabbix.org/wiki/Category:Specifications`.

It being a wiki, everybody is welcome to participate. See a mistake or something missing? Just go ahead and improve it. Want to write instructions for some process you found non-trivial to perform? Go ahead and create a new page. And if you are not sure about it, just ask on IRC, and somebody will surely help.

> There is also a Zabbix-related resource directory at `http://share.zabbix.com`. It does not host most of the content; instead, it usually links to templates or scripts on GitHub or a Zabbix website page. We won't look into it in any detail at this time, as the functionality is a bit limited, but it is suggested to visit it every now and then to check whether it has improved.

Using the Zabbix forum

The Zabbix forum is located at `http://www.zabbix.com/forum`. You can read it without registering, but for posting, you will need authenticated access, so register for a user account. The forum offers both a large collection of already solved problems and a chance that you will receive assistance with new problems.

While we've looked at the general suggestions for efficient and satisfactory communication, there are some forum-specific suggestions as well:

- Choose the appropriate forum for your question. If your problem is with the development version of Zabbix, it should not be raised in the forum concerning the Zabbix website.
- Choose wisely when to create a new thread and when to comment on an existing one. It is highly discouraged to ask different questions on an existing thread. On the other hand, it's better to search the forum before creating a duplicate thread about an existing problem.

- Enable new message notifications so that you can respond in a timely fashion if additional information is requested. That will help resolve the problem sooner.

Filing issues on the tracker

What if you have discovered a bug or have a bright idea on how to improve Zabbix? Zabbix uses an issue tracker to record such things and track the resolution process. To access the Zabbix issue tracker, navigate to `https://support.zabbix.com`. Here, you can register and log in to search existing reports as well as enter new ones.

When reporting a new issue, choose the correct project—project ZBX is used for bug reporting, and project ZBXNEXT for new feature requests. It is strongly suggested to search the tracker before filing a new report—perhaps the problem has already been reported and there is no need to create duplicate reports.

What if you have resolved the problem yourself and have a patch fixing some bug or implementing a feature? Just attach it to the corresponding report. You should discuss your approach with Zabbix developers before coding for all but the most simple cases—perhaps they are already working on it, or perhaps your approach will conflict with some other feature in development. Make sure to get familiar with the coding guidelines, too—they are available at `http://zabbix.org/wiki/Main_Page`.

> There is also a patch repository at `https://github.com/zabbix/zabbix-patches`, but it remains to be seen whether it becomes popular.

Meeting in person

All the discussed channels are great for communicating with other Zabbix users, getting help, and helping others. But there are also various ways to meet in person. A very popular and nice yearly event is the **official Zabbix conference**, but there are also various less formal events organized by local communities.

The Zabbix conference

The official Zabbix conference is a great event. It was first organized in 2011, and it usually happens in September. It is a chance to find out about the latest things happening to Zabbix, learn from a lot of very inventive Zabbix users, and have a bit of fun. It happens in the Zabbix birthplace and hometown—Riga, Latvia. There are two days packed with interesting talks, and the Zabbix team tries hard to make everybody feel welcome. If you have a chance, do try to join this event.

Local communities

Your local community might also be coming together. Check out the listing of various communication channels at http://zabbix.org/wiki/Usergroups. Join the user group, follow the news, and maybe even help in organizing events. Do not hesitate to add a new country to the list, too.

Following the development

So you have seen some interesting new feature mentioned on IRC and you want to try it out? Perhaps you want to check how exactly a particular change was implemented or comments on the way it was designed. Or perhaps you would like to produce a patch that depends on some changes being made in the development version. A lot of Zabbix development happens out in the open, and the main phases one could be interested in are:

* A specification being created
* Development starting in a separate feature branch
* A feature being merged to the main branches

> Specifications were public on http://zabbix.org/wiki/Main_Page before; now, they are not available anymore.

Providing feedback early is most likely to be helpful and has a higher chance of impacting the design. If you are interested in a specific feature, you could previously have followed the specification on http://zabbix.org/wiki/Main_Page, but that phase is closed now. Zabbix uses SVN for code versioning. The feature branches in SVN provide very early access to the code, and that is a great time to try out and test the features.

We talked about testing things out; let's find out how to get code that has not been released as a version yet.

Getting the source

When looking for the Zabbix development version, there are two ways to get it, each with its strengths and weaknesses.

Daily snapshots

On the Zabbix development download page, `http://www.zabbix.com/ developers.php`, there are daily snapshots of development versions provided. These usually have the same setup procedures as the released versions. The benefits of using daily snapshots include the following:

- Getting them is a simple download
- The source archive is already generated for you

The drawbacks include the following:

- There is no way to update only those parts of the development version that have actually changed
- There is no way to easily see what actually has changed
- You have no access to the feature branches
- There is no way to get an arbitrary older version

It is suggested to use daily snapshots if you want a simple, one-time peek at how Zabbix development is progressing.

Accessing the version control system

If you plan to follow Zabbix development for a longer time period or if you want to see how exactly a particular change was implemented, daily snapshots will quickly become cumbersome to use. There are no snapshots of the feature branches, so we have to use SVN if the feature has not been merged to the main branches yet.

> You can also browse the official SVN repository using a WebSVN instance at `https://www.zabbix.org/websvn/wsvn/ zabbix.com`. It won't allow you to do a local checkout, but for a quick check on a few files, it can be more convenient.

To access SVN repositories, specific software — a client — is needed. There are many different SVN clients for various platforms, and you can choose whichever seems most convenient to you. Here, we will use the official command line client. As this client is available on almost all Linux distributions, we may want to use it on our Zabbix test server. But before we start playing with it, we must know that the Zabbix source code repository resides at `https://svn.zabbix.com/`. In SVN, development is usually split into a trunk and branches. While the trunk represents the most recent development work, branches are usually used for stable version maintenance. Zabbix uses the same schema, and there are branches for stable version maintenance such as 3.0, while the development for the next stable version happens in the development section, the trunk. The changes do not happen in the version branches or trunk right away, though — they are first implemented in the development branches, which are usually located at `svn://svn.zabbix.com/branches/dev/ZBX-1`, with the correct `ZBX` or `ZBXNEXT` issue number at the end.

Let's say we are interested in the latest features and want to retrieve the trunk. To do this, run the following:

```
$ svn checkout svn://svn.zabbix.com/trunk zabbix-trunk
```

This will proceed to retrieve all the files in the trunk and place them in a directory called `zabbix-trunk`. As of writing this, Zabbix trunk checkout uses approximately 118 MB on disk, but the amount transferred over the network will be smaller than that. Once the process completes, you might be tempted to proceed with compilation, but that won't be easy to do as there is no configuration script at all. There's a convenient script to generate the configuration:

```
$ ./bootstrap.sh
```

After this completes, we should have the configuration script. Now, we can compile this development version of Zabbix, right? Not quite yet. Development repositories hold only a generic database schema and content description, so we will not be able to create the database. We will have to generate the actual schema and data files ourselves. For the Zabbix frontend, specific CSS files have to be generated, too. It is also suggested to create a package, one just like those downloadable from the Zabbix site, so let's do that. Before we can generate the database schema and package, we have to use the configuration script, though. But we can make it slightly faster and require fewer dependencies by omitting any features that are not required. This also enables the creation of a Zabbix package on another machine that does not have all the dependencies for the required functionality, such as SNMP or IPMI monitoring, installed. In the most simple case, run this:

```
$ ./configure
```

This will produce the files required for database schema and package generation. Now, we can proceed with schema and CSS generation:

```
$ make dbschema
$ make css
```

> We discussed the packages required for compilation in *Chapter 1, Getting Started with Zabbix*. For the make css step, you will also need the Sass Ruby gem.

With the database schema and CSS files generated, we are ready to create a package:

```
$ make dist
```

After this command completes, the source directory should have a new archive, named zabbix-<version>.tar.gz. Here, the version will be whatever name the development part has received. From now on, we are back to the known path, as this package is pretty much the same as the one you can download from the released version area or from the daily snapshots area.

But that was a lot of work to get the same thing we could have downloaded right away—why do it at all? Indeed, if you only want to grab the development version once, daily snapshots should be your choice. But an SVN checkout presents other benefits. Let's understand what those are.

Looking at the changesets

A collection of changes to a repository is called a **changeset**. A changeset that has been placed in a repository is said to be committed. We can list changesets that have been committed. For example, if we would like to know what was the last changeset that was committed to this part of the repository, we would issue this command:

```
$ svn log -r PREV:HEAD
```

The -r Subversion switch allows us to specify revisions—numeric representations of each change. PREV and HEAD are special references, being the previous version and latest version respectively. Sometimes, we might be instructed to test or use a specific version, called a **revision**. In that case, it is possible to retrieve it by issuing this command:

```
$ svn up -r 1234
```

Replace `1234` with the revision number you are told to use. This will update the whole checkout to that revision, and you should now run the commands discussed previously again, repeating the same process used after just having checked out. But sometimes, we might need to update only one or a few files to a specific revision — that can be done by specifying the path, like this, for example:

```
$ svn up -r 1234 frontends/php/history.php
```

You can specify both directories and files and get different revisions to test behavior changes or find the specific change that introduced a problem for you.

So you have tried out a development version, maybe several revisions. Some time later, you decide to find out what changes have been made to the trunk. First, the current revision should be figured out. While in the checkout directory, run the following command:

```
$ svn info
```

Look for the line that looks like this:

```
    Revision: 60013
```

With that number on hand, it is now time to update the local copy to the latest and greatest. From the local copy directory, run this:

```
$ svn up
```

This will proceed to update everything that has changed, compared to whatever copy you have. As only changes are pulled, this will result in much less data being downloaded, compared to downloading daily snapshots over and over again. Now, you can just proceed with building Zabbix as discussed before, or you can choose to view the exact changes developers have committed:

```
$ svn log -r 60000:HEAD
```

This command will display the exact changes pushed to the code repository, along with any comments that the developers decided to add. This can be used to determine what exactly was changed. But all this was about the forward-looking development version, the trunk — what if you want to see a particular bug fix for some problem in the stable version applied to that particular branch? Just as we grabbed the trunk from the code repository, we can also grab the branch:

```
$ svn checkout svn://svn.zabbix.com/branches/3.0
```

Instead of the trunk, we are now specifying the subsection branches. After that comes the specific branch, which can be any valid branch. What branches are there? We can list them:

```
svn ls svn://svn.zabbix.com/branches
```

While installing a branch version is pretty much the same as installing the trunk, there's one more use case with branches. If a particular bug is fixed in the branch and you want to benefit from that before the next stable version is out, it is possible to apply this single change to the installed copy. To do that, though, the change has to be first extracted in a format that is easy to reuse. Here, another command comes to the rescue. Remember svn log, which we used to look at changesets before? It showed the revision number for each changeset. If we now have this number, we can take a look at what files a particular commit modified:

```
$ svn log -v -c 60013
```

Here, we use the -c switch to specify a single changeset and -v to increase the verbosity level. In the Changed paths section, one or more files will be listed, for example, these:

```
M /trunk/ChangeLog
M /trunk/src/zabbix_server/escalator/escalator.c
```

When creating a patch, we might want to omit files that do not affect actual software behavior — the changelog in this case. Creating a patch would be done like this:

```
$ svn diff -c 60013 src/zabbix_server/escalator/
escalator.c > /tmp/zabbix.patch
```

Notice how we used Subversion's diff subcommand, specified a single file, and redirected output to a file. Now, the patch should be applied to our Zabbix installation. To do this, change to the Zabbix source installation directory, and execute this:

```
$ patch -p 0 -i /tmp/zabbix.patch
```

> Be careful with extracting patches like this. They will often work if the change was made soon after the release you are patching. If a lot of development has happened between the used version and the patch, the patch might depend on some other changes and not work properly.

The patch utility is instructed to use the input file zabbix.patch and use full path information as specified to apply the changes. After patching, we should evaluate areas the patch applies to — if it's the server, we should recompile and reinstall our server binary, the same with the agent daemon. If changes were performed on the frontend only, we'll usually want to apply the patch to the installed frontend directly, by changing to the frontend directory and applying it as root with this command:

```
# patch -p 2 -i /tmp/zabbix.patch
```

Note that in this case, we are instructing the `patch` utility to strip the first two directories from the path inside the patch. When we are patching the frontend, no recompilation is necessary, and all changes will be visible immediately. What if we applied a patch but it only made things worse? Thankfully, that is easy to undo by applying the same patch in reverse:

```
# patch -R -p 2 -i /tmp/zabbix.patch
```

If using this command for the frontend, again, no further action is required. If it affects binaries, we have to recompile them.

> Refer to the SVN documentation for more detailed instructions, or ask on the Zabbix IRC channel for Zabbix-specific Subversion repository questions.

Translating Zabbix

The Zabbix frontend is available in various languages, and that is a great achievement of the community — the Zabbix company does not do most of the translations. This is also a great opportunity to get involved and make Zabbix available in your language. Zabbix uses the online tool Pootle, which is a very easy way to get started. For more advanced contributors, po files can be downloaded and used with standalone tools. If you have decided to improve or create Zabbix support for your language, here are a few general suggestions:

- It can be a lot of work; be ready for that.
- Before starting, discuss the current state with existing translators for your language, if any.
- Think carefully about how the terms could be translated — how would you translate host, item, trigger, action, operation, and other entities?
- Don't try to translate the Zabbix manual right away — once the frontend has been fully translated and maintained for a while, manual translation can be considered. Translating and maintaining the Zabbix manual is a huge amount of work, and there is no language that has had a successful long-term translation of the manual so far.

> If a language you want to work on is available to translate but does not appear in the frontend language selection, it might be hidden. You can enable a language by editing the `include/locales.inc.php` file and changing the display property from `false` to `true`.

The exact steps and procedure for participating in the translation work may change, so I won't reproduce them here. Instead, go to `http://zabbix.org/wiki/Translating_Zabbix` and follow the steps there. It will likely include registering on the `http://zabbix.org/wiki/Main_Page` wiki, adding yourself to the translator table, subscribing to the translator mailing list, and asking for permissions on Pootle. The latter is probably best done on the Zabbix IRC channel, and that is also the best place to ask any questions about getting involved and the translation process.

Commercial support options

Community support is great. It is often speedy, correct, and friendly. However, even if it is like that always, there might be cases when you might need a more formal approach. Common cases when a formal agreement is pursued include the following:

- A company policy requires a support agreement for all systems put in production
- You want qualified help when implementing Zabbix
- The Zabbix installation will be managed by people who are not deeply involved and don't have great expertise in it
- You need some feature developed or improved

Approaching a commercial support provider is often the best solution in such cases, and it is possible to obtain such support from the company behind the Zabbix software. Visit the Zabbix website at `http://www.zabbix.com/support.php` to obtain more information. If you are ready to discuss commercial support in more detail, it's as easy as dropping an email to `sales@zabbix.com`. At the time of writing this, the sales team is very knowledgeable, helpful, and friendly—and usually lightning-fast to respond, too. There's no conflict of interest or personal gain for me; this is a completely truthful and honest endorsement.

In some cases, company procurement requirements might mandate that you use a local company for your support agreement—the partner and reseller list at `http://www.zabbix.com/partners.php` should help you choose one that is geographically close.

Index

custom scheduling 108, 109
custom script, using
  about 144-148
  custom mapping 148
  database lookups 149-154
  traps, filtering 148

D

daemon configuration parameters
  configuration cache 641
  history cache 641
  history cache index 641
  trend cache 641
  value cache 641
  VMware cache 641
dash 12
data
  reusing, on server 389
  sending 418-420
  sending, from file 421, 422
  sending, with agent daemon
      configuration file 420
  timestamped values, sending 422, 423
  using, in remote site 610, 611
data backups
  separating 650
database
  backing up 648, 649
  creating 13, 14
  data, using in remote site 610, 611
  existing data, modifying 614
  existing data, monitoring 615
  item, modifying 616
  modifying 611
  populating 13, 14
  querying 607-610
  Unix timestamp, displaying 615
  updating 616
  users, managing 612-614
Data Encryption Standard (DES) 123
data loss
  network problems 679
  overloaded monitored device 679
  overloaded Zabbix server 679

data visualization
  about 372
  challenges 372
  considerations 293, 294
  information, overloading 372
  non-interactive display 372
  specific section, displaying
      automatically 373
default speed 244
dependencies
  actions 226
discrete sensors
  bitwise trigger function, using 545-547
  monitoring 543-545
disk device discovery 561
downtime
  specifying 535, 536
dynamic index item OID 131
dynamic screens
  creating 360-362

E

embedded Perl code, using
  about 135, 136
  debugging 142, 143
  SNMP Trap Translator 144
  temporary file, handling 143
  values, filtering by originating host 141
  values, filtering by received data 136-140
encryption
  about 593
  certificate-based encryption 593
  concerns 602, 603
  pre-shared key (PSK) 593
engine ID, Net-SNMP
  authentication 123
  context 123
  encryption 123
escalations
  analogy, running 244
  handling 234-244
event log items 91
events
  details, viewing 214, 215
  event log, monitoring, on
      Windows 519, 520

generating 216, 217
hysteresis 216, 217
extended insert 649
external checks
certificate expiry time, searching 413-415
certificate validity, determining 416-418
performing 413
**Extra Packages for Enterprise
Linux (EPEL) 8**

F

file
values, sending 421, 422
filesystem discovery
about 442
custom thresholds, using with user
macro content 448-450
discovered graphs, including
in screens 445-448
LLD JSON format 442-444
flexible intervals
overlapping 107
fping
URL 97
Freenode
URL 701
frontend
exploring 33-35
raw data, extracting from 605, 606
user profile 35-37
frontend scripts 262

G

GCC (GNU Compiler Collection) 10
general version policy 651
global regular expressions
about 380-462
testing 463
usages, in default templates 464
global screens 366
global scripts
about 254, 255, 262
configuring 255-261
reusing, in actions 261, 262
global search
using 63, 64

graphs
about 43, 294
ad hoc graphs 295-297
controls, exploring 44-46
custom graphs 297, 298
simple graphs 294, 295
grpavg function
func parameter 394
group parameter 394
key parameter 394
param parameter 394
grpmax function 396
grpmin function 396
grpsum function 396

H

host 212
host groups 155-161
host inventory
about 161
data, editing manually 161-164
data, populating automatically 164, 165
host maintenance
about 166
ad-hoc maintenance 176
consequences 166
data, collecting 167-171
data collection, avoiding 171, 172
options 173
periods, creating 166
host maintenance period, options
daily maintenance 173
monthly maintenance 174-176
one-time only maintenance 173
weekly maintenance 174
host prototypes 563, 564
hosts 155-161
host screens 366
host technical name 334
hypervisors
discovering, automatically 559
monitoring 560-562

I

icon highlighting 336
icon mapping 344-347

www.ingramcontent.com/pod-product-compliance
Lightning Source LLC
Chambersburg PA
CBHW080339220326
41598CB00030B/4545